Religion in Society

Eighth Edition

Religion in Society

A Sociology of Religion

RONALD L. JOHNSTONE

Ball State University

Upper Saddle River, New Jersey 07458

Library of Congress Cataloging-in-Publication Data

Johnstone, Ronald L.
  Religion in society: a sociology of religion / Ronald L. Johnstone.—8th ed.
    p. cm.
  Includes bibliographical references and index.
  ISBN 0-13-188407-7
  1. Religion and sociology.   2. United States—Religion.   I. Title.

BL60.J63 2007
306.6—dc22   2005038026

Editorial Director: Leah Jewell
AVP, Publisher: Nancy Roberts
Senior Marketing Manager: Marissa Feliberty
Prepress and Manufacturing Buyer: Brian Mackey
Full-Service Project Management: Chella Sundaram/Integra Software Services, Inc.
Production Liaison: Cheryl Keenan
Editorial Assistant: Valle Hansen
Marketing Assistant: Anthony DeCosta
Director, Image Resource Center: Melinda Reo
Manager, Rights and Permissions: Zina Arabia
Manager, Visual Research: Beth Brenzel
Image Permission Coordinator: Cynthia Vincenti
Cover Art Director: Jayne Conte
Cover Art Designer: Bruce Kenselaar

This book was set in 10/12 Palatino by Integra Software Services, Inc.

Pearson Education LTD.
Pearson Education Singapore, Pte. Ltd
Pearson Education, Canada, Ltd
Pearson Education–Japan
Pearson Education Australia PTY, Limited
Pearson Education North Asia Ltd
Pearson Educación de Mexico, S.A. de C.V
Pearson Education Malaysia, Pte. Ltd
Pearson Education, Upper Saddle River, New Jersey

PEARSON
Prentice
Hall

10 9 8 7 6
ISBN: 0-13-188407-7

To Arline

Contents

PART II   THE SOCIAL ORGANIZATION OF RELIGION

might nonetheless send you on your way with the benediction "may force by with you." These same people might believe passionately in ain inalienable rights for all people. They will seek justice, equity, and dom from oppression for all people, holding such beliefs and aspira- ns as something so universal and important, and worthy of as much sion and conviction, as the most committed Christian believer who ives to bring a friend to Jesus. Might such believers, though not tradi- nally religious, be "religious" in much the same way as a typical hristian, Muslim, or Buddhist believer? And so, not only does everyone now at least a few things about religion, but also might everyone actually be religious" in one way or another?

But we are getting ahead of ourselves. We have not defined "religion" et. We have relied on some common knowledge and awareness that we all ave of what that pervasive phenomenon we call "religion" really is. So before we look at what sociology has to tell us about religion. We must consider what religion is and is not in a systematic way, to put us all "on the same page," so to speak. But even before defining "religion" we need to look in an introduc- tory way at what sociology is, in order to understand from the beginning the perspective on social reality (including "religion") that sociology brings.

THE TASK OF SOCIOLOGY

Very briefly, sociology is the study of the interaction of people in groups and of the influence of those groups on human behavior generally, as well as on society's other institutions and groups. Thus sociology has a twofold goal:

1. understanding the dynamics of group life—what groups are, how they function, how they change, how they differ from one another; and
2. understanding the influence of groups on individual and collective behavior. One fundamental assumption of sociology implied by this is that groups influence all human activity.

Throughout a person's lifetime, groups impinge on his or her biolog- ical "raw material," shaping it, modifying it, influencing it—*socializing* it, to use the sociologists' term. This process begins with the family and pro- ceeds through the hundreds of educational, associational, peer, and work groups that a person participates in and has contact with throughout his or her lifetime.

In both fundamental senses of the sociological enterprise—explaining group dynamics and explaining group influence—religion qualifies per- fectly as a field of sociological study and analysis. Leaving aside for now the question of whether religion is also (or even primarily) an individual

Preface

Considering the global context within which we live and the prominent role religion has in creating and now changing that context, I have felt it important to be more selective than ever in the treatment of topics and issues utilized as illustrations of sociological principles and theory. This has meant that I have deleted some sections that were in the seventh edition and I have added many. I believe most students are pragmatic and want to see and think about applications and implications of what they read and study, both for themselves and their world. A summary of some specific changes and additions follows.

1. New introduction and reorganization of Chapter 1.
2. Revised our working definition of religion, by emphasizing the element of the sacred and de-emphasizing the supernatural, thus including the so-called "Isms" as religious systems but essentially excluding them from later discus- sion in the book.
3. Added treatment of Durkheim's discussion of ritual and paid more attention to sociological theory at many points throughout the book.
4. Interchanged old Chapter 5 with Chapter 4, to introduce the church-sect typology earlier.
5. Expanded the chapter on religious conflict because religious conflict in all forms has implications for everyone, regardless of whether they have personal reli- gious commitment or not.
6. Updated the discussion of the Irish religious conflict, with discussion of the July 21, 2005 Sinn Fein directive to disarm and rely on negotiation and political process to resolve differences.
7. Made major additions to the chapters on "Religion and Politics" and "Religious Fundamentalism." These include:
   a. New Christian Right support for election of local school boards
   b. Updating of the U.S. Supreme Court decision on the phrase "under God" in the Pledge of Allegiance
   c. Expanded the explication of *Civil Religion* and its use by President G.W. Bush in light of the 2004 election
   d. Updated discussion of the public's approval/disapproval of abortion
   e. Expanded treatment of comparisons of Fundamentalists with Evangelicals.
8. Updated SES data by religious affiliation from NORC.

9. Both new and updated discussions in Chapter 11: "Women and Religion:"
   a. Additions to the ordination of women issue in the Catholic Church
   b. Updating on female seminary enrollees
   c. Expansion of discussion of Wicca/Neo Paganism
   d. Another option for fundamentalist women in megachurches
   e. Reaction of some Catholic women to the death of Pope John Paul VI.
10. Expanded discussion of the original intent of the First Amendment to the U.S. Constitution.
11. Added discussion of James Cone's concept of "environmental racism."
12. Expanded discussion of growth in Black Catholics.
13. New section on the "discrepancy between Catholic doctrine and practice."
14. Discussion of the accession of Benedict XVI to the papacy.
15. Included Baptist denominations in the section on Protestant denominations.
16. Introduced the newest major ecumenical group—Christian Churches Together in the U.S.A.
17. New discussion and data on the impact of differential birth rates in the growth of conservative denominations.
18. Added discussion of the impending loss of the Protestant majority position in the U.S.
19. Discussion of factors affecting growth and decline of various denominations.
20. Expanded discussion of the priest shortage in the Catholic Church.
21. Discussion of President Bush's "Faith-Based Initiatives."

This eighth edition is probably the most thorough revision in the thirty-year history of this text, but built of course upon the substantial revisions that constituted the sixth and seventh editions. With the exception of a few studies and data sets that I have retained from the 1960s to 1970s, because I have deemed them important for historical or theoretical reasons, research data have been thoroughly updated in the last two editions.

I am indebted to the following faculty for their helpful critical reviews of edition seven and their excellent suggestions for my consideration in creating the eighth edition: Alexander Riley, Bucknell University; James Wolfe, Butler University; Rick Fraser, California State University – Los Angeles; and Anson Shupe, Indiana University-Purdue University.

And finally, my enduring gratitude to Arline, who continues so steadfastly supportive beside me in this scholarly endeavor.

Chapter 1

The Sociological Perspective

Believers at worship.

Everyone knows at least a little about religion, even if they personally have no affiliation with any religious group. Religion is all around us. In the United States we are aware of the involvement of religion in the political process, particularly as observed in the recent two presidential election campaigns of George W. Bush. We have heard and learned much more about the religion of Islam than we ever did before 9/11. We cannot drive many blocks in any town or city, almost anywhere in the world, without passing a place of worship or monument to religion. In American public schools and Boy Scout troops, every child recites the phrase "under God" in the Pledge of Allegiance. Eventhough some will say they are not religious, do not belong to any religious group, and do not believe in God, phenomenon, it is obviously at least a group phenomenon. Thus, to the extent that religions organize themselves into groups—congregations, denominations, dioceses, cells, fellowships, and so on—an important task for sociology is the study of the structure and functioning of these groups simply *as groups*. In other words, we want to determine how and to what extent religious groups follow sociological laws governing group life in general. In what ways does a congregation, for example, operate like any other voluntary association—like, say, the League of Women Voters? Or how and to what degree do major religious denominations function like large bureaucracies—like, say, General Motors or the United States Army?

Insofar as religion is organized into groups, it exerts influence not only on its members, but also on nonmembers, and on other groups and institutions. Thus the second dimension of our preliminary definition of sociology—as a study of group influence—suggests that religious groups have at least the potential for influencing people, just as do groups that center around one's family, peers, or workplace. The question is not so much *whether* such influence exists but *to what degree, in what ways, and how it can be measured.*

CENTRAL SOCIOLOGICAL ASSUMPTIONS

Human Nature

A number of assumptions made in sociology center around the definition of human nature. Here we shall emphasize three of these assumptions.

First, and perhaps most obviously, a human being is a *biological organism*, a creature with physiological drives, needs, potentials, and limitations. Thus the socializing influence of groups is both directed at and limited by biological factors. Religion is, of course, among those socializing agents that attempt to influence or modify biological nature. For example, different religious groups have different approaches to, and provide different outlets for, sexual drives. And insofar as people in fact internalize these different emphases—whether they are permissive, compensatory, or restrictive—to that extent people will have different personalities and manifest different values and attitudes. In short, although the sociological perspective rejects notions of biological determinism, it recognizes as openly as possible that the human being has potentialities and limitations that are biologically provided.

Another sociological assumption regarding human nature, which is worth mentioning, is the apparently unique *ability of people to symbol*. By this we mean the ability arbitrarily to attach specific meanings to things, sounds, words, acts—meanings that are not intrinsic to the items themselves but that people have created. By establishing consensus on these meanings, groups are able to communicate and to accumulate knowledge. Using language as the prime symbolic mechanism, people can deal with abstract concepts and emotions, such as love, justice, and equality, as easily as they can ask someone to pass the potatoes at the dinner table.

The ability to express meanings symbolically is primarily responsible for the variety of groups, cultures, ideologies, and technologies throughout history. There is no activity in which people are engaged that does not involve acts of symbolizing—whether lecturing, voting, making love, or "being religious." Religion, in fact, consists entirely of symbols and of activities that are interpreted and mediated by symbols. This is true, whether the symbols have empirical referents or not. God, hell, salvation, Star of David, nirvana, guru, and mana—all have meaning to those initiated into a particular symbolic system. The meaning of each of these is not inherent in the word itself or in the combination of sounds, but is supplied by the believer. Even if divine truths have been revealed to people by a supernatural being, those truths have been expressed in human language, or are immediately translated into human language—otherwise the message would have no meaning for people.

Yet another primary sociological assumption about human nature is that *people become human only in groups*—admittedly a dramatic way of stating that the influence of groups on the human organism through socialization is crucial and far-reaching. We do not propose to debate the academic question of whether the newborn baby is, in fact, human. The point is simply that the newborn infant is not yet very much of what it is going to become, and that what it does become will be largely attributable to socializing influences. One of those socializing influences is religion, which affects everyone, whether or not they are born into a "religious" family, attend Sunday school, or are married by a member of the clergy, and so on. For religion also exerts an indirect influence on people, if only in an inverse way as a negative reference group, or through its influence on secular institutions.

Human Action is Directed toward Problem Solving

A fundamental assumption of sociology is that *every human action is in some form and to some degree a problem-solving act or mechanism.* Whether working at a job, getting married, planning a party, or genuflecting, the human being is engaged in the process of solving or resolving some existing (present) or anticipated (future) problem. The problem may be how to satisfy a biological need for nourishment, how to achieve victory on the athletic field, or how to get God to help you pass an exam this afternoon. In any case, the person perceives a problem that he or she must solve, either now or, if he or she fails to take appropriate action, in the future.

Religious behavior is problem solving like any other social activity. Praying, attending church services, observing religious laws, and having and talking about "mountaintop experiences," for example, are all religious activities that contribute in some way (at least from the perspective of the religious participant) toward solving a problem, either existing or antici- pated. Note that we are not suggesting (or denying) that religion, in fact, either solves problems or creates them. Rather, our point is that people often engage in religious activities *in the belief* that such behavior can solve problems or avoid them. Lest there be any misunderstanding, we must emphasize that throughout this book no attempt will be made to determine or question the truth or falsity, the efficacy or inefficacy, of religion in general, of any specific religion in particular, or of anyone's personal reli- gious beliefs. Engaged as we are in sociological investigation, we are concerned solely with what can be observed, including what people *believe* exists and happens.

All Social Phenomena are Interrelated

The final sociological assumption we need to clarify, before delving in detail into the sociology of religion, is that *all social phenomena within a given group or society are interrelated*. That is, all social phenomena are continually inter- acting, and every part becomes linked with every other, at least in an indirect way. More specifically, part A may not be influenced directly by part F, but F may be having some indirect influence through a chain of other factors or social phenomena called B, C, D, and E. Most important for our purposes, religion interacts with—is in a dynamic reciprocal relationship with—every other social phenomenon and process. Religion both influences them and is influenced by them; religion both acts and reacts, is both an independent variable and dependent variable, both cause and effect. This principle of the continual dialectic, involving religion and other social phenomena, is a central theme of this book, for determining the nature and extent of these mutual influences are key tasks in the sociology of religion.

We have now identified, in at least an introductory way, what sociol- ogy is. Now, more specifically, what do we suggest when we say that we are going to study religion as a social phenomenon, that is, take part in an activ- ity called the sociology of religion?

THE SOCIOLOGY OF RELIGION

Asserting that religion is a social phenomenon suggests several things. In the first place, the statement has a *nonevaluative intent*. Thus we are not going to be able to, nor will we want to, speak about the truth or falsity of religion. Speaking of religion in terms of the good, the true, and the beautiful may be worth- while and even stimulating for philosophers, theologians, and scientists, even sociologists, in some social situations; but such evaluative assertions take us beyond the scope of science. Sociology that claims to describe reality accurately demands that its practitioners approach their subjects—religion no less than any other (and perhaps more than most)—with all the neutrality and objectivity they can muster.

Of course, no sociologist can always (if ever) be perfectly neutral and objective with regard to his or her subject, let alone one so value-laden and emotionally charged as religion. Studies in the sociology of knowledge, as well as honest discussions that have punctured the myth of a truly "value-free" sociology, have been sufficient to discourage any such pretensions. Nonetheless, a conscious, deliberate striving for neutrality and objectivity must be present—indeed, it should be evident—in any sociological investigation.

The sociology of religion is also *empirical*—it can only study and reach conclusions about phenomena that are observable. In order to confirm or refute any particular theory, the sociologist must test that theory with relevant empirical observations or *data*. And since data are by their nature limited to the observable, the measurable, and the quantifiable, whatever elements of religion are spiritual or supernatural, in the sense that they cannot be seen with the eye or otherwise measured or recorded, are by definition beyond the purview of sociology.

Our characterization of the sociology of religion so far, as objective and empirical, can be summed up by stating that the sociology of religion is conducted according to the *scientific method*. By the scientific method we mean:

1. the systematic search for verifiable data (facts) firmly rooted in prior knowledge and theoretical formulations;
2. the production of evidence as opposed to hearsay, opinion, intuition, or common sense; and
3. the following of procedures that others can verify and replicate (reproduce under essentially identical conditions).

It is at this point that the sociologist of religion encounters probably the most strenuous objection from the religiously committed, which often runs something like:

> Since religion is related at its base primarily to the spiritual, the sacred, and often supernatural beings and forces—that is, to forces that are usually unseen—and involves matters of faith and feelings as well, anything the sociologist can say about religion, limited as he or she is to describing the observable, will be at best superficial and unimportant, at worst false and misleading.

J. Milton Yinger has supplied some useful imagery in speaking on this issue. He frames the objection to the empirical study of religion with the question, "How is it possible to see a stained-glass window from the outside?"[1] That is, the beauty and the message or picture of a church's stained glass window is visible only when one is inside and can see the sunlight shining through. Professor Yinger goes on to note, however, that the view from the inside constitutes only part of what can be learned about the window. Only from the outside, for example, can the viewer appreciate the exterior framework or context within which that window exists. Furthermore, there are, as Yinger suggests, pieces of information potentially important to understanding the significance of the window that have nothing to do with viewing it from the inside (or from the outside, for that matter): who built it, who installed it, who provides for its repair, who goes in to view it from the inside. We can also consider the reason why it was installed, what "outsiders" think of it, how it resembles or differs from other windows, whether the style of newer windows is the same or changing, and so on.

Rather than belaboring the obvious parallel that we are suggesting between this situation and the study of religion, it is enough to note that questions like these can be answered empirically, that they are important questions, and that the answers to them amplify our understanding. Granted, empirical data do not constitute the only information of any importance about religion. Nor can we claim that empirical or observable measures of religion reveal its "essence." Studying religion empirically places a certain restriction on our enterprise, but no more severe a restriction than is placed on the position of those who claim religion to be strictly concerned with spiritual matters and, therefore, off limits to empirical investigation. Each side of this issue can contribute to an understanding of the total phenomenon.

DEFINING RELIGION

In attempting to define religion, a common distinction made by sociologists has been between *substantive* and *functional* definitions. Substantive definitions attempt to identify and describe the "essence" or "substance" of religion—what religion *is* at its core. This has been very difficult to accomplish without also considering religion from the "functional" perspective of what religion *does* for people. Fundamental to explorations of the functional understanding of religion has been the observation that people desire to *know* more and to explain the mysterious elements that surround them literally everywhere and at all times—natural phenomena and events like thunder/lightening, floods, fire, sudden death, and so on, as well as questions of purpose, destiny, life's meaning, and the like. Throughout it all is a striving for comfort and hope, while in an ever-fragile life, that will help people understand and cope with danger, illness, tragedy, death, and uncertainties of many kinds.

Actually, the more one tries to understand and define religion, the more neither approach (substantive versus functional) is sufficient by itself to embrace what religion is, what it means to people, and what it does for them. Therefore, we will simply identify the major components of religion that are common to the social manifestations of what people have called "religion," and conclude with a one sentence working definition, as we begin our study of religion in society.

THE CHARACTERISTICS OF RELIGION

The English word *religion* has a Latin root; that much is certain. But there is disagreement over whether the Latin root word is *religare,* meaning "to bind together" (suggesting possibly the concept of a group or fellowship) or *relegere,* meaning "to rehearse, to execute painstakingly," referring probably to the repetitious nature of liturgy. Either word makes sense as a root, and each taps a dimension of religion that we will include in our definition. Yet it is clear that etymology by itself will not provide us with an ultimate answer to our problem of definition.

Religion is a Group Phenomenon

We will start with the concept suggested by the Latin word *religare*—the concept of the group or fellowship. Religion is first of all a group phenomenon. That is probably its most obvious physical characteristic, as we see places of worship all around us and have clear mental pictures of groups of people (congregations) assembling together in prayer, praise, and song in those local places of worship—or as we see hundreds of thousands of people enraptured below the Pope in St. Peter's Square as he gives his Easter blessing—or as we see hundreds of men kneeling in prayer facing Mecca on the floor of their mosque. As we will discuss in Chapter 2, religion essentially always becomes a group phenomenon, even when it seems to begin with an individual who has perhaps "had a vision" or feels he or she has a special insight to share with others.

We must quickly add that this is not to say that religion is not an individual phenomenon. Of course, it is that also. Every group is composed of individuals who incorporate into themselves as individuals what the group holds to be true and necessary to express and carry out. Certainly religion is an individual matter in any number of ways. It involves personal emotions and thoughts, insofar as one's religion is a matter of personal beliefs and behaviors and insofar as individuals are free to commit themselves to whichever religious system they prefer. It is individuals who absorb the beliefs taught them by the group; it is individuals who act on them and carry out their responsibilities and actions. In many religions, where there is a concept of an afterlife (heaven, nirvana, etc.), acceptance into that eternal reward is based in significant part on the individual's right belief and behavior. The group and its religion can tell individuals what they must believe, profess, and do; but in the end the individual must act according to his or her own volition.

Still, it would not make sense to expect that one could somehow systematically study every individual's personal religious beliefs. Sociology, being committed to systematic study of group behavior, has no such problem in that it concentrates on the group dimension of religion. But we will not totally exclude the individual in our discussions. In Chapter 5, for example, we will look specifically at the internalization of religion ("Becoming Religious"), which technically is within the sub-specialization in sociology called "social psychology." But even here our emphasis will be on the role of the group in the socialization process. Through all the chapters it should be clear that groups are indeed made up of individuals and we cannot think of one without the other. So, although our emphasis will be on groups, the individual is always there; and you, the reader, are there and should feel free to relate what you read and learn to *yourself as an individual*. What does it mean to you and for you? As we have stated above, all religions ultimately become an individual matter. But now, back to the group.

Sociologists are quite explicit in identifying the characteristics of a group. According to a definition that most sociologists would accept, a group has six major features. The first and most basic is that *a group is composed of two or more people (members) who have established certain patterns of interaction* including communication *with one another.* Such interaction does not necessarily take place continually, or even daily, nor does every member interact with every other member. Neither is this interaction necessarily face to face. The point is simply that the people who constitute a group—group members—are aware of one another (perhaps even know one another) and have established patterns of interaction characteristic of their group.

The second major feature of a group, according to our definition, is that *group members share certain common goals*—in fact, this is the reason they came together in the first place (although they may not have known it then). Thus the process of forming a group involves the fundamental sociological concept, introduced earlier in this chapter, that all human behavior consists of some sort of problem-solving activity. Saying that a group has common goals implies that individuals who are confronted with common problems have made contact and have agreed to work together toward the goal of solving those problems. Imagine, for example, five individuals, each deeply concerned about industrial-waste pollution in a certain trout stream, who through casual conversation (perhaps while trying to fish the stream) "discover" one another and subsequently form a group called STEP (Save Trout from Environmental Pollution), whose primary goal is reducing pollution in this and other trout streams. Thus what was originally the separate concern of five individuals has become a group concern, which in turn implies a certain common goal or set of goals that they share with one another.

Third, as a result of the above, *a group is guided by shared norms*. Once a group defines its goals, it then determines how to reach them; that is, the group specifies that such and such is what its members will do, as well as when, where, and how. All such specifications are norms—more or less formal expectations concerning appropriate behavior by one or all members of the group.

Fourth, *every group member has a role,* or set of functions, to fulfill. As such, a role consists of a set of specific norms the group wants carried out. The development of different roles within the group gives rise to what is known as *the division of labor.* Thus, whenever a member leaves the group or adopts a new role, the group may need to keep the division of labor in balance by recruiting someone else—either another member or an outsider—for that particular role.

Fifth, *a group functions collectively in accordance with a status system,* a hierarchy in which different amounts of power, authority, and prestige are accorded to different roles and to the individuals in them. Different groups, of course, have different criteria for establishing status rankings. Roles involving group coordination, decision-making, and interpretation, for example, which inherently carry the greatest authority and prestige, are often assigned to those individuals who are believed to perform these tasks most ably, although such other factors as seniority, wealth, and kinship can also be influential.

Sixth, *group members feel and express a sense of identification with the group:* "I belong," "This is my group." "Yes, I'm an active member of STEP." The degree of group commitment, dedication, and identification varies from member to member, and most groups are able to tolerate some such variability. But without a certain minimum amount of identification and commitment on the part of its members, a group will soon disintegrate.

These six characteristic features of a group obviously apply to religious groups no less than to any other kind. Thus, in studying religion as a group phenomenon, we already know many things to expect and even some questions to ask:

- How does a given religious group differ from all others in terms of these six aspects?
- What, for example, are the religious group's goals, its norms, its roles, its status criteria?
- Do the goals and norms change over time?
- How does the group handle conflict over changes in and challenges to the norms and goals?
- Do we see that the group has indeed changed over time?

- How committed to one another are the members of the group?
- Is the group growing and attracting new members?

And so on.

Religion Involves a Body of Beliefs

A second characteristic of religion is that it invariably includes or implies a body of beliefs. While beliefs are, of course, norms and have therefore implicitly been included in one of the six characteristics of groups identified earlier, they are of sufficient importance to include as a major characteristic of all religions. These are part of the religious sacred lore that has been handed down over the generations of the religion's existence. In preliterate societies, these beliefs are handed down from generation to generation by way of oral tradition.

All major world religions, and some minor ones, have their sacred book or books that spell out or at least provide the basis for determining the beliefs the group holds. Some examples are the Bible, the Qur'an (Koran), the Book of Mormon, and the Bhagavad Gita. Furthermore, every major religion has beliefs in addition to those contained in such "official" or basic writings—the interpretations and extensions of lesser prophets and of other successors to the founder(s) of the religion, for example. A prime instance is the Talmud, a commentary and clarification of the Old Testament accumulated over centuries by scholarly rabbis. Then, too, there is in every religion (and not just in those of preliterate societies) the oral tradition—unwritten explanations, in the form of sagas, proverbs, and myths handed down to each new generation by word of mouth.

Religion Involves a Set of Practices

A third characteristic of religion is that it universally involves specific practices, which consist of acting out certain normative expectations. One of the most obvious features of any religion—obvious because it consists of behavior rather than beliefs, attitudes, or perspectives—is the performance of ritual and the host of other activities generated by its beliefs. The gathering to worship, the rain dance, the sacrifice of animal or person, the ceremonial foot washing, the immersing in water at baptism, the vigil, the liturgical worship service form—all are examples of religious practices.

It is important to understand that there is nothing intrinsically religious in a given act—an act or practice becomes religious only when the group defines it as such. Thus, the act of eating a meal together may be no more than "filling one's belly," or it may be an *agape* (love feast) of the first-century Christians, or a ceremonial enactment of the Last Supper. One may wear a robe solely to fend off the cold, or (in medieval Europe to indicate one's academic rank, and to fend off the cold), or one may wear it to indicate that he or she is a holy person or messenger of God. Journeying to a distant town may be for the purpose of conducting business or shopping, or it may be for fulfilling the religious obligation of making a pilgrimage to a holy city at least once during one's lifetime.

Religion Involves Moral Prescriptions

A fourth feature of religion that, although certainly not unique to religious groups, is emphasized in all of them, is the moral dimension. This refers to the judgment a religious group or system makes that certain thoughts and ideas are good and worthwhile, to be encouraged, and to be positively reinforced, while other actions, thoughts, and ideas are bad, harmful, and to be rejected by the faithful. Another way of saying this, is that a religion advocates certain behaviors with the intention of encouraging its adherents to choose such behaviors in everyday situations. Frequently a "higher" source or basis for its morality is claimed:

> You should do something or refrain from doing it because God says so
> or it is in tune with cosmic forces, not simply because our group says so
> or because I, your leader, say so.

In other words, religion invokes the sacred or supernatural in order to influence the behavior of individuals, not only in extraordinary situations or in situations defined as religious, but in all the ordinary, routine ones as well. In many societies, especially small, perhaps preliterate ones, the consensus and moral authority of the group itself was more than enough to keep group members "in line." We need to keep in mind that in many traditional societies, such religious principles are viewed as *in the nature of things*. It would not enter members' minds to question them or violate them. We also need to keep in mind that the mere idea of moral principles as something separable from other norms of thought and behavior in the group—all of which are in the nature of things—are not open to question or challenge.

Religion Involves the Sacred

The final characteristic that we wish to include in our definition of *religion*, is its involvement with what Durkheim identified as the *sacred*,[2] what Rudolf Otto termed the *holy* or the *wholly other*,[3] and essentially what Mircea Eliade refers to as *sacred space* that is qualitatively different from all other *homogenous* space in which regular, everyday occurrences and activities take place.[4] There is a universal tendency for religion to urge awe, reverence, and fear with regard to certain things, beings, or situations and to distinguish them from the ordinary, the mundane—or, as Durkheim defines it, the *profane*. Old Testament Jews removed their sandals upon entering the temple, many Christians make the sign of the cross when praying to God, Hindus give cows the right of way,

Muslims undertake pilgrimages to Mecca, American Indians avoid disturbing holy plots of ground. All such behavior expresses the recognition of a sacred place or situation. In each instance, people acknowledge being in the presence of something special—something above and beyond them that demands adopting special attitudes, performing certain actions, and perhaps articulating special words and sounds as well.

For many people—for whole religious systems, for that matter—that "something special," the *sacred*, in fact involves the *supernatural*, a power or being not subject to the laws of the observable universe. Such a power may be personified by Jesus, by Vishnu, by Allah, or by any number of gods, devils, goblins, or spirits. Or perhaps it is simply a vague and diffuse power, such as that identified by the Polynesian term *mana* (which we shall discuss shortly).

In these beliefs, a dichotomy of reality is being expressed. On the one hand, there are the "profane" (ordinary) events and the visible environment of the routine workaday world. On the other hand, there is the invisible, largely uncontrollable, out-of-the-ordinary realm. To a greater or lesser degree, people can control and predict familiar everyday situations—the choice of daily tasks, conversations with others, the acts of eating and making love, the seeking of nightly rest, and so on. But most people seem to believe that there is more to life than such ordinary situations and events. What about the big bang in the sky last week and the twisting dagger of light that preceded it? What about my friend who dropped dead while running beside me? What about that place in the swamp where a whole hunting party was swallowed up in the mud? Such things are out of the ordinary; they cannot be taken for granted; they elicit fear, awe, and respect. We are here—in the presence of Otto's "wholly other"—an entirely different order of existence.

It should be emphasized that the experiences that people define as sacred vary considerably and the objects of their awe and reverence are infinitely diverse. Yet every society has its list of such awesome and mysterious things and events. Religion deals with them; religion provides explanations and answers; religion prescribes methods of placation and of expressing appropriate reverence. The sacred, the holy, the supernatural, together with people's relationship to them, thus constitute the prime subject matter of religion.

Although the term *sacred* may occasionally connote little more than "deserving or demanding respect," with no necessary thought of a supernatural power being involved, it is common for the two concepts to go together. That which is considered sacred is so, precisely because some supernatural force or activity arouses the feeling of awe that surrounds the sacred object, person, place, or situation. But they are not strictly synonymous concepts. And, while one might always observe sacredness when the idea of the supernatural is present, sacredness can occur without belief in the supernatural. So, in the interests of precision and clarity of the concepts of *sacred* and *supernatural*, we shall regard only the sacred as essential to religion.

This allows us to include several thought systems that most people would almost intuitively think of as religious systems, yet upon closer examination they are found to express no concept of the supernatural, particularly in the sense of a supreme being, such as the Christian God or Muslim Allah. We would mention, as examples, Jainism, Ethical Culture, early Buddhism, and early Confucianism. Further, we would also include strong commitments to such thought systems, philosophies, and world-views as socialism, Marxism, humanism, scientism, and nationalism, as well as "civil religion," a phenomenon we will discuss in Chapter 7, "Religion and Politics."

While we will not devote any significant space to discussing these "Isms" in the rest of this text, two quick examples will summarize how close these thought systems or world-views are to what we all would think of as traditional religions. First, communism: it has its "religious" elements—its prophets in Marx and Engels, its firm emphasis on orthodox socialistic beliefs, its ritual parades and celebrations, its sacred shrines, and a missionary zeal and unquestioning commitment of its strongest adherents. Similarly, with scientism, one sees a system of beliefs about the utility of scientific endeavors for the ultimate welfare of the world and its people, a set of practices required of all adherents—the scientific method, prophets of old—the founding fathers of modern science, sacred places—the laboratory, the computer, and "clean" room, supreme loyalty and commitment of its adherents, even the missionary zeal with which proponents try to win others to share their faith in scientific endeavor.

A WORKING DEFINITION OF RELIGION

In attempting to define religion formally, we shall go no further than to gather together the ingredients we have discussed, with but one exception. That exception is the inclusion of a term contributed by Peter Berger a generation ago that deserves to be included in most any definition of religion because of its succinct descriptive power. That is the two-word phrase "sacred canopy," which he used in his book title and also called a "sheltering canopy."[5] Berger used this term to describe religion's function as a protective cover shielding society from chaos and individuals from anomy (feelings of normlessness, rootlessness, nothingness). Religion thus serves to provide answers to peoples' questions and concerns over purpose, destiny, and mystery, as well as comfort and support in times of danger, bereavement, and death. One might say the canopy shields and shelters those who have huddled together as a group for mutual support and protection.

The definition we propose is simply this:

> Religion is a set of beliefs and rituals by which a group of people seeks to understand, explain, and deal with a world of complexity, uncertainty, and mystery, by identifying a sacred canopy of explanation and reassurance under which to live.

Let it be clearly understood that by employing this definition we are, for purposes of sociological investigation at least, adopting the position of the hard-hosed relativist and agnostic. That is, we are neither affirming nor denying whether what a group defines as sacred is or is not, in fact, sacred or true. We *are* asserting, however, that people in groups often identify certain beings, events, and objects as sacred. These beliefs, and the attitudes and behavior stemming from them, thus become the subject matter of the sociology of religion.

It should be clear by now that this definition is to be understood as neither the final nor the best definition of religion; rather, it is a pragmatic, functional one—one, moreover, that is reasonably in tune with what the majority of people consider religion to be. This latter point is particularly important, for it is unnecessary and unwise to deliberately define religion in a manner too different from the way that most people understand it.

THE DEFINITION APPLIED TO "MAGIC"

Before ending our formal treatment of the definition of *religion* (in a real sense, the remainder of this book represents an elaboration and explication of our definition), we need to apply our definition to the question of whether magic (not stage magic, of course, but magic in the original sense of using charms and spells to control supernatural forces) can best be regarded as a form of religion or whether it is clearly something else. Note that we discussed earlier whether the so-called "Isms" should be considered religions.

What is Magic?

By way of introduction to the issue of magic, we must consider the concept of *mana* (a Polynesian term), which is common in "primitive" religions, and vestiges of which appear in the religious systems of industrial societies as well. Purnell Benson notes, for example, that mana appears in numerous religions under various names—in Hinduism it is *darshan*; in Christianity it is *divine grace*; among American Indians it was called *manito* by the Algonquins, *wakanda* by the Sioux, *orenda* by the Iroquois, and *maxpe* by the Crow.[6]

Mana is a prime ingredient in magic. To those who believe in it, there exists in the world, everywhere, and in everything, an elemental force, a primary energy—mana. Mana even exists—it floats, so to speak—in the very air we breathe. Often it is just *there*, not directly attached to anything, simply waiting to be grasped, harnessed, used. Though mana is in people, in things, in animals, in plants, and in the atmosphere, it is impotent until someone or something, or a spirit perhaps, activates it by discovering the secret key that unlocks its energies.

Enter magic, which attempts to exercise power over people and things by controlling the ubiquitous mana. The practice of magic is not an expression of ignorance, as is commonly supposed, but a conscious, deliberate attempt to circumvent what might normally be expected to occur. That is, magic is typically used to undercut the predictable by marshaling sufficient mana—elemental force—to change what otherwise would be inevitable.

In those societies where magic is most likely to be practiced and condoned (the more "primitive" societies), people make little if any distinction between magic and religion—or for that matter among scientific knowledge, religious knowledge, common-sense knowledge, and magic. Knowledge is knowledge, be it scientific, religious, or any other. This lack of categories, of course, makes the task of distinguishing between magic and religion a bit more difficult.

Similarities with Religion

We may begin, however, by noting the similarities and the differences or contrasts that have been suggested in the long debate over the relationship of religion and magic. First, some similarities:

1. both are serious attempts to deal with and solve the basic problems people face;
2. both are based on faith in the existence and efficacy of powers that cannot be seen and can only be inferred by results;
3. both involve ritual activity, traditionally prescribed patterns of behavior; and
4. both are bona fide elements of the group's larger culture and have well-defined norms and taboos to follow and observe.

Bronislaw Malinowski describes other similarities. He notes that both religion and magic grow out of situations of emotional stress, such as life crises, failures, death, unrequited love, and anger turned to hate. In addition, both religion and magic pose escapes from such difficult, emotional situations that offer no solutions by other means. That is, both suggest a supernatural solution "in the atmosphere of the miraculous."[7]

Differences from Religion

Some differences or contrasts follow:

1. Religion more often centers on such overarching issues as salvation and the meaning of life and death, whereas magic is more likely to be employed in

grappling with current, concrete problems (counteracting a viper's bite, bringing rain, defeating the enemy, for example);

2. Religion is more often future-oriented, while magic is primarily concerned with the here and now (or at least the very near future);

3. Religion's orientation toward supernatural powers tends to be one of obeisance and supplication, involving sacrifice and prayer (such as asking the appropriate deity or spirit to act on one's behalf), whereas magic is more manipulative, more often suggestive of pride than of humility (the magician seeks direct control over things and events, even at times seeking to trick the deity or defeat the deity in a contest, if he or she can control enough mana); and

4. Religion is characteristically a group activity, with groups of people collectively engaged in rituals and worship, while magic is typically an individual affair—the magician against the world, so to speak.

Of course, it is important to recognize that the magician conducts his or her work within a group (the society), and that in a real sense it is the group that *allows* the magician to work. Thus, even though the magician works alone, his or her work is group sanctioned.

Are religion and magic, then, different phenomena, or two aspects of the same phenomenon? Or is one a subpart of the other? The last alternative is probably the most helpful way to see their relationship. Recalling our definition of religion, we find that magic fulfills each of our criteria—magic consists of beliefs and practices; it clearly is concerned with the sacred and the supernatural; and it is practiced by an individual. In fact, the relationship of magic to religion is virtually a classic example of specialization, for magic is typically practiced where the religious system considers it a legitimate and useful activity and encourages or at least allows its use. Thus, magic is probably best seen neither as a competitor with religion nor as an alternative to it, but as a specialized subunit of religion. In fact, rarely is religion without at least some magical elements, just as magic is seldom practiced entirely apart from a larger religious system that legitimates it.

Final Reflection on the Definition of Religion

As readers reflect a moment on our task of defining religion, they might sense some ambivalence. If so, we have achieved one of our purposes in this chapter. Frankly, as we write this, we face a dilemma that cannot be resolved to the satisfaction of all. The dilemma resides in the recognition that:

1. our definition of religion (the six characteristics) is not inclusive of all phenomena that may in some sense be "religious," and it tends to be "conservative" in the sense that the focus is inevitably upon what has been traditionally recognized as religious—the religious institution in society; and that

2. such traditional institutional forms of religion do happen to be a prominent feature of societies and, as such, merit analysis and understanding.

Thus, we have opted in this introductory text to concentrate on what is commonly regarded as religion and seems to fall fairly cleanly within our definition (a fantastically broad array of data and developments as it is). But we recognize and draw attention to the fact that there is most likely much more that can legitimately be called religion than this. Thus, in one sense we conclude this chapter, deliberately leaving the issue of defining religion somewhat open-ended. Yet we also proceed from a close-ended approach, as we pragmatically attempt to cover a manageable subject. That is, we will spend most of our time in this text discussing religion as included in our definition. But we strongly assert that when the discussion is ended, we will only have begun to talk about what could have been included from other perspectives or definitions.

A CONCLUDING HISTORICAL NOTE: THE DEVELOPMENT OF THE SOCIOLOGY OF RELIGION

A clearly identifiable interest in a formalized sociological study of religion goes back only about a hundred and fifty years, roughly coincident with the beginning of formalized sociology in general in the last half of the nineteenth century. The stimulus for sociological interest in religion seems to have been the reports of anthropologists during the early and middle nineteenth century, who encountered and studied "primitive" societies in Africa and Oceania. Two significant observations made by these social scientists were:

1. the existence everywhere of some form of religion; and
2. the fascinatingly wide variety of religious forms and behaviors.[8]

In other words, religion was observed to be as diverse as it was widespread. Such had always been true, of course, but as long as societies remained relatively isolated, the diversity and universality of religion were not fully appreciated. The advent of European colonialism and the consequent increase in world trade and commercial interaction after the Middle Ages, raised the frequency and intensity of intersocietal contacts and eventually led to ethnographical investigations by social scientists. As a result, more and more people began taking an interest in understanding and explaining the worldwide diversity of religion.

Following the initial flurry of social scientists' interest in religion (initiated by early anthropologists), sociological interest in and research on religion, with a few notable exceptions, lay somewhat dormant until fairly recently. David Moberg has suggested several reasons for this:

1. Some sociologists, discouraged by the close historical association of religion with philosophy and metaphysics, decided that religion could not fruitfully be studied empirically;
2. Other sincerely interested sociologists yielded to the opposition to sociological research on religion that came from many religious groups;
3. Those teaching in state universities were fearful of jeopardizing their positions, if they should somehow overstep the boundary separating church and state;
4. Others, convinced that religion was definitely on its way to extinction anyway, preferred not to waste their time; and
5. Still others, who had personally rejected religion, were reluctant to maintain any contact with it—even if only of a research nature.[9]

The notable exceptions included some of the early sociological giants, such as Émile Durkheim, Georg Simmel, and Max Weber, who devoted a significant portion of their scholarly energies to analyzing the role of religion in society. After Weber's publication of his *Sociology of Religion* in 1921, however, little research or theoretical development occurred in the sociology of religion until after World War II, when there was a dramatic upsurge in religious activity, particularly in the United States. Significant increases in church membership and attendance at religious services, extensive building programs, and the establishment of hundreds of new congregations each year, engendered serious talk of a religious revival.

Sociologists became interested. Here was a social phenomenon to explore and explain, a development that was particularly intriguing, in that many social scientists had long been predicting the eventual and even precipitous demise of religion, particularly in its institutional form. The sociologists' new research interest in religion, which began in the late 1940s and early 1950s, has continued essentially unabated to the present and is attracting some of the best minds in sociology. One reason for this is that these new developments in religion, which clamor for investigation and explanation, have continued at a rapid pace. Furthermore, the persistence of religion in its various forms has finally forced sociologists to renew the effort, initiated by early fathers of sociology, like Durkheim and Weber, of attempting to understand the nature and function of religion. For both these reasons, this book concentrates on systematizing sociological research and theoretical efforts that have appeared during the past thirty-five years or so—not because the newest efforts are necessarily the best ones, but simply because most of the empirical work in the field is of relatively recent vintage. Indeed, it appears that social scientists are beginning to fulfill in part the prophecy of the anthropologist James Frazer, who predicted some eighty years ago that the time would come when the religions of the world would no longer be regarded in terms of their truth or falsehood but simply as phenomena to be studied like any other expression of humanity.[10]

NOTES

1. J. Milton Yinger, *The Scientific Study of Religion* (New York: Macmillan, 1970), p. 2.

2. Émile Durkheim, *The Elementary Forms of the Religious Life*, trans. Joseph Ward Swain (New York: Collier, 1961), p. 52.

3. Rudolf Otto, *The Idea of the Holy*, trans. John W. Harvey (London: Oxford University Press, 1936), pp. 8–41.

4. Mircea Eliade, *The Sacred and the Profane*, trans. Willard R. Trask (New York: Harcourt Brace Jovanovich, 1959), p. 20.

5. Peter Berger, *The Sacred Canopy* (Garden City, NY: Doubleday and Company, 1967, 1969).

6. Purnell H. Benson, *Religion in Contemporary Culture* (New York: Harper & Brothers, 1960), p. 136.

7. Bronislaw Malinowski, *Magic, Science, and Religion* (Garden City, NY: Anchor Books, 1954; originally published by The Free Press, 1948), p. 87.

8. This pair of observations is suggested by J. Milton Yinger in *Sociology Looks at Religion* (New York: Macmillan, 1961), pp. 11–12.

9. David O. Moberg, *The Church as a Social Institution* (Englewood Cliffs, NJ: Prentice Hall, 1962), p. 13.

10. James Frazer, *The Gorgon's Head* (London: Macmillan, 1927), pp. 281–282.

Chapter 2

The Sources of Religion

Religion emerges anywhere/everywhere.

We now approach what is admittedly a speculative, but at the same time a fascinating, issue in the sociology of religion—the question of the origins and sources of religion. When we realize that the question is phrased not so often, "Where does religion come from?" but instead, "Why are people religious?" we see that the question of origins and sources is a relatively common one—one that has intrigued philosophers throughout the centuries and scientists more recently. When people observe what we have come to think of as religious behavior and become curious about why people are doing or saying what they are, they are raising a question that, by implication, goes far beyond the immediate event and the persons involved in it. Ultimately, the question is: From where did these ideas and practices come?

Or, to be more ultimate yet, how did the idea of a God, or supernatural and sacred forces and entities, originate in the first place? The answers to such questions, whether immediate or ultimate, have been many and varied, although we will soon discover that they can be organized fairly conveniently into relatively few categories.

The question of religion's origin *per se* is no longer actively pursued by social science, for any evidence of an origin or origins has been lost in prehistory. Attempts to reconstruct origins by examining contemporary preliterate societies have, in fact, served only to delay slightly the admission that such evidence, if it ever existed, is lost in antiquity. It is important to recognize that the scientific method is limited in this regard; in fact, it is incapable of establishing absolutely verifiable conclusions about past events on the basis of present or even known past realities. Thus, even when substantial evidence appears to support an attractive theory, any hypothesis regarding religion's origins is doomed to remain forever tentative. There will be more on this problem later in the chapter.

Yet despite such limitations in the pursuit of religion's origins, we propose to explore the question briefly. We do this because of the historical value and intellectual stimulation such a look at the past provides; but more important, such an exploration will serve to introduce us to several relevant contemporary issues in the sociology of religion, which we will discuss more fully later. These are such issues as the functional view of religion, the nature and extent of social influences upon religion, the possibility of changing roles for religion in society, and to some extent the conflict between theology and sociology regarding an analysis of religion.

With regard to prehistoric people, it seems reasonable to assume, on the basis of available evidence, that they seldom, probably never, had questions about the sources of their religious beliefs and practices. Their religious elements were such integral parts of their culture and normative system that they most likely saw them simply as "in the nature of things." Things were that way and always had been. Therefore, there was little likelihood that questions of religious origins would occur to these people. There were often myths and tales of the origins of human beings or of one's society in particular, but seeing religion as something distinct from the rest of one's beliefs, values, and practices in society was not likely.

REVELATION AS ORIGIN

With the beginning of Christianity and, before that, Judaism, part of the answer was extremely simple—God was the originator of religions. God created the world and the people in it; in the Garden of Eden he had already established some general principles and laws; he later spoke through selected prophets, and they recorded God's words and their own God-inspired commentary. God himself was directly at work instructing his people, and in the process was creating religion through the process of revelation.

This hypothesis or explanation of a divine origin of religion is not unique to Judaism and Christianity. Even Gautama Buddha, the founder of Buddhism, reports having experienced heavenly inspiration as he sat under the bo tree, practically at the end of his tether in his quest for truth. The insight around which he developed his religious system hit him out of the blue, so to speak; he had a "revelation." The revelation that inspired Mormonism was in the form of golden plates buried in a hill, called Cumorah, in New York State. John Smith said he received from God the key to translating and interpreting what was on the plates. Muhammad reported receiving visions (the revelation) from the angel Gabriel in a cave near Mecca.

All such cases report the belief that either God himself or some other cosmic, supernatural force intervened in history, altered the normal course of events, and deliberately added to what had been previously known and discovered. Whether by personal contact with the divine power, an experience with an intermediary, sudden inspired insight, or discovery of secret written messages, it is the direct intrusion of a supernatural power with new knowledge and insight for humanity.

In turn, of course, such religious leaders, as they speak and write for the followers that gather around them, are themselves sources of revelation for the religious system that has begun to develop. As they become defined as gods or, at the very least, spokespersons for divinity, what they utter is revelation. Leaders of cults and new religious movements, about whom we will hear more later, fit in here as they claim to bring new messages and interpretations from God. Jim Jones, instigator of the Jonestown mass suicide, claimed to carry new messages from God to the Peoples' Temple, and David Koresh was in the process of writing a new interpretation (inspired by God, he believed) of the Seven seals in the New Testament Book of Revelation as the Waco conflagration began. In other words, revelation for some religious groups need not be something only from ancient history but can be new, fresh, and contemporary.

It is important to realize that such revelational explanations, for the origins of religion, concern what believers consider to be the only "true" religion—that is, their own. Proponents of the revelation hypothesis usually refer only to their religion as the one revealed by God. Other religions exist, of course, but their source is something else, an inferior source, although it is likely that other religions are hard at work trying to find the very truth that God has given only to "us."

THE "NATURAL-KNOWLEDGE-OF-GOD" EXPLANATION

Christian theologians, claiming direct revelation from God for the gift of "true" religion as found in the Holy Bible, have always been intrigued by the existence of other religions. If God revealed himself directly only to the

Chosen People of Israel, they asked themselves: How did the religions of other peoples arise? The answer they settled on, based on scattered verses from the Bible, was the "natural-knowledge-of-God" concept: All human beings are born with a fundamental awareness of the divine, a rudimentary knowledge that God or some power is ultimately responsible for what they see around them. All other religions, then, are the result of people's striving to build on this fundamental awareness and make some sense out of it. The great diversity of religious systems is then relatively easy to explain. Because the initial awareness of God is so vague and diffuse, people are forced to call upon their imagination and experiences in developing these systems. And since the imaginations and experiences of people are so diverse, the religious systems they evolve consequently differ.

Associated with the natural-knowledge-of-God idea is the "witness-of-nature" concept: The wonder and complexity of nature reinforces people's innate knowledge of the divine and motivates them to seek explanations. What I see around me—the cycle of seasons, the wonder of the flora and fauna, the majesty of the mountains, the splendor of the sun by day and the moon and stars at night—must have been brought into existence by someone or some power, some god or gods. And perhaps that god has helpers for specific spheres and activities, such as the oceans, farming, lovemaking, and war. Eventually a complex system evolves from an original "seed of divine awareness."

Sociologists can obviously neither confirm nor refute such a hypothesis. As we shall soon see, however, except for the idea of inherent initial awareness, this attempt to explain the origins of religion is basically in harmony with modern sociological and anthropological concepts. That is, there is a recognition that people themselves create their norms and beliefs and thought systems in response to their experiences and surroundings, and that a fundamental factor in such experiences is their contact with the physical and natural environment. But more on such sociological views later in this chapter.

ANTHROPOLOGICAL EXPLANATIONS

We now turn from explanations of theologians to those of social scientists, who have attempted to explain the sources or origins of religion on the basis of empirical observations. We first focus on the anthropologists, particularly those of the nineteenth century, who were so instrumental in stimulating investigation of religion from the perspective of social science. They all believed that religion somehow arose in response to the experiences of people in the world in which they lived. As preliterate people encountered awesome, mysterious, even terrifying events—thunder and lightning, earthquakes, tidal waves and floods, illness, birth and death—they felt the need to understand their causes. Thus religious systems gradually evolved out of people's need to assign causes for so-called natural phenomena and other recurrent experiences.

Some differences in emphasis and focus among early anthropologists are worth noting. Max Müller, for example, is a representative of the "naturistic" school, which emphasized the role of physical acts of nature—natural events like storms, sunrises, tides.[1] Prehistoric people were fearful and almost completely defenseless and at the mercy of these events: Why do they happen and why to me in particular? Müller suggests that since prehistoric people saw other people cause events—push rocks, throw stones about, shoot arrows, fell trees, and so on—they reasoned that *everything* that happens must be caused either by other human beings or humanlike agents. What evolved then was the belief in spirits—invisible beings much like people in the sense that they possessed wills and abilities to bring about effects by their actions. It is these spirits who *cause* natural events. Thus prehistoric people might suggest that a spirit crashes giant circles of granite together and produces thunder; that a fire-breathing spirit spits out lightning; that spirits move about in the depths of the earth and cause an earthquake; that a spirit takes the sun out of its basket and puts it on a ledge in the sky each morning; and so on.

Early anthropologists discovered, among the "primitive" peoples they studied, an apparently universal belief in such spirits, a phenomenon termed *animism*—the belief that all sorts of inanimate objects, as well as living, growing things and moving creatures, possess a life principle or soul of some kind. Rocks, trees, animals, and people have spirits in them, whereas some spirits are freewheeling and unattached to specific things. All spirits, however, are conceived of in a thorough-going anthropomorphic fashion—that is, they have shapes, minds, feelings, and wills, though they are invisible beings. They are much like people in that they can be amenable to sound arguments or placating gifts, particularly when they are in a good mood. They can also be quarrelsome, nasty, and dangerous when upset or angry. They like flattery, loyalty, and deference. Therefore, one must be continually vigilant to stay on their right side.

Thus when a coconut fell nearby, the prehistoric person is less likely to have said, "The coconuts are ripe; it's coconut season again," and more likely to have asked, "Who threw it? What did I do now to make a spirit angry?" Or perhaps, "Great, I've received a gift from the coconut spirit again; may there be many more." Or tripping over a root in the path, they were less likely to curse their clumsiness and more likely to ask why the root's spirit reached out and grabbed them: "Was it only a playful jest, or a warning that worse may happen if I don't shape up in some way?"

Whereas Müller emphasized the external events of nature, Edward Tylor, who represents the "animistic" school, focused on such personal experiences as dreams and seeing one's reflection in the water.[2]

When I dream of sexual conquest, or felling the enemy on the field of
battle, or running from a tiger, what is happening is that the spirit that
resides in me (my soul) is out for the night—having a ball, displaying
his or her valor, or running into a bit of trouble. My image in the stream?
Why it is none other than my spirit looking up at me. See, when I smile,
it smiles; when I frown, it frowns.

Another representative anthropologist, Robert Lowie, focused on those
experiences that generate a sense of "mystery and weirdness" in people. For
Lowie, religion is not simply a matter of identifying spirits or distinguishing
body and soul. Rather, religion only arose when people's emotions became
involved and a sense of mystery pervaded people's observations of the
activities that spirits engage in.[3]

A recent critique of Tylor's work, by J. Samuel Preus, is that Tylor "could
not satisfactorily explain *why* religion not only survives but thrives, in modern as well as archaic times."[4] Tylor was probably hindered in anticipating
religion's survival in complex, scientifically—sophisticated societies, by the
widely—shared conviction that religion would not survive the evolution of
society and the rapid development of knowledge and technology into the
present day.[5]

Mary Douglas is a contemporary anthropologist who finds few true
universals in what we today would consider the arena of religion. For example, Douglas rejects the earlier anthropological idea that all "primitives"
were nature worshipers by asserting: "Indeed, in certain tribal places there is
a notable lack of interest in the supernatural."[6]

Clifford Geertz goes much further than his anthropological forebears,
who tended to concentrate on small preliterate societies. The early anthropologists, observing the animism of these peoples and the religions of spirits
that developed, in effect generalized to religion in general. Yet the religions
of small prehistoric societies in Africa or South America seem to be very
different from, say, Islam, as practiced by whole societies of millions of
people, or Christianity, as espoused by many large complex societies. Geertz
overcomes this gap and potential contradiction by distinguishing traditional
religion from rationalized religion. *Traditional religions,* which almost
assuredly will have a great deal of magic in them, are practiced in more
simple, prehistoric ("primitive") societies; *rationalized religions* are more
abstract and logical, with the divine power or essence more removed from
much of everyday experience. Such rationalized religions raise issues to
their cosmic level, as in: What is evil? and Where does suffering come from?
Traditional religions seldom look for the cosmic generalization; instead, they
are more situationally—oriented, as in: Who or what caused my son to die?
What has made me so terribly ill this year?[7]

Many more hypotheses developed by anthropologists could be cited, but
the above examples are enough to make the point that what we are calling

anthropological explanations for the origin of religion, focus primarily on people's belief in spirits and in what these spirits do. Such beliefs arise largely from needs of prehistoric people to explain natural events in the physical environment as well as their own experiences. In a real sense, this is a need for rationality of a sort, for a means of making coherent the many things people have no control over.

This is what social scientists call the *cognitive need* explanation for religion. That is, people want to know and understand the "what" and the "why" of the goings on around them. Explanations often evolve that place the source of mysterious events in the hands of supernatural beings and forces that reside in sacred spaces.

PSYCHOLOGICAL EXPLANATIONS

Another broad area of explanation, the psychological perspective, in general treats the origins of religion in terms of people's emotional needs—in other words, not so much like Müller and Tylor, who emphasized people's cognitive needs to explain the mysterious, but more in terms of their need to resolve and adjust emotionally to the mysterious and the disastrous, more like Lowie's emphasis. In this view, people seek to maintain emotional stability in the face of danger, insecurity, and disruption, particularly as they encounter illness, accident, and death: How can I keep going as my world (health, personal relationships, and so on) crumbles about me? Why do disasters happen to me and to those I love? Can I make any sense out of it all? How can I find strength to go on? Can I have hope for the future?

Erwin R. Goodenough expresses this perspective clearly when he describes religion as the response of human beings to constant threats to their safety, security, and future existence. In particular, people face great insecurity and anxiety related to the knowledge that they shall not only ultimately perish but that it could happen at any moment. He calls this the *tremendum*—a Latin word referring to "that which must be feared" or the "source of terror."[8]

As an extension of this, a common psychological explanation suggests that people seek solutions and answers for such frustration, anxiety, and fear, by trying to fit their experience into the larger framework of a divine plan with a long-range perspective: All things work out for those who love God; things will be better in the by and by; he died because God needed him more than we did; God is testing me to see if I am worthy; my sins have caught up with me, and I am being punished.

Psychologist, Walter Huston Clark, has borrowed W. I. Thomas's idea that people basically have four "wishes" or drives—for security, response, recognition, and new experience—and contends that these are reasonably comprehensive for understanding the psychological need and appeal of religion.[9] This leads us beyond the idea of emotional adjustment just expressed, although we are still dealing quite specifically with emotional needs that the individual strives to fulfill—specifically, according to Clark's approach, through religion.

Another psychologist, George S. Spinks, agrees with Clark by speaking of religion as actively fulfilling fundamental human needs but takes this idea a step further by emphasizing the uncertainties and terrors that continually threaten to overwhelm the individual.[10] As such, he and Goodenough say the same thing.

Sigmund Freud, the "father of psychoanalysis," sees religion stemming primarily from a sense of guilt derived, at least partly, from the Oedipus complex and the attempts by the male to reconstruct a father image after his "love affair" with his mother and his ritual "killing" of his father. Thus, for Freud, religion is a mechanism that allows people to sublimate many of the primitive instincts in people that society represses.[11]

Another perception that Freud uses extensively is the concept of projection. In projection, the god characters are really representations (projections) of wishes and conflicts within the person. God the Father, Christ, the stories of the original paradise and the "fall into sin," the ideas of the devil and immortality—these are all projections from the unconscious mind. Freud believed that gradually psychology would fathom the relationships.

Freud adds that a basic desire of people is to control some of the terrifying forces that surround them. A model for such control appears early in the lives of many persons—that model is the child's father. Thus, the family setting and role functions within the family (the patriarchal father role, in particular) becomes the basis for projection of "fatherly" qualities, both of authority and of problem-solving and answer-giving to the gods and supernatural powers that make up religious systems. We might add here, although getting a little ahead of ourselves, that Freud is really quite sociological in his perspective on this point. The group setting, and the role structure of that group, play significant parts in Freud's analysis.

In general, then, from the psychological point of view, religion serves an adjustment function. That is, it helps people survive frustration in trying to fulfill or serve drives and needs, and in trying to adapt to the frightening experiences that threaten their emotional integrity.

While we earlier credited anthropologists with the cognitive need explanation as an important component in understanding reasons for the development of religion, particularly its supernatural elements, this is an emphasis within psychology as well. Abraham Maslow said that a person has a "cognitive need to understand." Life needs to have a meaningful framework for the person to survive. Thus, a person "needs a religion or religious surrogate to live by, in about the same sense that he needs sunlight, calcium, or love."[12]

Erich Fromm notes that everyone has a religious need, "a need to have a frame of orientation and an object of devotion."[13] He states further that the question is not whether a person will have religion but whether it will further the development of humankind or hinder it.[14] There is no assurance that religion will be an ultimately beneficial force in one's life but it will give orientation and direction, and will provide an object of devotion. Fromm notes that need for religion does not specify the form it will take. Thus, people might worship items in nature, be it the moon, a tree, a cow, or a large black boulder, or handcrafted things, or a person who might be a saintly figure to emulate or a diabolical being to fear. For some, that object of devotion might lead its followers to a life of helpfulness to humankind; but others might be led by their object of devotion to a life of harm and destruction of those about them. Again, the form is variable; but the need for an object of devotion and allegiance is universal.[15]

SOCIOLOGICAL VIEWS

We now turn to the sociological treatment of the issue of religion's sources or origins. Actually, to continue using the term *origins* would be misleading. Certainly contemporary sociologists no longer use the term; nor did the early representatives of sociology whom we shall soon cite. A more appropriate term is *social correlates* (or simply *correlates*) of religion—that is, associations between various events and features on the one hand and religious forms and expressions on the other. As shall be evident throughout this text, one of the central concerns of contemporary sociology of religion is tracing the interaction of social factors with religion, not pretending or even hoping to discover "origins," but only influences on and modifiers of religion. In an important sense, it makes little difference today to most social scientists whence religion came. It exists almost everywhere and in great variety. Therefore religion merits our scrutiny and analysis. It is much more important for us today to assess the degrees and kinds of influence religion has in various social contexts and to understand the current direction of religion, regardless of religion's sources.

We will now look more specifically at what several major sociological theorists have learned in seeking the sources and background correlates of religion. Theirs is not so much the anthropologists' emphasis on personal experiences with the physical environment, or the psychologists' emphasis on personal emotional adjustment, but an emphasis on models of what transpires in group interaction processes. These models are, in a sense, copied and reiterated in the religious system. This excursion will make what follows in the rest of this text more intelligible.

Georg Simmel

In elaborating the sociological position, we shall first consider the contribution of the pioneering social theorist, Georg Simmel. Patterns of social interaction that are themselves nonreligious, Simmel asserted, exert a prime influence on religion. Many feelings and patterns of expression commonly termed "religious" are also found in other areas of life and, in fact, are basic ingredients of social interaction in general—exaltation, commitment, fervor, love, and so forth, are common to all forms of human experience and relationships. Faith, for example, is a common ingredient in relationships between individuals. Most of our interactions with people are founded on faith—faith that an approaching stranger will not shoot me as he passes; faith that the pilot of the plane knows how to fly, is not on a suicide mission, and is sober; faith that the cook at the drive-in has not laced the hamburger relish with arsenic; and so on. *Religious* faith, then (to continue the example), is a supreme form of a prime factor in everyday interaction. "In faith in a deity," Simmel writes, "the highest development of faith has become incorporate, so to speak; has been relieved of its connection with its social counterpart."[16]

Implicit in what Simmel says here is a crucial sociological assumption concerning religious origins—namely, that the **models** for many, if not all, religious sentiments, expressions, and beliefs, reside originally in society at large, in its patterns of interaction. In other words, society precedes religion. Before religion can develop, there must first exist general patterns of social interaction—that is, a society—that can serve as a model.

Émile Durkheim

Another pioneer, and Simmel's contemporary, Émile Durkheim, devoted much of his scholarly energies to studying religion and was particularly intrigued by the question of religion's origins and social correlates. Durkheim emphasized religion's role in influencing and reinforcing societal integration—in legitimating society's values and norms by providing divine sanctions for behavior that society defines as normative and by periodically bringing people together for ritual activities that strengthen their feeling of unity. Like Simmel, Durkheim believed that general patterns of social interaction provide models for religion. But Durkheim goes further in asserting (quite dramatically) that society's norms, roles, and social relationships are so closely reflected by religion that the latter is nothing more than these characteristics expressed in a somewhat different form. The extreme of this position is Durkheim's contention that the real object of veneration in any religion is society itself—that which is venerated may be *called* "God," but it is really society.

Totem   In talking about God and the society, Durkheim makes use of the concepts of *totem* and *totemic principle*. A totem is an object or a living thing, such as a bird, animal or plant, that a group regards with special awe, reverence, and respect. It is what has often been mistaken by outside observers of so-called primitive people as an object of worship—a false god or idol—in Christian terms. Durkheim says the object is not worshiped *per se*. What is important is what the totem *represents;* what it represents is worshiped. The totem is only a symbol of something more fundamental. Durkheim says:

> Thus the totem is before all a symbol, a material expression of something else. But of what?
>
> From the analysis to which we have been giving our attention, it is evident that it expresses and symbolizes two different sorts of things. In the first place, it is the outward and visible form of what we have called the totemic principle or god. But it is also the symbol of the determined society called the clan. It is its flag, the sign by which each clan distinguishes itself from the others, the visible mark of its personality, a mark borne by everything, which is a part of the clan under any title whatsoever, men, beasts or things. So if it is at once the symbol of the god and of the society, is that not because the god and the society are only one? . . . The god of the clan, the totemic principle, can therefore be nothing else than the clan itself, personified and represented to the imagination under the visible form of the animal or vegetable that serves as totem.[17]

Under-girding Durkheim's view that society personifies itself in the form of totems or gods to revere and worship (that is, society itself is the real object of worship), is his perception of the need of society to reaffirm itself, that is, affirm its legitimacy and worth. This involves, for Durkheim, the creation of an "ideal" society. That ideal society is literally the *idea* it has of itself—what it is like, what it stands for, where it has been, where it is going, and so on. This is more than the strictly *material* side of society that would include the people themselves, the ground on which they stand, the things they use, and the gestures they make. Integral to this process of maintaining the ideal aspect of society (its essence, so to speak), is religion that personifies the social ideal and is the primary mechanism for its maintenance.

Soul   As a further extension of this idea of the essential identity of God and society, is Durkheim's view of the idea of a person's soul. John Wilson points out that Durkheim saw in the belief of the soul "a symbolic representation of the relation between the individual and society."[18] The moral authority of the society is the reality that stands behind the concept of the soul. So, when people refer to their souls, they are referring (without, of course, being aware of it) to a social element within themselves. This social element will, of course, live long after the people themselves. One would have to think at this point of the Hindu and Buddhist concept of *samsara* (the endless sequence of rebirths in new forms to which all beings are subject) and the traditional Greek and Christian concept of the immortality of the soul.

Ritual   Now we need to introduce the concept *ritual*, which is always present in religion in the form of predictable, repetitious actions, sometimes sets of words and phrases, done/said collectively by a group as part of a scared event designed to remind, re-enact, instruct, worship/praise, and strengthen the commitment of participants. In describing the essentials of religion, Durkheim identified ritual as intimately—associated with the *sacred* (that which is set apart and viewed with awe and demanding one's most careful attention). It is during the ritual activities of people during sacred time where the emotions are most involved and strong passions are stirred. Durkheim says:

> Once the individuals are gathered together, a sort of electricity is generated from their closeness and quickly launches them into an extraordinary height of exaltation . . . probably because a collective emotion cannot be expressed collectively without some order that permits harmony and unison of movement, [their] gestures and cries tend to fall into rhythm and regularity, and from there into songs and dances.[19]

Durkheim uses the terms "ecstasy" and "effervescence" in describing ritual and a group's participation in ritual. We see dramatic evidence of such ecstasy and effervescence in contemporary ecstatic religious behavior within Pentecostal churches and various similar subgroups in all the major religions.

Durkheim was a pioneer in observing the centrality of ritual to religion, but he also recognized that ritual becomes a part of profane activities as well (the ordinary, mundane activities of life involved in taking care of family and providing food and shelter). And today many sociologists see ritual at the base of most, perhaps all, things social. This has included the origin and experience of language, of music, and of engaging in almost any interactive activity, such as eating a meal together.[20] Here one cannot help but think of the mingling of sacred time and profane time as some people "say grace" before and/or after family meals and people in some Asian societies offer a token offering of food to their ancestors before beginning the meal.[21] Ritual is everywhere. In fact, if Roy Rappaport is correct in asserting that "ritual [is] humanity's basic social act,"[22] then ritual is, of course, central to the actions of people also, as they participate in sacred acts as part of what we would call "religion"—to get back to Durkheim's first point about ritual's intimate association with the sacred.

Functionalism   We mentioned earlier that Durkheim saw religion as a *functional* element in society. That is, religion performs a beneficial function within society, for all religious acts (in Durkheims's view) tend to reaffirm society's legitimacy and to bind its members more closely together. His views of the functional (integrative) role of religion are well-illustrated in his discussion of the social functions of religious and ceremonial ritual, as summarized by Harry Alpert.[23] Durkheim sees four primary social functions of such ritual:

1. It serves a disciplinary and preparatory function—that is, ritual imposes a self-discipline that is necessary for social life. Members of society need to accommodate constraints, controls, and boundaries. Learning to follow religious rituals facilitates development of this ability.
2. Ceremonial ritual provides a cohesive function—that is, it brings people together, reaffirms their common bonds, and reinforces a social solidarity. By doing things jointly and repetitively, the members of the group strengthen their bonds of relatedness. "The essential thing is that men are assembled, that sentiments are felt in common, and that they are expressed in common acts."[24]
3. It serves a revitalizing function—that is, it makes members of the society aware of their common social heritage. It links them to the past: What we do has a history; we ourselves have a history. Such awareness can provide motivation and inspiration to carry on.
4. It serves a euphoric function. It aids in establishing a pleasant feeling of social well-being. This function takes on special significance when a group is faced with calamities, disappointments, losses of treasured members, and other threats to its stability. It helps straighten out the sharp curves and adds some rays of light in the dark tunnels of disappointment and despair.

It is appropriate at this point to mention an extension of functional theory by Robert Merton. He speaks about the possibility of "functional alternatives." That is, although a given action or role of a particular subunit in a social system may be seen as functional, it should not be concluded that such is the only action or performance that may be functional in that particular place and time.[25] This is of particular relevance to the identification of religious functions. The fact that religion performs certain functions and satisfies certain needs of society and its individual members does not necessarily mean that religion is either inevitable or absolutely necessary. Other systems or mechanisms could conceivably satisfy these needs as well or better. Actually, this may help explain why some persons are religious while others are not at all religious, at least not in ways traditionally—defined as such by that society. That is, while some people practice major religions, others avail themselves of nonreligious functional alternatives or of religious alternatives outside the mainstream of formalized religion.

Guy Swanson

More recently, Guy E. Swanson has adopted Durkheim's basic position but modified it in conducting an innovative piece of research. Starting with the

basic sociological assumption that all human ideas arise from the experience of people with their environment,[26] both physical and social,
Swanson attempted to discover examples of specific human experiences
that might give rise to certain forms of religious belief. In *The Birth of the
Gods*, his 1960 study, Swanson focused on religion's preoccupation with
the supernatural, in an attempt to determine the origin of this concept. Like
the early anthropologists, Swanson noted the predominance of spirits and
of the concept of mana in "primitive" religious systems. What are the
sources of the belief in such phenomena? Swanson suggests that spirits,
which he defines as "organized clusters of purposes" having a personal
identity and access to mana, grow out of, and consequently stand for,
social patterns already present in the society.[27] That is, as Durkheim and
Simmel both maintained earlier, society and its social norms, structures,
and patterns serve as the **models** for religion.

Swanson then asks what social relationships the experiences with spirits
correspond to. That is, what are the social correlates? He suggests four conditions or types of social patterns or groups:

1. social relationships in which there are evident connections between cause and
    effect, associated with the belief that spirits have a purpose and a will;
2. relationships regarded as persisting over the generations, which relate to the
    belief that spirits are immortal;
3. particular groups that are the source of particular spirits, which means that
    every spirit has a specific identity; and
4. groups that have distinctive purposes, associated with the fact that spirits
    differ in purpose and role.[28]

Using this general orientation to the source or basis of belief in spirits,
Swanson analyzes data drawn from preliterate and early historical
societies, in order to trace the relationship between certain kinds of belief
(such as monotheism, polytheism, and the beliefs in ancestral spirits, in
reincarnation, in the immanence of the soul, and in the efficacy of witchcraft) and various social conditions and relationships. That is, he sought
correlations between religious beliefs and practices, on the one hand, and
on the other, such social factors as the society's source of food, its amount
of food production, the degree of danger of attack from alien societies, the
size of the population, the degree of private property ownership,
the emphasis on communal versus noncommunal specialties within the
society, social stratification, the nature and frequency of unlegitimated
contacts with members of other societies, the variety and kinds of social
organizations, and so forth. In some cases Swanson found a surprisingly
high correlation between a set of social factors and a particular religious
belief or practice—that is, a particular belief was always (or almost always)
present *only* if certain social factors were also present, and always (or

nearly always) absent *only when* the same factors were absent. In all cases, he found fascinating and highly-suggestive correlations, whether of high magnitude or not. For example, witchcraft, Swanson discovered, tended to occur in societies where people must interact with one another on important matters with no clear norms, controls, and structures to guide them.[29] Thus, people resort to witchcraft apparently as a substitute, as a compensatory device for attempting to explain and above all to control what happens to them. Or to take another example: The belief in reincarnation is more likely to appear in societies where the pattern of settlement is dominated by "small hamlets, compounds of extended families, small nomadic bands, scattered rural neighborhoods, or other units smaller than a village."[30] The apparent logic underlying this is that there is a greater probability that a person will be regarded as living on through reincarnation where there are intimate, highly-interdependent, long-lasting relationships within a relatively small but fairly independent social unit— where, in other words, the social unit is thought to survive the members who constitute it at any given time. The individual and their idiosyncrasies within such groups are of considerable interest and importance. As Swanson points out, "The particular potentialities of each member are appreciated as limiting or facilitating the lives of all the others, and those effects persist after a member dies."[31] These effects are such things as "his technological inventiveness, his habit of shirking work, his fecundity, or the qualities of his voice in the ceremonial songs [that] have shaped adaptations of his fellows . . . [and that] continue after his death."[32] In other words, "the memory lingers on." Moreover, the social relationships and structure of the group provide a model for the development of a belief in personal reincarnation.

While Swanson himself admits that even strong positive correlations do not conclusively establish cause and effect relationships between social factors and religious beliefs, his achievement lies in having shown that *certain beliefs are extremely unlikely to occur and be accepted unless certain social factors, conditions, or relationships are present.* For example, it is extremely unlikely that a society lacking a certain degree and type of organizational complexity will accept belief in a monotheistic "high god" (one considered responsible for creating the world), even if the belief is suggested by a member of the group, revealed by a deity, or diffused from another society. Specifically, societies that accept such a belief have a hierarchical arrangement of three or more "sovereign groups" (groups having ultimate decision-making authority over specified areas of life).[33] Although Swanson stops short of asserting any causal relationship here and would simply affirm that this social structure is most likely the model for the emergence of monotheism much of the time, the relationship is strong enough to tempt the reader to begin thinking about necessary and sufficient conditions for the development of that particular belief.

RATIONAL CHOICE THEORY

As we conclude our brief look at various theories about the source(s) of religion, we look ahead to Chapter 3, where we will begin a summary of the sociological perspective on religion as sociology analyzes the reciprocal relationships of religion and the rest of the societal and other group structures within which religion exists and functions. But before we proceed with this, it is important to understand a way of looking at religion's place in society, as it is perceived by the people who practice religion and want some of the answers and services they believe religion provides. It is a theory that tries to deal seriously with not only the persistence of religion but also the observation that some form of religion appears to be ubiquitous among societies, even if some individuals deny the validity of the religions that surround them.

This perspective is called *rational choice theory* and has received a great deal of attention by sociologists in the last two decades. The concept is borrowed, in part, from the field of economics that poses a model of persons trying always to maximize their rewards and gains from the economy within which they find themselves, through making reasoned/rational choices to the best of their ability. That is what people always do. They seek a variety of goals from an array available to them and usually understand that certain effort (costs) will be needed on their part in order to reach them. As sociologists, we must stress immediately that this is not simply brainpower or IQ at work, but there are many sociological factors that enter into it as well. Readers of this book will think back to the norms and values, the role definitions and status arrangements of any and all groups that we outlined in Chapter 1 and will consider again in Chapter 5 when we talk about religious socialization. But we also must keep in mind that people as individuals have a unique set of social experiences as they proceed through a lifetime—other individuals and groups they encounter and with whom they interact, situations they experience, and their reception of the hundreds of thousands of stimuli coming from the physical environment, and the various forms of instructions as well as the mass media and advertising that bombard them in a lifetime. They also experience positive and negative sanctions from people; and they mimic the behavior of others and learn what works and what does not, as well as everything in between. And we could go on. But the idea is clear that people have a set of mental images stored in their brains with which they make decisions as rationally and sensibly as they know how.

Such decisions are made in all areas of life, including religion. That is, people make rational religious choices (decisions) that are rooted in all the learning and experiences that the person has already absorbed, just as much as they make economic, political, or social decisions to buy a bag of chips (economic), to keep one's opinion to oneself when one strongly desires to remain in good standing in a group where everyone seems to espouse a different opinion (political), or to ask that person in your sociology class out for coffee after class (social). Rodney Stark and Roger Finke succinctly summarize what rational choice theorists mean by the principle of human rationality as follows: "Within the limits of their information and understanding, restricted by available options, guided by their preferences and tastes, humans attempt to make rational choices."[34] When one adds the factors of supply and demand to the above, one has the necessary elements to explain a great deal of human behavior and the choices people have made that led to their behavior—including religious behavior and decisions (choices) that are as rational to the people who make them, as are scientific observations made by the most well-trained, knowledgeable scientist who analyzes data in her/his field of specialization. The religious ideas and the information about the unseen world that are available to people, proffer rewards and gains that are desirable to people—close fellowship with like-minded people, help in need, emotional support in trying times, a good life after death, and so on. Then there is one more factor. For every reward or gain there is a cost, whether it is changing one's lifestyle, tithing one's income for the religious group, perhaps enduring ridicule by former friends, giving up much of one's leisure time to activities required by one's religious group, and the like.

While rational choice theory does not deal at all with the original sources of religion, it picks up at the point where religious ideas and systems already exist in some form and people turn to those ideas and systems for answers, consolation, protection, promises, and solutions. Rational choice theory, by definition, presumes diversity within the broad field of religion. As such, rational choice of religious ideas and values did not come into play in the small prehistoric societies, which the early social scientists such as Durkheim, Müller, and Tyler studied in their quest for the origins of religion. We will have occasion to return to rational choice theory several times throughout the remainder of this book, to gain insight into how this theory helps us understand that part of social life we call *religion*.

CONCLUSION

Although the origins and ultimate sources of religion can never be known with certainty, research and speculation on these subjects have not been fruitless. The hypotheses we have summarized—the anthropological theories that emphasize people's interaction with nature; the psychological theories that stress people's fears, frustrations, and emotional needs; and the sociological theories that focus on the social context in which religion exists—at the very least contribute to our understanding of what religion is, why it has come about, and perhaps also why it persists.

In summary, then, it seems reasonable to advance the following propositions concerning the forces that sustain religion, if not give rise to it:

1. People are continually and universally threatened with failure, frustration, and injustice.
2. Religion becomes the attempt of people in groups to "relativize" such threats to their wholeness, by placing them within a context of a larger system or plan and often by "explaining" much that happens in terms of supernatural intervention into, and control over, earthly events.
3. At the same time, threats similar to those experienced by individuals also affect social relationships—and, in fact, society itself.
4. Religion arises as an attempt by society to cushion such threats (both to itself and to its members) by bringing people into a ritual fellowship of common belief and action. Thus, religion is a response to both individual and group needs.
5. The characteristic form of religious belief and interpretation in a given society is significantly conditioned by the type and complexity of social patterns and relationships that the group has developed over time.

NOTES

1. See F. Max Müller, *Anthropological Religion* (London: Longmans Green, 1892); idem, *Lectures on the Origin and Growth of Religion* (London: Longmans, 1878).
2. See Edward B. Tylor, *Primitive Culture* (London: Murray, 1871).
3. Robert Lowie, *Primitive Religion* (New York: Boni & Liveright, 1924), p. xvi.
4. J. Samuel Preus, *Explaining Religion: Criticism and Theory from Bodin to Freud* (New Haven: Yale University Press, 1987), pp. 208–209.
5. Ibid.
6. Mary Douglas, *Implicit Meanings: Essay in Anthropology* (London: Routledge & Kegan Paul, 1975), p. 73.
7. Clifford Geertz, *Interpretation of Cultures* (New York: Basic Books, 1973), pp. 171–175.
8. Erwin R. Goodenough, *The Psychology of Religious Experiences* (New York: Basic Books, 1965), p. 6.
9. Walter Huston Clark, *The Psychology of Religion* (New York: Macmillan, 1958), p. 67; William I. Thomas, *The Unadjusted Girl* (Boston: Little, Brown, 1923), pp. 4ff.
10. George S. Spinks, *Psychology and Religion* (Boston: Beacon Press, 1963), pp. 46–47.
11. Sigmund Freud, *The Future of an Illusion* (New York: Liveright, 1928).
12. Abraham Maslow, *Toward a Psychology of Being* (Princeton, NJ: D. Van Nostrand, 1963), pp. 57–64.
13. Erich Fromm, *Psychoanalysis and Religion* (New Haven: Yale University Press, 1950 [Bantam Book edition]), p. 25.
14. Ibid., p. 26.
15. Ibid., pp. 35–36.
16. Georg Simmel, "A Contribution to the Sociology of Religion," *American Journal of Sociology* 11, no. 3 (1905): 336–367.
17. Émile Durkheim, *The Elementary Forms of the Religious Life*, trans. Joseph Ward Swain (New York: Collier, 1961), p. 236.
18. John Wilson, *Religion in American Society* (Englewood Cliffs, NJ: Prentice Hall, 1978), p. 19.

19. Émile Durkheim, *The Elementary Forms of the Religious Life* (London: Allen & Unwin, 1912/1976), p. 216.

20. Robert N. Bellah, "The Ritual Roots of Society and Culture," in *Handbook of the Sociology of Religion,* ed. Michele Dillon (Cambridge, UK: Cambridge University Press, 2003), pp. 31–44.

21. Ibid., p. 41.

22. Roy A. Rappaport, *Ritual and Religion in the Making of Humanity* (Cambridge, UK: Cambridge University Press, 1999), p. 107.

23. Harry Alpert, *Emile Durkheim and His Sociology* (New York: Russell & Russell, 1961), pp. 198–203.

24. Durkheim, *Elementary Forms*, pp. 431–432.

25. Robert K. Merton, *Social Theory and Social Structure* (Glencoe, IL: Free Press, 1956), pp. 33–34.

26. Guy E. Swanson, *The Birth of the Gods* (Ann Arbor, MI: University of Michigan Press, 1960), p. 1.

27. Ibid., p. 18.

28. This typology is summarized from ibid., pp. 19–20.

29. Ibid., Chapter 8.

30. Ibid., p. 113.

31. Ibid., p. 112.

32. Ibid.

33. Ibid., pp. 62–65.

34. Rodney Stark and Roger Finke, *Acts of Faith: Explaining the Human Side of Religion* (Berkeley: University of California Press, 2000), p. 38.

Chapter 3

Religion as a Group Phenomenon

Religion is embodied in groups.

In Chapter 1 we made the point that, as a social phenomenon, religion exhibits patterns of interaction and process that duplicate many, if not all, patterns that all other social groups exhibit, and we emphasized explicitly that religion is a group phenomenon. We will now pick up on these fundamental sociological observations and expand them, as we look more specifically at the social organization of religion. That is, we want to see how religious ideas, regardless of their real or supposed source, become embodied in groups and how, in turn, these groups proceed to function, manifest similarities among themselves and with other groups, but also distinguish themselves both from one another and from other kinds of groups in society.

RELIGION AND THE CHARACTERISTICS OF A GROUP

In Chapter 1 we briefly defined *group* as two or more interacting people who

1. share common goals or aims that stem from common problems and a desire to resolve them;
2. agree upon a set of norms that they hope will help them to achieve their common goals;
3. combine certain norms into roles that they expect persons within the group to fill and carry out in the interests of the group;
4. agree (often only implicitly) on certain status dimensions and distinctions, on the basis of which they rate one another; and
5. identify with the group and express or exhibit some degree of commitment to the group, what it proposes to do, and how it proposes to do it.

Clearly, religious organizations meet all of these criteria. Religious groups are concerned with problems and with expressing aspirations, hopes, and goals. They all want to know why certain things happen (cognitive understanding of accidents, death, thunder, and so forth); some may want to express their dependency relationship with a deity (proper worship and ritual activity); some may want to devise methods of gaining rewards from the deities (techniques of prayer or magic); some may want to provide emotional support and encouragement for people in illness, disappointment, and other difficulties and inevitabilities of human existence; or some may want to achieve a proper existence after this present life (salvation). In each case we are observing goals and the process of establishing goals that will, of course, vary considerably from group to group.

Intimately associated with the establishment of goals, of course, is agreement on norms. To agree that it is an appropriate goal to appease a jealous god is to establish a norm—namely, that there is such a god, that so and so is his or her name, and so on. Any belief or assertion about the sacred, any explanation of what happens in that realm, any established practice or ritual directed toward the sacred, is a norm. Christianity, with its elaborate doctrines, dogmas, and theological tomes, clearly possesses an extensive normative system. Its historic emphasis on "right belief" becomes partially understandable in this context. Yet "primitive" religions that appear more to emphasize behavior—the ritual that involves proper steps and stages in the rain dance, the puberty rite, or the battle preparation—equally emphasize norms—norms of right behavior, perhaps, more than norms of right belief.

As immediately as norms follow goals, so do roles follow both. The group agrees on a leader (priest, shaman, rabbi, guru, prophet, pastor) and defines their duties. It specializes other functions into dancers, cantors, sorcerers, choirs, treasurers, acolytes, deacons, theological professors, executive secretaries of evangelism, directors of research and survey, public relations directors, news release writers, members of the commission on church literature, ushers, chairpersons of the annual spaghetti supper, and so on.

Partly, but not solely, as a result of such specialization of roles, status differences appear in religious groups. Quite naturally, the leader, the coordinator, the spokesperson, and the teacher of religious truths acquire greater status early on—greater prestige and respect, if nothing else—than the rank-and-file participant. The status of such persons also involves greater authority and, perhaps as a spin-off, greater power as well. Possibly greater wealth and more leisure may accrue. But there are other status distinctions, too. There are those members who appear to follow the norms of the group more closely than others. Such behavior will likely be recognized by many members, who will characterize those who are most assiduously normative as "very religious," "most sincere," "Zoroastrian of the Century," "Methodist of the Year," and the like.

Related to such ideas of status differentiation, is the factor of group identification. Identification and commitment are variables that range from low (if not zero) to high. Groups tend to tolerate variability here, though most strive for high commitment from all members. Of course, as we will point out shortly, the larger the group, the more likely the range of commitment and identification will increase.

The major point we are making is that, although the subject matter of religion may be unique and although it may claim a unique (namely, sacred, or perhaps supernatural) source for its norms and roles, yet as the religious group organizes itself and sets about doing what it feels it should be doing, it exhibits all the features of any and all other groups. At the level of organization and structure, it is no different from other groups. The focus of the goals may be different, the specific set of norms may be different, the combination of norms into particular roles may be unique, and the criteria for status assessment may vary. But the religious group, as any other group, will have all of these ingredients and must constantly work at resolving differences of interpretation and application of its goals, norms, and roles. It must adjust them, expand them, and so on, just as any group must. Just as nations, social clubs, political parties, or nuclear families differ among themselves, yet also exhibit similarities in the problems they must adjust to and the ultimate resolutions and patterns they exhibit, so religious groups, though unique in certain ways, show similarities among themselves and, in fact, with all other social groups.

This suggests, by way of practical application, that the problems and challenges that any group must deal with on a day-to-day basis, will be there for a religious group to deal with also. Just as a family has certain tasks to be performed—cooking meals, washing clothes, mowing the lawn, bringing home spendable income in the form of wages or salary—so a religious group needs someone to lead the group in worship, someone to clean up afterwards, someone to provide leadership in music, and someone to keep tabs on revenues and expenditures. Just as political parties meet in convention periodically to define and refine their platforms and address new issues facing the nation, so churches gather in convention to refine their theological position on various issues and address new issues that are brought before them. Just as a society devises a court and penal system to provide a fair hearing for those accused of deviation from society's norms, and to punish and attempt to rehabilitate those who are found guilty, so religious groups establish procedures to provide a fair hearing and to punish if the person is found guilty, perhaps to the point of excommunication if the individual persists unrepentant in his or her deviance—be it called heresy, immorality, or heterodoxy.

In short, a group is a group is a group.

RELIGION AND THE FIVE FUNCTIONAL PREREQUISITES OF GROUP LIFE

Recruitment and Reproduction

By way of a more systematic and thorough treatment of what we have suggested above, we can point out that religious groups, no less than other groups, are involved with meeting the challenges of the five functional prerequisites of group life identified by the anthropologist David Aberle.[1] First, any group must pay attention to the prerequisite of recruitment or reproduction to replace those members who die, defect, or become incapacitated. Societies accomplish this task through natural reproduction (births), acceptance of immigrants, or annexation of neighboring territories and populations. Other groups rely primarily on natural reproduction and recruitment of new members through voluntary affiliation with the group. Religious groups have historically not been unmindful of meeting this prerequisite for group continuity. In fact, many religious groups have explicitly urged maximum natural reproduction. Prohibitions against birth control, emphasis on conception as the only valid motive for sexual relations, and social ridicule or pity for the barren woman, all enter in here. Although the Old Testament injunction to be fruitful and multiply has more recently been interpreted simply as a predictive statement of what would naturally happen as men and women mated, it was historically interpreted as a divine command to reproduce as prolifically as possible. Some groups have explicitly urged their members to bear as many children as possible so, as to increase the numbers of God's chosen people. Many religious groups have also worked hard at adding to their numbers through recruitment of members from outside the group—by conversion or proselytizing. Jesus' injunction quoted in Matthew, "Go ye therefore, and teach all nations," has been followed to greater and lesser degrees throughout history. Since (and even before) Charlemagne "converted" the barbarians through mass baptisms in 722, Christian missionaries have been attempting to expedite conversion of nonbelievers and pagans. Actually, however, it was not until the eighteenth and nineteenth centuries, when the new worlds of the Americas, Asia, Africa, and the Pacific experienced extensive exploration and colonization, that Christian groups began subsidizing significant missionary activity.

All Christian groups continue today to support missionary work throughout the world, though such activity is somewhat curtailed because of political unrest in various nations, the development of political nationalism that is often accompanied by religious nationalism (e.g., in Iran, note the intimate relationship of the Islamic religion with the political revolution that deposed the shah), and declining financial support from parent denominations. Much of the current missionary activity is highly traditional in the sense of going out into the jungles and villages to meet the indigenous peoples where they are, and to establish congregations; however, increasing emphasis is being placed on work within the expanding urban centers, as one after another of the underdeveloped nations begins to industrialize. Along with this ministry to the urban centers, often goes increasing attention to a radio and television ministry designed to reach out to the masses.

With respect to contemporary mission work, almost everyone is familiar with the sight of pairs of young Mormon men in suits, white shirts, and ties plying the streets and neighborhoods of towns and cities in many countries, trying to find receptive ears for the story and message they have to tell. They are urged by their church to devote two years before marriage to full-time mission work, some in the home country, others in a foreign one.

Or look at the cult members, such as those in the Unification Church ("Moonies"), who divide their time between fund-raising from those they are unlikely to recruit and charming the rootless, uncommitted young people into social contact with the group and convincing them to stick around and find out more. There were few people indeed, in the 1970s and 1980s, who did not run into or at least observe such young people at work in airports and busy city streets.

Other major religions, such as Islam and Buddhism, have also actively courted nonmembers, not infrequently using force and political means when ordinary persuasion was insufficient. In fact, in Islam the political-military and religious motivations are so mixed as to be impossible to separate (which is true throughout the history of Christianity also, of course). Early in the history of Islam, the conquering of both near and far territories, for both booty and land, became an absorbing goal and activity. Subjugated peoples were, of course, also pledged to the religion of Islam. Buddhism used religious missionaries, monks, and teachers to spread their message. In fact, as early as two centuries after Gautama Buddha's death, the Indian emperor Asoka, who came to the throne in 273 B.C.E., conceived of Buddhism as a world religion and sent missionaries as far as Egypt and Greece.[2] These missions left no trace, however, and these attempts to spread Buddhism were apparently quite ineffective. In Sri Lanka (Ceylon) it was a different story. Buddhist missionaries sent by Asoka's son, Mahinda, in 240 B.C.E. were so successful that Buddhism quickly became the state religion of Sri Lanka and remains so until this day.[3]

A classic example of a group's failure to meet the requirement of reproduction and recruitment of new members is that of the American religious group called the Shakers, founded in 1787. One of their primary tenets was strict separation of the sexes and complete sexual continence. Therefore, a prime source of new members (natural reproduction) was deliberately eliminated. Sole reliance was placed on adult conversion to the faith. Perhaps in great part, because of the limited number of persons willing to observe sexual continence, the group had trouble gaining enough new members to maintain itself. Not surprisingly, the group today consists of a very few elderly people.

Socialization

A second prerequisite, that any group must be concerned with, is developing a process of training and educating new members—what we have been calling socialization. The norms and practices of the group must be taught to new members, whether they are children of current members, converts, or conquered subjects. Religious groups, of course, face this challenge continually. The doctrines and the rituals of the group must be inculcated in new members. They must know and believe certain bits and bodies of doctrine and ritual, first of all for their own good, and also in order to become and remain members in good standing. Further, they must know and believe certain things if they are to help preserve the group's beliefs and practices and to hand them down to succeeding generations of followers.

Accordingly, the teaching or educative function of religion becomes a major task for religious groups. It is not by chance, for example, that the full-time religious leader in Judaism, both ancient and contemporary, has the title *rabbi*, meaning "teacher." In "primitive" religions, of course, the socialization process was largely informal and accomplished through emulation, as the young watched the old and began to participate in the ritual activities and as they listened to the sagas and tales that elaborated the group's beliefs. However, religious systems that also emphasize various systematic cognitive elements of understanding and belief develop formal mechanisms for conveying such knowledge and for training in ritual performance: confirmation classes, Sunday or other church and Sabbath schools, and study groups of all kinds. Religious groups, that tend to rely on generalists called ministers or priests, may at some point add specialists to their staff known as ministers of education. An early development among American Christian denominations, for example, was to establish a publishing house to produce aids to ritual activities (e.g., hymnbooks) and educational material designed to aid the religious growth and maturation (socialization) of members.

Producing Satisfactory Levels of Goods and Services

A third prerequisite for the continued existence of all groups, is the production and distribution of a level of goods and services that will satisfy at least the minimal requirements or demands of their members. In the case of a total society, this task involves satisfying at least the minimal survival needs of its citizens for such items as food, shelter, and clothing. For voluntary associations, such as contemporary religious groups, it means giving members what they have come to the group to find or else running the risk of members losing interest and leaving. Presumably, members of religious groups receive certain expected benefits from their affiliation, or they will not stay, or would not have joined in the first place. Perhaps they are seeking eternal salvation, or comfort and reassurance, or good fellowship, or a vehicle through which they can help those in need. A religious group, therefore, must either "deliver the goods," so to speak—or at least convince its members that the goods are being delivered or will be in the hereafter— or see its constituency evaporate. Although this may sound almost crass, perhaps even sacrilegious when talking about religious groups, these very religions must "deliver" something that people want, or the people will go elsewhere.

Religious groups that we will be defining as *cults* or new religious movements (NRMs) in Chapter 4, which tend to be centered around a charismatic leader, are notoriously unstable and likely to disband as quickly as they formed, when the leader becomes discredited, dies or the competition promises more. Followers may decide they are not receiving what they were seeking or believe that they will more fully or more quickly receive what they seek from the competition that has appeared on the scene.

The relationship of most members to their religious group is, of course, not so tenuous or easily shifted as what we just described in cults. Certainly, lifelong adherents to a group must overcome apathy and inertia, if nothing else, if they wish to defect—yet defect they will (and do) if evidence accumulates and the conviction mounts that what was sought has not been found or is no longer being offered fully enough by the group.

Over the last forty-five years, researchers have been observing declining memberships in several major denominations in the United States (and increasing memberships in others). Interestingly, those with declining memberships tend to be more theologically and socially liberal; those with increasing memberships tend to be conservative on both counts. We will not, at the moment, evaluate the hypothesis that people are becoming increasingly disenchanted with liberal theology and the intrusion of liberal social and political views into the major Christian denominations and, as a consequence, are leaving such groups to join more traditional groups that emphasize personal comfort and the reassurance of absolute rather than relative truths. But we can certainly agree that most people who leave a religious group, whether or not they affiliate with another one, are expressing a dissatisfaction with the "goods and services" delivered by that group—it no longer provides them with what they want, or at least not enough of what they want to maintain their allegiance.

As we talk about goods and services and the possibility of choosing to leave one religious group for another that promises more of the goods and services one desires, we are reminded of the theory of rational choice that we introduced near the end of the last chapter. In rational choice theory we deal with concepts that are at their root economic. Stark and Finke talk about "religious economies." They make the point that the religious subsystem in a society is clearly parallel to the subsystem involved with the commercial/business (secular) economy. Both systems involve the interplay of supply and demand for products that people desire and value. Stark and Finke describe religious economies as follows: They "consist of a market of current and potential followers (demand), a set of organizations (suppliers) seeking to serve that market, and the religious doctrines and practices (products) offered by the various organizations."[4] In a real sense, religion is, or at least provides, a market (supply) of ideas, explanations, and messages from which people make choices.

The authors are quick to point out that employing terminology from the secular marketplace and the conjunction of economics and religion are not intended to belittle the goods and services (products) that people both gain and believe they gain from religion. But this economic concept, which consists of "products" and "supply and demand," is very helpful in understanding the relationship of persons with a group or organization that they value. They are in an "economic" relationship over religious products that people want (demand), which are provided from a supply that religion makes available.

Preserving Order

The fourth primary task that groups must perform is that of preserving order. Essentially, this task involves coordinative and supervisory roles, but above all it means motivating members to pursue group goals while employing and abiding by group norms. Within total societies, this centers in the political process and the exercising of governmental controls and sanctions—the range of rewards and punishments meted out for adherence to or deviation from the norms, as the case may be. On the positive side, it involves encouraging members to cooperate with one another and to supplement, rather than interfere with, the performance of others' roles. It involves providing a context for freedom of movement and action of individuals within limits agreed upon by the group. On the negative side, it may involve incarceration, the death penalty, or ostracism.

So far as religious groups are concerned, we think here of the three major types of church government established to reach the organization's goals. First, there is the *episcopal type* (e.g., Episcopal and Roman Catholic churches), in which authority rests with the congregations' clergy and with higher-ranking clergy, such as popes and bishops. Second, the *presbyterian type*, in which authority rests with representative committees of clergy and church members. Third, the *congregational type*, in which ultimate organizational authority resides in local church members and with their representatives meeting periodically in regional or national convention or assembly.

We also think of heresy trials and inquisitions, in which those accused of deviating from official doctrine or practice are sought out, tried, and punished. Fundamental here is the conviction that if such controls are not employed, radical changes may be introduced that would result in the alienation and loss of members to the point of ultimate dissolution and destruction of the group.

Maintaining a Sense of Purpose

The fifth primary prerequisite that groups must fulfill, if they hope to survive, is the maintenance of a sense of purpose among its members. This task is concerned with the sixth feature of groups mentioned in Chapter 1—namely, the identification factor. Groups must develop and maintain among members, a feeling of commitment to and identification with the group. Groups that fail continually to reinforce members' commitment, run the risk of takeover or collapse in the face of internal opposition or outside threat. A society, for example, needs citizens sufficiently committed to pick up arms and risk death on the battlefield in the face of enemy invasion. A religious group wants to be able to count on sufficient loyalty and commitment among its members, so that they are not swayed (or possibly even converted) by every fragrant new wind of doctrine or practice that blows by. They want members who take pride in their affiliation and who will resist the wiles of other groups or philosophies that may try to win them away. Most religious groups (except most Jews and Hindus), in addition, want members who will, in fact, try to bring others into their fold. "We've got a great group here and would like you to share its benefits with us!" Failing to maintain a sense of purpose can bring a group to the brink of destruction, just as can failure in any of the other four primary tasks already discussed.

THE EFFECTS OF INCREASING GROUP SIZE

Having examined one aspect of religion as a group phenomenon—in terms of the tasks that face all groups, not just religious ones—we now turn to a discussion of the pressures for change that religious groups (no less than other groups) experience. Of particular interest and significance is the effect on groups of increasing size. Important changes occur and new challenges develop as groups grow. Although a group may in one sense be successful by increasing its membership, serious problems may arise as a consequence. Paul Mott has summarized well the various developments associated with a group's increasing size.[5] We include only some of them—those with particular salience to religious groups.

Consensus Declines

As groups increase in size, the degree of consensus among members concerning goals, and especially norms, declines. In great part, a basic problem of communication and interaction is involved here. As groups grow, a point is reached when not everyone can interact with everyone else; nor can any one person interact with all others. Levels of understanding and commitment to goals and norms cannot be maintained. Not only can people not share as fully with one another and reach truly common understandings by involving everyone in decision and policy making, but problems of increasing diversity arise as more members come in. In fact, each new person is a potential disrupter, if not a potential revolutionary, inasmuch as the ideas they bring or those that they may develop, challenge fundamental beliefs of the group. Obviously the tight-knit, integrated, primary-grouplike relationship that may have existed at a group's inception and during its early development, begins to submit to increasing diversity and more specialized interests as different elements enter.

Increased Deviance

An almost inevitable outcome of increased diversity and reduced consensus, resulting from an increase in size, is increasing deviance from group norms. Since norms influence behavior, the introduction of diverse or conflicting norms results in diverse behavior. Some members may assent to many of the group's norms (they probably would not be members otherwise), yet not share others. For example, a religious group may have explicit norms defining alcoholic beverages as the devil's tools of destruction. The member who would still like a nip or two is more likely to depart from the group norm as the group grows larger. Perhaps the norm and its importance to the group has not been explained fully to them or is no longer reinforced through discussion and conversation; perhaps this person does not feel as closely united with the other members as they did when the group was small and thus does not feel so bad about disappointing them should they find out about their deviance. Actually, as the group grows larger, it becomes physically and emotionally impossible to feel or express as much concern about other individual members as was possible when the group was smaller and members more intimate.

Increased Formalization of Norms

As groups increase in size, the ratio of formal to informal norms increases. That is, when a group is small and the members can interact almost at will with one another and with the leader, norms and ideas can be shared with everyone in an informal way. But when the group grows to the point where not everyone can talk readily with everyone else and perhaps does not even know everyone else, the group will find it necessary to formalize its norms, principles, and beliefs, by writing them down. It is not coincidental that, almost without exception, holy books and bibles are written *after* the religion has been established for a while, has gained converts, and has moved beyond small group status. For one thing, the leader can no longer speak to everyone. So someone copies down some of his or her sayings and pronouncements and passes copies around to the membership.

Increased Role Specialization

A fourth development, as groups grow larger, is that roles tend to become more specialized and part-time roles tend to become full-time roles. Such specialization removes the nonspecialist from intimate contact with the tasks of various roles. Greater autonomy for roles develops. Members who originally were involved, to some degree in almost everything the group did and decided, now know less and less about what others are doing.

Greater Need for Coordination

As groups increase in size, there is greater need for coordination. As the number of roles increases, there is greater need for coordinators to interrelate those roles and ensure that they are performed in proper sequence. Nothing is wrong with that, of course. But in the process, the coordinators gain greater knowledge about the operation of the total organization than ordinary members possess; having by definition greater authority, they become increasingly isolated from the rank and file. Obviously, the original intimacy and democracy of the group fade fast in the face of this tendency. There are also, of course, increased opportunities for abusing one's power and perpetuating oneself in office, for example.

Mott lists thirteen developments within groups, related to increasing group size. The five discussed here, however, are sufficient to make the point that one measure of success that groups often use—namely, membership growth—sets them on an irreversible course involving change along a variety of dimensions. In Chapter 4, we will refer back to these dimensions in our discussion of the church-sect typology. First, however, we want to look more closely at one of the developments in groups related to increasing size—the bureaucratization trend that we identified earlier as an increase in the coordinative element in groups.

THE BUREAUCRATIZATION OF RELIGION

The Process

In the preceding section, we talked about the need for increased coordination, as groups grow larger. This introduced us to the concept of bureaucracy, which has as its essential feature the coordinating idea. That is, as specialized roles appear and as decisions need to be made, certain persons assume or are given coordinating roles. These people tend to be ranked in a hierarchy of authority. The whole idea is that greater efficiency should be achieved because someone is organizing the activities of others, so that the whole group does not need to meet and take a lot of time reaching a democratic decision. Further, these coordinators have a broader picture of what is being done and can presumably determine the most efficient sequence of activities.

Let us point out, however, that, although bureaucratization appears to be an inevitable trend in groups as they grow large and develop an increasingly complex division of labor requiring careful coordination, it may also create problems and have unintended and unwanted consequences. As Hammond and Johnson point out, a key issue in the Protestant Reformation of the fifteenth century concerned how authority was to be exercised within the church. Implicitly, this was a question of what to do about the church bureaucracy.[6] Certainly the Roman Catholic Church had long been organized along rather classic bureaucratic lines. An elaborate hierarchy of authority passed down through pope, archbishops, bishops, and priests, with other levels in between. Specialized training and experience were required of those who filled various specialized roles. Explicit rules were in effect for nearly every situation and role. An air of impartiality and impersonality pervaded relationships among leaders and between them and members.

But the leaders of the Protestant Reformation wanted greater involvement and a stronger voice for the laity. A key theological tenet stressed within early Protestantism was that every person could have direct contact with and access to God. No intermediary, such as church, pope, or priest was required. Some groups were convinced that no church authority should exist or exercise control beyond the democratic assembly of each local congregation—no level of authority above the congregation (except God himself) should require the member or the congregation to do anything. Congregationalists (now the United Church of Christ), Lutherans, and Baptists are among Protestant denominations that still espouse this principle, though in a modified form in each case.

How successful have such religious groups been in implementing this philosophy and thereby avoiding the bureaucratization that sociologists have documented in other types of groups? We gain some insight into the issue when we observe what happens when an individual or a local body of believers strives to maintain its autonomy but also finds it expedient to cooperate with other individuals or congregations in various joint ventures. Perhaps several congregations discover that training future pastors is a difficult task to accomplish alone, so they join together in establishing a theological seminary. Or they may want to send missionaries to foreign lands. A single congregation usually cannot afford to support a missionary, but several congregations can. So they establish a missionary society, board, or commission to handle the details, such as collecting mission contributions from the several congregations. Or they may want to produce lessons and literature for their Sunday schools, but local ministers do not have the time or perhaps they lack the specialized skill. Therefore, several congregations organize a Sunday school board and organize a commission on church literature to handle the planning, writing, editing, and publishing tasks.

Outcomes

The outcome of such developments is that, although no one particularly intends it, the local congregations lose some of their autonomy. The boards, agencies, or commissions assume some measure of authority and independence and, in turn, gain influence over the congregations. It is a reciprocal relationship—while local congregations may have established the goals and even some of the policies for such administrative groups, once in existence the latter turn around and influence the congregations. They train the ministers, organize and supervise the missionary endeavors, and write the Sunday school material. Thus, they become innovators and not simply implementers of policy.

The relationship between such boards and the local congregation and its members can, therefore, become somewhat uncertain. Such a situation is highlighted when one or more congregations discover they do not like the theological inclinations of their seminary's ministerial graduates or feel that heretical ideas are slipping into their Sunday school material. The congregation, of course, has the option of severing the relationship, but then it faces the problem of carrying on all these tasks by itself or linking up with yet another organization. The common reaction is to go along with the established pattern, even though the congregation loses some of its cherished autonomy in the process.

A method observed by Paul Harrison, in the American Baptist Church, that bridges the gap between national boards and local independent congregations, is the action of the executive who heads a board or agency. If the executive secretary or other administrator of a national board or commission has charismatic qualities, they can gain broad-based support among local clergy and laypeople that grants them greater flexibility and autonomy and ultimately substantial authority and influence over local decisions.[7] Of course, even without charisma, the denominational executive will have some measure of autonomous power because much of their day-to-day work is unseen and unknown by most of the constituency. As Harrison points out, most lay members have no knowledge of the internal operation of the larger church body, never attend national, state, or even local associational meetings, and most likely do not even know the names of their officials, let alone the policies they set.[8]

In other words, a bureaucracy, once formed, tends to take on a life of its own, initiates and implements policy partly of its own making, and may begin to direct the larger group, of which it is a specialized part, in new directions.

Iron Law of Oligarchy

Robert Michels's classic "iron law of oligarchy" can be seen operating in many religious groups. This refers to the tendency, as responsibilities and authority are transferred to leaders (a process seemingly inherent and inevitable in group life), for a number of developments in combination to lead to oligarchy (power and control becoming vested in a small number of leaders). Granting responsibility to leaders, for example, concentrates both skills and informal prerogatives in their hands. Leaders become more skilled than rank-and-file members in administration, coordination, manipulation, diplomacy, and so on, and they have access to information not available to others. Along with such skills and knowledge goes power. The gratitude and allegiance of members to their leaders, for doing jobs they would not care to do, also strengthens the leaders' positions of power and influence. Further, leaders tend to be self-perpetuating in their positions. They like their power and privilege, and they want to keep it. As a result, incumbents are hard to remove.[9]

Religious organizations are not immune to such organizational tendencies. In fact, they join on an equal footing with all other democratic organizations in this tendency. This is true regardless of how zealously a group may strive to remain a pure democracy. Even those religious groups that make a strong theological point that local and individual religious autonomy is sacred, are faced with the tendency to oligarchy. Of course, other religious groups, such as the Roman Catholic Church, stress a hierarchical authority pattern in the first place and have little problem living with the oligarchic tendency. Although there has been some change recently, with laypeople demanding more input into decision and policy making, the issue in such a group has traditionally been less one of laypeople wanting to curtail the power of bureaucratic church executives than of church officials trying to keep the laypeople from becoming too independent and free thinking. It is a struggle for power either way that is based on two characteristics of groups:

1. diversity on a number of dimensions within the group, and
2. the oligarchic tendency for leaders to accumulate power.

Internal diversity within a group makes effective total control next to impossible, yet oligarchic tendencies serve to override diversity in the interests of bureaucratic efficiency.

O'Dea's Five Organizational Dilemmas

Thomas O'Dea has taken into account these and similar tendencies within groups and has identified five major dilemmas that face religious groups, in particular if they persist over time, as religion becomes institutionalized. These are paradoxes that produce a variety of internal strains for religious and other normative organizations in particular.[10]

First, the *dilemma of mixed motivations*. This refers to the change that occurs in religious groups following the single-mindedness and sharp focus the group had at its creation. Initially, the group is clearly focused on particular important issues by the charismatic leader. But over time the group develops roles and statuses, and other concerns and interests begin to absorb peoples' attention. Privileges associated with leadership positions begin to supplement and dilute the "pure" motivations of the founder who focused on the mission of the group that they gathered around them. The question can always be asked as the group evolves over time: Why do leaders aspire to their positions? Is it to carry on the mission or is it to enjoy the privileges of leadership in the sense of prestige, power, reward, honor, and the like? Or is it a combination—that is, mixed motivations?

It is likewise with rank-and-file members, who are children of the founding members but did not share in the original conversion experience and may not have the enthusiasm or the insight and focus the original members had as they mobilized around their charismatic founder.

Second, O'Dea identifies the *symbolic dilemma*. Every religious group inevitably uses symbols and rituals to convey the meanings of experiences the group has had. People enjoy repeating acts that were part of meaningful experiences and events that occurred in the beginning. The symbols remind the participants of good times and experiences. But as time goes by and more people join who did not share in those original experiences, they find less and less meaning in the repetitious symbolic acts that become rote and routine—clichés at best, semi-magical at worst. So symbols that originally conveyed profound meaning and provided a rich memory of past experiences become essentially meaningless repetitive acts, with magical properties that pervert original meanings and interests and might alienate newer members of the group.

Third, there is the *dilemma of administrative order.* As the group grows in complexity and size, new roles and offices develop in response. But such bureaucratization often inhibits responding positively to change (calcified joints do not move well), as the group loses the flexibility it had at the beginning when the single leader made the decisions.

The fourth is what O'Dea called the *dilemma of delimitation: concrete definition versus substitution of the letter for the spirit.* His observation here is that religious messages must be shown to have applications for the everyday life situations and experiences of people, if religion is to have impact. The abstract needs to have concrete applications. That is, ethical insights are translated into a set of rules.[11] But, as leaders attempt to make rules to cover every contingency, the rules can become so absolute, specific, and legalistic as to stifle the "spirit" of the original teaching or ethical principles. Principles become absolutes and legalism takes over.

Fifth, the *dilemma of power: conversion versus coercion.* A religious group relies on an inner conviction of its adherents that its beliefs are both true and important. But as the group persists over time, it can resort to manipulation of those born into the group who might be trained to believe but do not develop the inner emotional conviction a conversion experience might have created. Further, a group that exercises such power internally might try to exercise power over others within the society in which it exists. In either case, it undercuts its original strategy of convincing people of the rectitude of the group's position and gaining their commitment through conversion.

RELIGIOUS LEADERSHIP

As we discuss groups, religious or any other kind, we cannot conclude without talking about group leadership. Certainly all groups have leaders, that is, those within the group who are looked to by the rest for creative ideas, advice, decisions, encouragement, and interpretation of the group's norms.

Such leadership can be exercised either as a shared, alternating responsibility by representatives of the rank-and-file members (laypeople) or by professional clergy who have specific, often very lengthy training, with titles like priest, minister, rabbi, guru, pastor, parson, reverend, prophet, shaman, and so on. While we will concentrate on the professional group, there is always lay leadership that, at the very least, supplements the professional, formal leadership of clergy. Some religious groups have only lay leadership. Groups, such as the Amish and the Society of Friends (Quakers), rely on members to maintain the group and to contribute to the enhancement of one another's knowledge, insight, and spiritual well-being, as they feel moved to do so.

While sociologists prefer to consider groups before they talk about the leaders of those groups (which is exactly our approach in this chapter), it is nonetheless true that leaders are important and fill a crucial role in groups. This is particularly obvious when we are talking about a charismatic leader—a subject we will take up shortly. But sociology tells us that most leaders are able to function legitimately—are able to lead—only as their actions and programs are firmly based in the group and its purposes and values. Note the adverb *legitimately:* It is true that a dictator or despot can rule and "lead" a group, if that person has sufficient firepower to keep the people in line and can keep them uneasy and frightened enough of informers and secret police to acquiesce. Yet most groups carry on with legitimate leadership that the current members have either chosen or accepted and, as such, have granted legitimacy both to the leadership role and to the person(s) occupying it.

For a group to proceed with its customary activities and make progress toward its goals, it not only needs some leaders to function as coordinators and "cheerleaders," who encourage the members to keep up their good work, but it also needs them to inspire and inform, to stretch their horizons and make relevant applications of the foundation principles to which they are committed. Thus, as James Wood points out, if leaders in churches can point to Scripture and relate what Jesus or St. Paul did or said and show how this is relevant to a current event or issue (perhaps facilitating racial integration through a bussing program or voting for some specific referendum or person, etc.), then the rank-and-file members are likely to consent to their leader's exhortations and deem them legitimate, even if the specific application of group principles that the leader proposes was not already in members' repertoire of actions and commitments.[12]

An important distinction among clergy leadership functions is that of prophet versus priest.[13] This distinction is made by Max Weber. He identified the religious functionary who carries out the ritual and repeats the sacred messages (the priestly function) and the religious prophet who proclaims innovation and a break with tradition, not on the basis of the official literature handed down through the generations (for Christians, the authority of Scripture) but because: "I, your prophet, say so; I bring a new message and new insight." To the extent that the prophetic leader can convince people to accept his or her word, we see charisma at work.

As with *prophet*, we have in *charisma* an overworked word. Currently, rock musicians, politicians, baseball players, business tycoons, movie stars, and many others "have charisma." As so used, the term suggests that the charismatic personage has special qualities that attract devoted followers, inspire high levels of emotion, and elevate the person so gifted well above the mundane level at which most of us function. Weber, however, restricted his use of the term to religion and in his own words called charisma "a certain quality" of a person by which they are "set apart from ordinary men" and possesses "supernatural, superhuman, or at least specifically exceptional powers or qualities."[14] And the prophet or prophetess with charisma "preaches, creates, or demands *new* obligations."[15] In other words, charismatic authority is revolutionary. A break with tradition is called for.

In contrast, most religious leaders are *priests*. That is, they are representatives of established religious systems with a body of teaching and ritual to perpetuate. They are functionaries who are prized more for their faithfulness than for their innovation.

But simply to distinguish between prophets and priests is not to say enough about the social functions of religious leaders, particularly those of priests, who are by far the most common type of religious leader. Although we have hinted that the role of priest is fairly predictable and functions in a fairly conservative social system, the role functions of these religious leaders vary. In a study of Methodist ministers and Episcopalian and Roman Catholic priests in England, three British social scientists identified seven subroles for professional religious leaders. They are listed in Table 3.1.

TABLE 3.1 Clergy Roles

Ranson, Bryman, and Hinings	Blizzard	Hall and Schneider
Administrator of church affairs	Administrator	Organizer and administrator
Celebrant of sacraments	Priest	Priest (leader of worship services)
Leader in the local community	—	—
Preacher of the word	Preacher	Preacher (giver of sermons)
Official (representative) of the church	Organizer	—
Pastor and father of the congregation	Pastor	Pastor (counselor)
Counselor (advisor and confessor)	—	—
—	Teacher	Teacher

Sources: Stewart Ranson, Alan Bryman, and Bob Hinings, *Clergy, Ministers and Priests* (London: Routledge & Kegan Paul, 1977), pp. 62ff,

Samuel W. Blizzard, "The Minister's Dilemma," *Christian Century* 73 (25 April 1956): pp. 508–510,

Douglas T. Hall and Benjamin Schneider, *Organizational Climates and Careers* (New York: Seminar Press, 1973), pp. 25–26.

What has been for years the classic list of clergy functions is that of Sam Blizzard, who identified six functions or subroles of American clergy. They are listed opposite their counterparts on the English list in Table 3.1. Blizzard called them "practitioner roles of parish ministers."[16] Hall and Schneider call them professional roles and refine the list to five (cf. Table 3.1). While the reader will recognize a great deal of consistency from list to list, always at issue for ministers is the question of the relative importance of these specific functions of the clergy role. Blizzard discusses how the clergy view the relative importance of these tasks and their order of preference in fulfilling them, yet reports a different ordering in actual practice. While the roles of *preacher* and *pastor* head both lists of importance and effectiveness, the role hit hardest in terms of clergy consensus about its relative importance is administration. The ordering in terms of importance that Blizzard finds in a survey of 690 ministers puts administration last. And it is next to last in their self-assessment of their effectiveness in carrying out that function. Yet administration consumes a higher proportion of their time than any other function. They reported two-fifths of their time spent on administration, but only one-fifth as preacher and priest combined, one-quarter as pastor, one-tenth as organizer, and one-twentieth as teacher.[17]

In the Ranson, Bryman, and Hinings study of English clergy cited earlier, the ministers in all three groups listed their role as administrator next to last in importance—only slightly more important than the role of official representative of the local and denominational church organization. But they too, like their North American counterparts, spend a great deal of their time as administrators.

It is significant to note, however, that a recent follow-up to the Blizzard study of 1955, by Sandi Brunnette-Hill and Roger Finke in 1994,[18] suggests that ministers are today spending considerably less time with administrative tasks. The average number of hours per week devoted to administration by mainline Protestant clergy in 1994 was slightly less than half (46 percent) the hours in 1955 (18.7 hours in 1994, 34.6 hours in 1955).[19] This decline is then reflected in an overall decline in total work week hours, from 69.3 in 1955 to 42.7 in 1994.[20]

NOTES

1. David Aberle, "The Functional Prerequisites of a Society," *Ethics* 60, no. 2 (1950): 100–111.
2. John B. Noss, *Man's Religions* (New York: Macmillan, 1949), pp. 175–176.
3. Edward Conze, *A Short History of Buddhism* (London: George Allen & Unwin, 1980), p. 42.
4. Rodney Stark and Roger Finke, *Acts of Faith: Explaining the Human Side of Religion* (Berkeley: University of California Press, 2000), p. 36.
5. Paul E. Mott, *The Organization of Society* (Englewood Cliffs, NJ: Prentice Hall, 1965), pp. 48–69.

6. Philip E. Hammond and Benton Johnson, *American Mosaic* (New York: Random House, 1970), p. 149.

7. Paul M. Harrison, *Authority and Power in a Free Church Tradition: A Social Case Study of the American Baptist Convention* (Princeton, NJ: Princeton University Press, 1959), pp. 74–77.

8. Ibid., p. 92.

9. Robert Michels, *Political Parties,* trans. Eden and Cedar Paul (Glencoe, IL: Free Press, 1949). First published in England in 1915.

10. Thomas F. O'Dea, *Sociology and the Study of Religion* (New York: Basic Books, 1970), pp. 243–251.

11. Ibid., p. 249.

12. James R. Wood, *Leadership in Voluntary Organizations* (New Brunswick, NJ: Rutgers University Press, 1981), p. 88.

13. Weber identified a third type of religious leader—the magician—who performs magic rituals and acts that are consistent with our discussion in Chapter 1 of magic as a subtype of religion.

14. Max Weber, *The Theory of Social and Economic Organization,* trans. A. M. Henderson and Talcott Parsons (New York: Oxford University Press, 1947), p. 358.

15. Weber, *The Theory of Social and Economic Organization,* p. 361.

16. Samuel W. Blizzard, "The Minister's Dilemma," *Christian Century* 73 (April 25, 1956): 508.

17. Blizzard, "The Minister's Dilemma," p. 510.

18. Sandi Brunnette-Hill and Roger Finke, "A time for Every Purpose under Heaven: Updating and Extending Blizzard's Survey on Clergy Time Allocation," *Review of Religious Research* 41(Fall 1999): 48–64.

19. Ibid., p. 54.

20. Ibid.

Chapter 4

The Church-Sect Continuum of Religious Organization

Religion as cult and sect.

Up to this point, we have explored ways in which religious groups are not only similar among themselves but also similar to other groups and social organizations. We now turn to some important distinctions among religious groups—distinctions that are fundamentally matters of organization—that is, sociological, not theological, differences. We begin with the *church-sect typology*—a way of identifying differences among religious groups. This typology was given its fullest early conceptualization by the theologian Ernst Troeltsch, but it was introduced into sociology by his teacher, Max Weber and has been used and expanded by numerous sociologists since their time.

The dichotomy of church and sect actually only identifies two polar types of religious organization. That is, the church and the sect occupy the ends of a social continuum that has several gradation points (other types of organization) in between. We will first contrast the polar types and then discuss three other types of religious organization that investigations, following those of Troeltsch and Weber, have shown to be important additions to the typology.

THE SECT

Demerath and Hammond suggest that differences between churches and sects can be observed from either of two perspectives, one concerning the internal characteristics of the organization, the other the external relationships of the group with the features of its social environment.[1] Focusing on internal differences, we can observe the following about sects:

1. A sect sees itself as a fellowship of the elect—that is, an embodiment of true believers.
2. Sects encourage spontaneity of religious expression, involving extensive group participation.
3. Sects de-emphasize organization and strive to maintain maximum democratic participation of members within an explicitly nonbureaucratic structure.
4. A sect is usually small and deliberately so.
5. Sects utilize laypeople as leaders. Frequently part-time, such leaders most likely have little or no formal theological training. Commitment to the principles avowed by the group is seen as more important than "book learning." The element of charisma is a common feature of leaders.
6. A sect emphasizes purity of doctrine and usually demands a return to original religious teaching. This involves a renunciation of the doctrinal perversions and aberrations that it accuses the established denominational religious groups of having allowed to intrude into true religion.
7. A sect emphasizes traditional ethical principles and strives to influence its members along a broad spectrum of behavior.
8. Sects tend to concentrate on other-worldly issues (salvation, deliverance, heaven, and hell) and discount or deprecate this world's concerns. Even their emphasis on ethics (point 7) is focused more on its relevance to ultimate other-worldly concerns and less on the relationship of person to person.
9. A sect gains new members primarily through conversion. It is initially a fellowship of adults, although eventually it must turn its attention to the religious socialization of children.
10. A sect draws disproportionately from the lower social classes in the society.

Implicit in many of the characteristics just outlined is the prime characteristic of a sect, namely, protest. Usually it is protest against both (1) established traditional religious forms and groups that sect members feel have strayed too far from pristine religion and (2) the surrounding secular society, which is viewed as embodying all kinds of evil. A sect thus reflects schism—a breaking away from and a rejection of established patterns, both religious and secular. At this point, we encounter most directly the external relationships of a sect to its surrounding social environment, which we mentioned earlier. The sect in its protest against the evils of the surrounding society engages in some kind of rejection of that social structure. The form may be withdrawal, in both a figurative and literal sense, from most of the typical activities people engage in. Communal groups, such as the Amish and Hutterites, would fit here and would be the most extreme form of withdrawal and rejection. They refuse to participate in the surrounding community, being nearly self-sufficient on their communal farms.

We might mention in passing that there are, of course, many other types of sects. Although we will not go into a description of the various types here, two typologies the reader may wish to explore are those of Elmer T. Clark and Bryan Wilson. Clark distinguishes the pessimistic-Adventist sects, the perfectionist-subjectivist sects, the charismatic-pentecostal sects, the legalistic-objectivist sects, and the communistic sects.[2] Wilson distinguishes the revolutionist, introversionist, manipulationist, thaumaturgical, reformist, and utopian sects.[3]

THE CHURCH

Before presenting the corresponding characteristics of the church type, we need to make it clear that the church (the sect also) is clearly what in sociology we call an ideal type. That is, the concept of church or sect or any of the other types of religious organization that we will describe later in the chapter, provides a summary or distillation of social characteristics and phenomena that frequently appear together and that, in combination, help to distinguish one set of organizations from another. It is a kind of model that expresses in pure, complete form the central characteristics of a pattern of organization or behavior. Although we do not expect to find all the characteristics of an ideal type in pure form in a particular organization at a given moment in time, we will expect to see most of them. In a sense, an ideal type is used for dramatic purposes, to heighten one's awareness of salient characteristics of a social phenomenon. For example, we listed ten characteristics of the sect. Yet a religious group may accurately be identified as a sect and lack one or two of the characteristics on the list or not reproduce all ten characteristics in full, "pure" form. Similarly, the church type represents one "extreme" form of religious organization that may have appeared at some time in history in essentially all its characteristics but probably never in pure form in all dimensions. That is, an ideal type is more a concept and less an empirical reality, though it is based on substantial empirical observations. Its value lies in providing a clear-cut base of comparison for what we observe empirically at a given point in time. Although we may be unable to observe an empirical example of a "church" at this point in history, we can understand more clearly what we do observe because of either its similarities to or differences from the ideal type we have as a base of contrast.

Within the category of "church" at one end of the church-sect continuum, J. Milton Yinger has distinguished two subtypes. At the very extreme is the Universal Church.[4] This type is truly all-embracing of the religious organization and expression in the society. It is the guardian and exponent of religion in that society and tolerates no religious competition. But part of its success in maintaining its religious dominance is its ability to tolerate considerable diversity within its ranks. Yinger notes that it integrates both sect and church tendencies "in a systematic way."[5] Further, it helps with the integration of the society and is, in fact, in close touch with the political and economic structures of the society and reinforces them. But it also satisfies many of the personality needs of individuals on all levels of the society. Yinger notes that the medieval Roman Catholic Church of the thirteenth century best illustrates this type. It was closely allied with the political structure and helped maintain a fairly well-integrated social structure, but it also tolerated considerable diversity, principally through its monastic structure.

We can summarize several characteristics as follows: The church

1. claims universality and includes all members of the society within its ranks, and has a strong tendency to equate "citizenship" with "membership";
2. exercises religious monopoly and tries to eliminate religious competition;
3. is very closely allied with the state and secular powers—frequently there is overlapping of responsibilities and much mutual reinforcement;
4. is extensively organized as a hierarchical bureaucratic institution with a complex division of labor;
5. employs professional, full-time clergy who possess the appropriate credentials of education and formal ordination;
6. almost by definition, gains new members through natural reproduction and the socialization of children into the ranks.

The other subtype of church was given the designation *ecclesia* (the Greek term for church) by Leopold von Wiese and Howard Becker.[6] The ecclesia shares the six characteristics of the universal church identified above but is less successful in incorporating diversity and does not have such full support from all levels of the society.[7] Yinger states that the ecclesia might be called "a universal church in a state of rigidification."[8] The traditional state churches of Europe, that we know of from the past six centuries or so, fit in here fairly well—but they tend to become almost an anachronism. That is, while still an official state church, other religious groups begin to operate and to be tolerated, though receiving no state tax support. As such, even the state-supported ecclesia becomes more like a denomination, though perhaps a special case. We turn now to the denomination.

THE DENOMINATION

The *denomination* is in a mediating position between the church and the sect, and as such is the most important addition to the original dichotomous church-sect typology. When the church loses its position of religious dominance and monopoly, denominationalism is the result. In fact, the moment the protesting, struggling sects that have been striving to attain autonomy are tolerated, however reluctantly, by the established church, the church is by definition dead and is immediately transformed into a denomination—that is, one religion among several. As some of the protesting sects evolve (we will discuss this evolutionary process later in the chapter), they too become denominations, and this type of religious organization—denominationalism—becomes a distinct, identifiable type.

A denomination can be defined as follows:

1. It is similar to the church, but unlike the sect, in being on relatively good terms with the state and secular powers. The denomination's most extreme stance in this respect would be "loyal opposition." It is at home in the halls of government and occasionally tries to exert some influence in that direction—something few sects try to do.
2. A denomination maintains at least tolerant and usually fairly friendly relationships with other denominations in a context of religious pluralism.
3. It relies primarily on birth for membership increase, though it will also accept converts; some groups even actively pursue evangelistic programs, although it is directed primarily to the unconverted, unchurched citizens, not persons who are presently members of other denominations.
4. A denomination accepts the principle of at least modestly changing doctrine and practice and tolerates some theological diversity and dispute—something a true sect will not do.
5. It follows a fairly routinized ritual and worship service that often explicitly discourages spontaneous emotional expression.
6. It trains and employs a professional clergy who must meet certain formal normative requirements before certification.
7. It recognizes competing demands from other affiliations upon its members' commitment and involvement; thus, it accepts less extensive involvement from members than a sect does but often expects more than the church (where, by virtue of the citizen-church member equation, it is recognized that many persons will be minimally or noninvolved members).
8. A denomination draws disproportionately from the middle and upper classes of the society.

Before proceeding to look at two other important types of religious organizations within the framework of the church-sect typology—namely, the cult and the institutionalized sect—we need to analyze further the relationship between sect and denomination. First, we want to look at the point of rupture when the sect protests to the point of breaking with the denomination or church. Second, we will trace the evolutionary pattern that most sects follow that eventually leads them to denominational status.

THE FORMATION OF SECTS

We stated earlier that the fundamental theme of the religious *sect* is protest—protest that leads to schism and a breaking away from the parent religious group, be it church or denomination. Such action, however, is not the only method of resolving conflict within a religious group.

Historic Alternatives to Sect Formation

One method historically employed by church-type religious groups—of which the Roman Catholic Church is the paramount example—is by allowing, often in fact encouraging, the formation of specialized groups within the larger body. If some persons feel they cannot worship properly in the established ritual form of ordinary local congregational groups (the reasoning goes), then allow them to form a subgroup or religious order within the larger body that emphasizes extensive contemplation and private meditation, or one that encourages active participation in social and political activities, or one that engages in spontaneous, emotional, pentecostal-type worship behaviors and experiences. Monastic orders within the Roman Catholic Church have served this purpose admirably. Even today, the tacit permission, if not encouragement, of pentecostal subgroups within such standard denominations as the Catholic, Lutheran, Presbyterian, and Episcopal Churches, is an excellent example of this tactic of channeling deviant and/or specialized groups within the overarching structure of the denomination.

Probably the most familiar method of resolving dissatisfaction within a denomination is simply for individuals or families to withdraw—either to drift from traditional organized religion altogether or to affiliate with another religious group that seems to satisfy their wishes and concerns more fully. How many present-day denominational switches are such expressions of religious protest, we do not know. Undoubtedly, many are relatively simple transfers of convenience, such as when a family moves and cannot find its denomination represented nearby; or when upward mobility (as opposed to ideological conflict) suggests to a person that they should forsake, say, their Baptist background and affiliate with a "higher-status" Presbyterian or Episcopalian congregation; or when an interfaith marriage leads one partner to switch to the other partner's religious group as a matter of form and convenience.

Another way of resolving religious conflict is for those who are dissatisfied simply to split off and form another denomination. We will soon emphasize that a prime ingredient in sect formation is the factor of social class. But if social class is not a particularly primary factor in a given controversy and the issue is more strictly political or ideological, then a denomination may simply split in two. The division of both the Baptists and the Presbyterians, into northern and southern denominations during the Civil War, are good examples of this process. The split within the Presbyterian Church in the 1930s over certain doctrinal issues is another example; not a sect, but another denomination (the Orthodox Presbyterian Church) formed as a result. Similarly, in nineteenth-century Europe, Reform Judaism separated from Orthodox Judaism, not as a sect but as a denomination.

Sect Formation

The final method of resolving religious group conflict is the one we keep referring to—the process of sect formation. What happens in this process and why? Ostensibly, the issue is almost invariably doctrinal or theological. Potential sect members are likely to talk about the loss of true Christianity in the parent denomination—about how doctrine has become liberalized and people are not living their Christianity the way they should. Some members finally opt out and form their own small group, in order to preserve or recapture the basics and the essence of true religion and save themselves from further theological contamination and perversion. Undoubtedly, most sectarians are sincere and truly believe that theological or doctrinal issues are the real issues. Yet one suspects there is more to it than that. The social scientist continually looks for latent factors lurking behind manifest behaviors, definitions of the situation, and rationalizations. We are thus particularly intrigued when we observe that sectarians are predominantly of lower-class social status. Aware that social status influences all manner of social behavior and attitudes, sociologists regard it as very likely that social status also relates in some way with the sectarian break from the denomination.

In his classic analysis of the interrelationship of religion and social structure, Liston Pope reviews several hypotheses that try to account for the phenomenon of sect formation. Most writers, he notes, pay serious attention to the status dimension or, at least by implication, suggest that lower social status is somehow significantly involved in the motivation for sectarian involvement.[9] For example, the "cultural shock" hypothesis of John B. Holt suggests that migrants to cities seek out or form sects as a means of preserving rural religious lifestyles and values and as a defense against the anonymity of the city and the urban denominational congregations.[10] Although such factors may be relevant for some persons, Holt's analysis does not account for the formation of sects in rural and small-town settings. Holt does point out, however, that persons attracted to sects, whether migrants experiencing cultural shock or not, are predominantly lower class.

A major explanatory perspective for many theorists, then, is to see sect formation as some form of compensation for those deficiencies epitomized by inferior social status. Pope notes that sects "substitute religious status for social status."[11] The sectarian is likely to say something like: "I may not be high society, but I'm on God's first string," or "I may not have a big house, a fancy car, and a college education, but I've got what's really important— I've got true religion." Pope observes: "They transmute poverty into a symptom of Grace."[12] Socially separated from those above them in the stratification system, they then emphasize separation from "the world" as a virtue. Although they feel excluded from fellowship with those of higher education and social and economic position, they in turn exclude from their fellowship those who dance, play cards, smoke, drink, and bet on the races. Unable to afford jewelry, they make wearing of any such adornment a sin. Pope again observes: "Excluded from secular society, they set up a religious society of their own, in which standards of membership are more rigid than those of the general culture that has ignored them."[13] Reaching heaven, which is the supreme, ultimate reward, becomes eminently more important than earthly success and the good life here and now, which is only temporal and not eternal.

THE IMPACT OF DEPRIVATION ON SECT DEVELOPMENT

To this point, we have been concentrating on a rather simplistic distinction between high and low socio-economic status. Charles Y. Glock has added specification to this general hypothesis, by introducing the concept of *deprivation* and making distinctions among five types of deprivation.[14] First, there is *economic deprivation*, which consists of limited income and access to the material necessities of life. It may be objectively defined and measured as well as subjectively experienced and perceived. That is, although people may technically not be categorized as living at the poverty level, they perceive themselves as poor. Such a perception can influence their behavior and attitude as much as, or more than, the objective facts of their existence.

Second, *social deprivation* refers to the relative absence of such societal rewards as prestige, power, social status, and opportunity for participation in various activities and organizations. This is frequently a concomitant of economic deprivation in the sense that low economic status most likely means low prestige or respect, little power or influence over others, and exclusion from much of the social and organizational life of the community. But social deprivation is not necessarily strictly correlated with economic deprivation. A person may be socially deprived yet be economically solvent, even successful. Social deprivation has been one of the main emphases of the Women's Liberation Movement. "Although I can buy all that my heart desires, I'm considered 'just a housewife' because it's my husband's income

I'm spending." "I may be receiving a very livable salary, but it's less than that of a man doing comparable work." And so on. Or social deprivation may be along age lines. Consider the very young and the very old, who have relatively little power and prestige, even though economically they may be facing no difficulty. Further, the minority-group member, such as a Chicano, black or American Indian, may be economically successful yet feel others regard them as a second-class citizen in other dimensions of status.

A third type of deprivation is *organismic*. This refers to the deprived condition of some in society along the dimensions of physical and mental health and biological-physical abilities. Some suffer from neuroses or psychoses; some are deaf or blind; some are paraplegics; some are mentally retarded; others suffer from one or more of an almost infinite variety of other conditions.

Another type of deprivation is what Glock calls *ethical*. This exists when persons come to feel that the dominant values and norms of the society no longer provide them with a meaningful way of organizing their lives. Ethically-deprived persons have trouble finding meaning in their lives and cannot decide where to go or how to proceed to find it. Above all, these persons seek a body of ethical prescriptions on how to organize their lives and want an alternative value system to inform and guide them.

Finally there is *psychic deprivation*, which affects the person who may enjoy the material rewards of society and may subscribe to society's norms but who nevertheless lacks an adequate share of psychic rewards—the person does not *feel* satisfied or really accepted in society. Such deprivation frequently accompanies social deprivation—for example, the black professional in American society who has superior specialized skill and education, who may be economically successful, but who still feels looked down upon because of skin color, and who, in many situations, is made to feel inferior or second-rate. Whereas social deprivation is more or less an objective measure or dimension, psychic deprivation is a psychological matter and thus highly subjective.

To relate these types of deprivation to the sources of sectarianism, we can first of all observe with Glock that the emergence of any protest movement or group—religious or otherwise—requires some feeling of deprivation on the part of the participants.[15] They face a problem that is either not being met by the groups they are presently affiliated with or is in some way produced by a group or groups with which they are affiliated (or both). Glock suggests, however, that while some felt deprivation is a necessary condition for protest group formation, it is not a sufficient condition—there are additional requirements. The deprivation must be shared with others, and these people need to find one another; a leader must emerge to suggest a solution; and no alternative existing institutional arrangements or processes must appear to be available.[16] When such factors combine, a protest group can get underway.

But what form will it take? For example, will it be a secular group or movement, or will it be a religious organization, such as a sect breaking away from a denomination? If the deprivation is either economic or social, it is likely that a religious route will be followed (1) when the nature of the deprivation is inaccurately perceived or inadequately understood—that is, when people do not realize that a prime factor in their unhappiness and frustration is their economic or social position relative to others, or (2) when, even though the nature of the deprivation is accurately perceived, people feel powerless to work directly at eliminating its causes.[17] In either case, persons may retreat into an emotionally releasing, rationalizing, other-worldly sectarian religious group and activity as a conscious or subconscious means of escaping from the harsh realities of economic or social deprivation. On the other hand, if people accurately perceive the problem and feel capable of attacking and resolving it through social change, then they are more likely to form a secular organization or attempt some other secular resolution. In other words, religious resolutions, such as the formation of sects, are essentially compensatory mechanisms for alleviating feelings of deprivation, while secular resolutions try to strike directly at the causes of the deprivation.

A striking example of both of these attempts can be seen in the black community in the United States. Historically, much black religious behavior and involvement has tended to be of the sect variety, quite clearly responding to economic and social deprivation in a compensatory way. More recently, however, as more blacks have become cognizant of the real nature of their problems, have rejected doctrines of inherent inferiority, and have become convinced that the system could be effectively challenged, the civil rights movement has flowered. Some young blacks in particular have increasingly turned to secular political organizations, or religious groups such as the Black Muslims, rather than to traditional black churches. More on this phenomenon and on black religion in general, appears in Chapter 13.

When social deprivation is not intimately associated with or reinforced by economic deprivation, another route may be followed that is neither sectarian nor secular—very simply, another religious denomination may result. Again we turn to the American black community for an example. The African Methodist Episcopal Church came into being, not as a sect, but as a denomination when freed blacks, many of them of essentially middle-class economic status, reacted to unequal participation privileges and unequal voice in the white-dominated Methodist Episcopal Church and broke away in 1796.

Rodney Stark has recently completed a large body of sociohistorical research into protest movements in Europe during the tenth to twelfth centuries, before the fifteenth and sixteenth century reformers began to achieve success. A fascinating finding in that research is the high percentage of leadership of these early attempts to reform the Catholic Church that were middle and upper class.[18] Historically, many of the protest movements (sectarian), instigated and led by middle- and upper-class citizens/members, that challenged the hegemony of the Roman Catholic Church in the first twelve hundred years of the Christian Era, could today have formed a new denomination. But such a solution to their dissatisfaction with dominant Roman Catholicism was totally intolerable to the Roman Catholic Church, whose universal response was to hunt down the heretics and stifle their protest by force of torture and death.

Although we have not discussed the cult as a specific type of religious group, we should mention at this point that either ethical or psychic deprivation is less likely to result in sectarian development and more likely, for reasons that will become evident later, to cause people to form, or be attracted to, a religious cult. It is, of course, also possible that ethical or psychic deprivation may precede secular solutions and the formation of nonreligious groups.

THE EVOLUTION OF SECTS

So much for the phenomenon of sect formation. We now turn to the issue of sect evolution and an investigation of the factors involved in the nearly universal tendency of sects (if they survive at all) to change and move away from their original "pure" state—in fact, to move toward eventual denominational status and to begin manifesting the characteristics of an organization from which they originally withdrew and which they earlier repudiated. We refer to the sect in its pure state as a religious group composed of the exclusive "elect" or select few, who practice what they see as "pure," authentic religion and who avoid secular involvement and contamination. Yet despite the good intentions and the sincere commitment to original and pure religion that give birth to a sect, we must begin with the empirical observation that only in extremely rare circumstances can a sect remain a sect.

Effects of Increasing Group Size

A major causative factor in the evolution of sect to denomination is quite nonreligious and very sociological. We refer here to the laws of increasing group size that we outlined in Chapter 3. For these laws to apply, we assume, of course, that the originally small sect grows. And even if a sect does not grow enough to call into play the laws of increasing group size, other nonreligious factors apply that we will discuss later. But assuming a sect adds to its numbers—as most do, since they usually want to spread their gospel and share their discovery of true religion—then some inevitable developments come about. More people automatically means a greater diversity of backgrounds. New members will not share precisely the same experiences of the original core group, and some will have significantly different personal objectives and goals that they expect the group to fulfill. Thus, problems of unanimity and total consensus arise, even though all may sincerely believe that they subscribe to the same goals and norms as everyone else. The foundation is therefore laid for ultimate modification of the sect's central goals and values.

As a group increases in size, subgroups inevitably develop. Although this phenomenon occurs the moment any few people form a group, it intensifies in geometric proportion as the group grows. Subgroups develop their own unique combinations of goals, norms, and roles, while still subscribing to the overarching ideology of the larger group and still respecting its structure. Subgroups not only provide internal diversity but also represent the distinct possibility that a particular subgroup may become increasingly deviant, gain more adherents, and ultimately dominate the larger group and assume guiding control. Obviously, under such circumstances the group will change.

We just mentioned deviance. As groups increase in size, deviance increases, largely through subgroup action. But that is not all. Tolerance of deviance increases, either because the deviance is unknown or unrecognized or because the task of enforcing strict normative behavior on the membership becomes more and more difficult. Clearly, the original conformity and unanimity is breaking down.

A prime need for groups, as they grow larger, is greater coordination. Strictly democratic decision-making in all matters becomes impractical and impossible. Responsibility for coordinating the activities of many persons and roles is centralized in specialists. A side effect will likely be a declining intensity of commitment and sense of involvement among ordinary members. Also, the distance between élite and rank-and-file members will increase. The person who sees original principles changed or lost will find it increasingly difficult to communicate their concern to the élites in the group. Not only will change remain unchecked, but also the individual who objects to change will become increasingly dissatisfied and disenchanted (while others, of course, will applaud the change).

A result may well be a legitimacy crisis, with some concluding that they must reject the authority of the leaders and coordinators. But perhaps they are voiceless or powerless. What to do? Go along silently but unhappily, or leave and form a new group—a new sect that can once again restore purity and truth to religion?

Universal Group Maintenance Needs and Process

But what if a sectarian religious group manages to avoid the problems inherent in organizational growth by simply not growing or, at least, by not growing to the extent that a bureaucratic structure develops and members become isolated from one another? Even with no growth or only limited growth, sources of change are present and begin to work. Almost immediately after formation, a formalization of norms begins and the group loses some of its spontaneity and flexibility. Then the group must answer two questions: (1) Where does authority lie? In a book? With a leader? In a doctrinal statement? That is, who or what is the ultimate arbiter? (2) What are correct beliefs? What are we going to teach our children and the adults who knock on our door and inquire about coming in?

With each development the group is becoming more stabilized as it formalizes its norms; structurally, it is becoming just a bit more like the group from which it severed itself. There is a little less chance for innovation; it is becoming a little more difficult to substantiate that the Holy Spirit is working through you to bring new insight. It becomes increasingly necessary to reconcile that which is newly-introduced with what the group has already established as normative in answering the two questions above.

Further, the group must provide for leadership succession. If the group begins with a charismatic leader, what happens if they die or are incapacitated or discredited as morally or otherwise unfit to continue as leader? Norms must, therefore, be established that outline the process of leader selection and succession. Perhaps it will involve a training program for potential leaders. Above all, it will require specification of the qualifications and duties of the leader. After all, if we bring in a new leader, they have to know what the duties are. At this point, something highly-significant has happened—the leader has become an officeholder. The leader's role has been routinized and formalized. And one observes the beginning of formal structure and ultimately, perhaps, of bureaucracy itself.

Also, any expansion beyond the few initial individuals or families will require attention to financial matters. A hall for meetings must be rented or purchased; some minimal equipment and fixtures must be provided; a checking account must be opened at a local bank. And again we see the spontaneous, flexible group becoming structured and routinized. It is taking the first step toward becoming the type of organization it disdained. "That church I used to belong to paid too much attention to everyday, worldly matters like meeting budgets, fund raising, and building maintenance. It didn't pay enough attention to spiritual matters—the really important things." So says the sectarian. Yet the sect itself must soon begin to have similar concerns, though at first on a smaller scale, of course.

Another factor contributing to change in the sect is the strong tendency within any group for higher-status persons to assume positions of power and to be elected to office. The sect is no exception. Low-status members of a group tend to defer to those with more education, a higher-status job, and greater prestige. The result tends to be a conservative influence on the group—conservative in the sense that such higher-status leaders are likely to want to modify and tone down extremes in the sect's stance and ideology. They have more at stake in the surrounding community and do not want their names associated with too weird a group. Thus, the sect begins to change, to accommodate itself, and it becomes more compatible with the surrounding culture.

A final important factor involved, in turning the sect around and leading it back toward the denominational form, is the upward status mobility of some of its members. Insofar as sect formation is primarily a lower-status phenomenon, what happens when some of these lower-status members improve their social and economic condition? They will either bring the group with them along the lines of modification and accommodation just discussed, or they will leave the group and affiliate with another group (more denominational in character) that is more compatible with their enhanced social status. If they stay, conceivably they could even force those in the group, who have not begun to change their status level and conditions, to pull out and form a new sect; this could be done consciously or unconsciously. What is involved here is effectively and poignantly stated by John Wesley, himself a founder of a sect—a sect that has become the Methodist Church in its various denominational forms:

> Wherever riches have increased, the essence of religion has decreased in the same proportion. Therefore, I do not see how it is possible, in the nature of things, for any revival of religion to continue long. For religion must necessarily produce both industry and frugality, and these cannot but produce riches. But as riches increase, so will pride, anger, and love of the world in all its branches. . . . Is there no way to prevent this—this continual decay of pure religion? We ought not to prevent people from being diligent and frugal; we must exhort all Christians to gain all they can, and to save all they can; that is in effect to grow rich. What way then can we take, that our money may not sink us into the nethermost hell?[19]

In other words, the sect has an inherent problem—in Marxian phraseology, a seed of self-destruction or change—that leads it out of its "pure" state and into something it rebelled against at an earlier point in time. And out of a sect grows a denomination. This is precisely what happened with Wesley's Methodists; indeed, it is a pattern that has also been followed by most of the other major Christian denominations today. Such groups as the Baptists, the Lutherans, the Presbyterians, and the Seventh-Day Adventists all began at one point as sects, but each has evolved to full-fledged denominational status today. David Harrell, who focuses on this manner of development in tracing the evolution of the Church of Christ sect, mentions that the evolution of some of these sectarian groups is directly related to the changing character of the membership of the group: "The cultured element in the movement . . . simply [begins] the search for a more sophisticated type of religion."[20]

Routinization of Charisma

Much of what we have discussed above, in tracing the difficulty for a sect to retain its level of protest and differentiation from its parent religious group, describes specific features of Max Weber's concept: *the routinization of charisma*. The sect begins with the emergence of leadership that may be one or a very few persons who have abilities to encapsulate many of the desires of those about them, to share their dissatisfactions, and propose solutions that will be in part at least new ideas or new combinations of ideas, that are conveyed in energized, convincing, enthusiastic ways. To do this the leader(s) must capture an emotional commitment from the others on the basis of a facility with appropriate language and hortatory skills that arouse them to decision and action. The leader is engaging, persuasive, and enthusiastic and is able to arouse similar enthusiasm to go forward with action defined as appropriate to solve their problem with the larger group, which they believe has deviated from traditional, true values and practices.[21]

We, of course, have been applying Weber's concept of the routinization of charisma to religious groups. But he applied the concept both to religious and nonreligious groups and tended to follow closely W. E. H. Lecky's application of the concept to a process that occurs in any group. Lecky says: "An enthusiasm is kindled, a group of adherents is formed, and many are emancipated from the moral condition of their age. Yet the full effects of such a movement are but transient. The first enthusiasm dies away, surrounding circumstances resume their ascendency, the pure faith is materialized, encrusted with conceptions that are alien to its nature, dislocated, and distorted, till its first features have almost disappeared."[22]

The person with charismatic qualities pulls people out of the routine and mundane, predictable ways of viewing and doing things. Although sectarians break away from their religious group, almost invariably with leadership from a charismatic fellow member, the focus is not on totally new and "far-out" theology. Rather, what is radical is the decision and act of pulling away from their original religious home, in order to get back to the traditional ways and original norms and practices of their religion as the leader and they now define them.

We shall shortly see that the factor of a charismatic leader for the group becomes even more central in the formation of a *cult*. In fact, it is most clearly seen in the formation of a *cult*. But it certainly applies also as sects begin, because leadership is always necessary for religious groups to form and continue. Of course, in the early religions of preliterate peoples, we do not know and obviously cannot observe the formation of religious groups in that situation and time. But we need to remember our earlier point that what we call "religion" was not viewed by prehistoric peoples as a separate institution in society, as we do now as more complex and larger societies have evolved. Leadership in such early societies was much more a function of the whole group and part of the "nature of things," without the focus on leadership that has characterized both standard religions and the emergence of new ones (as well as sect and cult formation during recorded history).

THE INSTITUTIONALIZED SECT

Another important type of religious organization is what Yinger calls the *established sect* and what others call the *institutionalized sect*.[23] It has been necessary to develop this concept to cover a route that sects occasionally take as an alternate to the predominant sect-to-denomination pattern. There is, of course, yet a third path that many sects follow—the sect-to-oblivion route. In fact, most sects do not survive long. Internal rivalries and personality clashes, problems with leadership succession, the geographic mobility of members, urban renewal that disperses constituencies and removes facilities—all conspire to make most sects transitory. Those that survive tend to evolve into denominations. However, some become institutionalized sects.

Characteristics

Such groups manage to retain elements of their radical protest and a strong commitment to ideology, while avoiding the accommodation and modification that would turn them into a denomination. Some denominational characteristics, however, usually become incorporated into the group—the group becomes somewhat bureaucratized; its norms and procedures become formalized; some of its members gain higher social status. Yet it does not become a denomination, even though it is no longer a pure sect. An institutionalized sect is halfway between the denomination and the sect on the church-sect continuum. What is of crucial significance, however, is that it is in a state of arrested development—the evolutionary process has been brought to a standstill.

Some examples will help clarify this type of religious organization. Religious cooperative and utopian groups, such as the Amish, the Hutterites, the Dukhobors, and various Mennonite groups, are excellent examples. The Quakers (Society of Friends) are a well-known group that also qualifies as an institutionalized sect. These groups are like the pure sect in the sense of being relatively small in numbers, engaging in protest against both the way religion has been routinized in denominations and the society itself, and emphasizing democratic involvement of members and thereby avoiding extensive bureaucratization. In fact, most such groups do not employ full-time clergy.

Members of institutionalized sects are unlike members of ordinary sects, in that their socio-economic status is often higher. Furthermore, their religious expression in worship is less emotionally charged, and they are more concerned about education than the newly-formed sect, which is primarily a fellowship of adults.

What we see in the institutionalized sect is essentially a case of "arrested development," in which a group neither moves all the way along the evolutionary path from sect to denomination nor disappears. How might we account for the arrested development of the institutionalized sect? The cooperative religious groups provide a very significant element in suggesting an answer to this question.

The Amish Example

Groups, such as the Amish, have avoided unsettling influences from the surrounding society and from other religious groups, by the rather dramatic tactic of withdrawing to a considerable degree from the surrounding society. As mentioned at the beginning of this chapter, this includes physical or geographic isolation, to the degree that such is possible in a modern society, by establishing themselves exclusively in rural environments. In the process, their members collectively become nearly self-sufficient, depending on the outside world for little, except machinery, fuel, and building materials. Thus, their members engage in only minimal contact with people outside their group. Such groups further increase their isolation by forbidding television sets and radios and by limiting the education of the children to elementary school. By specifying a very simple lifestyle and adopting distinctive clothing, they deliberately set themselves apart from others and maintain a readily discernible identity, besides avoiding the interaction with the outside world involved in keeping up with new styles. By deliberately minimizing contact with the outside, by making a virtue out of their uniqueness, and by carefully socializing their children, they contribute significantly to their protracted period of "suspended animation." Some of these groups have existed for hundreds of years with very little change and show essentially no signs of accelerating their pace of change today.

The Quaker Example

The Quakers, on the other hand, have not physically isolated themselves. In fact, among their members are many high-status, highly-educated professionals. Quakers, moreover, are politically and socially motivated and involved, as exemplified by their support for two social action and lobbying groups in Washington, DC. Yet the Quaker sect, which originated in the mid-1600s, has not become a full-fledged denomination. The Methodist Church and the Society of Friends today are quite different kinds of organizations, although both started out as sectarian movements. Yinger contrasts these two groups in making a very important theoretical suggestion, concerning why one group will proceed along the continuum to denominational status, while another will stop short at the institutionalized sect stage. He states that differential status improvement could not be a cause, since members of both groups have moved up the class ladder in fairly equal proportions. There does seem to be some difference, however, in intensity of persecution. Quakers were more vigorously opposed and persecuted everywhere than were Methodists. Conceivably then, the Quakers could have developed a stronger feeling of cultural isolation and thus greater internal solidarity.

But at best, Yinger suggests that such could only be a proximate cause. The really important question is: Why were the Quakers more vigorously opposed than the Methodists? Answering this question requires examining the nature of the group's original protest. Yinger's suggestion is that those sects that emphasize problems of individual anxiety, sin, and salvation tend to evolve into denominations, while sects whose concern is focused on social evils and injustices will become established or institutionalized sects.[24] Radically different kinds of protest distinguished the early Methodists from the early Quakers. The Wesley brothers and other early Methodists were concerned primarily with individual morality and worked to rescue people from their sin. Quakers, however, attacked society and called for political reforms, for an end to societal injustice and discrimination, and for an end to poverty. Certainly society could more easily tolerate, even encourage, the Methodists' emphasis, yet feel threatened by the Quakers' beliefs, a fact that goes far in explaining why one sect was persecuted vigorously and the other not nearly so much.

The point here is not so much that, as a result of societal persecution and opposition, a group such as the Quakers may be forced back on its own resources and develop higher group identification and morale. The point is that such a group finds its feeling of estrangement from society intensified— it feels less at home in society and is less likely to evolve to full-blown denominational status, one characteristic of which is a relatively cozy, supportive relationship with the governing structure of the society. The stance the Quakers adopted placed them in a role more like that of an antagonist and less like that of even "loyal opposition," as we understand that term from British parliamentary politics.

In a sense, the physical isolation of the cooperative, utopian religious groups is matched by the political and social isolation of the Quakers. Moreover, the institutionalized cooperative sects are also in opposition to much that exists in society, which is viewed as basically evil and as a source of contamination. Many of these groups do not even vote in national or local elections. Institutionalized sects, such as the Quakers, on the other hand, do not express their opposition to society by withdrawing; they become activists and try to change society. In either case, however, such groups are inhibited in moving along the path to standard denominational status.

THE CULT

The final type of religious organization to consider is the religious cult. A *cult* is similar to a sect in its rejection of the religious patterns and formulations of denominations—or of whatever the society's dominant form(s) of religion happens to be. Cult members were either not attracted to dominant religious groups in the first place or, like sectarians, became disenchanted with commonly-accepted religious forms. The cult differs from the sect, however, in that it does not call for a return to the original, pure religion, but rather emphasizes the new—a new revelation or insight provided by a supernatural power, say, or the rediscovery of an old revelation that had been lost and unknown for many years (and which is, therefore, new to this age). Thus, cults tend to be out of the mainstream of the dominant religious system in a society. Although there will usually be some overlapping of ideology and terminology, cults deliberately contrast themselves with dominant traditional religious groups. As might be expected, cults frequently employ new terminology and symbols. The discourses of some groups, such as the Great I Am, are hardly intelligible to the uninitiated. The themes of cults tend to be mystical and esoteric. Furthermore, a cult is more likely than any other type of religious group to be centered around a charismatic leader—that is (as introduced earlier in this chapter), a person who is believed to have been given special revelation or knowledge and the ability to open the door of truth and insight to the uninitiated. Father Divine, Daddy Grace, Mary Baker Eddy, the Reverend Jim Jones, the Reverend Moon and certainly Bo and Peep (also known as Tiddly and Wink, Winnie and Pooh, and, at the end, Do and Ti) of the Heaven's Gate mass suicide in 1997, are such types.

Cults also have a strong individualistic emphasis, stressing peace of mind and getting the individual in tune with the supernatural, while exhibiting relatively little concern with social change. Cults tend to be urban-centered, in part because they have traditionally not attracted great hordes of people and therefore need a large population to draw from, but probably also in part because cults tend to attract the disenchanted, those persons looking for meaningful attachments to counterbalance their anonymity—persons who are probably more likely to be found in urban settings. Cults seldom develop much of an organizational structure, often tend to remain small and informal, and can be quite casual about membership requirements. They may not even require followers to sever their other religious affiliations.

Cults tend to be rather transitory and short-lived. Being dependent on a charismatic leader, they tend to dissolve when the leader dies, disappears, or is discredited. Occasionally, however, a cult persists, develops a structure and means of leadership succession, grows in size, and actually moves toward denominational status. In a study of cults in Alberta, Canada, W. E. Mann found the following characteristics of members: Anglo-Saxon by ethnic

FIGURE 4.1 The Church-Sect Continuum

background, more female than male, individuals rather than family units, avid readers with above average educational attainment, highly mobile, and although of comfortable financial means, seeming to lack full middle-class acceptance.[25] Although a few writers have placed the cult beyond the extreme end of the church-sect continuum, another way of viewing it is to see it as an alternate to the sect at one end, that may move on to the continuum at some point and give evidence of evolution toward denominational or quasi-denominational status. Figure 4.1 shows what we are suggesting. The dotted line associated with the cult indicates the possibility that it may change, not die, and get on the evolutionary road toward denominational status. A classic example is Christian Science, which began as a cult (with Mary Baker Eddy as its leader) but today exhibits most of the characteristics of a standard denomination. Similarly, the Nation of Islam (Black Muslims), which originally met all the criteria of a cult—it began as a small group with a charismatic leader (Elijah Muhammed) who preached a new doctrine of black supremacy and Islam (out of the mainstream of Christianity), emphasized individual self-help rather than societal reform, and was primarily urban—is now showing definite signs of moving toward a denominational pattern.

It must be noted that cults are rather commonplace today. Faith-healing cults continue to abound; cults that center around Eastern religious ideas and individual gurus have gained in popularity; interest in the occult and the formation of groups around the practice of the occult have increased; and segments of the drug culture that celebrate the use of mind-expanding drugs as a religious enterprise continue to emerge. The cult phenomenon is very much alive and well, although individual cults themselves may be extremely transitory as they flower today and wither tomorrow.

Jim Jones's Peoples Temple as Cult

To illustrate some of the points we have made concerning cults, we will look specifically at the Reverend Jim Jones's Peoples Temple, as a representative religious cult. Although Jim Jones started off traditionally enough as an ordained minister in a standard denomination (Disciples of Christ), he and members of his congregation began to pull away from the parent denomination as they migrated from Indiana to northern California and as such exhibited some characteristics of a sect, at least for a short time. But the Reverend

Jones's message was not a return to the original true faith of the denomination of his ordination but a *new message* totally centered in the leader himself. And Jim Jones became "god" in classic cult fashion. The date is November 1969; the place is the Peoples Temple Christian Church in Ukiah, California. The Reverend Jim Jones is preaching:[26]

> The King James Bible is full of contradictions and errors. . . . If there were a God in Heaven, do you think he would let me say these things about his Holy Word? If there is a God in Heaven, let him strike me dead![27]

Was this a "new message?" If not new, it was unusual—to say the least—from a Christian pulpit. Note that Jones is not calling for a return to the original message or intent of Scripture as a sectarian would. He simply discredits the Bible and substitutes a new message. As Jones continues, he sounds more and more like a cult leader:

> I have seen by divine revelation the total annihilation of this country and many other parts of the world. San Francisco will be flattened. The only survivors will be those people who are hidden in the cave that I have been shown in a vision. Those who go into this cave with me will be saved from the poisonous radioactive fallout that will follow the nuclear bomb attack. This cave is what led our church to migrate to this little valley from Indianapolis, Indiana. I have been shown that this cave goes deep into the earth. All the members of my church will stay in it until it is safe to come out. We have gathered in Redwood Valley for protection, and after the war is over we will be the only survivors. It will be up to our group to begin life anew on this continent.[28]

In a cult, a charismatic leader[29] not only brings a new message but is also frequently deified—or something very close to it. For example, Father Divine openly called himself God and his followers regarded him as such. By way of another example, in the Unification Church it is very difficult to distinguish when references to God are to God, as commonly viewed in Judeo-Christian terms, or to Reverend Moon himself. Often it does indeed seem to be Moon.

We note the same pattern with Jim Jones.

> Jim looked around the room again and in a loud voice called out, "Wilson." The room became silent.
> "Yes?" This time it was a middle-aged black woman sitting near the front.
> "You have been having a dull pain in your stomach even as you sit here today."
> "Yes."
> "To give you more faith I want you to know that I can see a bottle of aspirin in your bathroom medicine chest. It's sitting beside a prescription bottle that was given to you by a Dr. Edwards."

Mrs. Wilson, who had been speaking softly, suddenly shouted out, "Yes, Lord!"

"Who can know these things?" Jim asked with a sweet smile.

Tears were flowing down her cheeks as she answered, "Only God could know."

"You have a cancer in your stomach. You don't even know it is there but by the power of love I will make it pass."

Mrs. Wilson went into the restroom with one of the women, that Jim indicated was a nurse, and a few minutes later they returned. The nurse was holding a mass of smelly flesh covered with blood in a handful of tissues. Jim asked the nurse to take it around to show those who might be skeptical. He took his dark glasses off for a moment as he looked lovingly at the woman and said, "This is the cancer that left your body, and I tell you that it will never return. Praise God!" And praise she did, along with everyone else in the room. But the praise was not for God, it was all directed toward Jim Jones.[30]

He began to hint broadly that he was none other than "God Almighty." In a secret meeting he told us that he knew his previous incarnations. He bragged that he had been Buddha, the Bab, Jesus Christ, and, most recently, Lenin. "Of course," he warned them, "this is highly confidential and you aren't to tell anyone else. The members might not understand, especially about that last incarnation."

When he realized that his staff members were awed by this revelation, he decided that the rest of his members would probably be impressed, too. In the next Sunday service he announced that he was going to tell those who were present one of his greatest secrets. With a great deal of ceremony he announced, "I have lived on this earth before. I have come for a special mission and you who are following me are my chosen people. Most of you have been with me during some of my previous incarnations. I lived thousands of years ago as Buddha. Then I spent a short incarnation as the Bab, the person who founded the Bahai faith. I have lived on earth as Jesus the Christ, and my last incarnation was in Russia as Vladimir Lenin." He spoke with such authority and sincerity that we all believed him.[31]

Although the charisma of the leader is important in maintaining a cult, it is also necessary that the group have important goals and aspirations. The group needs more substance than hero worship by itself. The ostensible goals of the Peoples Temple are epitomized in Jim Jones's words, as follows:

I have the answers to the problems of society. Someday I will be the ruler of the United States. I will eliminate racism, political oppression, ecological imbalances, and the problem of the super rich and the super poor. I will make the whole country become like our community. I call this "Apostolic Socialism."[32]

It probably needs to be said at this point, in all fairness, that much of the time the group strenuously opposed racism, was itself highly-integrated racially, and provided for the care of scores of lost, homeless, and desperate people. It hardly needs mentioning, of course, that some of these were among the followers who lost their lives in Jonestown.

In the following vignette, we note the introduction of the idea of mass suicide that became the ultimate test of dedication to the "Cause," as identified by Jones in the preceding quote. The year is 1973, five years before the deaths at Jonestown.

One afternoon the P.C.[33] counselors received an emergency message. "Come to the church immediately for a special meeting." We dropped what we were doing and left as instructed. When we arrived it was obvious that Jim was very upset.

He began, "Eight people left the church last night. They cut the telephone wires so Tom couldn't call to warn us." He was speaking in a low voice as though he were afraid the walls might hear what he was saying. "No one knows why they left, but Jim and Terry Cobb, Wayne Pietila, Micki Touchette, and four others all disappeared. Don't worry, though, I'll find them." Jim tried to sound confident, but then he shook his head in despair. "These eight people might cause our church to go down. They could say things that would discredit our group. This might be the time for all of us to make our translation together." He had mentioned the idea of a "translation" a few times before, but no one had ever taken it seriously. His idea was that all the counselors would take poison or kill themselves at the same time, and then he promised we would all be translated to a distant planet to live with him for eternity. The few who believed this fairy tale said they'd be happy to do it anytime. Now, however, faced with death, it became obvious that there were many who didn't want to

"What about the other church members, and our children?" Linda Amos asked.

"Oh, yes, that's the problem. Those who would be left behind." Jim was speaking slowly and deliberately now, and it seemed that he was trying to formulate his ideas as he spoke. "Perhaps we could devise a plan where the children would be sent to another country first." I relaxed as I realized that his plan wasn't as well thought out as I had feared. Since he hadn't worked out these important details, I was sure he couldn't insist that we all kill ourselves right now.

"I want to take a vote today to find out how dedicated you all are," Jim said. "Life is a bore. Surely no one here is enamored with his existence. You've seen too much reality in all the hours of counseling at the P.C. meetings. How many of you here today would be willing to take your own lives now to keep the church from being discredited? Perhaps this way we will go down in history as revolutionaries. We could leave a note saying that we were doing this as a sign that we want peace on earth, or that we couldn't exist as an apostolic socialist group, or something like that."[34]

And so the seed had been planted. On November 2, 1978, all that was left for over nine hundred people was potassium cyanide, a few bullets, and Jim Jones's promise of an immortality that comes with dying for a cause you believe in. And a religious sect-become-cult had flourished, but now is gone.

David Koresh's Branch Davidians as Cult

David Koresh is a cult leader of more recent memory who met his death along with eighty-five others, including seventeen children, in his Mr. Carmel community near Waco, Texas, 19 April 1993. Although his message never became so deviant from what we might call a legitimate branch of Christianity as that of Jim Jones, David Koresh certainly saw himself bringing a new message that would unlock many secrets of the Bible and usher in a new age. He claimed his message, that was gradually unfolding, was from God himself and was given only to him as God's final emissary and chosen leader of the faithful.

Like Jones and many other cult leaders of the past, he defined himself as divine, as *a* Christ. That is, just as Jesus Christ was the special Son of God, so Koresh was a special son of God, selected finally to reveal to the world the meaning of the Seven Seals identified in the Book of Revelation. Koresh maintained that the "lamb" referred to in Revelation is not Jesus, as Christian interpretation has maintained through the nineteen centuries following the writing of the Book of Revelation, but a "second Messiah," namely, David Koresh himself. At many other points in Scripture, Koresh identified himself as the true referent, though traditionally it has been seen as Jesus.

David Koresh was a ninth-grade dropout and not a recognized minister of the Seventh-Day Adventist Church with which he identified. But he was a knowledgeable student of the Bible and could quote at length and cross-reference thoughts and Scripture passages with great agility. He identified himself as the seventh messenger of Revelation 10:7, sent to unlock the mysteries of the Seven Seals when God told him to do so. Koresh believed he received God's final approval to proceed with writing his exposition of the Seven Seals on 14 April, five days before the destruction of the Branch Davidians.[35] He began immediately to decode the messages of the Seven Seals and promised to come out and turn himself over to the authorities when he was finished. Apparently he completed his work on the First Seal in those last days before the conflagration, as a survivor brought out with her a computer disc of the typescript.

Whether he would have come out when all seven expositions were finished will remain unknown, of course. To be sure, he had made similar promises before and failed to follow through. But this time it would most likely have been different. James Tabor, a biblical scholar trusted by Koresh, says, "There is not the slightest doubt in my mind that David Koresh would have surrendered peacefully when he finished his manuscript."[36]

It is tragic that the Bureau of Alcohol, Tobacco, and Firearms lacked sufficient theological insight themselves and failed to take advice from those who did, to be aware that the Seven Seals were the point of it all. Koresh truly believed his mission in life was to decode those seals. And now, finally, he had both the insight and the divine authorization to do so (so he believed).

James Tabor and Eugene Gallagher repeatedly make the point that for those who know something about biblical apocalypticism—belief that the end times are near and the signs are in the Bible (particularly the Book of Revelation) to be read, interpreted, and understood—what Koresh said and did do not seem as weird as his actions and words would suggest to those unfamiliar with the apocalyptic vision.

A key to understanding the stalemate that lasted fifty-one days and ended in death for so many, is that each side defined the situation very differently. The Bureau of Alcohol, Tobacco, and Firearms and the Federal Bureau of Investigation defined it as a hostage/barricade rescue situation, which suggested a set of standard tactics and procedures. However, the Branch Davidians believed they held no hostages, had erected no barricades, and did not need to be rescued from anything except unlawful outside attack. Tabor and Gallagher summarize their point of view as follows: "They understood themselves to be a religious community or *family* that had been brutally attacked, without provocation, by agents of the United States government."[37]

A lack of understanding of the theological message and mission of David Koresh and the Branch Davidians was a serious problem—a problem exacerbated by failure of the authorities to seek out and listen to people who could inform them about both the theology and the character of groups such as this. As Michael Markun says: "The single most damaging mistake on the part of federal officials was their failure to take the Branch Davidians' religious beliefs seriously."[38]

The second serious problem, as noted by numerous scholars, was that those who did have the ear of the authorities were anti-cultists (cult busters) and deprogrammers who saw cults almost solely in pejorative terms. The counsel received from these advisers was full of dire predictions about outcomes if David Koresh was not stopped now "because that's the way cults are." There was no special knowledge or insight into this particular cult on the part of those giving that advice.

OTHER NON-AMERICAN CULTS

Both the Peoples Temple and David Koresh's group of Branch Davidians are native-born American cults. It is important to note, however, that such groups emerge elsewhere as well and can develop out of any religious system (as they have time and time again throughout the centuries). In very recent years, there are numerous examples around the globe—not just cults forming (there are always hundreds, perhaps thousands of them worldwide), but cults that have involved violence and mass suicides/murders and/or governmental intervention and intrusion into their activities.

In early spring, 2000, the world was shocked to read of some 979 citizens of Uganda who died (some murdered, some from suicide), while being members of a cult called Movement for the Restoration of the Ten Commandments of God that had two charismatic leaders, Cledonia Mwerinde and Joseph Kibwetere. This was an apocalyptic group that had predicted the end of the world on 31 December 1999. There is evidence that this was less suicide than murder by the leaders, because when "doomsday" did not occur as the new millennium began, followers began to demand return of their property and possessions that they had given to the group and its leaders upon their instructions: Some 530 members were burned alive in the group's principal location in Kanungu, Uganda. The rest were murdered and buried in several common graves on various properties owned by the group.

It should be noted that this group, although in an East-African country, was led by two excommunicated Catholics and drew heavily from Catholics who were unhappy with their church though not necessarily separated from it. And the context in which this occurred was a country ravaged by infection and death from AIDS and the reigns of terror conducted by dictators, Idi Amin and Milton Obate. Characteristically, the group forbade sex, cosmetics, and short skirts, and urged fasting, prayer, and hard work. All property was communal; all earnings were handed over to the leaders; and absolute sexual abstinence was required.[39]

A cult of a different order is the Falun Gong in China. This is a group also of recent origin—1992—which has attracted a large following, estimated to be in the millions. This group has its religious origins in Buddhism and Taoism and promotes health and morality while practicing prescribed slow motion exercises. At the core of its theology is the founder's (Li Hungzhi) teaching that he can provide his followers with a "dharma wheel," which he describes as a miniature of the cosmos that he installs telekinetically in their abdomens. It rotates inside them, throwing off bad karma and gathering good *Qi*. The name Falun Gong means "great law of the dharma wheel." Apparently some followers have relied on their internal *falun* and failed to get well. Accordingly, on 22 July 1999, the Chinese government banned Falun Gong and accused its leadership of directing more than 1,600 followers to decline modern medical treatments, consequently condemning them to what amounted to suicidal acts.

In issuing a warrant for the arrest of Li Hungzhi, the Ministry of Public Security accused him of spreading superstition and malicious fallacies to deceive people, resulting in the deaths of many practitioners. Further, the governmental Xinhua News Agency stated there were many cases of people committing suicide, having psychiatric illness, or refusing to see doctors because they believed that Falun Gong could heal serious illness.

On 26 December 1999, four Falun Gong leaders were sentenced to up to eighteen years in prison. At the same time, six leaders of underground Protestant groups were sent to a labor camp for one to three years, as part of a government crackdown on cults.[40]

One more contemporary example of a cult is a group that is familiar to every reader—Osama bin Laden and his al Qaeda organization. While many would perhaps not immediately think of bin Laden and his group as a religious cult, probably seeing it as a political group which it is also of course, a close look at its characteristics reveals a good match with the cult phenomenon we have been discussing. Certainly there is the charismatic leader in the person of bin Laden. There is strong devotion and commitment to him and his ideology on the part of followers that can lead to the ultimate test of commitment—a suicide mission.[41] There is strong emphasis on religious devotion and motivation, but to a tangential or deviant form of religion that does not represent its mainstream attachment (Islam in this case) and becomes obsession. That is to say, while the two most strongly motivating concepts in the al Qaeda theology—jihad (struggle, war) and the promise of immediate transport to heaven upon one's death in jihad—are taken from traditional Islam, they are uniquely defined and practiced under bin Laden's direction. In other words, bin Laden's theology is not faithful to orthodox Islam.

Gilles Kepel notes that bin Laden invites the world to see a clear parallel between the Prophet Mohammed's flight to Medina in Year One of the Hegira, prior to recovering Mecca and revealing Islam to the world, and bin Laden's own flight to the mountains of the Hindu Kush in Afghanistan. This is the point of departure for the return to the Middle East to cleanse it of Western influence.[42] Throughout it all, bin Laden echoes a theme of many cults—proposing a radical response to the state of affairs in which we find ourselves—in the name of religion. Throughout it all streams his plea to his fellow Arabs to expel the Americans from the Islamic peninsula—the land of the two most holy places of Islam (Mecca and Medina).[43]

An Alternative Term

In concluding our discussion of cults, it needs to be stated that most sociologists now avoid using the term. This is because the term *cult* has become almost synonymous with a sinister, diabolical, brainwashing, authoritarian, irrational organization. As such, the word has lost much of its usefulness, particularly in communicating with the general public, because the violence and frequent suicidal tendencies and outcomes of some cults have come to dominate people's thoughts whenever the word is heard or read. Many scholars have argued persuasively for avoidance of the word because it lacks scientific precision. And there is now consensus within the sociology of religion to speak of New Religious Movements (NRMs) and eschew the "C" word, cult. While that is fine for many of the groups we have called cults, that have formed in the last thirty years or so, there are other groups that we have called cults in the past for which we now lack a name. Here we refer to the largely urban groups with an out-of-the-ordinary emphasis or focus that seem to attract people who have relatively few primary group ties in the city and like to explore new and novel ideas. Frequently these groups are not too concerned about membership and whether those who show up are deeply committed, and their connection with the leader is not so strong or deep as with the more dominating and communal cults of Jones, Koresh, and bin Laden. Perhaps these nonviolent, less intense, and demanding groups should be called *traditional cults* and leave the designation New Religious Movement to describe more narrowly the examples identified earlier, which are indeed usually "new" and always demanding of total commitment, even to the point of mass suicide as absolute devotion and obedience to the leaders are demanded.

REFINEMENTS OF THE CHURCH-SECT TYPOLOGY

Although the church-sect typology, which has been presented and applied in this chapter, is time-honored and although we continue to see it as helpful, particularly in its descriptive capacity, the concept has had its critics. In fact, a very substantial literature on this topic has emerged in the last fifty years.[44] Some of the critics suggest refinements; others suggest alternatives.

Actually, in a very real sense of the term, much of what we have presented in this chapter has been in the nature of refinements of the original church-sect typology. The concepts *denomination, institutionalized sect*, and *cult (New Religious Movement)* are all refinements of the original typology proposed by Troeltsch and Weber, though Weber uses the term "cult" in an archaic way as "any religious group," not a subcategory or type of religious group, as sociologists and others do today.

Another approach, by way of refinement, has been to elaborate the list of characteristics of sects and/or churches. For example, Liston Pope makes twenty-one distinctions between the church and the sect, in his classic study of the religious life of Gastonia, North Carolina.[45]

Benton Johnson went in the opposite direction and suggested that there is really only one essential distinction between a church and a sect. That distinction is whether a religious group accepts or rejects its larger social environment. The sect rejects; the church or denomination accepts.[46] This distinction is, of course, highly-compatible with all of our discussion in this chapter. Johnson is simply trying to distill everything into its essence. The sect opposes, challenges, and rejects much of what it sees in the surrounding society and its culture; the church or denomination compromises, reinforces, and accepts most of that same society and culture.

Before Johnson's single-variable measure (1963), Yinger (1957) had proposed two criteria for differentiating churches from sects: degree of inclusiveness-exclusiveness of the group and degree of attention paid by the group to the task of social integration as opposed to satisfaction of personal need.[47] By 1970, Yinger added Johnson's criterion and changed his earlier second criterion to emphasize the degree of bureaucratization and success in integrating a variety of subunits into one structure.[48]

Roland Robertson has suggested two criteria: the basis of legitimacy as perceived by the leaders of the religious group and the principle of membership implemented by the group.[49] The legitimacy measure contrasts views of religious leaders: (1) the view that one's group is only one among other sets of acceptable or valid religious vehicles (religious pluralism); and (2) the view that one's group is the only valid religious form (unique, true religion). The membership principle contrasts "relatively demanding standards of admission and/or religious performance" (exclusivism), with low standards of acceptance (inclusivism).[50]

Another interesting modification has been contributed by Stephen Steinberg. He has analyzed the emergence of Reform Judaism from its "parent," Orthodox Judaism, not as the formation of a sect but as a "church movement." Note that earlier in this chapter we described the emregence of Reform Judaism as a breaking away from a parent denomination not as a sect but as a full-fledged denomination. That is, Reform Judaism did not object to any "perversion of true religion" embodied in Orthodox Judaism but to the continued insistence by Orthodox Judaism on retaining the "old ways"—the Reform movement sought to "modernize" Judaism. Building on Benton Johnson's single-variable distinction between church and sect that we described earlier—in which a religious organization accepting the surrounding social environment is defined as a church and one rejecting it as a sect—Steinberg points out that the rebel group (Reform Judaism) did not follow the common route of the sect by rejecting its social environment but accepted and accommodated that environment.[51] Although Steinberg notes that conditions giving rise to such a "church movement" are rare, such a development is well worth noting. Further, our understanding of the dynamics of such a development is enhanced by our understanding of what "normally" happens along the church-sect continuum.

NOTES

1. N. J. Demerath III and Philip E. Hammond, *Religion in Social Context* (New York: Random House, 1969), pp. 70–71.
2. Elmer T. Clark, *The Small Sects in America* (Nashville, TN: Abingdon, 1949).
3. Bryan Wilson, *Religious Sects* (New York: McGraw-Hill, 1970).
4. J. Milton Yinger, *The Scientific Study of Religion* (New York: Macmillan, 1970), p. 257.
5. Ibid.
6. Leopold von Wiese and Howard Becker, *Systematic Sociology*, on the basis of Leopold von Wiese, *Beziehungslehre und Gebildelehre* (New York: John Wiley & Sons, 1932), pp. 624–628.
7. Yinger, *The Scientific Study of Religion*, p. 262.
8. Ibid.

9. Liston Pope, *Millhands and Preachers* (New Haven: Yale University Press, 1942), pp. 133–134.

10. John B. Holt, "Holiness Religion: Cultural Shock and Reorganization," *American Sociological Review* 5, no. 5 (1940): 740–747.

11. Pope, *Millhands and Preachers*, p. 137.

12. Ibid.

13. Ibid., p. 138.

14. Charles Y. Glock, "The Role of Deprivation in the Origin and Evolution of Religious Groups," in *Religion and Social Conflict*, eds. Robert Lee and Martin Marty (New York: Oxford University Press, 1964), pp. 24–36.

15. Ibid., p. 29.

16. Ibid.

17. Ibid.

18. Rodney Stark, *For the Glory of God* (Princeton, NJ: Princeton University Press, 2003), Chapter 1, "God's Truth: Inevitable Sects and Reformations, pp. 15–119.

19. Quoted in H. Richard Niebuhr, *The Social Sources of Denominationalism* (New York: Meridian Books, 1957), pp. 70–71.

20. David E. Harrell Jr., *Emergence of the "Church of Christ" Denomination* (Lufkin, TX: Gospel Guardian Company, 1967), p. 28.

21. Max Weber, *The Theory of Social and Economic Organization*, ed. and trans. by H. M. Henderson and Talcott Parsons (New York: Oxford University Press, 1947), pp. 363–364.

22. W. E. H. Lecky, *History of Rationalism*, vol. 1, p. 310 (New York, 1867) quoted in H. H. Gerth and C. Wright Mills, *From Max Weber: Essays in Sociology* (New York: Oxford University Press, 1958), p. 53.

23. Yinger, *The Scientific Study of Religion*, pp. 266–273.

24. Ibid., pp. 266–268.

25. W. E. Mann, *Sect, Cult, and Church in Alberta* (Toronto: University of Toronto Press, 1955), pp. 5–8, 37–40.

26. All quotations are as attributed to the Rev. Jim Jones by Jeannie Mills. Reprinted by permission of A & W Publishers, Inc., New York, from Jeannie Mills, *Six Years with God: Life Inside Rev. Jim Jones's Peoples Temple*. Copyright 1979 by MBR/Investments, Inc.

27. Mills, *Six Years with God*, p. 121. Reprinted by permission of A & W Publishers, Inc.

28. Mills, *Six Years with God*, p. 122. Reprinted by permission of A & W Publishers, Inc.

29. A charismatic leader, as introduced in Chapter 3, is a person thought by his or her followers:

    1. to possess special qualities superior to ordinary people, sometimes to the point of seeing the leader as divine;

    2. to have access to special knowledge or revelation;

    3. to be directed to lead their followers down a new, perhaps revolutionary, path; and

    4. to be able to create a special relationship with their followers—what amounts to a "calling" to them, of a level of trust, love, and obedience that they had not known before.

30. Mills, *Six Years with God*, pp. 123–124. Reprinted by permission of A & W Publishers, Inc.

31. Mills, *Six Years with God*, pp. 180–181. Reprinted by permission of A & W Publishers, Inc.

32. Mills, *Six Years with God*, p. 218. Reprinted by permission of A & W Publishers, Inc.

33. The peoples council—the inner core leaders comprising some thirty to fifty people.

34. Mills, *Six Years with God*, pp. 230–231. Reprinted by permission of A & W Publishers, Inc.

35. James D. Tabor and Eugene V. Gallagher, *Why Waco? Cults and the Battle for Religious Freedom in America* (Berkeley: University of California Press, 1995), p. 15.

36. Ibid., p. 21.

37. Ibid., p. 104.

38. Michael Barkun, "Reflections after Waco: Millennialists and the State," in *From the Ashes: Making Sense of Waco*, ed. James R. Lewis (Lanham, MD: Rowman & Littlefield Publishers, 1994), p. 41.

39. "Body Count Reaches 979 in Uganda Cult Deaths," Fox News, April 27, 2000 "Uganda Sect Members Speak of Doom," MSNBC News, April 3, 2000, accessed through *www.rickross.com*. Joshua Hammer, "An Apocalyptic Mystery," *Newsweek*, April 3, 2000.

40. Joe McDonald (Associated Press), "Chinese Defy Ban on Sects," *Ann Arbor News*, July 23, 1999, p. A4, and "Key Sect Members Sentenced to Prison," *Star Press*, Muncie, IN, December 27, 1999, p. 3A.

41. But the reader must be aware that not all cults demand suicide of their members.

42. Gilles Kepel, *Jihad: The Trial of Political Islam* (Cambridge, MA: Belknap Press of Harvard University Press, 2002), p. 318.

43. Ibid.

44. See, for example, Benton Johnson, "A Critical Appraisal of the Church-Sect Typology," *American Sociological Review* 22, no. 1 (1957): 88–92; idem, "On Church and Sect," *American Sociological Review* 28, no. 1 (1967): 64–68; idem, "Church-Sect Revisited, *Journal for the Scientific Study of Religion* 10, no. 2 (1971): 124–137; Erich Goode, "Some Critical Observations on the Church-Sect Dimension," *Journal for the Scientific Study of Religion* 6, no. 1 (1967): 69–77; idem, "Further Reflections on the Church-Sect Dimension," *Journal for the Scientific Study of Religion* 6, no. 2 (1967): 270–275; N. J. Demareth III, "In a Sow's Ear," *Journal for the Scientific Study of Religion* 6, no. 1 (1967): 77–84; Allan W. Eister, "Toward a Radical Critique of Church-Sect Typologizing, *Journal for the Scientific Study of Religion* 6, no. 1 (1967): 85–90; J. Kenneth Benson and James Dorsett, "Church-Sect Replaced," *Journal for the Scientific Study of Religion* 10, no. 2 (1971): 138–151; James A. Beckford, "Religious Organization," *Current Sociology* 21, no. 2 (1975): 5–170, particularly 96–102.

45. Liston Pope, *Millhands and Preachers* (New Haven, CT: Yale University Press, 1942), pp. 122–124.

46. Benton Johnson, "On Church and Sect," *American Sociological Review* 28, no. 4 (1963): 539–549.

47. J. Milton Yinger, *Religion, Society, and the Individual* (New York: Macmillan, 1957), pp. 147–148.

48. Yinger, *The Scientific Study of Religion*, p. 257.

49. Roland Robertson, *The Sociological Interpretation of Religion* (New York: Schocken Books, 1970), pp. 123ff.

50. Ibid., p. 124.

51. Stephen Steinberg, "Reform Judaism: The Origin and Evolution of a 'Church Movement'" *Journal for the Scientific Study of Religion* 5, no. 1 (1965): 117–129.

Chapter 5

Becoming Religious

Religious socialization in process.

As we look at the impact of religion on society and the people who constitute society, we shall begin at the beginning. That is, we shall look at the process by which people become religious in the first place. We assume that newborn infants have no "religious instincts." While they may have certain needs for which religion might, among other institutions as well, provide some satisfactions—such as security, protection, explanation, reinforcement (see Chapter 2)—they are not born with a ready-made religious system within them just waiting to bloom. However, it is possible that, as Durkheim has been interpreted to have suggested and Randall Collins asserts, infants could be born with a predisposition to seek and welcome ritual and effervescence in their lives. What those situations will be and the context within which effervescence will be experienced are socially conditioned and produced by the group into which an individual is born. That is, the infant must be taught; it must learn the contents of its family's religious system just as it must learn language, table manners, and how to drive a car. This learning is what we know as socialization. Thus, we continue to work with the simple but basic observation that religion is a group phenomenon and that a member of a religious group is either born into it or joins it at some later stage in their life; in either case, they are taught the norms of the group and integrated into the life of the group. In this process the group socializes (it teaches and trains), and the individual internalizes the norms (they learn). Throughout this chapter we shall move back and forth between these two foci of the socialization or learning process.

ELEMENTS IN RELIGIOUS SOCIALIZATION

We begin with the group and the desire to socialize new members. The group desires to bring a person (a member) into a committed, functional relationship with other members of the group, so that the new member knows what the group stands for, can fill a role within the group, and help it reach its goals. Some of this process is nonstructured and occurs through informal contacts and interactions with other members; much of it is structured and formal, channeled through educational agencies and processes.

In primitive societies (that is, preliterate societies, usually with a hunting and gathering economy), religious socialization, as with nearly all socialization, is primarily informal. Children gradually learn the beliefs and understandings of the group through conversation and by hearing their elders recount the sagas and tales passed down through the generations. In a similar manner, children learn practices associated with and growing out of religious beliefs. But through it all, religious socialization is seldom distinguishable from general socialization in primitive societies, inasmuch as their members seldom distinguish the religious from other spheres of thought or knowledge.

There is, nevertheless, some degree of organization and planning in the socialization of primitive religion. For example, Wallace distinguishes two forms, in addition to individual expression, in which primitive religion is manifested: the shamanic and the communal. A shaman, sometimes described by outside observers as a witch doctor or medicine man, is one who is believed to possess greater access to and control over mana and who performs service rituals for people. Obviously, viewing shamanic activity is a learning experience for the neophyte. Similarly, with the communal form of religious expression conducted both by natural subcommunities (such as nuclear families, larger kinship groups, and affinity groups such as those determined by age or sex) and by the total community acting in concert, there are rites of passage from one stage in the life cycle to another (such as puberty rites or tribal totem celebrations) in which everyone gathers around the symbol or symbols of their common origin and loyalty, in order to reaffirm their unity as well as their common past.[1] Certainly a great deal of socialization and learning takes place at all these levels of primitive religion. Nor do these forms of socialization disappear as societies evolve. A child observes the family religious activities so common in orthodox Buddhist and Confucian religious systems, and the congregational worship activities in the Judeo-Christian heritage. And the child learns.

However, although informal socialization still exists and remains influential in both agrarian and industrial societies, with the greater specialization of roles and differentiation of activities in these societies, religious socialization becomes more formalized. Religious teachers deliberately teach neophytes specifically religious norms, and formalized religious ceremonies are conducted during which neophytes learn about religious activities and gradually begin to participate in them.

The socializing or educative intent of religious groups is summarized in a classic manner by Jesus: "Go therefore and make disciples of all nations . . . *teaching* them to observe all things whatsoever I have commanded you."[2] This refers to socialization pure and simple—transmitting knowledge as well as training in appropriate ritual and other activities. Most religious groups view this process as a lifelong one. Worship services in the Western tradition are in significant ways of a socializing nature, extending or expanding on what is already known. A sermon, for example, expounds and explains, not simply exhorts and directs. The various communal ceremonies of most religious groups, in fact, are fundamentally socializing experiences. In addition to adoring the deity through giving praise and performing rituals believed to please them, joint activities perform a reinforcement function, reminding participants of their beliefs and of how they are to conduct themselves before a deity and as they approach a sacred place or function.

Worship services and ceremonial gatherings may also bring about the conversion or full commitment of newcomers, another aspect of socialization. When people hear something or learn something that moves them to attach themselves to the group, socialization has begun; now formal educational processes take over. The person's commitment is also reinforced through new informal socialization contacts.

Thus several things are involved in religious socialization. First, the group convinces the newcomer to make a commitment to the group and what it stands for, often with little knowledge or contact. (By *newcomer* we mean either a potential convert or the child of a group member.) Second, there is the core process of building on that commitment through teaching the newcomer the norms of the group—its beliefs and appropriate behaviors and rituals. (Note that these stages are interchangeable—that is, people may be involved in the process of learning norms for some time before being converted or committing themselves.) Third, the group tries to extend its influence over the person to those situations where they are not in direct contact with the group or its members. That is, the group tries to influence *all* values that form the foundation for a person's actions; this is essentially the morality dimension that many suggest is an integral feature of religion. Finally, there is the reinforcement and encouragement aspect of continuing socialization. One reason religious groups encourage their members to continue participating in ceremonies, attending education classes, and listening to sermons after having learned the "basics" of religion, is to strengthen and reinforce the members' commitment.

METHODS OF RELIGIOUS SOCIALIZATION

Formal Methods

We have already touched on the socialization methods of religious groups. At this point we need merely to systematize them. There is, first, the formal mechanism that most religious groups establish—an educational system. All groups establish explicit teaching activities, which may take the form of a guru gathering a few persons around him, an evangelist on a tree stump or platform, a Bar Mitzvah or Bat Mitzvah preparatory class, or a Sunday sermon. The teaching function has been an integral and important part of religion from the beginning of the major religious systems that exist worldwide today. Certainly the founder of any religion or religious group teaches as they try to get their message and vision across. Once established, the religious group uses diverse methods, both formal and informal, to communicate its ideas and the body of its knowledge, beliefs, and practices to the neophyte member. The effectiveness of such socialization is a major topic of this chapter and is discussed at several points in the chapters that follow.

Informal Methods

Another way in which socialization takes place is informally—through interaction with the members of a religious group. Such socialization or learning from others occurs in all kinds of groups, of course. The general socialization of children into the society that occurs through interaction with peers, for example, is of primary importance and is well documented. And it is popular knowledge that what you learn from associates in a work group through casual conversation and "around the water cooler," so to speak, is at least as important—if not more so—than the socialization that occurs through participating in formal orientation programs or by studying job descriptions.

Informal socialization in the family is, of course, one of the main reasons children are likely to follow the religious lead of their parents throughout childhood at least, unless some really significant event or experience has intervened to send them down a different path. Early socialization, as well as subsequent experiences, combine to make up the mental material with which a person chooses a particular religious or an irreligious path at a later time.

Those who have been introduced elsewhere to major sociological concepts and theories will recognize the above as an application of *symbolic interactionism*. That is a widely-held theory of socialization and learning, which holds that the primary and certainly most effective and long-lasting method of teaching what the group stands for and wants done, is through imitation and emulation, through mimicking and role taking. That is, we observe, then we do. Children mimic the behavior of adults and other children around them. This theory objects in particular to another widely held theory called the *behavioral learning theory*. It suggests that people learn what the group wants by being rewarded for "appropriate" behavior and punished for "inappropriate" behavior—positive and negative reinforcement.

Interestingly, many religious groups recognize the importance of informal socialization and consequently often deliberately encourage it. A term frequently used by religious groups in this connection is *fellowship;* members of religious groups are encouraged "to fellowship" with fellow members. Such formal mechanisms as religious youth groups, men's clubs, women's auxiliaries, and senior citizens' groups are organized in great part with the hope and expectation that members of the larger organization—for example, the congregation—will develop friendships and maintain ties outside formal religious contexts. What is involved here is recognition of the importance of reinforcement—through continued and frequent contact with others of your religious group, the formal norms and beliefs you have been taught and have accepted will be reinforced and, as it is often expressed, "your faith will be strengthened."

Considerable empirical evidence has been gathered that tends to support this strategy, though it is difficult to determine which is cause and which is effect—whether such contact strengthens one's faith, or whether those of strong faith seek out such fellowship in the first place. Thus studies have shown that the person, whose close personal friends are mainly members of their religious group, tends to be more orthodox in their beliefs, and a more regular participant in their religious organization. Glock and Stark, for example, constructed an index of "religious experience," based on whether respondents were certain of having "a feeling [of being] somehow in the presence of God," "a sense of being saved in Christ," and "a feeling of being punished by God for something you had done." Almost invariably, regardless of Christian denomination, respondents with a greater number of best friends, who were also members of their congregation, scored higher on this index.[3]

An intensive extension of the fellowship mechanism for religious socialization occurs through marriage. Religious groups urge endogamy— that is, marriage within the group—assuming (rightly) that a marriage between two persons from the same religious group will encourage both persons to participate and remain with the group. Intermarriage with a person of another religious group introduces the risk of losing your member to the other group, and may reduce the level of participation and commitment of your member, even if they do not defect. There is, of course, the possibility of gaining a new member through intermarriage of one of your members with an outsider. Some groups, in fact, appear to be net gainers through this process. Yet few groups wish to advocate such an approach because of the risks involved. Thus, religious groups have traditionally forbidden (or all but forbidden) interfaith marriage. Until recently, Roman Catholics, for example, could not be married by a priest in church if the non-Catholic partner refused to join the Catholic Church or would not sign a statement agreeing that any children born of the marriage would be reared as Catholics. Many Orthodox Jewish families ostracize children who marry Gentiles. In the face of high rates of interfaith marriage, most groups have been relenting on this issue, although the official stance of discouraging interfaith marriage remains.

MEASURING THE IMPACT OF RELIGIOUS SOCIALIZATION

And so religious socialization goes on in both formal and informal ways, which simple enough. But how effective is religion in this socialization process, and how do we measure its effectiveness? Also, how do we measure religiosity in the first place?

"Religiosity" usually describes the intensity and consistency of a person's practice of their religion. A person strongly committed to a religious system is concerned about him or herself, first of all, but concerned about others in the group as well.

Certainly individuals who are committed to a particular religious system are concerned about whether they meet their group's criteria for being religious: Am I a true believer? Have I committed the unpardonable sin? Are there any signs and indications that tell me whether I measure up or not?

Christian theologians talk about "marks" of Christianity, and theologians of every belief pore over sacred scriptures trying to distill the essential characteristics and behavior that sets the true believer apart from all others.

"Do you believe in Jesus Christ as your only Savior?" "Do you bow toward Mecca at the specified five times daily?" "Do you belong to the Catholic Church and attend mass at least the minimum prescribed number of times a year?" "Do you abstain from pork, keep a kosher kitchen, and study Torah faithfully?"

Denominational administrators seek "indicators" of religiosity for the purpose of evaluating their programs. If, for example, certain congregations in their jurisdiction participate in a "Religious Enrichment Seminar" and consequently increase their contributions to the denomination's general fund, administrators may reason that this is a program to be urged on all the other congregations. Or, if people who attended the denomination's parochial schools now attend church more often, contribute higher proportions of their income, and participate in the organizational life of the congregation more extensively than those who did not attend such schools, then such schools are most likely regarded as accomplishing their religious purpose. This is despite the fact that those attending such schools are more likely to come from staunch, active member families who have, throughout the child's life, instilled such values quite apart from the parochial school.[4]

Researchers in the sociology of religion also continually search for valid ways of defining the concept of "being religious"—what we will be calling religiosity from now on. Sociologists are specifically interested in identifying what constitutes religiosity for the purpose of measuring it in relation to other factors: Is the religious person different from a nonreligious person in any other respects? And if so, how? Is the religious person more humanitarian or less so? Are they more prejudiced or less? More economically successful or less? More likely to be politically liberal? Better "adjusted"? And so on.

One place to start, in our attempt to define religiosity, is the definition of religion that we arrived at in Chapter 1: Religion is a set of beliefs and rituals by which a group of people seeks to understand, explain, and deal with a world of complexity, uncertainty, and mystery, by identifying a sacred canopy of explanation and reassurance under which to live. Thus, we could say that anyone who is a member of a religious group, who believes certain things about the sacred and perhaps the supernatural, and who engages in certain activities associated with these beliefs, is a religious person, and that everyone else is not. Would that it were so simple!

Some religious groups have approximated this approach in trying to distinguish the religious from the irreligious person. Historically, the Roman Catholic Church has maintained that any member who participated in a specified minimum number of ritual activities was a saved member of Christ's church, and that all others were not. Lutherans tended toward this approach also, identifying the true church and its members, wherever the sacraments were correctly administered and the people accepted Jesus Christ as Savior.

Such neat definitions, however, leave several questions unanswered. Should any distinction be made, for example, between those who evidence maximum participation in the group's ritual activities and those who just "get by" with minimal participation? Or are such extremes to be considered equally religious when compared with others who do not participate in these activities at all? And what about the person who occasionally participates in the ritual but has not made a membership commitment? Are they, therefore, not religious? Or what about the person who participates occasionally, and who is a member, but actually is a disbeliever or at least doubts some of the group's central beliefs? Some people are more sincere in their religious beliefs than others; some are more enthusiastic in their ritual participation than others. Some "leave their religion at the church/ temple/tabernacle/mosque door" as they leave the worship service, while others consciously attempt to apply it in all life situations. Are all of these people religious? And if so, are they equally religious? And what about those who share a group's belief but prefer to meditate and worship on their own?

Our definition of religion is less helpful than we might hope in determining people's religiosity because of a fundamental principle of sociology, namely, that almost any characteristic that can be attributed to a given social phenomenon exists at some point on a *continuum*. That is, such characteristics typically are neither totally present nor totally absent, but exist to a greater or lesser degree along a range from high to low. For example, among business organizations classified as bureaucracies, some organizations are more highly bureaucratized than others. Organizations may, therefore, be ranked from high to low along a continuum called *bureaucratic complexity*. Nations, to take another example, can be arranged along a continuum called *industrialization*, or people along continua called *authoritarianism, prejudice, self-motivation*, and so on.

Similarly it is likely that people, if not organizations, may be located at various points on a continuum, called *religiousness* or *religiosity*. People intuitively assume this when they make statements and comparisons, such as those that began this chapter. Our problem here, however, is how to *operationalize* the concept of religiosity—how to translate such feelings into terms of observable characteristics that will permit us to make meaningful comparisons among people. Realize, of course, that we embark on this process, not in order to make invidious comparisons among people or to judge them, but solely in order to be able to determine the impact of the different ways in which people feel and express their religiosity.

Sociologists take two basic approaches to defining religiosity and applying it to their research. The first approach centers on people's affiliations with religious organizations or groups, according to which sociologists attempt to predict and observe differences in people's behavior and attitudes. Technically, this approach focuses not so much on religiosity (which involves something going on inside the individual) as it does on the organization itself. This is appropriate because, whenever we talk about the effect of religion on people's behavior, we are assuming a religious group's influence somewhere along the line. The second approach to identifying religiosity deals with individuals and tends to disregard religious affiliations, except as a possible control variable.

SOCIOLOGICAL DEFINITIONS OF RELIGIOSITY: GROUP AFFILIATION

First, we will look at the group affiliation approach. There are two principal variants—simply a matter of how specific the researcher wishes to become. The first is to categorize people according to major religious families, such as Protestant, Catholic, and Jewish (in Western societies), or Hindu, Muslim, Buddhist, and Christian (in Asian societies), or any number of other relevant sets of affiliations. Extensive research using such religious distinctions has been fruitful in showing different attitudes and behavior among such major groupings. Data from national surveys between 1972 and 1984 reveal that whereas only 11 percent of conservative Protestants, 23 percent of moderate Protestants, and 31 percent of Catholics believe homosexuality is not immoral, 64 percent of Jews and 90 percent of Unitarian-Universalists hold this tolerant view of homosexuality.[5] In the same surveys it was found that, while 91 percent of Unitarian-Universalists and 76 percent of Jews believe abortion should be available to women without restriction, only 9 percent of the members of the Assemblies of God—a conservative Protestant church— agree with that view.[6] In a Gallup Poll survey, 72 percent of Southern Baptists say religion is very important in their lives; only 37 percent of Episcopalians and 25 percent of Jews so assert.[7]

Data from the National Opinion Research Center's 1996 General Social Survey show a wide range of opinions from members of one set of religious groups to another on the issue of allowing incurable patients to die. The proportions that agree that such patients should have the right to choose death range from 42 percent of Evangelical Protestants, to 71 percent of Mainline Protestants, to 73 percent of Catholics, to 79 percent of Liberal Protestants, to 86 percent of Jews.[8] In 1992, other data from the General Social Survey show similar differences among broad religious categories on the question of support for the U.S. Supreme Court's prohibition of prayer in public schools. Proportions supporting the Court's prohibition ranged from 30 percent of Evangelical Protestants, to 40 percent of Mainline Protestants, to 43 percent of Catholics, to 86 percent of Jews.[9]

By the early 1960s, however, many sociologists began to point out that, while research showing differences among such major groupings as Protestants, Catholics, and Jews may be revealing, it also tends to hide almost as much as it reveals, for these categories are still so broad that they obscure significant internal diversity. The primary objection focused on the Protestant category, which includes fundamentalists and other extremely conservative groups as well as theologically liberal groups that reject much of traditional Christian doctrine. Similar problems were seen to exist for the Catholic and Jewish categories as well—there are both liberal and conservative Catholics, and there are Reform, Conservative, and Orthodox Jews.

Moreover, in surveys, even fairly large (and expensive) samples do not include enough members of, say, the various subcategories of Protestantism to make meaningful comparisons. For example, suppose you wanted to analyze social differences among various religious groups in the United States and, at some point, decided to make specific comparisons between Unitarians and Mennonites—two groups nearly at opposite extremes on a continuum called *Protestantism*. Suppose you had been able to afford to survey a fairly large sample of 1,000 persons representative of the United States population. Suppose also that your sampling techniques had worked perfectly and you had picked a truly proportionate representative sample. You would then find when you went to your sample, theoretically at least, exactly eight-tenths of one Unitarian and nine-tenths of one Mennonite. You would also get only one-and-eight-tenths Seventh Day Adventists, nine Mormons, and eleven members of the United Church of Christ—hardly a sufficient number of any of these groups (not to mention a host of other small religious groups) to reach valid conclusions about any of them.

Mainline Protestant church bodies, however, such as Presbyterians, Methodists, Lutherans, Baptists, and Episcopalians, each have many more members; consequently they can provide sufficient numbers in national or area samples of a thousand or more persons to justify making comparisons among them. Thus evolved the second stage of utilizing religious affiliation as an independent variable, when major subcategories of Protestants began to be studied. The research team of Charles Glock and Rodney Stark, of the University of California at Berkeley, who were among the first to use this approach extensively, found significant differences among major Protestant denominations that one might have thought existed only among smaller groups that tend to hold more extreme views. For example, Glock and Stark discovered that on such a fundamental doctrinal question, as the divinity of Jesus, the proportion of members of major Protestant bodies who accept without reservation the traditional view—namely, that Jesus is the Son of God—and admit to having no personal doubts about it are as follows: 40 percent of Congregationalists, 54 percent of Methodists, 59 percent of Episcopalians, 72 percent of Presbyterians, 74 percent of Disciples of Christ, 74 percent of American Lutherans, 76 percent of American Baptists, 93 percent of Missouri Synod Lutherans, and 99 percent of Southern Baptists.[10] Differences among the same Protestant groups, on the question of miracles, is even more dramatic. The proportion of those who believe that miracles actually happened as described in the Bible are as follows: 28 percent of Congregationalists, 37 percent of Methodists, 41 percent of Episcopalians, 58 percent of Presbyterians, 62 percent of the Disciples of Christ, 62 percent of American Baptists, 69 percent of American Lutherans, 89 percent of Missouri Synod Lutherans, and 92 percent of Southern Baptists.[11] Certainly the religious group with which one is affiliated makes a big difference. It teaches and stands for certain beliefs, principles, and values, and while it inculcates them into its members, it will also attract people who already hold like-minded ideas. The results are distinctive groups that differ in a long list of dimensions.

It is perhaps becoming obvious that we are straying from a strict definition or understanding of religiosity. We have indicated some of the major ways in which researchers have attempted to operationalize the concept of religiosity—that is, identify a quantifiable measure that seems to measure or "get at" something of what religion is—in order to assess its effect or impact on people's behavior.

The two types of measurement, which we have already looked at, are in reality subtypes of the affiliation measure that focuses on the religious group to which a person belongs. In such cases, how do we know whether a person is religious? We may simply consider a person religious if they profess to be a Protestant, a Catholic, a Jew, or a member of any other religious group, while the nonmember would be considered nonreligious, or at most less religious than the member. Although ultimately we may want to talk about the religiosity of individual people, we wind up focusing on the general or central tendencies of groups and differences among those groups—an important focus indeed, but hardly the whole package. At most, the focus on group differences measures the effect of formal religious differences among groups, primarily differences in belief and doctrine. What we lack are measures of differentiation in intensity or sincerity of belief and degree of religious interest, as well as how religion affects a person's daily behavior. Such ideas are closer to the concept of individual religiosity, which presupposes a difference of degree of commitment and interest in religious ideas, religious answers or solutions, and religious participation.

SOCIOLOGICAL DEFINITIONS OF RELIGIOSITY: THE INDIVIDUAL APPROACH

We now focus on major attempts by sociologists to measure religiosity, defined more narrowly as the degree and type of commitment to religious values and norms.

Although it has not always been recognized, there is great diversity within each group discussed in the preceding section, a fact illustrated by the historical development of the attempts to measure differences related to religious group affiliation. While research that contrasted the major categories of Protestants, Catholics, and Jews exposed numerous differences, such broad and inclusive categories have been recognized to be just that—inclusive of a great deal of internal diversity, as numerous studies, including those by Glock and Stark, have documented. Implicit in the data from such studies, though not always discussed, are great differences within each of the subgroups as well. For example, although only 28 percent of Congregationalists but 92 percent of Southern Baptists believe in miracles, there nevertheless exists within each of these groups internal differentiation—differentiation which is even more obvious within the other Protestant groups that fall between the Congregationalists and Southern Baptists, as reported earlier in this chapter. In other words, although 72 percent of Congregationalists do *not* believe in miracles, 28 percent *do* believe in them; although 42 percent of Presbyterians do not believe in miracles, 58 percent do believe in them; and so on. How do we explain such internal diversity? Why do some members of a group accept one belief, practice, or social perspective, while other members do not?

Measures of Individual Ritual Participation

Such questions have led some researchers to ignore, at least temporarily, formal group differences and regroup—or more accurately, recategorize— people on other bases, such as types of commitment, intensity of belief, and so on. An early attempt along these lines, one which has subsequently been widely used, is based on *ritual participation,* or the frequency with which people attend the formal religious services of their religious group. Thus, those who report attending weekly or nearly every week might be categorized as demonstrating a "high" degree of religiosity; those attending once or twice a month would perhaps be categorized as showing a "moderate" degree; and those attending less often would be classed "low" on this scale. Refinements of this measure into a five-point scale (with the addition of "moderately high" and "moderately low" categories), and even a seven-point scale, have been used. Other factors, such as frequency of participation in other activities sponsored by the religious group, have been included by some researchers. Commonly, when Protestants and Catholics are major components in the study, frequency of attendance at the sacrament of Communion, or the Lord's Supper, is used as a measure of religiosity. Quite obviously such measures attempt to assess variations in the intensity of commitment and the importance of religion to the individual.

But many researchers have objected that such a procedure does not really measure religiosity, that attendance statistics tell us nothing about how a given individual *feels* about attendance. A person's regular attendance may be simply a result of habit, and so it may mean relatively little to them personally. Or, a person's regular attendance may be due to family or other group pressures—they may not want to disappoint grandmother, or to give an employer cause to question their morality. Or perhaps a person attends regularly because they look forward to the opportunity to socialize with friends after services.

Other Measures of Individual Religiosity

Such objections have spurred attempts to measure religiosity by other means. One method has been to ask people about their prayer life—focusing again, however, as with church attendance, on frequency. The reasoning here is that if a person reports engaging frequently in personal private prayer (where "frequently" is usually defined as at least daily), then religion is most likely more meaningful and important to them than it is to one who prays only occasionally or one who never prays except in groups, as in formal religious services.

Other measures that try to probe just a little more deeply into the subjective feelings and commitments of people, rely on respondents' ability, in interviews and questionnaires, to categorize themselves in terms of their personal commitment to religion and to evaluate how important religion is to them personally. These measures, occasionally composites or indexes based on more than one question, vary from one study to another, but usually are based on questions such as, "How important would you say religion is in your life—very important, somewhat important, not very important, or not at all important?" Or, "All in all, how important would you say your church or synagogue membership is to you?"

Evaluation of Individual Measures of Religiosity

All the attempts to operationalize the concept of religiosity, that we have mentioned in this section, have in common the fact that each relies on a single measure, or on a single set of measures—for example, combining frequency of church attendance with frequency of Communion attendance, or frequency of personal prayer with extent of involvement in the total organizational life of a congregation. Such measures of religiosity have revealed significant differences among people. For example, at the beginning of the Civil Rights Movement in the 1960s, it was found that among white southern college students, those who attended church were somewhat more prejudiced against blacks than those who never attended—although there were also strong indications that among the churchgoers, those who attended more frequently were less prejudiced than infrequent churchgoers.[12] Or, to cite another brief example, among American middle-class men, those who attend church more regularly, tend to be more upwardly mobile.[13]

Differences of this sort, however, have not been so great or so consistent as some researchers had anticipated. The primary reason, according to recent research, seems to be that religiosity is not a one-dimensional phenomenon. That is, not all people are religious in the same way. A person may rank high in religiosity on one dimension or measure, but low on another or several others. Thus, if certain behavior is correlated with a high score on one scale of religiosity but a low score on another, then entirely different conclusions could be reached concerning the impact of religion on that behavior, depending on which measure of religiosity was used. One's conclusions about the impact of people's religion on their behavior and commitment could therefore be inaccurate and misleading.

SOCIOLOGICAL MEASURES OF RELIGIOSITY: MULTIDIMENSIONAL MEASURES

Several researchers, taking a multidimensional view of religion, have either combined several specific measures into a composite of some kind or utilized several discrete measures. The rationale for such approaches is that religion is not a single, uniform entity that can be apprehended by any single measure; rather, people can "be religious" in various ways.

In works published in 1951 and 1954, Joseph Fichter distinguished four ways in which a person could be a Catholic.[14] Based on attendance at mass, participation in confession, sending children to parochial school, other involvement in church subgroups, and expressed religious interest, Fichter constructed the typology of *nuclear Catholic, modal Catholic, marginal Catholic*, and *dormant Catholic*. Nuclear Catholics go beyond minimal requirements of membership, are active in parish life, and attend Holy Communion at least weekly. Such "ideal" members in Fichter's second (1954) sample were found to comprise only 5.7 percent of all Catholics.[15] Modal Catholics comprised about 70 percent of the membership and were described by Fichter as follows:

> Since the modal parishioner holds a position midway between the nuclear and the marginal Catholic, he may be said to live up to his religion in a "middling sort of way." He generally observes the Friday abstinence and knows the difference between Advent and Lent. His name is likely to be on the roster of the Holy Names Society at some time during his life, but he hardly ever attends a meeting. He attends Sunday Mass most of the time but has difficulty "catching Mass" when holy days of obligation occur during the working week. His children fill the parochial schools, and he has a kind of aloof respect for priests and nuns.[16]

The marginal Catholics (about 20 percent of Catholics) consider themselves to be members of the Catholic Church and tend to be so considered by the church itself, yet may not have attended mass during the past year, may not have received Holy Communion or participated in confession, and the children in the family do not attend Catholic parochial school.[17] The dormant Catholic is one who was born into a Catholic family, baptized as a Catholic, may have been married by a priest, and perhaps asks for a priest's services as death approaches, yet is not a formal member of a Catholic congregation.[18]

It should be fairly clear from earlier comments that Fichter's typology is a simple one, in the sense that his measure of religiosity essentially involves only ritual and formal participation in a religious organization. Excluded are several dimensions we have hinted at earlier and others we will identify as we proceed. Yet his typology made an important contribution, particularly in that it stimulated others to expand and improve on his work.

Glock and Stark found that people can be religious in several ways and that the same person can exhibit more than one way of being religious at the same time. Glock first identified four dimensions: the *experiential*, which attempts to measure the degree of emotional attachment to the supernatural; the *ritualistic*, which counts the rate of participation in the group's activities; the *ideological*, which refers to the degree of commitment to the religious beliefs of a person's group; and the *consequential*, which refers to the impact of religious commitment and involvement on an individual's general behavior.[19] Later, Glock added a fifth dimension—the *intellectual*—which measures the degree of knowledgeability about the formal beliefs of a person's religion.[20] Still later, Glock, together with his colleague Rodney Stark, subdivided the ritualistic dimension into two parts: ritual and devotion. *Ritual* includes such formal religious activities as attending religious services and taking Communion—what can be called public activities. *Devotion* includes such behavior as praying and studying sacred books and religious writings.[21]

These above formulations have stimulated considerable research and elaboration by social scientists. An important outcome has been a consensus that religiosity is clearly multidimensional. Thus a person may score high on one dimension and be termed "very religious," yet score low on one or more other measures and be identified as only "slightly religious" or even "irreligious." For example, people may know religious teachings or doctrines inside and out, yet seldom or never attend religious services, never engage in devotional activities, disbelieve what they know intellectually about their religion, and evidence no effect of religious knowledge on their behavior.

It is important to be aware of the many ways in which people can be religious, because by relying on only one—for example, "religious knowledge" or "participation in religious activities"—we might seriously misrepresent the level of religiosity inherent in people.

Consider these research findings. Schroeder and Obenhaus, for example, noted in a study of an Iowa town that among church members with above average intellectual ability and a strong commitment to and involvement in church life, less than half were able to relate a reasonably accurate version of the story of the good Samaritan—one of the most well-known stories in the New Testament.[22]

In my study of Lutheran youth, only 8.7 percent of those sampled who attended church services regularly and also attended a parochial school, could correctly identify Nathanael as one of Jesus' disciples, and only 25 percent correctly identified Enoch as the Old Testament character, who is described as never experiencing physical death.[23] Similarly, in a 1970 nationwide survey of adults, only 15 percent correctly identified five prominent biblical figures (Moses, Daniel, Jonah, Peter, Paul). In fact, a greater number of respondents (17.5 percent) were unable to identify even a single figure, and less than half (46.4 percent) were able to identify three.[24]

If we relied solely on religious/biblical knowledge to measure degree of religiosity, then few would be identified as having even a moderate level of religiosity. This applies also to using the frequency of church/synagogue attendance as a single measure of religious participation, involvement, and commitment. In one national survey, fully 34 percent of those who were members of religious groups attended religious services, never or, at best, seldom (less than once a month), and 53 percent attended less than once a week.[25] Gallup poll data corroborate those percentages. In a sample representing all adults (not just members of churches/synagogues), about 60 percent of the U.S. population eighteen years of age and older do not attend church or synagogue on any given weekend.[26] Yet some, and perhaps many, of those not in attendance would describe themselves as "religious people."

Actually, these data from polls probably overestimate church attendance rates. A recent study of Hadaway, Marler, and Chaves raises serious questions about the accuracy of people's self-reporting of church attendance as gathered by polling organizations such as Gallup. These researchers acquired data consisting of on-the-spot counts of people in Protestant and Catholic churches, and found church attendance rates of both Protestants and Catholics to be about one-half of those commonly reported. After identifying all churches in a selected sample county (Ashtabula County, Ohio) and checking average actual church attendance (some by direct observation on Sunday mornings), church attendance in Protestant churches was only 19.6 percent of the membership in those churches.[27] Data for Catholics were based on reports of actual attendance at Catholic churches in a sample of eighteen Catholic dioceses in all parts of the United States and show a pattern similar to Protestants. While virtually all studies of church attendance show higher rates for Catholics over Protestants, the actual rates are approximately half those recorded by polls—28 percent versus the 51 percent reported by Gallup.[28] Actually, when various adjustments are made, the authors believe the Catholic rate is more like 25 percent. As such, the Catholic rate is even more similar to the Protestant rate, in being less than one-half the self-reported rate.[29]

INTERNALIZATION OF RELIGION

We have been focusing primarily on the agents and processes of religious socialization, and in assessing the effectiveness of such socialization we have focused on the group. We now turn to the obverse of socialization—namely, internalization. What are some of the processes involved, stages of development, and differences in outcome for individuals who are being socialized?

In considering the process of the internalization of religion, we are immediately required to distinguish between those who internalize the religious concepts and practices of a group from birth and those who undergo a conversion experience at some later point in life. We first look at the most common pattern—that of "growing up religious" within a particular religious context.

"Growing Up Religious"

A fundamental observation is that individuals internalize the religion of their group essentially in the same way they learn the language of their culture, or their sex role, or the lifestyle of their social class. The process is intimately tied up with the development of one's personality and the evolution of one's concept of self. People internalize—make a part of themselves—what they hear, see and both consciously and subconsciously consider applicable to them. The person hears words, is introduced to concepts, and is confronted with various phenomena at the intellectual, or cognitive, level. But they also—especially initially—emulate or imitate what they see. In a sense, the person absorbs many patterns, norms, and values through the experience of seeing them exemplified by parents, peers, and others long before they confront them intellectually.

Just as children learn to talk before they are exposed to the rules of grammar and spelling, so they attain an orientation toward the sacred (and, if they are Christian, perhaps a concept of self as a sinner) long before they confront such issues in the form of religious doctrines and propositions.

This orientation fits into the broad framework of the development of the self—a process in which religion plays a part. Early in the process of this development, the child becomes aware of himself or herself, not simply as an "I" or subject—the center of the universe, so to speak—but also as a "me," an object with certain characteristics that others react to and interact with. They begin to learn how others expect them to behave if they are to interact successfully as well as to satisfy their personal needs. Children begin to see themselves from various perspectives and in various roles—male or female, son or daughter, friend or stranger, American or foreigner, and so on. As they are exposed to religious influences in the family and in the family's religious group, they also acquire the rudiments of a religious self. They begin to regard themselves as related, not only to the so-called natural and social worlds of things and people that they see and interact with, but also as related to an unseen world of the sacred. They begin to have an orientation toward the sacred, however, *that is defined and then instilled by the group*. As they begin to see themselves in relation to that other world, they expand their image of self accordingly.

At this point, depending on the specific religious group context, great diversity may appear. One child begins to see himself as a worthless sinner utterly helpless in the face of God, while another sees herself as a special object of creation with great worth and potential. For most, a combination of both perspectives applies. In any case, the individual becomes aware of unseen powers in the universe. To some extent, this may be comforting knowledge, a convenient way of explaining much that is incomprehensible. To some extent it may be frightening, particularly as they consider or learn the ways in which they can incur the wrath of those supernatural powers and even be punished by them.

In short, then, what children learn about themselves from religious group sources supplements what they are learning about themselves from interaction with playmates, television, siblings, and so on. Initially, this learning is almost exclusively through informal observing and intuiting, only later to be supplemented by more formal cognitive learning. Most children, in any society, derive some of their self-concept from religious sources, even if they are born into families who espouse no formal religious group affiliation. For everyone is, at least indirectly, influenced by religion, through contact with other people and institutions.

It will be obvious to some readers that the foregoing description of the process of internalizing religion leans heavily on the symbolic interaction perspective in sociology, a basic premise of which is that people relate to things, events, and other people, on the basis of the meanings they assign to them. These meanings, in turn, develop within the person during the process of social interaction, while the religious institutions themselves contribute to the construct of meanings that people develop. Obviously the particular set of observations and interactions that a given individual makes and experiences, has a crucial influence on whatever religious meanings develop within them.

Gaining Religious Identity

Although religious socialization primarily aims at providing a person with an appropriate stance in relation to the sacred and instructs her or him in the nature and function of the sacred world, another important socialization process involves teaching the child their religious identity. David Elkind has conducted research that indicates that even this process is complex. Children, he contends, proceed through certain stages in learning who they are religiously. Thus, a child of five who says, "I am a Catholic" understands that identification differently from a child of nine or twelve. Elkind found that from the age of five or six, most children know their religious identity and will freely admit they are, say, Protestant, Catholic, or Jewish. But such identity for them is not at all what it is for older children or adults. The young child tends to confuse religious identity with nationality and racial designations. Their religious identification is a name with no clear referent.

By eight or nine years of age, however, children have a more concrete conception of their religious identity. They can distinguish religious from nonreligious designations and can attach behavioral description to various religious groups. Yet, it is not till the age of ten to twelve that an abstract dimension of religious identification is added—only then do youngsters begin to speak of cognitive elements such as beliefs and try to explain why particular religious groups engage in certain activities.[30]

The Role of the Family

As mentioned earlier in this chapter, much religious socialization occurs outside the formal structure of the organization, with a significant portion taking place in family interaction. Religious groups recognize this. Some have programs that focus on trying to help parents perform this task, while others at least point out the importance of the family. However, John L. Thomas, a Jesuit sociologist, found through research in the late 1940s that the kind of religious socialization that the Catholic Church hoped parents would conduct for their children was not, in fact, occurring on the scale expected. Thomas stated that although persons professionally involved in promoting organized religion agree that an important function of the family is the inculcation of religious beliefs and practices in their children, he found that the religious training of the Catholic preschool child at home fell far short of traditional expectations.[31] Family influences are nevertheless significant in the sense of reinforcing and filtering religious influences from elsewhere, particularly from formal agencies such as parochial schools.

In a more recent study of Mormons, Marie Cornwall found that although family religious socialization did not have as many direct influences on their children's adult religiosity as she expected on the basis of prior research, nonetheless, family religious socialization did have significant effects, as it operated through the intervening variables of significantly affecting church attendance and fostering the development of a circle of friends made up of fellow Mormon young people. These variables, in turn, had significant impact on adult religiosity.[32]

But the family was not devoid of direct influences either. In fact, there was a consistent direct influence of one major measure of family influence (home religious observance) on personal dimensions of religiosity, which were identified as religious knowledge, spiritual commitment, and frequency of personal prayer.[33]

Analysis of data from Catholic, Southern Baptist, and Methodist middle-class youth, by Dean Hoge and Gregory Petrillo, points out that positive impact on participation in religious activities comes, not from socioeconomic factors, types of school attended, level of religious knowledge, or level of activity in school or community—rather, relationships with other people predominate. First, parents have a very strong positive impact so far as a young person's church attendance is concerned. Second, peers of the young people had a strong influence on their participation in youth programs and having positive attitudes toward those programs.[34]

In my own study of the impact of parochial schools on the religious beliefs, attitudes, and behavior of young people, the family influence turned out to be the pivotal variable. What appeared upon first-level analysis to be significant differences in religious commitment, religious knowledge, orthodoxy of belief, and participation in religious activities and functions that were traceable or related to the amount of exposure to parochial school education, disappeared when we controlled for different levels of religious training and environment in families. In fact, it was only in those families that lacked religious unity (mixed religious marriages), where attendance by parents at religious functions such as Sunday worship was spasmodic or nonexistent, and where there was little or no overt religious instruction and reinforcement in the home, where the parochial school could come through and make up for some of those religious deficiencies in the family. Otherwise, the parochial school did not add significantly to what was already happening so far as religious socialization was concerned in families that were themselves unified, active, and supportive of the religious values, beliefs, and behavior of the denomination with which they were affiliated.[35]

Such immediate influences, while children are living with parents in the home, are common. For example, Potvin and Sloane found that young people whose parents attended church regularly are five times more likely to score high on a variety of religious practices (including church attendance) than adolescents whose parents attended church infrequently or not at all.[36]

A more recent study, by Gerald N. Stott confirms this finding. In a study of Southern Baptists and Mormons in the St. Louis area, he found a very low correlation between the religious involvement of parents and the religious involvement of their children as *adults*, if that is the only relationship one looks at. However, he discovered something else that has been affirmed in other studies as well; that is, that there is a strong positive relationship between both the religiosity of one's spouse and the religious affiliation of one's best friend as an adult and one's own level of religious activity as an adult.[37]

Such data, of course, emphasize the importance of the primary groups in which an individual lives and moves—parental family group as a child and adolescent, marital group consisting of the individual and their spouse, and close friendship groups.

RELIGIOUS CONVERSION

As stated at the outset of the preceding section, the process of internalizing religion and developing the religious self is, so far as can be determined, essentially similar to the process of internalizing other knowledge, beliefs, and skills, and merely adds another dimension to one's initial concept of self. A more dramatic form of religious internalization is that of conversion.

We shall not delve deeply into the conversion phenomenon itself, which is strongly psychological in nature and for the most part nonempirical. We cannot, for example, determine whether a particular individual's conversion is, in fact, a personal experience with God Himself, in which the Holy Spirit enters the person and leads them to certain convictions. We can, however, provide some sociological insight into the context within which conversions occur, point out that conversion is not wholly a psychological phenomenon, and note that it does not occur in a wholly religious context as distinct from a social one.

The Group Context

First we must note the somewhat obvious yet important fact that conversion, as a form of behavior or process, is affected by the group within which it occurs. That is, what constitutes conversion, what one can expect to experience, and even whether one should expect a conversion experience at all, are matters defined by the religious group one belongs to or happens to be under the influence of at the moment (during an evangelistic service, for example).

In a study of young people in the fundamentalist Swedish Mission Covenant Church, Hans Zetterberg found a number of group influences on the conversion phenomenon, which he defined as itself a stage in the social role of membership. For one thing, every member had a clear background of being religiously influenced before entering the group and undergoing the conversion experience; in fact, eight of every ten converts came from families in which at least one parent was already a member of the group. Second, conversion does not necessarily imply a change in one's way of life—the convert already has "pious habits and right belief." Conversion is simply a signal of a more conscious acceptance of this life. Third, a clear majority of conversions occur under conditions that are created and manipulated by the group (revival meetings, church camps, and the like). Fourth, although a sudden change in lifestyle may be the stereotype of conversion, such conversions are relatively unlikely. Zetterberg found that only 16 percent of his sample had conversions of this type. Much more likely is "sudden role identification," in which a person, who has been undergoing socialization by the group, suddenly feels certain of their salvation (although behavior does not change noticeably because they had been living the role of the converted for some time). The other type of conversion is "role assimilation," in which the person gradually becomes sure of their saved condition over an extended period of membership.[38]

Borhek and Curtis are even less impressed with the common stereotype of conversion as a sudden reversal or change of direction and commitment on the part of an individual. They suggest that the actual conversion (such as might occur in a revivalist service) is a *rite de passage* "differing from other such rituals only in the fact that the participant may be largely unconscious of its ritual, conventional character."[39] They suggest further that conversion experiences are often "so highly conventionalized, that it requires real effort not to view them as rituals *learned for the occasion*."[40]

The Age Factor

A second major point about conversion is that—in its dramatic form, at least—it is primarily an adolescent phenomenon. It is understandably no accident that the Jewish boy has his bar mitzvah and the Jewish girl her bat mitzvah in early adolescence. Similarly in most liturgical Christian churches, confirmation is in early adolescence, and in nonliturgical churches, baptism and/or profession of faith occur at this time. Walter H. Clark cites two early studies in the psychology of religion by E. D. Starbuck (1899) and E. T. Clark (1929), that found the most common age for conversion of males to be about sixteen, and for females about fourteen or fifteen.[41]

David Elkind makes the point that, until adolescence, the child "knows much more than he understands about his religious identity."[42] Gordon Allport describes adolescence as the time when the person must transform his religious attitudes from secondhand to firsthand fittings of his personality.[43]

There is some indication that sexual guilt feelings and anxieties among people who have only recently begun to struggle with their sexual development, desires, and propensities are strongly influential here. The traditional stereotyped conversion in a tent meeting or evangelistic service almost invariably includes a discourse and series of prayers and altar calls that have touched on "sexual sins" more than any others and have been designed to produce admission of guilt for what are essentially universal feelings and urges. Thouless states: "The typical adolescent conversion may be regarded psychologically as the sudden emergence into consciousness of a previously repressed system of feelings belonging to the sex instinct, which is now admitted into consciousness because it is sublimated, purified and directed to a religious end."[44]

That conversion should frequently occur during adolescence is probably not surprising, considering the hormonal changes, opportunities for new experiences, and intellectual awakening that occur at this stage in the life cycle. Religion may be one among many other new ideas and systems to embrace. Or religion that began to be internalized many years earlier may have developed to a peaking point at this time. It is certainly no mere coincidence that a majority of the followers of new religious movements (cults) are young people. For example, E. Burke Rockford, Jr. found that well over half (57 percent) of those who joined the Hare Krishna group (International Society for Krishna Consciousness) were between 18 and 23 years of age. Only 20 percent were older than 25.[45]

Not all conversions occur during adolescence, of course. But something akin to the psychological and emotional dislocations that occur during adolescence happen at other times in people's lives as well. Catherine Robins, in analyzing conversion of women into the East African Revival—a large-scale Protestant revival movement—notes that among Kiga women from Southwest Uganda, it is common for a "life crisis" to have precipitated conversion.[46] She notes that among Hima women from the same region, a common precondition for conversion appears to be a marital crisis, whether that means being forced into an unwanted "arranged" marriage or finding oneself in a marriage that is dominated by a conflict of Christian values with traditional values that allow, for example, a husband's male kin sexual access to his wife.[47]

Stages in Conversion

Our third sociological observation about conversion focuses on its socialization aspect. In describing the process of conversion into a small NRM called the Divine Precepts (popularly known as the "Moonies"), John Lofland distinguishes between (a) predisposing conditions—attributes of persons prior to contact with the group—and (b) situational contingencies—social factors and influences in operation after contact with the group is made.[48]

Predisposing Conditions   The first of three predisposing conditions is tension and emotional dislocation, which those who later became converts perceived themselves to have been enduring at fairly high levels for some time. Such tensions could have resulted from failing grades in college, a broken love affair, career uncertainties, and the like. Second, the potential converts for various reasons did not avail themselves of more conventional mechanisms for solving problems and reducing tension. Such tension-relieving mechanisms could have been psychological counseling, immersion in political or public service activities, or pure avoidance-escape techniques, such as drug or alcohol use, as a means of temporarily blotting out or dulling the impact of unpleasant reality.[49] Third, having found no psychological or socio-political avenue for releasing their tension, they sought a religious solution in conventional religious organizations and/or in reading self-help and other religious literature—all without significant resolution of their tension and emotional discomfort.

An interesting aside here is that Eileen Barker has found that those who become Moonies tend to come from families for whom religion is important.[50] At a more general level, Snow and Machalek observe that people are more inclined to believe than to doubt.[51] If we can then suggest that this propensity to believe is most apparent among those with a religious background, what we are seeing is people with a religious background encouraged to seek out a *religious* solution, even if it is with a group others might label a cult.

Situational Factors According to Lofland, after the search, four situational factors appeared. These are what Lofland stresses as factors that are for all practical purposes "outside" the individual, highly *sociological* in nature. The first he calls the *turning point*—that is, when the preconverts first encounter the Divine Precepts cult, they had reached or were about to reach a crisis in their lives, for whatever they had done before had been disrupted, was completed, or had failed. In other words, some serious change in their social environment had occurred. Second, there developed or already existed an *affective bond* between the potential recruit and one or more group members. That is, a social relationship of some meaning and significance had developed for the potential recruit (convert). In this case the relationship was with a member and committed affiliate of a particular group. Third, the preconvert's affective relationships outside the cult were either weak or ineffectual. Again, something of significance had happened to the potential convert's social relationships that had preceded involvements with the cult. In this case they did not amount to much; they did not constitute much by way of competition. Fourth, total conversion required a period of intensive interaction, often abetted by residence in the group's communal dwelling. Here, of course, we are talking about social interaction, pure and simple— interaction that can be intensive, thorough and probing, and can, as a result, be very effective in producing changes in people (conversion).

Conversion Career What has just been described, then, is not some sudden, instantaneous experience, but a process—what James Richardson and Mary Stewart call a conversion *career*.[52] In describing conversion as "career" we would observe that it is progressive (that is, it involves stages and a progression from one level to another), and it has a background of predispositions within a person that are based on prior socialization experiences. Thus, when conversion occurs, we can observe a blending of situational and social-environmental prerequisites, psychological needs, receptivity on the part of the individual, and, above all, active socialization efforts by members of the group to which the person is converting.

Refinements Lofland has not been without his critics.[53] Some suggest the process is more complex and has more stages. Others suggest that people progress toward conversion with certain stages missing. Lofland himself, and his colleague Norman Skonovd, have suggested that not all conversions are alike and, as such, the stages in conversion will have greater or lesser importance and visibility, depending on which type (motif) of conversion is being experienced. They distinguish six motifs.[54] First there is the *intellectual* motif, where people consciously investigate religious alternatives and almost "convert themselves." At least they consciously and actively put themselves into interaction with members of a particular group and essentially "ask for" group influence and socialization to take over.

Second is the *mystical conversion*, which Lofland and Skonovd say is the most familiar conversion motif, where there is a high level of emotional arousal. The person is conscious of change coming on with a rush and they are "taken over" by a particular religion's god. This is the "born again," "Damascus road" conversion. Third, there is the *experimental* motif, where a fairly long time of "trying out" the new religion is involved. There is a gradual learning and familiarization process. The fourth is the *affectional* motif, where positive relations with members of a particular group over a somewhat extended period (usually several weeks or more) integrate the newcomer into the group. Fifth is the *revivalist* motif, which is similar to the second motif (mystical), except that it occurs in public and dramatically as the convert in ecstasy heeds the altar call and publicly demonstrates their rejection of evil and acceptance of the new way. Sixth is the *coercive* motif, rather rare, yet alleged with some frequency by those opposed to particular religions. It is identified by such negative designations as "brainwashing," "programming," "mind control," and the like. The individual feels compelled sincerely to confess guilt and embrace a new ideological system.

Despite critiques and modifications, there is virtually universal agreement on at least two prerequisites to conversion, so crucial in Lofland's theory: (1) the existence of prior affective bonds between a recruit and one or more members of the group and (2) intensive interaction and involvement with the group in order to facilitate conversion. As such it is likely that the person converts not for doctrinal reasons (for what the group's teachings are), but because of the supportive acceptance of the group of fellow human beings who express warmth, acceptance, and support.

DECONVERSION

Within the context of considering conversion, it is appropriate to look also at its opposite, deconversion. People not only affiliate with a religious group through conversion, they also disaffiliate and repudiate their former commitment. While there are a variety of terms to describe what happens—for example, defection, disaffiliation, and apostasy—we will employ the fairly neutral term deconversion, which implies an actual decision to leave.

As we have learned, most conversions involve a process that extends over a period of time and proceeds through stages; it is not a sudden, spur-of-the-moment phenomenon. Likewise, research shows that deconversions follow similar patterns. The leader is the focus point in most religious groups, cults in particular, and it takes time to interact with that leader, fall under their "spell," and place full trust and confidence in them. Expectedly then, it takes some time to disentangle oneself from the leader when going through the deconversion process.

Janet Jacobs has gathered instructive data from people who have left religious cults,[55] and has found an evolutionary quality to the process of deconversion for 80 percent of the people.[56] She emphasizes a "multi-phase exit" that involves two separations. First, one disengages from the social manifestations of the group—group activities and interactions and exchanges with the members. Second, one disengages from the leader and breaks the emotional attachment one has had to that person.

Most often the dissatisfaction and disillusionment with the group itself—the first step in the ultimate deconversion process—is described as "conflict over social life." This would be conflict over intimate relations, prescribed sex roles, and personal lifestyle—in other words, restrictions on one's freedom and personal life. Often this disgruntlement involves dissatisfaction with mid-level organizers, and not the leader. People can apparently survive in this stage of partial defection for some time. Jacobs notes that "partial deconversion can be understood as a state of consciousness on the part of devotees in which the leader assumes a separate and divine quality that is distinct from the mundane aspects of religious commitment associated with the regulation of group life and the social demands of affiliation."[57] Some members actually leave at this point. They never actually reject the leader, but they find the group structure too constricting and alienating. Of the subjects studied, 43 percent defected without repudiating the leader, but the remaining 57 percent rejected the group, its restrictions, and the leader. However, the rejection of the leader was emotionally wrenching and painful for these people. Jacobs notes that most followers of a cult, both male and female, express love for the leader. While the sojourn with the group might have become intolerable, the love and respect for the leader might still exist. Yet we must not lose sight of the fact that over half (57 percent) of Jacob's sample rejected both the group *and* the leader.

There were four primary areas in which leaders were perceived as deviant. Mentioned most often (by 60 percent of respondents) was psychological abuse. Next, at 45 percent, was emotional rejection. Spiritual betrayal (33 percent) and physical abuse (31 percent) round off the list.[58]

We noted above that Jacobs found that dissatisfaction with the leader is not everything. Nearly half of the defectors leave without rejecting the leader. Other factors are involved. Stuart Wright describes several factors or sources of disillusionment with the group that can also be significant. One is discovering inconsistencies between a leader's behavior and the ideals they profess. But there are three other possible precipitating factors:

1. a breakdown of isolation and insulation from the outside world, which provides opportunities for comparisons and contrasts to be made by the member;
2. unregulated development of a strong relationship with another member within the group, with whom you can discuss things candidly; and
3. a perceived lack of success in achieving the goals of the group to change and improve the world.[59]

It should be noted that there is a wide range in the amount of time required for members of these new religious movements to defect. While most will eventually leave (Saul Levine found that almost 90 percent of converts to cults and cult-like groups will actually leave within two years of their original commitment),[60] Jacobs found the average stay for her respondents was four and a half years, and over half stayed more than two years.[61] One gets a clear picture of a lot of movement both in and out of these groups. It is clear also that disillusionment and subsequent defection from one group does not discourage a majority of these people from later joining other similar groups. Stuart Wright found that 78 percent of his sample of voluntary defectors from the Unification Church, the Hare Krishna Movement, and the Children of God, eventually reconverted to another group.[62] And Jacobs found that among her respondents, who were all defectors, half had moved on to another similar group.

Two points seem clear: (1) disappointment with one group does not keep people from trying others; (2) underlying needs of these peripatetic types have not been met by other activities or affiliations in the meantime.

But not all disaffiliation is from cults. More numerous in the aggregate and, probably at least as important, are defections from more mainline religious groups. It is important to note first that the number of people who disaffiliate appears to have increased recently. John Condran and Joseph Tamney cite an increase in the number of people in national opinion polls who claim no affiliation. Those numbers have increased from 3 percent and under through the 1950s (2.7 percent claiming no religious affiliation in 1957) to 7.1 percent in 1982.[63] One must infer here, of course, that some people who, at points in the past, would have claimed affiliation with a religious group now do not, thereby implying disaffiliation. And who are these people? Kirk Hadaway and Wade Roof summarize a number of profile studies by noting that disaffiliates (apostates) are "most likely to be young, single, male, highly educated, liberal, and mobile, while studies of the reasons apostates give for leaving emphasize maturation, objections to church teachings, irrelevance, and lifestyle conflicts."[64]

DEPROGRAMMING

A second means of disaffiliating from new religious movements was what came to be known as deprogramming. Deprogramming involved physical withdrawal from the confines of the religious group, often forcefully by parents and other loved ones who hired self-described deprogrammers, who "rescued" the son or daughter from the clutches of the NRM and began a process of isolation and cleansing of the psyche that was designed to reverse the "brainwashing" that had occurred during the conversion to and participation in the NRM. Such deprogramming techniques were successful in some cases, though were widely regarded as serious violations of the civil rights of adult sons and daughters and the process is almost unheard of today.

CONCLUSION

The process of becoming religious is not a unique or unusual process. It is simply socialization by a group into a body of norms, which provides a set of meanings and interpretations that individuals internalize and relate to the large body of other meanings they possess. The process and ultimate outcome of religious socialization is not unlike learning the role and meaning construct of becoming a French citizen, Cuban mother, or center for the Celtics. The elements common to all who participate in a social group are learned. Yet a unique pattern emerges, for each individual has a unique combination of interactions and observations that eventuate in their meaning construct. Powerful social influences and factors impinge on the individual and are internalized. Thus, although psychological processes are involved, what we observe is not something internal to the individual that "comes out," so to speak. Rather, we see something created and induced "from without" through socialization.

But people also disaffiliate from groups. They sometimes leave. In other words, the group no longer provides the satisfaction it promised or perhaps once did provide for an individual. Or perhaps the leader becomes discredited, or another group looks more inviting. Often, like conversion, the process leading to defection is gradual. We have made the point more than once that the conversion/deconversion activity in religious groups is not unlike the joining and leaving by members from other groups. However, we do observe a difference when talking about NRMs (cults), as contrasted with the mainline denominational groups. On the average, there are more (a higher percentage of) defections from cults than from other groups, and even other religious groups. The reason is simply that by definition a cult's center of existence is its charismatic leader. If the leader becomes discredited in the eyes of some, many will leave. Even if not wholly discredited, as the infatuation with the leader loses its intensity, people drift away. In fact, the vast majority of recruits have left within the first year of two.[65]

NOTES

1. Anthony F. C. Wallace, *Religion: An Anthropological View* (New York: Random House, 1966), pp. 86–91.
2. Matthew 28:19–20 (Revised Standard Version). Emphasis added.
3. Charles Y. Glock and Rodney Stark, *Religion and Society in Tension* (Chicago: Rand McNally, 1965), p. 164.
4. Ronald L. Johnstone, *The Effectiveness of Lutheran Elementary and Secondary Schools as Agencies of Christian Education* (St. Louis: Concordia Seminary Research Center, 1966).
5. National Opinion Research Center data reported in Wade Clark Roof and William McKinney, *American Mainline Religion* (New Brunswick, NJ: Rutgers University Press, 1987), pp. 211–212.

6. Ibid.

7. George Gallup, *Religion in America 1984*, Gallup Report No. 222 (Princeton, NJ: Princeton Religion Research Center, 1984), p. 23.

8. National Opinion Research Center data abstracted from Table 1 of Jenifer Hamil-Luker and Christian Smith, "Religious Authority and Public Opinion on the Right to Die," *Sociology of Religion* 59, no. 4 (1998): 382.

9. National Opinion Research Center data abstracted from Table 2 of Michael Corbett and Julia Mitchell Corbett, *Politics and Religion in the United States* (New York: Garland Press, 1999), p. 268.

10. Charles Y. Glock and Rodney Stark, *Christian Beliefs and Anti-Semitism* (New York: Harper & Row, 1966), p. 7.

11. Ibid., p. 10.

12. R. K. Young, W. M. Benson, and W. H. Holtzman, "Changes in Attitudes toward the Negro in a Southern University," *Journal of Abnormal and Social Psychology* 60, no. 1 (1960): 131–133.

13. Gerhard E. Lenski, *The Religious Factor* (Garden City, NY: Doubleday, 1961), p. 103.

14. Joseph Fichter, *Southern Parish* (Chicago: University of Chicago Press, 1951); idem *Social Relations in the Urban Parish* (Chicago: University of Chicago Press, 1954).

15. Ibid., p. 24.

16. Ibid., p. 41.

17. Ibid., pp. 61–62.

18. Ibid., p. 69.

19. Charles Y. Glock, "The Religious Revival in America," in *Religion and the Face of America*, ed. Jane Zahn (Berkeley: University Extension, University of California, 1959), pp. 25–42.

20. Charles Y. Glock, "On the Study of Religious Commitment," *Religious Education* 62, no. 4 (1962): 98–110.

21. Rodney Stark and Charles Y. Glock, *American Piety: The Nature of Religious Commitment* (Berkeley: University of California Press, 1968), p. 15.

22. W. W. Schroeder and Victor Obenhaus, *Religion in American Culture* (New York: Free Press, 1964), p. 147.

23. Johnstone, *The Effectiveness of Lutheran Elementary and Secondary Schools as Agencies of Christian Education*, p. 100.

24. Ronald L. Johnstone, project director, national survey data gathered by the National Opinion Research Center for the Lutheran Council in the U.S.A., 1970.

25. Ibid.

26. Constant H. Jacquet Jr., ed., *Yearbook of American Churches, 1989* (Nashville: Abingdon Press, 1989), p. 277.

27. C. Kirk Hadaway, Penny Long Marler, and Mark Chaves, "What the Polls Don't Show: A Closer Look at U.S. Church Attendance," *American Sociological Review* 58, no. 6 (Dec., 1993): 744.

28. Ibid., p. 746.

29. Ibid., p. 747.

30. David Elkind, "Age Changes in the Meaning of Religious Identity," *Review of Religious Research* 6, no. 1 (1964): 36–40.

31. John L. Thomas, "Religious Training in the Roman Catholic Family," *American Journal of Sociology* 62, no. 2 (1951): 178–183.

32. Marie Cornwall, "The Influence of Three Agents of Religious Socialization: Family, Church, and Peers," in *The Religion and Family Connection*, ed. Darwin L. Thomas (Provo, UT: Religious Studies Center, Brigham Young University, 1988), p. 226.

33. Ibid.

34. Dean R. Hoge and Gregory H. Petrillo, "Determinants of Church Participation and Attitudes among High School Youth," *Journal for the Scientific Study of Religion* 17, no. 4 (December 1978): 359–379.

35. Johnstone, *Effectiveness of Lutheran Elementary and Secondary Schools.*

36. Raymond H. Potvin and Douglas M. Sloane, "Parental Control, Age, and Religious Practice," *Review of Religious Research* 27, no. 1 (September 1985): 10.

37. Gerald N. Stott, "Familial Influence on Religious Involvement," in *The Religion and Family Connection,* ed. Darvin L. Thomas (Provo, UT: Religious Studies Center, Brigham Young University, 1988), pp. 258–271.

38. Hans Zetterberg, "The Religious Conversion as a Change of Social Roles," *Sociology and Social Research* 36, no. 1 (1952): 159–166.

39. James T. Borhek and Richard F. Curtis, *A Sociology of Belief* (New York: John Wiley, 1975), p. 98.

40. Ibid., emphasis added.

41. Walter H. Clark, *The Psychology of Religion* (New York: Macmillan, 1958), p. 207.

42. Elkind, "Age Changes," p. 40.

43. Gordon W. Allport, *The Individual and His Religion* (New York: Macmillan, 1957), p. 32.

44. Robert H. Thouless, "The Psychology of Conversion," in *Conversion,* ed. Walter E. Conn (New York: Alba House, 1978), p. 143.

45. E. Burke Rockford, Jr., *Hare Krishna in America* (New Brunswick, NJ: Rutgers University Press, 1985), p. 47.

46. Catherine Robins, "Conversion, Life Crises, and Stability among Women in the East African Revival," in *New Religions of Africa,* ed. Benneta Jules-Rosette (Norwood, NJ: Ablex Publishing Corporation, 1979), p. 197.

47. Ibid., p. 199.

48. John Lofland, *Doomsday Cult* (Englewood Cliffs, NJ: Prentice Hall, 1966), pp. 31–62

49. To this list Richardson, Stewart, and Simmonds would add what they call the "conventional" responses of "muddling through," or doing other typically conventional things, such as moving, changing jobs, taking a holiday, getting married, and getting divorced, before taking the more dramatic route of affiliating with an offbeat religious cult. Cf. James T. Richardson, Mary White Stewart, Robert B. Simmonds, *Organized Miracles* (New Brunswick, NJ: Transaction Books, 1978), pp. 238–239.

50. Eileen Barker, *The Making of a Moonie* (Oxford, England: Basil Blackwell Publisher, 1984), p. 217.

51. David A. Snow and Richard Machalek, "Second Thoughts on the Presumed Fragility of Unconventional Beliefs," in *Of Gods and Men: New Religious Movements in the West,* ed. Eileen Barker (Macon, GA: Mercer University Press, 1983), p. 41.

52. James T. Richardson and Mary Stewart, "Conversion Process Models and the Jesus Movement," in *Conversion Careers: In and Out of the New Religions,* ed. James T. Richardson (Beverly Hills, CA: Sage Publications, 1978).

53. David A. Snow and Cynthia Phillips, "The Lofland-Stark Model: A Critical Reassessment," *Social Problems* 27, no. 4 (1980): 430–447.

54. John Lofland and Norman Skonovd, "Conversion Motifs," *Journal for the Scientific Study of Religion* 20, no. 4 (1981): 373–385.

55. Janet Jacobs, "Deconversion from Religious Movements," *Journal for the Scientific Study of Religion* 26, no. 3 (1987): 294–308.

56. Ibid., p. 299.

57. Ibid., p. 300.

58. Ibid.

59. Stuart A. Wright, "Defection from New Religious Movements," in *The Brainwashing/Deprogramming Controversy,* eds. David G. Bromley and James T. Richardson (New York: The Edwin Mellen Press, 1983), pp. 106–121.

60. Saul V. Levine, *Radical Departures: Desperate Detours to Growing Up* (New York: Harcourt Brace Jovanovich, 1986), p. 93.

61. Jacobs, "Deconversion from Religious Movements," p. 297.

62. Stuart A. Wright, "Post-Involvement Attitudes of Voluntary Defectors from Controversial New Religious Movements," *Journal for the Scientific Study of Religion* 23, no. 2 (1984): 172–182.

63. John G. Condran and Joseph B. Tamney, "Religious 'Nones': 1957 to 1982," *Sociological Analysis* 46, no. 4 (Winter 1985): 415.

64. C. Kirk Hadaway and Wade Clark Roof, "Apostasy in American Churches: Evidence from National Data," in *Falling from the Faith*, ed. David G. Bromley (Newbury Park, CA: Sage Publications, 1988), pp. 29–46.

65. James Beckford, "Conversion and Apostasy: Antithesis or Complementarity?" Paper presented at conference on "Conversion, Coercion, and Commitment in the New Religions," Berkeley, CA, June 11–14, 1981. Reported in Stuart A. Wright, *Leaving Cults: The Dynamics of Defection* (Washington, DC: Society for the Scientific Study of Religion Monograph Series, no. 7, 1987), p. 2.

Eileen Barker, "Resistible Coercion: The Significance of Failure Rates in Conversion and Commitment to the Unification Church," in *Conversion, Coercion, and Commitment in New Religious Movements*, eds. Dick Anthony, Jacob Needleman, and Thomas Robbins (New York: Crossroads Press, 1983).

Chapter 6

Religious Conflict

Religio-political action.

During their reading of the text so far, many readers will have sensed an emphasis on what is known, within the field of sociology, as *structural-functional* theory. This has been the emphasis, in part because much that religion is and does has purposes and functions that help people adjust to and accept the vagaries and vicissitudes of life. It is also in part because, to the extent that people are enabled to continue carrying out their social roles in a reasonably competent manner, the society itself is aided. Here we are thinking about such functions as providing a sense of belonging, suggesting answers to questions of deep concern, promising ultimate release and salvation, and providing a sense of life purpose.

CONFLICT THEORY ACCORDING TO KARL MARX

Another major theory in sociology is in sharp contrast—namely, the *conflict* perspective. This perspective recognizes that there is another side of the coin. Religion not only might provide solace and comfort and explanations for complex and puzzling issues, but can also create or at least enhance stress, anxiety, worry, guilty consciences, and sexual "hang-ups." This perspective also emphasizes the competition and antagonisms, even outright physical conflict, that exist among individuals and subgroups in a society, even among religious people and their groups. Additionally, the conflict perspective features the availability within religion of considerable power and influence, which can be used to control and exploit others.

As we begin our discussion of conflict theory, particularly as it applies to religion in society, we must immediately take note of the founding father of this perspective. Karl Marx, over a century ago called religion the "opium of the people." As such, religion in its organized form was in direct competition with Marx's socialist political philosophy, which defined religion, although a powerful force in its own right, as an enemy of a socialistic revolutionary state. But apart from the sedating and misdirecting effects of religion, people and the groups of which they are a part in a capitalist society are in competition and, as such, in a conflict situation. They are continually seeking their advantage in a world of limited resources. Any cooperation and integration that might develop among these competitors is a result of expediency and self-interest and, therefore, tenuous.

Agents of Control

In addition to identifying the competition (conflict) that exists among individuals and groups, Marx emphasized the use made of religion by the dominant and powerful in society:

1. to encourage acceptance of one's lot in life regardless of its lowly and unpleasant character,
2. the performance of one's job as competently and energetically as possible, and,
3. a looking forward to one's ultimate reward in heaven or nirvana.

Conflict theorists speak of control and manipulation of the masses, in a community or society, by the powerful élite with their middle-class supporters. Marx observed that religion, with its emphasis on doing one's duty and obeying the laws of the land that are viewed in turn as the laws of God, serves as a narcotic drug administered by the élites to the less-privileged in society, to keep them docile and accepting of the *status quo*.

Only Two Classes

In this connection, Marx asserted that, despite their seeming complexity, societies could be reduced to two social classes that are inherently in conflict with one another. These are the owners of the means of production (the bourgeoisie) and those who work for the owners and have only their muscle and energy to sell (the proletariat). The owners are out to extract as much work and product from the workers, with as little expenditure in the form of wages, as possible. The workers, of course, want more than a starvation wage and at least some share of the product of their labor. Thus you have class conflict—the eternal conflict in society—eternal, that is, according to Marx, until the workers can prevail and inaugurate worldwide socialism and, over time, create a perfect classless society.

From Ownership to Power

We should mention, somewhat parenthetically at this point, that today many conflict theorists prefer to emphasize the concept of power instead of ownership. If power is defined as "the probability that one actor within a social relationship will be in a position to carry out his own will despite resistance,"[1] then having power (or having little to none) becomes crucial and narrows human relationships to the bare essentials. It is still a conflict between the haves and the have-nots. But now management and supervisory people in the large corporations and public institutions can be included with the haves, whereas they would often have to be included as have-nots if actual ownership of the means of production were a requirement. In other words, Marx was looking at early industrial society. We are now in a post-industrial, service-oriented society in which positioning on the basis of specialized training and skills in a bureaucratic hierarchy is all-important.

Resignation and Misdirection

But to return to the place of religion in society according to conflict theory, a major observation by conflict theorists is that while one cannot say that religion *per se* creates the problems faced by the proletariat—the poverty, the misery, the inequality, the shortened life expectancy, to name a few—for a great many people, a religious expression or interpretation is their sole response to the injustice. That could be a response of resigned acceptance, of hope for greater reward in the life of bliss that will follow this present life, which is admittedly worse than it could be, and of bowing to the will of God, which far surpasses our own short-sighted, selfish understanding and perspective. And, of course, the point made here by conflict theorists is that such a religious response is missing the real point of the issue and therefore fails its followers.

A second major point of conflict theory is that religion deflects the actions of the downtrodden from striking at the root sources of their oppression. Here we would observe the common themes of most religions, that one must accept one's lot in life, carry out the duties that one is assigned, and find emotional release through acceptable channels, such as participation in an expressive, emotional-release type of religious service. As such, Marx calls for the abolition of religion to eliminate the "illusory" happiness of people, so that true happiness can be achieved.[2]

Those at the other end of the economic scale will thank God that they have a more favored position in life. They might carry food baskets to the poor at Christmas time, but they will not raise their wages, allow them into a profit-sharing plan, or give them the training or opportunity for a better job.

We should mention here that conflict theorists view religion as they would any other institution in society and as such are not particularly "picking on" religion. It is assumed that, in every institution and social relationship, a fundamental conflict of interest is in operation. It is assumed that one will observe exploitation, misdirected energies, false comfort, and much that sounds like "pie in the sky, by and by" almost anywhere one looks. Such a perspective from conflict theory might well elicit angry rejoinders from many believers. Yet conflict theory is at least partly right in the sense that, at their core, all religions try to make their members feel better and more secure, as they face a future that is uncertain for everyone. Members have a conviction that they know the real truth about most things, that they know what they should do (rituals) to please the supreme being(s), and that they can look forward to a better future whether in heaven, by reincarnation, or by the good memories of them retained by those they leave behind. Both pro-religionists and anti-religionists will grant that religion does succeed to some degree in pacifying and making hopeful many whose reward in this life is very minimal. We introduced this idea in Chapter 4 and will discuss such functions of religion further in Chapters 8 and 9. But for now we will simply grant that there is very likely truth on both sides of functional/conflict theory. We want now to examine religion in conflict, in an effort to understand that which might seem to be an inherent contradiction—namely, violence in the name of and for the sake of religion. What we will look at is so-called "real-life" conflict that exists and needs to be recognized, whether one subscribes to conflict theory or to structural-functional theory as the best starting point for understanding social life.

Our first observation is that the religious conflict we have seen recently, in such places as Northern Ireland, Iran, Yugoslavia/Serbia, the Near East, Indonesia, and India, is far from new and can be observed throughout all of history. We will point to a few examples, which will lead us to an analysis of contemporary religious conflict, later in this chapter.

RELIGIOUS CONFLICT IN HISTORY

If we go back to the history recounted in the Old Testament, we read about a continual series of wars and battles. These were essentially what can be called political skirmishes of one society or tribe against another, as they fought over land and resources. A fundamental reason for such warfare was the fact that the Israelites, following their escape from Egypt, were trying to occupy land that was already inhabited by others. Of course, they believed they were God's chosen people who were simply following God's instructions and proceeding with God's special blessing and assistance. In that sense, it is certainly appropriate to speak of religious conflict, particularly when the Old Testament continually speaks about doing battle, not simply against Israel's political enemies, but against worshippers of false gods and graven images who, as such, were God's enemies.

In the Middle Ages, we observe one armed religious conflict after another. They were frequently defined by the participants as "holy wars" because they often took the form of crusades marching through Europe and the Near East to Palestine to defeat the infidels (the Muslims), who had occupied God's sacred ground (Palestine) that should be in Christian hands. The conflict then was Christian against Muslim—a religious conflict. But first, we will look briefly at the internal religious conflict within the Catholic Church during the middle ages.

Internal Catholic Conflict

There were frequent European wars and programs involving the Roman Catholic Church, which often tried to suppress heresy with the sword. One might think of the well-known Inquisition or the relentless near-extermination of the Cathars, Waldensians, and other Catholic revolutionary sectarian groups in southern France, just before and after the turn of the thirteenth century. Inasmuch as these groups were branded as heretics, the church felt justified in uniting with secular authorities to annihilate them. In 1179, the Third Lateran Council even proclaimed a crusade against these French Christians, probably the first occasion when this tactic was used against people who viewed themselves as orthodox Christian believers. Pope Innocent III, who ruled from 1198 to 1216, is acknowledged to have initiated the final steps in eliminating these reform groups. More crusading armies were organized. And thus, as Kenneth Scott Latourette says, "Religious zeal . . . combined with quite secular motives, sectional jealousies, and the desires of the nobles of Northern France to reduce the power of the South and to profit by its wealth."[3]

Many years of warfare ensued, resulting in a great deal of bloodshed and cruelty. It has been reported that, when Beziers was entered by a crusading army, the Papal Legate was asked if the faithful Catholics should be spared. He expressed fear that the heretics would feign orthodoxy to escape the sword. So he said, "Kill them all, for God knows his own." And thus the heretics were subdued through nearly total annihilation. These were people who would today have felt fairly comfortable in much of Christendom, even in some Roman Catholic churches. They believed that laymen and women could preach and administer the sacrament of the Lord's Supper and that a liturgy in Latin made no sense because people could not understand it. They believed masses and prayers for the dead were of no effect and that purgatory was not really a place to which souls journeyed after death, but rather consisted of the trials and tribulations that people endure in their lifetimes.

The Crusades

We have just been talking about the military crusades directed against the Cathars and Waldensians. But the better-known crusades were those directed against Muslims. And although the crusades evolved out of a variety of motives, some of which were purely economic and political, several clear religious motives were articulated.

First was the goal of liberating Palestine from the control of "infidel" Muslims. Second was a desire to create some protection from the Muslim Turks for the beleaguered Byzantine Empire centered in Constantinople. Third was a desire of several popes in succession to heal the breach between the Western, Latin branch of Catholicism and the Eastern, Greek branch.

While Jerusalem was "rescued" for Christian occupation twice (in 1099 and 1229), in 1244 it fell to Muslim siege and was to remain in Muslim hands until the twentieth century. But crusades were not organized solely to rescue Jerusalem. They were also directed against Muslims in Spain, against "pagans" in what is now northern Europe, and against Christian groups that a given Pope might judge to be enemies of the faith.

And so with the Crusades we have a nearly perfect example of religion that is not just an accessory to conflict but its initiator. Although some Christians raised voices against the cruelty, the squandering of life and property, the condoning of violence, and excess of all types, a majority of Christians accepted such eventualities as the will of God. In fact, the Latin phrase *Deus vult*! ("God wills it!") was the crusaders' battle cry.

CONTEMPORARY EXAMPLES OF RELIGIOUS CONFLICT

As we now turn to more contemporary examples of religious conflict, we need not look far. Almost every continent has a well-known example to display. We will identify several and then look more closely at one of them. In Europe, we have witnessed the Catholic-Protestant guerrilla war in

Northern Ireland. This conflict has been going on for more than seventy years, with greater intensity since 1970, yet with a great deal of effort by the British government and both sides to the conflict during this same period, to bring about a resolution. At this writing the historic signing of the Northern Ireland peace agreement, which was ratified by citizen vote in May 1998, still holds despite sporadic acts of violence that have threatened but not broken the fragile peace that began the process of forming a coalition government. That process has been slow and interrupted more than once. But the date of 28 July 2005 might well turn out to be the most significant date of all in the lengthy conflict between Protestants and Catholics in Northern Ireland. On that date, the Catholic Irish Republican Army (IRA) made the striking official announcement that it was renouncing violence and mandating its membership to lay down and fully deactivate their arms and henceforth rely on peaceful, political processes to resolve issues and grievances. Members are to "assist the development of purely political and democratic programs through exclusively political means."[4] The statement appears to be unambiguous. Of course, the goal is more than peace between Irish Catholics and Protestants. It is a united Ireland and independence from British rule. It will still take some years for everything to be worked through. But this statement delivered by a long imprisoned IRA leader, Seanna Walsh, shows genuine promise.

In the Union of South Africa, until recently a white minority held power over the black population majority and enforced apartheid, basing both their philosophy and their practice on an interpretation of the Bible by the Dutch Reformed Church of South Africa.

In the eastern Mediterranean, Israelis (Jews) and Palestinians (Muslims) have fought a guerrilla terrorist war since the modern re-creation of Israel in 1948. Under new leadership for the Palestinians, following the death of Yasser Arafat in 2004 and with continuing world pressure, there is some optimism that continuing discussions between the opposing ethnic-religious groups will eventually bring about resolution, though violence continues.

In the former Yugoslavia, the Christian (Eastern Orthodox) Serbs, under the direction of Slobodan Milosevic, have murdered their Muslim neighbors and fellow citizens and destroyed their neighborhoods and villages. Only massive intervention by the United States and NATO in 1998–99 ended the worst of the so-called "ethnic cleansing" in the Balkans.

In the southern Philippines, Muslim extremists massacred more than a dozen Roman Catholic Christians in 1994. A militant Christian group, the Ilaga, threatened reprisal against the Muslim militant group blamed for the massacre—the Abu Sayyaf.

In India, a minority religious offshoot (sect) of Hinduism—the Sikh religion—garnered many headlines beginning in the 1980s. Two Sikh bodyguards of Prime Minister Indira Ghandi assassinated her on 31 October 1984. Hindu and Muslim citizens retaliated with countless individual and mob acts of violence against Sikhs, which ended with at least 2,700 killed and thousands left homeless.[5]

In 1999, in the predominantly Roman Catholic East Timor region of Indonesia, self-styled Muslim militia, with the tacit approval of the Indonesian military, killed hundreds, probably thousands, of East Timorese (including fourteen Roman Catholic clergy) and drove 300,000 citizens from their homes, as they attempted to gain political independence. This violence perpetrated by the Indonesian Muslim militia was vigorously denounced by Muslims living in Timor's nearest country to the south, Australia, through their spokesman, Abbas Ahmed, president of the Australian Federation of Islamic Councils.[6]

Other attacks by Muslim extremists against Christian institutions, such as schools and hospitals, occurred in Pakistan in August 2002; and in Nigeria, dozens of citizens were killed in violence between Christians and Muslims in the capital city, Jos, in 2001.[7]

But the Far East also has religious-based conflict between Hindus and Muslims. In December 1992 it was reported that nearly 700 people died in a Hindu-Muslim conflict, which was centered in the primarily Hindu town of Ayadhya. Escalation of the conflict occurred after Hindu extremists demolished an ancient Muslim mosque. Following that act, many night-time raiding parties from the Hindu and Muslim subcolonies in Bombay's massive slum district attacked one another with knives, hatchets, Molotov cocktails, and light bulbs filled with acid.[8]

In November 2002, Indian security forces used rocket launchers to end a siege of two Hindu temples by Islamic militants in Kashmir. Twelve people were killed and some fifty injured, most of them Indian Hindus. In fact, Hindu-Muslim violence has been almost commonplace since independence from England was achieved in 1948. Paul Brass observes that riots between Hindus and Muslims, as well as what he calls pogroms against Muslims "have been endemic in India since Independence."[9] He adds that hardly a month goes by in which a Hindu-Muslim riot does not take place that is noted in the press, with smaller conflicts probably occurring daily somewhere in the country.

Also in India, conflict between Hindus and Christians escalated in the late 1990s to the highest level during the half century of India's independence. According to the Indian Home Ministry, attacks upon Christians rose from 7 in 1996, to 24 in 1997, to 86 in 1998. The attacks are based on objections to conversion activities by Christian groups from Hindu nationalists, in regions where the political party Bharatiya Janata is dominant.[10]

Even in the Americas, some of the Hindu diaspora from India have clashed with Christians in the Caribbean countries of Trinidad and Guyana over conversion attempts by Evangelical Christian groups.[11]

Clearly what is old is also new and up to date in religious conflict. And such interreligious conflict has not been restricted to any one or two major religions. Christians, Hindus, Muslims, Sikhs, and others have all been both perpetrators and victims, depending upon the circumstances of time and place. Although there is evidence that true progress in peace negotiations between warring religious groups has occurred in several places, new conflicts break out a continent or two away at the same time as religious conflict is mitigated somewhere else. We now turn to a closer examination of the Sikh-Hindu-Muslim case in India and Pakistan.

Sikh-Hindu-Muslim Conflict

Sikhism is a minority religion in India, with its 15 million adherents constituting only about 2 percent of the population in the country. It was founded in the early part of the sixteenth century, as an offshoot sect of Hinduism, by a man who came to be known as Guru Nanak. Much like Gautama Buddha many centuries before him, Nanak claimed a special vision and mission and devoted the last forty years of his life to spreading the Sikh message.

The Early Years   Sikhism originated in the Punjab region in northern India and is still centered there. In fact, the modern state of Punjab is the only Indian state in which Sikhs constitute a majority of the citizens and voters. Punjab is between and to the south of the two parts of Pakistan, where Islam has long been dominant. So Sikhism had not only to contend with its parent religion, Hinduism, but also even more significantly with Islam, which by its nature is a confrontational religion not averse to violent tactics to secure conformity. In fact, Sikhism sought deliberately to be a mediator and to bring closer together the religions of Hinduism and Islam.

Nanak was the first of ten gurus who helped Sikhism evolve to its mature form, over a period of approximately two hundred years. During these formative years, the new religion was under frequent attack by Muslim rulers, who viewed Sikhism as a heresy that needed to be exterminated. The reason for Sikhism's founding and development as a conscious bridge between Hinduism and Islam was hardly attractive to Muslim leaders, who demanded loyalty to traditional Islam.

Such persecution and violence help explain two distinctive features of the Sikhs—namely, a tradition of bravery and martyrdom and disproportionate representation in the Indian military. Proud of their heritage, Sikhs are easily identifiable by the five Ks: *kes* (long hair wrapped in a turban with a full beard as well), *kach* (short trousers), *kara* (a steel bracelet on the right wrist), *kangha* (a comb), and a *kirpan* (a curved dagger). While such uniformity helps in maintaining a strong sense of community, many have observed that it also provides ready targets for one's enemies.

It is the religious concept of martyrdom, Murray Leaf notes, that is significant in explaining the Sikhs' relationship to violence. In Leaf's words, martyrdom "provides an explicit and accepted ethical balance or counterpoint to the kinship idea."[12] By this he is suggesting that, while the Sikhs emphasize family and kinship ties and obligations, the logical extension of which could be self-centeredness or at best family-centeredness (in which individuals would sacrifice the welfare of the larger community for the benefit of the kinship group), the Sikhs consciously strive to do the opposite. They believe that if all would behave in self-centered ways, then all would suffer. Therefore martyrdom, in which individuals sacrifice their individual well being, perhaps their own life, has been viewed very positively by Indian Sikhs. The virtue to be defended is self-defense—and "self" is understood to mean one's family and, by extension, the Sikh community with which one is associated.[13] So, although violence seems to follow the Sikhs, it began as defensive violence, not aggressive, initiating violence.

Consistent with such dedication and faithfulness to their own, Sikhs are known by their skill and industriousness and have proven to be valuable allies. Although they number only about 2 percent of the Indian population, Sikhs constitute at least 15 percent of the nation's army and nearly as large a proportion of governmental bureaucrats (a recent president of India, Zail Singh, was a Sikh). They have a strong work ethic and have been highly successful, whether as businessmen, farmers, or soldiers. Their loyalty to the British during the Sepoy Rebellion in 1857, when most Indians revolted, was rewarded by generous grants of land in the most fertile region in India—the "land of the five rivers" (Punjab).

After India's Independence from Great Britain   Problems arose for the Sikhs after India secured its independence from Great Britain in 1949. At that time, when Pakistan was separated from India, the boundary lines cut across Punjab and severed millions of Sikhs from their homes in Pakistan. Considerable violence against both person and property was exchanged between Pakistan Muslims and Indian Sikhs, just as in the old days of three hundred to four hundred years before. The Sikhs began to demand a Sikh homeland, complaining that "the Muslims got Pakistan, the Hindus got India, but Sikhs got nothing."

Although slow to do so, the Indian government finally conceded and produced a compromise solution of dividing Punjab into two states—Punjab, in which Sikhs were a 52 percent majority, and Haryana, where their typical minority status was maintained. Soon a religio-political party (the Akalis), dating from the 1920s, resurfaced with renewed vigor and commitment to achieve more gains for Sikhs. In an effort to weaken the Akalis, the Indian central government supported the leadership of a Sikh charismatic preacher, named Jarnail Singh Bhindranwale. But Bhindranwale turned out to be a poor choice, because he promoted a return to Sikh fundamentalism in the manner of Iran's Ayatolla Khomeini promoting a return to Muslim fundamentalism. Bhindranwale also similarly advocated violence to secure Sikh independence. In the first half of 1984, three hundred people in

Punjab were killed. Many were themselves Sikhs, who either had opposed Bhindranwale or were Indian governmental employees. Soon terrorist Sikhs began random killing of Hindus for no reason other than their Hindu religious affiliation. As the violence escalated, Bhindranwale and his followers holed up in the Golden Temple compound—the most holy shrine of the Sikhs. The smoldering Sikh rebellion of two years' duration came to a head as Indira Ghandi, the prime minister, ordered Indian troops to end the terrorism by attacking the Golden Temple in Amritsar with an army of 4,000 troops. As they surrounded the 72-acre compound and tried to induce surrender with machine gunfire, the Indian military forces were met with surprisingly strong resistance from totally dedicated men bearing sophisticated weaponry. The army eventually had to resort to tanks and howitzers to penetrate the fortress. It took two days; but of course the Indian army prevailed, killing Bhindranwale and Major General Shubheg Singh, the mastermind behind the Sikh rebellion of the previous two years. Five months later, the Sikh bodyguards assassinated Ghandi and the retaliatory violence was resumed.

The key to understanding the Sikhs' actions probably lies in their minority status and its attendant identity crisis. It is important to remember that the partition of India in 1947 opened wounds that had festered for decades. In that partition, when western Punjab, the cradle of Sikh culture, became a part of Muslim Pakistan and millions of Sikhs were displaced from their land and villages, it must have seemed like the days three to four hundred years earlier, when the Sikhs tried to defend themselves from Muslim rulers.

In the Sikh-Muslim conflict we have a classic instance of a religio-political clash, in which a religious group shows itself to be a political ethnic group as well. In striving to maintain its religious identity and distinctiveness, it perceives a need for political autonomy as the framework within which to carry on its ethnic tradition. Its reality, its identity as a political group, religious group, and ethnic group, places it in conflict with both the overarching state interests and with other religious and ethnic groups and often leads, what was religious idealism, into lawlessness and violence almost for its own sake. During the years of peak violence (1981–94) when religious ideals were overwhelmed by violent retribution for injustices both real and imagined, Mark Juergensmeyer comments: "distinctions between valid and inappropriate targets become blurred, virtually anyone could become a victim of the militants' wrath."[14] He says further that, by January 1988, more than 100 people a month were being killed in battles among radical Sikhs, police, and fellow citizens caught in the crossfire. A religion that had preached nonviolence could now support the use of force "for a righteous cause." He quotes a prominent Sikh leader, Simranjit Singh Mann, as saying that violence in the cause of justice was not "a moral decision," but "a strategic one."[15] Such an intermingling of religious, political, and ethnic identities is what makes the elimination of conflict so doubtful. In other words, we have not heard the last of religio-political conflict—in India, in the Near East, in the Balkans, and elsewhere.

The Primacy of Particularism

When we look at religion and conflict, we are struck by an irony that is essentially endemic in group life, namely, the final characteristic of groups, which we identified in Chapter 1 as the creation and maintenance of a sense of group identity among the members. On the positive or functional side, we think of group identification, faithfulness, dedication, even sacrifice of property and life, to defend the name and existence of one's group. But the obverse of the coin, as we consider this feature of the group from the conflict perspective, is fanaticism, blind allegiance, "my country (group), right or wrong," and conflict with other groups that remain unimpressed by your claims of superiority and exclusive rights.

At a relatively weak level, we encounter ethnocentrism and the almost quaint claims that "my group is just the greatest thing around." At a more problematic level, we see *particularism* and claims of exclusive rights and a corner on truth. In a general sense, particularism refers to strong, undivided and unambiguous commitment, and devotion to one particular party, system, world-view, etc. Glock and Stark note that at the religious or theological level, it is the "belief that only one's own religion is legitimate."[16] They go on to quote the philosopher Eric Hoffer, who has provided a succinct yet very descriptive portrait of the particularistic "true believer:" "The true believer is apt to see himself as one of the chosen, the salt of the earth, the light of the world, a prince disguised in meekness, who is destined to inherit the earth and the kingdom of heaven too."[17] Here we will see invidious comparisons with the "unenlightened," hear some name-calling, and find overt attempts to convert others to one's group. At a more serious level we note discrimination, segregation, and ghettoization. But at an even more seriously problematic level, we find out-and-out conflict that reaches the level of violence, even genocide. This is a level, as we have seen, that is reached by antagonistic religious groups with more frequency than most religionists would care to admit.

We should point out here that even sociologists of the functional persuasion will admit that conflict is not always bad and can even lead to beneficial results. Certainly the civil rights movement in the United States involved conflict—sometimes physical conflict with fire hoses, clubs, mobs, guns, injuries, and deaths. But the end result has been improvement in race relations and the opening of doors of opportunity for blacks and other members of minority groups. Also, the collective bargaining movement among American workers involved a great deal of violence, equipment and building damage, and loss of life during the last few decades of the nineteenth century and into the fourth decade of the twentieth century. Yet today, this conflict, which represented a fundamental difference of interest between the workers and the owners/managers has been normalized as both parties tend to play by the rules of the game. People now sit around a bargaining table to settle most labor issues in a peaceful, normative manner, though it must be noted that many unionists worry that their leaders have become too "cozy" with corporate management and have lost their assertive edge.

INTRARELIGIOUS CONFLICT

To this point, we have mostly considered interreligious conflict, that is, conflict between religious groups or, in some cases, of a religious group with the state. But another important type of religious conflict is what we call *intrareligious conflict*, which is defined as conflict *within* the religious group.

Introduction   At an initial and superficial level of thought, one might not expect to see much of this. People who join together in a religious group to worship God agree with one another. As such, they would certainly not be in conflict. Yet if we take the sociological perspective and our knowledge of social functioning at all seriously, we would actually expect less than perfect consensus from the very beginning, because religious groups are in many ways like all groups (see Chapter 1). They always have subgroups with special interests; local subunits (congregations) are exposed to different stimuli and influences, exist in a unique social environment and, therefore, evolve somewhat differently from other subunits. This occurs, despite the fact that they all formally subscribe to the same creed. Such conflict within a religious group can become extremely significant and emotionally consuming, because in the minds of the participants, the issues are often perceived as having life-and-death eternal significance. This is basically what the Reformation and, later the Counter-Reformation, were all about. If right belief and right behavior are necessary for eternal salvation, then differing interpretations of right belief and right behavior become crucial. And so doctrinal controversies have been nearly perpetual in most religions. As we saw in the last chapter, conflict over correct interpretations of a group's sacred writings can result in sectarian withdrawal of one or more subgroups from the parent group. Such ruptures and splits can be seen in all major religions—Christianity, Islam, Hinduism, and Judaism, to name the best known. In North America, most of the major Protestant denominations have experienced splits—whether into northern and southern branches over the issue of slavery in the mid-nineteenth century or over right doctrine as in the Presbyterian, Lutheran, and Baptist denominations in the twentieth century.

We will discuss the controversy over slavery in Chapter 9. But now we will now look briefly at the conflict within Christian groups over doctrine, belief, and practice.

Controversy Over Right Doctrine

Always at the heart of doctrinal issues is the age-old question of how to interpret the Bible (whether literally or metaphorically, whether a product of "verbal inspiration" or not). We encounter such questions as whether the birth of Christ was a real "virgin birth," whether Jonah actually lived and survived a sojourn in the belly of a "great fish," whether the miracles recorded in the Bible really happened as described, whether the water of the Red Sea did in fact part to form two walls with a dry path between them on which the Israelites could walk and thus escape Pharaoh's pursuing army, and so on. While these are old question and ancient battles, within some denominations they are being fought for the first time.

We must note that even denominations that appeared to resolve the fundamentalist-modernist issue years ago, by camping on the liberal side of the fence, do not show the internal unanimity today that one might expect. Thus, although most Congregationalists, Methodists, and Episcopalians do not accept without reservation that Jesus was born of a virgin or that miracles actually happened just as the Bible says they did, some in these denominations do. On the question of Jesus' virgin birth, for example, 39 percent of Episcopalians accept the doctrine without reservation. Similarly, 21 percent of Congregationalists, 34 percent of Methodists, and 41 percent of Episcopalians accept the biblical account of miracles as completely true.[18] That is, although such denominations may have essentially resolved the fundamentalist-modernist controversy (if only in the sense of tolerating a diversity of views and beliefs), some of their members still hold to traditional beliefs and might even feel reasonably comfortable in another, theologically more conservative denomination.

Then there are groups that have continued to maintain an official position supporting traditional beliefs and interpretations of Scripture and whose members (according to survey data) have consistently expressed high levels of concurrence with these doctrinal formulations, but in which an erosion of doctrinal solidarity appears to have begun. Two prime examples are the Lutheran Church–Missouri Synod and the Southern Baptist Convention. Both groups have long proclaimed their adherence to a conservative version of Christianity and continue in an official way to subscribe to traditional doctrine—essentially what we will later call fundamentalist doctrine. However, voices throughout both of these groups and others have challenged and questioned the official traditional positions by using a more open-ended approach to many historical definitions and understandings of Christian doctrine without necessarily denying them outright.

Example One—Southern Baptists

Looking specifically at the Southern Baptist Convention, we note that a powerful biblical inerrancy subgroup within the denomination has worked hard over the last thirty years or so to reduce the influence of the "moderate" voices that urge more open-endedness. Their aim has been to "clean up" the theological instruction at Southern Baptist seminaries and enforce its views of scripture and traditional doctrinal understanding upon seminary trustees and faculty. The inerrancy proponents have sought to cut short the drift toward "liberalism" they sense has been occurring in this large denomination. A major goal for the 1980s was to control the election of president of the church body. At stake each year is the president's authority to appoint members to two powerful boards, which in turn select people for the boards of directors of various agencies and seminaries in the Southern Baptist Convention. These annual conventions comprise representative members of local congregations, in numbers ranging between thirty thousand and forty thousand. In 2005, these conventions had for twenty-seven consecutive years selected a conservative president, often in hotly-contested battles. But the margin of victory for the conservatives has increased fairly steadily over this time period, not necessarily because there is an increasing shift to the right among Southern Baptist clergy and laity, but because once the balance was tipped in the conservatives' favor nearly three decades ago, the more liberal Southern Baptists (moderates) began to withdraw from the confrontation and began boycotting the annual conventions. With respect to the 1992 convention in Indianapolis, Victoria Rebeck observed: "Moderates stayed away from the convention in droves."[19]

Further, a substantial number of moderate Southern Baptists have considerd withdrawing from the Southern Baptist Convention to form their own denomination. As of 1994, there were more than 1,200 congregations in this group calling itself the Cooperative Baptist Fellowship, with an expectation of 2,000–3,000 churches, in five to ten years as an independent denomination.[20]

In 1999, the conservative president of the Southern Baptist Convention, the Reverend Paige Patterson, agreed that at some point a split within the Southern Baptist Convention will come when congregations affiliated with the Cooperative Baptist Fellowship and others leave.[21] He predicted a maximum of 3,500 of the denomination's 40,000 congregations could break away.[22] The number will depend in part on the outcome of a bold move by the Baptist General Convention of Texas (the largest Southern Baptist state convention), which voted in 1998 to amend its constitution and give itself more autonomy. This was in reaction to the resolution of the delegates to the 1998 national convention of the Southern Baptists in Salt Lake City, which affirmed not only the heterosexual marriage of a man and a woman as the sole form of marriage established by God, but also that wives should "submit . . . graciously" to the leadership of their husbands.[23] The Texas state convention adopted a contrary resolution, which stated that men and women have "biblical equality" in the family.[24] Some months later, the Southern Baptists of Virginia also rejected the 1998 Southern Baptist Convention statement on wifely submission.[25]

Adding credence to the possibility of a significant split in the Southern Baptist Convention, was the announcement in late March 2000, that almost immediately after the 1998 Southern Baptist Convention, four Texas Southern Baptists took the first legal step toward establishing a breakaway denomination. They incorporated and registered the name "Baptist Convention of the Americas" with the Texas secretary of state.[26] But apparently that change was not necessary to meet their goals. The entire Baptist General Convention of Texas has moved to the left and is fairly rapidly distancing itself from the Southern Baptist Convention. Already at its convention in October 2000, they were able to withdraw funding of some $5 million intended for the Southern Baptist Convention. Four million dollars of that cut was funding they would otherwise have provided for support of six Southern Baptist seminaries. They did so in the belief that those schools exemplify "doctrinaire fundamentalism," restrict academic freedom on their campuses, allow undue intrusion by trustees into academic affairs, and have high faculty turnover.[27]

By state convention time, 2001, the Texas conservatives who continued solidly in the parent Southern Baptist Convention withdrew to hold their own separate convention at the same time the Southern Baptists of Texas, now with a large majority of moderates (5,730 local churches to 930 in the conservative camp), held its convention.[28]

The 2001 convention of the Southern Baptist Convention made it clear that it had held its course and seemed careful not to propose controversial issues. Rachel Zoll of the *Associated Press* observes: "The lack of contention at the two-day meeting partly reflected the increasing conservative control of America's largest Protestant denomination."[29]

In February 2002, the Southern Baptist Convention began to require that all 5,180 foreign missionaries affirm a revised doctrinal statement called "The 2000 Baptist Faith and Message Statement," that by its nature and intent would separate the moderates from the conservatives. Moderates feared this requirement would break the strongest bond that yet remained between moderates and conservatives, namely, support of foreign mission work.[30] In early June, at its 2002 annual meeting, the Southern Baptist Convention reaffirmed its conservative stance and gave it new meaning as they questioned the integrity of the *Today's New International Version* of the New Testament (the complete Bible translation including the Old Testament, released in 2005) and expressed "profound disappointment with the International Bible Society and Zondervan Publishing House for this inaccurate translation of God's inspired Scripture." Specifically, the Convention objected to the International Bible Society's translation "erasing gender-specific details . . . in the original language."[31] It also heard a former Convention president, Jerry Vines, state that "Islam was founded by Muhammad, a demon-possessed pedophile." This statement was defended by the newly elected president of the Southern Baptist Convention, Jack Graham, as "accurate."[32]

Example Two—The Lutheran Church–Missouri Synod

The Lutheran Church–Missouri Synod has continued to have particularly fractious doctrinal controversy and conflict since the early 1970s, when conservatives assumed control of the church body's presidency and leadership on many of its denominational boards and commissions, as well as geographic districts, particularly in the Midwest and openly criticized the faculty of its flagship seminary in St. Louis, Missouri. The church's 1973 convention in New Orleans (called by some the "Second Battle of New Orleans"), after much debate, approved as binding on all clergy and seminary professors a highly specific and conservative statement of faith, and approved the censure of dissident faculty members at the St. Louis seminary. They also set in motion procedures for purging theological deviants. The result was a walk-out by all but five faculty and a high number of students to form the Seminary in Exile (Seminex) and soon a quasi denomination of "exiled" clergy, students and congregations, called E.L.I.M. (Evangelical Lutherans in Mission) evolved. Over the course of the next ten years, a significant number of these clergy affiliated with other Lutheran denominations and many seminarians sought calls in those same denominations after completing their theological training in the Seminary in Exile, which continued its work in facilities provided by St. Louis University, a Roman Catholic institution. Several geographical districts within the church body also provided a safe haven for many of the dissident moderate clergy and laypeople.

   The conflict did not die and has occasionally resurfaced publicly, most notably through actions and rhetoric following the terrorist attack on America on 11 September 2001. The precipitating act was the participation of the Rev. David Benke, President of the Atlantic District with headquarters in New York City, in the city's ecumenical convocation in Yankee Stadium called *A Prayer for America*, on 23 September 2001. He had permission from the church body's President, Gerald Kieschnick, and saw his participation as an opportunity to witness to what Christians believe is central to its faith and hope. But since he joined with Muslim, Jewish, Sikh, Hindu, and other Christian clergy with whom the Lutheran Church–Missouri Synod is not in fellowship, that is, is not in agreement on a long list of theological points, several of his fellow clergy officially charged him with violation of the

Constitution of the Lutheran Church–Missouri Synod which outlaws "unionism and syncretism of every description." Those terms refer to participation with other faiths in events and activities by virtue of which some participants and observers might infer all participants are of one mind and in theological agreement.

Those charges were taken seriously by the vice presidents of the Lutheran Church–Missouri Synod. In what many argue was an irregular, or at least unwise procedure, they left the decision about suspension to one member of the group of vice presidents—the Rev. Wallace Schulz. On 25 June 2002, he did indeed suspend David Benke from the Lutheran ministry. But several months later, after an appeal by the Rev. Benke, the church body's Commission on Constitutional Matters issued a ruling, which essentially said the whole process of filing charges and issuing a suspension was out of order from the beginning. He had acted with the specific approval of the Synod president, who was acting on the basis of a document accepted by the immediate past convention of the church body. As such, the charges against Benke were unconstitutional. Eventually the Commission's finding above, that Pastor Benke's suspension was unconstitutional, was also affirmed by the church's Dispute Resolution Panel and Benke was reinstated and later also re-elected president of the church body's Atlantic District with no opposition.

Yet one more observation remains clear. The denomination is at least as deeply divided as at any time since the 1973 New Orleans convention, though the moderate president of the church body was re-elected in 2004 and the cadre of conservative vice presidents was replaced. Nonetheless, a high percentage of both clergy and lay people, as well as the members of various church boards and committees, remain committed to the conservative religious values that came to the fore in 1973. Intrareligious conflict in the Lutheran Church–Missouri Synod will continue to surface in the future.

Example Three—The Episcopal Church

There are similar divisions in the Episcopal Church. But the conservatives are less numerous than in the Southern Baptist Convention and the Lutheran Church–Missouri Synod, and they are coming to the fore much later than in those denominations. Nonetheless, at the end of August 1995, a group of Episcopal priests published a 40-page, nearly 250-count indictment of Presiding Bishop Edmond Browning and a core of some 76 supporting bishops. The booklet, titled "Catalog of Concerns: The Episcopal Church under Edmond Lee Browning," lists what are described as "inept, unbiblical, and sometimes immoral actions," of Browning.[33] The document expresses concerns about support in the church body for the ordination of homosexual priests and apostate, heretical beliefs and teachings of some of the Episcopal clergy. Michael McManus quotes Bishop James Stanton of Dallas, Texas: "The issue is order . . . The schismatics are departing from the historic faith. They are having it their way and getting away with it. Bishops of this church do not want to fight. They are trying to be nice and Episcopalian."[34]

The Episcopal intradenominational conflict has recently coalesced around the issue of homosexuality, particularly as it pertains to Episcopal clergy and whether an Episcopal priest can be allowed to maintain an open, committed homosexual relationship as an ordained priest or if a candidate for the priesthood who is in such a relationship can be ordained.

The controversy over the ordination of Episcopal priests, who are openly gay or fully supportive of gay rights, to ordination and gay marriage, was seriously exacerbated in 2004 when two actions took place. First, Gene Robinson, an openly gay Episcopal priest, was elected by the New Hampshire diocesan convention of the Episcopal Church. Second, an international commission established by the worldwide Communion of Anglican and Episcopal Churches issued its response (the Windsor Report) to the election of the New Hampshire bishop and the blessing of same-sex relationships by some Canadian and American dioceses. As this report emphasized the strong desire to preserve the worldwide Episcopal communion, it also seemed to demand that the Episcopal Church in the United States "apologize" for its actions.[35]

In the absence of an apology along the lines of "We were wrong," from the North American bishops and dioceses who sanctioned both the consecration of same sex marriages and the election of Bishop Gene Robinson, the leaders of the 77 million Anglicans worldwide meeting near Belfast, Northern Ireland on 24 February 2005, asked the North American churches to withdraw from the Anglican Consultative Council for three years. This is seen by some as a prelude to a permanent split in the worldwide Anglican/Episcopal federation, though there appears to have been no follow-up as of this writing in mid-2005.[36]

Sociological Observation

And so the theme of intradenominational conflict has become a familiar one—one that crosses many denominational lines and is not restricted to conservative churches. Yet it appears that in no denomination, in which such debate and conflict flourishes, do the conservatives recognize the sociological realities that any large group faces, particularly as it grows. Any such group will inevitably have greater deviance and will find itself tolerating more deviance. In fact, we would suggest that the appearance of diversity and controversy in such groups is not nearly so amazing as the fact that these were forestalled or at least kept hidden for so long. The point is that unanimity does not and cannot exist and that diversity will only increase, unless one faction accumulates sufficient power essentially to split the group formally into two groups or to force out the more extreme and vocal deviates.

Local Intracongregational Conflict

Then there is the intragroup conflict that is probably the best-kept secret of all, the conflict that occurs at the local level—within participating congregations where members find themselves on opposite sides of issues. Sometimes it is a liberal/conservative split on doctrinal questions. Sometimes it is a personality conflict between a minister and a congregation. Sometimes the dissension is about changes in forms and style of worship, or struggles over budget, or how to respond to membership losses. Sometimes the rift is over social issues, epitomized in the 1960s and 1970s by many clergy and laypeople, both Jewish and Christian, actively participating in the civil rights movement and the anti-Vietnam War movement. Such commitments and participation were challenged by other clergy and laypeople, who were convinced that such issues as civil rights and war were social and political issues and as such of little concern to religious groups. Such issues were not to intrude into religious institutions or absorb the time of clergy who had other things to do with their time—administer comfort and counsel to their flock while leaving social activism to secular authorities and professionals. Currently the debate is often over abortion rights of women or the acceptance of openly gay persons into church membership.

Actually, few readers will be unaware of at least one such incident in their community. In some instances, a pastor is transferred prematurely (suggesting that representatives of the congregation have got to the bishop or district president); in other instances, the controversy becomes more public, with padlocks on church doors, possessions removed to the sidewalk, suits and countersuits, even deputy sheriffs restraining some among the parties to the controversy; in still other instances, congregational representatives extend a vote of "no confidence" to the minister, who then puts his or her name on a list of preachers available for a call and an opportunity to start over somewhere else.

But often the disagreements are more substantial than conflicts of personalities or style. They may represent wide discrepancies between the theology of pastor and people or disagreements on how much time and money the local church should devote to social service programs, or conflict over "gifts of the Spirit" (charismatic gifts) and speaking in tongues. And of course the same conflicts as those occurring at the denominational level in the Southern Baptist, Lutheran Church–Missouri Synod, and Episcopal examples discussed earlier, find local embodiment among congregations in those and other denominations.

CHALLENGES TO SOCIETY FROM RELIGIOUS GROUPS

At this point, we wish to introduce yet another type of religious conflict. Although this is certainly not new, it may seem new with each generation. That is the conflict that results when religious institutions or their representatives challenge one or more sociopolitical aspects of the community or society of which they are a part. Here there has been much in recent memory. Here is where many would say religion has been and can be at its finest. Here we see religious groups initiating verbal if not physical conflict with the political or economic institutions of the surrounding society. Other religious groups may be supportive, opposing, or neutral. So it is possible that conflict with other religious groups might emerge also at this point, yet it is not necessary or inevitable.

Within recent memory in the United States, some religious groups, leaders, and members have been active in the civil rights movement, the anti-abortion right-to-life movement, and the peace movement. Not that the activism was always or even most of the time initiated by religious groups, but at an early point they became active and significant influences in the movements overall.

Other occasions, in which religion in the United States has been a challenge to the *status quo* and has participated in conflict with societal laws, structure, and institutions, would be the Prohibition movement in the first third of the twentieth century, and the "blue laws" that have pervaded American society since its founding and are not totally abolished everywhere today—laws that prohibited ball games and shopping on Sundays, restricted how close an establishment selling alcoholic beverages could be to a church or school, or legislated whether alcohol could be sold at all, or whether it was legal for physicians to prescribe birth control devices to patients, let alone that people could buy condoms and spermicides over the counter (the Comstock laws). All are distinctive and well-known examples of religion wanting to have and indeed having an impact on the society that encompassed it. But in these examples, the influence was in a restrictive, conservative direction, in contrast with the more liberating approach of civil rights activists who appealed to religious precepts to reinforce social forces that would provide equal opportunity and access for those who had long been discriminated against and restricted in opportunities to follow their talents and abilities. Among the efforts of religious groups to put restrictions on societal norms, laws, and behavior, are such areas as women's right to an abortion or the rights of people to same-sex marriages to medical insurance benefits and various other legal rights that accrue to heterosexual married couples. These topics will be introduced again in later chapters as we discuss fundamentalism the political action of right-wing Christians, and some of the programs and proposals of President George W. Bush.

CONCLUSION

While religion is a favorite rallying point and an organization that has a large number of potential recruits, and while it enables some to define their people as purveyors of truth but the other religion(s) as plotting to subvert that truth and perpetuate falsehood, thereby adding fervor to the defense of the cause, the heart of the matter in the examples we have examined is political. Although these groups in name and purpose are religious, they also exist as political groups. While no one wants to suggest that the Protestant-Catholic conflict in Northern Ireland, or the Sikh-Hindu-Muslim conflict in India, or the enduring conflicts in the former Yugoslavia, and in Israel are not really religious conflicts at all but are political conflicts purely and simply, by the same token the conflicts should certainly not be taken at face value. That is, they are not wholly religious conflicts that are concerned only with discovering divine truth and worshipping the true god in a correct manner. They all involve religio-political groups that transcend the purely theological character and content of those religions.

But to go further, we must observe and keep in mind that many people throughout the world believe, as we have seen in the last several pages, that there are elements endemic to religion in general, and to Christianity in particular, that should precipitate social involvement and reformistic activity and leadership from the ranks of both clergy and laypeople.

NOTES

1. Max Weber, *Economy and Society* (New York: Oxford University Press, 1947), originally published in 1922.
2. Karl Marx, "Contribution to the Critique of Hegel's Philosophy of Right," in *Marx and Engels on Religion*, ed. Reinhold Niebuhr (New York: Schocken Books, 1964), p. 42.
3. Kenneth S. Latourette, *A History of Christianity* (New York: Harper & Brothers, 1953), p. 456.
4. Brian Lavery and Alan Cowell, "I.R.A. Renounces Use of Violence; Vows to Disarm," *New York Times*, July 29, 2005, by internet access, July 29, 2005.
5. William McCord, "Success Takes Its Toll: The Punjab Paradox," *New Leader* 67, no. 10 (October 19, 1984): 14.
6. "Clergy Targeted in Timor Violence," *Christian Century* 116, no. 26 (October 6, 1999): 930.
7. "Police Arrest 12 in Attacks on Christians," *Muncie Star Press* (August 18, 2002), p. 3A; "Religious Violence Erupts in Nigeria," *Muncie Star Press* (July 10, 2001), p. 3A.
8. "India Riots' Death Toll Nears 700," *Mt. Pleasant Morning Sun* (December 10, 1992), p. 14.
9. Paul R. Brass, *The Production of Hindu-Muslin Violence in Contemporary India* (Seattle: University of Washington Press, 2003), p. 6.
10. *New York Times* (January 23, 1999), reported in *Religion Watch*: 14, no. 4 (February, 1999), p. 7.
11. *Religion Watch* 16, no. 2 (December, 2000): pp. 6–7.
12. Murray J. Leaf, *Song of Hope: The Green Revolution in a Punjab Village* (New Brunswick, NJ: Rutgers University Press, 1984), p. 181.

13. Ibid., pp. 184–85.

14. Mark Juergensmeyer, *Terror in the Mind of God* (Berkeley, CA: University of California Press, 2000), p. 89.

15. Ibid., p. 92.

16. Charles Y. Glock and Rodney Stark, *Christian Beliefs and Anti-Semitism* (New York: Harper & Row, 1966), p. 20.

17. Eric Hoffer, *The True Believer* (New York: Mentor Books, 1951), p. 93. Glock and Stark, ibid., pp. 9–10.

18. Glock and Stark, ibid., pp. 9–10.

19. Victoria A. Rebeck, "Southern Baptists Draw Line on Local Autonomy," *Christian Century* 109, no. 21 (July 1–8, 1992): 637.

20. *Christian Century* 111, no. 21 (July 13–20, 1994): 678.

21. "SBC Will Split, Predicts Patterson," *Christian Century* 116, no. 36 (December 22–29, 1999): 1247.

22. Ibid.

23. "Controversy and Conflict in the SBC," *Christian Century* 116, no. 1 (January 6–13, 1999): 19.

24. Ibid.

25. "Briefly Noted," *Christian Century* 116, no. 34 (December 8, 1999): 1194.

26. Associated Press, "Incorporation Papers Filed for Rival Baptist Denomination," *Muncie Star Press* (March 25, 2000), p. 2D.

27. "Texas Baptists End Most of Their Support for 6 Seminaries," *Chronicle of Higher Education* (November 17, 2000), p. A53; "Texas Baptists Break with Denomination," *Muncie Star Press* (October 31, 2000), p. 4A.

28. "Dueling Baptists Conduct Conventions," *Muncie Star Press* (November 3, 2001), p. 3D.

29. Rachel Zoll, "Baptists Avoid More Controversy," *Daily News*. Ball State University (June 14, 2001), p. 2.

30. Knight Ridder Newspapers, "Southern Baptist Missionaries Being Asked to Sign Faith Statement," *Muncie Star Press* (February 27, 2002), p. 5C.

31. Eric Reed, "Southern Baptists Blast TNIV," *Christianity Today* 46, no. 10 (September 9, 2002): 17.

32. "Baptist President: Comments Accurate," *Muncie Star Press* (June 13, 2002), p. 3A.

33. Michael McManus, "Episcopal Church Division Growing," *Muncie Star Press* (September 2, 1995), p. 8A.

34. Ibid.

35. *Christian Century* 121, no. 23, pp. 8–9.

36. An Associated Press article, *Muncie Star Press*, February 26, 2005, p. 2A.

Chapter 7

Religion and Politics

Separation of church and state?

Although politics is nearly as variously defined as religion, there is consensus about at least two characteristics. First of all, politics (like its corollary, government) consists fundamentally of norms—that is, ways of reaching decisions, procedures for carrying out certain tasks, and expectations about rights and privileges. Second, politics is mostly concerned with the societal norms that stipulate how and by whom coercive power shall be used in the pursuit of societal goals.[1] The employment of coercive power by government appears necessary, primarily because the available supply of rewards that people strive for, both individually and collectively, is limited. Such rewards include money (or other means of obtaining goods and services), prestige, honor, respect, power, love, affection, and the like. Although such rewards are not necessarily in scarce supply, their supply is finite. That is to say, it is relatively rare for any person to feel satiated so far as his or her share of such rewards is concerned. Most people want at least a few more dollars and a few more things than they presently possess. And universally, people could use a little more love, affection, and respect, even if they are not specifically seeking fame or power over others.

The resulting discrepancy between supply and demand inevitably places people into a competitive position with respect to garnering their desired share of available rewards. Politics and government are the social systems or institutions developed in a society, to regulate the process of reward seeking and to reduce the disruptive tendency inherent in the competition for rewards, which could result in a war of all against all. Thus, we understand the concept of politics to be the norms that designate the ultimate coercive power and the process by which the norms that regulate the exercise of power and authority are implemented. This accords well with Harold Lasswell's classic definition of politics as who gets what, when, and how—that is, the process of determining the distribution of society's rewards and of balancing power relationships and claims.[2]

It is important to note that religion has an influence on politics. Religion is neither silent nor impotent so far as affecting political life is concerned. Certainly it is not always effective in swaying opinion or in reaching its desired outcome. And certainly religion may speak with different voices, depending on the religious branch from which the instruction comes. Further, many in the society will be dismayed and distressed at the outcome religion sometimes achieves. This may be because the debate itself might be rancorous, confrontational, divisive, even deadly (e.g., abortion clinic personnel shot dead by a right-to-life Protestant fundamentalist) and it may be perceived to be harmful. The outcome engineered by religious forces could be perceived negatively because the outcome itself is defined as "bad" as, perhaps, when an "enlightened, experienced, progressive" U.S. Senator is defeated by a challenger whose credentials are no more than a sincere rooting in fundamentalism.

What are some of these areas of impact of religion on political life? We would mention such outcomes as approval of the Prohibition Amendment in 1919, patriotic support for World War I and World War II, the anticommunism crusade of the 1950s, the civil rights movement in the 1960s. While each is a complex case study in itself, about which many volumes have been written with many more yet to come, they are listed here to stimulate discussion and inquiry by the readers. Some were pursued by the right, some by the left, and certainly some by numerous religious organizations and people speaking with a fairly united voice. We mention them simply to note that religious groups, movements, and coalitions have influenced the political process and outcome in the broader society.

THE RELATIONSHIP OF RELIGION AND POLITICS

What, then, is the relationship of religion to politics? We should expect, considering the broad scope of our definition of politics, which implies a great diversity of processes, norms, and behavior, that there will be a variety of ways in which religion relates to the institution of politics.

This certainly has been the case. But we shall not go into all of the many types of relationships. We shall simply outline the range of possibilities and then discuss the most common pattern.

At one end of the continuum is the *pure theocracy. Theocracy* literally means, "rule by God." Thus religious leaders are seen as ruling all of society in God's name and ostensibly according to His wishes. Actually, the state as a distinct entity does not exist in a theocracy. The rule of Israel by God's prophets in the Old Testament period is an example of the pure theocracy. A prophet, such as Samuel, was seen as God's spokesman regarding, not only religious matters, but political and governmental matters as well. Interestingly enough, the people chafed under this arrangement—they pleaded embarrassment in the face of surrounding societies who were under the rule of kings and appealed for a similar "separation" of church and state.

Closely related is the *modified theocracy*. In this case, while the state is subordinate to the religious institution and its leaders, even in temporal affairs, the state nevertheless exists as a separate entity. The state is seen here as the enforcement agency of religion, an agency necessary because of the tendency of people to deviate from societal norms but to depend on religion for its authority. Most medieval European societies dominated by Roman Catholicism were of this type. Similarly, John Calvin's Geneva and the early Massachusetts Bay Colony are good examples. Further, the relationship of Buddhism to the government of Sri Lanka (Ceylon) from the third century B.C.E. until the nineteenth century C.E. was that of a modified theocracy. Only a Buddhist could become king, and his chief function was to protect and promote the faith. On the other hand, the Buddhist monks not only instructed and advised the royal court and conducted the king's coronation in the temple, but they held enormous political power in their influence and control over the masses. They could incite or prevent rebellion. No king could rule without their support.

It is worth noting that the inclusion of the state within the religious system, or at a minimum some kind of control over the state by religion, is not simply a quaint, antiquarian phenomenon or legacy from pre-industrial times. It is an almost universal feature of the utopian and millenarian groups and movements of the nineteenth and twentieth centuries—groups that endeavored to establish models of the perfect Kingdom of God—in addition to such a group as Jim Jones's Peoples Temple and the Jonestown experiment in Guyana.

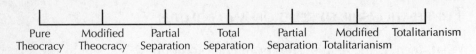

Pure	Modified	Partial	Total	Partial	Modified	Totalitarianism
Theocracy	Theocracy	Separation	Separation	Separation	Totalitarianism	

FIGURE 7.1 A Continuum of the Possible Relationships of Church and State

At the other extreme is a *totalitarian* system, in which religion is either controlled by the state as a tool or enforcement arm of the state, or is outlawed altogether. A pure form of a totalitarian system is more theoretical than real, although the goal of the Bolshevik revolution in the Soviet Union in 1917 was such. What religion they could not eradicate entirely, they intended to control and manipulate.

Midway between the extremes of theocracy on the one hand and totalitarianism on the other, is the concept of *total separation*. In this arrangement, the arenas in which religion and politics operate are entirely distinct with no overlap. There one must assume that religion serves the soul and the state serves the body—or that religion is entirely an individualized, subjective, internalized phenomenon, while politics and the state serve the group, deal with externals relative to survival, and are entirely secular. Such total separation has never been achieved, and thus remains purely a theoretical possibility. While separation of church and state is almost a slogan in the United States and is a clearly stated goal in the U.S. Constitution, the United States has never come very close to achieving total separation and it is safe to say it never will.

Certainly *partial separation* is the most sociologically sound option. Inasmuch as both religion and politics are social institutions and consist of subgroups, norms, and people, they interact with one another, they sometimes overlap in their functions, they often involve the same people and they seek commitment and involvement from the same people. It is, of course, partial separation that describes the system with which we are most familiar in North America and Europe. But partial separation is itself a variable and tends to fluctuate toward one extreme or the other, as implied by the range outlined in Figure 7.1. This figure presents, in graphic form, the options we have been discussing. That is, the middle, neutral position would be "total separation." The relationship between church and state could then go in either direction, toward total religious control and domination at one end (pure theocracy), or total state control at the other extreme (totalitarianism), with various intermediate points on the way.

THE INFLUENCE OF RELIGION ON POLITICS

We would expect, then, that the relationship of religion and politics would take a wide range and variety of forms. What that relationship will be and how much influence there will be, will depend on many factors. We will mention two in the forefront, put forward by Robert Fowler.[3] First, the theology of the group will define its stand on political involvement. Basically, the issue is how a group's theology defines participation in the political process—is it a legitimate arena in which the believers ought to work? And beyond pure theology, yet closely allied with it, is the tradition of the group with regard to participation in social action endeavors. Although we will discuss the issue of the involvement of churches in social action in Chapter 12, we can simply observe here that religious groups vary greatly in their degree of support for members (particularly the clergy) to be directly involved in social action activities. Certainly their stance as a group will affect the behavior of individuals within the institution.

The second factor that affects the degree of a religious group's political involvement, according to Fowler, is the level of rank-and-file support for the involvement of leaders in social action activities, along with the degree of unity among the group. This becomes crucial because a low level of unity and support from lay members and clergy will negate even the clearest of theologies supporting social action. The history of the religious controversy over support for and involvement in the civil rights movement, begun in the 1960s, is a graphic case in point. (More discussion of this in Chapter 15.)

We now continue our discussion of religion and politics, by looking at specific ways in which religion affects, or tries to affect, politics. That is, we shall be asking to what extent and in what ways religion can be seen to be an influence on political action and outcomes.

Religion and Voting Behavior

A widely-recognized point of religious influence over politics is that of people's voting preference and behavior. The supporters of almost every candidate for public office at all levels, can be heard during the campaign talking about trying to get the "Catholic vote," the "Jewish vote," the "Baptist vote" or, more recently, the "Evangelical vote." Such interest gives very explicit recognition to the correlation that exists between religious affiliation and commitment on the one hand and voting behavior on the other. That there should be a correlation is exactly what would be expected, of course, if religious affiliation and commitment mean anything at all. What one believes with respect to that which is good, true, and desirable, as well as what God intends for people and society, could be expected to influence the choices one makes in the political arena. That is, religion should affect people's voting patterns.

As we prepare to present evidence in this area, we must mention one problem that we will have in interpreting the data. Although we will see significant differences by religious affiliation and commitment, the differences cannot be traced totally and simply to religion. For example, we will later see a fairly strong relationship between religion and social class. That is, certain religious groups tend to have disproportionate numbers of certain classes as members. If, in a particular instance, the members of a denomination tend to be predominantly working class and also vote overwhelmingly for Democratic candidates, we have two correlations with political activity at work—both religious affiliation and social class. We want to be alert, from the beginning, to such a problem of interpretation. But first some data.

Basic Patterns in the United States   If we consider party preference and voting behavior we find, as most Americans are aware, that, historically, Protestants have been more likely to be Republicans and Catholics more likely to be Democrats, with Jews even more likely than Catholics to be Democrats. Data from a variety of opinion polls reaffirm these relationships. Combined National Opinion Research Center (NORC) data accumulated from 1972–2002 show in Table 7.1 the differences in political preference by religious affiliation that have become well-known to most citizens. The historic pattern has been basically reaffirmed here though not so dramatically as in days gone by. The upward mobility of many Catholics (see Chapter 10) and the growth of the number of political Independents in all religious groups, have brought the proportions who identify with either the Republican or Democratic parties closer together. But note in particular that Jews continue to distinguish themselves from both Protestants and Catholics in their affiliation with the Democratic Party.

In Great Britain, one sees such differences as well. For example, in 1974, polling by the Gallup organization found a moderately high correspondence between membership in the Church of England and support for the Conservative political party: 67 percent of Conservatives were members of the Church of England, whereas only 58 percent of Labourites belonged to the Church of England. There was a similar pattern, but reversed, for Catholics: 15 percent of Labourites are Catholics, whereas only 9 percent of Conservatives are Catholics.[4]

TABLE 7.1   Political Party Affiliation by Religious Membership

	Protestant	Catholic	Jew	Other Religions	None
Republican	39.0%	30.2%	18.1%	26.2%	22.9%
Democratic	48.0	54.6	70.5	50.6	49.2
Independent	11.9	14.0	9.2	19.1	24.8
Other party	1.1	1.2	2.2	4.0	3.0

Source: 1972–2002 General Social Survey Cumulative Datafile, National Opinion Research Center, University of Chicago, through internet access 22 March 2005.

Fluctuation Over Time   While we can definitely say that religious affiliation does correlate with political preference and voting behavior, in the sense that Protestants are more likely to favor the Republican Party, Catholics and Jews the Democratic Party, such correlations fluctuate over time. Sometimes other factors assume greater influence over voters' behavior than does religion. For example, we go back to the mid-nineteenth century. From the 1860s to 1893, the religious factor, reinforced by the ethnic factor, had a very powerful effect on voting. For the most part, what mattered was not geographic region, such as north versus south, social class, or urban versus rural residence, but whether one was Protestant or Catholic. Protestants tended strongly to vote Republican; Catholics tended just as strongly to vote Democratic.

But then a strictly economic factor intruded and rendered the religious factor relatively ineffectual. The economic factor was the deep economic depression of 1893. While the Democrats were clearly in the ascendancy until the depression of 1893 began, elections in 1893 and 1894 voted them out and brought the Republicans in. Religion had very little to do with it.[5] It was economic conditions and the inevitability of placing blame for economic collapse on the political party in power at the time.

While the dominance of economic influence over religious influence, at a particular point in time, is a striking finding in itself, it is nearly as important to note that even when religion seemed to be such a powerful predictor of political party affiliation and voting behavior, it was probably at no time as purely religious as it might have appeared to be. That is because religion was almost always intimately bound to ethnicity and national origin. Remember that the last half of the nineteenth century was the period of greatest migration from Europe to the United States. Those immigrants remembered their religion as well as their homeland. The result was that they had two important reasons to stick together—ties that were both ethnic and religious. Then, too, they tended to have the same kinds and levels of jobs, and they lived in the same neighborhoods. The religious factor, then, was really more than religion—at least an ethnic-religious factor. Regardless, the power of economic considerations superseded that of religion when something like an economic depression occurred.

However, by the turn of the century the religious factor regained some influence. For example, we can look back and see pietistic Protestantism sway the mood of the nation toward the approval of the Prohibition Amendment to the Constitution in 1919 in the face of strong Catholic opposition. There were simply more Protestants than Catholics in the nation. But the influence of religion continued strongly in the aftermath of the Great Depression, beginning with the stock market crash of 1929, when Protestant leadership got trounced at the polls by Franklin D. Roosevelt and the new Democrats. Catholics voted overwhelmingly for Roosevelt in all four of his elections (as high as 76 percent in 1936).[6]

We have noted earlier that, since the mid-nineteenth century, when substantial immigration of Catholics into the United States began, they have tended to lean, often substantially, in the direction the Democratic Party has taken. While this is explainable in part by their coming into working class jobs and adopting the perspective of the labor movement, now that Catholics are integrated all along the social class and status range, passing in the aggregate a number of Protestant groups in the process, the direction in the aggregate away from the Republican Party and toward the Democratic Party remains.

Looking at differences in party identification between Catholics and Protestants, the spread between Catholics and Protestants was 13 percentage points in 1952 (43 percent of white Protestants, 56 percent of Catholics identified with the Democratic Party). As we look again at Table 7.1, we note that the spread has dropped to 9 percentage points in 2002

The conclusion reached by Kenski and Lockwood, based on these and other data, is that there has been some erosion of support for the Democratic Party by Catholics since the 1960s.[7] Nonetheless, Catholics remain more likely than Protestants to vote Democratic.

While this has less to do with class politics, inasmuch as Catholics have converged with white Protestants in terms of education, occupational status, and income, it probably has more to do with theological and philosophical outlooks—the complexities of which we cannot go into here. Suffice it to say that this affinity of Catholics with the Democratic Party makes sense when we realize that more Catholics than Protestants subscribe to liberal political and social views, despite the very conservative position of the Catholic Church on many core Christian doctrines.

Kenski and Lockwood note the CBS/New York Times exit poll data of 1986, which identified 17 percent of Catholic voters describing themselves as liberal compared with only 12 percent of white Protestants, and 41 percent of white Protestants viewing themselves as conservative compared with only 32 percent of Catholics.[8]

It is equally important to note that, while more Catholics than white Protestants identified themselves as liberal, they too, along with white Protestants, were less likely than others (black Protestants, Jews, and those with no religious affiliation) to describe themselves as liberal.[9]

Voting for a Catholic for President   The religious issue emerged as extremely significant in the two presidential elections involving a Catholic candidate. The first was Al Smith in 1928, the second John F. Kennedy, in 1960. Protestant bias against Catholics had long been a part of American politics. While it peaked in the mid- to late 1800s, the pattern of deep suspicion of Catholics by Protestants remained a prominent fact of religious and political life well into the next century, even beyond its midpoint (more discussion of this topic in Chapter 12). It was certainly very strong in 1928, when the Democratic candidate Al Smith was resoundingly defeated by Herbert Hoover. The fear harbored by many Protestants was that a Catholic President would have primary allegiance to the Pope and would act as an agent of the Vatican against the interests of Americans.

In 1960, the attacks against John Kennedy, on the basis of his religious affiliation, were initially just as virulent as those against Al Smith thirty-two years earlier. All the old fictions about Catholics were trotted out and distributed to millions. Many Protestant leaders openly opposed Kennedy. Even some Catholic leaders questioned his loyalty as a good Catholic when his public statements distinguishing his politics from his religion sounded too "secular." However, very early in the campaign, Protestant leaders in most denominations publicly rejected the old anti-Catholic bias and public opinion began to change. When all was said and done, the long-standing bias of Protestants against a Catholic presidential candidate was shattered fairly early in the campaign, never to be raised seriously again. Not only did enough Protestants break ranks and vote for Kennedy, but his nearly three years in office demonstrated quite clearly that Protestants had little to fear after all regarding Vatican control over the White House.

Wide Range Within Protestantism   While in the foregoing discussion we have concentrated on the broad religious categories of Catholic, Jew, and Protestant (distinguishing black from white), we do need to mention, as we shall discuss at greater length in a later chapter, that there is a great deal of further variation within each category. In Table 7.2 we not only see differences among Catholics, Jews, and Protestants, but also sizeable differences within Protestantism. In fact, to group all Protestants together is to mask very important differences within that broad category.

Note that the data in Table 7.2 are arranged so identification with the Democratic Party steadily decreases as one moves from the 82.3 percent of African-American Methodists and Baptists to the 37.4 percent of Episcopalians and Presbyterians who identify with the party. Conversely, with the exceptions of those affiliated with other religions or with no religion, identification with the Republican Party proceeds in the opposite direction.

Of course, there is more indicated in Table 7.2 than religious affiliation as a factor in political party identification. Clearly race is a factor. African-American Methodists and Baptists are much more likely than white Methodists and Baptists to identify with the Democratic Party and vice versa for affiliation with the Republican Party. Region also is a factor. The African-American Methodists and Baptists, as well as the Southern Baptists, who constitute the majority of white Baptists in Table 7.2, are concentrated in the South, where the Democratic Party traditionally was dominant, though recent elections have demonstrated a dramatically clear trend in the opposite direction, as white Evangelicals in the South have shifted towards the Republican Party.

TABLE 7.2 Political Party Preference among Major Religious Groups (cumulative data from the General Social Survey, 1972–1996)

Political Party Preference	Black Methodists & Baptists	Jews	White Baptists	Catholics	Other Religions	No Religion	White Methodists	Lutherans	Episcopalians	Presbyterians
Democratic Party	82.3%	73.4%	60.2%	50.6%	51.4%	50.6%	44.3%	42.1%	37.4%	37.4%
Independent	6.1	8.3	10.3	19.1	18.0	22.5	9.2	11.0	8.9	8.6
Republican Party	11.3	15.7	28.6	26.2	20.2	24.2	45.5	46.9	52.4	53.2
Other Party	0.3	2.6	0.9	4.1	3.9	2.7	1.0	1.0	1.3	0.8

Note: Democratic and Republican party preferences include those who identify strongly, moderately, and weakly with the party. Data have been grouped by the author. Note that there are small differences in data between Tables 7.1 and 7.2: This is because the data in Table 7.1 are GSS cumulative data from 1972 through 2002, but the data in Table 7.2 are cumulative from 1972–1996.

Source: 1972–1996. General Social Survey Cumulative Data File, National Opinion Research Center, University of Chicago, through Internet access, April, 2000.

Conclusion   In summary, while religious commitments impact political attitudes, beliefs, and membership, they are not foolproof predictors of individual voting behavior. While one will be correct more often than not in predicting that a certain Presbyterian or Episcopalian will vote Republican and hold convictions consistent with much of the Republican platform, there is almost a one-in-three chance that the Presbyterian or Episcopalian will vote Democratic. One's chances to be accurate are, of course, much greater if one predicts that an African-American Baptist will vote Democratic (82.3 percent) or that an American Jew will vote Democratic (73.4 percent). Yet there is a one-in-ten chance that the African-American Baptist will vote Republican and a one-in-six chance that the American Jew will vote Republican. Nonetheless, religious affiliation is a factor to take into account in predicting or explaining political behavior, in the aggregate, though, not at the individual level without knowing more about the person than simply religious affiliation.

Legislation of Morality

Another significant area, in which religion influences the political structure, is in the "legislation of morality." American state and local governments have been riddled with so-called blue laws, many of which are still on the books—and most of which reflect strong religious influence. Laws restricting Sunday business activity, laws specifying how close to schools and churches bars and taverns may operate, laws restricting the sale of intoxicating beverages, laws regarding the sale and distribution of birth-control devices—all these laws evidence strong influences by religious groups. Some are carryovers from Puritan colonization; some are related to concentrations of Catholic immigrants; some are traceable to conservative Protestantism, which has been influential throughout our history.

To be more specific, in the area of the legislation of morality, we shall look at several historical relationships between religion and the political process and structure in the United States.

Prohibition and Birth Control   The struggle over "demon rum," that eventually resulted in ratification of the Eighteenth Amendment (1919), which prohibited the sale of most intoxicating beverages in the United States, is a clear example of the influence of religious groups in the political arena. The Prohibition amendment was largely the work of a well-organized church lobby, the Anti-Saloon League. The league was organized in the Calvary Baptist Church in Washington, DC, in 1895, and although other temperance societies that lacked a clear religious connection cooperated with it, churches were the primary source of its membership, support, and leadership. Leo Pfeffer reports that between 1911 and 1925, an annual average of thirty thousand local churches, predominantly Baptist,

Methodist, Presbyterian, and Congregational, were affiliated with the league.[10]

Pfeffer notes that the Anti-Saloon League did not deny that it was a political organization. When confronted with that charge, a league representative replied, "The Church is a machine and the League is a machine within a machine."[11] Pfeffer goes on to say:

> Its effectiveness as a machine, as of any political machine, is measured by the fruits thereof; and the fruit of the League was the adoption of the Eighteenth Amendment within six years after the League formally launched its campaign for national prohibition. Though the League was less successful in retaining the victory it had won, its influence was respected and feared by many.[12]

The adoption of prohibition is a prime example of Protestant influences on the political system, while Catholics have an analogous influence with reference to birth-control legislation. Since Catholic doctrine maintains that any "artificial" interference with conception is inherently evil and sinful, the Catholic Church has worked long and hard to resist attempts to repeal or modify existing laws that prohibit the sale of birth-control devices or dissemination of information regarding their use. Earlier in American history, Catholics were not alone in this stance—the "Comstock law," actually a set of laws passed by Congress in 1873, prohibiting mailing, transporting, or importing "obscene, lewd, or lascivious" materials, had support that also included Protestants and some groups that were at least ostensibly secular. Birth-control information and devices were interpreted as being included among the prohibitions detailed by these laws. Soon thereafter, twenty-two states passed "little Comstock laws" that imposed strictures ranging from New York's restriction on physicians' freedom to prescribe lawful contraceptives (and then only "for the cure or prevention of disease"), to the Massachusetts ban of the publication of information and the distribution of material dealing with contraception, to Connecticut's absolute ban on birth control, extending even to the private use of contraceptive devices.[13]

Abortion Rights   But we do not need to look only to examples from history. There is a perfect example of an attempt to "legislate morality" occurring as we begin a new millennium. That is the controversy and debate over abortion rights and the attempts by a variety of religious groups to influence legislatures and the Congress to repeal the liberalization of abortion restrictions that followed testing of abortion rights in federal courts in the 1970s. What we might call the modern period of the abortion debate began with the landmark U.S. Supreme Court decision titled *Jane Roe v. Henry Wade* that, in 1973, prohibited governmental interference with a woman's right to terminate a pregnancy through abortion, except under narrowly defined, exceptional circumstances. This momentous U.S. Supreme Court decision overturned a Texas law that made it a crime to have an abortion. And, of course, the decision overturned similar laws in other states. The controversy has escalated since 1973 to the point of murders of four physicians and three clinic workers, plus several other physicians and clinic workers wounded between 1993 and 1998. And there is hardly a more emotionally-charged issue than this one that puts so many people on one side or the other, with almost no neutral meeting ground in between. In other words, many people, from a wide variety of religious persuasions, disagree with the U.S. Supreme Court's judgment in *Roe v. Wade* and work strenuously to get it overturned.

Many felt this happened in 1989 in the *William Webster v. Reproductive Health Service* case, in which the U.S. Supreme Court, by a narrow margin of five to four, let stand a Missouri law that required medical tests to determine if the fetus was viable, that is, capable of survival outside the womb. While some claim the Webster decision has invalidating internal inconsistencies, at a minimum it refueled the debate.[14] State legislatures have been encouraged to reduce the applicability and impact of *Roe v. Wade* by supplemental legislation. The Webster decision conveyed the message that the U.S. Constitution allows states to place some restrictions on abortion practices.

Abortion in U.S. History   It is of interest that in early American history, based on British common law, there were no prohibitions against abortion until "quickening," when a woman first perceived movement by the fetus itself. In practice, abortion was thus unsanctioned until the fourth or fifth month of pregnancy.[15] It was not until 1821 that any state (Connecticut) enacted a law against abortion. Even then, such state laws prohibited "post-quickening" abortions, not abortions during the first four or five months. And even then, state laws prohibiting abortion beginning in 1821 were not so much a condemnation of abortion as they were expressions of concern with women's health.[16] Abortions were extremely dangerous. The 1821 Connecticut abortion law prohibited only the use of poisons to induce abortions and addressed only post-quickening abortions. Death from abortion procedures used by medical personnel was common. Lawrence H. Tribe reports a 30 percent death rate from infections after abortion surgery in mid-nineteenth century New York.[17]

Nonetheless abortions, particularly those up to the fourth or fifth month, continued. The birth rate for white women declined by 50 percent between 1800 and 1900; with birth-control methods to prevent conception still very primitive, abortion was obviously employed with some frequency.

The involvement of religion in the abortion debate, during the nineteenth and the first half of the twentieth centuries, while significant, does not appear to have been as great or as strident as more recently. Much of the opposition to abortion by Protestants was either primarily expressing concern about the immoral behavior that produced an unmarried woman's pregnancy, which in turn created an interest in abortion as a solution, or concern with the high death rate among women receiving abortions. Among Roman Catholics, it was not so much that abortion was wrong because it ended human life (that of the fetus) and could even be considered murder as one would hear today, but more that abortion was an artificial method of birth control and interfered with the true purpose of one's sexuality and sexual activity, namely, procreation. Thus, contraception of any kind, including abortion and even masturbation, was forbidden by the Catholic Church.

With additional encouragement from the medical profession, that became increasingly opposed to abortion, first on medical grounds (risk to women's health) but also on moral grounds, from the mid-nineteenth century to the turn of the century, more than forty antiabortion laws were passed in the states.[18] The distinction between quick and non-quick fetuses dropped out of much of this legislation and a definition of abortion at any stage as illegal and probably immoral became a widely accepted norm. Yet *therapeutic* abortions were acceptable and continued to be performed—with therapeutic defined as "to preserve the life and health of the woman." Although poverty and psychological concerns were deemed by some to be appropriate therapeutic concerns, and although many abortions were performed for those able to afford a skilled practitioner, the cultural consensus was negative toward abortion.

Increased Leniency on Abortion and Roe v Wade Decision   But gradually sentiments began to change in the direction of greater acceptance of abortion—traceable to no single factor but with several relevant developments having taken place. These include the advances in medicine that resulted in a reduction of the death rate for legal abortions, from one hundred per one hundred thousand legal abortions to three out of one hundred thousand between 1955 and 1972, and a growing willingness by doctors to include psychological health as a factor in defining the appropriateness of an abortion.[19] There was also social concern about the discrimination against the poor in the availability of legal and safe abortions. There was concern over population growth and a feeling of obligation to lead the way and put our own house in order, by putting a curb on our own population growth. And, of course, the developing women's movement and the assertion of women's rights to make decisions affecting their own bodies gained just about everyone's attention. And here you have the background for the *Roe v. Wade* decision in 1973.

We have reminded readers more than once of the spirited debate going on between the two sides in the abortion issue: the antiabortion forces who refer to themselves as "Pro-Life," versus the supporters of the right of the woman to make the individual, personal choice of whether to abort a fetus carried within her body, often called the "Pro-Choice" position. These appear to be the two ends on a continuum of attitudes toward the permissibility of an individual's choosing to abort a fetus. It is important to know that while supporters for these two extreme positions grab the headlines, relatively few Americans actually hold either of these extreme views.

Citizen Opinion on Abortion   Research has shown that relatively few Americans are either totally in favor of abortion in any and all circumstances or totally against abortion in all circumstances. The National Opinion Research Center has excellent data going back to 1972, that posed six possible reasons for a pregnant woman to seek an abortion. Respondents to the survey can select from none to all of the six reasons and be defined as totally *pro-life* by rejecting all six, *situationalist,* defined as allowing abortion in certain circumstances or situations, that is, accepting from one to five of the six reasons, or totally *pro-choice,* that is, accepting all reasons as valid for electing to end a pregnancy.[20]

The six conditions under which an abortion might be justified were divided into two groups for analysis purposes—*elective* abortion circumstances and *traumatic* abortion circumstances. The elective abortion circumstances are: (a) the woman is married and does not want more children, (b) she is not married and does not want to marry the man, and (c) the family has a very low income and cannot afford more children. The traumatic circumstances are: (a) there is a strong chance of serious defect in the baby, (b) the woman's own health is seriously endangered by the pregnancy, and (c) she became pregnant as a result of rape.

It is interesting and certainly worth knowing that a majority of Americans cannot place themselves at either extreme, but are "situationalists"—in other words, abortion is neither always wrong nor always a pure free individual choice but *depends on the situation.* In fact, a majority of Americans (53 percent) are situationalists; a substantial 39 percent are totally pro-choice (approve abortion in all six instances); only 8 percent are totally antiabortion (pro-life).

Another important statistic is that 76 percent of those surveyed supported abortion under all three of the "trauma" circumstances.[21]

What the data suggest is, that while the extremists at both ends of the range of opinion and conviction about the appropriateness and morality of abortion get the most attention and publicity, the majority of citizens hold more moderate opinions, that center around the conviction that while abortion is not an easy, casual solution to a "problem," it is appropriate in certain circumstances.

A very recent poll by ABC News and *The Washington Post* (2004) reports data quite consistent with the Cook, Jelen, Wilcox data from 1992 discussed earlier, though the gap, between those who approve abortion in at least some cases and those who oppose in most or all cases, might have narrowed somewhat. The ABC poll did not provide the detailed options that were in the

TABLE 7.3   U.S. Citizen Views of the Legality of Abortion (2004)

Views Percent
Legal in all cases 23.9%
Legal in most cases 32.7
Illegal in most cases 23.4
Illegal in all cases 17.8
Don't Know or No Opinion 2.2

Source: ABC News/*Washington Post* Poll ("Religion and Politics, 2004"), Gary E. Langer, Director of Polling, accessed online from The American Religion Data Archive (ARDA), Pennsylvania State University (www.TheARDA.com), March 14, 2005.

Cook, Jelen, Wilcox study. Nonetheless, it is clear that the majority of U.S. adults approve of abortion in most or all cases—56.6 percent, and 41.2 percent disapprove in most or all cases. The "situationalists" in the Cook, Jelen, Wilcox (53 percent) are probably mostly accounted for in the two middle groups of respondents in the ABC study and account for 56.1 percent of respondents in this recent poll. It is actually fairly striking that the two percentages—53 percent and 56 percent are so close after twelve more years of heated debate and controversy.

However, the criteria for the situationalists are not identical to the broad definition of "in most cases" in the two middle categories in the ABC poll. Also, it is important to note that the total percentage of those totally against abortion (pro-life) is greater in the more recent poll—17.8 percent versus 9 percent in the 1992 study. But again, respondents in the earlier study had more options, three of which were "trauma" situations that were described for respondents. The more recent respondents were not reminded of the various reasons a woman might choose an abortion. So the "increase" from 8 percent "pure" pro-life respondents in 1991 to 17.8 percent in 2004 should not be seen as an actual increase of that magnitude, though it certainly could have increased somewhat.

Similarly, with the fully pro-choice respondents—a decline of 15 percentage points from 39 percent fully pro-choice in 1992 to 23.9 percent in 2004. Nonetheless, the clear conclusion from the 2004 data is that a majority of respondents are still some kind of situationalists (56.1 percent). This is, statistically speaking, the same as the 53 percent situationalists in 1991, though, as we have already discussed, the percentages are not perfectly comparable.

And so, the debate will continue to be waged in the courts and many public places, though "pro-choice" of some form continues to be the majority opinion.

School Prayer and Religion in Public Schools   School prayer is another contemporary issue that from one perspective can be viewed as a legislation-of-morality issue, but can also be seen simply as an example of the ongoing saga of citizens and the Supreme Court trying to balance the First Amendment's nonestablishment clause with the provision of opportunities for the free exercise of religion. Many thought the issue had been settled back in the 1960s, when two landmark decisions were handed down by the U.S. Supreme Court. The first, in 1962, was the *Engle v. Vitale* case that prohibited the State of New York from requiring a prayer written by the State to be recited by students and teachers at the beginning of each school day. The second, in 1963, was the *Abington School District v. Schempp* case that struck down the requirement for Bible reading and prayer to begin each school day in Pennsylvania public schools. Proposals to provide for prayer in public schools, by way of a constitutional amendment, have circulated ever since. In addition, since 1992 the issue of prayer, as part of graduation and baccalaureate exercises, has been front-page news as several Supreme Court cases have addressed the issue.

In a major speech intended as a landmark directive, President Clinton hoped to settle the issue by providing guidelines for prayer and other religious expressions in an address at James Madison High School in Vienna, Virginia, on July 12, 1995. The *Religion News Service* summarized the main points of President Clinton's directives as follows:

- Students have the right to pray individually and in groups during the school day. However, students do not have "the right to have a captive audience listen, or to compel other students to participate."
- Students may read the Bible or other scriptures, say grace before meals, and pray before exams "to the same extent they may engage in comparable nondisruptive activities."
- Students may discuss religious topics with their peers, but school officials should intercede if student speech is deemed to constitute harassment.
- School officials cannot authorize organized prayer at graduation ceremonies or organize religious baccalaureate ceremonies.
- Teachers and school administrators cannot solicit, encourage, or discourage religious activity while in their roles as government employees.
- Public schools can teach about religion, but they cannot provide religious instruction. For instance, courses dealing with the history of religion, comparative religion, and the Bible as literature are permitted.
- Students may express their religious beliefs in homework, artwork, etc., when such expression relates to a school assignment.
- Students have the right to distribute religious literature when other literature unrelated to school activities is permitted for distribution.
- Students may wear religious messages on their clothing if they are allowed to wear comparable nonreligious messages.
- Student religious groups have the same access to school facilities as comparable student groups.[22]

The President drew heavily from an eighteen-point statement signed by thirty-five organizations, representing a wide range on the political spectrum.

The statement, "Religion in the Public School: A Joint Statement of Current Law" has been defined by some as "a tool of predominantly liberal political organizations to sabotage the movement for a school-prayer amendment."[23] They, with others, continue to support the movement to produce a religion-equality amendment to the constitution. One such amendment proposed by Congressman Gerald Solomon reads: "Nothing in this constitution shall prohibit the inclusion of voluntary prayer in any public school program or activity. No person shall be coerced by the United States or by any State to participate in such prayer. Neither the United States nor any State shall prescribe the content of any such prayer."[24]

Nonetheless, most people, on both sides of the school prayer issue, would accept President Clinton's summary of permissible behavior with respect to religion in public schools. Yet some will continue to worry about later attacks and will continue to push for a "prayer amendment."

We have been making the point that controversy and debate over what are appropriate applications of the First Amendment's principles of religious freedom and the separation of church and state have, if anything, increased over the years, despite the willingness of the Supreme Court to hand down opinions. In part, this is because changes always occur in the makeup of the Court itself, the societal and political climate or context, and the way issues are defined. In this connection, we will mention a decision handed down by the U.S. Supreme Court in June 1995, that very few scholars would have predicted. This decision will fuel for a very long time the debate over the extent of support for religion and its activities that the state and its institutions are allowed to provide. The decision, called the Rosenberger Ruling (*Rosenberger v. Rector and Visitors of the University of Virginia*), determined that the University of Virginia must provide funds derived from student fees collected from all students to any recognized student organization. Included would be religious organizations whose express purpose is to promote a particular religious perspective.

The case arose from the denial by the University of Virginia of a request for $5,862 by Ronald Rosenberger and a group of undergraduates who wanted to cover printing costs of their journal *Wide Awake: A Christian Perspective at the University of Virginia*. The purpose of the journal was "to challenge Christians to live, in word and deed, according to the faith they proclaim, and to encourage students to consider what a personal relationship with Jesus Christ means."[25]

The students based their appeal on the Freedom of Speech clause of the First Amendment. This clause prohibits government from interfering with people's expression of their personal ideas and beliefs. On the other side, the University of Virginia cited a long list of Supreme Court decisions that prohibit governmental action, which would provide tangible benefits to any particular religious group or perspective.

While this case pits against each other two basic principles that our Constitution supports—free speech and freedom of religion/freedom from establishment of religion—almost anyone with any acquaintance at all with Supreme Court decisions regarding state support for religious activities would have quickly determined that such support violated separation of church and state. That is based on the direction of the Court over the last three-quarters of a century.

Lawrence White notes that this ruling essentially tears down the primary precedent used by the Supreme Court for nearly twenty-five years— the *Lemon* v. *Kurtzman* case where the principle forbidding "excessive governmental entanglement with religion" was first used.[26]

However, in the continuous ebb and flow of Supreme Court decisions, in late 1999 the Court declined to hear several cases on appeal that requested state aid to religious schools in school districts in which there was no public high school. Separate cases were submitted from Maine and Vermont. The Supreme Court's refusal to hear these cases meant that the lower court decisions to allow the states to differentiate private from parochial (religious) schools—providing school district subsidies in the former, denying such for the latter—were allowed to stand.[27] The Court let stand a Vermont Supreme Court ruling that it would be a violation of the state constitution for a public school district to pay for any student's tuition at a Catholic school.

Clearly, it is difficult to always predict accurately what decision the Court will make on a church-state issue or whether the Court will even agree to hear a particular case. While not hearing a particular case technically does not establish legal precedent, such a decision does allow existing practice to stand. In these cases, we have instances of maintaining separation of church and state. But, as we will see in the following section, within three years the Supreme Court essentially reversed its stance of prohibiting state support for education of students in religious schools.

School Vouchers   On 27 June 2002, the U.S. Supreme Court approved a school voucher system for public school students to attend alternative private or religious schools of the family's choice, with a portion of the prevailing tax allocation per student following the student. There is one observation about this Supreme Court decision on the Cleveland, Ohio school voucher system about which there is high consensus, regardless of whether one feels the decision was good or bad. That is, it was a landmark decision. It has changed the terrain upon which the church-state debate with regard to public education will be waged. Until 27 June 2002, the six-year Cleveland practice of transferring as much as $2,200 of school district funds to qualified students' private schools of choice, was conducted with protesting lawsuits over head. But now it is fully allowed. The opportunity is designed primarily for economically disadvantaged students, whose public school education has been demonstrated to be seriously inadequate and ineffective.

There are two other states where education vouchers are in use with criteria similar to those in Cleveland. These are Wisconsin and Florida. In

Milwaukee 10,800 students qualify and carry $5,054 to the private school of their choice; in Florida, only 47 students qualify and are credited with $3,400 in tuition money.[28] In all three cases, not all of the state's per student allocation goes to the private or religious school a student chooses. Depending on the state, from one-third to one-half of the per-student allocation stays in the public school district.

Without a doubt, this Supreme Court decision is what many citizens have been waiting for. In fact, already the next day, proponents of the voucher system in California and the District of Columbia, took first steps to establish the same system in those jurisdictions. To be specific, Fredreka Schauten of the Gannett News Service reports that U.S. House of Representatives Majority Leader Dick Armey, a Republican from Texas, was preparing shortly to introduce a pilot voucher plan for low income residents in Washington, DC[29] residents. Probably many will be successful, though not without opposition during a complex, protracted process. But the real point here is that *for the first time* a public education jurisdiction will be allowed to provide school vouchers to parents who meet certain qualifications to send their children to a religious school, with public funds covering much of the cost. This Supreme Court decision will be encouraging in the extreme to proponents of a voucher system.

As suggested above, extension of this ruling will come slowly and with difficulty and challenges every step of the way. Several of the most formidable factors to hinder extension beyond this specific ruling for Cleveland are:

1. Over two-thirds of the 50 states have prohibited such school voucher systems in their state constitutions.
2. A majority of Americans oppose school vouchers.
3. In two recent test cases (California and Michigan) in 2000, ballot referenda to allow a school voucher system were soundly defeated. Further, at least 26 states have failed to provide first-step legislation favorable to education vouchers.[30]
4. Public school teachers' unions are large, powerful, and unified in opposition to school voucher systems.

However, on the other side of the coin, besides the precedent set by the 27 June 2002 Supreme Court ruling (there is little in the field of law more powerful than *precedent*) are two factors that loom significant:

1. At least eight states (California, Colorado, Kansas, Maryland, Minnesota, Missouri, Pennsylvania, Texas) are often described as having waited for just such a decision by the Supreme Court and will likely move to implement similar school voucher programs in their jurisdictions.
2. Although it was a split vote of 5–4 in the Supreme Court, there is a lot of Republican support for school voucher systems. Several new Supreme Court justices will likely be appointed in the next few years by a Republican president with confirmation from his Republican Congress, where there is already

considerable support for the school voucher concept. A strong hint of what is likely to transpire, even in the relatively near future, is seen in the approval by Congress in 1997 of a school voucher system for the District of Columbia, only to see it denied by President Clinton's veto.

Election of Local School Boards   Closely related to our discussions above, regarding prayer in public schools and state support for religious and other private and voucher schools, is the organized attempt within the Christian Right to elect supporters of the Christian Right education agenda to local boards of education. The strategy is simply to work within the political systems to elect those who, it is believed, will move school boards and systems to make decisions and establish policy desired by many in the Christian Right. Accordingly, strategies have been operationalized from California to New Hampshire to Florida to restrict sex education, eliminate references to homosexuality in elementary and secondary classrooms, and promote American Culture as superior to other cultures.[31]

However, despite substantial effort, this strategy has not been particularly successful except in a few instances. Melissa Deckman has found that candidates who ran for school board positions as Christian Right candidates and with strong Christian Right support, were no more likely to win than the non-Christian Right candidates in the case-study school board elections she studied.[32] In fact, although not statistically significant, the Christian Right candidates were slightly more likely than non-Christian Right candidates to lose such elections. Further, the Christian Right has had some difficulty finding and convincing their type of candidates to train for and run in local school board elections. In addition, Deckman notes a clear reluctance for Christian Right candidates to openly support Christian Right objectives in campaigns, apparently fearing such advocacy would "turn off" more voters than it would attract. Deckman's conclusion is: "In terms of Christian Right activism this study finds that the impact of Christian Right organizations is somewhat limited at the school board level."[33] Moreover, the Christian Right nationally has put relatively few resources into local school board election campaigns, despite what at first thought might be a reasonable path for them to follow in attempts to get their way and put education back on the "right" path.

God in the Pledge of Allegiance   One final church-state issue of recent interest. That is the question of the legitimacy of the phrase "under God" in the Pledge of Allegiance to the Flag. This phrase was not originally in the Pledge written in 1892 by Francis Bellamy and officially adopted by Congress in 1942, but was inserted in 1954 during President Eisenhower's first term. This was at the peak of national concern over the possible spread of "Godless Communism" in America—the time of the post-World War II revival of religion, which will be discussed at greater length in Chapter 12. In the year 2000, Michael A. Newdow filed suit on behalf of his daughter against the school district in Elk Grove, California, Congress, and the president (Clinton) stating that they, as atheists, objected to the phrase "under God" in the Pledge of Allegiance that children recited in school every day because it was an unconstitutional blending of church and state. A federal judge dismissed the case. But on appeal, the phrase was declared unconstitutional by the Ninth U.S. Circuit Court of Appeals in June 2002, but automatically put on hold by Court rules for forty-five days to allow for challenges or appeals. Both Governor Gray Davis and school officials in Elk Grove promised to appeal and did so. The appeals were heard by a three-judge panel of the 9th U.S. Circuit Court of Appeals in San Francisco, who declared that the phrase in the Pledge was indeed unconstitutional when its recitation was required in public school classrooms.[34] The case was then appealed to the U.S. Supreme Court, which heard the case in March 2004. The Supreme Court decision came on 15 June 2004, as they dismissed the challenge on the grounds that the father lacked proper legal standing to sue on behalf of his daughter, because his divorce had not given custody of his daughter to him but to his wife. And so the substantive constitutional issue of the phrase "under God" in the Pledge was not resolved and the Pledge of Allegiance can continue to be recited in public schools on a voluntary basis. Mr. Newdow has since joined with other parents and students to sue the school system again, but with no assurance that this new action will receive the substantive decision from the U.S. Supreme Court that they and many others were hoping to see the first time around.

While the case was wending its way through the courts, on 8 October 2002, the U.S. House of Representatives passed Bill 401–5, affirming the legitimacy of the phrase in question and the importance of its remaining in the Pledge.[35] For good measure, they also declared overwhelming support for the statement "In God we Trust" as the national motto (just in case anyone had ideas of challenging that, and of course some do). While some have perceived this as a joke, there is a fundamental issue of the separation of church and state here, especially in a nation, which is not so unified religiously as it once was or that many think it still is.

The *Christian Century* provides interesting perspective and commentary in response to the Circuit Court's and Congress' actions described above:

> The only way "under God" can be construed as constitutional is by arguing that the words do not really carry the kind of theological weight Goodwin (the Circuit Judge who authored the majority opinion) ascribes to them. Probably for many Americans the phrase "under God" in the pledge is not loaded with much religious meaning; it merely lends a pleasant aura of sanctity to the nation and its ideals . . . [But to] the extent "under God" has real religious meaning, then, it is unconstitutional. And the phrase is constitutional to the extent that it is religiously innocuous. Given that choice, we side with the Ninth Circuit. And we see no need— especially not for Christians—to defend hollow references to an innocuous God.[36]

CIVIL RELIGION

As we continue to look at the relationship between religion and politics, we need to consider a concept that has wide attention among those trying to understand how religion and politics affect one another. That is the concept of *civil religion*.

Definition and Origin of the Concept

Briefly, the idea of civil religion refers to the view of some people, that the foundation of their society and the events that mark its progress through history are parts of a larger, divine scheme of things. The political structure and the political acts that flow out of that structure have a transcendental dimension—God is at work in our nation, and as such we have a destiny and our efforts have meaning consistent with God's divine plan. Marcela Cristi states that "civil religion may be considered a belief system or, a surrogate religion, that expresses the self identity of a collectivity."[37] That sounds a lot like something our definition of religion in this book would include. More on that later. The term was coined by Jean-Jacques Rouseau, in his book *Social Contract* in 1762. Civil religion, in his words refers to "civic faith to be created and imposed by a sovereign as a way of promoting civic virtues and political unity."[38] Its modern interpretation and description, introduced by Robert Bellah, draws more heavily on Durkheim's theory of religion than Rouseau's. As Bellah describes civil religion, it is very close to Durkheim's view of religion as integrative and cohesive—as a reinforcing mechanism for pulling together the units of a society. This is in contrast with Rouseau's view that civil religion can easily be an instrument of power and coercion in the hands of political élites to bring a society to work cohesively together toward goals established by the political élites. That is, civil religion is not so much an expression of unity that arises spontaneously from within the group, but a consciously manipulative, if not outrightly coercive means of moving a society in certain directions dear to a political leader's heart. Cristi provides an extended example of the conscious use of civil/political religion in the seventeen years of totalitarian rule in Chile by Augusto Pinochet from 1973–90, during which he urged a political religion among Chileans, by frequently invoking the name of God and defining his rule as following God's design.[39] Not that this political religion was totally or even primarily responsible for maintaining control, at least the political religious rhetoric buttressed the primary mechanism of terror and torture. In her review of Cristi's book in the *Journal for the Scientific Study of Religion*, Laura Olson adds her own trenchant example of "political religion" in a totalitarian society—that of the Taliban's five years of "extremist interpretation of Islamic law in Afghanistan,"[40] following the retreat of Russia in 1992 and the ascendancy of the Taliban in May, 1997, until unseated by the United States and its allies in 2001/02.

Bellah's Modern Application

But, getting back to the Bellah-Durkheim form of civil religion with which we are most familiar in democratic societies, we shall focus briefly on his theory. He describes civil religion as a substratum of common religious understandings that are quite pervasive in society, American society in particular.

> Although matters of personal religious belief, worship, and association are considered to be strictly private affairs, there are, at the same time, certain common elements of religious orientation that the great majority of Americans share. These have played a crucial role in the development of American institutions and still provide a religious dimension for the whole fabric of American life, including the political sphere. This public religious dimension is expressed in a set of beliefs, symbols, and rituals that I am calling the American civil religion.[41]

Bellah goes on to point out that America's civil religion is certainly not Christianity in anything like the specific sense, such as would necessitate belief in Jesus Christ and the Atonement, but rather it is more "unitarian" in the sense of regarding God as a sort of single supernatural being. But this God is not to be understood simply in the deistic[42] tradition of an aloof Maker who set the world in motion and then left it to shift for itself. No, "he is actively interested and involved in history, with a special concern for America."[43] At the heart of civil religion within the United States, as Bellah describes it, is the idea that America is the promised land God has led people to—out of the land of bondage (Europe). Thus, this nation is to be dedicated to order, law, and justice as God would have them carried out. Bellah quotes extensively from Washington and Jefferson, as well as from John Kennedy and Lyndon Johnson, pointing out the idea of America as charged with a divinely-ordained mission to fulfill in bringing about God's will for humankind. Out of the trauma of the Civil War emerged new themes of sacrifice and rebirth. Lincoln's Gettysburg Address was replete with Christian symbolism, without being specifically Christian (e.g., "those who here gave their lives, that that nation might live"). Lincoln's own "sacrificial" martyrdom enhanced the concept. Memorial Day ceremonies and to a lesser extent the ceremonies of the Fourth of July, Veterans Day, Thanksgiving Day, and Washington's and Lincoln's birthdays provided ritual vehicles for the civil religion.

John A. Coleman formalizes a definition of civil religion and lists three central characteristics of American civil religion. He defines *civil religion* as "the set of beliefs, rites, and symbols, which relates a man's role as citizen and his society's place in space, time, and history to the conditions of ultimate existence and meaning."[44] Three characteristics, according to Coleman, typify American civil religion:

1. The nation is the primary agent of God's meaningful activity in history. This belief gave rise to the doctrines of manifest destiny and world obligation.
2. The nation is the primary society in terms of which individual Americans discover personal and group identity. Like the historic church, through the doctrine of the melting pot, America was called to be "catholic."
3. The nation also assumes a churchly feature as the community of righteousness.[45]

Civil Religion and President George W. Bush

As Bellah noted originally, Civil Religion has both "priestly" (conservative orientation and support for the *status quo*) and "prophetic" (change and challenge) orientations. In other words, its core message can be used effectively by those at both ends of the conservative-liberal political continuum. And it tends to have broad, cultural resonance without sectarian divisiveness.[46] It is in this context that we can understand what was the balance-tipping message of George W. Bush's 2004 campaign for the presidency that not only gathered strong Republican support but also enough support from others of different political persuasions to hand him the election. That crucial message was that America was really doing God's work in handing the people of Iraq democracy and freedom—which is God's intention for all people. The United States was doing God's work. President Bush utilized very effectively what are clear Civil Religion themes. And we cannot help but remember Rousseau's view of civil religion as an ideal in the hands of the élites.

Now that we have mentioned President Bush and the 2004 political campaign's utilization of Civil Religion imagery and emphases, and knowing that there was strong conservative Christian support for President Bush, we must note that Civil Religion must not be viewed as synonymous with Christianity, conservative, or otherwise. In fact, following Bellah's bringing Civil Religion as a concept to the attention of sociologists and others, many Christians were abhorred by the thought that the Civil Religion Bellah described might become a substitute for the "real thing"—what was for them "true," authentic religion—Christianity (or for others, Islam, Judaism, Hinduism, and so on). But it must be noted that even those who thought that Civil Religion is a **good** thing, will often understand that America's brand of Civil Religion comes out of Christianity ("Our God [Christian] has singularly blessed us") and is in reality in close alliance with Christianity. America's Civil Religion is then in this view really none other than an extension of Christian thought, ethics, and values.

Certainly George W. Bush espouses a contemporary version of American Civil Religion when he talks about bringing democratic values to Iraq and in turn to the rest of the Middle East, and freedom to all nations still governed by dictators (as he emphasized in his 2005 inaugural address). For President Bush, Democracy needs to be spelled with a capital "D" inasmuch as it is more than a form of governing. It is the way God wants all people to live and it is part of America's mission from God to bring this form of government to others. But President Bush's vision also seems to include at some ultimate level and time also the Christianization of Muslims, just as America is not only a democratic nation specially blessed by God, but it is a Christian nation, although having sometimes strayed from God's path in some ways (e.g., continuing to allow abortions in violation of God's command), he will help America return to God's ways.

Such a mixing in people's minds of fairly standard civil religious ideals and rhetoric with such specific Evangelical values, such as uncompromising opposition to abortion and support for the Constitutional prohibition of same-sex marriages, might over time weaken the impact of a Republican appeal to traditional Civil Religion ideals. This might help explain why even some Republicans, who supported George W. Bush in his re-election campaign, are showing some reluctance to support every item on his agenda as he reveals them.

Certainly the New Christian Right wants to expand on the American values held dear in American Civil Religion, by including a full ban on abortion and a constitutional amendment explicitly forbidding same-sex marriage, for example. But to push for such an expanded definition of American civil religion amid widespread opposition, is to weaken the societal value of American civil religion as accepted and reiterated (without the name attached) for more than 200 years. Or perhaps the inclusion of an international political dimension to American civil religion is to some a logical extension of the concept. God has particularly favored us; now we need to extend the favor to others.

RELIGION AND POLITICS IN THE THIRD WORLD

Although religious issues periodically surface as political issues in every society of the world, a politico-religious phenomenon virtually unknown in the United States but fairly common in the Third World (the developing nations of Asia, Africa, and Latin America) is the emergence of religious political parties—that is, political parties whose constituency is a particular religious group and that pursue both religious and political ends. Donald Smith distinguishes three kinds of Third World politico-religious parties.[47] There are, first of all, the *communal parties*, such as the Hindu Mahasabha, the Jana Sangh, and the Sikhs in India, which exist within a national context of religious pluralism. Their self-styled function is to "protect and promote the largely secular economic and political interests of their respective communal groups."[48] Such political parties are organized manifestations of communal conflict and violence of the sort that might erupt between Hindus and Muslims if the latter were alleged to have killed sacred cows or if a Hindu procession was accused of disturbing Muslims in their mosques at prayer—violence of the sort paralleled in the West by the protracted Protestant-Catholic conflict in Northern Ireland. An excellent example of the Third World communal party is the Freedom party, led by S.W.R.D. Bandaranaike, that pledged itself to restore Buddhism to its rightful place in the national life of Sri Lanka (formerly Ceylon). The focus of its attack was Christianity, particularly the Roman Catholic Church, which was felt to be favored by governing authorities. Bandaranaike succeeded in becoming prime minister in the election of 1956, but was assassinated three years later. The subsequent administration under his wife found its power considerably weakened through expedient compromises with Marxists.

The second type of religious political party is the *sect-based party*. Smith cites the Ummah in the northern Sudan as a prime example. Although the northern portion of the Sudan is solidly Muslim, the Ummah is a minority political party that derives its constituency from the Ansar sect within that branch of Islam. In other words, unlike the interreligious conflict inherent in the communal parties, here intrareligious conflict between a sect and the parent religious group finds expression in political action and party formation.

The third type is the *ideological religious party* that, Smith notes, functions in societies in which religious minorities are politically unimportant. Such parties are not oriented to conflict with other religious groups but desire to speak to the ideological assumptions that undergird and shape the society. They may be conservative and attempt to preserve traditional patterns, such as many Latin American conservative parties, particularly of thirty and more years ago. Or they may be modernizing or reforming, as they challenge aspects of the fundamental societal ideology. Examples of the latter are the Christian Democrats in Chile and the Masjumi in Indonesia.

The Third World Islamist Movement

Beginnings of Islamism   Although we will discuss what has been called *Islamic fundamentalism* in the next chapter on religious fundamentalism, our current discussion of "Religion and Politics in the Third World," is the appropriate place to introduce Islamism and the Islamists. These are terms that identify modern politico-religious movements in Islamic societies, which Western nations have found so vexing. As described by Gilles Kepel,[49] these Islamists have a three-pronged platform that can be credited to three spokespersons and Islamism theorists who became regional leaders during the rise of Islamism in the second half of the twentieth century. Each of these leaders moved the movement forward, with major emphases on one of what became the three central ideas of the new movement referred to now as Islamism. These ideas are sequential, evolutionary perspectives.

First, Sayyid Qutb in Egypt, the leader of the Muslim Brothers, who was hanged as a revolutionary by President Gamal Abdel Nasser in 1966.

His emphasis was that Islamic nations must reject their strong nationalistic emphases and commitments and begin to think collectively of a world community that first of all unites all Muslims but then ultimately overcomes all those who do not worship Allah and creates a true world community of Islam. One major reason the Islamists opposed nationalism, was that they believed within the nationalistic Muslim societies that people were basically ignorant about historic, true Islam. For too many Muslims, their sense of history was restricted to their country and did not extend to the dispersed broader Muslim community spanning North Africa, the Near East, and Asia. Qutb urged a clean break with the established political and social order, not the theological foundation of Islam. As such, he attracted displaced, unemployed urban youth but alienated the Muslim clergy and the middle class.

The second core value of the Islamists came from Mawlana Mawdudi of Pakistan. He stressed that in de-emphasizing nationalism and identifying more broadly with Islam as a world religion, true Muslims must avoid the trap of thinking of Islam primarily as an Arab religion, as the Western world certainly did. Rather they should think of Islam as inclusive of a vast territory spanning the north of Africa, the Near East of course, but also much of Asia (primarily Southeast Asia). Actually, the traditional *Arab* world included only one-fifth of Muslims worldwide. Mawdudi advocated establishing an Islamic republic as a gradual project that would proceed step by step. This more moderate, gradualist approach attracted the Pakistani middle classes but did not generate much enthusiasm among the masses. It would take too long to see tangible results.

Third, is the contribution of the Ayatollah Ruhollah Khomeini in Iran. He introduced the necessity of revolution and violence in carrying out and hurrying along the unification of the Muslim world and ultimately even the rest of world. He alone was able to create a functional coalition of all the interested parties: the disinherited, the middle classes, radical intellectuals, and clerics. As a consequence the Islamic revolution succeeded in Iran and so far only there.[50]

Now we proceed to a definition of *Islamism.* It is the commitment to the idea of Islam as a world religion that rises above the nationalistic interests of individual Muslim nations and unites in a worldwide Muslim effort to spread the religion of Islam to the rest of the world that as yet is unenlightened. There are two primary themes to remember: First, all current Islamic nations must be united, and, second, the goal is the ultimate triumph of Islam as the world's religion.

It was this three-fold emphasis of Qutb, Mawdudi, and Khoumeini, that Osama bin Laden absorbed as a young Muslim intellectual, developing his own plan and tactics to carry on their vision through terrorism, which would demoralize and ultimately topple the West and its allies and achieve both Islamic unification and the ultimate worldwide triumph of Islam. He had no country and its citizens to answer to (even declared unwelcome in his country of birth and education, Saudi Arabia); he was not a Muslim cleric and therefore had no traditional theology to either guide or limit him; he was extremely wealthy from his father's and then his own extensive construction business in Saudi Arabia (the family accumulated great wealth during the dramatic growth of the oil industry and its immense monetary return to the country and region); and his revolutionary message to the disenfranchised and unemployed youth stressed a bright future for Muslims, if they would only attach themselves to him. This message began to attract followers in significant numbers.

Jihad!   So bin Laden now controls the al Qaeda, which is a pan-Islamic political party that is not particularly absorbed in national politics but committed to the penultimate and ultimate goals of Islamism, namely, unification of *all* Islamic states and ultimate victory over *all* those outside the Islamic fold. And the familiar rallying cry has become *Jihad!*

Jihad does, at one level or by one of its definitional nuances, mean "holy war against our enemies." But that is not its primary meaning, despite its being claimed by bin Laden and his al Qaeda to be justification for a first strike, aggressive war against the West, the United States in particular as the greatest "Satan."

The Arabic word *jihad*, identified by Rudolph Peters as the verbal noun of the verb jahada, means "to strive, to struggle, to exert oneself."[51] Peters explains this as follows:

> The word has a basic connotation of an endeavor towards a praisewor-
> thy aim. In a religious context it may express a struggle against one's evil
> inclinations or an exertion for the sake of Islam and the *umma* (the
> Muslim community), e.g. trying to convert unbelievers or working for
> the moral betterment of Islamic society ("jihad of the tongue" and "jihad
> of the pen").[52]

J. Harold Ehlens notes that jihad in the Qur'an generally means "working urgently for a certain godly objective."[53] On the other hand, the Qur'an also says: "O prophet! Strive vigorously against the infidels and those who are inauthentic in their faith, and be very aggressive against them. Hell is where they are at home, and their strategies are evil."[54] Or, the following quotation that in Ehlen's words "seems particularly applicable to the present moment in history and is probably one of the sacred scriptures which has directly inspired bin Laden and his al Qaeda minions."[55] Chapter 46:16 of the Qur'an, as translated by Ehlens, reads: "Shortly you will have the opportunity to make war against an immensely powerful nation. You will continue the war until they give up. God will bless you greatly."[56]

But there is no doubt that today in a very real sense a major feature of jihad is what we call "war," or as it is embellished, "holy war." We must also realize that this should not really sound unfamiliar in the West.

Parallels in Other Religions   Certainly the Old Testament Jews were constantly engaged in war, sometimes defensively but even then as a response against those who opposed the Jews' takeover of their land. And what was the biblical exodus from Egypt other than a march to reclaim the land of Abraham (roughly today's land of Israel)? It was a war against those who had moved in during the generations when the Israelites had lived in Egypt. Oh, maybe God told them it was rightfully theirs. But it was aggressive action to gain territory, even so.

Throughout this book, we make passing references to war and violent aggression in the name of Christianity. After all, for most of history, Christianity was not denominationally organized even close to what we know it to be today. What we now call the Middle Ages, had dominant state churches that tolerated little deviance and had great political power. An outgrowth was the proliferation of the Crusades that spanned the eleventh, twelfth, and thirteenth centuries. These endeavors caused untold hardship and the loss of millions of lives. Then think of the militaristic tone and message of many Christian hymns (e.g., "Onward Christian Soldiers,"). The war imagery is common. And the continuing war against the devil often included death for those who were defined as in league with him, whether they were or not.

Other world religions too, especially in the hands of warlords and special interests, have perpetrated violence and waged war. The Hindu-Muslim conflicts are not at all one sided (that is, instigated by Muslims). In short, aggression, violence, and war have not been the province only of Muslims. To decry "jihad" and think of it as different, even unique, and totally unbecoming of a group that calls itself religious is not by definition to discredit it. Someone might point out that Islam is different, because it is and always was a politico-religious group from the Third World. But violent aggression is not really any more at the heart of Islam than acts by Christians, such as murders of abortion clinic personnel, or mass killing of innocent people in a medieval crusade, or convincing followers to join in mass suicides by the hundreds or thousands are at the heart and core of Christianity.

When the West condemns the Islamists with justifiable indignation for the more than 400-day hostage situation in Iran and the terrorist action in Kenya, Tanzania, New York City, Washington, DC, and Pennsylvania under bin Laden, of terrorist bombings of passenger trains in Spain and London, followers of Islam respond by recounting the horrors of 300 years of Crusades and the repression by European colonialism, as well as American manipulation of Arab governments, in the interest of keeping the oil flowing west to North America at a reasonable price. In other words, we can understand why so many Muslims hate the West and pray for its fall from power and influence. We know that their theology includes: (1) broad, variously interpreted concepts such as *jihad*, and (2) a mandate by the Qur'an to reform Muslim societies in every age. Both ideas are subject to continued reinterpretation. As Nasim Jawed says so forthrightly: "it matters far less what the scriptures say and far more what the believers in those scriptures interpret them to mean."[57] He adds that "religious histories are replete with examples of finding new messages in old texts and assigning new meanings to scriptural and traditional concepts."[58]

Conclusion

In a real sense, it all boils down to such facts as these:

1. Islam as a religion is at least on its surface more a politico-religious organization than Christianity is (or thinks it is) today and is highly likely to use religion as justification for the political actions of Islamic countries or factions within them (e.g., the al Qaeda);
2. Islamic peoples are trying to come out from under many generations of colonial rule and influence;
3. Islamic nations in the main even today are at the economic level only of "developing" countries, yet with citizens desiring to enjoy the economic benefits of modernity.

There is, therefore, a natural push to oppose those nations defined as the exploiters and appropriators of their treasure, possibly even destroy them.

We are left with three major conclusions:

1. Islam is a religion with strong political influence and is, toward the totalitarian end of the church-state continuum, which we described earlier in this chapter.
2. In the face of the necessity to accept the sovereignity of Islam in those societies where the citizens have accepted it, other religions and societies must accept their religion as it is.
3. When political aspects or applications of Islam threaten our existence and way of life, we try to respond appropriately trying to separate the political from the religious without denying their rights to their religious views.

Obviously, keeping such distinctions in mind is a mighty challenge but such challenge certainly makes clear why the relationship of religion and politics is such an extremely important focus of study.

We continue this focus in the next chapter as we turn to Religious Fundamentalism.

Final Note

Probably the major point to appreciate in this brief look at religion and politics in the Third World, is the widespread tendency of citizens in these societies to refuse to relegate religion solely to the private sphere of individual faith and practice. The politico-religious conflict that ensues is aided by the onrush of social change and the inevitable challenges to traditional ideologies that social change involves. Such developments may upset traditional delicate compromises and stalemates among religions, which may lead to intergroup conflict, or religious groups may organize themselves politically to uphold traditional values in some cases or promote other values in other cases. The point, then, is that in many Third World societies, religion and politics are less clearly separated than in, say, the United States.

A prime reason for this, as Smith points out, is that Third World societies began much more recently to question the view of government as ordained by God and of government leaders as gods or direct agents of God.[59] These societies have not become as secularized as most societies of the West. As we have seen, in our look at recent developments with Islam as a politico-religious entity, the process of secularization is occurring only with great difficulty and is perhaps the major reason for the rise of Islamism, the contentiousness both within Islam and between Islam and other religions, and the popularity of a leader like bin Laden.

Religion in developing countries, especially where Islam is dominant, will be a fascinating story for sociologists and for everyone long into the future.

NOTES

1. J. Milton Yinger, *The Scientific Study of Religion* (New York: Macmillan, 1970), p. 408.
2. Harold Lasswell, *Politics: Who Gets What, When, and How* (New York: Meridian Books, 1958).
3. Robert Booth Fowler, *Religion and Politics in America* (Metuchen, NJ: The Scarecrow Press, 1985), pp. 168–173.
4. George H. Gallup, *The Gallup International Public Opinion Polls*, vol. 2 (New York: Random House, 1976), p. 1306.
5. Discussion based in part on Fowler, *Religion and Politics*, Chapter 3.
6. Ibid., p. 52.
7. Henry C. Kenski and William Lockwood, "The Catholic Vote from 1980 to 1986: Continuity or Change?" in *Religion and Political Behavior in the United States*, ed. Ted G. Jelen (New York: Praeger, 1989), p. 136.
8. Ibid., pp. 113–114.
9. Ibid., p. 114.
10. Leo Pfeffer, *Church, State, and Freedom* (Boston: Beacon Press, 1953), p. 200.
11. Quoted in Pfeffer, *Church, State, and Freedom*, p. 200.
12. Ibid.
13. David M. Kennedy, *Birth Control in America* (New Haven, CT: Yale University Press, 1970), p. 218.
14. Lawrence H. Tribe, *Abortion: The Clash of Absolutes* (New York: W. W. Norton, 1990), p. 21f.
15. Ibid., p. 28.

16. Ibid., p. 29.
17. Ibid.
18. Ibid., p. 34.
19. Ibid., p. 36.
20. Reported in Elizabeth Adell Cook, Ted G. Jelen, and Clyde Wilcox, *Between Two Absolutes: Public Opinion and the Politics of Abortion* (Boulder, CO: Westview Press, 1992), pp. 32–35.
21. All the data above reported in Cook et al., *Between Two Absolutes*, pp. 35–37.
22. Dale Hanson Bourke, in Religion News Service. Reported in *Christian Century* 112, no. 23 (August 2–9, 1995): 734–735.
23. Jennifer Ferranti, "Clinton: Room for Religion in Nation's Schools," *Christianity Today* 39, no. 9 (August 14, 1995): 57.
24. *Church and State* 47, no. 2 (Feb., 1994): 9.
25. Lawrence White, "The Profound Consequences of the 'Rosenberger' Ruling," *The Chronicle of Higher Education* 41, no. 44 (July 14, 1995): B1.
26. Ibid., B2.
27. "Court dismisses church-state cases," Religious News Service. Reported in *Christian Century* 116, no. 29 (October 27, 1999): 1022–1023.
28. Linda Greenhouse, "Supreme Court, 5–4, Upholds Voucher System that Pays Religious Schools' Tuition," *New York Times* (June 28, 2002): © New York Times Company, 2002. Provided by www.lexis-nexis.com.
29. Fredreka Schauten, "Supreme Court Upholds Ohio Voucher Plan," *Gannett News Service* June 28, 2002): 1. © Gannett Company Inc., 2002. Provided by www.lexis-nexis.com.
30. Michael A. Fletcher, "Voucher Movement May Boost Choice Movement," *Washington Post* (June 30, 2002): A7. © The Washington Post, 2000. Provided by www.lexis-nexis.com.
31. Melissa M. Deckman, *School Board Battles: The Christian Right in Local Politics* (Washington, DC: Georgetown University Press, 2004), p. XII.
32. Ibid., p. 128.
33. Ibid., p. 170.
34. David Graves, Associated Press, "Court Rules 'Under God' Unconstitutional," *Ball State Daily News* (June 27, 2002), 1.
35. "House Reaffirms 'Under God' in Pledge," *The Muncie Star Press* (October 9, 2002), p. 3A.
36. "Taking On the Pledge," (editorial), *The Christian Century* 119, no. 15 (July 17–30, 2002): 5.
37. Marcela Cristi, *From Civil to Political Religion* (Waterloo, Ontario: Wilfrid Laurier University Press, 2001), p. 3.
38. Jean-Jacques Rousseau, *The Social Contract and Discourses*, trans. G. D. H. Cole (London: J.M Dent and Sons, [1762] 1984).
39. Cristi, *From Civil to Political Religion*, pp. 165–180.
40. Laura Olson, book review of Cristi, *From Civil to Political Religion*, in *Journal for the Scientific Study of Religion* 41, no. 3 (2002), pp. 592–593.
41. Bellah, "Civil Religion in America," pp. 3–4.
42. Deism is a belief in a god who is somehow responsible for setting the world in motion but subsequently has left it to find its own way with no divine direction or intervention.
43. Bellah, "Civil Religion in America," ibid., p. 9.
44. John A. Coleman, "Civil Religion," *Sociological Analysis* 31, no. 2 (1970): 76.
45. Ibid., p. 74.
46. Bellah, "Civil Religion in America," ibid.
47. Donald E. Smith, *Religion, Politics, and Social Change in the Third World* (New York: Free Press, 1971), pp. 140–169.
48. Ibid., p. 140.

49. Gilles Kepel, *Jihad: The Trail of Political Islam* (Cambridge, MA: Belknap Press of Harvard University Press, 2002), pp. 23–42.

50. Ibid. The above discussion relies heavily on Kepel.

51. Rudolph Peters, *Jihad in Classical and Modern Islam* (Princeton, NJ: Markus Wiener Publishers, 1996), p. 1.

52. Ibid.

53. J. Harold Ehlens, ed., *The Destructive Power of Religion: Violence in Judaism, Christianity, and Islam*, Vol 3, *Models and Cases of Violence in Religion* (Westport, CT: Praeger, 2004), p. 45.

54. *Qur'an*, Ch.66:9 as translated by J. Harold Ehlens and quoted in Ehlens, ibid., p. 46.

55. Ehlens, Ibid., p. 47.

56. *Qur'an*, Ch.46:16 as translated by J. Harold Ehlens, ibid.

57. Nasim A. Jawed, *Islam's Political Culture: Religion and Politics in Predivided Pakistan* (Austin: University of Texas Press, 1999), p. 147.

58. Ibid.

59. Smith, *Religion, Politics, and Social Change*, pp. 1–2.

Chapter 8

Religious Fundamentalism

Come back to the Fundamentals!

Having presented some evidence in the previous chapter, concerning extreme points of view on such contemporary issues as abortion rights and school prayer, we are prepared to consider the religious phenomenon of fundamentalism. *Fundamentalism* is a religious perspective and movement that originated around 1900 within American Protestantism. It was a self-conscious effort among conservative Protestants to curtail the spread of "liberalism" in American religion and secularization in American culture and society.

However, over time the term has been applied more broadly to include movements within other religions—first Islam, then Judaism, Hinduism, and Buddhism—to name the major religions of the world. Each has fundamentalist tendencies and identifiable fundamentalist movements within them.

As such, fundamentalism has become a major consideration in describing religion in society and the impact of religion on society. In such analysis, fundamentalism is immediately recognized as much more than a collection of theological views. It is a social phenomenon in the sense that its sources are more than purely religious; they are cultural or sociological as well.

Fundamentalism should also be regarded as a social phenomenon, in that it has impact on the surrounding society in which it exists. And here, of course, we find ourselves on familiar ground, as throughout this book we observe and analyze religion from the dual perspective of social forces and features affecting religion and, reciprocally, religion's independent impact on that surrounding social structure.

THE CONCEPT OF FUNDAMENTALISM: ITS ORIGIN AND USE

Fundamentalism has been added to the vocabulary of a great many more people worldwide, through the increased attention to activities identified as fundamentalist by journalists and social scientists. The term itself is certainly not new. In 1920, it was coined by a journalist, Curtis Lee Laws, with the Northern Baptist journal *The Watchman Examiner*. But its use and applicability have been extended beyond the conservative Protestants in America, whom Mr. Laws labeled "fundamentalists," early in the twentieth century. Jewish fundamentalists began to organize with the initiation of Jewish resettlement in Israel in the 1920s, but they became particularly noticeable after the achievement of Jewish statehood in 1948. Muslim fundamentalism emerged as an identifiable movement and named as such in the 1970s, when the Shah of Iran was deposed and the religious leader, the Ayatollah Khomeini, assumed control (though, in retrospect, historians see fundamentalist movements in Islam well before Khomeini).

The First Application

Fundamentalism is a title worn with pride by those Christians who have been placed by others under that title. The ultimate source of the term was the publication, beginning in 1910, of the conservative Christians' (Evangelicals) manifesto in twelve volumes, titled *The Fundamentals*. This publication was the capstone to a series of Bible conferences held by Christian conservatives throughout the country between 1876 and 1900, which Gasper views as "embryonic stirrings" of the fundamentalism movement.[1] *The Fundamentals* included the basic (fundamental) Christian doctrines that many said one must accept and believe. But *fundamentalism* is a new designation for those Jews, Muslims, Sikhs, Buddhists, Hindus, and others, whom sociologists, historians, philosophers, and other scholars include under that title today.

Reaction against Modernity

Although fundamentalism has been recognized as such for nearly a century, it is nonetheless a relatively recent phenomenon, if we put it in the context of the many centuries of recorded history that have preceded us. This is so because most scholars agree that fundamentalism is usually a reaction to events and changes that have occurred in the modern world—a constellation commonly called modernity. Fundamentalism is, then, reactive and wants to restore what has been lost or discarded in the face of changes that modernization has made. To return to the "good old days" requires, first, the realization that you have moved beyond those days and that change has occurred.

There were no fundamentalists, in a pure sense, prior to modernization. Modernization has been ushered in through the tremendous growth in technology that includes most of what we see and use around us—the telephone, radio, automobile, television, computer, Internet, electric power, space exploration, and the marvels of modern medicine, from antibiotics to human organ transplants to cataloging the human genome. Most of what we see, use, and depend upon day by day did not exist for use by anyone one hundred and fifty years ago.

Fundamentalists use all of this technology. As such, they have become moderns along with everyone else—all save those few such as the Amish, who eschew electricity and still use horse and buggy for transportation. All the rest of us are moderns. Yet to be modern is not necessarily to go the next step and become *modernists*, which would imply not only an embracing of the products of modernization, but also taking on a feeling of freedom and new life as one rejects much of the old—old world views, old prejudices and biases, old beliefs and explanations of reality (e.g., accepting evolution as a replacement for the literal Biblical version of a six-day creation). It is at that point, where the enthusiastic modernist rejects not only the old technology but also the old world-views and explanations of reality, that the fundamentalists part company with the modernists. Fundamentalists want to return to the old core beliefs and principles.

Fundamentalism is a predictable response of some people in any culture one wants to name, to one or more manifestations of modernity. Peter Berger summarizes modernity as a set of five developments. Each of them poses a dilemma for the citizen wherever modernity develops.

Berger's Five Features of Modernity

First, there is the development of abstraction. By that he means a pulling away from the solidarity, concreteness, and sense of relationship with others that one pictures in smaller communities of lifelong residents, where one's work was a direct and nearby part of one's life. One thinks of stability, predictability, security, and *Gemeinschaft* relationships. One sees the movement to large cities of many uprooted anonymous people who work in large bureaucracies or work at machines that do what had for millennia been done by people taking pride in their careful handiwork. Such abstraction and reduction of the significance of the individual citizen in deference to the anonymous city, workplace, and governmental authority, produced what Emile Durkheim called *anomie* and Karl Marx called *alienation*.

Second, is the development of an emphasis on futurity. For most of history, people's concentration has been on the present and the past, with very little attention paid to the future. It was for the most part predicted to be much like the present and the past or, if different, totally out of our control to modify in any way. People believed there was, therefore, little point in thinking much about the future.

But with the coming of modernity, the future becomes a major focus for both thought and activity. This affects individuals in their day-to-day living, which requires keeping appointments and getting to work "on time"; it affects people as they perceive themselves on a "career" path that may put them into several different jobs and many new locations along the way; and it affects whole societies that develop annual plans, five-year plans, and long-range goals to strive to achieve in the future. Even the stock market is future-oriented, as investors buy stocks with both eyes to the future growth in value they hope to see, or they sell with the prediction that the future promises no more growth for their stock, or that the market as a whole is about to move down or even crash. Through it all is a continual focus on the future and an abiding conviction that one can affect it, even control it.

Third, we observe the process of individuation, which is in reality the other side of the first concept discussed—that of abstraction. The weakening of the supportive community that sustained the individual, and its replacement by the distant megastructures of modern society, have left individuals much more alone and in need of belonging somewhere than before, when belonging was an endemic part of culture for most people. The prospect of individual anomie increases greatly.

Fourth, there is liberation. The element of choice is introduced to many areas of life, that in earlier generations were viewed as governed and determined by God, by fate, by nature, by the all-powerful king, or by the constellation of the stars. Peter Berger says, "Tradition is no longer binding; the *status quo* can be changed; the future is an open horizon."[2] While this opening up of options and choices can be exhilarating and liberating, it can also bring terror and anguish in the face of uncertainty and the choices that one must make all around.

Fifth, there is the secularization that we have mentioned before and will discuss at greater length later. Here again, we think of it as providing alternative answers and explanations for phenomena and events, which in an earlier day were explained as God given, directed, and ordained; now religion and religious explanations have been relegated to restricted spheres of life, and science and reason are used to explain most of what we wonder about.[3]

In the face of such liberation and secularization, which come with modernity, the answers fundamentalists provide are attractive to many people. Fundamentalism says that the liberation from tradition and the secularization that relegates God to being simply one among several explanations for reality, must be resisted and overcome.

Distinguishing Religious from Political Fundamentalism

At this point, after an introduction to fundamentalism that promotes awareness of its currency and its ubiquity, but before looking at the three most frequently encountered examples of fundamentalism for most readers, we hasten to point out a distinction between what we might call religious fundamentalism (or traditional fundamentalism) and political fundamentalism. We do not mean to suggest that a fundamentalist must be one or the other. We want mainly to suggest that political fundamentalists have added political activism to their agendas and are no longer solely religious in their message and objectives.

Actually it did not take long, even in the beginning of the fundamentalist movement, before the political dimension was added to the fundamentalist agenda. In part, that stems from the source of fundamentalism, which we have suggested lies largely in a reactionary response to modernity. Inasmuch as modernity has important manifestations in social structure and inevitably seems to produce a loosening of traditional social structures, it is not surprising that some would want to reform and improve the social structure while bringing people back to the true, fundamental religion.

Everyone is aware of the strong political character of Islamic fundamentalism. In fact, to the outsider the Iranian dictatorship of the Ayatollah Khomeini in the 1980s might have looked totally political and not religious at all. One does not usually think of Protestant fundamentalism as highly political—nonetheless, the political dimension appeared early and has been continued. One early example in the United States was religious involvement in the temperance movement that led to the Eighteenth Amendment in 1919, which then ushered in the Prohibition era in the United States. That was a very effective political movement that had strong religious roots.

More recently, we have seen the active involvement of fundamentalists in the defeat of liberal U.S. senators and representatives, in electing people to Congress, who are committed to fundamentalist values, in electing George W. Bush twice to the U.S. Presidency, and in becoming highly-assertive in the battle over abortion and same-sex marriage. In short, religious fundamentalism often expresses itself on political issues and pursues political ends.

We now turn to a brief overview of the fundamentalist branches of the three religions, best known by the readers of this text: Protestant fundamentalism, Jewish fundamentalism, and Islamic fundamentalism.

Protestant Fundamentalism

We begin with the religion that contributed the term *fundamentalism*, namely, Protestant fundamentalism.

The Early Issues

The primary stimuli for the emerging fundamentalist concern were, first, what the fundamentalism proponents viewed as increasing secularism in the society. This is connected with the advancement of science and the increasing confidence in the inductive scientific method of attaining truth—at the expense of deduction from a standard repository of truth such as the Bible. Of concern to them also were such developments as the dissemination of the Marxist social philosophy, the spread of the accounts of Darwin and others concerning the evolution of people and their world, and the increasing independence of society's institutions from religious influence. In short, the traditionalists—or Evangelicals, as they are commonly called—were disturbed by the erosion of religious influence throughout the rest of the society and its institutions. Second, they felt that the Christian religion was being betrayed from within. The increasing emphasis on social service and the social gospel by individuals and groups within the broad Christian community was a significant part of their concern. For one thing, they felt that when social service was emphasized, the traditional redemption/salvation emphasis was of necessity neglected, or at best put in a secondary position. For another, they felt some were rejecting the traditional message of Christianity altogether and substituting the social gospel in all particulars. This was liberal ideology as opposed to their conservative religion—this was liberal Christianity that attempted to incorporate secular values into the Christian structure. What further alarmed the Evangelicals was the development of a form of biblical scholarship known as *higher criticism*, an approach to the Bible asserting that it is a collection of human documents subject to the same principles of textual criticism as any other group of documents—a perspective that originated in German theological schools and universities in the mid-1800s and was subsequently adopted at many leading seminaries in the United States.

In an effort to combat this "creeping liberalism" and restore Christianity to what they regarded as its original nature and message, many Evangelicals coalesced around the publication, beginning in 1910, of *The Fundamentals* (mentioned above). *The Fundamentals* exposited five central doctrines and an additional four that could more or less be inferred from the central five. The five were:

1. the verbal and inerrant inspiration of the Bible,
2. the virgin birth of Jesus Christ,

3. the substitutionary atonement of Jesus Christ (Jesus taking the punishment for sin in people's place),
4. the bodily resurrection of Jesus Christ from the dead, and
5. the imminent second coming of Jesus Christ.

The four related doctrines were:

1. the deity of Jesus Christ,
2. the sinful nature of humanity,
3. salvation by faith through the free grace of God, and
4. the expectation of the bodily resurrection of true believers on the Last Day.[4]

Much attention was also paid to refutation of errors, such as the theory of organic evolution and higher criticism of the Bible, and to ways of relating to such heretical religious groups and movements as Roman Catholics, Mormons, Jehovah's Witnesses, Christian Science, and spiritualism.

Fundamentalism became more conscious of self when the assumptions of conservative Protestantism—which had served as the dominant, pace-setting religion throughout the previous two and one-half centuries of American history—began to be threatened. First, many immigrants—particularly Roman Catholics and Jews—arriving in the last half of the nineteenth century, created a sense of uncertainty for those who would come to be known as fundamentalists. At the same time, industrialization and the erosion of the centrality of farming and small business patterns, which had prevailed during the first two and one-half centuries of the country's existence, were having an impact. Until this time, fundamentalists, while not terribly conscious of their political nature, were nonetheless comfortable with notions of this as a Christian nation, which puts Christian principles of morality and civility into practice.

James Speer describes such devolution of fundamentalism, between 1870 and 1920, as movement from a "church" to a "beleaguered sect."[5] But following this period of adjustment and consolidation of its concerns, fundamentalism came back with a flurry of activity following World War I, opposing the teaching of evolution in schools and supporting prohibition. In fact, fundamentalism probably reached its zenith in 1925. This was the date of the Scopes "monkey trial," in which the fundamentalists hoped that their political spokesman and three-time candidate for the presidency, William Jennings Bryan, would defeat religious modernism, as epitomized in the teaching of evolution in the public schools. Even though Scopes was found guilty of teaching evolution contrary to Tennessee law, the farcical nature of the trial and the "bad press" the prosecution received, turned the legal victory of the fundamentalists into a public relations defeat, and the cohesiveness of the movement began to dissipate. By the following year, attendance at their annual meeting had fallen off. By their 1930 convention, "none of the scheduled speeches contained any reference to modernism or evolution."[6] They began to fight among themselves, and a host of subgroups formed. It is of perhaps more than parenthetical interest that Mr. Scopes was a high school coach and a part-time biology teacher, who may never actually have taught evolution in a biology class, though personally he subscribed to evolution over the six-day creation story.

The Post-World War II Fundamentalism Revival

Following World War II, many evangelicals/fundamentalists joined the anti-communist crusade that linked them with right-wing political groups. These political groups supported the reckless inquisition by Senator Joseph McCarthy and the destruction, or at best the long interruption, of careers for many people. The movement was based on such ideas as opposition to communism and socialism in almost any form; support for traditional free enterprise and capitalism and its corollary limited government; commitment to traditional morality, which would exclude and condemn such persons as "liberated" women, homosexuals, and civil libertarians; and frequently an expression of anti-Semitism as well. The Radical right and its history in the United States is a fascinating topic in itself. But what is of primary interest to us in this text, is the relationship and intermingling of radical right political philosophies and activities with fundamentalist Protestant religion. Particularly intriguing is the intimate association of fundamentalist Protestant theology with right-wing politics among many of the anticommunist crusaders in the 1950s and 1960s. As Janson and Eismann state:

> Ultraconservative leaders have had considerable success, simply by preaching anticommunism, in rallying not only religious fundamentalists concerned about heresy but also political, economic, and social fundamentalists concerned about the liberal trends that are threatening their values.[7]

Some of the radical right groups actually tried to remain aloof from religion—Robert Welch's John Birch Society, for one. Welch did not reveal his personal religious convictions, if any, and said that he did not care what religion a person was. His ultimate appeal was not to religious beliefs but to what he viewed as fundamental American values. Other prominent right-wing political groups, however, made an intimate connection between the two. Fred C. Schwartz's Christian Anti-Communist Crusade, Billy James Hargis's Christian Crusade, and Carl McIntire's "20th Century Reformation Hour" were major groups, with deep roots in Protestant fundamentalism. As Hargis said, "I fight Communism . . . because it is part of my ordination vows, of my creed."[8] In his publication, *Christian Crusade*, he states:

> Christian Crusade's fight against Communism is Christ's fight. Christ is using this Movement. The very fact that Christian Crusade has existed

through fourteen years of opposition from powerful forces in high and low circles is proof that it is of God . . . I know we are on the right track, getting the job done for Jesus.[9]

In discussing the connection between religion and politics, which tends to exist among radical right groups, Murray Havens states that most of these groups "would substitute for religious tolerance an insistence on uniform acceptance not only of Christianity but of their particular highly dogmatic version of Christianity."[10] Their urging of Protestant fundamentalism merges smoothly with appeals for maximum cultural conformity based on small-town and rural America, an explicit anti-intellectualism, and a defense of the *status quo* so far as economic and racial disparities are concerned.

It is interesting that while most authors, who have analyzed radical right groups, note the congruence and close association between right-wing political views and fundamentalist Protestant religion, not all of them carry out much analysis of the relationship. However, John Redekop discusses several intimate connections. One is a simplistic dualism. The fundamentalist sees only two categories, good and evil, with nothing in between. The radical right-winger of the 1950s saw fellow citizens as either Americans or communists, one or the other. Tolerance is only for those who do not believe strongly in anything. Hatred of evil is, therefore, perfectly logical, and heresy hunting perfectly legitimate. A second characteristic as described by Redekop, of both fundamentalism and radical right political philosophy, is a conspiratorial view of the world. Satan conspires to detour people from the path of righteousness; communism does the same. Communism actually becomes the Devil personified—or better, politicized. As a result, all political discussion takes on a strong moral fervor. Thus, politics becomes a crusade, and one's patriotism proof of a mature Christianity.

The third connection identified by Redekop is the individualistic emphasis in fundamentalism (individual salvation) and a corresponding disapproval of social action and public welfare programs, which matches the radical right's *laissez-faire* economic and political ideology. Individuals are more important than society and are capable of satisfying their wants and needs in the free enterprise marketplace. Governmental intervention here is morally wrong. Communism is, therefore, readily viewed as the epitome of evil.[11]

Although Murray Stedman is most likely correct when he contends that "there is no apparent dictate in the inner logic of fundamentalism that would necessarily predispose its followers to political authoritarianism"[12]—that is, not all fundamentalists are or will become radical right-wingers—there is nevertheless a ready alliance between the two. When they coincide, as they frequently do, the connection is easy to understand, for the religious and the political views reinforce one another. It should be noted that this connection had been highly explicit in an earlier generation as well. In the early 1920s, the spellbinding evangelist Billy Sunday convinced a lot of people that there was an extremely clever satanic plot afoot in the world, which true fundamentalist Christianity had to combat. The world conspiracy consisted of kaiserism (the First World War had just ended), bolshevism (the Communist Revolution in the Soviet Union occurred in 1917), evolutionism, higher criticism (modern biblical scholarship), and liberal theology in general—a mixture of certain theological, political, and scientific elements—all evil in their own right, according to Billy Sunday and his followers.[13]

It might be suggested that anticommunism was, in a sense, an interlude for fundamentalism, as it climbed aboard the anticommunism bandwagon. But communism was so tempting in that it was everything the fundamentalists hated. It is equally important to realize that many of the movements and ideas that fundamentalists oppose today were not serious issues then. Most people were perfectly content to discriminate against "fags"—a derisive old term for male homosexuals; abortion was clearly illegal and not widely sought; minorities were "in their place" at the back of the bus and in menial service jobs "where they belonged"; and women, too, knew their place—helpmate to a man who gave her his name and a regular paycheck. If, for some reason, the woman needed a job, she could be a nurse assistant to a male doctor but seldom a doctor herself, a teacher but seldom a principal or superintendent, a secretary but seldom an executive, a lab assistant but seldom a professor.

But, as citizen interest in the shrill variety of anticommunism of the 1950s declined, fundamentalism in its original religious form was still around and could return with a clearer focus on spiritual matters and an emphasis on personal regeneration.

The New Christian Right: Late Twentieth Century Developments

Nonetheless, by the mid-1970s, the political aspirations of fundamentalism were again stirring, as fundamentalists brought to mind again their core beliefs and remembered from where they had come. Such remembrance would in their view suggest possible political action to improve their country—a way of thinking that would affect profoundly both individuals and the corporate body of the nation. Such a waxing and waning of fundamentalist interest in political action expresses an inherent ambivalence among these religious groups. This ambivalence is best understood by the juxtaposition of two important themes in Calvinism, which is the religious parent of fundamentalism. One is that the individuals should separate themselves as much as possible from the evil world because it can contaminate and infect them spiritually. Politics is particularly suspect in this regard. Therefore, Calvinists concentrate on regeneration and making the people in a society moral, attempting to perfect the society one person at a time. The other theme is that of theocracy. That is, if a group of well-informed believers can achieve God's design for humanity by controlling the governance of a social system, then they should do so.

The so-called New Christian Right is an expression of the latter view. Fundamentalists and evangelicals saw opportunities to have a profound effect on the nation through controlling the outcome of elections, which could set the stage for later legislation and enforcement of morality as they defined it. In other words, the fundamentalists could see opportunities to apply their religious convictions to the political scene and perhaps eradicate some immoralities and create a more moral, godly society in the process. This would be just as they had kept "demon rum" boxed in somewhat for fourteen years in the early part of the century, by facilitating in a significant way the passage of the 18th Amendment that survived from 1919 to repeal in 1933.

In June 1980, the Reverend Jerry Falwell founded Moral Majority[14]— an organization with at least five primary messages and emphasis:

1. America is in a state of terrifying moral decline;
2. moral decay in this country will result in the fall of America and the rise of atheistic dictatorships if not stopped;
3. this nation is a chosen instrument of God for good in the world;
4. Christian citizens have a moral obligation and duty to vote;
5. as they vote they are to put into office candidates who pledge to support the religious principles of the Moral Majority.

It was reported that within sixteen months, Falwell's group claimed to have signed up 72,000 ministers and 4 million lay members, with chapters in every state, and had expectations of raising $5 million for support of political campaigns in 1980 alone.[15]

In addition to coming out foursquare in support of the Republican candidate, Ronald Reagan and the Republican platform he represented (they had a hand in building it), the New Right groups collectively opposed three major developments: the legalization of abortion on demand, the spread of pornography, and the tolerance of homosexuality. Three causes they championed were as follows: providing for prayer and Bible reading in public schools, nullifying the Equal Rights Amendment, and defeating liberal senators and members of Congress who were viewed as aiding and abetting moral decay. These groups set as one target for 1980 the defeat of six liberal senators.

Five of them did indeed go down in defeat in November 1980: George McGovern of South Dakota, Frank Church of Idaho, John Culver of Iowa, Birch Bayh of Indiana, and Gaylord Nelson of Wisconsin. Only Alan Cranston of California retained his seat in the Senate. During the campaign, not necessarily with the endorsement of the national organization, epithets such as "baby killer" and accusations of promoting homosexuality were commonplace at the local level. Birch Bayh's comment is typical of those concerned about the New Religious Right movement. He said, "The cause of liberty is not served by organizations that brand public officials as being immoral or anti-God simply because they may hold different views . . . These hate groups now have tasted blood . . . Step out of line one time, and they'll chop your head off."[16]

Many have referred to the platform of these groups as "single issue politics." While "single issue" may be an overstatement, at most their platforms include but a few items. What they overlook is the broad array of political issues a member of Congress or a president is called upon to deal with. Further, critics point out that with their emphasis on abortion or homosexuality or prayer in public schools, there is total silence with respect to providing justice for all, care for the needy, protection of minorities, and the like. Various religious groups have gone so far as to condemn publicly, or at least raise questions about, their tactics and program. Among others, these include some Methodist and Lutheran groups, the National Council of Churches, the American Jewish Committee, and the Jesuit publication *America*.

In all fairness, however, it should be pointed out that more liberal church people and the groups they represent, although not so well-financed or perhaps with as much support, have also been known to wage single issue campaigns—anti-Vietnam War protesting, antinuclear demonstrations, participation in the 1960s civil rights movement, and supporting the American Civil Liberties Union, are examples of these campaigns.

The Impact of the New Christian Right

What nearly everyone has wondered, with respect to American fundamentalists, is how influential and powerful they might be or might become. Are they now, or will they become, a significant political force? The answer is that they have proven themselves "significant." However, without a cultural context of crisis, such as that following the moral failures of President Clinton and the fears following 9/11, the New Christian Right would not have had the opportunities to become as influential as it is has become. Without the stumbling of the Democratic Party in the aftermath of events in President Clinton's second term, the New Christian Right would not have been able to boost George W. Bush into the Presidency in 2000 and provide him the opportunity to promote his expanded version of traditional American Civil Religion. And without the crisis of 9/11 and continuing terrorist threats, the New Christian Right could not have engineered President Bush's re-election in 2004. There simply are not enough of them and they are not likely to attract hordes of new believers. Stephen Johnson and Joseph Tamney observed already in 1982 that survey data from Middletown, concerning the 1980 presidential election, showed that Ronald Reagan won the election, not because of unified support from fundamentalists, but from highly-educated political conservatives, that is, traditional Republicans, and from people who felt that controlling inflation was the most important issue of the election.[17] In other words, conservatives come in a number of varieties and are not all alike. But sometimes they can coalesce around particular issues. Nonetheless, they will not all gather around the extreme set of issues put together by the fundamentalists.

A fear that evolved in the late 1970s and early 1980s, was that Protestant fundamentalists might control a great many elections. But evidence fairly quickly showed that a fundamentalist was far from an automatic victor in political contests, particularly at the federal level. If the person is not in other ways a wholesome candidate, with some desirable planks in their platform to provide broad appeal, there will not be enough votes from the fundamentalist extremists to elect the person. In such cases, there needs to be a substantial number of votes from more moderate, traditional Republicans and Independents as well. Johnson, Tamney, and Burton analyzed the campaign and vote for a U.S. Congress seat from Indiana where the Republican candidate—a fundamentalist who campaigned on three fundamentalist moral issues—was defeated very emphatically. They note that while there is a pool of voters who, besides being politically and economically conservative, have a strong commitment to a traditional moral code centering on conservative family issues (called social traditionalists), they are few in number. "Such people can decide a close election, but they cannot form the nucleus of a winning constituency."[18]

It had become clear that Christian fundamentalists were not the force they were once thought by many to be. The fundamentalists began to recede in the late 1980s. Their candidate for president, Pat Robertson, did not become popular with the voters and withdrew during the primaries in 1988; several of NCR's prominent televangelists were discredited (Jimmy Swaggert and the Bakkers); the Moral Majority, founded in 1980 and renamed the Liberty Federation in 1986, ceased to exist in 1989; and a focus of theirs—prayer in public schools—had declined in national interest.

But, an Evangelical Christian George W. Bush, was elected President of the United States in 2000 (though barely) and re-elected in 2004 again in a close race against the Democratic candidate, John Kerry. And there is a Republican majority in both houses of Congress. The New Christian Right has felt greatly rejuvenated in the twenty-first century and has been emboldened to continue to pursue issues it holds dear.

So, indeed, the New Christian Right has maintained strong influence in the second election in the Third Millennium, but may have over-reached itself in the afterglow of the re-election of President G.W. Bush in 2004, as it and the Republican Party defined their victory as a "mandate" that was more optimistic than realistic. What we appear to have is another rejuvenation of the New Christian Right and its favorite positions on issues that will again wane as their minority status in the American population becomes evident once again.

Nonetheless, one primary issue stubbornly refuses to be submerged: the abortion issue. This debate continues vigorously and is in the forefront of political debate. It remains a vital issue because it is not only a concern of fundamentalists. Significant numbers of other religious groups, particularly Roman Catholics, share both concern and position with the fundamentalists on this issue. And, of course, there is now another galvanizing issue—that of same-sex marriage that will be a prominent political issue at local, state, and national levels for years to come.

Focus on the Abortion Issue

Protestant fundamentalists have been active in the abortion controversy for many years. This is not simply following the *Roe v. Wade* decision in 1973, but earlier as well. But the right-to-life movement, bolstered by Protestant fundamentalists, gained momentum once abortion on demand was legalized by the *Roe v. Wade* decision. Few citizens in America are unaware of the opposition of Christian fundamentalists to abortion. Television and the daily and weekly press inform us frequently of the demonstrations, marches, and picketing of abortion clinics by the right-to-life groups; television ads against abortion blanket the country; and flyers and brochures are handed out everywhere.

Until 1993/94, these activities remained mostly nonviolent, except for occasional shoving matches between a few pro-life and pro-choice protagonists or passive resistance to arrest that has required police to drag or carry pro-life protesters to waiting police vehicles for transport to jail.

In all fairness, it is important to note that the majority of pro-lifers subscribe to nonviolent tactics. And most have condemned the violence directed against abortion clinic personnel that began in 1993. Nonetheless, the killings of a Florida medical doctor and his escort by Paul Hill, have brought to light some explicit support—at least in principle—for physical violence against those performing abortions. The Reverend Michael Bray, himself convicted of destroying seven abortion clinics in the mid-1980s, became a spokesman for Paul Hill and those who were convinced they had Biblical authorization for their murderous violence against those performing and protecting abortions. Reverend Hill used a verse from Psalms 91: "You will not be afraid of the terror by night, or of the arrow that flies by day" as affirmation that his act was divinely sanctioned.[19] The editor of *Religion Watch* summarizes a report by Lauri Goodstein in the *Washington Post* (13 August 1994) by noting that radical pro-lifers have become more public. They identify the killing of abortion personnel as "justifiable homicide" and cite as their authority the Bible, the Holocaust, the fight to end slavery in the last century, and the concept of a "just war."[20] This submovement among prolifers deliberately "went public" when thirty-two activists signed a petition at the request of Paul Hill, expressing their view that killing abortion personnel is justifiable homicide.

Religion Watch goes on to summarize Goodstein's article, by pointing out that groups exist within the pro-life ranks that support the extreme tactic of homicide. Advocates for Life Ministries are the most visible. And a new group, American Coalition of Life Activists, which split off from the group Operation Rescue, has refused to condemn Hill's action and continues to speak positively of him, despite the group itself not explicitly approving murder of abortion doctors.[21] A fringe of radical pro-lifers certainly exists. But it is important to note that all major pro-life groups have publicly condemned Paul Hill's extreme actions.

A few months after the Hill killings, there was another occasion of fatal violence. In Brookline, Massachusetts, on 30 December 1994, John C. Salvi III killed two receptionists and wounded five other people who worked at or were present at an abortion clinic. He escaped and went on to Norfolk, Virginia, where he shot out windows in an abortion clinic. He was arrested there. The Associated Press reports a demonstration of support for Salvi in Norfolk, organized by Pro-Life Virginia, where speakers and signs thanked Salvi for what he did in Brookline.[22] Mr. Salvi was convicted of first degree murder in 1996 and sentenced to life in person where he subsequently committed suicide.

Brief Reflection

A few words of reflection before going on to Jewish Fundamentalism: In Protestant Fundamentalism, we continue to see the classic fundamentalist perspective, which is to restore traditional Christian religious values as the rules and norms by which citizens live. Abortion is, of course, not the only issue, though it is certainly the most explosive. In fact, as the campaigning of candidates of all parties, but particularly the Republicans, rolled up and down and across the country, and as the political campaigns preceding the 2000 Presidential election evolved, the abortion issue became a litmus test that many voters faithfully used to judge the attractiveness of various candidates. Some candidates gained favor and others lost favor to a very significant degree on this factor alone. But there also continued to be the traditional doctrines that were put together in *The Fundamentals* back in 1910—the virgin birth, divine inspiration, Jesus' resurrection from the dead, and so forth. And they continue to be excited about either replacing or paralleling evolution with creationism in the public schools, they seek prayer in the public schools, and they vigorously oppose homosexuality.

The Distinction between Evangelicalism and Fundamentalism

One more point about Protestant Fundamentalism before we move on to other fundamentalisms—that is to distinguish between evangelicalism and fundamentalism, which are designations used interchangeably by some. A major reason the terms are often used interchangeably is that both are movements or sets of groups that are appropriately called conservative Christian or conservative Protestant, and both subscribe to the same core beliefs and would equally defend the list of orthodox beliefs mentioned earlier, which are at the heart of fundamentalism. But there are differences within an array of subcategories of conservative Christianity known as fundamentalists, evangelicals, and even some conservative subgroups within mainline Protestant groups, such as Orthodox and Bible Presbyterians and the Wisconsin Synod and Missouri Synod Lutherans. While the latter mainline Protestant groups tend not to associate with or self-identify with the fundamentalists and evangelicals, and although they are not particularly active politically, they certainly qualify as conservative Protestants and contribute to the confusion that surrounds the application of the designations "conservative Christian," "fundamentalists," "evangelicals," "new Christian right," and "born-again Christian."

Nonetheless, it still makes some sense to think primarily of the fundamentalists and the evangelicals as the major group components of the New Christian Right. As we discussed earlier in this chapter, fundamentalism arose around the turn of the nineteenth into the twentith century, in direct response to liberalizing theological tendencies within mainline Protestantism and gained considerable national attention in the 1920s. Christian Smith identifies the evangelicals as a more recent movement, dating from the early 1940s, when a group of moderate fundamentalists, grown weary of that tradition, began to pull away with reform in mind. Smith identifies three primary motivating ideas that were central. First, they believed that traditional fundamentalism, in its zealous attempt to restore and preserve doctrinal purity, was seriously neglecting the primary Christian task of spreading the Gospel of salvation (the word *evangelical* comes from the Greek noun *evangelium*, meaning gospel/good news). Second, led by many scholars and intellectuals among them, they wanted to bring a "distinctive and respectable Christian voice" to the major intellectual debates of the day. But they were frustrated with the anti-intellectualism of their fundamentalist heritage, even embarrassed by it. Third, they believed that conservative Christians should be politically active in convincing others that "Jesus Christ was the answer for the world's social, economic, and political problems."[23]

Thus we see the evangelical wing of theologically conservative Protestantism as a reforming movement being led by respected conservative intellectuals that emerged out of fundamentalism, with a dual focus on preserving doctrinal orthodoxy but also engaging the world, both to bring it the Christian Gospel of salvation but also to improve its social and moral order.

The Christian Right we see today is therefore an amalgam of old-line fundamentalists and more socially engaged, yet doctrinally orthodox evangelicals who continue to argue among themselves on various issues and only fairly recently have come to see opportunities to have an impact on the political process in America. And it remains challenging to separate the two movements, because they now proceed in mostly parallel lines. Although we can clearly distinguish Billy Graham (evangelical) from Jerry Falwell (fundamentalist) and distinguish the fundamentalist base of a hundred years ago from the more politically engaged evangelicalism of today, it is also appropriate to see them merged as the *New Christian Right*. That designation is appropriate and enables discourse about political events and influence, so long as we know and keep in mind that Christian fundamentalism and evangelicalism are not true synonyms.

JEWISH FUNDAMENTALISM

As mentioned earlier, there are fundamentalist tendencies and movements within all the major religions of the world. If we see fundamentalism in some significant degree to be a reaction among religious faithful to modernity and secularization, then as a society modernizes, fundamentalism will emerge regardless of the religious system that is dominant in the society.

Samuel Heilman and Manachem Friedman describe fundamentalist Jews in ways that are both similar to and different from descriptions of Protestant fundamentalists. They are similar in that they believe the fundamental truths of their religion are unchanging and their religion, as lived and applied today, is part of an unbroken tradition that began with the Old Testament prophets and moved through history until today.[24] But they are quick to note that an important ingredient is not necessarily implicit in what has just been described as unchanging doctrine and practice. That is "a refusal to endorse or legitimate contemporary Western culture."[25] Ian Lustik provides an excellent definition in his discussion of fundamentalisms. What distinguishes them anywhere and in any religious context "is their relative unwillingness to compromise with reality in seeking to implement sweeping changes in society ordained by whatever transcendental sources of ultimate value they acknowledge."[26] This certainly fits as a definition of American Fundamentalism, especially as it has evolved over the past century. Though it began with strictly religious reforms in mind, it soon began to want to impose those traditional religious values, and what they saw as direct implications from them on their fellow citizens—the Prohibition Amendment, ban on abortion, and so on.

Similarly with Israel, particularly as seen with the Gush Emunim (to be discussed shortly), whose return to orthodox Jewish theology directed them to take part in restoring the boundaries of traditional Israel. It bears mentioning that Leon Wieseltier prefers not to describe any recent development in Judaism as fundamentalist. He would call them Jewish restorationists.[27] While that term picks up nicely the theme of restoring the old land boundaries of ancient Israel, it lacks the implication or flavor of the religious dimension that "fundamentalism" implies in worldwide understanding.

The Origins

A designation commonly accorded these fundamentalist Jews is "ultra-orthodox." But Heilman and Friedman feel that a Hebrew word *haredi* (*haredim* in the plural) is more apt. Its literal meaning is "those who tremble" at God's word. It came to refer to anyone who was punctilious about his or her religion. More recently it has been used to identify Jews who, in their beliefs and lifestyle, went further than simply *orthodox*.[28] In the pages that follow, we will use it interchangeably with *Jewish fundamentalists*.

It is helpful to know (as outlined in Chapter 14) that what we commonly refer to as Jewish Orthodoxy is itself a relatively recent phenomenon and emerged as a self-conscious reaction to what some perceived to be an erosion of traditional Judaism, with the birth of Reform Judaism in central and Western Europe in the last third of the nineteenth century. The Orthodoxy movement was a reaction against the erosion of traditional Jewish life, customs, and ideas that supporters of Reform Judaism were leading away from. An emphasis on the past and one's cultural tradition embedded in that past, was giving way to a focus on the future and to embracing change and "progress."

Many of the Orthodox talked about getting along with Gentiles and, of necessity, interacting with them in a mutually productive way. But in the process, Orthodox Judaism was becoming a religious denomination (one religious group among many) and the old way of life was disappearing. The *haredim* emerged to oppose the rampant acculturation of Jews within the Gentile world and the loss of traditional culture, beliefs, and practices. They stressed separation from the Gentiles as much as possible, and absolute devotion to and dependence upon a rabbi, whose authority was firm and unquestioned. As they did so, they felt they were following God's demands and remaining committed to the fundamentals of the religion God had established with his chosen people of old, the Jews.

The Subgroups

Two groups of *haredim* opposed much of the Zionist philosophy that gained strength from the 1920s through the Second World War and progressed to the establishment of the Jewish state of Israel in 1948. Some *haredim* were against the focal goal of Zionism, namely establishment of the Jewish state. This was true of the Eda Haredim (the Pious Community).

The Eda Haredim   The Eda Haredim gained strength and momentum following the establishment of the state of Israel. Their opposition was in significant part, because of the secular nature of the Zionist movement.

By way of contrast, another prominent fundamentalist group, the Agudat Israel, felt it could best reclaim Jews for the orthodox way by working from within the system. And they could claim some successes. For example, the Agudat Israel obtained from the David Ben-Gurion government, an agreement that safeguarded the Sabbath as a national day of rest and provided religious education, both public and private, as a citizen's right, as well as other controls by Orthodox religion throughout the society.[29]

The Eda Haredim were more confrontational and were ready to do battle with modern culture wherever they perceived contradictions with traditional religious practices and dicta. They opposed drafting young women for the Israeli army and supported deferment for students in Orthodox schools and seminaries (yeshiva); they opposed archeological digs that they claimed desecrated ancient cemeteries; they wanted bus shelter walls stripped of posters they considered too sexually explicit; and they opposed the sale of books they defined as heretical in neighborhood stores.[30]

One is struck almost immediately with parallels to the Christian fundamentalist groups in the United States, who at various times have objected to certain books on assigned reading lists in public schools or available in public libraries, television programs defined as offensive, the Equal Rights Amendment before Congress and state legislatures, pornographic magazines on display in drugstore magazine racks, the operation of abortion clinics, and so on.

As with American Protestant fundamentalists, there are many subgroups among the Jewish fundamentalists. It is hardly a unified movement. It is also not extremely large. The *haredim* are a rather small minority of Orthodox Jews, who are themselves a minority among Jews and who comprise only 12 percent of American Jewry and 20 percent of religious Jews in Israel. Thus, of about 12 million Jews worldwide, at most a half million could be called fundamentalists.[31]

The Gush Emunim   Then there are the Jewish fundamentalists who hold to Orthodox beliefs and ritual, but embrace Zionism as a major focus of their lives and activities. The Gush Emunim, a fundamentalist group with a rather short but lively and continuing history, is frequently in the news and is widely known. Although its roots were in a secretive youth movement of the 1950s (Gahelet),[32] it began in the mid-1970s and has been deeply committed to direct political action and violence. It has become, in the words of Gideon Aran, "one of the most resourceful, determined, and efficient groups in Israeli politics."[33] If one were to observe that such an assertion sounds like the Gush Emunim is really a political party or radical political action group, one would miss its essence, which is avowedly and self-consciously religious, as it transforms religiously committed people into "people with a proud, active high-voltage religion."[34] A tenet of their system is that nothing should be considered outside the boundaries of religion.

As such, the group goes beyond where most fundamentalist groups would venture in promoting with full-powered religious fervor something that many would suggest is actually its competition, namely, the secular political ideology of Zionism. While that overlap may, at one level be its genius and the source of its attractiveness to some people, it borders on a rare, if not impossible, union of opposites. In this context, it is easy to understand Aran's depiction of Gush Emunim as radical. He points out that it is radical in at least three senses:

> First, in settling the Greater Land of Israel, it disregards, as a matter of principle, Arab rights and interests. Second, it consistently, although indirectly, strives to impose religion on secular sectors, using power to dominate state and society and make them abide by the movement's particular norms. Third, the subtlest and deepest sense of Gush Emunim's radicalism refers to the symbolic system, which shapes its worldview. Gush Emunim's revolutionary notion of Judaism presents Zionism as an integral component of religion, if not its axial one. Gush Emunim claims that just as there is no Zionism that is not religious, there can be no Jewish religion that is not Zionist. Moreover, it argues that Zionism is the core and essence, the critical criterion of Judaism. The traditional definition of Judaism is broadened to encompass nationalism, perceived as an elevation and perfection of conventional religious Judaism. These three levels of Gush Emunim radicalism coalesce in the perception of ultimate sanctity in a militant regional policy.[35]

While Israel is essentially a modern secular society, with political leaders frequently drawn from ranks of nonreligious Jews, the Gush Emunim has made religion a significant moral and political factor, despite numbering only a few thousand members. It was formed in 1974, in the aftermath of the Yom Kippur War of October 1973. It was clearly committed to conservative religious principles and because of them dictating, as they saw it, Israel must gain sovereignty over what can be identified as the original "Land of Israel." Its goal was to establish small Jewish settlements all along the West Bank of Judah and Samaria, as their contribution to their ultimate goal of fulfilling Israel's geographic destiny. This goal they called religious, though others might appropriately call it political.[36] Although they steadfastly maintain their religious nature and eschew any designation as a political party or organization, they are recognized by others as a political force performing political functions nonetheless. In a real sense, then, they continue to follow the urgings of two early leaders, Rabbi Abraham Isaac Kook and his son, Rabbi Zvi Yehuda Kook, who "called Zion away from the drift of secularism and back to its spiritual moorings."[37]

And so, in the groups that make up the Eda Haredim and the Gush Emunim, one observes the two major branches of Jewish fundamentalism. While they have common purposes in restoring Jewish religion to its roots and traditions, they hold opposing views of the state. The former deprecate the state and push it into the background in importance and allegiance. The latter elevate the state and would extend its purview of influence.

ISLAMIC FUNDAMENTALISM

In analyzing Islamic fundamentalism, it is important to note something we have pointed out before in our discussion of various forms of fundamentalism—there are always two foci. The one can be viewed as a religious focus and it contains the perspectives and the language and terminology that constitute the fundamentalist religious rhetoric. The other is more purely political. While other fundamentalisms always include both the religious and political dimensions, such a dual emphasis and application is particularly prominent in Islam and the societies where Islam is dominant.

Ambivalent Responses to Modernity

The Islamic response to modernity has been profoundly ambivalent. On the one hand, modernity challenged long-held religious traditions and practices as, for example, maintaining the traditional place of women in society. Yet modernity brought the promise of swift movement from a Third World country to at least, in some ways, a first world country, because many Islamic countries had the wherewithal (oil) to buy into modern technology in a significant way. In addition, Muslims were not averse to success and being able to buy the luxuries that industrialization and modernization could provide and produce.

But when success was not great enough or did not come quickly enough, and the divine promise of earthly success was not being fulfilled, there could be two causes some Muslim leaders were quick to suggest. Either people had drifted too far from divine precepts and needed to be led back into line by religious leaders, or outside interference and involvement, particularly from the western nations with their technology, needed to be resisted and overcome. But which would it be?

Ninian Smart[38] talks about three ways Muslim societies have responded to modernization and the innovation of science and technology. One was to accept the idea that technology and economic advances of industrialization were related to secular, Enlightenment values. Therefore, there is little need for religion. It might even hold us back. So, throw off the dead hand of religion. This was the response of Muslim Turkey. That is, join the West.

The second response described by Smart, was to adopt a Muslim equivalent of liberal Protestantism. That involves replacing part of the Muslim tradition called Sharia, which is the law that covers both public and private life, with Western-style law. Religion is still honored and practiced, but selectively—what we have seen in Muslim Egypt.

The third option is to conclude that the reason Islamic nations have fallen behind the West in developing technology and harnessing natural resources, was the faithlessness of so many Muslims, and that the way to restore the old Muslim glory was to restore genuine Muslim piety.

But this option, which one immediately recognizes as the response of classical fundamentalism, can follow several distinct directions. The first is much like that of a sect, which wants to return to the true, authentic, pure religion of the past that gets back to the basic principles, practices, and beliefs that the founder described. For example, in Egypt there is a group that calls itself "The Society of Muslims": but is identified by the press and the public as "Excommunication and Flight." The group gained this identity by "excommunicating" most Egyptian Muslims, whom they accused of idolatry. By idolatry, they meant that most Egyptians had forsaken traditional Muslim piety, belief, and commitment and now "worship" usury, fornication, prostitution, mixing the sexes in public functions, and drinking alcohol. Some of this fundamentalist group isolated themselves from these evils by withdrawing ("flight") to caves on the edge of the desert, thereby also avoiding payment of taxes and conscription into the military.

But even among these Excommunication and Flight fundamentalists, a subgroup formed. Its constituents desperately sought the purity of original Islam but also pursued a strategy of violence against the government, which allowed the above-named abandonments of traditional Islam. Their acts of violence included kidnapping and assassination of government officials.[39] In other words, political reform was being called for. That is, there were two linked goals—religious reform and political reform.

The Ayatollah Khomeini: Fundamentalist or Populist Politician?

This pairing could not be more evident than in the fundamentalism represented by modern-day Iran and the leadership of the late Ayatollah Khomeini. While much of the rhetoric has been religious and has called for a return to pure, original Islam, the motivation for such rhetoric stems in large measure from opposition to western forces, which exerted economic and political influence and that has shored up repressive political regimes. It is more than an appeal to return to the fundamentals of religion; it is also a call to restore political and economic independence and rule by the citizenry.

We can certainly see why the Ayatollah Khomeini would be called a fundamentalist, as he led his people to return to and restore original Islam. But it was what we might call a more mid-range, third fundamentalist path, in contrast with the two options followed by the Egyptian Society of Muslims described above. He came to power, not so much because he proposed "fundamentalist" concerns, but because he emphasized a host of highly sensitive economic, social, and political issues. In doing so, he developed a new Islam that could be described as the Iranian version of political populism.[40] Ervand

Abrahamian says that Khomeini's populism had more in common with Latin American charismatic political leaders, and even the likes of Hitler and Mussolini, than with traditional Shiism and conventional Islam.

In support of this argument, Abrahamian continues:

> They all contained much radical-sounding rhetoric, but no concrete pro-grams for the redistribution of wealth. They all vociferously attacked the political establishment, the comprador bourgeoisie, and the foreign pow-ers, but remained conspicuously silent on the question of middle-class property. They all claimed to be waging war on "international ideas" and returning to "native roots"; but in actual fact they borrowed heavily from the outside world—especially from Marxism, which they perceived as a "cosmopolitan Jewish conspiracy." They saw "foreign plots" every-where, particularly among ethnic minorities, political dissenters, and university intellectuals. They all used mass institutions and a plebiscite style of politics to mobilize the public, but at the same time distrusted any form of liberalism, political pluralism, and grassroots organizations. What is more, Khomeini's populism—like populism the world over—disparaged democracy, built the state into a behemoth, reveled in the cult of death and martyrdom, and elevated the leader to the status of a demigod towering above the nation. The title *Imam,* which the revolution endowed on Khomeini, reflects this attitude, for, until the 1970s, Iranians considered this title to be sacred and used it only to refer to the Twelve Imams of early Shiism. In fact, the true fundamentalists in Iran consider it blasphemous to use this title for Khomeini.[41]

Muhammad's Predictions about the Need for Recurrent Reform

It is of interest that a call for reform in Islam is not just a contemporary phe-nomenon. John Esposito mentions the reform movements begun by the Muslim theologian Abu Hamid al-Ghazali in the early twelfth century and the jurist Taqi al-Din Ahmad Ibn Taymiyyah in the early fourteenth century.[42] Such reformers talked about the need to abort the "socio-moral corruption of Muslim society," return to the fundamentals of Islam, and restore an errant community.[43] In fact, a traditional word of the prophet Muhammad himself says: "God will send to ummah (the Islamic commu-nity) at the beginning of each century those who will renew its faith."[44]

It is possible that we are observing in Islam, a contemporary manifesta-tion of the recurring call for a return to the fundamentals of religious faith for the Muslim faithful, which the prophet Muhammad predicted long ago. But with such a call to return to Islam's religious base, there is the political dimen-sion and the powerful stimuli of modernization and other conditions, which encourage the emergence and sustenance of fundamentalism. Bruce Lawrence refers us to urban, upwardly mobile, well-educated males who are patriarchal, ascetic, anti-Western, and fervently devoted to the Qur'an, and who are also unemployed or underemployed engineers, medical professionals, or governmental bureaucrats, who seek purpose and goals from the past, in order to face the uncertain future.[45] But they live in a Third World society that has difficulty facing up to the implications of Western modernity, unable to dispel feelings of inferiority. Manning Nash goes on to say: "Until Muslims have strong and prideful identities, we can confidently expect manifestations of fundamental Islam, with varying degrees of vigor, disruption and political success."[46] Lawrence pursues this idea as follows:

> It is such shortfalls, between the first world and the third world, between the West and Islam, between dignity and displacement, that produce Islamic fundamentalists who also are often the terrorists of airport notoriety. They want to achieve power in this world. Confident that Allah will direct their deeds and increase the number of "truly" loyal Muslims, they are willing to perish in cars, buses, or trucks, on tarmacs or battlefields because they are bound by their ideals. They are certain not only of their own celestial reward but also of the ultimate terrestrial triumph of their viewpoint.[47]

The Uniqueness of Islam's Politico-Religious Fundamentalism

It is clear that as we talk about Islamic fundamentalism, we always come face to face with the reality that we are viewing a "fundamentalism" that is different from Christian fundamentalism and much of Jewish fundamentalism. The difference rests in the observation, made in Chapter 7, that Islamic fundamentalism and Islam itself are each much more politico-religious entities than are other major religions. As we discussed in Chapter 7, in classic Islam the state was God's state and all law was God's law. There could be no other. ". . . there was no church as an autonomous institution. Church and state were one."[48] It is this co-mingling of church and state in Islam and its status at the pure theocracy end of the church-state continuum, that makes the application of the term *fundamentalism* to Islam not quite parallel with fundamentalism in other religions. In other words, in Islam the fundamentalist call to return to the pure religion of the past is not so much theological as it is political. Yet it is a call and movement to bring back a number of virtues and features of the politico-religious culture of the past and put them into practice today. But what dominates among the radical Islamists is a focus on but one meaning of jihad (you may want to refer to the discussion of the various meanings of *jihad* near the end of Chapter 7) and the adoption of terrorism as an end that justifies the means, in order to destroy the evil influences of democracy and Western culture and replace them with a Muslim world order.

It is extremely important always to keep in mind that the most heinous activities perpetrated by the most radical Islamists—the Palestinian suicide bombers, the al Qaeda terrorists, and their radical fellow travelers—are actions not so much by religious fanatics or ideologues, but political revolutionaries.

For them, hatred of the West, the United States in particular, comes first; Islam and its scripture come second as a very convenient rationale for terroristic violence, as they invoke the name and authorization of god almighty, namely, Allah himself. A French sociologist, Farhad Kohosrokhavar, has published a recent book, *Les Nouveaux Martyrs d'Allah*, which is based on his study of the Iranian revolution, as well as interviews with Muslim extremists currently held in French prisons. In a recent interview, he noted that Islamic radicals and terrorists were not originally pious Muslims who were merely carrying out the dictates of their faith. Rather, their hatred of the modern world developed first.[49] Then the traditional religion of Islam was mined for justification, rationalization, and reinforcement for their terroristic jihad against the West.

As we try to put together the Islamist ideology in Chapter 7, with the concept of Islamic fundamentalism here in Chapter 8, we must agree with Nasim Jawed that fundamentalism is not a fully relevant term to apply to Islam.[50] While we can perhaps understand that the radical Islamism of Koumeini, Osama bin Laden, the al Qaeda, and the Taliban in Afghanistan can grow out of traditional Islam, it would be misleading to imply that such radical movements and leaders are legitimate, though admittedly at the outer limits of authenticity. Islam is not a religion of terror just as Christianity is not a religion of terror, despite what individuals or subgroups have done or yet will do, while claiming the name of Islam or Christianity. Jawed describes this range of interpretations and applications of Islam both succinctly and clearly.

> The Islamic faith, like all other major religions, can provide intellectual and emotional underpinnings for democracy as well as despotism, universal brotherhood as well as sectarianism. Much depends on the Muslim interpretation of Islam. Interpreted positively, with generosity of mind and spirit, the Islamic values of equality, justice, and compassion can contribute to the harmony of the civil society and thus contribute to the strength of the civic order, in theory infusing both with a sense of moral responsibility and civic virtue. Interpreted narrowly, however, Islam, like any other faith, can be used by zealots, bigots, and despots to justify discrimination, intolerance, and oppression.[51]

THE FUTURE

As we look to the future, we need to be aware that fundamentalism will continue to be with us, regardless of region, or regardless of what religion is dominant in the culture. Fundamentalism will not go away. But fundamentalism also will not "win" in the end. It has neither enough adherents to do so now, nor enough potential converts or recruits out there to provide overpowering numbers. While it will continue to manifest itself where it has already appeared and will surface in new places from time to time, fundamentalism will not attract significantly higher proportions of adherents than it already has. One reason is that the notoriety of fundamentalism is traceable in significant part to coverage by the press and the electronic media. Fundamentalism is not a theology, such as Protestant theology, Islamic theology, or Sikh theology. It is an ideology. And, as Bruce Lawrence points out, the press is "an instrument of ideologues."[52] He continues, "Fundamentalists not only want a platform for their ideas; they need outlets to enhance their influence and to register their success. Reporters, on the other hand, need stories, and fundamentalists provide lively headlines: threats from them or fears about their influence help to sustain both viewer ratings and magazine subscriptions."[53]

NOTES

1. Louis Gasper, *The Fundamentalist Movement* (The Hague: Mouton, 1963), p. 11.
2. Peter Berger, *Facing Up to Modernity* (New York: Basic Books, 1977), p. 77.
3. Ibid., pp. 71–80.
4. *The Fundamentals: A Testimony to the Truth*, vols. 1–12 (Chicago: Testimony Publishing Company, n.d. [c. 1919]).
5. James A. Speer, "The New Christian Right and Its Parent Company: A Study in Political Contrasts," in *New Christian Politics*, eds. David Bromley and Anson Shupe (Macon, GA: Mercer Press, 1984), p. 30.
6. Norman F. Furniss, *The Fundamentalist Controversy, 1918–1931* (New Haven: Yale University Press, 1954), p. 56.
7. Donald Jansen and Bernard Eismann, *The Far Right* (New York: McGraw-Hill, 1963), p. 239.
8. Billy James Hargis, television address, Fresno, CA: KAIL-TV, October 25, 1964. Quoted in John H. Redekop, *The American Far Right* (Grand Rapids, MI: William B. Eerdmans, 1968), p. 17.
9. Billy James Hargis, *Christian Crusade*, January–February, 1962, p. 3. Quoted in Redekop, *The American Far Right*, p. 18.
10. Murray C. Havens, *The Challenges to Democracy* (Austin, TX: University of Texas Press, 1965), pp. 82–83.
11. Redekop, *The American Far Right*, ibid., Chapter 10.
12. Murray Stedman, *Religion and Politics in America* (New York: Harcourt Brace Jovanovich, Inc., 1964), p. 129.
13. Erling Jorstad, *The Politics of Doomsday* (Nashville: Abingdon, 1970), p. 24.
14. While the Moral Majority is technically a political organization, not a religious group, its major leadership, membership, and support came from the New Religious Right.
15. George J. Church, "Politics from the Pulpit," *Time*, 116 (October 13, 1980): 28.
16. "Religious Right Goes for Bigger Game," *U.S. News and World Report*, 89 (November 17, 1980): 42.
17. Stephen D. Johnson and Joseph B. Tamney, "The Christian Right and the 1980 Presidential Election," *Journal for the Scientific Study of Religion* 21, no. 2 (June 1982): 123–131.
18. Stephen D. Johnson, Joseph B. Tamney, and Ronald Burton, "Factors Influencing Vote for a Christian Right Candidate," *Review of Religious Research* 31, no. 3 (March 1990): 301.
19. Mark Juergensmeyer, *Terror In the Mind of God* (Berkeley: University of California Press, 2000), p. 23.
20. Reported in *Religion Watch*, ed. Richard P. Cimino, vol. 9, no. 10 (September 1994): 3–4, from *Washington Post*, August 13, 1994.

21. Ibid.
22. *Muncie Star Press,* January 2, 1995, pp. 1, 5.
23. Christian Smith, *American Evangelicalism, Embattled and Thriving* (Chicago: Univerity of Chicago Press, 1998), p. 10.
24. Samuel C. Heilman and Menachem Friedman, "Religious Fundamentalism and Religious Jews: The Case of the Haredim," in *Fundamentalisms Observed,* ibid., p. 197.
25. Ibid., p. 198.
26. Ian Lustik, *For the Land and the Lord: Jewish Fundamentalism in Israel* (New York: Council on Foreign Relations, 1988), pp. 5–6.
27. Leon Wieseltier, "The Jewish Face of Fundamentalism" in *The Fundamentalism Phenomenon,* ed. Norman J. Cohen (Grand Rapids, MI: William B. Eerdmans Publishing Company, 1990), p. 194.
28. Heilman and Friedman, ibid., pp. 198–199.
29. Ibid., pp. 234–235.
30. Ibid., p. 240.
31. Ibid., p. 198.
32. Bruce B. Lawrence, *Defenders of God* (San Francisco: Harper & Row, 1989), p. 137.
33. Gideon Aran, "Jewish Zionist Fundamentalism: The Bloc of the Faithful in Israel," in *Fundamentalisms Observed*, eds. Martin E. Marty and R. Scott Appleby (Chicago: University of Chicago Press, 1991), p. 295.
34. Ibid.
35. Ibid., p. 296.
36. David Neuman, "Introduction: Gush Emunim in Society and Space," in *The Impact of Gush Emunim,* ed. David Neuman (New York: St. Martin's Press, 1985), p. 1.
37. Lawrence, *Defenders of God,* p. 137.
38. Ninian Smart, "Three Forms of Religious Convergence," in *Religious Resurgence,* eds. Richard T. Antoun and Mary E. Hegland (Syracuse, NY: Syracuse University Press, 1987), p. 228.
39. Richard Antoun, *Understanding Fundamentalism: Christian, Islamic, and Jewish Movements* (Walnut Creek, CA: AltaMira Press, 2001), p. 74.
40. Ervand Abrahamian, "Khomeini: A Fundamentalist?" in *Fundamentalism in Comparative Perspective,* ed. Lawrence Kaplan (Amherst: University of Massachusetts Press, 1992), p. 111.
41. Ibid.
42. John Esposito, *Islam and Politics* (Syracuse, NY: Syracuse University Press, 1984), p. 31.
43. Ibid.
44. See John Voll, "Renewal and Reform in Islamic Tajdid and Islah," in *Voices of Resurgent Islam,* ed. John L. Esposito (New York: Oxford University Press, 1983), Chapter 2.
45. Lawrence, *Defenders of God,* p. 197.
46. Manning Nash, "Fundamentalist Islam: Reservoir for Turbulence," in *Journal of Asian and African Studies* 19 (Spring 1984): 78.
47. Lawrence, *Defenders of God,* ibid.
48. Bernard Lewis, "Muslims, Christians, and Jews: The Dream of Coexistence," *New York Review of Books* (March 26, 1992): 49.
49. Jean-Francois Mayer, "Islamic Martyrs Multiply," in *Religion Watch,* ed. Richard P. Cimono, 17, no. 12 (October 2002): pp. 6–7.
50. Nasim A. Jawed, *Islam's Political Culture* (Austin: University of Texas Press, 1999), pp. 129–133.
51. Ibid., p. 150.
52. Lawrence, *Defenders of God,* p. ix.
53. Ibid., p. x.

Chapter 9

Religion
and the Economy

Religion in the Economy.

In line with an underlying principle made explicit throughout this book, namely, that religion is in a continuous reciprocal and interdependent relationship with society and its institutions, we now turn to one of society's most important institutions (some would say, *the* most important)—the economy.

We can initially observe that religion, although often legitimately viewed as a semiautonomous social system (societal institution) paralleling other institutions, is itself in various ways a part of the inclusive economic system of a society—it is an employer; it buys and sells; it owns property; it contributes to the gross national product (the amount spent annually on all goods and services). A brief look at religion as an active participant in the economy constitutes the first section of this chapter. The major section that follows looks at religion's influence on economic relationships in a society. We will, then, in a third section, conclude with an assessment of how and to what degree religion has an impact on the economy and vice versa.

RELIGION AS AN ECONOMIC INSTITUTION

Two obvious ways in which organized religion plays an economic role in most societies is as an employer (providing the economic livelihood for religious professionals and their families) and as an owner of property and a builder of facilities. Although there are no precise figures available concerning the number of persons employed by religious organizations, we do know that as of 1987, there were at least 530,763 members of the clergy in the United States.[1] But even this figure is not comprehensive, inasmuch as not all religious groups report statistics to the National Council of Churches. Conservatively, we would therefore estimate that there are at least 650,000 clergy members in the United States alone. Add to this the members of Catholic monastic orders; the tens of thousands of church secretaries, janitors, and sextons; employees of religious publishing companies; parochial school teachers, as well as clerical and secretarial staff for area, state, regional, and national denominations and ecumenical organizations; social workers employed by religious welfare agencies, and the like—and a total of well over one million families deriving part or, for many, all of their family income from religious organizations would be a conservative estimate.

In 1957, church property and endowments in the United States were valued at $13.7 billion.[2] Although there was some decline in new construction by religious groups between 1965 and 1975, the value of expenditures for such new construction has increased each year from 1975 to 1987, the last year for which data are available. Total new construction in 1987 was $2,753 million ($2,340 million in 1982 adjusted dollars).[3]

Probably even more impressive are the figures for contributions to religious groups. In 2003, the American Association of Fund-Raising Counsel estimated contributions to religious groups at $86.39 billion, or 35.9 percent of total charitable giving of $240.72 billion. Religious organizations received the most of any category (education was second at $31.59 billion and foundations third at $21.44 billion).[4] While it is not the largest business in this country or the world, religion is nonetheless a significant element in the economy, as an owner of great amounts of property and as an agent for the collection and distribution of many billions of dollars annually.

Religious organizations also engage in economic activities and enterprises that are not intrinsically religious—they own and derive income from apartment and office buildings, parking lots, factories and, of course, stocks and bonds held as endowments by local congregations, national denominations, and church workers' pension funds. Until 1969, many such "for profit" enterprises owned by churches went untaxed, because religious groups were unique among incorporated organizations in not being required to pay income taxes on "unrelated business income."[5] But the Tax Reform Act of 1969, which was actively supported by such associations as the National Council of Churches and the U.S. Catholic Conference, closed this infamous loophole. Most "horror stories" of tax preferences and abuses predate 1969 and the five-year grace period that followed. But even before the federal law went into effect, most religious groups, particularly at the local level, held no investments beyond the buildings and property in which they worshiped and performed their educational functions. They earned no "unrelated business income."

With respect to taxes on the property owned by churches, there is great variation by state and municipality. Generally, property used primarily for religious worship and education is not taxed, though some churches contribute a sum annually in recognition of the police and fire protection accorded them by the community. Land used to turn a profit for the church is often placed on the property tax rolls.

RELIGION AS A SHAPER OF ECONOMIC ATTITUDES AND BEHAVIOR

Throughout history, religious groups have faced a dilemma with regard to attempting to influence economic attitudes and behavior. On the one hand, churches have tended to treat poverty as a virtue and discourage the faithful from becoming encumbered by material goods and concerns. Certainly the Bible extols poverty in such statements as "Blessed are the poor, for they shall inherit the earth" or "How hard it is for a rich man to enter the kingdom of heaven." Buddhism extols the mendicant monk, who travels light and remains free from economic concerns, in order to engage in a life of contemplation.

Yet any religious group, particularly as its organization begins to get the least bit complex, requires funds to operate. The group then begins to get involved in economic affairs, whether it wants to or not. It finds itself grateful for substantial contributions from wealthy members. It may exact a tithe from its adherents. As at least some members rise out of poverty, it does not kick them out but perhaps even extols them for their industry and frugality. It is this tendency of religious groups to become actively engaged in economic activities, that is one of several stimuli to the formation of sects. We observed in Chapter 4, that sects tend to turn poverty into a virtue. This is what Max Weber calls a "theodicy of disprivilege" or "theodicy of escape,"[6]—that is, a rationalization and justification of one's disprivileged economic and social status as an advantage, so far as salvation is concerned. True riches and enhanced status will accrue in the hereafter, when it really counts—when it is for eternity, not just sixty or seventy years of toil and trouble on this earth.

Just as children say, "That's the dumbest toy I ever saw—I didn't want that crummy old thing anyway" of the toy they grab from another child but have to return after a stern parental reprimand, so the sectarians of low socioeconomic status are likely to define what is denied them as evil, or at least as unimportant and undesirable. Wealth, fancy clothes, "highfalutin" manners and language? Who needs them! Actually, Weber identifies three different forms that release from earthly disprivilege might take: the expectation of a better life in the hereafter (paradise or heaven); hope for oneself, or at least for one's progeny, in a new world to be created by God for the faithful, called the Messianic Age or the millennium; hope for another life or rebirth in this world that will be better or higher than the present one (the concept of transmigration of souls in Hinduism, for example).[7]

On the other hand, there is the "theodicy of good fortune" identified by Weber. Here there is theological justification for superior economic and social status. "The fortunate is seldom satisfied with the fact of being fortunate. Beyond this, he needs to know that he has the *right* to his good fortune . . . that he 'deserves' it."[8] Good fortune wants to be "legitimate" fortune. Religion legitimates the favored conditions of "religious men, the propertied, the victorious, and the healthy. In short, religion provides the theodicy of good fortune for those who are fortunate."[9]

Here we find ourselves drifting into the perspective, in which religion is seen as influenced by forces outside itself—in this case, by economic factors, which are seen as influencing religious doctrine. There is, of course, much evidence supporting this point of view, and we will look at the matter more closely in the third section of this chapter. But first let us examine how and to what extent religion affects economic attitudes and behavior.

David Moberg mentions several ways in which religion, to varying degrees of intensity and significance, affects economic attitudes and behavior. First, insofar as such personal and business virtues as honesty, fair play, and honoring one's commitments are essential in economic life, and to the extent that religion is successful in inculcating such virtues in its members, religion has an impact on the economy. Second, religion on occasion stimulates consumption. Religious holidays implicitly encourage material consumption by followers, even if it is only special candles to light and special foods to eat. Third, in emphasizing one's work as a "calling," religion (Protestant Christianity in particular) has glorified and elevated work at one's job, however menial it may be. To the extent that people internalize this view, it is likely to increase productivity. The individual worker may think along the following lines: "I'm working for God, not just for my employer or for myself. Therefore, I'd better put out a little more and do the best job possible."[10]

Vogt and O'Dea provide interesting evidence related to this point.[11] Although located in the same natural environment, the communities of Homestead and Rimrock (fictitious names) evidence quite different social systems. Rimrock, which stresses cooperative community effort and achieves great productivity as a consequence, appears to be strongly influenced by the Mormon ideology held by most of its citizens. Homestead, with its individualistic orientation and less successful farming endeavors, evidences the influence of competition and divisive Protestant denominationalism, which inhibits community-oriented cooperative efforts.

A fourth way in which religion may influence the economy, is by explicitly endorsing certain economic systems or certain types of economic or business activities. For example, Liston Pope notes that religious leaders were influential in helping establish the cotton mill industry in Gaston County, North Carolina, around the turn of the twentieth century. This was accomplished directly through supportive sermonizing and pronouncements that helped create public approval of the textile enterprise. Religion also indirectly influenced economic endeavor in Gaston County, by supporting Prohibition. With the advent of Prohibition, economic capital that had been invested in distilleries was released for investment in the textile mills. Mill workers were also slightly more likely to appear for work on Monday mornings in good condition, now that weekend "benders" were somewhat less likely to occur. Above all, religion helped the mills (and thus influenced the economy) by exerting moral influence over the workers, encouraging them to do a good day's work and to do what the boss told them.[12]

Weber's *Protestant Ethic and the Spirit of Capitalism*

Probably the greatest single contribution to the discussion of the impact of religion on the economy, is Max Weber's seminal study *The Protestant Ethic and the Spirit of Capitalism*, which has stimulated massive amounts of research and discussion since its publication in 1905. Weber's thesis is that Calvinistic Protestantism, as a theological belief system, exerted an important influence on the emergence and growth of capitalism as a mode of economic organization. Quite explicitly, Weber was trying to answer Karl Marx's assertion that society's normative system, including such phenomena as religious values and principles, in fact consists of epiphenomena produced, or at least conditioned in a primary way, by factors in the economy. Weber was essentially saying that, at the very least, the influential relationship between religion and the economy is a two-way street. Accordingly, he set out to show how religion, as embodied in Calvinism, affected the economy, as represented by capitalism.

The Prime Elements in Calvinistic Theology

In order to see the relationship hypothesized by Weber, we first need to understand a bit of Calvinistic theology. At the center of Calvinistic theology is the concept and goal of the *glory of God*—everything people do should somehow add to God's glory. Since God does not exist for people, but people for God,[13] it is not too surprising that an early Calvinist theologian has been quoted as saying that he would eagerly and joyfully be damned in hell if that would somehow glorify God.

A second central doctrine of Calvinism is that of *predestination*. This teaching speaks of the foreknowledge and, above all, the fore-ordaining by God of all people either to eternal salvation or eternal damnation. In Lutheran theology, the attempt had been to use this doctrine as a source of comfort and encouragement to the believer. The emphasis was on God's foreknowledge. God knows in advance who will become a true and faithful follower and believer and who will not. Those whom he foresees as believing, he then predestines to heaven. God does not, however, explicitly predestine to hell those whom he foresees as rejecting him of their own free will; rather, they seal their own fate, so to speak, by rejecting opportunities to become a believer. Thus, people who "see the light" later in life, even after a life of sin and godlessness, will be saved because God foresaw their ultimate conversion and had predestined them to eternal life.

In Calvinism, however, God appears a bit more arbitrary. With less emphasis on God's foreknowledge, Calvinism sees God as assigning some to one fate, some to the other. An important implication of Calvinism's version of predestination was that a person has to proceed all alone down the path of life, to meet the destiny decreed for him or her for eternity.[14] No priest, no church, no sacrament, nothing human can avail to the contrary. This is because what God has decided beforehand cannot be changed. Of course, someone who is damned should still belong to a church and observe the sacraments, because in such activities God is glorified. This is one's obligation as a human being. But it will not do the person any good, so far as his or her eternal destiny is concerned. Such activities will not change God's mind. This is so because Christ died only for the "elect" (those predestined to salvation).[15] Obviously this view is a radical departure from Catholicism, which emphasized the church, the sacraments, and the priesthood, as channels of God's gifts of hope and salvation to humankind.

A social consequence of this combination of predestination and obligation to glorify God was the encouragement of a rather extreme kind of individualism. Not only are you on your own in the sense that no other individual or group can help you change the direction of your predestined end, but you must be careful lest your relationships with people become too strong and important. You must not get carried away in involvement with, and commitment to, husband, wife, children, or friends. Your primary task is to glorify God.

We now add one more element to complete the basic theological ingredients, as Weber saw them, which provided the foundation for the Protestant (Calvinist) ethic—the concept of the *calling*. This is a concept, elaborated by Luther, which emphasized using one's secular occupation, whether farmer, artisan, soldier, king, or housewife, to glorify God and to help your neighbor, by doing a good job and faithfully carrying out your tasks. This concept taught people not to despise or belittle their job or role in life—it taught them instead to see their work as a "calling" by God. Calvinism picked up this concept and placed even greater emphasis on hard work; whatever your calling, you must carry out its duties to the best of your ability and with your last ounce of energy.

Implications for the Individual

We have to realize that the Calvinist was placed in a rather uneasy position with the combining of these three theological elements. They were to glorify God by working to the fullest in their calling, all the while aware that they had been predestined—yet not knowing whether to heaven or to hell. Hence, a highly important question in the person's mind was: Is there any way I can know or at least infer that I am one of the elect? Catholics had little problem with this question. If they were members of the church and performed at least the minimal ritual and confessional requirements, they had nothing to worry about. Lutherans also were little worried about predestination. Since predestination was viewed as based on God's offer of salvation, they had every reason to believe that they were numbered among the elect. Furthermore, they were promised the inner working of the Holy Spirit, who would develop in them a consciousness and conviction that they were specially chosen by God. True, they could "fall from grace"—but only if they lost their faith and rejected God's offered hand of deliverance. So as long as one believed and did not reject, one did not need to worry. In fact, they could be confident of salvation by God's grace.

Calvinists, however, did not have such assurance. They could not truly know or be convinced. But the Calvinist could make inferences from essentially empirical evidence—evidence of an ability consistently to perform well, of success in their calling, of the feeling that God seemed to be providing them with opportunities and was working through them. Would God be likely to choose to work through someone who was not one of the elect? The upshot was that the three theological elements mentioned earlier, in combination with a desire to know whether one was predestined to salvation, produced a tremendous drive toward action. This resulted in what Weber calls "ascetic Protestantism"—a life of strict discipline. Hard work in one's calling is the best discipline. Work is not only the best prophylactic against a sensual, immoral life but also the best means for glorifying God. Time, then, becomes infinitely valuable. Thus, one must avoid idle conversation, unproductive recreation, or more sleep than absolutely necessary in order to have maximum time for work.

Now, if you work harder than people around you, if you put in more hours at your job, if you live frugally and ascetically, you will likely be economically more successful than those around you. This is not bad. In fact, it is good—in two ways. First, this might be inferential evidence that you are one of God's elect. Second, God is being glorified. In the meantime, however, you may become rich. Now what? One dare not use such wealth for personal sensual pleasure—to buy wine, sexual favors, and frolic. It should not be used to buy early retirement from one's calling. What alternative is there, then? The answer is *investment*—investment of capital to produce more goods, which create more profits, which in turn represent more capital for investment, *ad infinitum*—which is the heart of entrepreneurial capitalism. The option of giving away the surplus in philanthropic activity was seldom recommended, inasmuch as the poor might then be distracted from doing their duty in their calling to menial but important tasks.

Implications for Economics

This returns us to Weber's thesis, regarding the effect of religious norms and patterns on economic relationships and institutions. Attempting "to ascertain whether and to what extent religious forces have taken part in the qualitative formation and the quantitative expansion of [the] spirit of capitalism over the world," Weber concludes that Calvinism was indeed just such a force. However, Weber is quick to warn that no one should be so foolish as to maintain that capitalism or the spirit of capitalism could, therefore, only have developed as a result of the Reformation or that it is a direct product of Calvinism.[16] Rather, he essentially maintains that Calvinism served an important stimulating and reinforcing function for capitalism. Calvinism did not create capitalism nor was it even absolutely necessary for the triumph of capitalism. Rather, Calvinism encouraged capitalism and, if nothing else, hastened its development in those societies where Calvinism wielded an influence.

Weber was much more careful than some of his followers in hypothesizing about the relationship between Calvinistic Protestantism and capitalism, a point not always appreciated by those critics who represent him as arguing that the former "caused" the latter.

Alternatives to Weber's Hypothesis

At this point, we will briefly consider some of the alternatives to, and modified versions of, Weber's thesis, which have been suggested. Kurt Samuelsson cites four early objections to Weber's position, raised by Felix Rachfahl four years after Weber first made it public, in a series of articles in 1905. Rachfahl first questions the validity of representing ethical-religious motivation as a crucial factor in economic activity. More reasonable factors, he suggests, are such things as the desire to enjoy life, solicitude for the family, and the urge to work for the common good, or for the nation and its welfare. Second, Rachfahl points to several limiting conditions imposed by Calvin on economic activity that, taken together, do not at all condone a free-for-all capitalism. Third, the differences between Catholicism and Calvinism, with regard to economic activity, should not be exaggerated. Catholic monastic orders, such as the Franciscans and Jesuits, were not so different from Calvinism in this respect. Fourth, Weber's distinction between Catholic and Protestant countries and cities, with regard to economic activity, are not so neatly associated with one religion or the other as Weber seems to suggest. Some supposedly Protestant capitalistic cities, for example, had strong Catholic influence.[17]

R.H. Tawney also emphasizes Rachfahl's fourth point, observing that capitalism had clearly existed in medieval Italy and Flanders (both Catholic areas) and that the capitalistic spirit was "only too familiar to the saints and sages of the Middle Ages." He goes on to point out that Catholic cities were the chief commercial capitals of medieval Europe and Catholic bankers its leading financiers.[18]

Another hypothesis is that the social situation of Calvinists, rather than their theology, encouraged their entrance into capitalistic ventures. Calvinists constituted a religious minority almost everywhere except Geneva, and in some countries and communities they were barred from governmental positions and professions, such as medicine and law. Where else to turn but to business enterprises? Thus, we observe a process similar to that affecting Jews during the Middle Ages, who undertook money-lending and money-handling positions partly by default—because Christians did not want to "dirty their hands" with such activities or break the church's laws against usury. Just as it did not mean that Jews had some kind of genetic advantage over Gentiles, so far as financial matters were concerned, so there was nothing particularly significant in Calvinist theology that was more conducive to the development of capitalism than Catholic, Lutheran, or Presbyterian theology.

Personality factors might also be suggested. Perhaps the very persons who were most energetic and independent, who were most willing to take business risks, were those most attracted by Calvinism as a theological system because of its stress on individualism and effort. That is, perhaps at least some people choose a religion because it meshes with their own value system and commitments. As such, it would be incorrect to suggest that religion produced particular economic attitudes, for example.

Tawney, questioning Weber's concept of capitalism itself, does not see Calvinism fitting into the free-for-all capitalism of the eighteenth and nineteenth centuries. Rather, Tawney credits Calvinism with providing a business ethic to a "world of small traders and handicrafts."[19] The huge fortunes required and created by capitalism were not produced merely by thrift, Tawney notes, but by exploitation, by deliberately creating "opportunities," and by cornering markets in raw materials.

As one scans four centuries of Calvinist theological writing, one is impressed with the dilemma mentioned earlier in this chapter—the dilemma of a fundamental distrust in wealth and a belief in its likely insidious undermining of fundamental Christian principles, such as "keeping oneself unstained by the world," as opposed to the religious group's need for money, in order to survive and the need to justify its members' accumulation of wealth. In this connection, some have stressed the distinction between early and later Calvinism—the theology of Calvin himself contrasted with that of later followers and interpreters. John McNeill points out that John Calvin had a profound mistrust of economic success, and he suggests that to argue that Calvin characterized the prosperity of believers as inferential proof of their election to heaven is to misinterpret completely the evidence we have of Calvin's thought, as reflected in such statements as: "Wherever prosperity flows uninterruptedly its delight corrupts even the best of us . . . Prosperity like wine inebriates men . . . Property is like rust or mildew."[20]

Indeed, only later did Calvinists rationalize economic success and interpret economic gain as a sign of virtue. It is interesting that Weber quotes extensively from Richard Baxter, a late seventeenth-century Puritan-Calvinist theologian, writing approximately 150 years after Calvin. Weber also quotes Benjamin Franklin, who was not only considerably removed in time from Calvin but was not a Calvinist theologian at all. Thus it was Baxter, not Calvin, who made such statements as, "Be wholly taken up in diligent business of your lawful calling . . . It is for action that God maintaineth us . . . Keep up a high esteem of time and be every day more careful that you lose none of your time . . . [and] if vain recreation, dressings, feastings, idle talk, unprofitable company, or sleep be any of them temptations to rob you of any of your time, accordingly heighten your watchfulness."[21]

Toward a Resolution of the Issue

While still other critiques of Weber's hypothesis could be introduced, enough have been summarized to make the point that the link between Calvinism and capitalism, if one exists at all, is far from a unitary causal one. Of course, Weber himself spoke not of cause but of strong encouragement and support—what we today tend to call *reinforcement*. Actually, most of Weber's critics grant some such supportive role for Calvinism. This is the position taken by Tawney, who says that the "capitalistic spirit," though "as old as history, found in certain aspects of Puritanism a tonic which braced its energies and fortified its already vigorous temper."[22] And Rachfahl, the first to criticize Weber's hypothesis, points out several indirect ways in which the doctrinal positions of Protestant theologians influenced economic matters. He concludes that despite important weaknesses in Weber's interpretation, the basic contention that Calvinism had an important influence upon economic activity is valid.[23] Rachfahl's observations are the following:

1. Protestantism permitted the intellect to be devoted to worldly pursuits, whereas in Catholic countries many of the best minds went into the priesthood.
2. Protestantism introduced education to the masses.
3. Protestantism reversed the tendency toward indolence and distaste for work, associated with Catholic renunciation of the world.
4. Protestantism encouraged independence and personal responsibility for one's fate—something downplayed in Catholicism.
5. Protestantism created a "higher type of morality" than did Catholicism.
6. Protestantism distinguished politics from religion more clearly than did Catholicism. This freed persons to engage in more diverse economic activities and, by tolerating a greater diversity of views, ultimately resulted in economic change.[24]

Although some of these points tend to make false or at least strained comparisons, in combination they constitute the essence of the observation made more recently by Hammond and Demerath. These writers suggest a way of salvaging Weber's thesis without having to accept all that he says. They note that the advent of Protestantism—that is, the fact that it appeared at all—implies a weakening and ultimate breakdown of medieval Catholic control, resulting in greater freedom to experiment with new political and economic forms, one of which was capitalism.[25] In other words, there is a third variable out there, or a whole set of other variables, that affected *both* Calvinism and capitalism and provided fertile soil in which both could grow.

In a very real sense, then, the success of Protestantism represented the destruction of the church type of religious organization (discussed in Chapter 4) and the introduction of religious pluralism, which is intimately associated with political, and ultimately with economic, pluralism as well. That is, people were beginning to face options and make choices—political and economic choices as well as religious ones. The positive influence of Protestantism on capitalism, is, of course, only an indirect one and must take second place to primary developments—the discovery and colonization of the New World, the expansion of trade, the second agrarian revolution that increased food production and so resulted in a labor surplus available for commercial and manufacturing occupations, the Enlightenment, political revolutions, and ultimately the Industrial Revolution itself.

Guy Swanson analyzes the relationship of Protestantism and capitalism along somewhat the same lines as Rachfahl and also as Hammond and Demerath, by seeing the general "loosening" of the social structure as the important ingredient. But for Swanson, religion is essentially the middle variable in a three-variable chain that begins with political structure and ends with social structure, of which capitalism is only one aspect. Comparing the social structures of various European states in late medieval Europe, he notes that important differences in political structure preceded and served as a base for different religious commitments (Protestantism or Catholicism). Thus, societies that remained Catholic tended to have one primary source or center of decision-making. By contrast, Protestantism was more likely to appear in those societies in which there were a variety of decision-making sources. Thus, political diversity encouraged Protestantism, and together they encouraged capitalism.[26]

Whether one agrees with Samuelsson that there is "no support for Weber's theories" and that "almost all the evidence contradicts them,"[27] or with others who hold out for at least an indirect relationship of some kind between Calvinistic Protestantism and the growth of capitalism, one conclusion seems clear: Although religion has some impact on the economy, it is likely to be indirect and to be effective only as a supportive, reinforcing ingredient in concert with others in a complex causal chain.

An ASSESSMENT OF THE RELATIONSHIP BETWEEN RELIGION AND ECONOMICS

It is clear that religion is, among other things, an economic institution—in the sense that it participates in the economy and is an economic "force" as a buyer and seller of goods and services, in the sense that it is an employer, and in the sense that it influences the buying habits of believers. Even in such relatively simple, small ways, as creating a market for devotional and "peace of mind" literature, and supporting industries that produce religious artifacts, such as religious vestments, statues, medallions, church pews, and baptismal fonts, religion has an impact on the economy of the society.

Religion's Influence on the Economy

It is important to realize, however, that the economic influence or impact of religion is seldom radical or revolutionary. It is unlikely to send the economy in new directions. The buying-and-selling and economy-stimulating role of religion in the society is both stable and predictable. It creates few new markets and demands few innovative products. Religion is a relatively stable employer, which neither stimulates nor retards economic swings of recession, depression, or inflation. It does, however, tend to respond to economic change. During the Great Depression of the 1930s, in the United States, thousands of seminary graduates of all denominations went without calls to religious vocations because congregations could not afford to hire and pay them and denominations could not afford the cost of establishing new congregations that would need clergy leaders. During the period of economic expansion, beginning in the late 1940s and continuing through the 1950s, when new congregations proliferated and when established congregations expanded their membership and programs, seminaries could not launch enough graduates into the religious sea. Demand was greater than supply.

Of course, some religious leaders occasionally exert a significant influence on the economy of the society. A prime example, though not consciously directed toward economic change, consists of the attempts by religious groups to reinforce traditional moral values. Sometimes religious groups or persons attempt to ban the sale of certain "immoral" books or curtail the distribution of pornographic films. When this happens, an obvious indirect influence on the economy is made. The most dramatic and economically influential instance of this, in recent times, is the movement leading to enactment of the Prohibition amendment in 1919. Conservative religious forces are generally credited with pushing this amendment through the states. The economic impact upon specific segments of the economy (liquor producers, wholesalers, retailers, bootleggers, and the like) was significant, though the impact on the overall economy was not that great. Eventually, minor readjustments by subunits in the economy were required, not major changes in its direction or form.

The Economy's Influence on Religion

Although we have been concentrating, in this chapter, on ways in which religion impinges on the economy, we do not mean to imply that there is no relationship between religion and the economy that proceeds in the opposite direction. In fact, many have suggested that the primary or most frequently observed relationship between religion and the economy is that of the economy influencing religion. Probably the most extreme view along these lines is the familiar perspective of Karl Marx, who saw religion—and all normative features of society, for that matter—as growing out of and reflecting economic factors and relationships. For Marx, religion was little more than a tool in the hands of the society's élite for pacifying the masses and maintaining prevailing economic patterns and the respective relationships of owners and nonowners to the means of production. First, there is the economy and a stratification system that reflects the relationship of various people to the means of production within that economy; then comes religion, both reflecting these economic relationships and reinforcing them. Although we do not subscribe to the whole of Marx's point of view, some of this perspective is implicit in Chapter 4's discussion of the importance of lower socio-economic status in sect formation. Certainly differential economic status is associated with different needs of all kinds, religious needs included. We need only recall Weber's distinction between the theodicies of escape and of good fortune, to see a relationship between economic status and religious perspective and expression.

It can hardly be accidental that most religious groups in a society implicitly, and often explicitly, support prevailing economic norms and institutional patterns. For example, one would hear few if any sermons on any given Sunday in the United States decrying capitalism. Social norms—in this case, economic norms—get absorbed into all institutions and most groups in a society, religious groups included. Although one could find as many precedents, examples, and specific injunctions in the New Testament for communal ownership, sharing of wealth, and giving to the needy till it truly hurts, as one could find for a capitalistic economic structure and private accumulation of wealth, it is not by chance that Christian churches in nonsocialistic lands usually support a capitalistic ideology. Very simply, the dominant economic norms of a society tend to be reflected by religion in that society.

We have referred before to Liston Pope's *Millhands and Preachers*. He provides some fascinating documentation of the impact of economic factors on religion. For one thing, he discovered that religion prospers as the economy prospers and expands—new churches are founded, old ones add members, and all groups tend to prosper as the economic base of the community expands, attracts workers, and provides wages for those people. Pope observes that in the mill towns in Gaston County, the mills provided land and built churches for the workers and often subsidized ministers' salaries, but at a price. Mill management expected and usually received religious support and reinforcement of their policies and ideology. At the very least, the mill churches and clergy kept silent on economic issues, sticking to "religious" concerns, thereby, of course, implicitly supporting economic policy and practice.[28]

In summary, we must repeat that although religion is definitely involved in, and a part of, the economy of the society in which it exists, its overall impact is relatively slight. Primarily, it reinforces economic norms and patterns through participation, as one among many buyers and sellers of goods and services. Although occasionally religion challenges specific aspects of economic relationships or the activities of specific economic units, its challenges tend to be of slight impact in the long run.

NOTES

1. National Council of Churches of Christ in the U.S.A., Office of Research, Evaluation, and Planning, *Yearbook of American Churches, 1987*, ed. Constant H. Jacquet Jr. (Nashville, TN: Abingdon, 1987), p. 247.

2. David O. Moberg, *The Church as a Social Institution* (Englewood Cliffs, NJ: Prentice Hall, 1962), p. 169.

3. National Council of Churches of Christ, *Yearbook*, p. 280.

4. Website, American Association of Fundraising Counsel (*www.asfrc.org*), piechart of "2003 Contributions by Type of Recipient Organization," accessed March 16, 2005.

5. Dean M. Kelley, *Why Churches Should Not Pay Taxes* (New York: Harper & Row, 1977), pp. 17–18.

6. Max Weber, *The Sociology of Religion*, trans. Ephraim Fischoff (Boston: Beacon Press, 1963), p. 113.

7. Max Weber, "The Social Psychology of the World Religions," from *Max Weber: Essays in Sociology*, ed. and trans. H. H. Gerth and C. Wright Mills (New York: Oxford University Press, 1958), p. 275.

8. Ibid., p. 271.

9. Ibid.

10. Moberg, *The Church*, pp. 170–174.

11. Evon Z. Vogt and Thomas F. O'Dea, "A Comparative Study of the Role of Values in Social Action in Two Southwestern Communities," *American Sociological Review* 18, no. 6 (1953): 645–654.

12. Liston Pope, *Millhands and Preachers* (New Haven, CT: Yale University Press, 1942), Chapter 2.

13. Max Weber, *The Protestant Ethic and the Spirit of Capitalism*, trans. Talcott Parsons (New York: Scribner's, 1958), pp. 102–103.

14. Ibid., p. 104.

15. Ibid.

16. Ibid., p. 91.

17. Kurt Samuelsson, *Religion and Economic Action: A Critique of Max Weber*, trans. E. Geoffrey French (New York: Harper & Row, 1961), pp. 8–9.

18. R. H. Tawney, *Religion and the Rise of Capitalism* (Gloucester, MA: Peter Smith, 1962), pp. 84, 316.

19. Tawney, *Religion*, p. 31.

20. John T. McNeill, *The History and Character of Calvinism* (New York: Oxford University Press, 1954), p. 222.

21. See Weber, *The Protestant Ethic*, pp. 262, 260, 261.

22. Tawney, *Religion*, pp. 226–227.

23. Quoted in Samuelsson, *Religion and Economic Action*, p. 10.

24. Ibid.

25. N. J. Demerath III and Phillip E. Hammond, *Religion in Social Context* (New York: Random House, 1969), p. 150.

26. Guy E. Swanson, *Religion and Regime* (Ann Arbor: University of Michigan Press, 1967).

27. Samuelsson, *Religion and Economic Action*, p. 154.

28. Pope, *Millhands*, Chapters 8 and 9.

Chapter 10

Religion and the Class System

Expressions of religion vary by social class.

In Chapter 4 we introduced the topic of the relationship between religion and social class (social stratification), in outlining differences between denominations and sects. In fact, we observed that one of the dominant features of sectarian religion is its close association with lower- or working-class problems and life situations, together with the responses of persons of low social status to those problems and situations.

In generalizing from investigations into the relationships between religion and social class, sociologists have made the primary observation that there are important differences in religious meaning related to social class/status. That is, religion tends to perform at least somewhat different functions for people in different classes. Or, put another way, people tend to seek or construct different things in religion depending on their social class position.

Such assertions that stress the importance of social class with regard to religion should not really surprise us, inasmuch as nearly every beginning student of sociology becomes aware that one of the most significant variables in social life is social class/status. Although not strictly determinative, one's social class/status position dramatically influences one's behavior, attitudes, and aspirations—that is, both what one thinks and what one does throughout life. Depending upon peoples' social class origins and lifetime position in the stratification system, they will find their lives affected in a multitude of ways—voting propensities, likelihood of psychosis, amount of travel, attitudes toward social issues, age upon marriage, size of family, sexual behavior, even life expectancy. Small wonder, then, that important relationships between social class and religion have also been found. Differences by social class levels can be seen in differential affiliation with various religious groups, type and degree of involvement in the activities of religious groups, perceptions of the purposes and functions of religion for people, motivation for joining and belonging to religious groups, religious knowledgeability, and the like.

DIFFERENCES IN RELIGIOUS MEANING AND EXPRESSION AMONG SOCIAL CLASSES

A classic distinction, regarding differences in the functions of religion by social class, is that made by Karl Marx. In defining religion as the "opium of the people," he was actually drawing an implicit distinction between the religion of the bourgeoisie (property-owning capitalist) and that of the proletariat (working class). For the proletariat, in Marx's view, religion is a sedative, a narcotic that dulls people's sensitivity to and understanding of the plight of their life situation; it provides an escape from the harshness of reality. But more, as Marx wrote: "Religion is the sigh of the oppressed creature, the mind of a heartless world, as it is the spirit of unspiritual conditions . . . the removal of religion as the illusory happiness of the people is the requirement for their real happiness."[1]

By way of contrast, for the bourgeoisie and élites in society, Marx contended, religion serves both as a tool of oppression—a means of placating and keeping the proletariat in line—and as a rationalization and justification for the élite's own position of power and privilege. Inasmuch as Marx viewed the normative aspects of social life as deriving from the most fundamental fact and relationship in society—namely, the economy—religion becomes really nothing more than an expression of prevailing economic relationships and thus, in the capitalistic economy, a means of preserving and reinforcing class distinctions. The intertwining of capitalism and prevailing religions is so complete, and the alienation of people from their true destinies so truly reflected in religion, that Marx's associate, Engels, could predict that religion would disappear when the prevailing capitalistic economies disappeared.[2]

Although Max Weber objected to the unidirectional nature of the relationship that Marx portrayed, between the economy and social norms and values (including religion), and although he wrote *The Protestant Ethic and the Spirit of Capitalism,* in large part to refute or at least modify or offer an alternative to Marx's theory, Weber actually held much the same view of differential functions of religion for the various social classes. We have already spoken of Weber's distinction between the religion of the underprivileged and that of the privileged, underlying the concepts *theodicy of despair or escape* and *theodicy of good fortune.*[3] In the first case, one thinks of the proletariat, for whom religion promises release and some kind of eventual "salvation" if they can only endure and remain faithful. Interestingly, according to Weber, the need for compensation and hope in the face of an adverse existence is relatively seldom colored by resentment or rebellion. In other words, some of the underprivileged appear to be satisfied that hell is reserved for wealthy sinners (recall our earlier discussion of the sect in Chapter 4). The privileged classes, however, learn and express religious justification of their good fortune and emphasize their "blessings" as evidence of the favor with which God looks upon them. Wealth and privilege for them are not detrimental to their salvation, but an indication not only that all is going well for them now but that it is likely to continue to be so in any future life.[4]

Liston Pope discovered similar differences by social class, in his study of Gaston County, North Carolina. This county became an important textile mill center in the 1920s and 1930s, attracting thousands of unskilled and semiskilled laborers for the mills. Early during this period, a division of residents between "uptown" people and mill workers was made—a distinction roughly corresponding to Marx's bourgeoisie and proletariat and to Weber's privileged and underprivileged. Religious behavior and ideology differed rather markedly between these two major segments of the population. Pope described the religion of the mill workers as follows:

> In the theology of the mill worker, the world is a great battlefield on which the Lord and the Devil struggle for each individual soul. The "blood of Jesus" and the reading of the Bible turn the tide of victory toward the Lord. As one mill minister summarized it, "You have to carry a bucket of blood into the pulpit to satisfy these people." The principal sins, in the eyes of mill villagers, are such uptown "worldly amusements" as playing cards, dancing, gambling, drinking, and swimming with members of the opposite sex.
>
> . . . But the worker also looks to his church to find transvaluation of life, which may take the form of reassurance or of escape, or both. By affirmation of values denied in the economic world, the church provides comfort and ultimate assurance; in its religious services it often affords escape temporarily from the economic and social situation in which workaday life must be spent. The difficulties of life for the mill worker in this world help

to explain the noteworthy emphasis on otherworldliness in his churches. Most of the hymns and sermons in village churches point toward a more placid state and have little concern with mundane economic or social relations . . . A well-loved stanza, typical in ideas of many others, says:

> While some live in splendid mansions,
> And have wealth at their command,
> I'm a stranger and a pilgrim
> Passing through this barren land.[5]

In short, religion for mill workers provides a relief or escape from the harshness of their lives. For an hour or two, once or twice a week, they can transcend the mundane, and focus on a future that promises to be far better than the present.

Pope points out, by way of contrast, that "if religion in the mill churches is largely an escape from economic conditions, religion in the uptown churches is to a considerable degree a sanction of prevailing economic arrangements."[6] Pope reports that major sins for the uptown church members include sexual immorality, breaking one's word, not paying one's debts, engaging in "shady business," and failing to carry out one's civic and social obligations.[7] Although religion attempts to invade the personal life of the mill worker, religion is not to meddle in the private lives of the middle- and upper-class town residents. Pope suggests that "greater economic security breeds personal independence."[8] According to Emile Pin, such independence and individualism are also major features of the religion of the bourgeoisie. Pin states that individualism characterizes essentially every aspect of the life of the bourgeois, "who has reached, through his own efforts, a worldly 'salvation,' does not depend on religion to regulate his existence, but rather appeals to it only to assure the continuation of this salvation in the other world."[9]

Pope points out that for the privileged classes in Gaston County, religion is, for the most part, a specialized sphere of life. Their religious attitudes, as he observes them, are:

- that a man ought to belong to a church, and should attend as often as convenient, and should bear his part of the financial burden;
- that churches are essential to the welfare of the community;
- that there is no use in getting all wrought up or emotional about religion;
- that if a person lives as decently as he can, that's all that God can expect of him;
- that a minister ought to be a good fellow in his private life, joining civic clubs, attending baseball games, etc.;
- that a minister ought to be a leader in all community enterprises, such as projects sponsored by the Chamber of Commerce;
- that religion ought not to meddle in politics, except where moral issues, such as prohibition, are involved;
- that Holy Rollers are ignorant, and are to be pitied;
- that mill churches meet the needs of mill workers very satisfactorily.[10]

Pope summarizes by saying, "The role of the uptown minister, and of his church, is not to transcend immediate cultural boundaries but to symbolize and sanction the rightness of things as they are."[11]

DIFFERENTIAL DENOMINATIONAL AFFILIATION BY SOCIAL CLASS

As would be expected, differences in the meaning and expression of religion by social class are reflected in denominational affiliation—that is, denominations differ in their social class composition. An indication of class differences is suggested in Table 10.1. From National Opinion Research Center data, gathered from a representative national sample of U.S. adults over a 32 year period, we see that there are dramatic differences by denomination in the proportion of members who have completed at least four years of college.[12] Jews are clearly more likely than any other major religious group in the United States to have graduated from college. Specifically, they are over two and one-half times as likely as Roman Catholics, and nearly five times as likely as Baptists to have reached that educational level.[13]

More detailed and expanded data, also from the National Opinion Research Center samples in the 1970s through to 2004 (presented in Table 10.2), reaffirm the higher status position of Jews, Episcopalians, and Presbyterians, with Catholics and several major Protestant groups trailing behind. Note that the data in Tables 10.1 and 10.2 are cumulative over a 32-year period and as such do not show us possible year-over-year changes in rankings among religious groups during that time period. Also, by pooling data from the 1970s, when fewer people graduated from college than do

TABLE 10.1 Proportion of Denominational Membership in 1998 Who Have Graduated from College

Denomination	Percent Graduated College
Jewish	49%
Episcopalian	38
Presbyterian	31
No Religion	20
Roman Catholic	18
Lutheran	17
Methodist	12
Baptist	10

Source: 1972–2002 General Social Survey Cumulative Datafile (National Opinion Research Center, Chicago), compiled from Internet access 24 March 2005.

TABLE 10.2   Status Differences along Two Dimensions among Major U.S. Religious Groups

A. Highest Educational Level Attained

| | Denomination | | | | | | |
| | B^* | L^* | M^* | C^* | P^* | E^* | J^* |
Educational Level							
Less than High School	35.7%	20.9%	22.1%	24.0%	15.0%	11.3%	10.9%
High School Graduate	50.9	57.3	55.4	34.8	48.6	44.9	19.7
Some College	3.6	4.6	4.0	23.8	6.3	5.6	26.8
College Graduate	7.0	12.3	13.2	11.8	21.0	24.0	27.0
Graduate and Professional School	2.8	4.9	5.3	5.6	9.1	14.2	15.6
(Minimum of "Some College"	13.4	21.8	22.5	41.2	36.4	43.8	69.4

B. Family Income by Denominational Affiliation

| | Denomination | | | | | | |
Income Range	B	M	L	C	P	E	J
Less than $12,500	21.3%	17.8%	12.8%	12.2	8.2%	13.2%	5.5%
$12,500–34,999	36.8	30.3	36.8	32.5	24.6	24.6	21.1
$35,000–59,999	23.6	24.1	23.3	25.4	19.4	18.9	24.2
$60,000–109,999	14.7	20.9	20.5	21.2	30.9	26.4	21.1
$110,000 and above	3.6	6.9	6.6	8.7	16.9	16.9	28.1

*The capital letters represent Baptists, Lutherans, Methodists, Catholics, Presbyterians, Episcopalians, and Jews respectively.

Source: 1972–2002 General Social Survey Cumulative File (National Opinion Research Center, Chicago). Data compiled through Internet access, March 24, 2005.

now, the percentages in the tables are slightly lower than we would see in a sample of Americans of this size surveyed today. Note further, that a salary of $110,000 in 1972 both seemed much larger and certainly had far greater purchasing power that $75,000 does today (until recently $75,000 was the inclusive upper limit income category in the NORC surveys).

Nonetheless, two observations stand out boldly from these data. First, measures of socioeconomic status (SES), i.e., achieved educational levels and annual family incomes, show dramatic differences among denominations. Second, Jews, Episcopalians, and Presbyterians, on average, consistently rank higher than those who belong to other denominations, even those that most would consider "mainline" Protestant groups. It is probably also appropriate to mention once again that the culture of groups tends to attract disproportionately from a society's social classes.

The factors underlying such class differences among denominations are many. In part, it is a self-selection process of like seeking like—of people affiliating with a church whose current members are reasonably similar to themselves. There is the theological dimension also—the theological celebration of success in this world in some religious groups versus the emphasis on otherworldly salvation in others. In large part, the class differences by denomination are a product of history. The highest status denominations in Tables 10.1 and 10.2, with the exception of the Jewish groups, have been well-established in this country for the longest periods. Thus, their members have had greater opportunities to accumulate family wealth and enhance their status. On the other hand, Lutherans and Roman Catholics are composed, for the most part, of more recent arrivals in this country, who have had less opportunity for upward mobility. The Lutherans also are predominantly rural in their constituency and hence likely to rank lower on such dimensions of status as education, cash income, and occupational prestige. Sectarians, we have earlier noted, are almost by definition more likely to be of low SES, than members of established denominations. For example, Christian Smith and Robert Faris report (also using GSS data) that members of several Pentecostal religious groups, that tend toward lower SES, are less likely on average than members of the major groups cited in Tables 10.1 and 2, to have graduated from college—only 7 percent have completed college.[14]

It is clear though that no religious group is completely class-exclusive—that is, there is a range of classes represented in every religious group. Class exclusiveness, however, is often more pronounced at the local congregational level. Thus, if a third of all Congregationalists, for example, are lower class, we would not infer that a third of all the members of every local Congregational church, or even a majority of them, are from the lower class. What it does mean is that there are some congregations with a majority of lower-class members, others with a majority of middle- and/or upper-class members. This should not be surprising inasmuch as congregations tend to attract a majority of their members from the neighborhoods in which they are located, and neighborhoods tend to be fairly class-exclusive.

This phenomenon is clearly in evidence in Pope's study of Gaston County. In 1939, Pope tallied thirty-four rural churches, only five of which had a significant minority (a minimum of 20 percent) of mill workers and none of which had a significant minority of uptown members. Similarly, of seventy-six mill churches, only one had a significant minority of rural members and only eight a significant minority of uptown members. Uptown churches were less likely to be so predominantly of one class. Yet in only seventeen of thirty-five were even 20 percent of the members mill workers, and in only three were there significant minorities of rural members. In total, only 23 percent of the churches in Gaston County had significant minority membership, and only 6 percent lacked a majority group of at least

66.6 percent.[15] Clearly, then, a religious group is very likely to represent the class constituency of the geographic area in which it is located.

Demerath has pointed out that although there is a mixture of social classes in national denominations and in their local congregations, the members of these classes may not be looking for or receiving the same things out of their affiliation and participation.[16] Demerath first reports Fukuyama's 1960 study demonstrating differences in religiosity among Congregationalists by social class. Fukuyama's data, reported in Table 10.3, show that the higher social classes are more likely than the lowest social class to express their religion in cultic and cognitive ways, whereas the lowest social class is more likely than the others to express religion devotionally (the differences along the creedal dimension are not significant). Demerath dichotomizes the possible relationship to one's religious group for his sample (Lutherans) into "churchlike" and "sectlike" religiosity. Some of his findings are included in Table 10.4, which indicates quite clearly that the lower the Lutherans' social class position, the less likely they are to exhibit a churchlike attachment to religion. As would be expected, a corresponding opposite relationship is observed with respect to sect-like commitment. The progression for high sect-like commitment from the upper through the middle, working, and lower classes is 10 percent, 15 percent, 25 percent, and 35 percent, respectively.[17]

All these data indicate that social status appears to have an effect upon the meaning and expression of religion for people. This is not only evidenced by the fact that people of one status level tend to be members of particular denominations or sects, but people within a particular denomination, and even within a local organization, are both looking for and finding different things.

TABLE 10.3   Proportion of Congregationalists Scoring High on Selected Measures of Religiosity, by Social Class

	Socioeconomic Status		
Measure	High	Medium	Low
Cultic	53%	43%	35%
Cognitive	28	24	15
Creedal	27	28	31
Devotional	16	23	32

Note: Cultic = measure of church attendance and organizational participation

Cognitive = measure of knowledge of religious doctrine and congregational affairs

Creedal = measure or personal allegiance to traditional doctrine

Devotional = measure of personal prayer and expression of reliance on religion beyond the church itself.

Source: Adapted from Yoshio Fukuyama, "The Major Dimensions of Church Membership," Review of Religious Research 2, no. 4 (1960), 159.

TABLE 10.4   Churchlike Religiosity among Lutherans, by Social Class

	Socioeconomic Status			
*Degree of Churchlike Commitment**	*Upper*	*Middle*	*Working*	*Lower*
High	51%	45%	32%	24%
Moderate	20	20	19	19
Low	29	35	48	57

*Based on frequency of church attendance, participation in parish organizations, and member-ship in outside organizations.

Source: N. J. Demerath III, *Social Class in American Protestantism* (Chicago: Rand McNally, 1965), p. 87.

Religion and Social Class in India

That the meaning of religion and participation in religious activities varies among social classes is, of course, not unique to western Christianity. Such differences are noted particularly in Hinduism. The division into social classes of Brahmins, Kshatriyas, Vaisyas, Chudras, and "outcasts" or "untouchables," correlates quite closely with differences in the historical meaning and expression of Hinduism as a religion. The fact that originally only the two upper classes were literate and could read and become familiar with the holy books, predetermined important differences. For example, even today the upper classes tend to be monistic—they believe in one Absolute, with all other gods a part or expression of the One. The common people tend to be polytheists and believe in many local gods and spirits, tend to identify the image or statue itself with the divine living reality, and believe in a heaven and hell, which the higher classes do not. The upper classes believe more firmly in the doctrines of samsara (the transmigration of souls), karma (the principle of cause and effect—what you sow you reap), and dharma (the standard of determining whether you move socially upward or downward in the next life). The upper classes are more firmly committed to the belief that if you follow the rules of your caste you can move upward, from one life to another. This could be all the way to an ultimate goal of being released from the nearly endless cycle of transmigration of souls and realizing unity with the Brahman or Absolute (attaining Nirvana). John Noss notes that the masses have never had a clear conception of the finer points of Hinduism such as the various "ways" of salvation and release from the miseries and responsibilities of life (Way of Works, Way of Knowledge, Way of Devotion). He says that the masses go about being religious in the traditional manner of their local area. They practice and reflect animism, fetishism, shamanism, demonolatry, animal worship, and devotion to local spirits and godlings, often without the "higher" worship of the supreme deities in the Hindu pantheon.[18] Noss goes on to say that in some areas. Hinduism can hardly be recognized as such; a primitive animism takes its place. This sub-Hinduism is common among the millions of "untouchables."[19]

Along a similar vein, Buddhism, in its original form, found little response among the masses. But they gradually became interested, as Noss observes, not in the theologian Gautama Buddha, but in the man.[20] Worship of the person and the idea of salvation through various saviors, became popular with the lower classes.[21] In fact, some of the untouchables, in trying to improve their degraded lot in life, adopted Buddhism, which promised some relief and release from the desperate, unredeemable character of their existence.

If we look a little more closely at the religious situation in India, we discover that Hinduism and Indian culture (including its caste system) are almost one and the same. Hinduism is a comprehensive religion in the sense that there is really nothing that the Hindu does of a cultural nature—whether brushing one's teeth, preparing food, encountering people in the street, or any other act—that does not have religious significance and some kind of religious prescription wrapped around it. "Hinduism is a culture and a religion at the same time . . . religion and life are synonymous."[22]

At least this is the heritage of India's past—a caste-based society in which strict separation of classes was both a cultural and religious dictum. In 1950, however, the Democratic Republican Constitution of India was adopted. This constitution, much like that of the United States, emphasizes justice, liberty, and equality—and not just in a political sense but also in a social sense as well. Article 15 of the Constitution states that caste cannot be a basis for discrimination or any restrictions on access to stores, restaurants, village water sources, and the like. Further, any traditional practices based on untouchability are categorically forbidden.

However, castes continue to be identified, and such a system, though in a somewhat modified form, will continue for many years to come. This is so and will continue to be so, in part because the caste system is so deeply embedded in Indian culture and society that it is a primary source of identification for people. As such, it is a rallying point, a source of members of caste-restrictive political parties, a power bloc for economic and political action, an audience for caste journals and newspapers, the body of membership in particular craft unions, and the constituency of voluntary associations of various types. Such goes on quite irrespective of religious sanctions one way or the other and of a constitution that prescribes that caste be ignored and transcended.

It is worth noting, too, that with respect to the origin of caste, the role of religion is almost assuredly one of reinforcement rather than cause. While there is not now, and probably never will be, total consensus on the precise cause or causes of caste in India, it is likely that several factors together provided the basis. While a common belief among the populace is that the castes "issued from the mouth, arms, thighs, and feet of Brahma," it is also widely understood that race has played a part. Sir Herbert Risley states that in eastern India "a man's status varies in inverse ratio to the width of his nose."[23] Others emphasize occupational sources of caste. That is, various occupations were status ranked differentially by the people themselves; subsequently, specific occupations and occupational categories became castes. Still others point to the separateness of ancient tribes, as well as the differences between invaders and the conquered, as early sources of castes. And so on. But the point is simply that cultural and highly sociological factors have contributed to a rigid class (caste) system that, while integral within Indian religion, is not necessarily of religious origin. Further, a democratic constitution and continuous religious denunciation of caste today do not eradicate overnight or even in a generation or two what has been so integral a part of a society's political, religious, and social structure.

SOCIAL STRATIFICATION WITHIN RELIGIOUS GROUPS

If we define social stratification as a hierarchical arrangement or ordering of people in a group according to criteria or standards determined and accepted by that group—a definition implicit in this chapter so far—then it is easy to see that such stratification is an integral part of religion. Although many religious groups preach the equality of everyone before God, this often implies only equality among the specially favored people in their own group. Religious groups are historically notorious for their clear distinction between the "ins" and the "outs," the believers and the nonbelievers, the saved and the unsaved. Moreover, stratification appears, even within the group itself. Stratification is endemic in two senses. First, there is the distinction between prophet and people, or leader and followers. Those who are considered to have special insights or who are credited with special revelation, are accorded elevated positions relative to those who listen and follow. The person with deeper knowledge of sacred things (rituals and writings)— the teacher or priest—is ranked higher than those who are their pupils and followers. Second, there is the recognition that, even among the followers, some follow the norms of the group more closely than others and are more holy, more knowledgeable, more dedicated than the "average" or "majority" of followers or members. Even though the majority of rank-and-file members may not personally aspire to such status, they tend to acknowledge its validity and give honor and respect to those who embody most perfectly the virtues and knowledge that the group has defined as praiseworthy. Such distinctions are readily observed in the panoply of saints in the Roman Catholic Church—persons who have gone an extra mile or two in perfecting the expression and application of the Catholic faith.

The great majority of Buddhists also recognize the elevated status of the numerous monks and "holy men," who have proceeded farther along the path in search of the ultimate goal—the elimination of desire—than has the ordinary follower of the Buddha.

Jehovah's Witnesses speak of the 144,000 (a number mentioned in the Biblical Book of Revelations) higher-caste believers who will be rewarded with "heaven," while others will simply be inhabitants of "paradise." Although the sacred number of 144,000 appears to be taken more figuratively than literally today, particularly as the world membership in the group has far surpassed that number, the idea of a greater reward for the few who are most holy remains.

As Glenn Vernon suggests, probably the best known "celestial caste system" is that of the Roman Catholic Church, with its four levels of heaven, hell, purgatory, and limbo for persons after death—heaven for the purest believers, hell for the nonbelievers, purgatory for the believers who still need some "cleansing" before entering heaven, limbo a place to which people went before Christ's work of redemption was completed and from which he thereafter liberated them.[24]

Other groups talk of the visible church on earth—the voluntary association including not only sincere believers but also some nonbelievers and hypocrites, who are professed but insincere members—as contrasted with the invisible church, which is composed of true believers whom only God can know by looking within their hearts and assessing their sincerity.

We have already mentioned the religious stratification in Hinduism that is so intimately associated with the societal stratification as well. Lower-caste persons are not just lower-class socially but religiously as well. To move upward in successive lives, through the process of samsara (transmigration of the soul), into higher castes in the social sense, is to move upward religiously as well. One would thereby not only enjoy more and more of the amenities of life but would also come ever closer to the ultimate goal of union with or absorption into the timeless or eternal Brahman, thus finding release from the cycle of transmigration. In this connection, Charles Eliot reinforces a point made earlier in this chapter, that it is the caste structure of Indian society that influences Hinduism, not vice versa. He states that many Hindu religious leaders have declared unequivocally that there ought to be no social distinctions among believers. But caste continually reasserts itself. Social structure and precedents, Eliot concludes, are stronger than theology.[25]

STRATIFICATION, RELIGION, AND RACE

We now turn to a somewhat extended example of how stratification and religion interrelate, when a third variable, race or ethnic background is introduced. Here again we shall see the reciprocal-interaction relationship between religion and other features of the society.

Although each of the major religions of the world has tended officially to welcome all comers into its fellowship of faith, in practice most have, at some time or other, discriminated against racial or ethnic groups living in the same society. Of course, we need to emphasize that the religious element in such discrimination is usually inextricably bound up with political and economic factors as well. This point will be amply demonstrated as we proceed.

One quick example, before proceeding with our primary one: The interaction of political and religious factors is dramatically seen in India and Pakistan, where the centuries-old conflict between Hinduism and Islam culminated in the 1971 war over Bangladesh (formerly East Pakistan). When East Pakistan was still a part of the larger nation, the government located in the western portion, which has a Muslim majority, systematically discriminated against Hindus within both West Pakistan and East Pakistan, which has a Hindu majority. Thus a basic ingredient of the military and political conflict was the religious antagonism between Muslims and Hindus.

We need to think once again of the examples of religious conflict presented in Chapter 6—the Inquisition in medieval Europe, the Thirty Years' War in seventeenth-century Europe between Protestant and Roman Catholic forces, the long-term Protestant-Catholic conflict in Northern Ireland, and, along a somewhat different line, the prejudice and discrimination in the name of religion that has been directed against blacks throughout American history. We shall focus just a bit on this last phenomenon particularly, because it so well portrays the intimate connection of the three variables mentioned above—religion, race, and social class.

By definition, slaves in any society which approves of slavery are at the very bottom of the stratification system.[26] But the phenomenon of slavery presented a problem for the Christian religion. In fact, it became a dilemma in the sense that Christian theology had developed the principle that, although slavery itself was not forbidden by God, a Christian should not hold another Christian in bondage. The dilemma arose when that principle came in contact with the conversion principle—that is, the mandate to "make disciples of all nations" and convert everyone possible.

The Early American Experience with Slavery

Early in colonial American history, the question arose concerning what to do about the religion of black slaves. One mandate said: Convert them to Christianity. But the other said: You should not hold a fellow Christian in slavery. Therefore, what to do? Some slaveholders quite expectedly opposed the conversion of slaves. Unconverted they presented no problem, since the slaveholder would not be keeping a fellow Christian in slavery. But theologians and clergy members said it was the Christian's obligation to teach the slaves Christianity and convert them. Some Southerners and others resolved the issue by defining blacks as less than human. They said in essence: "We do not convert dogs, kudus, or zebras; therefore, we do not need to convert blacks—as a lower animal form, they lack a soul to be saved."

And so the controversy went on. But ultimately a compromise was reached. Religious leaders abandoned their original position and said that the church would no longer maintain the position that conversion required emancipation. This meant that the church could save souls and the slaveholders their investment. This compromise led to substantial missionary activity among slaves, who were rapidly converted to Christianity. The mass conversions of slaves occurred in significant part, of course, because once the owners decided their slaves should espouse Christianity the slaves themselves, as property and with essentially no personal or civil rights, had little choice in the matter.

The Methodist Example

The process of this religious about-face is well documented for the Methodist Church and merits a somewhat extended examination as an example of social-class and economic influences on religious ideology and practice. In its beginning, American Methodism quite naturally looked to its English founder John Wesley for guidance on the issue of slavery. They did not look in vain. Among Wesley's *General Rules*, prepared in 1739, was a rule forbidding "the buying or selling of the bodies and souls of men, women, or children with an intention to enslave them."[27] And in 1772 he denounced the slave trade as "the sum of all villainies."[28]

Early Prohibitions   Accordingly, the Methodist Episcopal Church, organized in Baltimore in 1784, proposed and adopted the following six special rules designed to destroy slavery among its members:

1. Every slave-holding member, within twelve months, was required to execute a deed of manumission.
2. All infants who were born after these rules went into effect were to have immediate freedom.
3. Members who chose not to comply were allowed to withdraw within twelve months.
4. The sacrament of the Lord's Supper was to be denied to all such thenceforward.
5. No slaveholders were to be admitted thereafter into church membership.
6. Any members who bought, sold, or gave slaves away, except on purpose to free them, were immediately to be expelled.[29]

This, then, was the official stand of the Methodist Church on the question of slavery.

Gradual Accommodation/Erosion of Principle   Thus, during these early days of Methodism in the United States, there appeared to be no great problem with slavery. Apparently no members were slaveholders, and moreover, Wesley's principles were in force. Slavery, however, seems to have found its way into the Methodist Church during the Revolutionary War, probably without the knowledge of John Wesley or his American assistant, Frances Asbury.[30] It seems to have entered gradually and unobtrusively. In this connection, it is important to note that rather lax church administration prevailed at this time. By 1778, every English missionary preacher had returned to the mother country except Asbury, and the latter restricted himself primarily to the small state of Delaware. The job of expanding the church was thus committed to young, inexperienced, poorly-educated men. Almost all of these young ministers had been born and reared in a slave culture and appeared to have no clear understanding that slavery was wrong. Daniel DeVinne states that the forty-eight preachers who had been received into the ministry during the Revolutionary War, belonged almost exclusively to this class.[31] Further, the early work of these Methodist preachers was primarily in the slaveholding states. Out of a national membership of about fourteen thousand, only about two thousand resided in non-Southern states.[32]

It is not surprising, then, that the formal resolutions of Methodist conferences and conventions during the last decade of the eighteenth century, although disapproving slavery, became ever more modified in tone.[33] Hiram Mattison reports that by 1808 "all that was related to slaveholding among private members [that is, laypersons] was stricken from the Methodist body of rules and regulations and the following put in its place: 'The General Conference authorizes each Annual Conference to form their own regulations, relative to buying and selling slaves.' "[34] It is important to note that it was the buying and selling of slaves that each conference was to regulate, not the holding of slaves. Apparently the possession of slaves, at least by laypeople, now had the church's tacit approval. By 1840, the ownership of slave property was extended to ministers.[35]

Crisis and Resolution   A crisis developed in 1844, when a bishop of the Methodist Church, the Reverend James Andrew, was found to be a slaveholder. This necessitated a clear decision. Either do something with Bishop Andrew or openly tolerate slaveholding in the highest positions of the church. Was the Methodist Episcopal Church a slaveholding church, or was it not? The issue was essentially resolved that same year when the Methodist Episcopal Church split into what amounted to Northern and Southern branches—the former condemning slavery, the latter citing Scripture to support it.

What we observe quite clearly here, is the influence of social and situational factors upon the institution of religion. To summarize briefly: Early

American Methodist activity and growth were in the South, where the question of slavery and slaveholding became an issue almost by definition. As the plantation system grew and as it became economically profitable to own slaves, Methodist laypeople, preachers, and finally bishops acceded to the practice. Bishop Asbury, residing in Baltimore, had little knowledge of or control over his fellow Methodists scattered throughout the South. Also, the Methodist ministers during this period were little educated, poorly-informed, and Southerners by background, orientation, and ways of thinking.

And so, quite apart from official theological statements or the moral convictions and commitments of church leaders, social factors exerted their influence on the religious group. Economic pressures, organizational features, and characteristics both of the members and lower-level leadership combined to override theological and moral mandates. Because religion exists in society and in the subcommunities and regions of that society, it finds itself influenced by the norms and structure of that society and its subunits.

Other Denominations and Slavery   Presbyterians followed a similar route. Murray states that most colonial Presbyterians viewed slavery as permitted by God and tended to accept the customs of the areas in which they settled.[36] As slaveholding became more economically significant, the battle lines between North and South were more clearly drawn. This was true of religious groups, no less than other groups and institutions in the society. Actually, although some Southern Presbyterians vigorously opposed slavery, it was not only the issue of theological liberalism but also the controversy over slavery that resulted in the "schism of 1837" between "old-school" and "new-school" Presbyterians.[37] This schism was sealed by the coming of the Civil War, as the Northern and Southern Presbyterians went their separate ways.

With the outbreak of the Civil War in 1861, all the major Protestant denominations either officially split into Northern and Southern branches or allowed local political policy to dictate the church's position. For example, C.F.W. Walther, leader of what is now known as the Lutheran Church–Missouri Synod, saw the slavery issue as a matter for government, not churches, to decide. In doing so, he relied on a strict interpretation of the principle of separation of church and state: Church members are to respect and abide by the laws established by the political process in the governmental units of which they are citizens.

Into the Present

Slight variations of this principle appear to have guided much religious thinking on the slavery issue and thus set the stage for the relative noninvolvement of religious groups in civil rights struggles following the Civil War. Most religious groups, at both the national and local levels, remained on balance silent on the issue of black civil rights for nearly ten decades. It was a stand of aloofness that relegated first the issue of slavery, then equal rights for blacks, to the political and social realm, and asserted that it was "not the business of the church" to interfere in such social and political (that is, nonreligious) matters.[38] It is, in fact, this very silence that prompts our excursion into the question of the relationship of white Christianity in the United States to black Americans. White churches have tended to reinforce the class and caste gap between whites and blacks, sometimes by lending active support to claims of blacks' inherent inferiority and to justifications for their second-class citizenship, but most often by remaining silent and thereby giving tacit approval to racial segregation, discrimination, and prejudice. Further, racial or ethnic differences, which became closely associated with class differences, were reflected in religious differences. In other words, white churches were for whites, black churches for blacks. Kyle Haselden asserts that "long before the little signs—'White Only' and 'Colored'—appeared in the public utilities, they had appeared in the Church."[39]

In the 1950s and 1960s, however, nearly every major religious group issued official statements and passed resolutions at their national conventions, favoring equality for blacks and calling for an end to discrimination and segregation, although not always issuing clear calls for integration as such. Also during this period, white faces in clerical collars became highly visible in sit-ins, marches, and demonstrations, as numerous white clergy and some laypeople as well provided leadership and helped fill the ranks of participants in the civil rights struggle. They sincerely wanted to tell the nation and the world that the white Christian churches were concerned and committed, and they wanted, by example and exhortation, to bring their fellow white church members along. Yet their voices and presence do not seem to have been representative or typical of the churches from which they came.

A fairly strong antiblack animus remained within the white Christian denominations. In a nationwide survey conducted at the end of the first decade of the civil rights movement (1967), nearly half (44 percent) of the white respondents registered basic disapproval of the black civil rights movement in this country.[40] However, more recent data from the General Social Survey, which are cumulative since 1972 and benefit from interviews as recent as 2002 with representative samples of Americans, show changing attitudes with respect to racial issues. For example, in the most recent GSS survey ending in 2002, only 23.1 percent of respondents said there "should be laws against marriage between blacks and whites."[41] Thirty-three percent of these same respondents admitted that ten years earlier they held this view against racial intermarriage but had now changed their minds. Implicitly there is some progress here.[42]

Actually, it is generally believed that the 44 percent of laypeople who expressed disapproval of the civil rights movement in 1967, represented a decline from earlier periods. Paul Sheatsley, of the National Opinion Research Center, believes that various polls conducted since the 1940s indicate a steady, unambiguous increase in positive sentiment toward civil rights issues.[43] While an improvement over attitudes expressed in earlier polls, a Brink and Harris poll in 1966 found that 52 percent of white Americans would be upset if blacks moved into their neighborhood, and 76 percent of whites who live in neighborhoods into which blacks would like to move would be upset at such a development.[44] More recent data from Gallup polls (1978), suggest continuing improvement in such attitudes. For example, in response to the question, "If blacks came to live next door, would you move?" only 4 percent said they definitely would move (with an additional 9 percent saying that they might move). A full 84 percent said they would not move (the remaining 3 percent expressed no opinion).[45] A follow-up question, that posed a more "threatening" situation, elicited more willingness to move. Fifty-one percent of white respondents said they either definitely would or might move if blacks came to live in great numbers in their neighborhood. Yet 45 percent said they would not move.[46]

A related question, from current data available from the General Social Survey (GSS), shows continuing progress. A full 75 percent of Americans disagree with the statement, "Whites have a right to keep blacks out of their neighborhoods if they want to, and blacks should respect that right." Only 11 percent strongly agree with the statement.[47]

Another question, from the earlier Gallup survey, asked respondents if they would vote for a qualified black candidate for president if nominated by their political party. A full 77 percent said they would—a proportion that has been steadily growing from the 38 percent who said they would vote for such a candidate when this question was first asked in 1958.[48] Current data from the GSS show the proportion of Americans who would vote for a black presidential candidate stands at 85.3 percent.[49]

Religion, Social Class, and Racial Attitudes

Quite obviously, religion in the United States has not reversed, even to the degree it has tried, its long history of maintaining major class distinctions between whites and blacks. There are, however, important differences in this regard among major religious groups. Jews, for example, express far less suspicion of and animosity toward blacks than do Protestants and Catholics, with Catholics slightly less likely than Protestants to express such suspicion and hostility. For example, in the mid-1960s, Jeffrey Hadden found that only 43 percent of Jewish laypersons would be upset if their rabbi participated in civil rights activities, but 68 percent of Catholic laypersons and 77 percent of Protestant laypersons would be upset if their priest or minister joined in civil rights activities, such as marches or sit-ins. Similarly,

59 percent, 30 percent, and 27 percent, respectively, of Jewish, Catholic, and Protestant laypersons, agreed that Martin Luther King was an outstanding example of making Christianity relevant and meaningful.[50]

The social class of respondents also appears to be extremely relevant here. It appears that traditionally the lower the social class of people, the more likely they have been to express suspicion and resentment toward blacks. Using level of educational achievement as the independent measure of social class, we observe some dramatic contrasts in Hadden's sample. For example, the proportion of respondents who believed that "clergy should stick to religion and not concern themselves with social, economic, and political questions" declines rapidly with increasing amounts of education. Specifically, while 63 percent of those with only "some high school" agreed with the above view, the proportion declines to 47 percent of high school graduates, 38 percent of those with some college, and only 23 percent of those who had graduated from college.[51]

One must note, of course, that not all religious persons of low educational attainments or low social status are opposed to black progress or express measurable prejudice against blacks. In fact, David Harrell has noted that some Southern whites, of working- or lower-class social status, have related well to blacks at the same class level, express little or no racial prejudice, and engage in integrated religious activities.[52]

It has frequently been suggested that part of the reason for prejudice against blacks, particularly by whites of at least moderately low SES, is the latter's fear of economic threat and of a potential undermining of their only "claim to fame," so to speak—namely, having higher status than at least one other category of people (the blacks around them). Christian antagonism toward Jews has some of this same flavor—not strictly a class phenomenon, but an uneasiness and resentment in the face of Jewish economic, educational, and political success and influence, which is frequently seen as disproportionate to their numbers in the population.

Recent data strongly suggest that amount of education is still a powerful factor in predicting prejudical views against blacks by whites. The data in Table 10.5 show dramatic differences related to a major component in determining social class, namely, level of education attained by respondents. On the question of favoring laws against racial intermarriage, the difference between those with less than a high school education and those with graduate or professional education beyond a bachelor's degree is striking—45.3 percent of those with less than a high school education, but only 4.9 percent of those with graduate education, favor laws against racial intermarriage. The progression is continuous through all five educational categories. Of course, it should also be noted that it is clearly a **minority** of respondents in each of the five educational categories—even in the lowest educational category who favor such racist laws.

TABLE 10.5   White Attitudes on Racial Issues by Level of Education Attained

	Less than High School Graduate	High School Graduate	Some College	College Graduate	Graduate Work beyond College
A. Favor Laws against Racial Intermarriage					
Agree	45.3%	19.9%	8.5%	6.2%	4.9%
Disagree	54.7	80.1	91.5	93.8	95.1
B. Believe Whites Should Have Right to Live in a Segregated Neighborhood					
Agree	40.0%	23.5%	13.7%	12.4%	9.9%
Disagree	60.0	76.5	86.3	87.6	90.1

Source: 1972–2002 General Social Survey Cumulative Data File. National Opinion Research Center, University of Chicago, through Internet access, 1 April 2005.

The same pattern can be seen on the question of whether whites should have the right to live in an all-white neighborhood. Again there is a thirty-point spread between the two educational extremes, and each category reflects the same pattern as before. That reflects an inverse relationship between education and acceptance of the white-neighborhood-for-whites-only principle. It is also important to note that in just the last six years, those in the lowest educational categories, who believed whites should have the right to live in an all-white neighborhood, dropped 9 percentage points (from 49 percent in the 1972–96 cumulative GSS to 40 percent in the 1972–2002 cumulative GSS).

A fitting conclusion to this chapter is to state the obvious, yet highly significant, point that religious affiliation *and* social status factors, education in particular, are important in predicting social attitudes and behavior. It is not so much a question of which comes first, but that these important social variables can be mutually reinforcing.

NOTES

1. Karl Marx and Friedrich Engels, *Toward the Criticism of Hegel's Philosophy of Right*, trans. Glen Waas (Paris, 1843), quoted in Robert Freedman, *Marxist Social Thought* (New York: Harcourt Brace Jovanovich, 1968), p. 230.
2. Friedrich Engels, *Anti-Dühring* (Moscow: Foreign Language Publishing House, 1954), pp. 438–440, quoted in Freedman, *Marxist Social Thought*, p. 228.
3. See Chapter 8.
4. Max Weber, "The Social Psychology of the World Religions," in *From Max Weber*, trans. and eds. Hans Gerth and C. Wright Mills (New York: Oxford University Press, 1958), p. 276.

5. Liston Pope, *Millhands and Preachers* (New Haven, CT: Yale University Press, 1942), pp. 88–90.

6. Ibid., p. 92.

7. Ibid.

8. Ibid.

9. Emile Pin, "Social Classes and Their Religious Approaches," in *Religion, Culture, and Society,* ed. Louis Schneider (New York: John Wiley, 1964), p. 411.

10. Pope, *Millhands and Preachers,* pp. 93–94.

11. Ibid., p. 95.

12. While not by itself a perfect indicator of social class, education, particularly if it involved attendance at college, reflects class differences fairly well.

13. Note that there are numerous sub-denominations of Methodists and Baptists, which have been combined in each of these two categories. These individual denominations among Baptists range from 19 percent college graduates in the National Baptist Convention USA to 8 percent of the American Baptist Church USA (Southern Baptists are at 13 percent college graduated). Similarly with the Methodists—24 percent of the United Methodists (largest Methodist denomination) have college degrees, but 9 percent of members of the African Methodist Episcopal Zion denomination have graduated from college.

14. Christian Smith and Robert Faris, "Socioeconomic Inequality in the American Religious System: An Update and Assessment," *Journal for the Scientific Study of Religion* 44, no. 1 (March 2005), p. 98.

15. Pope, *Millhands and Preachers,* pp. 70–71.

16. N. J. Demerath III, *Social Class in American Protestantism* (Chicago: Rand McNally, 1965).

17. Ibid., p. 88.

18. John B. Noss, *Man's Religions* (New York: Macmillan, 1949), p. 243.

19. Ibid., p. 244.

20. Ibid., p. 171.

21. Ibid., p. 188.

22. Trevor Ling, *Buddha, Marx, and God* (London: Macmillan, 1966), p. 211.

23. Herbert Risley, "The Tribes and Castes of Bengal," quoted by N. Presad, *The Myth of the Caste System* (Petna: Prakashan, 1957), p. 26.

24. Glenn M. Vernon, *Sociology of Religion* (New York: McGraw-Hill, 1962), p. 380.

25. Charles Eliot, *Hinduism and Buddhism,* vol. 2 (London: Routledge&Kegan Paul, 1921), pp. 176–178.

26. This is not the place to discuss whether norms that condone slavery run counter to "human nature" or violate fundamental human rights to such things as life, liberty, and the pursuit of happiness. Although we happen to agree that involuntary servitude is in direct violation of universal human rights, we need not debate the issue to understand the sociological points that this chapter is making.

27. Quoted in W. W. Sweet, *The Methodist Episcopal Church and the Civil War* (Cincinnati, OH: Methodist Book Concern Press, 1912), p. 15.

28. Quoted in Charles Swaney, *Episcopal Methodism and Slavery* (Boston: R. G. Madger, 1926), p. 1.

29. Sweet, *The Methodist Episcopal Church,* p. 16.

30. Daniel DeVinne, *The Methodist Episcopal Church and Slavery* (New York: F. Hart, 1857), p. 12.

31. Ibid.

32. Ibid.

33. Lucius Matlack, *History of American Slavery and Methodism from 1780 to 1849* (New York: Lucius Matlack, 1849), pp. 33ff.

34. Hiram Mattison, *The Impending Crisis of 1860* (New York: Mason Brothers, 1859), p. 30.

35. Ibid., p. 34.

36. Andrew E. Murray, *Presbyterians and the Negro—A History* (Philadelphia: Presbyterian Historical Society, 1966), p. 12.

37. Ibid., pp. 103ff.

38. Ralph Moellering, *Christian Conscience and Negro Emancipation* (Philadelphia: Fortress Press, 1965), p. 76.

39. Kyle Haselden, *The Racial Problem in Christian Perspective* (New York: Harper & Row, 1959), p. 29.

40. Jeffrey K. Hadden, *The Gathering Storm in the Churches* (Garden City, NY: Doubleday, 1969), p. 127.

41. National Opinion Research Center, *1972–2002 General Social Survey Cumulative File* (Chicago: Data compiled through Internet access, 2005).

42. Ibid.

43. Paul B. Sheatsley, "White Attitudes toward the Negro," *Daedalus* 95, no. 1 (1966): 217–238, quoted in Hadden, *The Gathering Storm*, p. 130.

44. Reported in Hadden, *The Gathering Storm*, p. 130.

45. George H. Gallup, *The Gallup Poll: Public Opinion 1979* (Wilmington, DE: Scholarly Resources, 1979), p. 214.

46. Ibid., p. 215.

47. National Opinion Research Center, *1972–2002 General Social Survey*, ibid.

48. George H. Gallup, *The Gallup Opinion Index* no. 160 (Nov. 1978): 26.

49. National Opinion Research Center, *1972–1996 General Social Survey*, ibid.

50. Hadden, *The Gathering Storm*, pp. 136–137.

51. Ibid., p. 145.

52. David E. Harrell Jr., *White Sects and Black Men in the Recent South* (Nashville, TN: Vanderbilt University Press, 1971).

Chapter 11

Women and Religion

She is the Pastor.

In an age of turmoil over the roles and rights of women, it is small wonder that religious organizations worldwide have themselves become microcosms of the women's role and rights debate. An examination of the sociological relationship of women and religion, from both a historical and contemporary perspective, will be the focus of this chapter.

By way of a beginning, we will explore, in at least an introductory way, the context within which women have had and continue to have their relationship to religion, and within which they express themselves religiously. This is, of course, the society and the subgroup context within which both women and the religious institutions themselves live out their lives.

THE RELATIONSHIP OF WOMEN TO RELIGION AS SOCIETIES EVOLVED

As we try to reconstruct life in early hunting and food gathering societies, at least one characteristic appears to be universal. The contribution of women's work to the food supply, and hence their importance to the community, was equal to and perhaps greater than that of men. As such, the power and status of women were not appreciably lower when compared with men. Further, female participation in and responsibility for what we would today call "religious" activities, were on a fairly equal plane with men.

Hunting and Gathering Societies

While it is true that biological gender factors determine that at least some of women's work will almost assuredly be different from men's work, such work was not usually seen as less important. Because of recurrent pregnancies that were in most cases necessary and desirable in hunting and gathering societies, in order to replenish a population continually devastated by a high death rate, a woman's work needed to be close to camp and hut, and she herself needed to be accessible to nursing children. As such, her activities centered around gathering edible plant life—roots, fruits, and berries—in the vicinity of the camp, as well as caring for the children and carrying out routine camp chores. The men hunted and traversed the more distant territory of the society's domain. While each contributed to the food supply, the women's contribution was usually the more stable and predictable portion and as such was almost by definition the most important. Thus, her status was usually essentially equivalent to that of men.

Horticultural Societies

As horticultural societies evolved, following the discovery of the cause-effect relationship between seed planting and harvest, women's role receded but little. The gardens that had now been created fell most often upon the women to tend (the gardens were, after all, on the edge of the village), while men continued to wander in search of game. Even today, in the rural areas of developing countries, women and girls provide 60 percent of household food. Again, the stability of women's contribution to the food supply contributed to their maintenance of status. Concomitantly, matrilineal lines of descent were nearly as common as patrilineal, and sexual freedom, whether prenuptial or postnuptial, was frequently as great for women as for men. In short, there was relatively little status differentiation by sex.

With the domestication of animals and eventually the invention of the plow, men's roles in the food production process began to exceed those of women. For one thing, the arduousness of breaking and tilling the ground, as well as breaking and controlling the large animals that provided the energy, required the greater physical strength of men.

Industrial Societies

Eventually, as technology expanded and as industrialization transformed society, women became increasingly economically dependent upon men. Although they played important roles in childbearing and childrearing and in food preparation and home management, they were drawn further away from direct access to the means of production. Not only did they not own the means of production, they participated only minimally in the production process. As such, their economic dependency increased, and their status decreased.

Although the beginnings of industrialization, in the form of cottage industries, brought women back, at least for a while, into the mainstream of the productive process, the persons involved—the men, the women, and the children alike (remember that abuses in the area of child labor began in the home cottage industry, not the factories, mines, and mills that followed after)—were all sufficiently enslaved by the cottage industry process as to do little for the status of these women. They were all members of an exploited class, dependent for bare subsistence upon the middlemen who provided the raw materials and accumulated the finished products for resale and their own profit.

It was only later, as the work of at least some women was moved out of the home—first in the textile industry, then in primary education[1]—that women began to participate in a more direct and obvious way in economic production. However, such a shift involved sufficiently few women, and jobs were sufficiently economically exploitative, that there was still no significant improvement of women's status. However, it is in these early days of industrialization that the pioneer voices of women's liberation could be heard. The first major feminist tract in the United States, *The Vindication of the Rights of Women*, was published in 1792. The first American feminist convention, led by Lucretia Mott and Elizabeth Cady Stanton, well-known nineteenth-century feminists, was held in 1848.[2]

But before we get too close to the present and too far away from our quick overview of the past, we want to parallel the relationship of women to religion and their roles in the religious patterns and institutions, with the various stages of societal evolution.

THE HISTORICAL PATTERNS

In Ancient Cultures

There is considerable archeological evidence that a great mother goddess was the supreme deity in a great many ancient societies. In fact, Merlin Stone states quite categorically: "At the dawn of religion, God was a woman."[3]

Although evidence is insufficient to be certain that such was indeed true *everywhere*, a great deal of supporting evidence does exist.

The anthropologist, Edwin James, documents the prominent position of female deities throughout the ancient world, from the Indian subcontinent and Mesopotamia, through all of the Near East and Greece and Rome, to Western Europe and the islands of the Mediterranean.[4] There were female creator gods in China, Australia, Africa, Babylon, and Egypt. Legends in Japan identify the sun goddess, Amaterasu Omikami, as the supreme deity and founder of the Japanese imperial family.[5]

Egypt is one of the better-known ancient societies in which female deities not only appeared early but also remained prominent. Already by 3,000 B.C.E., the goddess Nut—probably derived from the more ancient Nekhebt, a goddess in early Upper Egypt—was described as having existed before anything else appeared in the world and as actually having created all else that has come into being. In fact, she first placed the familiar sun god, Ra, in the heavens.[6] At the point of recorded history, however, Ra (Re) appears to have become first among a pantheon of gods.[7] Ra represented the sun in all its fullness, combined all the forces of nature, and held absolute control over the Nile valley. Yet he appears to have been preceded by a powerful and creative mother goddess, as we have mentioned.

It was Nut's daughter, Isis, who became the most popular and important goddess in Egyptian history—a highly beneficent deity, who personified all that was vital in motherhood—a goddess who remained important for a long period of time.[8]

It is also worth noting that in early Egypt the queen was intended to have greater power than the king, and in marriage the wife was to have authority over her husband, with husbands agreeing to be obedient to their wives.[9]

What appears to have been the most important deity to the various Eskimo tribes was Sedna, a female deity. Tales relate how she sent her children across the seas to become ancestors for other cultures, what we know as European cultures in particular. When her father tried to sacrifice her to appease an evil spirit by throwing her into the sea, even cutting off her fingers as she grabbed at the side of the boat, her fingers became the seal and walrus and other sea animals crucial to the Eskimos' survival. As Sedna sinks to the bottom of the sea she becomes "Mother of the Sea Animals." One can readily infer her supreme importance from such depictions, when one realizes the centrality of the seal and walrus to the Eskimo food, clothing, and tool supplies. When taboos are perceived to have been violated and she withholds the sea animals, shamans must get very busy performing appropriate rituals to appease her.[10]

Even in the region of Palestine, where Old Testament Judaism ultimately triumphed and not only excluded female deities (without even having a vocabulary word for "goddess") but severely restricted women's participation in religious activities, mother and other goddesses abounded in prehistoric times. Prominent among them were Anat, the "Lady of the Mountain" and consort and sister of Alevan-Baal; Asherah, the arch rival of Anat, who with the god El bore seventy gods and goddesses; and Astarte, a Philistine goddess of procreation and fecundity.[11]

That the female should be so prominently featured and credited with primary religious responsibilities in the earliest societies, should not really surprise us, if we remember observations made at the beginning of this chapter. For one thing, the female bears the most obvious productive responsibility. It is she who actually bears the children. Thus, from mother of children to "mother of the tribe," "mother of humankind," and so on, would be fairly logical and easy extensions. Further, some reinforcement for the importance and centrality of "mother" would be observed in those societies that were uncertain concerning the source of conception in the first place, not really perceiving the male role and the serial relationship among coitus, conception, and birth. Men were most often perceived to be very much on the fringes of this process of reproduction and birth.

As hunters and gatherers discovered horticulture and as they began to rely increasingly on cultivation and gardening for their food supply, female goddesses continued to be prominent in the religious thought systems of these people. This is most likely related in a significant way to the fact that women were, in most societies, the principal gardeners. However, the male gods did begin to assume greater prominence in horticultural societies. Many of the female goddesses became merely consorts and assistants or specialist supervisors over particular functions. The primary gods gradually became male—Ra in Egypt, Elyan and Bel in Syria, Yahweh in Israel, Zeus in Greece, and so on.

In Eastern Religions

We have entered a time period when the religious roles of men began to wax, those of women to wane. That is, while there still were positive roles for female deities and for ordinary women as members of the religious community as well, the role and view of women and religion became ambivalent. An excellent summary of the ambivalence, the change, and the ultimate subjugation of women religiously can be seen in India. In early Indian religion at the time of the Vedas (about 1000 B.C.E.) there were not only numerous female goddesses, but women generally enjoyed comparative freedom of movement and participation. However, by 500 B.C.E. and the flowering of classical Hinduism, women as a category had clearly been relegated to second-class status. There was even a common belief that no woman of any caste could, as a woman, gain salvation through the attainment of Nirvana. In a later life she would first have to be born a man.

For a time in the early years of Buddhism, women's status saw a beginning of modest restoration. Buddha himself (born 563 B.C.E.) preached the Four Nobel Truths and the Eightfold Path to all who would listen, including women. Falk reports that women received a great deal of respect in the home, were allowed to manage property, give it away, and probably inherit it as well.[12] They were not forced into marriage—certainly not into child marriages as was later so common in Hindu practice. Nor did either societal or religious dictum force women to become recluses if widowed. "Most important, they were able to leave the world, study the sacred teachings of Buddhism, [and] become preachers and teachers in their own right."[13] The reference here is to female monastic orders. These were established fairly early, and monasticism became an alternative to marriage for some Indian women. But there was a fascinating ambivalence, and Buddhism changed within three to four centuries to closely mirror Hinduism. On the one hand, the Buddhist teaching on karma—with the goal of spiritual perfection, which would eliminate the differences among living beings—maintained that continued spiritual development should result in a gradual sloughing off of sexual differences and limitations. To such goals, monks and nuns alike would strive. They had virtually identical spiritual paths and charges, and dressed alike as well.

But another sexual model dominated in the society (the Hindu conception of dharma)—an image of everything "in its place" and following its "nature," role, and order. Failure to coincide with one's dharma invites disaster for all concerned. The woman's dharma is to be a childbearing wife and mother. Thus, for a woman to follow a monastic role was to violate her dharma. Consistent with such a view was the positive portrayal within Buddhism of laywomen who were mothers. Their deeds and virtues could be recounted and extolled because they were following their dharma. And so, Buddhism, Hinduism, and the society itself, all agreed that women's proper role was domestic.

Denise Carmody suggests that the change is associated with the view of women as dangerous temptations—one side of the ambivalent view of women that we shall discuss later. Women in the monastic orders, even though in separate ones, were viewed by some as threats to male celibacy.[14] Buddhist literature at the time warned against the ravenous sexual appetites of women and the obstacle to the perfection of male monks that they represent.[15] Thus, what Carmody calls a "deeply misogynistic strain"[16] infects both Hinduism and Buddhism. "Unless a woman is neutralized by marriage to a controlling man, Hindu imagination conjures up for her such images as the snake, death, the underworld, hell's entrance, the prostitute, and the adulteress."[17]

The record of Confucianism and Taoism in China is much like that of Hinduism and Buddhism in India. There is evidence of early respect for women generally, together with female goddesses and opportunities for women to participate in religious activities. But by the time of Confucius (500 B.C.E.), women were relegated to a distant second behind men.

In Islam, where the common image is one of male dominance in religion, as well as most other areas of life, Muhammad himself elevated the status of women in Arabian culture by providing women a share of their family's inheritance, caring for destitute widows, and banning infanticide, which usually had meant killing female newborns.[18]

In Japan, it appears that women were provided a little more formal religious involvement and for somewhat longer than in the other ancient Asian societies. There is considerable evidence to suggest that early Japan was actually a matriarchy, with female shamans playing a prominent role in religious activities.[19] However, with the importation of the Confucian ethic, the depreciation of women began, and women eventually lost their civil rights. It is interesting to note, though, that a curious ambivalence so far as the ideal of womanhood remained. On the one hand, there was the ideal of the court lady who epitomized elegance and romance and presided over a mannered, erotic, leisured, and artistic court life.[20] On the other hand, some women were urged to overcome their female frailty and match males' fortitude and bravery.[21] They were trained already as children to repress their emotions and to be able to use the dagger that they were given at the onset of puberty.[22]

Once all of the major religions had reached their maturity,[23] they all strongly resembled one another, both in their depiction and treatment of women and in the degree and type of religious involvement granted their female adherents. Women were defined as inferior to men and dependent on them; the religious tasks open to them were peripheral or at best serving in nature.

In Judaism

Even to this day, Orthodox Jewish men can be heard to repeat a morning prayer that says, "Blessed art thou, O Lord our God, King of the Universe who has not made me a woman." Jewish women have traditionally been discouraged from studying the holy Torah or even learning Hebrew.

Women have not counted in the *minyan* (the quorum of ten males required for public religious services), cannot read Torah publicly or lead public services, and must frequently sit in special locations in the synagogue, separated from men.[24]

In Christianity

Within Christianity, building as it did on a Jewish base, we find a long history of second-class citizenship for women. St. Paul sets the stage and tone for nineteen centuries that follow as he says:

> A woman must be a learner, listening quietly and with due submission.
> I do not permit a woman to be a teacher, nor must woman domineer

over man; she should be quiet. For Adam was created first, and Eve afterwards; and it was not Adam who was deceived; it was the woman who, yielding to deception, fell into sin.[25]

Closely associated with the Pauline view of women as inferior to men are other themes that were enunciated early in the Christian tradition and reinforced throughout much of its history.

1. Celibacy, continence, and virginity are the better ways for persons of both sexes.
2. Sexual drives, if sexual restraint is not possible, must be released only within marriage and then for the procreation of children.
3. Women tempt and seduce; they are below man, yet they drag him down by their sexual attractiveness and wiles.
4. Women, as inferior to men, are to stay in the background of religious activities. (Note again Paul's assertions in 1 Tim. 2:11.)
5. Women who want to be religiously active can join specific religious orders established for that purpose. As celibates they can come closer to God, thereby benefiting both themselves and the men around them by withdrawing from interactions that could lead to infractions of God's moral code.
6. Leadership and decision-making are reserved for men.
7. Preaching and interpretation of the Scriptures are reserved for men.

In fairness to Christianity, it should be noted that Jesus himself treated women and men more evenhandedly than many of his followers did. His recorded miracles include women as well as men as recipients—the daughter of Jairus and Peter's mother-in-law benefited no less than the man born blind or the man possessed by demons, for example. Women were singled out for their expressions of strong faith as frequently as men (e.g., the woman with a hemorrhage, the Samaritan woman, and the beggar woman). Although Jesus did not practice affirmative action in the selection of his twelve disciples, he did number several women among his close friends. He violated the Sabbath to help women (e.g., Luke 13:10–13), and he rejected one taboo after another in speaking to the Samaritan woman at the well (John 4:7–30)—taboos against associating with impure persons (in this case doubly so—both as a woman and a Samaritan)—and then using her as a religious messenger to her townspeople. Carmody summarizes by saying:

> Jesus treats men and women simply as individuals who need his help, or as coworkers, or friends. He offers women no separate but equal way of works; he compiles no segregating list of feminine virtues. In the face of considerable opposition, and with the consequence of provoking scandal, Jesus associates with the outcasts and marginal people of his day; the poor, sinners, tax collectors, lepers—and women.[26]

That there is this model in the New Testament, as a contrast to the Pauline reinforcement for the established societal model of second-class citizenship for women, is probably a primary reason that many women continue to work for reform within the Christian denominations—one of the options or routes being followed by women today (to be discussed later in this chapter). In fairness to Paul, however, there are many scholars who would attribute the New Testament books that tend to subjugate women and urge their second-class nature to writers, other than Paul. Many scholars would suggest that only Romans, 1 and 2 Corinthians, Galatians, and Philemon, are genuinely authored by Paul. It should be noted that these books are least likely, of the nonhistorical books of the New Testament, to support inferior status for women. In fact, a favorite text for sermons preached at ordination services of women candidates for the ministry, continues to be the text chosen by the Reverend Luther Lee at the ordination service of the first woman ordained in the United States (Antoinette Brown) in 1856—Galatians 3:28: "There is neither Jew nor Greek, there is neither slave nor free, there is neither male nor female; for you are all one in Christ Jesus." The second of the dual texts used by Reverend Lee was the prophecy in Joel 2:28, which was quoted by Peter in the story of Pentecost and recorded in Acts 2:17: "Your sons and daughters will prophesy."[27]

Summary

By way of a brief summary of the roles of women in traditionally religious societies, we turn again to Carmody. She notes first a subordinate role, as a woman gained status only through her relationship to a man—"by being the daughter of this father, the wife of this husband, the mother of that son."[28] Second, there is the dependent role. Carmody notes that Buddhist nuns were expected to serve even the newest and youngest monk; Christian wives were instructed to be silent in the churches and obedient to their husbands, as their "heads," just as Christ is the head of the Church; Muslim women were veiled through purdah from the eyes of all but their own husband.[29] Third, there was assumed intellectual inferiority. For example, Jewish women were denied opportunity to study the Torah; Chinese women did not study the Confucian classics; Hindu women did not study the Vedas.[30] In short, all the major religions were decidedly patriarchal, reflecting the cultures within which they arose.

CONTEMPORARY RESPONSES

As we look at the contemporary religious scene so far as the responses and participation of women are concerned, we see a broad array of options that are available—challenges, if you will—all of which have proponents, all of which are in process and practice, all of which have precedents as well.

Introductory Summary

In an attempt to provide some organization to what might at first glance seem a bewildering and unrelated set of options, we would suggest that there are three primary categories of response on the part of women to the question of their relationship to religion. Each category of response has in turn at least two subcategories.

The first we shall call the tradition-affirming response. Here we encounter two major subtypes: (1) The subordinate female religious role along the lines of the New Testament admonition for women to "keep silent" in the church and refrain from having any religious authority over men; and (2) the specialized religious role for women as best typified in the female monastic orders within Roman Catholicism.

Second, there is the tradition-reforming response, in which there is continuing strong commitment to the religious institution, but at the same time there is a call for significant change (reformation) with respect to the traditional role and functions of women. Here two particular movements or emphases stand out. One is the movement to open ordination to the ministry to women. The second is a position that is newer and somewhat more inclusive than the ordination issue. That is the "radical obedience" position articulated by the women's rights leader and theologian Rosemary Radford Ruether by which she urges rethinking and reforming the traditional roles and perceptions of women, but without either destroying the church or pulling women out of the institution.

Third, there is the revolutionary response that calls for such change in the substance of religion as traditionally expressed and organized as to be truly revolutionary. Here we include two subthemes. First, the call to "exodus" from traditional religious institutions as expressed by the Roman Catholic writer and theologian Mary Daly. Second, the proclamation of female superiority and the rejection of male dominance and direction of religious patterns through the resurrection of ancient practices and beliefs of witchcraft.

Tradition-Affirming Responses

Traditional patterns of religious involvement for women are certainly the most highly supported of all the options. That is to say, female religious orders continue to gain novices, and ladies' guilds and societies in both denominations and sects continue to flourish. This is not to say that membership in religious orders is not down from past numbers (actually membership has declined at a dramatic rate), or that ladies' guilds and women's missionary societies are flourishing at their peak post-World War II levels. But it nonetheless remains true that, because of the inertia of tradition, if nothing else, great numbers of women continue to express themselves and find some level of satisfaction in avenues of religious expression, which have been sanctioned by long-standing tradition.

Religious Orders   We earlier mentioned the option for women of monastic orders, particularly with reference to Buddhism. The viability of this option within Christianity for a great many centuries is well-known. The provision of a structure, through which women could perform distinctly "feminine" tasks, such as nurturing and healing the sick, caring for the poor and needy, or teaching the young in schools, was well-suited to use women's skills and energy in constructive ways and yet did not at all challenge the established religious patriarchy. One might even suggest, at the risk of sounding facetious, that these women, celibate as they were required to be, were therefore not only closer to God but constituted that many fewer temptations to the men in society.

We referred earlier to the high regard for virginity and celibacy that existed in the early centuries of the Christian Church. This resulted already in the second century C.E. in the consecration of young women to remain unmarried and live either with the parental family or occasionally alone, to fulfill a life of contemplation and devotion. Some widows were consecrated as deaconesses to live lives of service. Gradually, communities of these celibate women developed and what we would properly think of today as a monastic order or convent emerged. This occurred at least as early as the fourth century C.E. Both male and female monastic orders began to multiply and we encounter such founders and advocates as Saint Antony, Saint Pachomius, and Saint Basil in the fourth century, and Saint Augustine, Saint Benedict, and Saint Caesarius in the fifth century. Their female counterparts and contemporaries were the sisters of Saint Pachomius and Saint Benedict, Bathilde at Chelles, Rodegund at Poitiers, Joan at Bourges, and Bridget in Sweden. They opened houses of learning, work, and devotion, which were based on various elaborations of the three universal vows of chastity, poverty, and obedience.[31]

New orders continued to be established throughout the world. Taking vows of a nun (sister) became, in the Roman Catholic Church and much later in a few Protestant denominations, a goal for young women that was highly valued by both the women themselves and their fellow church members. Thus, for millions of women down through the centuries, the celibate, impoverished, obedient life of the nun has been a highly legitimate religious route for women to follow, although the number of women entering such orders continues to dwindle.[32] It is, without question, about as traditional a choice as there is—chaste, virginal women doing "women's work" of teaching, healing, serving the needy, and baking bread.

Traditional Christian Role   The other traditional religious role for women is one with which the reader is probably very familiar. This is the role that for all but a very few has placed women in the background of religious activities—in most Christian denominations, for example, without vote in congregational matters and excluded from the pulpit and from behind the communion rail, women have typically been in charge only of chicken dinners and the pre-Christmas bazaar. This traditional role within Christianity, as well as some flavor of a contemporary woman's reaction to that traditional role *vis-á-vis* the traditional male role, is ably described in the following excerpt from Sharon Emswiler's essay "How the New Woman Feels in the Old Worship Service." While this describes her experiences in the early 1970s and, as we shall show in succeeding pages, there has been significant change in some denominations, her description of her participation in a typical worship service in a Protestant church continues to be experienced in many religious groups today and describes dominant patterns in most other denominations until very recently. As such, Emswiler's description represents the experience of millions of women in churches today and certainly also tens of millions of their mothers before them.

> I enter the sanctuary and am directed to my seat by an usher, always male, except on "Ladies' Day," that one day in the year when women are given the opportunity to "play usher." As I sit and meditate I listen to the organ prelude. If the church is a small one, I notice that the organist is a woman. However, if the church is a large, prestigious one, with an expensive organ, the position of organist is most often filled by a man.
>
> The minister (or ministers)—male, of course—then appears to begin the service, accompanied by a layperson (male) acting as the liturgist of the morning. The call to worship is given, setting the worship service in motion. One such call to worship that sticks in my mind from a service I attended contains the line, "To be is to be a brother." Hearing those words, I instantly carry them to their logical conclusion: "I am not, and never will be, a brother. Therefore, I am not. I do not exist." The service is off to a great start!
>
> The congregation now rises for the first hymn and I find myself singing a song such as "Men and Children Everywhere" (I wonder in which group I am to include myself), "Rise Up, O Men of God," or "Faith of our Fathers." If it is near Christmas, the selections might be "God Rest Ye Merry Gentlemen" or "Good Christian Men, Rejoice"; while the Easter season offers such choices as "Sing with All the Sons of Glory" or "Good Christian Men Rejoice and Sing." Other possible hymns in the service might include "Once to Every Man and Nation," "Now Praise We Great and Famous Men," "Brother Man, Fold to Thy Heart," "As Men of Old Their First Fruits Brought," or "Turn Back, O Man."
>
> If the service is of a more contemporary style, I go in the hope that the hymns will speak to me in a way that the traditional ones do not. But here, too, I discover that while the folk tunes have a great appeal to me, I am asked to sing songs with titles like "Be a New Man," "Sons of God," "Come, My Brothers," "Brothers, Get Yourselves Together," and "Brother, How's Your Love."
>
> As I sing I try to imagine that these songs are speaking to me, but I am not accustomed to thinking of myself as a "man" or a "brother"; and the

identification is difficult, and most often impossible. The only way I can find to identify with these masculine words is to attempt either to deny or set aside my femininity. But I do not want to deny that part of my personhood; I want rather to affirm it. I want my femaleness recognized and affirmed by the Church also. As the worship progresses through the prayers, creeds, and sermon, the same language form keeps recurring—always the masculine when referring to people, always the masculine when referring to God. While I sing and during prayer I change the word "men" to "people"; "mankind" to "humankind"; "sons" to "children"; "Father" to "parent," but I feel as though I am outshouted by the rest of the congregation. My words are swallowed up by theirs.

Listening to the minister preach his sermon for the morning, I am aware that he is not really attempting to address me or my sisters in the congregation. His illustrations all revolve around men and speak overwhelmingly to the masculine experience in our society. Suddenly, I feel as though I am eavesdropping on a conversation labeled "For Men Only." Or worse yet, I feel that the suspicion I had after the call to worship is true. I do not exist! I look down at my hands and arms and feet. I can see them; they are very real to me. But I feel that somehow I must be invisible to this preacher who has designed this service and now stands in front of me, speaking of "the brethren" and telling his congregation to be "new men."

Following the sermon, the worshippers are invited to participate in the celebration of the Lord's Supper. As the large group of male ushers marches down the aisle to receive the communion elements and distribute them to the congregation, I am suddenly struck with the irony of the situation. The chicken suppers, the ham suppers, the turkey suppers in the church are all prepared and served by the women. But not the Lord's Supper! Yes, it is prepared by the women, but the privilege of serving the Lord's Supper in worship is reserved for the men. This particular morning I find it very difficult to swallow the bread and drink the wine, knowing that within the Body of Christ, the Church, the sisters of Christ are not given the same respect and privileges as are his brothers.[33]

Such a "men only" or "men first" pattern is, as mentioned earlier in this chapter, not unique to Christianity. It has been characteristic, in some cases to an even more extreme degree, in all the major world religions. Nor is it dead. Far from it. For one thing, a great many women continue to assume such female subordinate religious roles and postures as proper and divinely ordained. Entire denominations continue to espouse such perspectives and make them tenets of doctrinal assent. In fact, a resurgent movement within many fundamentalist and conservative church bodies and congregations, calling for a return to the "Christian family," holds as the ideal family structure a patriarchal one in which women and children assume nurturing and obedient roles respectively behind a dominant, decision-making, sanction-disseminating husband-father. Consistent with this perspective, though not necessarily essential to it, was the "total woman" concept espoused by Marabel Morgan and made popular in the 1970s.[34] The central ideas of the total woman concept were that a woman could expect a much happier and more satisfying life if she worked hard at pleasing "her man" and remained in the traditional niche set aside for women.

Modifications of the Traditional Christian Role   Feminist critics would say that women who espouse this "traditional" role of women generally, and in traditional religion in particular, have been deluded and do not recognize such traditional forms of religion as a tool of preserving patriarchy, suppressing women's energies and talents, and imbuing them with "false consciousness," in which hope for a better life is deferred toward expectation of heaven.[35]

This should not suggest that these women are not aware, from their personal experience and observation, that women's roles and place in all the major world religions has been (and remains) subordinate to men. In the Christian case, they have learned well the directive from St. Paul to "keep silent in the churches." But many have found ways to assert themselves and rise above the limitations their religions place upon them, by participating independently in other groups within their religious tradition, where they can find strength and delight in religious discussions and experiences that are not dictated by men—experiences that give them spiritual and emotional strength. One such group is the Women's Aglow Fellowship International.[36]

Griffith describes the women in this group as seeing themselves as filling a nurturing role in church and society, as they demonstrate themselves to be "more supportive, loving, and spiritual than men."[37] They deny the suggestion by their feminist sisters that they are "[blind] to their own sociopolitical, religious, and domestic disempowerment, the hazardous result of seeing the world only through Jesus-colored glasses."[38] Griffith goes on to say, "Yet Aglow and like-minded women defy characterization, perceiving themselves not as blind victims but as clear-sighted dissidents opposing basic elements of the wider culture: its materialism and greed, for instance, along with its apathy, self-indulgence, and ubiquitous violence."[39]

But there is also evidence on the other side of this issue. In many denominations, women have been and are assuming both more visible and more significant roles in religious life. Ordination to the ministry and receiving calls to be pastors, priests (Episcopal), and rabbis constitute dramatic evidence of this (to be discussed later in the chapter). But even short of ordination, women in some denominations serve on church boards, become deacons and elders in local churches, and assist in the distribution of holy communion.

Thus, what we have referred to, as the traditional secondary and subordinate role for women in religious activities, is certainly not extinct. In fact, one could hardly even say it is dying. While, as we will document in the concluding two sections of this chapter, there are numerous challenges and alternatives to such traditional views of women's religious roles, and a significant number of women have adopted alternative definitions and modes, such challenges have actually at the same time stimulated a resurgence of support for traditional female religious roles. A quick browsing through any religious bookstore that specializes in conservative, fundamentalist or "born again" Christian literature, will immediately reinforce this observation.

Reformation Responses for the Female Religious Role

Here we shall look particularly at two ways in which women want to continue within the traditional religious organizations but, at the same time, are dedicated to reforming those organizations and their traditional patterns. Parallel to a grand tradition in British politics, these would be women of the "loyal opposition." That is, they want to remain members in good standing of a standard religious group, yet are equally committed to changing certain aspects, tenets, or practices of that group or, in their terms, "updating" them.

Any woman who seeks to change a local congregation's constitution that prohibits women from voting on congregational matters, serving as an elder or deacon, or assisting with the formal worship service in any visible way, is part of this reformational response. Any woman, who lobbies within her denomination for change in that religious group's stand on abortion or birth control, is part of this response. But in the interest of brevity, we shall focus briefly on only two emphases—first, the movement toward the ordination of women as bona fide "clergymen," and second, the perspective espoused by the women's rights leader and theologian Rosemary Radford Ruether and identified in her own terms as "radical obedience."[40]

Ordination of Women   The ordination of women issue, though not entirely new, is certainly of relatively recent origin so far as the span of history is concerned. As we mentioned earlier, the first American woman to be ordained into the ministry was Antoinette Brown, a Congregationalist, in South Butler, New York, in 1856.[41] Olympia Brown followed in 1863. But such nineteenth-century ordinations were rare. Most members of churches, and their leaders as well, must have agreed with the argument against the ordination of women expressed by a seminary professor at Oberlin Theological School in 1849. He argued categorically against the ordination of women because women are "emotional, physically delicate, illogical, weak-voiced, vain, dependent, and most important, divinely ordained to be homemakers."[42]

It took until the twentieth century, and only in the last half of that, before any significant number of religious groups have allowed the ordination of women. For example, it was not until 1956 that the United Presbyterian Church in the United States began to ordain women. The Church of the Brethren ordained its first woman in 1960. The Lutheran Church in America approved the ordination of women in 1970. The first Jewish woman in Reform Judaism in the United States to become a rabbi,

Sally Priesand, was ordained in 1972. The first female rabbi in Conservative Judaism was not ordained until 1986. And it was not until 1974, that the first women were ordained in the Episcopal Church in the United States and not until 1987, that Episcopalians in Great Britain (the Church of England) first developed guidelines on how to open the priesthood to women.[43]

A logical consequence of the ordination of women is consideration of their consecration as bishops in faiths that have such roles—namely, Roman Catholicism, Eastern Orthodoxy, and some Protestant denominational families, such as Anglicanism, Lutheranism, and Methodism. In the Episcopal (Anglican) Church in the United States, that action occurred for the first time in February 1989, when Barbara Harris was consecrated as a bishop in Boston. Ms. Harris is not only a woman, but she is black as well. Neither the Anglican Church of England nor the Roman Catholic Church sent formal representatives to the rites, though sixty American Anglican bishops were present. Lutherans now have 22 female bishops worldwide, including 7 in the United States and 1 in Canada as of summer 2002.[44]

The provocation for raising the question of the ordination of women has been largely a social one. It is clear that when women, participating in the antislavery movement in the 1830s to 1860s, discovered that while their leadership and oratory were often eagerly sought out, they were not allowed to use a pulpit or church platform as a place from which to speak, their consciousness as well as their level of indignation were raised. Women, such as the Grimké sisters (Angelina and Sarah), Margaret Prior, Lucy Stone, and Lydia Child, led the way. When Lucretia Mott and Elizabeth Cady Stanton were excluded, on the basis of sex, from the World Anti-Slavery Convention in London in 1840, they began to lay plans for a new movement devoted to the cause of women.[45]

As feminism in general, and the woman's suffrage movement in particular, gained momentum at the end of the nineteenth and beginning of the twentieth centuries, culminating in the Nineteenth Amendment in 1920, which provided women the right to vote in U.S. elections, some religious groups saw the incongruity and permitted women to head churches as ordained ministers (primarily in Baptist, Methodist, and Pentecostal churches). But probably more common was the alternative of being a female religious entrepreneur who possessed charismatic leadership qualities and gathered bands of local followers in sectarian groups, particularly in urban settings. Some of these women attained national and international notice and followings. Note such women as Mary Baker Eddy, founder of Christian Science, and the evangelist Aimee Semple McPherson.

An interesting example of early women in the ministry comes from the fringe of Protestantism in the Unitarian and Universalist churches. They were among the first denominations to ordain women and by 1890 they had ordained seventy women. But relatively few of them actually served in full-time, paid pastorates. Cynthia Tucker notes that they were called only to small, barely viable congregations that male clergy would not take, or they were married to ministers whose positions overshadowed their own. Tucker observes that they "were a largely unnoticed presence whose existence came to be known primarily through the efforts of a still smaller group who banded together on the frontier in the 1880s and 1890s."[46] Here were small, struggling congregations that could neither attract nor afford full-time male clergy with families to support. The population base in the frontier towns was far too small to provide great numerical success for what were definitely fringe groups that originated within American Protestantism.

Nonetheless, the door to ordination and religious leadership remained closed to most women. As we have mentioned, it was only very recently that the barriers have been knocked down in many of the major religious groups. Continuing in opposition are such major religious groups as the Orthodox Churches, the Lutheran Church–Missouri Synod, the Roman Catholic Church, Orthodox Judaism, and over a hundred of the 262 official Christian denominations in the United States that report statistics to the National Council of Churches. Of course, none of these is without both male and female voices that challenge the sex-based restrictions to ordination. Even such a stronghold of religious patriarchy as the Roman Catholic Church, is beginning to discuss the topic. Books, papers, and special conferences are beginning to accumulate. And the National Conference of Catholic Bishops has considered proposals to countenance the ordination of women to the priesthood but has rejected it under strong urging of Pope John Paul II through the 1990s and continuing opposition from Pope Benedict XVI.

In contrast, the Church of England (Anglican Church) has made the decision to ordain women priests. On 12 November 1992, it joined twelve of the twenty-eight self-governing parishes in the worldwide Anglican communion. Needed to approve was a two-thirds majority of all three houses of the church's General Synod. Votes to approve were 39 to 13 by bishops, 176 to 74 by clergy, and 169 to 82 by lay representatives. Interestingly, a switch of only two votes among the lay delegates would have blocked approval.[47]

Professional Careers for Women Compared   With respect to those women who have been ordained in the United States, three sets of data are instructive. First, there continue to be relatively few ordained women. The 1960 United States Census listed 4,727 women as "clergymen." This was 2.3 percent of all clergy. This proportion compares with 3.7 percent of all lawyers and judges, and 7 percent of physicians and surgeons. By 1970 the proportion of clergy who were women had increased to 2.9 percent. But lawyers-judges and physicians-surgeons categories had increased even more—to 4.9 percent and 9.7 percent, respectively. In the 1980 census, the increase of women clergy was more substantial. Their increase was an even doubling of their proportion of all clergy—from 2.9 percent in 1970 to

5.8 percent in 1980 (from 6,674 to 16,434). Again, this increase still lagged behind that of women lawyers and judges by a considerable margin. Women lawyers-judges grew as a proportion of all lawyers-judges from 4.9 percent to 14 percent—nearly tripling their share. The number of women physicians also grew, but not by as much on a percentage basis: from 9.7 percent in 1970 to 13.4 percent of all physicians in 1980.

By the 2000 United States census, growth in the proportions of female lawyers/judges and medical doctors had not grown as fast, though the proportions were still increasing. Female lawyers and judges had grown to 275,022 (29.7 percent of all lawyers/judges); female medical doctors had grown to 200,601 (27.9 percent of all medical doctors). The proportion of female clergy continued to lag fairly far behind, at slightly less than half the proportion of women in law and medicine—50,922 female clergy accounting for 13.8 percent of all clergy. Nonetheless, the increase for women in the clergy ranks has been substantial, growing proportionately six-fold in forty years (1960–2000). This compares to a proportional four-fold increase in medical doctors and an eight-fold increase for lawyers/judges, over the same forty years. But, as noted in the 1960 data, the percentage of female clergy started noticeably lower than lawyers/judges and particularly lower than medical doctors—a proportion that, in 1960, was only one-third as great as the percentage of women in the profession of medicine.[48]

Ordaining Women Still New in Many Denominations   So far as women clergy are concerned, we must remember that most Judeo-Christian denominations do not ordain women, but also that of those who do, several have opened the door of ordination to women only in the last decade or two. Therefore, the number of ordained women in some denominations remains small. In a study for the National Council of Churches, Constant Jacquet found in a study of female clergy in Protestant churches between 1977 and 1986, that despite the fact that about eighty denominations ordained women by that time, female clergy were still clustered in preponderant numbers in a few denominations. The two religious groups with the greatest number of female clergy—the Assemblies of God, with 3,718 female clergy, and the Salvation Army with 3,220—are neither large nor at the core of mainline American denominationalism. On the other hand, the only other groups with more than a thousand female clergy are mainline denominations—the United Methodist Church (1,891), the Presbyterian Church U.S.A. (1,519), and the United Church of Christ (1,460). The proportion of females to the total number of clergy in various denominations is still low, except for the Salvation Army (62 percent of Salvation Army clergy are women). Of mainline Protestant denominations, only the United Church of Christ, at 14.5 percent is above 10 percent, and most are in the 4 to 6 percent range (Methodists, Episcopalians, American Baptists, and Lutherans).[49] Within Judaism, as of 1993, Simon, Scanlan, and Nadel reported that approximately

4 percent of Jewish rabbis were women, most of them educated at Hebrew Union College, a Reform Jewish seminary.[50]

The Ordination of Women Issue in the Catholic Church The situation in the Roman Catholic Church shows both change and "business as usual." The business as usual is that the Roman Catholic Church does not ordain women to the priesthood, nor will it do so any time soon. But following Pope John XXIII and the Second Vatican Council that he convened (concluded in 1965), women were allowed, for the first time, to enroll in schools of theology to prepare for ministry. Within a relatively short time (by 1988), approximately one-fourth of students enrolled in Catholic theological schools were women.[51] These women are allowed to serve as "parish administrators" or "pastoral associates." Other titles used are: pastoral coordinator, pastoral minister, pastoral director, parish life coordinator.[52] As such, they perform many of the tasks that ordained priests and ministers are asked to carry out: teaching members at all age levels; conducting some portions of the liturgy; providing premarital counseling; making calls on the sick, lapsed members, and prospective members, and some preaching. Although they are not allowed to preach the major homily following the reading of the Gospel, they do preach at other points of the service or do so following the Gospel reading after the supervisory priest has himself said a few words by way of introduction. But the major responsibility they cannot perform is consecration of the Eucharist. This must be performed by a visiting priest, who is the parish administrator's supervisor. Further, they cannot baptize, preside at a marriage or funeral mass, or hear confession.

And we must note again that parish administrators are not ordained. They remain part of the laity, whether they are sisters (nuns) in religious orders or regular lay members of a Roman Catholic parish. While they serve much like those in the ancient role of deacon, which goes back to New Testament times, unlike male deacons they cannot aspire to ordination and permission to celebrate the Mass, which includes consecration of the Eucharist. While Edward Echlin, in his book on the history of the diaconate in the Roman Catholic Church, explicitly calls for women to be admitted to the diaconate, in order to fill increasing needs for their service, and even strongly hints that their role could be redefined and expanded as needed in the future,[53] that is unlikely to happen. What is more likely is a broadening of the limits on what religious functions the parish administrator or a deacon can perform, yet without actually ordaining women. For example, instead of requiring that an ordained male priest always bless the host (bread/wafer) for holy communion each time the Eucharistic distribution is made, an ordained priest could bless enough communion wafers and wine to last several weeks or months, or in essence "deputize" the pastoral assistant or deacon to carry out the Eucharistic acts in the stead of and by the ordained authority of the supervising priest.

Female Clergy Underrepresented in the Parish Ministry   Nearly half (46.6 percent) of professional level staff positions in Catholic dioceses, however, are held by women.[54] This is a two percentage point increase between 1995 and 1998 and shows, if nothing else, that women's service within the traditionally male-dominated Roman Catholic Church is increasing in all areas of church life, except ordination to the priesthood itself.

The second set of data shows that of the ordained women at work in the denominations that permit them, the proportion in the parish ministry is quite low. In 1951, only half (51.8 percent) of the ordained Protestant women were serving as pastors of churches (including those in an assistant minister capacity). Of the thirteen denominations that have over one hundred female clergy and provide sufficient data, the proportion of female clergy serving in a pastoral capacity within a local congregation had not increased much by 1986. Data abstracted from Jacquet's study show only 55 percent, with a range that runs from 20 percent (Church of the Nazarene) to 99 percent (the Christian Congregation denomination).[55] Actually, the overall percentage of 55 percent is not so out of line as it might at first appear. The total proportion of all clergy in the denominations that report statistics to the National Council of Churches who are in the parish ministry is only 61 percent.[56] Although female clergy are included in that proportion, the proportion for males alone is barely above 62 percent. Of course, the male clergy, who are not parish pastors when interviewed, have in most cases been parish pastors at one time. Although they are now hospital or military chaplains, seminary professors, executive secretaries of denominational agencies and commissions, directors of religious social service organizations, and so on, in most cases they started out in the pastoral ministry.

What might be suggested here is a moderate tendency to separate or isolate women clergy into specialized roles, much like the more radical clergy were, according to Phillip Hammond and Robert Mitchell's study,[57] and to assign them to nonparish roles, such as the campus ministry or to various administrative roles within denominational and ecumenical bureaucratic structures. Another partial explanation may be that the role of parish minister has been a male role for so long that women may find some difficulty in filling it without at least some redefinition of the role taking place. That women can fill the role well, though with perhaps some necessary redefinition of the role, is well-attested in Priscilla and William Proctor's book, *Women in the Pulpit*.[58] Chaim Waxman notes that even in Reform Judaism (the most liberal branch of Judaism) the "ordination of women . . . can provide the necessary title but it does not guarantee a job." Waxman also notes the turning of some of the few ordained Jewish women to Jewish community service, since no synagogue pulpits are open to them.[59]

It should be mentioned that Orthodox Jewish scholar, Blu Greenberg, in 1993 referred to a growing movement of Orthodox women who are learning the Torah and Talmud in a variety of institutes, study groups, and university programs. Such women could be candidates for the rabbinate. She notes, in conclusion, that some highly respected Orthodox rabbis see no barriers in Jewish Law to the ordination of women.[60] Actually, in 1997, occurred the first ordination of a woman (Haviva Ner-David) as an Orthodox rabbi by a respected rabbi in Jerusalem. But at the time Ner-David said the ordination would likely be more symbolic than actual because it was unlikely that an Orthodox synagogue would employ her. To even hope to serve as a rabbi, she believed she would need to submerge some of her feminist ideals and neither read Torah nor lead prayers in a mixed congregation.[61]

Acceptance of Women Clergy   With respect to predicting the future of women filling the clergy role and finding acceptance by laypersons, studies in several denominations are now available. We shall look briefly at three. First is Larry Kersten's study of Lutherans in 1968 before any Lutheran women had been ordained in the United States. Kersten found that a substantial majority of laypersons in the two more liberal Lutheran denominations (73 percent of the Lutheran Church in America and 68 percent of the American Lutheran Church) were in favor of women being allowed to become ordained ministers.[62]

In a study of attitudes toward women clergy, using a representative sample of United Presbyterian laypersons, Edward Lehman found a generally favorable attitude toward women clergy, but with some qualifications. For example, although fully 82 percent of laypersons said that a woman's temperament was as well-suited to the ministry as that of men, a third of the sample still tended to think of women pastors in a stereotypical way, with respect to carrying out the dual functions of pastor and wife-mother.[63] Also, nearly two-thirds of the respondents indicated that, in the face of local church resistance to calling a woman as pastor, they would choose a man over a woman,[64] that is, ignore affirmative action principles. A number of factors correlate with this bias: sex (men were more likely than women to express such bias), age (older members more likely than young), education (the higher the education the more open), church size (the larger the more likely to be biased), and involvement (the greater the involvement by members the less supportive of women clergy).[65]

There is clear evidence that once a female minister is allowed to carry out the activities of a minister, people generally evaluate the performance as satisfactory. Yet two-thirds will still say they prefer a man, even going so far as to believe that their female minister is an atypical success—a woman with very special abilities.[66]

Lest the reader come away with a negative conclusion about how people view female ministers, we hasten to note that Lehman concludes that, while there are negative and stereotypical views of women in the ministry in churches and a "resistant minority has a powerful voice in the current debates,"[67] still the predominant response of church members to women in ministry is positive.[68] And Lehman concludes: "If women are allowed to function as ordained clergy in local congregations, they will succeed as fully as men."[69]

Jacquet provides some interesting data regarding opportunities for female clergy to serve as sole or senior pastors of congregations. Nationally, only 20 percent of female clergy are serving in the traditional parish ministry as "head pastor," whether alone or in charge of one or more other ministers in a large congregation. The range is almost incredibly wide: from 2 percent (21 of 860) of female clergy as head pastor in the Reorganized Church of Jesus Christ of Latter Day Saints, to 99 percent (289 of 290) of women clergy in the Christian Congregation denomination.[70] It is of interest to note that the denomination with the greatest number of female clergy (the Assemblies of God, with 3,718 women clergy) has a very low proportion of its women clergy as heads of pastoral staffs—only 7 percent.[71] The denomination with the second highest number of female clergy is the Salvation Army, which also has a low proportion of its female clergy as heads of pastoral staff—only 18 percent. Actually, the denomination with the second highest proportion of female clergy acting as head pastor, is the Lutheran Church in America (now merged with the American Lutheran Church to form the Evangelical Lutheran Church in America) with 55 percent. All other denominations are below 50 percent, with most in the 23–32 percent range.[72]

Ministerial Job Satisfaction   With respect to satisfaction so far as their ministries are concerned, Hale, King, and Jones found, in a study of nine hundred Methodist clergywomen, a great many with feelings of acceptance, success, and satisfaction. Yet, for 15 to 20 percent, the ordained ministry has confronted them with serious problems and provided them with little satisfaction.[73] Actually, a third of Methodist clergywomen reported "considerable" to "much" difficulty at all but one of seven stages in reaching a mature ministry. The least problematic was handling the course of study at seminary (only 22 percent reporting at least "considerable difficulty").[74]

The question of levels of satisfaction expressed by female clergy is one that needs more attention by denominational leaders. There does seem to be a problem. In her sample of women clergy, Joy Charlton[75] found that half of the women in her sample had left the ministry during a fifteen-year period. While this was a small study, involving only a few clergywomen from two denominations (Methodist and Lutheran), it was well conceived and executed and provides a type of data rarely found, namely, longitudinal data following the same sample over a span of several years.

The 50 percent dropout rate appears to be high and is certainly higher than for male clergy. Women appear to be leaving at a faster rate and at a younger age than men. If the same high dropout rate is occurring in other denominations, the growth rate for women clergy will be slower than the growing numbers of women attending seminaries might suggest.

Suggestive of a reason or set of reasons for the 50 percent dropout rate, is Charlton's discovery that while almost none of her sample aspired to be feminists while in seminary training, after fifteen years all wanted to join the feminist ranks, though they felt their role would not permit it. It would appear that acceptance of female clergy in congregations is certainly not universal and is far from wholehearted and unconditional. Although data from Lehman showed that stereotypical views of women clergy as less well-suited for ministry than men and associated doubts about their effectiveness are held by only a minority of parishioners, the attitudes and actions of that minority of 15 percent[76] is certainly enough to leave women clergy with less than full satisfaction.

Enrollment in Seminaries by Women   Further indications of the future increase in women ordained to the ministry come from seminary enrollment data—our third set of data. From 1972 to 1987, the enrollment of women in Protestant seminaries in the United States and Canada increased 356 percent. The corresponding change for males was only 36 percent. The number of women enrolled in Protestant seminaries increased from 3,358 in 1972,[77] when they accounted for 10.2 percent of seminary enrollees, to 15,310 in 1987, when they constituted 27 percent of enrollment. By 1992, the number had increased to 19,926. This was 31 percent of seminary enrollments. A decline of 128 students (64 less than one percent) in 1993, is the first numerical decline since women began to enroll in theological schools to a significant degree.[78]

But since that one aberational year of decline, the enrollment of women in Protestant seminaries has continued to increase year by year (by as much as 7 percent in 1998). In 2003, the most recent year that data are available, the percentage increase was 8 percent during the two-year period since 2000. This increase has yielded a total of 27,920 female seminarians as of 2002.[79]

During all this time, women have continued to gain on men as a percentage of enrollees at Protestant seminaries, but recently only very slowly. Although the gain since 1972 is substantial—from 10.2 percent of total seminary enrollment in 1972 to 35.5 percent in 2003—in the latest fifteen year period from 1988–2003, the increase is only 6.21 percentage points, moving from 29.29 percent to 35.5 percent of seminary enrollments.[80] This increase is small compared with the increases in female enrollees and graduates in the professions of medicine and law, cited earlier in this chapter. There are two straightforward reasons the women's recent gain on the male enrollees is small. First, it is clear that the trend of increasing numbers of female seminarians has slowed substantially since the 1970s and 1980s. Second, the number of male seminary enrollees has also increased slightly, thus making it more difficult for female enrollees to make significant percentage gains.

However, it is still clear that women have become a significant presence in most Protestant seminaries, averaging over a third of the enrollees. But this has not had a negative impact on male enrollment, which also has increased. An obvious conclusion at this point, is that in the future the ranks of Protestant clergy will, on the one hand be clearly diverse so far as gender is concerned, yet, on the other hand, the ministry will not become a primarily female role, except possibly in a few denominations. The numbers cited above are totals and do not reflect fairly significant differences by denomination. The enrollment of women in a few Protestant seminaries has already passed 50 percent.

At Roman Catholic theological schools, Ruth Wallace reports that enrollment of women was approximately 25 percent in 1988.[81] But, as noted earlier, such education does not lead to ordination to the priesthood for these female students.

It is interesting that the ordination question is not an issue only within Christianity. We noted earlier that all the major world religions reversed earlier positions of forcing women to withdraw into the background and refrain from trying to assume leadership positions. So it was definitely a newsworthy item in 1994 to learn that Hindus in Trinidad had recently ordained their first woman priest. This elicited criticism from orthodox Hindu groups, who asserted that Hinduism does not permit such a role for women. But a reform movement, the Arya Samaj, claims that the Hindu scriptures, the Vedas, permit women priests. This group has ordained female Hindu priests in North America, South Africa, India, and other Asian countries.[82]

While it appears that the acceptance of females in the clergy role is already fairly high and will undoubtedly increase over time, an intriguing question remains. That is, are there differences in ministerial style between men and women?

Differences in Ministerial Styles by Gender?   Some studies suggest that differences in managerial styles, between male and female business persons, might be reproduced among clergy leaders. A study of pastoral associates in the Catholic Church, by Ruth Wallace, suggests that women serving as pastoral associates tend to follow a collaborative style, while their predecessor male priests were perceived to be more hierarchical and patriarchal.[83]

A study of thirty-five female rabbis and twenty-five female Protestant ministers, by Rita Simon, Angela Scanlan, and Pamela Nadell, found high consensus among the female clergy, that they "carry out their duties as ministers and rabbis differently from male colleagues of comparable age and background." They described themselves as: "less formal," "more engaging," "more approachable," "more people-oriented," "more into pastoral care," "more personal," "more likely to reach out to touch and hug," and "less concerned about power struggles." They also considered their sermons "more personal," "more emotional," "conversational," "casual," "more relational," and "more spiritual."[84]

Research by Edward Lehman suggests something different. To make his point, he first describes what might be called traditional differences between the ministerial styles of male and female ministers, as widely believed to be the case. The masculine style is a familiar one and fits a traditional clergy role, often described as "patriarchal." Lehman describes this style as involving "a ministry steeped in impersonal hierarchies, segmental relationships, hyper-competitiveness, power over nature, rigid theology, legalistic ethics, and exclusion of women and minorities."[85] In contrast, the feminine role "incorporates personal communities, holistic relationships, egalitarianism, empowerment of laypeople, democratic decision-making, cooperation with nature, open and flexible theology, existential ethics of responsible sharing and inclusion of women and minorities." While these differences sound stereotypical, some research supports such descriptions. However, Lehman points out that these studies were conducted on single-sex samples and did not directly compare and contrast male and female clergy at the same time and in similar settings.[86]

Lehman interviewed both male and female clergy in four denominations and found that most clergy characterized themselves in relatively feminine terms, particularly with respect to dimensions of interpersonal style. While there are, of course, some differences among ministers with respect to ministerial style, gender is not necessarily the crucial factor in determining or predicting these differences. Actually, he concluded that male and female clergy exhibit relatively similar styles of ministry. Both men and women exhibit each style, and one style is not more characteristic of either men or women.[87]

We conclude at this point, as we wait for more evidence to be gathered, that we probably have a classic example of the role itself dictating the behavior of the role-taker more substantially than the gender and other personal characteristics of the individual. However, there are likely some differences in emphasis and style associated with gender that are not only worth noting but also possibly worth encouraging.

Reforming Role II: "Radical Obedience"

We referred earlier to a second reforming approach so far as the relationship of women to religion is concerned. That is the approach of "radical obedience" urged by Rosemary Radford Ruether. The term is Ruether's own. She remains within the Christian Church (Roman Catholic), speaks out explicitly against some of the more radical options espoused by some women, the feminists among them in particular (options that we shall discuss in the final section of this chapter), yet wants reformation of existing structures, not their dissolution and death. We shall neither attempt nor pretend to fully present Rosemary Ruether's position and advice, but will offer a few summary indications of her position.

While appealing for reform, rather than revolution and rejection of the core of Christianity, Ruether notes how women have in the past exercised some leadership and made contributions "from within" the body of the church.[88] Religious orders of nuns and sisters, who are set apart for special religious work, constitute an example known by everyone. But martyrdom has not been sex exclusive, and women have been recognized as contributing prophetic gifts in this process. Further, at times when reform movements, such as millennialism, have gained popularity, women could step into leadership positions because the very nature of the movement called into question some of the traditional expectations and patterns of family, religious organization, and society. She also mentions the important difference between religious organizations that have stressed lay leadership in contrast to formally-trained and sanctioned clerical leadership as in the Roman Catholic Church. She notes that those "who have the gifts, rather than those authorized by the traditional institutions, are acclaimed as leaders. In this situation women too can emerge as leaders."[89] Further, she notes that the Pentecostal groups and traditions have provided more opportunities for women, because the "gifts of the Spirit" could come to anyone, male or female. As such, the person and the message should have been heeded without particularly noting the sex of the person who was seen as a vehicle for the Holy Spirit.

Her conclusion, at this point, is that women should appropriate such patterns and precedents from history to vindicate their moving forward within religious institutions in the present in order "to reshape and enlarge the vision and life of the church today."[90]

Integral to this "reshaping" must be reevaluation of both traditional and contemporary Mariology (the theology surrounding the Virgin Mary within Roman Catholicism).[91] Here she speaks of the need to excise the concept of passive femininity, in which women are made to be "specialists in self-abnegating, auxiliary modes of existence,"[92] while men remain dominant and superordinate. Nor is it enough for men to adopt a "feminine side," particularly when such a feminine side is viewed as in the "nature" of women, but only auxiliary and supplemental to men.[93]

While Ruether is here enunciating, in almost a classic manner, the contemporary feminist demand for a true balance and transposition of so-called male and female qualities, rights, and expectations, she continues her assertions and appeals for action within the context of *reform*, "radical" for some though it may be.

Revolutionary Responses

Among various proposals for resolving the issue of traditional inferior roles and status for women in the major world religions, and Christianity in particular, we shall focus on what seem to be the two major options at the moment: (1) the religious exodus proposal, and (2) the resort to witchcraft.

Religious Exodus   The principal spokesperson for the religious exodus proposal is Mary Daly, who first caught public attention in 1968 with the publication of her book *The Church and the Second Sex*. In the book she was highly critical of the sexist perceptions, views, and practices of Christianity (Roman Catholicism in particular). But she called for reform, not revolution, in the sense of destroying the old to inaugurate a new order. But fairly quickly she moved to the point, not of revolution in the strictest sense of the term, perhaps, but of *exodus* from the institution—turning one's back on the old and marching out to establish something new. She articulated this position already in 1971, in her now famous Harvard Memorial Church Sermon, in which she spoke of the women's movement as an "exodus community." She speaks of women building a new community, as they are bonded in sisterhood. This sisterhood includes a number of qualities that lead eventually to the exodus. It is revolutionary as it destroys the credibility of sex stereotyping. It is revolutionary as it creates new definitions of God and invalidates patriarchal religion. It is antichurch in the sense that the institution called church remains sexist and wedded to patriarchal religious concepts. It is church itself, as it becomes a community "with a mission to challenge the distortions in sexually unbalanced society, to be a counter force to the prevailing sense of reality by building up a new sense of reality."[94] It is, finally, an exodus community that goes away from the land of its fathers. In that sermon, Daly then called to women to follow what had probably already been a spiritual break, by giving physical expression to their exodus community by leaving, that is, literally walking out of the church building.

In her book, *Beyond God the Father,* Mary Daly calls for the death of God, as he has been known within the Judeo-Christian tradition—that is, as male. This concept should be replaced with one of God more like that proposed by theologian Paul Tillich—ultimate meaning and reality, a process more than a "person."

She then makes even clearer what she means in her "postchristian" introduction to a second printing of her first book, *The Church and the Second Sex.* In a fascinating review of her own book of seven years earlier, she describes how far she has moved from those embryonic beginnings, how she had referred to her sisters in the movement as "they," not "we," and above all had viewed the movement as one of *reform*, not the exodus-revolution she has now come to espouse. In a subsequent book, *Gyn/Ecology*,[95] she refers to her first book as written by a "reformist fore-sister" (herself) whose work she had to refute. She has not retreated in any way from the revolutionary position she took thirty years ago, when she wrote with regard to institutional religion: "When you can say 'No' to the institution you can say a clearer and more effective 'Yes' to real movement, the movement of your sisters—past, present, and future."[96] She has continued to expand a new vocabulary with which to analyze what she believes is an unsalvable male-dominated (patriarchal) social system and language. As such, her followers are almost

exclusively women and remain relatively few. Rosemary Ruether agrees with
much of Daly's problem analysis but believes she and her movement have
fallen into a trap she calls "sectarian closure." Ruether describes this trap as
"an exclusivist view of truth" granted to and held by a privileged few women
(the elect).[97]

Witchcraft, Goddess Spirituality, and Paganism   Another revolutionary
expression, so far as the relationship of women to religion is concerned, is
articulated by Naomi Goldenberg. Like Mary Daly, Goldenberg traces the
rapid evolution of her own perceptions. She identifies her problems with
traditional religion beginning, when she tried to visualize women as rabbis,
priests, and ministers, but suddenly wondered how they, as women, would
or could represent a male god.[98] She saw this as an impossible incongruity.
She now sees in witchcraft a solution to the ancient problem of the
subordination of women religiously and otherwise.

In witchcraft, traditional historic religion is essentially turned upside
down. Female is defined as superior; although goddesses have male consorts,
and although those male beings are called gods, the goddess is more highly
valued and ranks higher in prestige and power.[99] What makes witchcraft
very different from most religions, particularly in the West, is not only the
superiority of women it upholds, but the radical break it makes with the view
of religion always implying an "other"—a god or other supernatural force or
power that is "out there," so to speak. Witchcraft places divinity within—not
a new idea at all of course (one thinks of pantheism, deism, Reform Judaism,
to only begin a long list). Its radical, revolutionary nature is in the substitution
of inner divinity for any and all traditional religious systems and expressions.

Some of the flavor of this inner divine power, residing within the
female and superior to that in the male, as well as a feel for some of the rage
and defiance against traditional religion that women in the witchcraft movement feel, is found in Goldenberg's description and analysis of an evening
service of the first national conference on women's spirituality held in
Boston on 23 April 1976, attended by several hundred women. Goldenberg's
description is as follows:

> The keynote speeches and opening rituals were held in a church in the
> heart of Boston. After listening attentively to two addresses on the theme
> of "Womanpower: Energy Re-Sourcement," the audience became very
> active. In tones ranging from whispers to shouts, they chanted, "The
> Goddess Is Alive—Magic Is Afoot." The women evoked the Goddess
> with dancing, stamping, clapping and yelling. They stood on pews and
> danced bare-breasted on the pulpit and amid the hymnbooks. Had any
> sedate, white-haired clergyman been present, I am sure he would have
> felt the Apocalypse had arrived.
> This episode during the Boston conference cannot be described as joy-
> ful. Women felt angry and bitter in a church that represented the worship

of a male god. It did not matter that this particular denomination had a more liberal outlook than most. In fact, the women were angry at all religions of the fathers and took this opportunity to mock and defy those religions in a church they had rented for the occasion. The anger was not pretty but it certainly was justified. Why not be enraged with the whole Judeo-Christian tradition for centuries of degradation of the bodies and images of women? Why not display your breasts in a place that has tried to teach you that they are things to be ashamed of, features that make you unlike God or His son? Proclaiming that the "Goddess Is Alive" in a traditional church setting is proclaiming that woman is alive, that being female is divine. The women in Boston were raising up their images as fleshly female beings to defy their culture's image of God as an immaterial male spirit. At this opening of the Boston conference the Goddess represented fierce pride in female physical presence and fury at the abuse that presence has taken from male religious authorities. The Goddess was never symbolized as an idol or a picture in this or any other ritual. Instead, She was seen as the force which had motivated each woman to be present at the first national gathering in Her honor.[100]

The ideas, introduced in Naomi Goldenberg's description, have expanded greatly in the last thirty years. Although the themes of goddess and witchcraft remain robust, and although the foundation motivation coming from dissatisfaction with traditional religion remains as a firm base for discovering or creating new forms of women's religion, few were probably prepared for the diversity of concepts, insights, and resources in this area that have proliferated. Therefore, we must expand our discussion of this revolutionary response of women, both to religion as it stands organized around them and to religion as it is an expression of the individual's analysis of internal needs and the interpretation of interactions and experiences with nature and with other people.

Marilyn Gottschall states that the goddess movement has evolved in America, over the past twenty-five years or so, as a grassroots gathering of women, who "have felt alienated from mainstream religious and political institutions."[101] Its roots and sustenance, she says, have come from New Age spiritualities, from the American neopagan movement, from feminist critics of mainstream patriarchal religious traditions, and the thousands of women across the country, who felt a deep spiritual longing that seemed not to be satisfied through traditional religious contacts, affiliations, and practices.[102]

As such, the expressions of the goddess movement are highly idiosyncratic. Gottschall says that "Goddess spirituality is highly individualistic with personal belief and practice at its center."[103] She agrees with Cynthia Eller, that feminist spirituality features a spirit of rugged individualism, in which "each woman is breaking her own spiritual path."[104] Of course, it is almost inevitable that these individual practitioners will link with one another and engage in much sharing of ideas, experiences, and rituals. Ritual is of great importance to the women's spirituality movement. Ruth Barrett says that participation in ritual highlights important changes or passages of life, whether they are emotional transitions or physical crossroads.[105] Further, "it is often through women's rites that they connect to and honor the deepest parts of themselves, bringing their inner knowledge to conscious awareness."[106]

Of sociological interest is the observation that, like most New Religious Movements, the followers of Wicca/Neo Paganism tend to be young, highly-educated, white, middle class, and mostly women.[107] The groups are quite independent and have no central bureaucracy that determines doctrine or practice. Its roots are old, dating to paleolithic times. But modern witches do not aim to mimic or reproduce old practices just because they are old. Neopaganism is devoted to nature and its maintenance. This is where Gaia comes in—Gaia, the ancient Greek Mother Earth goddess, from whom all other gods come. The focus of many ritual practices in neogagan festivals are directed at sustaining the *ga* (Greek for *earth*) which we all share and for which we have responsibility. Equally important at festivals is the neopagan focus on the self—its discovery and unfolding, its sustenance, and its expansion. Festivals provide opportunities for the "real self" to be revealed and expanded.

Sarah Pike notes that as neopagans become one with the world through the healing that takes place at festivals and rituals and, in turn, they send energy back to the earth. She says: ". . . the healing power that they conjure up is more powerful because of its collective amplification than if they were working individually . . . Self-expression and self-transformation accomplished within the framework of a religious community more effectively heal or change the world as we know it, as well as transform the self."[108]Hence, the focus and importance of the many festivals local groups sponsor every year.

It should also be noted that ritual practices in the goddess movement tend to focus on women's "mysteries." These are the five blood mysteries of birth, menstruation, birth/lactation, menopause, and death. Barrett describes these mysteries as woman's ability to create life, sustain life, and then return to the earth out of which all things come. "Women's Mysteries celebrate the Earth's seasonal cycles of birth, death and regeneration, and women's likewise cyclical nature."[109]

There may be as many as several hundred thousand women[110] who would identify themselves as participants in one or another of these groups that might be identified as a goddess group, as a part of neopaganism, as a part of wicca or the practice of witchcraft, Gaians, or simply, spiritual feminism. Although some of these terms might connote negative images in the eyes and minds of observers outside, they are benign. There is no linkage here to Satanism or demonism, to suicidal cults, to witches spinning evil spells and curses while dancing about boiling cauldrons of mysterious brew. Rather, at a most elemental level, these are women with prior religious experiences and affiliations who no longer find them satisfying and who have become feminists. At its core is the conviction that womanhood has great worth and power in its own right.

The goddess movement at its heart is an expression of extreme dissatisfaction with conventional religion. It encourages separation from the group (church, denomination, synagogue, and the like) and concentrates on the individual and her ideas and inherent self-worth, which consciously moves from male-centered to woman-centered religion, and which moves away from devotion to a god outside to the goddess inside the woman herself. There is great stress on the extreme value of the female body, mind, and experience, which is certainly at least the equal to those of the male. It is in reality the religious/spiritual dimension of feminism itself.

While outright goddess worship may not yet be of extreme significance in terms of numbers and is not about to replace all of traditional religion in American society or elsewhere, the movement is highly significant for what it says about the dissatisfaction of many women with the limiting options provided them in conventional religious organizations and expressions. The issue of the ordination of women, for example, begins to lose some of its potency as a significant social or religious issue, in the face of women pointing to the goddess dimension or force in all religion as well as to the goddess dimension within each of them. These women do not seem to need a traditional religious organization to practice their religion and are not concerned about ordination to the ministry.

Reformation Responses Revisited

At this point it is appropriate to return to the "reforming responses" some women are making, so far as their denominational affiliation and commitments are concerned. These are women who have moved far from "tradition-affirming" religious responses but are clearly not in the ranks of those women making true "revolutionary" responses. They are *reformers*, but admittedly not on the far end, the most radical end, of the reforming responses.

To more clearly understand their position, we have inserted the revolutionary religious response of women as described in the preceding section, before putting forward the most contemporary form of the reforming responses. These are not goddess-wicca-Gaia practitioners; yet they await opportunities to reform their denominations on women's issues or perhaps find themselves, in some cases, simply at a way station on the path to goddess-wicca-Gaia feminist religion. Susan Greenwood makes this same distinction between the reforming and revolutionary responses in her chapter on "Feminist Witchcraft," noting that reinvented feminist witchcraft began in the 1970s and that two different branches of feminist spirituality emerged. One consists of those who desire to reform orthodox religion without resorting to actual witchcraft. The other consists of "those who looked to pre-Christian primordial goddesses that inspired a perception of the universe as organic, alive, and sacred."[111] Feminist witchcraft is endemic in this latter view.

"Defecting in Place"   But there is another less radical option that some women have taken. About this option, that for the most part remains within the Christian reforming tradition, Miriam Winter, Adair Lummis, and Allison Stokes have coined a very well-chosen and descriptive name—"defecting in place."[112] This is a position taken by a growing number of women, who remain with their denomination but seek or create a special place for themselves, in which they find spiritual sustenance, encouragement, and acceptance. In briefest terms, the authors in their book's subtitle, describe these new groupings as "Women Claiming Responsibility for Their Own Spiritual Lives."[113] Inevitably these women find one another and form women's support groups within churches. Certainly women's support groups are not a new phenomenon; women have gathered together throughout history for study of the Bible or other sacred texts, discussion, prayer, and sharing. But the women who, by the authors' phrase, "defect in place" are doing the Bible study, discussing theological and religious issues, and praying—all from a feminist perspective and through a feminist lens. They are always aware of the sexist and male-oriented interpretations of Scripture and theology with which they grew up and want it brought into line with modern feminist perspectives and insights. It is important that we discuss them as feminists, although they have to this point held back from the exodus option espoused by Rosemary Ruether and so many others, including the goddess-wicca-Gaia groups. Winter, Lummis, and Stokes refer to these groups of women as "feminist spirituality groups,"[114] though not all these women are currently affiliated with such a group. But most have been part of a spiritual (not necessarily feminist) support group in the past.[115]

Feminist Spirituality   Winter, Lummis, and Stokes summarize the results of this study of their sample of women from women's spiritual groups with seven major conclusions. We shall summarize them briefly. First, feminist women distinguish between religion and spirituality. They seek the right to have their own spiritual experience of God within them with greater theological independence and ritual spontaneity.[116] Second, as an extension of the above, they claim responsibility for their own spiritual lives. This is not to put ultimate trust in themselves, but in the "God/Goddess who is the ultimate authority."[117] Third, they seek out and join with other feminist women to explore and nurture their spirituality. This is a logical and natural step, once they realize their feelings of loneliness amidst denominational theology and the religious practice of congregations.[118] Fourth, this feminist spirituality is different from other more traditional forms of Christian spirituality. Its distinguishing feature is claiming "the right to image and name the God of one's own experience."[119] This is a god who, if not clearly female, has a strong maternal side and is welcoming to all, dispensing justice and liberation to everyone who is open to such inclusiveness. Fifth, this feminist spirituality often leads to a new understanding of "church," that is free of patriarchal restrictions, as they become part of the new people of God. Sixth, these feminists often express alienation from the traditional institutional church, because the church demands faithfulness to the tradition and to suppression of one's individuality. Seventh, while the majority of feminist women in Winter, Lummis, and Stokes' study have chosen to remain in the church, they are remaining on their own terms.[120]

The authors describe this last observation from their study as follows:

> This brings us to what is our most remarkable finding. Many feminists of faith, however alienated or angry, are not pulling out of the churches, but instead are "defecting in place." While women in our study hold fast to the truth of their own experience, either alone or with other women, and insist upon honoring their own inner voice, they remain committed to their faith communities, to congregations and denominations. The need for continuity, for community and connection, the desire to remain a part of a tradition in which one has one's roots is significant for many women. So they choose to remain in a way that will not violate their integrity. At the same time, deep within is the hope that the values they profess will one day be accepted and that the institution will change.[121]

And so there is an alternative to the extremes of "tradition affirming" and patriarchal theology, as usual on one hand and the "exodus" form of the revolutionary response on the other. Yet one might suspect that the fact that many of these "defecting in place" women are but a step away from rejecting their traditional religious affiliation altogether; after all, "defecting in place" is a gerundial phrase from a very strong verb. However, Winter, Lummis, and Stokes make another interesting observation: "When the environment is socially and ritually inclusive and sensitive to women's concerns, it is possible to remain and be somewhat nurtured despite feelings that are suppressed."[122]

A Fundamentalist Option   We also need to be aware of Barbara Brasher's contention that many fundamentalist Christian women are neither leaving their churches nor "defecting in place." They are establishing solid women's support groups within fundamentalist churches that do not challenge fundamentalist theology and church structure that is primarily in the hands of men, but they establish "a parallel symbolic world in which they can be full participants."[123] This symbolic world is connected to the somewhat parallel men's groups that have long existed within the control structures of churches, but with the addition of special women's ministries and professional staff that offer free counseling, child care, continuing education, and inexpensive weekend retreats, in addition to the satisfaction of group association and support from other like minded women.[124] This option is probably most likely to occur in full flower in megachurches (a phenomenon that will be discussed in Chapter 14) that have the resources to provide staff and organizational help to maintain the program.

So the future is not clear as to outcomes of the issue of feminism in the churches. Certain denominations can hold many feminist members if they become more willing than they have been to modify their theological positions on women's issues. For example, if the Roman Catholic Church would de-gender its liturgical language and allow full ordination of women to the priesthood, the church would hold those many women who still cherish important parts of their Catholic heritage and do not really want to leave. Yet such a massive reversal of theological position, that would allow the ordination of women in the Roman Catholic Church, will not come soon. So the position of feminist women in the Roman Catholic and other denominations will continue to be seriously ambiguous.

FEMALE-DOMINATED RELIGIONS

It has been implicit in the evidence presented in this chapter, that around the globe and throughout most of recorded history, women have participated in the religion of their society or, in pluralist situations, have participated in one of each individual's choosing, but always in roles of less prestige and influence than those available to men. Leadership positions open to her have been low-level ones of application (service) and implementation, not policy making or theology writing or determining direction for the group.

Nonetheless, there have been societies, here and there and from time to time, where women have been leaders and have formulated theology. Two questions are, therefore, immediately obvious. First, in what ways are religions developed by and/or directed by women different from those dominated by men? A second question emerges from that: How might religions, that we know of, change as these traditionally male-dominated religions find women more and more assuming leadership positions? Susan Sered has made a substantial contribution to our understanding of religions dominated by women. She has done this by presenting data on twelve instances where the religion of a people or the religion of a subgroup within a larger society is controlled by women. These are ancestral cults among black Caribs in contemporary Belize, the indigenous religion of the Ryukyu Islands, the *zar* cult of northern Africa, the Sande secret society of Sierra Leone, matrilineal spirit cults in northern Thailand, Korean shamanism, Christian Science, Shakerism, Afro-Brazilian religions, nineteenth-century Spiritualism, the indigenous *nat cultus* of Burma, and the Feminist Spirituality Movement in the twentieth-century United States.[125]

She notes that these are all well-chosen for four reasons. First, they are all unmistakably dominated by women, so far as both leadership and membership are concerned. Second, there is no discrimination against women, as regards either leadership or participation. Third, members are clearly self-aware that this is a women's religion. Fourth, there is awareness that the group is independent of a larger, male-dominated societal religion.[126]

Sered found three sets of factors that were usually found as context for the development or fostering of women's religions. The first is gender dissonance. This is an experience "in which culturally accepted notions of gender are either highly contradictory and/or rapidly changing."[127] The second is matrifocality. This suggests that there is noticeable cultural emphasis on the maternal role. Such an emphasis is often accompanied by either matrilineality and/or matrilocality. The third is a relatively high degree of personal, social, or economic autonomy for women.[128]

As these three conditions come together and women either establish a new religion, transform an existing one, or simply join an incipient group and swell its ranks, one can expect several developments. There will be focus on religious beliefs concerning motherhood, touching on its many aspects. These would include religious prescriptions, proscriptions, and counsel concerning sexual activities and its relationship to fertility, concerns about child-care, and the creation of a religious perspective that is maternal in the sense of concern about nurturing and protection.[129] In other words, there will be a clear emphasis on activities, issues, and responsibilities, that traditionally fall to women because of their function as the bearers of children.

Second, there will be explicit attention paid to the issue of patriarchy and its appropriateness in particular areas of life. This consideration will take place, regardless of whether patriarchy is universally applicable throughout the society or covers certain areas only.

Third (and this is regarded by Sered as the most important finding of her study), the effects of gender on the form and content of religion will not be so great as some might expect it to be. Women's religions are not highly different from men's religions. They seem to stem from similar needs, respond to similar conditions, and engage in similar activities, regardless of which gender dominates. Sered says that religions dominated by either men or women will "worship supernatural beings, perform rituals of thanks and appeasement, utilize techniques that induce altered states of consciousness, and provide devotees with persuasive explanations for the ultimate conditions of existence."[130]

Nonetheless, sometimes women's religions emerge. We earlier identified the three conditions under which a female-dominated religion will possibly develop: namely, gender dissonance, matrifocality, and relatively high autonomy for women.

The first of these—gender dissonance—is clearly observed in mid-nineteenth-century America, where and when Shakerism, spiritualism, and

Christian Science either emerged or gained increasing favor. Certainly patriarchy flourished and the so-called cult of true womanhood emphasized
female passivity, frailty, and dependency. And, as Sered stresses, women felt
very inadequate, if not totally powerless to carry out their social mandate to
provide for children's health and welfare.

This was a time when some women were beginning to press for added
rights and opportunities to demonstrate competence. The idea of women's
suffrage gained support. Women became leaders of the abolitionist movement. Louisa May Alcott's book, *Little Women*, provided glimpses for many
women, of women's capabilities beyond traditional roles. As we have seen
earlier in this chapter, a few women actually achieved ordination in established, mainline churches. However, their parishes tended to be isolated,
small congregations in the frontier west, out of sight of most members of the
denominations.[131]

Such beginnings, of course, created tension. Women began to see what
might be possible for them in the sense of full participation in the diversity of
roles offered by society. But resistance and objections also increased as road-
blocks and obstacles were raised to impede their progress. And there one has
the ingredients for genuine gender dissonance. This occurs, as Sered points
out,[132] not when oppression of women was of greatest intensity, but when sex
roles and understandings of gender differences were changing and there
were rising expectations of women as they saw what might be possible.

The second and third factors associated with providing a receptive cultural environment, in which women's religion might find fertile soil in which
to root, are the existence of matrifocality and a fairly high degree of autonomy
for women. With respect to matrifocality, there is focus on the central importance of the mother role in the household. This results in a more egalitarian
relationship between the sexes. In addition, in matrifocal societies there is
fairly equal valuation of male and female economic and ritual statuses.[133]

Susan Sered provides an illuminating summary of how this works out,
in her description of the place of women in Belize, where we find black Carib
religion, one of the twelve examples of female-dominated religions listed
earlier. Sered says:

> Black Carib women are quite independent of men. Their labor and sexu-
> ality are not treated as the property of men, nor are women under the
> authority of men. Women choose their own spouses and leave unsatis-
> factory ones at will. They control their own money and own their own
> property. Spouses generally keep their finances separate. The kinship
> system is officially bilateral, yet although all kin are expected to help
> each other, it is primarily women who are responsible for the networks of
> reciprocity. Most daughters stay in the same communities in which they
> grew up. Most marriages are among residents of the same village, and
> women show a marked preference for living with their own rather than
> with their spouses' kin.[134]

In short, "Women's religions are most often found in societies in which women control important resources, in which families are focused upon mothers, in which kinship is matrilineal."[135]

PREDICTIONS

On the basis of our look, with the help of Susan Sered, at religions in which women dominate, other recent research, and trends in enrollment at seminaries, we will venture a few predictions.

Proportion of Female Clergy Will Increase   First, and most obviously, the proportion of women in the clergy ranks will increase. This increase will ultimately lead to women becoming a majority of clergy in some denominations. This will occur first in those denominations with a head start—the United Church of Christ, the Assemblies of God, the United Methodists, and a variety of small sectarian groups.

But the growth will not be in a straight linear fashion. We earlier discussed seminary enrollments of men and women and noted that the rate of gains of women's seminary enrollment on men has been growing only very slightly for nearly two decades now. At this rate of gain, the twentieth-first century would be past its midpoint before female seminary graduates would exceed male graduates. Also, if Joy Charlton's findings apply more broadly than her sample and there is indeed a higher rate of attrition for female clergy, increasing enrollment by women at seminaries or even rates of ordination will not shift the balance to women as quickly as one might have predicted. We should also not assume that the ministry would continue to be an attractive career goal for women, young women in particular.

Some Denominational Holdouts   Second, a few denominations will hold out and might not concede on the issue of women's ordination, even in this century. However, one denomination that will surprise many is the Roman Catholic Church. It will begin to ordain women, though probably in a special way or by creating a new clergy category. They are actually moving steadily in that direction right now. As we saw earlier, more and more Roman Catholic women are becoming "parish administrators" and "pastoral assistants," as the church endeavors to provide ministry to parishes without a priest because of a shortage of young men aspiring to the priesthood.

Mark Chaves points out that an important observation from the sociology of organizations is directly relevant here. He says: "Fundamental to this approach is the insight that organizational characteristics are often generated by an organization's efforts to respond to external, institutional pressures that may be only related tenuously to the organization's pragmatic activity."[136] That is, social changes, whether they are legal/regulatory, ideological or demographic (few male candidates for the Roman Catholic priesthood, for example), might require an institution to modify traditional policy, reinterpret and manipulate its policy to mesh more successfully with social changes within the institution and its members' existence.[137]

An influential group of Roman Catholic scholars, both priests and laymen, the Canon Law Society of America, concluded in October 1995, that ordaining women as deacons (deaconesses) in the church would be appropriate and consistent with both Catholic theology and past practice. While deacons/deaconesses are not priests, they are but one step below priestly status. In much of the church's history, ordination as a deacon was preliminary to becoming a priest, at least for men. Deacons have authority to do all a priest does—administer baptisms and communion, preach sermons, officiate at marriages, conduct funerals and other rites—except celebrate the mass. The study and recommendations note that ordination of women as deacons would clearly recognize the sacramental nature of their work and their standing in the church. The study is being circulated among American Catholic bishops and recommends that ordaining women to the diaconate would be "desirable" for the Catholic Church in the United States.[138]

While female deacons were an integral part of the early church, by the eighth century, the female diaconate had almost disappeared.[139] It is clear, however, that interest in the female diaconate is being revived and there is more active interest in the male diaconate as well, particularly for second career Catholic males. A distinctly attractive feature of the diaconate in the Roman Catholic Church is that deacons can be married and remain so, though if one's spouse should die, the deacon cannot remarry. Likewise, an unmarried deacon cannot marry.[140] However, in October 2002, a highly influential panel, the Advisers to the Vatican Congregation for the Doctrine, found no historical or theological basis for ordination of women as deacons.[141]

Nonetheless, if one couples the growing shortage of priests with the decline of nearly equal proportions of young women for sisterhood in the various religious orders in the Catholic Church, at some time in the future there will be opportunities for young Catholic women to follow through on their desire to serve the Church but in a more prominent, influential way through the priesthood. This desire of some, perhaps many, Catholic women to be ordained and accepted into the priesthood is rather poignantly registered in the press release of the Women's Ordination Conference ("A voice for women in the Roman Catholic Church) following Pope John Paul II's death on 2 April 2005. In their press release that day, the group's executive director Joy Barnes wrote in part: "We honor Pope John Paul II for his prophetic preaching about women's dignity, yet we acknowledge that during his papacy, the church took significant steps backward in the struggle for women's equality. He kept women from the highest leadership positions in the church . . . he barred them from ordination."[142]

Another prediction here, that is probably a necessary condition for opening the Roman Catholic priesthood to women, is that the marriage of priests will be approved within the Roman Catholic Church within the next half-century. But we hasten to add that we make such predictions with two very important qualifiers up front. One is that a Pope of more theologically liberal and open stance than Pope John Paul II and his successor Pope Benedict XVI must be selected within those fifty years to pick up the strands of change begun by Pope John XXIII over four decades ago. Second, if rational choice theorists are correct and people continue to make rational choices with respect to their religious convictions and affiliation, those Catholics who want to allow priests to marry and to ordain women, at least at the deacon level, might break away from traditional Catholicism to form a "Reformed Catholic Church." If such would come to pass, traditional Catholicism could remain much as it is now or could even move back a step or two toward staunchly held official theological positions inherited from the past.

Evangelicals Will Concede   Third, evangelical and fundamentalist Protestantism, which has been a prominent holdout in the ranks of Protestantism, will move toward the ordination of women as well. We base that prediction on evidence of research, which suggests that feminism is slowly gaining ground within the fundamentalist ranks. While this change has not affected public pronouncements, at the local and individual levels there is change. Julie Ingersoll cites an example of a woman in a fundamentalist church, who taught the adult Bible class and stated unequivocally that the original Bible passages that require women to "remain silent in the churches" and not assume religious leadership, *must be interpreted in their cultural context*.[143] This is precisely the view that fundamentalism has been opposing. A few women have been ordained to the ministry in Southern Baptist congregations, despite adamant opposition to such ordination by its denominational leaders and the denomination as a whole. This has occurred only because individual congregations have much more autonomy and authority than in the vast majority of denominations, but these scattered, localized ordinations of women will gradually increase.

There is also growing evidence that fundamentalist women are adept at compartmentalization and do not necessarily uphold traditional fundamentalist doctrine on the submissiveness of women. Carolyn Pevey found that fundamentalists appeared to accept traditional fundamentalist doctrines but said that for themselves they did not apply particularly well. They tended to see themselves as independent, as unique in not accepting the doctrine of female submissiveness. Pevey found that all the Southern Baptist women in her sample would agree with a statement that women should be submissive, but some would reserve a private interpretation for themselves.[144]

More Clergywomen in Administration   Fourth, as more women enter the ministry in most denominations we will naturally expect to see them moving into administrative positions within church bodies and as professors at seminaries—positions of influence on the future of the churches. They are already moving into more and more positions of influence on denominational committees and boards that influence policy in denominations. As such, moves to positions of denominational influence accelerate, all interested persons, whether inside or outside the religious groups, will want to explore much more deeply and definitively whether there are discernible differences in style and substance so far as the ministry of women compared with men is concerned.

APPLICATION OF RATIONAL CHOICE THEORY

If we apply rational choice theory to the changes in women's roles within the Judeo-Christian tradition that we have discussed in this chapter, particularly the predictions here at the end of Chapter 11, one descriptor dominates, namely, caution. The caution is that changes that we predict will continue— changes such as significant inroads of women into the ranks of ordained clergy in most denominations, but with several very notable exceptions, and exploring by women from many denominational backgrounds new age ideas of gaia, wicca, and goddess religion—will not proceed inexorably to the same end. That is, as rational choice works its way within individuals and groups, people will make choices. Some will participate in reform of the religious group they are in and the group might change. Such groups could even be among the current adamant holdouts to women's ordination, such as the Roman Catholic Church, the Southern Baptists, and the Lutheran Church–Missouri Synod. Other believers will stay with the original group, as it steadfastly holds to the traditions of the group to the point that the reformers give up the fight and either create a new form of the original group or simply join an existing group that has already adopted the practice and teaching the reformers want—ordination of women, marriage of priests, and so forth.

But in a very real sense, we are "getting ahead of the story" of this book. We have yet to consider a major sociological concept called *secularization*. And we have not yet considered a great body of data and literature about membership losses and shifts among denominations. In addition, we will need to re-introduce some ideas from the discussion of religious conflict in Chapter 6. Yet the conclusion of this chapter on women and religion is a most appropriate place to be somewhat explicit about where we are going before we conclude this book.

Conclusion

Without belaboring issues or repeating ideas that have already been presented, one additional remark by way of conclusion seems appropriate. That is an insight contributed by Denise Carmody. She notes that there has been a worldwide tendency to view women as either much better or much worse than men, implying that only men have normal, mid-range humanity. So women have been placed on pedestals of purity, loveliness, and virginity. Correspondingly they have been denounced as evil witches, seducing sirens, and treacherous whores.[145] She adds, "What they have not been, historically, is equal sharers of humanity whose social and religious offices have been determined principally by their talents."[146] In a nutshell, this seems to be the central issue for society and the central issue for religion as well.

Notes

1. Jo Freeman, *The Politics of Women's Liberation* (New York: D. McKay, 1975), p. 14.
2. Ibid., p. 13.
3. Merlin Stone, *The Paradise Papers* (London: Quartel Books, 1976), p. 17.
4. Edwin O. James, *The Cult of the Mother-Goddess* (New York: Barnes & Noble, 1959).
5. Dorothy Robins-Mowry, *The Hidden Sun: Women of Modern Japan* (Boulder, CO: Westview Press, 1983), p. 5.
6. Stone, *Paradise Papers*, p. 52.
7. Jacquetta Hawks and Leonard Woolley, *Prehistory and the Beginnings of Civilization* (New York: Harper & Row, 1963), p. 724; E. O. James, *The Ancient Gods* (New York: Putnam's, 1960), p. 71.
8. James, *The Ancient Gods*, p. 85.
9. Reported by Diodorus and quoted in Stone, *Paradise Papers*, p. 53.
10. Adolph Jensen, *Myth and Cult among Primitive People* (Chicago: University of Chicago Press, 1963), pp. 141–144.
11. James, *Cult of the Mother-Goddess*, pp. 69–77; Hawkes and Woolley, *Prehistory and the Beginnings of Civilization*, p. 736.
12. Nancy Falk, "An Image of Woman in Old Buddhist Literature: The Daughters of Mara," in *Women and Religion* (revised edition), eds. Judith Plaskow and Joan Arnold (Missoula, MT: Scholars Press, 1974), p. 105.
13. Ibid.
14. Denise Carmody, *Women and World Religions* (Nashville, TN: Abingdon, 1979), pp. 49–50.
15. Ibid., p. 50.
16. Ibid., p. 51.
17. Ibid.
18. Jean Holm, "Introduction: Raising the Issues," in *Women in Religion*, eds. Jean Holm and John Bowker (London: Pinter Publishers, 1994), p. xii.
19. Carmody, *Women and World Religions*, p. 84
20. Ibid., pp. 82–83.
21. Ibid., p. 84.
22. Ibid.

23. By "maturity" we mean only a further point along an evolutionary plane and intend no value judgment whatsoever.

24. Gail B. Shulman, "View from the Back of the Synagogue: Women in Judaism," in *Sexist Religion and Women in the Church,* ed. Alice L. Hageman (New York: Association Press, 1974), pp. 147–149.

25. I Timothy 2:11–14. *New English Bible* (New York: Oxford University Press, 1976).

26. Carmody, *Women and World Religions,* p. 115.

27. Rosemary Skinner Keller, "Women and Religion," in *Encyclopedia of American Religious Experience,* eds. Charles Lippey and Peter Williams (New York: Charles Scribner's Sons, 1988), p. 1555.

28. Ibid., p. 16.

29. Ibid., pp. 16–17.

30. Ibid., p. 17.

31. Suzanne Cita-Malard, *Religious Orders of Women,* trans. George J. Robinson (New York: Hawthorne, 1964), p. 15.

32. In the United States the decline in the number of nuns in just ten years has been 18 percent—from 128,378 in 1979 to 104,419 in 1989. Cf. Felician A. Fay, ed., *1990 Catholic Almanac* (Huntington, IN: Our Sunday Visitor Publication Division, 1990), p. 427.

33. Sharon Neufer Emswiler, "How the New Woman Feels in the Old Worship Service," in *Women and Worship: A Guide to Non-Sexist Hymns, Prayers, and Liturgies,* eds. Sharon Neufer Emswiler and Thomas Neufer Emswiler (New York: Harper & Row, 1974), pp. 3–5. Copyright © 1974 by Sharon Neufer Emswiler and Thomas Neufer Emswiler. Reprinted by permission of HarperCollins Publishers, Inc.

34. Marabel Morgan, *The Total Woman* (Old Tappan, NJ: Fleming H. Revell Company, 1973).

35. R. Marie Griffith, *God's Daughters: Evangelical Women and the Power of Submission* (Berkeley: University of California Press, 1997), p. 203.

36. Ibid.

37. Ibid., p. 200.

38. Ibid., p. 210.

39. Ibid., p. 211.

40. Rosemary Ruether and Eleanor McLaughlin, "Women's Leadership in the Jewish and Christian Traditions: Continuity and Change," in *Women of Spirit,* eds. Rosemary Ruether and Eleanor McLaughlin (New York: Simon & Schuster, 1979), p. 19.

41. Margaret B. Crook, *Women and Religion* (Boston, MA: Beacon Press, 1964), p. 235.

42. Carole R. Bohn, "The Changing Scene: Women Come to Seminary," paper presented at the meeting of the American Academy of Religion, Dallas, Texas, 1980, p. 7, quoted in *Women of the Cloth,* eds. Jackson W. Carroll, Barbara Hargrove, and Adair T. Lummis (San Francisco: Harper & Row, 1983), p. 11.

43. Kenneth Slack, "Women's Ordination: The Fight Is On," *The Christian Century* 102, no. 38 (*December* 4, 1985): 1108–1109.

44. "Canadian Lutherans Elect Woman Bishop," *Christian Century* 119, no. 16 (July 31–August 13, 2002): 18.

45. Dorothy C. Bass, "Their Prodigious Influence: Women, Religion, and Reform in Antebellum America," in *Women of Spirit,* eds. Rosemary Ruether and Eleanor McLaughlin (New York: Simon & Schuster, 1979), p. 296.

46. Cynthia Grant Tucker, *Prophetic Sisterhood: Liberal Women Ministers of the Frontier, 1880–1930* (Boston: Beacon Press, 1990), p. 3.

47. Graham Heathcote, Associated Press, "Church of England Gives Approval to Women Priests," *Muncie Star,* November 12, 1992, p. 1A.

48. These data from U.S. Bureau of the Census, *Statistical Abstracts of the United States: 1963,* 84th Edition (Washington, DC: 1963), p. 232; *Statistical Abstracts of the United States: 1981,* 102nd Edition (Washington, DC: 1981), p. 403; *Statistical Abstracts of the United States: 2001,* 121st Edition (Washington DC: 2001), p. 380.

49. Constant H. Jacquet Jr., *Women Ministers in 1986 and 1977: A Ten Year View* (New York: National Council of Churches, 1988), p. 4.

50. Rita J. Simon, Angela J. Scanlan, and Pamela S. Nadel, "Rabbis and Ministers: Women of the Book and the Cloth," *Sociology of Religion* 54, no. 1 (Spring 1993): 115, 117.

51. Ruth A. Wallace, "The Social Construction of a New Leadership Role: Catholic Women Pastors, *The Sociology of Religion* 54, no. 1 (Spring 1993): 33.

52. Ruth A. Wallace, *They Call Her Pastor* (Albany: New York University Press, 1992), p. 128–129.

53. Edward Echlin, *The Deacon in the Church* (Staten Island, NY: Society of St. Paul, 1971), p. 133.

54. "Women Are Advancing in Catholic Church Jobs," *The Ann Arbor News*, July 10, 1999, p. A10, from the Associated Press.

55. Jacquet, *Women Ministries*, p. 7.

56. Constant H. Jacquet Jr., *Yearbook of American and Canadian Churches, 1987* (Nashville, TN: Abingdon Press, 1988), p. 247.

57. Philip E. Hammond and Robert E. Mitchell, "Segmentation of Radicalism—The Case of the Protestant Campus Minister," *American Journal of Sociology* 71, no. 2 (September 1965).

58. Priscilla and William Proctor, *Women in the Pulpit* (Garden City, NY: Doubleday, 1976).

59. Chaim I. Waxman, *America's Jews in Transition* (Philadelphia: Temple University Press, 1983), p. 217.

60. Reported in *Religion Watch*, ed. Richard P. Cimino, vol. 9, no. 3 (January 1994): 6, from *Moment*, December, 1993.

61. Reported in *Religion Watch*, ed. Richard P. Cimino, vol. 12, no. 5 (March, 1997): p. 2 of "Findings and Footnotes" insert.

62. Lawrence L. Kersten, *The Lutheran Ethic* (Detroit, MI: Wayne State University Press, 1970), p. 125.

63. Edward C. Lehman Jr., *Women Clergy: Breaking through Gender Barriers* (New Brunswick, NJ: Transaction Books, 1985), p. 31.

64. Ibid., p. 51.

65. Ibid., pp. 80–109.

66. Ibid., pp. 274–275.

67. Ibid., p. 285.

68. Ibid., p. 284.

69. Ibid., p. 294.

70. Jacquet, *Women Ministers*.

71. Jacquet, *Yearbook*, p. 263.

72. Ibid.

73. Harry Hale Jr., Morton King, and Doris M. Jones, *Clergywomen: Problems and Satisfactions* (Lima, OH: Fairway Press, 1985), p. 13.

74. Ibid., p. 15.

75. Joy Charlton, "Dropping Out/Staying In: Revisiting Women Ministers in Mid-Career" (paper presented at the 1994 annual meeting of the Religious Research Association and the Society for the Scientific Study of Religion, Albuquerque, NM, November 5, 1994).

76. Edward C. Lehman Jr., *Women in Ministry* (Melbourne, Australia, Joint Board of Christian Education, 1994), p. 59.

77. The first reporting by the Association of Theological Schools that identified gender of seminarians was in 1972.

78. Kenneth Bedell, ed., *Yearbook of American and Canadian Churches, 1995* (Nashville, TN: Abingdon Press, 1995), p. 280.

79. Eileen W. Lindner, ed., *Yearbook of American and Canadian Churches 2003* (Nashville, TN: Abingdon Press, 2005), p. 389.

80. Ibid.

81. Ruth Wallace, "The Social Construction of a New Leadership Role: Catholic Women Pastors," *Sociology of Religion* 54, no. 1 (Spring 1993), citing William L. Baumgaertner, ed., *Factbook on Theological Education 1987–1988* (Vandalia, OH: Association of Theological Schools in the U.S. and Canada, 1988), pp. 90–92.

82. Reported in *Religion Watch*, ed. Richard P. Cimino, vol. 9, no. 5 (March 1994): 8, from *Hinduism Today*, February, 1994.

83. Ruth A. Wallace, *They Call Her Pastor* (Albany: State University of New York Press, 1992), Chapter 4.

84. Simon et al., "Rabbis and Ministers," p. 120. It must be noted that these are all self-perceptions and are not corroborated by conclusions reached by outside observers or researchers. Also it is a small sample. Nonetheless, these are probably observations with some validity.

85. Edward C. Lehman Jr., *Gender and Work: The Case of the Clergy* (Albany: State University of New York Press, 1993), p. 4.

86. Ibid., p. 39.

87. Ibid.

88. Rosemary Radford Ruether, "Women's Leadership in the Jewish and Christian Traditions: Continuity and Change," in *Women of Spirit*, eds. Rosemary Ruether and Eleanor McLaughlin (New York: Simon & Schuster, 1979), pp. 19–28.

89. Ibid., p. 21.

90. Ibid., p. 28.

91. Rosemary Radford Ruether, *New Woman/New Earth* (New York: Seabury Press, 1975), pp. 56–59.

92. Ibid., p. 57.

93. Ibid.

94. Mary Daly, "The Women's Movement: An Exodus Community," *Religious Education* 67 (September/October 1972): p. 332.

95. Mary Daly, *Gyn/Ecology: The Metaethics of Radical Feminism* (Boston: Beacon Press, 1978), p. xi.

96. Mary Daly, *The Church and the Second Sex* (New York: Harper & Row, pub., 1968, 1975), p. 39.

97. Rosemary Ruether, *Women and Redemption* (Minneapolis: Fortress Press, 1998), pp. 215–221 and end note 40, p. 344.

98. Naomi Goldenberg, *Changing of the Gods: Feminism and the End of Traditional Religions* (Boston: Beacon Press, 1979), p. 3. Copyright © 1979 by Naomi R. Goldenberg.

99. Ibid., p. 103.

100. Goldenberg, *Changing of the Gods: Feminism and the End of Traditional Religions*, pp. 92–93. Copyright 1979 by Naomi Goldenberg. Reprinted by permission of Beacon Press.

101. Marilyn Gottschall, "The Mutable Goddess," in *Daughters of the Goddess*, ed. Wendy Griffin (Walnut Creek, CA: AltaMira Press, 2000), p. 59.

102. Ibid.

103. Ibid., p. 63.

104. Cynthia Eller, *Living in the Lap of the Goddess: The Feminist Spirituality Movement in America* (New York: Crossroad Publishing Co., 1993), referenced in Gottschall, ibid.

105. Ruth R. Barrett, "The Power of Ritual," in *Daughters of the Goddess*, p. 185.

106. Ibid.

107. Helen A. Berger, *A Community of Witches* (Columbia, SC: University of South Carolina Press, 1999), p. 8.

108. Sarah M. Pike, *Earthly Bodies, Magical Selves* (Berkeley: University of California Press, 2001), pp. XXI–XXII.

109. Ibid., p. 186.

110. Helen A. Berger, ibid. She suggests 300,000 as of 1999.

111. Susan Greenwood, "Feminist Witchcraft," In *Daughters of the Goddess*, p. 138.

112. Miriam T. Winter, Adair Lummis, and Allison Stokes, *Defecting in Place* (New York: Crossroad Publishing Co., 1995).

113. Ibid.

114. Ibid., p. 146.

115. Ibid., pp. 145–146.

116. Ibid., p. 194.

117. Ibid., pp. 194–195.

118. Ibid., p. 195.

119. Ibid.

120. Ibid., p. 196.

121. Ibid., pp. 196–197.

122. Ibid., p. 196.

123. Brenda E. Brasher, *Godly Women, Fundamentalism and Female Power* (New Brunswick, NJ: Rutgers University Press, 1998), p. 27.

124. Ibid.

125. Susan Starr Sered, *Priestess, Mother, Sacred Sister* (New York: Oxford University Press, 1994), p. 3.

126. Ibid.

127. Ibid., p. 43.

128. Ibid.

129. Ibid., pp. 7–8.

130. Ibid., p. 8.

131. Tucker, *Prophetic Sisterhood*.

132. Sered, *Priestess, Mother, Sacred Sister*, p. 44.

133. Ibid., p. 47.

134. Ibid., p. 51.

135. Ibid., p. 60.

136. Mark Chaves, *Ordaining Women* (Cambridge, MA: Harvard University Press, 1997), p. 3.

137. Ibid.

138. New York Times News Service, "Women Deacons Legal, Canon Law Experts Say," *Chicago Tribune*, November 12, 1995, sect. 1, p. 13.

139. Echlin, *Deacon in the Church*, p. 133.

140. Ibid., p. 123.

141. *The Lutheran* 15, no. 2 (December, 2002): 52.

142. Women's Ordination Conference website (www.womensordination.org), April 4, 2005.

143. Julie Ingersoll, "Gender Issues in Evangelicalism as Conflict over Sacred Space" (paper presented at the 1994 annual meeting of the Society for the Scientific Study of Religion, Albuquerque, NM, November 4–6, 1994).

144. Carolyn Pevey, "Submission and Power among Southern Baptist Ladies" (paper presented at the 1994 annual meeting of the Society for the Scientific Study of Religion, Albuquerque, NM, November 4–6, 1994).

145. Carmody, *Women and World Religions*, p. 17.

146. Ibid.

Chapter 12

Major Historical Developments

Religion front and center in early America.

In this chapter, we will discuss six specific themes or developments in the history of American religion, proceeding chronologically. Moreover, this discussion can be viewed within the context of two more general themes, which the reader will find helpful to keep in mind as we proceed—first, that the outward manifestation or pattern of religion has constantly changed during almost four centuries, since the initial European settlement of the American continent, and second, that the relationships between religion and other features of the social structure have also changed.

INTOLERANT BEGINNINGS

The first theme or stage in the history of religion in America, we call the period of intolerant beginnings. Many of the early colonists were themselves religious dissenters and minorities, extolled by our history books for their courage and principles in struggling for religious freedom and liberty, even to the extent of making perilous voyages in search of a place where they could practice their religious convictions unhampered. Yet many of these same seekers of religious freedom were inclined to deny to others what they demanded for themselves. Those who asked that others be tolerant of their views were themselves intolerant of the divergent religious views of still others.

During the colonial period, the settlers, though speaking of a new world and a new age, had reproduced an ancient pattern of officially established religion, which was supported by law and governmental authority. The state-church pattern predominated. Nine of the thirteen original colonies recognized officially established religious systems. Persons who dissented were frequently expelled from these colonies or, at best, accorded only second-class citizenship if allowed to remain.

The situation is well summarized in the following excerpt from the U.S. Supreme Court's opinion in the historic 1947 *Everson* decision:

> Catholics found themselves hounded and proscribed because of their faith; Quakers who followed their conscience went to jail; Baptists were peculiarly obnoxious to certain dominant Protestant sects; men and women of varied faiths who happened to be in a minority in a particular locality were persecuted because they steadfastly persisted in worshipping God only as their own consciences dictated. And all of these dissenters were compelled to pay tithes and taxes to support government-sponsored churches whose ministers preached inflammatory sermons designed to strengthen and consolidate the established faith by generating a burning hatred against dissenters.[1]

These examples were particularly obvious in Massachusetts Bay Colony and Virginia. As the Puritan settlers in Massachusetts established what, for all intents and purposes, was a state church, the colonial government was expected, as part of its service to its citizens, to support the Congregational Church and its clergy. The Congregationalist meeting house was used for both governmental and religious activities. Colonial law compelled all people to attend church services, regardless of their personal beliefs, and denied equal rights to the "unorthodox." Citizens were subject to trial by the colonial government for what the church called sins but the government called crimes—heresy, blasphemy, and idolatry.

Anne Hutchinson, whose history is one of the better-known examples of such victimization, was interestingly enough not a representative of a dissenting or deviant religious group in the Massachusetts Bay Colony where she resided. Although what she taught was defined as deviant, heretical doctrine, she was technically a Congregationalist, like all the other (acceptable) residents of Boston. Her heresy lay in her stress on a "covenant of grace"—a religion in which a person could have direct access to God's love and grace—in opposition to the "covenant of works," which stressed obedience to the laws of church and state. In 1638, both she and her doctrines were tried and condemned—her teaching as heresy and she as a blasphemer of God and seducer of the faithful.

Earlier, in 1636, Roger Williams and four companions, having been banished from the same colony, settled in "Rogues' Island" (that is, Rhode Island) and established a community there as a haven for Quakers, Baptists and other deviant and dissenting religious groups. Even in this tolerant colony, however, approximately a century later, a law was passed restricting both citizenship and eligibility for public office to Protestants.[2]

Quakers were particularly obnoxious to the colonists in Massachusetts, as reflected by laws there, specifying that any of that "cursed sect of heretics" who entered the colony were to be jailed, whipped with twenty stripes, and then expelled from the colony. Four Quakers were even hanged. Some were branded or had ears cut off. In at least one case, the children of Quaker parents were sold into slavery upon authorization of a Boston Court.

In Virginia, Anglicanism was established as the official church, but in a somewhat different form than Congregationalism was established in Massachusetts. Whereas in Massachusetts the church tended to control the government, in Virginia the government tended to control the church. In Virginia, all citizens were required to attend Anglican services and were taxed to support the Anglican church, no non-Anglican religious group could hold services, no Catholic or Quaker could hold public office, and no one who did not believe in infant baptism could even become a citizen of the colony.[3] Early Virginia laws, later reduced in severity, specified that anyone convicted a third time for failure to attend religious services was to spend six months in the galleys and that a third offense of working on the Sabbath was punishable by death.

THE CONSTITUTIONAL COMPROMISE

The First Amendment Clause

With the Revolution and the adoption of the Constitution, the colonial pattern became subject to forces that led to significant change. In the First Amendment, American society took the official stance that "Congress shall make no law respecting an establishment of religion, or prohibiting the free exercise thereof." As such, the early pattern of state churches and their implicit intolerance was repudiated for the nation as a whole. It was not until the passage of the Fourteenth Amendment, in 1868, that this prohibition of an established governmentally supported religion or church was applied at the state level. Theoretically, any state could have had an official state religion up to that time, and several entered the Union with an official, state sanctioned and supported church. But none did after 1833, when Massachusetts rescinded its state-church commitments, the last state to do so.

A major factor in this "constitutional compromise" was the strong influence of James Madison and his followers, who were passionate about diffusing power in the nation. To give an advantage to any group was to ask for abuse. Just as you should have the checks and balances of three branches of government, or the balance of federal power with state and local power, so you would not favor the establishment of a single religious group or perspective, that is, give it relatively unrestricted power.[4]

Another significant influence, in moving from state churches in the colonial beginnings of the nation to toleration and pluralism as it established its Constitution, was the simple fact that no single religious group could claim anything near the majority of supporters throughout the thirteen states necessary to establish it as the officially sanctioned religion of the new nation. Not that particular groups (Congregationalists, for example, who probably had the greatest number of members of any group) would not have wanted such status; it was simply that none had sufficient numbers to gain a majority vote. Every state had a goodly number of dissenters and minority religious group members; there were even substantial numbers of "free thinkers" who professed no formal religious affiliation. Therefore, only one practical solution appeared feasible, and that was to cut off churches both legally and financially from government support. Hence, the clause in the First Amendment, specifying that "Congress shall make no law respecting an establishment of religion."

Certainly the absolute prohibition of a federally sanctioned church was a dramatic and innovative part of the U.S. Constitution. This is so, even if one knows that this was a decision driven by very pragmatic political strategizing. It is also of interest to note that the single sentence referencing religion, that constitutes the First Amendment, is the only reference to religion in the entire U.S. Constitution. John K. Wilson notes that, while none of the framers personally objected to or ignored religion (they all held membership in one of the many denominational and sectarian options available), they "did not think that the new national government should be formally dependent upon religion to cultivate the loyalties of citizens."[5] Further, they gambled that "religious institutions and activities could be separated from state functions"[6] and both government and religion could survive, even thrive as separate institutions.

Looking at the situation from a slightly different angle, every religious group, whether dissenting or firmly established, now found itself occupying a minority status in the context of all thirteen states, and so each was quite naturally concerned with keeping government from interfering with what it wanted to do and teach religiously. What if another religious group should later gain a majority—what would happen to us? Hence the second clause dealing with religion in the First Amendment stating that Congress shall make no law "prohibiting the free exercise thereof."

With disestablishment came voluntarism and the rise of denomination-alism. People could join any religious group of their choice, or they could choose to join none at all. They could even form antireligious groups. Thus, religious groups now had to find ways of becoming self-supporting. Competition for members and for scarce resources developed, and religious innovation was implicitly encouraged as a consequence.

It is difficult to overstate the significance and the dramatic impact of this severance of religion from state auspices. Sanford H. Cobb, an expert on the history of religious liberty, maintains that the American pattern of reli-gious freedom was "the most striking contribution of America to the science of Government."[7]

As dramatic and innovative as the Constitution was, with respect to the social organization of both religion and government, it appears that these arrangements provoked relatively little struggle. Martin Marty notes that in only three of the thirteen original states was there much resistance to these First Amendment provisions.[8] Further, "in most other colonies the change was made as if with a sigh of relief, in a spirit of tidying up, and with only whimpers of reaction."[9]

What Did the Framers of the Constitution Intend?

This is not to suggest, of course, that the First Amendment resolved all the issues. Part of the problem is its brevity and vagueness. As Joseph Tussman states:

> The First Amendment in its attractive brevity leaves much unstated and seems to take much for granted. Even its spirit is elusive. Is it a practical expression of "a religious people"? Or is it a tolerant statement of com-mitment to a secular experiment? Does it indeed put us "under God"? What is "establishment" and what is an "exercise" of religion? The Amendment does not explain itself.[10]

Although it would be of great help, it is impossible fully to "get into the mind," of the framers of the Constitution and discover their intentions. Were they flaunting sociological realities, or were they acknowledging them? That is, were they trying to do something that cannot be done—namely, separate religion from politics and government in society? Or, recognizing that inter-action and overlap between the two is inevitable, were they simply trying to avoid excesses as the two spheres commingled?

Although throughout American history people have pointed to the First Amendment as evidence of an "official endorsement" of religion and have suggested that we are, therefore, fundamentally a religious people, it is not all that clear that the Founding Fathers were so much encouraging religion as they were trying to place some limitations on its power and influence. Clearly they did not want a repetition of early Massachusetts Bay Colony or Virginia at the national level. We need to remember that many of the Founding Fathers and framers of the Constitution were freethinkers and sons of the Enlightenment, who had personal reservations about traditional Christian orthodoxy and practices, though not discouraging religion altogether, as mentioned earlier. Further, at the official birth of the new nation, relatively few of its citizens were formal members of churches.[11] Quite clearly the early emphasis seems to be one of limitation of religious power and influence rather than support and encouragement of such influence. If this is so, it represents quite a shift from the strong religious (Christian) influence in the early days of the colonies. Yet note the action of the Supreme Court fifty years later (1844) as it interprets the First Amendment. In 1831, Stephen Girard, a wealthy Philadelphian, provided in his will for the establishment of a college for orphans—on condition that, although the orphans were to be taught the "purest principles of morality," no clergy members representing any religion whatsoever were to teach at, hold office in, or even visit the proposed institution. Daniel Webster, in challenging the will, stated: "No fault can be found with Girard for wishing a marble college to bear his name forever, but it is not valuable unless it has a fragrance of Christianity about it . . . A cruel experiment is to be made upon these orphans to ascertain whether they cannot be brought up without religion."[12]

The Supreme Court upheld Girard's will, interpreting it as bearing no animosity to Christianity, but only to clergy, since nonclergy were left free to teach Christian principles. In fact, regarding the requirement that teachers in the school "instill into the minds of the scholars the purest principles of morality," the Court commented: "Where can the purest principles of morality be learned so clearly or so perfectly as from the New Testament?"[13] In other words, Christianity should be taught—by lay Christians instead of clergy if necessary. Quite clearly there was a Christian bias abroad in the land, and it was certainly encouraged by the Supreme Court's interpretation of the Constitution.

John Wilson notes that religion was involved with many of the divisions that were capable of rendering the new republic inoperable. But, "by defining religious differences as beyond the reach of the national government to address or resolve, religion itself became a means of registering or even dramatizing differences of opinion in ways that they did not necessarily threaten the common life. In a word, religion has provided American society with an idiom in which it can acknowledge and accept social differentiation."[14] In other words, the republic would run high risks, if groups should try to leap over the line of separation and compel government to use its power to enact and enforce religious dictums and practices supported by some religious faction(s) but just as adamantly opposed by members of other religious groups.

We probably all think immediately of the fractious issues so familiar to most citizens today—abortion, gay marriage, and euthanasia. It seems that the genius of the Constitution, in allowing great differences of religious opinion to flourish in the land without fracturing the unifying nature of the republic itself, is seriously jeopardized by trying to cross the line separating the arena of discussion and debate over religious or other issues from the arena of political decision-making, by trying to force a single viewpoint through legislation based on a one-sided religious opinion.

Two summary observations can be made at this point: First, despite the constitutional prohibitions against the establishment of a state church, the history of our society evidences strong favor toward religion—Christianity in particular. Second, opinion regarding how and to what extent the state is to be allowed to exercise its support for religion has fluctuated. Although we lack the space to document this point in detail, some semblance of a pendulum motion has been in operation throughout our history, in terms of degree of involvement in and support for religion on the part of the state and political elements.

Some Challenges

The United States' original Protestant-Christian bias was not seriously challenged during the nation's first century, perhaps century and a half. But the Protestant hegemony was seriously challenged by waves of Roman Catholic and Jewish immigrants in the nineteenth and early twentieth centuries and later by agnostics and secularists. Mormons demanded the right to practice polygamy as a free exercise of their religion, but ultimately they were denied it. John T. Scopes was convicted of teaching evolution in a Tennessee high school, in contradiction to fundamentalist Christianity and, although a loser in court, was granted by many a "moral" victory because of the national publicity and lampooning of the prosecution by the press. Prohibition, a fundamentalist Christian sponsored constitutional amendment, came and went. Oregon required that every child be educated in its public schools, but the Supreme Court declared religious (parochial) schools a valid alternative (1925). And so, seemingly a great pendulum has swung in an arc between strong conservative Christian influence on national policies, and a rejection of such influence in favor of religious neutrality. But note that the pendulum has never swung in such a wide arc as to include opposition to religion, *per se*, especially its right to engage in debates alongside the political process.

To a great extent, the problem centers around balancing the requirement of nonestablishment of religion and its inherent neutrality stance, on the one hand, with providing opportunity for free exercise of religion on the other. When the state emphasizes neutrality, some are quick to accuse the state of antagonism to religion. When the state encourages free exercise, it is accused of "establishment of religion." For example, if the state says it cannot allow observance of Christmas in public schools lest it thereby favor Christianity, objectors claim that their freedom to act out their religious convictions wherever they may be is infringed upon. If Christmas observances are allowed, members of non-Christian religions or those with no religious affiliation or commitment, cry "foul" and "establishment of religion." Quite obviously, the First Amendment provides the political system with a built-in dilemma that will never be fully resolved. And so the problem of separating religion from other social phenomena, which we earlier branded as sociologically impossible in the first place, is now merely compounded.

The Frontier Challenge

We mentioned in the preceding section, that the Constitution's disestablishment of religion demanded innovation on the part of religious groups if they were to thrive—or perhaps just to survive. This need to innovate was significantly compounded by the opening of the frontier and increased westward migration. In a sense, the frontier almost immediately presented opportunities for religious groups to "test their mettle," so to speak. Here was territory. Here were people moving in to it. And no one religious group had a monopoly on either.

Frontier Conditions

A number of characteristics of the frontier, and the people who ventured there, are of direct relevance, both to the response and to the success or failure of religious groups in the frontier environment. One obvious feature was a sparse population located in small, widely separated settlements. This situation fostered loneliness among frontier settlers and the need for emotional outlets. These factors gave rise to an essential requirement of frontier life—a spirit of independence and self-sufficiency. If frontier settlers were going to make it, they had to do it on their own. Further, in the absence of external restraints, of social-control mechanisms for monitoring people's behavior, the task of checking antisocial behavior fell to control mechanisms internal to the individual. Overarching all this was another factor—namely, the constant threat of physical danger and insecurity, whether from disease, accident, inadequate food supply, Indian raids, or fellow citizens turned brigand. A final feature of the frontier worth mentioning, is the fact that the challenges and risks of the frontier effected selective migration. Those who traveled westward were not a representative cross-section of the inhabitants of the eastern seaboard. Rather, the trails west tended to fill up with those who had less at stake on the east coast—specifically, those of lower socioeconomic status (SES) and with little education. Not all of the latter traveled west, of course, but primarily those with an adventuresome spirit, a willingness to work, and long-range aspirations. At least those were the ones who survived and stayed.

Responses by Organized Religion

The established social institutions on the east coast, particularly the churches, were generally ill-equipped to meet the combination of challenges that were just described. The established eastern churches, which were of the denominational type, tended to require a trained, professional full-time clergy member to head a self-supporting congregation. They were used to meeting in a specially dedicated, permanent facility, containing the standard accoutrements—pews, hymnbooks, a pulpit, and perhaps a keyboard instrument. Transplanting this pattern to the frontier was infeasible, if for no other reason than that a sparse population with little ready cash could not support such a standard religious organization.

Recognizing this problem, some eastern ecclesiastical leaders and organizations turned to sponsoring revivals and camp meetings (occasional gatherings of large groups of people at a central location for several days of spiritual exhortation and instruction)—techniques that were actually better suited to such emerging sectarian groups as the Methodists and the Baptists. As a result, for a brief period after the Revolution, there occurred what came to be known as the Second Great Awakening. The First Great Awakening began in 1734 in New England, with the evangelistic preaching of Jonathan Edwards, George Whitfield, and others, and spread through the colonies in the 1730s to 1750s. This second general religious revival was epitomized in the Cane Ridge, Kentucky, camp meeting of 1801, where twenty thousand persons are estimated to have attended. Considering the sparse population of "the West" at that time, this is an extremely impressive number, which says a great deal about the eagerness of people for human contact, for an emotional outlet, and probably for many if not most, for religious participation and expression as well. The Second Great Awakening was relatively short-lived, however, and produced no durable institutional forms.

It should also be noted that the Congregationalists and Presbyterians made a serious, rational attempt to deal with the challenges of the frontier, particularly the sparseness of the population. In 1801, they formed a Plan of Union to create a noncompetitive missionary effort to the frontier and divide the more settled area between them. The Congregationalists were to stay north of a line extending west from New England; the Presbyterians would stay south of that line. The plan was unsuccessful, primarily because it failed to include the Baptists and Methodists who soon became the inheritors of the frontier.

The Baptist and Methodist Solutions

Both the Methodists and the Baptists quickly distinguished themselves on the frontier with innovative strategies for bringing religion to Americans heading west to find and build a better life. Thus, the Methodists, who had numbered approximately nine thousand in 1776, grew to become the largest religious group in the country by 1850. Baptist growth was nearly as great. There is no doubt, then, about their rapid success. But why? What exactly did they do? The answer is basically two-fold: (1) Both groups developed innovative organizational structures for reaching widely scattered people, and (2) as sects they had rejected many traditional denominational patterns and seemed capable of adapting to and growing up with the frontier while proclaiming a traditional, unadorned Gospel. As a consequence, they enjoyed a response among frontier settlers that the established denominations could not elicit.

First, regarding strategy, the Methodists employed the technique of the *circuit-riding preacher.* Initially these were men with some theological training, who were commissioned as missionaries to the frontier by John Wesley in England or by Bishop Asbury, John Wesley's representative in the colonies and then in the states. Their strategy was simply to go from house to house preaching the Gospel in the family setting, delivering sermons from a tree stump or wagon bed when a larger group could be gathered, creating "Methodists" as they went. They asked for little more than food and shelter from those who received them. Periodically they would return on their circuit to rally the faithful, solemnize marriages, and conduct baptisms. They traveled hundreds of miles a year along circuits that took a minimum of three or four weeks, and often a month or two, to complete.

The Baptists settled on a different, though equally successful, approach—the *lay preacher,* a farmer or craftsman for six days, a preacher for one. The success of this technique required only a concentration of a few families on adjoining farms or in a small village. The genius of the Baptist plan was that it required no recruitment from the outside. Anyone, with a "call" from God to preach and with some oratorical and pedagogical ability, could do it. The people whom such lay preachers gathered together began to think of themselves as Baptists.

And so the Baptist and Methodist sects grew. But these groups had more going for them than their strategies for overcoming the problem of sparse populations. The preachers were like their flocks—largely uneducated and independent of spirit—and knew "where the people were coming from," so to speak. They could communicate. And they encouraged emotional response and involvement in everyone. Religion for them was not a spectator sport. Revival services were frequent and they were popular, for they met people's need for emotional release. The democratic slant of these sects— which included the concepts that anyone could interpret Scripture as God directed him (no women were in the clergy role yet) and that parents were responsible for the spiritual welfare of their own children between visits by the circuit rider or Sunday gatherings for worship—agreed with the individualism and self-sufficiency of the frontier settlers. The typical emphasis of these sects on internal controls, in the face of all manner of temptations to sin, meshed well with the societal need for such internal controls in the relative absence of external ones.

Later Religious Responses

As the harshness of the frontier waned, as towns developed, and as social structures became more stabilized, further developments arose in the religious life of the frontier. For one thing, the Methodists and the Baptists consolidated their gains, for as people improved their lot and their communities became more firmly established, they did not suddenly forsake the religious group that had been serving them well. In great part, such continuity was maintained because the Methodist and the Baptist religious groups evolved and developed along with the frontier. Originally sects, they became full-fledged denominations. More attention was paid to theological training, colleges and seminaries were established throughout the South and Midwest, circuit riders became resident clergymen, and part-time Sunday preachers became full-time ministers.

As more middle-class business and professional people came west, the established eastern denominations followed and built their churches in the growing towns. Some of the upwardly-mobile early settlers joined these "higher status" Episcopal, Presbyterian, and Congregational churches, though not in sufficient numbers to seriously erode the membership gains the Baptists and Methodists had already made.

As the nineteenth century neared and passed midpoint, groups of Lutherans from Germany and the Scandinavian countries came to settle and tame the farmland of the Midwest and the north-central United States. They brought their churches with them and by virtue of different language and religion remained relatively isolated from those Protestants who had preceded them. Catholics came also in substantial numbers and established their ethnically oriented churches in both urban and rural areas. Thus, the frontier was becoming religiously diverse, primarily through the immigration of groups from outside the United States.

A pair of unique frontier phenomena must yet be mentioned. One was the emergence of two new denominations that were born essentially as denominations and did not follow the sect-to-denomination evolutionary route. These were the Disciples of Christ and the Churches of Christ. Both groups downplayed denominational differences and stepped into the developing towns and cities as the frontier moved ever westward, picking up some of the people left behind as many of the Methodist and Baptist preachers moved on to follow the scattering pioneers. These groups formed what today are often called "community" churches or "nondenominational" churches, which preach an "average" Protestantism and express little interest in the denominational "brand name" that a member may have had before. Many of these preachers were dissident Methodists, Baptists, and Presbyterians, who did not wish to be regarded as forming yet another denomination, but did so nonetheless.

The other unique frontier religious phenomenon was the Church of Jesus Christ of Latter-Day Saints (Mormons), founded by Joseph Smith in western New York State in the early 1840s. This group, regarded by some outsiders as neither Protestant nor even Christian, experienced serious opposition from an alliance of established Protestant denominations and growing Protestant sects, who otherwise only competed among themselves. To escape harassment that often reached violent proportions, the Mormons moved from New York to Ohio to Missouri to Illinois and finally to Utah. But even the Mormons, who were probably viewed as a religious cult in the beginning, evolved. Today the Mormon church is generally acknowledged to belong among the ranks of standard religious denominations, even though it is more aggressive in proselytizing than many of the latter.

THE ORDEAL OF PLURALISM

Anti-Catholicism

Although there had never really been any doubt, by the beginning of the nineteenth century, the new American nation saw itself as definitely a Protestant domain. This is probably one important reason why citizens generally accepted so graciously the radically new concept of separation of church and state enunciated in the First Amendment. Of the approximately four and one-half million citizens at the birth of the nation, estimates suggest there were only about twenty thousand Roman Catholics—a small minority indeed. Not that they were ignored. In fact, they were almost universally mistrusted. Small wonder, then, at the chagrin, uneasiness, and outright fear many citizens experienced and expressed as substantial immigration of Roman Catholics from Ireland, Germany, and Eastern Europe began in the 1830s.

The First Amendment's protection of the free exercise of religion was now to be put to its first test. The concept of *religious pluralism*, of freedom of religious expression and conviction, and of tolerance of religious diversity to which Protestants had paid lip service, now became a bitter pill for the many spokespeople for and supporters of the view that the United States was God's Protestant kingdom on earth. Not only were substantial efforts expended in trying to amend immigration laws to keep Catholics out of this country or, failing that, to convert them to Protestantism and thereby dilute their "poison," but also the society witnessed several decades of physical abuse directed against Catholics in the middle of the nineteenth century.

Martin Marty points out that the anti-Catholic agitators had deep reservoirs of suspicion from which to draw. He summarizes the historical setting as follows:

> The original colonists had felt themselves beleaguered, with French Catholics to the north and Spanish-Portuguese Catholics to the south. They had emotionally protected themselves against Catholic intrusions into the thirteen colonies. Where possible they isolated the Catholics, mostly in Maryland. Where necessary they began to accept them, as in the case of prestigious families like the Carrolls. But with few Catholics on the scene, it had been easy for colonial parsons to exaggerate stories of Catholic superstition and horror; no one was around to refute them. People could thus constantly reaffirm the prejudices their fathers had brought with them from England and elsewhere across the Atlantic.
>
> As the 20,000 or 25,000 colonial Roman Catholics grew to a body of 40,000 at the beginning of the [nineteenth] century and multiplied forty times by 1850 to 1,606,000, there were ever-increasing levels of animus and threat in the Protestant rhetoric.[15]

The "Protestant Crusade"

Reacting to this dramatic upsurge in Catholic immigration were a few outspoken propagandistsm such as Samuel F.B. Morse, who painted visions of a foreign conspiracy, based in the Vatican, to take over America. By mid-century, the nativist Know-Nothing political party was formed, with anti-Catholicism as one of its unifying themes. At this point we observe the blooming of what R.A. Billington terms the "Protestant Crusade."[16] At the heart of this "Crusade" were Protestants who felt threatened by the waves of Catholic immigration and were willing to believe almost any accusation or innuendo about Catholics. Occasionally they reacted, both impetuously and violently. There was, for example, Louisville's "Bloody Monday"—5 August 1855—in which more than twenty persons were killed and several hundred wounded. This was a conflict between Protestants and Catholics—the former having been aroused by a "no-popery" campaign carried on by the *Louisville Journal* within the context of the Know-Nothing political philosophy. The Philadelphia riots of 1844 represented an earlier case of anti-Catholicism that saw Catholic churches destroyed and the homes of Catholics burned, not to mention considerable bloodshed.

The Philadelphia Catholic Trustee Conflict

It appears that Roman Catholics in this country may have unwittingly and quite coincidentally provided some fuel for the Protestant fires that were smoldering. Consider, for example, the Philadelphia trustee conflict of the 1820s within the Roman Catholic Church, which revolved around the question of whether church property should be controlled by trustees representing laypeople or by the bishop of the diocese. The issue dated back to 1808, when St. Mary's Cathedral had been erected by the congregation and control of the property had been vested in a board of lay trustees, instead of the bishop as was usual. The long battle, during which the priest of the congregation was excommunicated, ended in 1830. The church was placed under an interdict, which caused members to abandon it for other churches and thus forced the trustees, left without financial support, to submit to the bishop.

This Philadelphia controversy did American Catholicism much harm. It attracted the hostile attention of the entire nation, inspired a great deal of "bad press" and negative literature, and left the impression in the minds of many Protestants that Catholicism was the sworn enemy of democratic institutions and thus a dangerous influence in the United States.[17] Some Protestants wondered if perhaps the Pope did desire to take over the United States. Ironically, the Philadelphia episode, in fact, marked an attempt by Catholic laypeople to pattern their church after typically American Protestant autonomous churches and to establish an independent Catholic church in America.[18]

Opposition by Catholics to the reading of the "Protestant" King James Version of the Bible in New York public schools, Protestant resentment and suspicion of the Catholic parochial schools as "un-American" and subversive, Catholic bloc voting as evidence of considerable political strength, "native American" resentment of "cheap" Irish-Catholic labor—all are factors that have contributed to anti-Catholicism in this country.

By the Civil War, anti-Catholic sentiment had lost much of its intensity. And the war itself certainly diverted energy and attention away from the issue. After the war, Catholic immigration proceeded steadily and then soared in the late 1800s, with the arrival of waves of southern and eastern European Catholics. By now, lacking evidence of any "papal plot," American Protestants established a somewhat uneasy but workable peace with their Catholic fellow citizens. The flames of conflict have been kindled sporadically ever since, however, over such issues as public aid to parochial schools, birth control and abortion, and official government or presidential representation to the Vatican. But as we will observe in Chapter 14, the animosities have been greatly reduced.

Anti-Semitism

A Brief History   The issue of religious pluralism and the challenge to Protestant domination was not limited to Catholic-Protestant relations. Significant numbers of Jews also immigrated to the United States between

1880 and the First World War. Until that time, there had been relatively so few Jews in this country—in 1815, for example, there were only about three thousand—that they were not regarded as a threat to established Protestantism. Although Jews had been excluded from full political participation in some of the colonies (e.g., Virginia) by trinitarian belief requirements, and although the depiction of Jews in the denominational literature of that period would today properly be termed anti-Semitic, the small number of Jews elicited little explicit reaction from their fellow citizens. Anti-Semitism in this country began in earnest with the substantial immigration of Russian Jews in the 1880s, when the Ku Klux Klan made anti-Semitism one of its major stances. Many of the Jews who immigrated to the United States after 1880, although often quite secularized (and sometimes politically radical), retained their ethnic identity, settling almost exclusively in urban areas and engaging in mutual assistance in establishing business enterprises. Other ethnic groups and Protestant "native Americans" began to resent their presence, and anti-Semitism began to surface. Jews thus found it necessary to establish various defense organizations, of which the Anti-Defamation League of the B'nai B'rith is the best known.

Anti-Semitism came to be a significant feature of American life—one that though considerably diminished is still alive today. Anti-Semitism probably reached its zenith in the 1920s and 1930s, when anti-Semitic newspapers and radio columnists proliferated and reached out into many American homes. Such strident anti-Semitism has been relegated to the fringes of our society today, and many of the most blatant forms of anti-Semitic discrimination in housing, education, employment, and voluntary-association membership have been eliminated. Yet the Anti-Defamation League annually reports on hundreds of public acts of denigration, denials of access, invitations to only second-class participation in groups, and even violence that occur in the United States. There continue to be swastikas spray painted on synagogue walls, vandalism of property, assaults against Jewish persons, and fire bombings of Jewish businesses and places of worship. And there are still sometimes a few public figures, who try to gain a following by expressing anti-Semitic slogans and opinions.

Anti-Semitic Attitudes   Various studies conducted over the past several decades prompt two observations. First, anti-Semitic feelings and opinions are harbored by many Americans, though most of them keep their thoughts to themselves. A survey conducted by the opinion-polling firm of Marttila and Kiley for the Anti-Defamation League, in 1992 found that 61 percent of Americans were at least somewhat anti-Semitic in terms of their beliefs and private opinions. Second, the overt acts and public displays of virulent anti-Semitism have been significantly reduced compared with earlier periods of American history.[19]

Studies by Glock and Stark and by Bernard Olson, have shown a connection between conservative Protestant theology and anti-Semitism, though the nature of this connection and its intensity are not clear.[20] A serious difficulty arises in trying to separate what we might call *social anti-Semitism*—hatred of Jews as social beings, as persons—from *religious anti-Semitism,* which from the conservative Christian viewpoint is the concept that Jews need salvation and that it will be denied them until they accept Jesus as Savior. Unfortunately, these two "types" of anti-Semitism, although undoubtedly intermingled in many cases, are not adequately distinguished in existing measures and indexes of anti-Semitism.

Other Targeted Religious Groups   Other groups, of course, come in for their share of aspersion and harassment. We have already mentioned the Mormons, who were literally forced to flee for their lives to new territory, ultimately standing their ground in the Utah Territory. Similar, though not so violent, harassment has been directed against Jehovah's Witnesses in many communities. It is interesting, from the sociological perspective, to note that both these groups traditionally engage in vigorous conversion and missionary activities. That is, they implicitly reject the pluralism concept that includes respect for every other group's autonomy and right to be and do as it chooses. Whereas adherence to the spirit of pluralism demands that one accept diversity—in fact, that one champion it—these groups actively seek to bring everyone into their ranks—an aggressive stance that undoubtedly encourages resentment. Even German Lutherans who, during World War I, persisted in using the German language in their worship services and conversation, were harassed in some communities.

The outcome of the religious pluralism controversy in this country has, however, been the triumph of pluralism and the peaceful acceptance of religious diversity by nearly all. This, of course, has not stopped many religious groups from actively proselytizing and openly criticizing the theology of other religious groups. But the practice of taking the process a step further by associating what appears theologically inadequate or incorrect from one's religious perspective with "un-Americanism," inferior citizenship, subversion, and the like, has been significantly reduced.

RELIGIOUS SOCIAL CONCERN

The second half of the nineteenth century marked the beginning of a highly significant controversy within American Protestantism that continues today—a fundamental argument over the proper focus of Christianity. In simplest terms, should the focus be the salvation of souls or the improvement of society? Although few if any proponents of either alternative would have asserted that Christianity should be exclusively devoted to one or the other goal, the controversy tended to place most Christians, theologian and layperson alike, into one camp or the other.

The Social Gospel Defined   This period, beginning in the late nineteenth Century, is known for the emergence of the so-called *social gospel* and the rise of such proponents of socially concerned Christianity as Horace Bushnell, Walter Rauschenbusch, and Washington Gladden. These were people who argued that Christianity is neither fulfilled nor true to its origins and history unless and until it immerses itself in alleviating the world's miseries and social pathologies—social problems that emerged with advancing industrialization, increasing urbanization, and the appearance, even then, of decay in portions of the mushrooming cities. These spokesmen contended that their emphasis on social responsibility was the old, authentic emphasis of the Bible. They pointed to the prophets in the Old Testament Scriptures and to Jesus in the New Testament Gospels, who evinced great concern for the physical and social needs and problems of people. On the other side, those who stressed the more individualistic salvation-centered focus for Christianity tended to emphasize the New Testament Epistles of Paul on the atonement of Jesus and his rescue of people from the wrath of a just and judging God.

Although we will look more thoroughly into this controversy in its present-day form in Chapter 15, we want at least to highlight the emergence of the "new" emphasis in Christianity (or, as many contended, the resurgence of the original one) that loomed so significantly as the nineteen century merged into the twentieth. Although it did not turn American religion completely around, for some individuals and groups, it did radically change the focus and purpose of religion; at the very least, it added a new dimension.

The establishment of hospitals, orphanages, and settlement houses, and the formation of groups, such as the Salvation Army, occurred after the Industrial Revolution was solidly under way and many of the latter's excesses and abuses were clearly seen adversely affecting great numbers of people. It is important to note, however, that the emphasis of religious people, during the period of western industrialization, was primarily an individualized one. That is, the primary concern of religious leaders was with helping individuals. First of all, they wanted to save the individual's soul. But then, out of compassion for those persons living a materially disadvantaged existence, they began establishing institutions and mechanisms for the purpose of helping the body. Again, just as the concern was for the souls of individual people, so the concern was for individual bodies. The social service activities of salvation-oriented religious groups, already begun in the 1820s, continued into the early part of the twentieth century. The emphasis was essentially that of John Wesley in the eighteenth century—concern for individuals, that is, replacing individual vices with individual virtues, changing the direction of individuals from hell to heaven, making physically healthy bodies out of ill and broken ones.

Later, religious leaders such as the aforementioned Bushnell, Rauschenbusch, and Gladden, began to direct primary attention away from salvation and toward physical and social well being; above all, they began to shift the focus from individual vices to societal ones. That is, they saw the locus of social problems not in individuals but in society and in institutional structures and patterns beyond the immediate control of individuals. To these social reformers the goal was one of "Christianizing" the social order, of applying the teachings of Jesus to the social and economic institutions of the society, of reforming the social environment in which people lived and worked. They expounded what came to be known as the social gospel.

Those who followed in the footsteps of the earlier, individual-oriented religious leaders, became increasingly uneasy with the social gospel, which they felt operated at the expense of individual salvation—the pre-eminent responsibility of Christianity, in their view. Influential evangelistic preachers who emphasized individual salvation, such as Dwight L. Moody and Billy Sunday, thus began challenging the social gospel and, in fact, essentially carried the day so far as rank-and-file preachers and church members were concerned. Martin Marty reports how the flamboyant evangelist Sunday took on the most noted advocate of the social gospel still at work in the parish ministry, Washington Gladden:[21]

> The setting of their encounter was Columbus, Ohio, where Gladden had piled up a record of achievement in a socially oriented ministry over three decades. But when Sunday came to town to carry on one of his pro-evangelistic and apparently "antisocial" revivals, Gladden quietly opposed him, and after the revival, Gladden was more outspoken over the meager returns he saw garnered from Sunday's raucous efforts. But Gladden was attacked by the vast majority of Columbus's ministers of all Protestant denominations. They rose to the defense of Sunday's approach and clearly identified with the conversionism of the revivalist.[22]

In their attempts to discredit the social gospel, the individual-oriented evangelists began to pull back from and react against social service and welfare activities, which they had earlier engaged in and rededicated themselves to efforts to win souls and raise levels of individual morality, by means of such tactics as emphasizing the evil of "demon rum" and supporting the Prohibition movement. The social gospel wing of American Christianity did not disappear, however. It continued with minority support in the major denominations and through the various agencies of the Federal Council of Churches (now the National Council of Churches) that had been founded in 1908 primarily by social gospel forces.

Thus, the social gospel movement did not wither away; in fact, it has continued to exert significant influence in American religion up to the present. It enjoyed a resurgence, with its involvement in the civil rights movement, in the 1950s and 1960s and in the war on poverty of the 1960s and 1970s, although with what still appears to have been a minority of church member support. There will be more on this issue in Chapter 15.

Reconciling the great diversity of opinion and practice regarding social versus individual emphases is, of course, not uniquely a problem of religious institutions. Religious groups have, in fact, always reflected the historical ambivalence in American society at large regarding rugged individualism, self-sufficiency, and individual responsibility versus social concerns, welfare, and mutual responsibility for one's fellow human beings.

THE POST-WORLD WAR II REVIVAL

Following World War II, the United States experienced what came to be known as a religious "revival." Beginning in the late 1940s and extending into the 1950s, church membership and attendance soared, contributions to religious organizations poured in, literally thousands of new congregations were established and quickly became self-supporting, and the value of new construction by religious groups increased dramatically, year after year. Some data will document this growth. Between 1940 and 1950, membership in churches rose from 49 to 57 percent of the population, and by 1959 it had reached 63.6 percent.[23] Gallup poll data show a comparable increase in church attendance—whereas only 36 percent of the sample in 1942 reported having attended a church service during the week preceding the interview, by 1957 the figure had risen to 51 percent.[24] The value of new construction of religious facilities totaled $28 million in 1935, during the depth of the Depression, and had increased to $59 million by 1940. But the really big increase was still to come—in 1950 the value of new construction was $409 million, and by 1965 the figure reached $1.2 billion. The religion business was indeed a booming one.

Further, there developed, what William Lee Miller has called our national "piety along the Potomac," which included Bible breakfasts, congressional prayer groups, and a president named Eisenhower who made numerous religious allusions in his speeches and was himself baptized in the White House following his inauguration.[25] Postage stamps and folding money suddenly began to include "In God We Trust" on their faces. We inserted the phrase "under God" into the Pledge of Allegiance. Popular music and movie extravaganzas followed religious themes. Books of a religious, devotional, or inspirational nature proliferated, and many even made the bestseller lists.

The opening passage of this section referred to a religious "revival." At least this is what many called it. Many churchmen who saw their churches filling up, who saw massive building programs quickly underwritten with cash and pledges, who noted their denominations annually opening new mission congregations numbering in the dozens and even hundreds, can hardly be blamed for speaking in such terms. Finally, their sermons and various other efforts, in a lifetime of dedication to religion, were bearing some tangible fruit. Religion was really "catching on" and getting through to people. Observing these phenomena sociologically, however, we should be more cautious in assessing what was going on. As A. Roy Eckhardt observes, there was "a manifest upsurge of *interest* in religion."[26] Whether this reflected a true revival in the sense of increasing dedication and commitment is difficult, if not impossible, to determine.

What we do know is that the period following World War II found many more people within our national boundaries, as millions of service-men and women returned home and as the baby boom of the 1940s got underway. A fantastic building boom accompanied the population growth, as many new and some older families moved to the suburbs in search of a place to start a new life. Church facilities, that had barely sufficed during a Depression and a world war (when there was relatively little new construction), clearly came up short in the face of population and residential expansion. New church facilities were built where the new people now were. In some cases, this meant a net gain, as the old facilities in the city remained and new facilities were built near the edges of the spreading suburban fron-tier. In other instances it was a trade. The downtown and inner-city churches were abandoned for the new, as a majority of the people moved out, or the former were sold for a few cents on the dollar to the sects that emerged to serve the migrants (primarily blacks), who replaced the mobile, more afflu-ent whites who left—a prime example of human ecological succession.

We do know that the United States was trying to piece itself together again after a long, harsh Depression and an expensive, grief-filled war. No doubt countless people were seeking moorings, eternal verities upon which they could start building something new. Paul Hutchinson wrote in 1955 about the "cult of reassurance," which he described as

> a flocking to religion, especially in middle-class circles, for a renewal of confidence and optimism at a time when these are in short supply. It is a turning to the priest for encouragement to believe that, despite every-thing that has happened in this dismaying century, the world is good, life is good, and the human story makes sense and comes out where we want it to come out.[27]

Further, there was in the postwar years the unsettled state of mind caused by the specter of the atomic bomb and the uneasiness of what was termed the "menace" of communism. Many people were undoubtedly seek-ing a firm base on which to stand and a clear perspective from which to eval-uate what was happening.

Yet we cannot help but return to our prior comments about the growing population, and above all the suburban migration trends. Without a doubt, something quite sociological and not particularly religious was going on, as people got involved in building churches and attending them once they were built. These people were in a new place; they had left their neighborhoods of many years, perhaps even of their childhood; they were temporarily without friends or voluntary-association outlets and involvements; they were looking for human contact. A ready place that developed early in the suburban development, to resolve some of these needs and problems, was the church. In a real sense, the idea of religion, as an integrating mechanism in society, has definite meaning and relevance here—religion provided social contacts, outlets, and activities for people that were quite apart from strictly religious functions or concerns.

At the height of the religious "revival," Will Herberg suggested another partial explanation for the rise of religious interest. His suggestion revolves around the third-generation hypothesis, which says that while the children of immigrants strive to deny their heritage in their struggle to "match up" to what they perceive to be true American standards and characteristics, the grandchildren (the third generation), quite secure in their Americanism, look for further identity, for a heritage and a link with the past. This, Herberg feels, is available for nearly all Americans in religion, specifically the three equally alternative religions of our contemporary society—Protestantism, Catholicism, and Judaism. Since, in the latter half of the twentieth century, we in the United States constitute essentially a nation of third-generation or later-generation Americans, it is, therefore, not surprising to see a renewal of interest in religion—a heightened interest not strictly for "religious" reasons, but for social and psychological reasons as well, as people try to identify what they are besides "just an American."[28]

Certainly some reservations are in order, concerning how paramount religious identity is for the majority of people. If asked, "What are you?" would not more people respond in terms of their occupation than their religion? It is nevertheless likely that, for some people at least, religious identity has come to serve as an important link with the past and as a source of present identity.

At this point we refer back to our discussion in Chapter 5 and a problem inherent in the measurement of religiosity. Most of the discussion of religious revival has centered around rather low-powered measures, such as church attendance and membership. There has been little assessment of changes in intensity of religious feeling or meaning, changes in what people believed in and are committed to (ideological dimension), or changes in behavior as a result of religious influences (consequential dimension). Thus, even if we could agree that a religious revival occurred in the United States from approximately 1945 to 1965, we may be referring to little more than what Eckhardt noted—an increased *interest* in religion. And this may be something of an overstatement. For example, what does an increase in church membership mean? In part it reflects the fact that requirements for church membership have in many groups become progressively less demanding and restrictive. That is, it appears to be easier to become a church member. Further, the high degree of geographic mobility of people during this period in our history, coupled with the tardiness of most local congregations in clearing their membership lists of dropouts and people who have moved away, have undoubtedly resulted in some—in certain cases perhaps considerable—duplication hidden in comprehensive church membership figures. That is, it is likely that some people were counted two or three times within a given year's totals.

There is no point here in going further in expressing our uneasiness with unqualified assertions of a post-World War II religious revival, for we have made our basic point.[29] That is, although there appears to have been a definite upswing in religious interest in the postwar period, the upswing may not have been so great or significant as some have supposed. In a sense, religion became more highly visible. It was no longer contained solely within the walls of religious organizations. It hit the jukeboxes, the movie theaters, and the drugstore paperback bookracks. Religion was popularized, and it impinged on everyone's consciousness—much as any fad does. Just as any fad, however, some of the glitter and popularity began to fade. Glock and Stark even suggest that, solely in response to wide publicity given church membership growth in the late 1940s, there was "generated a commercial interest in producing and promoting religious literature, songs and plays with a religious motif, and commodities having religious connotations."[30] That is, commercial interests saw a new market, and the resultant visibility of religion through commercial exploitation tended to exaggerate the level of religious interest actually felt and expressed by people.

Although we could now proceed to examine developments in American religion following the postwar religious "revival" and thus bring our discussion up to date, we shall delay such an examination until Chapter 15. In that chapter we shall go into greater detail concerning the contemporary religious scene and what developed out of the postwar religious "revival" period. We now proceed in the next chapter to discuss unique religious patterns on the American scene, namely, African-American religion and Native American religion.

Notes

1. *Everson v. Board of Education*, 333 U.S. 1.
2. Evarts B. Greene, *Religion and the State* (New York: New York University Press, 1941), p. 51.
3. Anson Phelps Stokes and Leo Pfeffer, *Church and State in the United States* (New York: Harper & Row, 1964), p. 7.
4. Robert B. Fowler, *Religion and Politics in America* (Philadelphia: American Theological Library Association and Scarecrow Press, 1985), pp. 234–235.

5. John K. Wilson, "Locating Religion in American Politics" in *Religion and American Politics: The 2000 Election in Context*, ed. Mark Silk (Hartford, CT: Center for the Study of Religion in Public Life at Trinity College, 2000), p. 8.

6. Ibid.

7. Quoted in Martin E. Marty, *Righteous Empire* (New York: Dial Press, 1970), p. 36.

8. Ibid., p. 37.

9. Ibid.

10. Joseph Tussman, *The Supreme Court on Church and State* (New York: Oxford University Press, 1962), p. xiii.

11. According to the first U.S. Census in 1790, only 5 percent of U.S. citizens reported being members of churches.

12. Quoted in Tussman, *The Supreme Court*, pp. 5–6.

13. Quoted in ibid., p. 6.

14. John K. Wilson, ibid., pp. 16–17.

15. Marty, *Righteous Empire*, pp. 127–128.

16. Ray Allen Billington, *The Protestant Crusade, 1800–1860* (Gloucester, MA: Peter Smith, 1963).

17. Ibid., pp. 38–40.

18. Will Herberg, *Protestant, Catholic, Jew* (Garden City, NY: Doubleday, 1956), p. 140.

19. Jerome A. Chanes, ed., *Anti-Semitism in America Today* (New York: Birch Lane Press, 1995), pp. 8–14.

20. Charles Y. Glock and Rodney Stark, *Christian Beliefs and Anti-Semitism* (New York: Harper & Row, 1966); Bernard Olson, *Faith and Prejudice* (New Haven, CT: Yale University Press, 1963).

21. Most of the social gospel advocates were seminary professors, editors, authors, and the like, who remained largely unknown to the rank-and-file church member.

22. Marty, *Righteous Empire*, p. 183.

23. Benson Y. Landis, ed., *Yearbook of American Churches, 1964* (New York: National Council of Churches of Christ in the U.S.A., 1964), p. 290.

24. Ibid., p. 283.

25. William Lee Miller, "Piety along the Potomac," *The Reporter*, August 17, 1954, p. 25.

26. A. Roy Eckhardt, *The Surge of Piety in America* (New York: Association Press, 1958), p. 17.

27. Quoted in ibid., p. 28.

28. Herberg, *Protestant, Catholic, Jew*, pp. 272–275.

29. Additional questions are raised by Charles Y. Glock, "The Religious Revival in America?" in *Religion and the Face of America*, ed. Jane Zahn (Berkeley: University Extension, University of California, 1959); Seymour Martin Lipset, "Religion in America: What Religious Revival?" *Columbia University Forum* 11, no. 2 (1959); and W. H. Hudson, "Are Churches Really Booming?" *Christian Century* 72, no. 51 (1955): 1494–1496.

30. Charles Y. Glock and Rodney Stark, *Religion and Society in Tension* (Chicago: Rand McNally, 1965), p. 78.

Chapter 13

Black and Native American Religion in America

Black Americans expressing religious convictions.

In Chapter 10, we introduced the subject of religion and the African American. We focused both on the historical issue once facing American Christians, of whether to convert black slaves to Christianity, and on the more recent issue of the relationship of white churches to the black civil rights movement. In this chapter, we wish to pick up at the historical point, when the issue of the conversion of slaves had been resolved and trace the development of the black church as a social institution. In doing so we will work within three major sections: an overview of the historical development of the institution, an examination of the role of militancy versus social pacifism so far as the black church is concerned, and a discussion of contemporary religious issues and developments within the black church and the black community, together with an assessment of the continuing role of religion in the black community. We will then review the impact of white colonization on Native American religion, consider some dominant features of Native American religion, and review the forms Native American religion has taken today.

THE HISTORICAL DEVELOPMENT OF THE BLACK CHURCH AS A SOCIAL INSTITUTION

Following the consensus in the United States, around the turn of the nineteenth century, that slaves should be converted to Christianity and still remain slaves, the early pattern of worship services found black slaves and whites in the same congregations—the blacks usually occupying the balcony, the whites the main floor. Such joint worship was deemed advisable because white masters could then keep an eye on their "possessions" and be reassured that their slaves were not listening to a different message—such as a call to insurrection.

The Deculturation Process

Whether slaveholders were always fully conscious of it or not, for blacks conversion to Christianity and joint worship served as part of the deculturation process. At the very least, religious conversion served as a useful follow-up and capstone to the deliberate efforts by slave traders and owners to deculturate the slaves, to strip them of their African culture and heritage. This was accomplished by such tactics as breaking up families and prohibiting any two slaves from the same African village or tribe to be sold to work on the same plantation. One highly significant concomitant of this tactic was that the slaves usually shared no common language and thus could only converse in the English language that they had to learn. In short, much of the original culture of these people was stripped from them in less than a generation.

Obviously, slaves could not successfully preserve and practice many shared religious patterns either. Christianity, which was substituted for the ancient religions, itself became an agent for subduing and pacifying the slaves. What slaves heard preached was submission to authority, obedience, obligation to perform one's duty, commitment to nonviolence, and the promise of splendid eternal rewards in heaven for all who led proper lives and made appropriate commitments during one's earthly sojourn. "Some God has made to be masters, some to be slaves. But we'll all receive a grand reward in the hereafter"—this is what has been referred to as "pie-in-the-sky by and by."

Kenneth Stampp has summarized well the use to which religion was put, with regard to controlling the behavior of slaves:

> Through religious instruction the bondsmen learned slavery had divine sanction, that insolence was as much an offense against God as against the temporal master. They received the Biblical command that servants should obey their masters, and they heard, too, that eternal salvation would be their reward for faithful service, and that on the day of judgment God would deal impartially with the poor and the rich, the black man and the white.[1]

Stampp also mentions an eighteenth Century book titled *Suggestions on the Religious Instruction of the Negroes in the Southern States*, written by Charles C. Jones and published by the national Presbyterian Board of Publication. Stampp cites Jones as advising missionaries to ignore the "civil condition" of slaves and to pay no attention to complaints against their master. In preaching to slaves, ministers should condemn "every vice and evil custom," urge the "discharge of every duty," and support the "peace and order of society." They should, in sum, teach the slaves to give "respect and obedience [to] all those whom God in his providence has placed in authority over them."[2]

Emerging Independence of the Black Church

The early pattern of joint worship of masters and slaves in the same church did not remain the common one, probably in large part because the white masters wanted one message for their slaves, another for themselves. Therefore, another early pattern on the larger plantations was for the owner to provide special religious leaders and preachers for the slaves. These were not always white preachers, but occasionally trusted slaves who had a "gift" for preaching. Also fairly early, the Baptists and Methodists began missionary activities among the slaves, and they enjoyed considerable success—for many of the same reasons that they succeeded with white settlers on the frontier (see Chapter 12). Thus, the early pattern of joint worship in the same congregation was gradually replaced by segregated worship in white and black "congregations." Strictly speaking, except in the North and in a few border cities, slaves did not form their own independent congregations, largely because of laws forbidding slave assemblies. Informally, however, on many plantations, essentially autonomous slave churches developed under "trusted" slave ministers. Of course, their services and activities were carefully monitored by the master or his overseer. Nevertheless, such congregations of slaves set the stage for the eventual emergence of the black church as the major formal group or organization over which blacks, after Emancipation, had essential control. Thus, we can begin to understand the importance and centrality that black religious organizations have assumed in the black community to this day.

Although for various reasons whites began to tolerate separate religious groups and activities for blacks, it was not without some apprehension. Richard Wade points out that as late as 1847, "many citizens" in Charleston expressed their discomfort over permitting religious institutions for blacks, particularly as it resulted in separate congregations. They feared the independence, the absence of the control and authority of the master, the taste of freedom it provided, and the opportunity for black leaders to emerge and learn skills.[3]

In the North, after some initial integrated worship, free blacks began to pull out and form their own congregations and, soon, their own denominations. In fact, the earliest all-black denominations, the African Methodist Episcopal Zion Church and the African Methodist Episcopal Church, organized in 1796 and 1816, respectively, were founded by free blacks, who had experienced harassment and "balcony segregation" in white congregations.

The Functions of the Black Church

After the Civil War and Emancipation, with most legal restrictions against black assemblies lifted, there occurred a mass withdrawal of blacks from racially mixed congregations, and even denominations, in order to form their own churches. What had begun as an outlet or escape and a focal institution for their lives under slavery, continued to serve the same functions after Emancipation. Although the following evaluation by Richard Wade concerns the functions of religion for blacks under slavery, the pattern then established continued after Emancipation.

> Slavery had stripped [blacks] of any meaningful pattern of life beyond that of the master and their bondage. The family could furnish none. No tradition could provide roots into a history without servitude. Neither today nor tomorrow offered any expectation of a life without the present stigma. Deprived of nostalgia for the past and unable to discover any real meaning in the present, the blacks sought relief and consolation in a distant time. In the church, with their own kind, amid songs of redemption and the promises of Paradise, a lifeline could be thrown into the future.[4]

The prominent black leader and sociologist, W.E.B. DuBois, states that once blacks assumed complete control over their church following Emancipation, the local black church became the center of its members' social life, the primary medium of communication and information exchange, and even the organizer of entertainment and amusement. With regard to the last function, he lists such activities and functions as concerts, suppers, socials, fairs, literary exercises and debates, cantatas, plays, excursions, picnics, and celebrations.[5]

A Community Center   Gunnar Myrdal describes the black church as a "community center par excellence."[6] In most black communities, the church was the only institution where blacks not only enjoyed autonomy and freedom from the prying eyes of whites but also had access to facilities in which to conduct social activities.

But to note such a function as this is only to begin to list the important roles of the religious group or institution in the life of African Americans. First there is the economic function: "A study of economic co-operation among Negroes," DuBois has stated, "must begin with the church group."[7] Many black churches early formed mutual-aid or "beneficial" societies designed to help members survive financial crises associated with illness or death of family members. These were actually incipient insurance companies. In rural communities, the emphasis seemed to be particularly on burial "insurance" to provide the members with a "decent Christian burial."

Vehicle of Education   The black churches have also played a significant role in education over the years. Frequently, black ministers established a school along with a church. Just as the original purpose of slave education had been to communicate the Christian Gospel and enable slaves to read the Bible, these minister-educators sought to raise the spiritual understanding of their people. When the Julius Rosenwald Fund aided in building over five thousand schools for blacks in the South during the first third of the twentieth century, black churches played an important role in supplementing those funds. E. Franklin Frazier notes that southern blacks contributed 17 percent of the total cost of $28 million (Rosenwald Fund, 15 percent; white friends, 4 percent; taxes, 64 percent), and that they raised much of their share through church suppers and various other church-sponsored programs.[8]

There was also impetus among the black denominations, following the Civil War, to erect educational institutions independent of white philanthropy. This plan was primarily motivated by the desire to provide a better-educated ministry—a project Frazier feels was not eminently successful, since the black denominational schools "never attained a high level as educational institutions . . . [and] have generally nurtured a narrow religious outlook and have restricted the intellectual development of Negroes."[9] Frazier also notes that the authoritarian demeanor and anti-intellectualism exhibited by many black ministers have tended to inhibit the black churches from making a strong, positive contribution to education.[10] In other words, although certainly contributing to educational advancement for blacks, the black church has not been as significant an influence in this sphere as it might have been.

Supporting the significance of the black church's role in educating blacks, however, Wade mentions that some of the pre-Emancipation opposition to independent black churches—or, for that matter, opposition to Christianity for blacks at all—centered around the observation that some blacks were becoming literate in the process of their religious instruction. Many whites feared black literacy as much as black independence in their religious activities.[11]

Opportunity for Political Expression   A third area of influence and involvement on the part of the black religious institution has been politics. During the Reconstruction period, several black ministers and bishops in the South became federal and state officials, state legislators, and U.S. congressmen, and one was elected a U.S. senator. With the end of Reconstruction and the resumption of white supremacy, however, blacks were virtually eliminated from public political life, and the black church then became, as Frazier observes, "the arena . . . of political activities" for black citizens.[12] As the sole major institution over which they had complete control, the church became the major context within which ambitious individuals could aspire to leadership and achieve distinction and status. In particular, the black church turned out to be the most likely source of power, upward mobility, and economic success for black males. Thus, black churches soon overflowed with aspiring ministers, apprentice ministers, and "jackleg preachers," who literally waited in the wings for a chance to preach, prove their ability, and gather a following or congregation for themselves.

In the South, the church also presented the only outlet of political expression for the black rank and file, which was denied the franchise in local, state, and national elections. The only place they could vote and make significant choices was in their church—as they elected local officers and denominational representatives and engaged in debate over policies for their local church.

We must note also that as the franchise was granted or returned to blacks, particularly in the North, black churches became more politically involved than most of their white counterparts. Candidates for political office were frequently invited to speak in black churches during or after Sunday services, ministers urged their followers to vote for particular candidates, and partisan campaign literature was made available in church buildings—all to a greater extent than in white churches, most of which counseled keeping politics and religion separate.

Although no hard data on the frequency with which black churches were involved in politics are available from the distant past, 1963 data on black clergymen in Detroit reveal that 45.5 percent allowed political candidates access to their churches, 62.7 percent permitted distribution of campaign literature from their churches, 67.8 explicitly encouraged their members to work with the political parties in their neighborhoods, and 30.5 percent even told their members for whom they should vote. Further, 24.4 percent of black clergymen in Detroit had at some time actively worked for a political party at the local level.[13]

It is noteworthy that the more militantly committed black clerics are to the civil rights movements and its goals, the more likely they are to engage in the political behaviors just cited. We will focus on important differences among contemporary black clergymen later in this chapter. At this point, we simply wish to document that the black church has been and continues to be a fairly active political organization. Although no comparable hard data for white churches are available, every indication is that, on the average, white churches have traditionally not been so politically involved. There has been some change here recently, as we have seen some clergy and churches become politically active over the abortion and gay marriage issues, and electing "right-minded" political candidates. Of course, an important part of the reason many local churches, both black and white, avoid introducing partisan politics into their midst, is the risk that political activism would jeopardize their continued tax-free status.

A Refuge in a Hostile White World   Finally, we must say that permeating all of the preceding functions of the black church is the fundamental function of representing what Frazier calls "a refuge in a hostile white world."[14] The black church has provided a structural context for interaction, in which blacks could not only express their deepest feelings and longings but also attain some measure of status (in God's eyes, if in no one else's). Earlier, religion provided black slaves some catharsis as well as hope for eventual freedom, even though they were now in temporal bondage. Later, in a similar way, the "emancipated" blacks, after a brief opportunity to participate somewhat freely in the wider society during Reconstruction, were soon again excluded from participation in the white person's world except as inferiors. They were disfranchised, given a skimpy and inferior education, and accorded far less than justice by a court system that operated with a double standard of justice. These "emancipated" blacks needed escape and hope, as much as their enslaved parents and grandparents before them. Where could a black person find refuge amid such hostility and discrimination? The place was predominantly their church, which whites left alone.

Most of what we have been describing in the foregoing paragraphs, applies most appropriately to the black church since the days of Reconstruction. During slavery, when the black church had to be the "invisible institution," there were many calls for freedom in black religion. Although it is difficult to distinguish whether calls for freedom in black slaves' religion were for ultimate spiritual freedom in heaven, or for temporal freedom from bondage, or perhaps a subtle and even unconscious combination of both ideas, there is evidence that black religion did encourage slaves' hopes of physical freedom. The leaders of the better-known slave uprisings, for example, used ample biblical imagery and justification for their actions. Consider, for example, the rebellions led by Denmark Vesey in 1822 in Charleston, South Carolina, and by Nat Turner, himself a black minister in Southampton County, Virginia, in 1831. Moreover, some of the northern black churches, composed of freed blacks, stood squarely for slaves' freedom as they worked for the Underground Railroad.

But following the Civil War, when the issue was no longer slavery but the pervasive racism that kept blacks securely "in their place," whatever small amount of past protest and calls for freedom there had been receded in the face of escapist and otherworldly emphases. It is this post-Civil War pattern of black religion, which nurtured the stereotype of the black church that so many whites cling to—the revivalist or sectarian emotionalism and escapism that an accommodating "Uncle Tom" minister, albeit a fiery and eloquent preacher, supervised and promoted. Here one sees the subservient, peace-making, don't-rock-the-boat style of black ministers, who knew only too well that their job was to keep their place, encourage submission and fatalistic acquiescence on the part of their congregations, and preach an otherworldly gospel. If they did their job well, their choir would receive an invitation to sing in white churches during the year, and they could look forward to a little free coal for the church and parsonage in the winter.[15]

The black church became overwhelmingly a haven where blacks could exercise autonomy but where there appeared to be little challenge to the *status quo*. In fact, the following observation by an anonymous black preacher probably conveys even more truth than humor: "Come weal or woe, my status is quo." Rare was the black minister who took up the banner of change or social revolution, at the risk of losing a fairly comfortable position, whose advantages included high personal status and power, and income as great if not greater than that of most other blacks. Black ministers were also occasionally accused of being "bought off" by elements in the white power structure, as they were accorded the courtesy of speaking for or representing the black community and serving as the funnel for the table crumbs of white philanthropy.

With little impetus for challenge and change coming from black ministers, who did reasonably well for themselves under a system of racism, and with the rank-and-file black church members finding solace, escape, recreation, and temporal autonomy in the black church, it is not surprising that the black church proceeded through the decades of segregation and discrimination tacitly approving, or at least certainly not openly challenging, prevailing social structures and patterns. Not that there were no voices of protest coming from the black church and its clergy. Not that black religion was totally acquiescent in the face of a dominant racism. On the contrary, there were definite protests and other forms of aggressive reaction in the name of religion. In fact, although we have been stressing the accommodating, otherworldly, withdrawal response of black religion—essentially the sect approach—in the face of white racism and exclusion from the society's mainstream, there has always been a mildly aggressive and persistent reaction stemming from within the ranks of black religion.

In this tension between acceptance/acquiescence/withdrawal on the one hand and rebellion on the other, we see one of the classic dilemmas or dialectics identified by C. Eric Lincoln and Lawrence Mamiya—that of the dialectic between accommodation versus resistance.[16] The black church was the primary mediating and socializing institution in the black community and it was counted on by both blacks and whites to teach some economic rationality and other cultural survival skills. However, as the primary source of leadership in the black community, there were also constant pressures to provide leadership, which could expose the injustices and organize some challenge to the system that dominated and continued to subject the black community to second-class status.

MILITANCY IN THE BLACK CHURCH

The Father Divine Style

Four types of black religious aggressiveness in the face of racism can be distinguished.[17] One is typified by the Father Divine Peace Mission, which flourished in the 1930s and early 1940s. Here was a religious group that provided blacks with food and occasional job opportunities during the Great Depression, as many blacks migrated to northern cities in search of employment. Although the Father Divine Peace Mission presents a fascinating study in theology (Father Divine was viewed as God Himself), our interest here is in the group's commitment to a social service that fed and housed thousands of needy persons over a period of years. Although, of course, this approach did not strike significantly at the root causes of problems facing African Americans, and worked only locally at the remedial level of treating symptoms, there was here and in similar groups a clear manifestation of aggressiveness in the name of black religion. We are forced to conclude, however, that the net impact of such food and lodging efforts benefited only a relatively few needy people.

The Black Nationalism Style

Another example of aggressiveness in the name of religion in the black community is similar to the foregoing, but more far-reaching and enduring. That is the self-help philosophy and activities of Black Nationalist religious organizations, best represented (most recently, at least) by the Nation of Islam (Black Muslims). Here is a group dating back to the early 1930s, which stresses black supremacy, advocates racial separation, and maintains rigid membership requirements (religious dietary laws and moral discipline). Major emphases are to build and support black institutions by pooling economic resources and "buying black," to secure an education, learn skills, work hard, cultivate self-discipline, and, in general, engage in cooperative self-help—all in the name of religion (in this instance a version of Islam whose validity other branches of Islam tend not to recognize). They believe Allah chose the Nation of Islam to be special messengers to blacks to return to Allah, black like them, whose time would come in the next period of history, when the rule and oppression of white "devils" would end.

As a group they have not gained the numerical success many predicted. In fact, their numbers may be smaller today than in the 1960s. They have periodically attained front-page news status: when sports superstars joined the ranks—Cassius Clay became Muhammad Ali and Lew Alcindor became Kareem Abdul-Jabbar; when Malcolm X defected from the group and was later assassinated by one of the faithful; when in the 1990s one of the Black Muslims' two major leaders, Louis Farrakhan, felt it necessary to rein in the national spokesman for the group, Khalid Abdul Muhammad, for speeches on college campuses that were too inflammatory and too negative toward whites, Jews in particular; or most recently with Farrakhan's sponsorship of the "Million Man March" in Washington, DC on 16 October 1995. Considerable credit can justifiably be given to the Black Muslims for their success in rehabilitating ex-convicts and improving the economic welfare of their adherents. While the movement has not attracted hordes of African Americans into its ranks, its success with those it has brought in is worthy of attention.

The Individual Aggressive Style

A third example of black aggressiveness in the name of or from the ranks of religion, would be the numerous examples of individual black ministers from the more standard black denominations, who either took it upon themselves to extract philanthropy from the white community or became involved as individuals in political activities that concerned blacks. An excellent example of the latter activity is seen in Detroit in the late 1930s and early 1940s, during the bitter labor struggle to unionize the Ford Motor Company. Using various ingenious techniques, Henry Ford and his aides had long kept a substantial contingent of blacks out of the labor movement. Although Ford, as early as 1910, established the policy that at least 10 percent of his employees would be blacks, all prospective black employees needed a letter of recommendation from a black minister attesting to their moral fiber and (at least implicitly) antiunion commitment. Black ministers were expected to emphasize not only what a benefactor Henry Ford was to blacks, but what a disaster unionization would be for black workers. By a system of judiciously placed contributions and periodic visits, Henry Ford kept many black clergy "in line." Three "maverick" black ministers, however, became outspoken leaders of the unionization movement and acted on the conviction that unionization would benefit their fellow blacks. The Reverends Horace White, Charles Hill, and Malcolm Dade were convinced that accommodation and an otherworldly gospel should be replaced or at least supplemented by challenges to existing structures and concern with the problems and opportunities of this world. Such religious leaders in the black community appear to have been rare, yet their presence merits noting in our summary of aggressive social action emanating from black religious sources.

Organized Militancy

In a fourth example of aggressiveness from the black church, the action centers in the clergy but is more organized and represents a greater proportion of black clergy. The emergence of black clergy organized for social protest action directed against institutionalized racism, occurred at the height of the civil rights movement in the early 1960s. In various urban communities, such as Baltimore, Detroit, and St. Louis, black clergy organized what amounted to economic boycotts, called "selective buying" campaigns, against firms that were guilty of blatant discrimination against blacks in employment and promotion and whose representatives refused to discuss the issue.

For example, the usual procedure in Detroit was for a committee of the larger clergy group, which called itself The Negro Preachers of Detroit and Vicinity, to request an audience with executives of the company suspected of discrimination, to discuss their policies and to check into the proportion of blacks employed at various levels in the organization. Following this initial contact, the committee would return with specific requests. The hope was that the company would cooperate, by hiring a number of qualified black workers at various levels within the organization as requested by the black preachers. The company was then given a few weeks to implement this proposal, after which time (they would be informed) an economic boycott of their product(s) would commence if compliance with the request was not forthcoming. If, after a three-to-four-week period, the company still delayed and resisted, the committee would contact every black preacher in the community and ask that they cooperate and help their black brothers and sisters in the community, by reading a letter to their congregations the following Sunday morning. That letter urged their members not to buy the products of a specified company and said, among other things: "Our eyes are open! Never again will we stand by and see doors closed in the faces of our people. We cannot, therefore, in good conscience, remain silent while members of our congregations support a company's prejudice with our dollars."[18]

A more recent political action, originating in black churches, was organized opposition by black denominations to the nomination and appointment of the black jurist, Clarence Thomas, to the U.S. Supreme Court in 1991. At least two major black denominations, the Progressive Baptist Convention and the National Baptist Convention, officially opposed the nomination and took their message of opposition, representing between twelve and fifteen million black Baptists, directly to Capitol Hill.[19] They believed Thomas was too accommodating to the dominant white society and would not represent well the majority of African Americans. But it became clear very soon that their attempt to block the nomination was to no avail.

Types of Black Religious Leaders

Of course, not all the black clergy in the Detroit area participated in the boycott campaigns just described. And not everyone who participated did so to the same degree or in the same manner. In fact, Detroit's black clergy can be divided into three fairly distinct types: militants, moderates, and traditionalists. The *militants*, who constituted approximately 20 percent of the black clergy, were persons deeply committed to civil rights goals, who demonstrated, marched, and picketed during the civil rights movement of the 1960s. They comprised the central planning unit of the boycott organization. These ministers tended to be young and highly educated, came from higher than average social status backgrounds, tended toward theological liberalism, served larger than average black congregations, assumed an independent stance in their voting behavior, and emphasized social as opposed to otherworldly concerns. It should be noted in passing, that the designation *militant*, as used throughout this chapter, refers to aggressive action to secure constitutionally guaranteed civil rights in an integrated society, not the more separatist militancy espoused by some black leaders after 1964.

Second, there were the *moderate* black clergy. Though committed ideologically to improving the lot of blacks in American society, they were gradualists and were more conciliatory and accommodating than the militant black clergy. On the average, they were likely to be older than the militants and not so highly-educated (a third of the moderates had no formal education beyond high school). Moderates lent support to the Detroit boycott activities by reading the letters from the boycott committee to their congregations, but by and large they refrained from helping plan strategy. In Detroit, 27 percent of black religious leaders fit into this category.

The third category, the *traditionalists*, were passive with regard to challenging the prevailing social order and were spiritually rather than socially oriented: "My job is to preach the Gospel and do spiritual work." They tended to be older men, who had little formal education (approximately three-fifths did not go beyond high school), came from low social status backgrounds, and served small congregations, often only as part-time ministers. These preachers, who constituted slightly over half of all black religious leaders, actually served fewer people in their combined congregations in Detroit than did their militant counterparts; thus, although they were not directly supportive of the boycott actions, neither could they prevent a clear majority of black church members from hearing about them.

An obvious conclusion we can make, on the basis of these observations about the three distinctive types of religious leaders in the black church during the height of the Civil Rights Movement in the 1960s (based on our Detroit data but likely applicable to at least the urban North, if not the urban South as well), is that the traditional otherworldly pattern of black religion has been effectively challenged. Militant social action and civil rights-oriented religious leaders and perspectives have emerged and gained substantial followings among members of black churches. Clearly, it would be both misleading and blatantly inaccurate to speak of *the* black church today. The range of internal diversity is great. The militant civil rights perspective has made significant progress within black religious institutions. Yet it is equally important to note that the traditional black religious emphasis on otherworldliness and accommodation persists.

Black Female Preachers

As mentioned in Chapter 11, an increasing number of black women are seeking ordination and opportunities to serve churches as pastors. What has been true of white women and predominantly white Protestant churches can be observed in black churches as well—growing numbers of women taking steps to become ministers, and opposition and difficulty in reaching that goal in many (actually, most) denominations. The black Baptist churches have been most resistant to ordaining women to ministry.[20] While there are substantial numbers of black women attending and graduating from black denominational seminaries, relatively few are called to be ordained and to serve in the formal ministerial role within the denomination in which they have been trained. This is particularly true of the black Baptist churches and the Church of God in Christ, but it can also be observed in the black Methodist denominations. A result is to find many of these women crossing the line into predominantly white denominations—the United Methodist Church in particular—to receive a call to serve predominantly black congregations in that primarily white denomination.[21]

J.D. Roberts is critical of black Baptist churches, which he describes as "the last frontier of male domination."[22] He observes that relatively few black Baptist churches are placing black women on their influential boards of deacons. He goes on to suggest that black theologians have a duty to attack such sexism in black churches.[23] Further, those who inhibit the entrance of black women into the ordained ministry are asserting authority they do not have, inasmuch as, in Robert's words, "It is God alone who calls humans, male and female, to minister in his redemptive cause."[24]

The Dilemma Posed by Black Militancy

Because of the rapid developments in the civil rights struggle and the emergence of countless "secular" local and national organizations combating racism and discrimination in various ways, the centrality and dominance of the black church have been challenged fairly seriously since the 1960s. It has been noted that young blacks, in particular, are becoming increasingly disenchanted with the churches and are less and less likely to find satisfaction there. Increasingly they have turned to other types of organizations that appear to deal more directly with their life situations and with the social problems they face. We are reminded of Glock's theory, introduced in Chapter 4, concerning relative deprivation and various possible responses to it. Recall that in the cases of economic and social deprivation, according to Glock's theory, responses are more likely to be secular than religious, if the causes of the deprivation are not only accurately perceived but also deemed capable of relief and change. Such seems increasingly to be the case with blacks, with young blacks in particular, perceiving greater potential to help bring about change coming from secular organizations than from the traditional religious ones.

Such organizations do not, of course, sound the death knell for the black church. For one thing, many people in a religious organization—whether black, white, or other—will remain there if for no other reason than simple habit—inertia. Also, for many, disaffiliating requires a more dramatic stand than they are willing to make. Further, many people over time come to regard their associations and relationships with others in an organization (such as a church)—as well as with the organization itself—as so meaningful and important, that these considerations alone prevent them from being readily convinced to substitute a new organization and commitment. But most important is the continuing satisfaction members receive in terms of what brought them to the church in the first place and kept them faithful, namely, comfort, hope for the future, purpose in life, and emotional outlet. This is the supply/demand equation of rational choice theory; that is, the church supplying resources needed by the people who come. Thus, the historic centrality and importance of the black church in the life of the black population and community alone makes it particularly unlikely that black church members will easily or quickly forsake this organization. Also, there still is a large proportion of the black population for whom the social environment has changed little, despite the progress achieved by the civil rights movement and subsequent affirmative action programs. If the sectarian nature of much black religion has served in the past, to provide release and escape for low status blacks, it might be expected to continue to do so today.

Note, however, that such comments about continuity of function within organized religion do not necessarily apply to those young blacks, who find escape in any of the three "strategies for survival" described by Lee Rainwater:

1. the expressive lifestyle of living "cool" and "working the game" on the people around you;
2. the violent strategy of more or less blindly striking back at the social structure that holds you down; or
3. the depressive strategy of withdrawal, perhaps into drugs—"I don't bother nobody; don't nobody bother me."[25]

Nor do such functions seem to apply well to those blacks who, in increasing numbers, are escaping the ghetto, securing advanced education, and entering previously closed or severely restricted occupations.

Observing young blacks' relative lack of enthusiasm for traditional black churches prompted black writer Joseph R. Washington essentially to predict, at the height of the civil rights movement in the early 1960s, the eventual demise of the black church—although in 1967 he retreated from that position and strongly urged the black church to become involved with the black revolution, because it had the potential to be of significant help, since it still had contact with many blacks.[26] Here is it important to mention, yet again, that rational choice theory becomes helpful. It would say that the black church has historically provided a great deal that its members want in terms of associational needs, emotional needs, and even cognitive needs. So long as such needs remain, people with those needs will continue to patronize those groups that they believe and feel meet at least some of their needs.

NEW THEMES IN BLACK RELIGION

Black Theology of Liberation

Although militant black clergy have issued calls for change and have had some successes in the attainment of civil rights goals among blacks, the black church as a whole appears to has had only limited influence in the civil rights area. There has been almost no challenge from the black community to the contention, expressed more than once in this chapter, that black religion has concentrated on "religious" matters and salvation concerns to the neglect of social action and reform. Thus, it is of more than passing interest that one black theologian, James Cone, has published a proposal for a "black theology of liberation" in which he contends that Christianity is, in essence, a religion of liberation and that the struggle of the oppressed for political, social, and economic justice is integral to Jesus Christ's message.[27] Cone condemns the black and the white Protestant churches in the same breath: "Both have marked out their places as havens of retreat, the one to cover the guilt of the oppressors, the other to daub the wounds of the oppressed."[28] Cone is calling for the reform of black theology and of the black church. The view that such reform is crucial in the face of social change is shared by Joseph Washington, who states in a review of Cone's first book that "the future of the black church is in its critical participation in the future of black power—which is, the future of black people."[29] Undoubtedly, there is less room today in the black church than in the white church for dual religious tracks—the one proclaiming traditional salvation goals, the other championing social reforms.

Cone chides the black church for emulating the white church and for feeling good when praised by whites. In reality, he asserts, the black church, just because it is black, is automatically among the rejected. He suggests that the black church must accept its true role as sufferer and follow the natural course of being black.[30] One thing this requires is excising the "most corrupting influence among the Black churches"—namely, "their adoption of the 'white lie' that Christianity is primarily concerned with an other-worldly reality . . . The idea of heaven is irrelevant for Black Theology. The Christian cannot waste time contemplating the next world,"[31] for that reward is not a legitimate motive for action. In fact, it is a denial of the Christian faith, in addition to being a gigantic "put-on" devised by whites to keep blacks in their place.

The Reverend Albert Cleage, another black theologian, also expresses this view when he describes the gift of Christianity to the black slave by the white master:

> The religion which the master gave to his slave was designed for pacifi-cation and to support the authority of white supremacy. He said, "This is a picture of God. This is a picture of Jesus. They are both white as you can plainly see. Here are Biblical characters. They are all white. But they love you in spite of your evil Blackness, and they offer you salvation in the great beyond! You have to live such a life here on earth, that after death, when you cross over Jordan, there will be a reward for you. Sometimes you think that all the suffering that you are doing down here is passing unnoticed by God, but it is not! God is watching everything, every minute of every day. And every bit of suffering you have down here is written down in God's big book, and eventually on the other side of Jordan there will be a reward, milk and honey and golden streets." So Black people had only to accept the authority of the white world to inherit a glorious reward in heaven.[32]

The point emphasized again and again by Cone and Cleage, is that the black church must purge itself of such otherworldly reward perspectives and join the black power movement. Black pride and social justice must become the dominant guiding concepts, both in the ideology or theology and in the activities of the black church. Integral to this process, at least for Cleage, is acceptance of the fact that the Jesus of Christianity was in reality black. Cleage defines Jesus as a revolutionary black leader seeking to lead a black nation to freedom.[33] But more than that, Cleage reflects the ideas of Marcus Garvey, who in the late 1920s organized the African Orthodox Church and developed an entire black hierarchy of black God, black Jesus, black Madonna, and black angels.[34] The Reverend Cleage was, for many years, pastor of the Shrine of the Black Madonna, formerly the Central Congregational Church, in Detroit.

Cone, too, speaks of God as black, but more in a figurative sense. God must be known as He reveals Himself in His blackness, by which Cone means that "either God is identified with the oppressed to the point that their experience becomes his or he is a God of racism."[35] Cone is referring, in other words, to total identification of God with black people and their plight. "Because God has made the goal of Black people his own goal, Black Theology believes that it is not only appropriate but necessary to begin the doctrine of God with an insistence on his blackness."[36] And again, "The blackness of God means that God has made the oppressed condition God's own condition."[37]

An intriguing observation, applicable to the "radical" black theology of Cone and Cleage, though suggested earlier by Washington, is the conviction that the black church not only must re-orient itself, but that it is capable of doing so. In one sense, such a belief or assumption appears sound inasmuch as the church is still by far the largest social institution in the African-American community and is in contact with the greatest number of people. On the other hand, whether it can turn itself around and make a radical change in direction and focus is problematic. It is undoubtedly true that significant numbers of influential black preachers have at least begun the switch. It is also true, as Cone points out, that the black church and its clergy have retained some of the theme of freedom and injustice from their slave religion heritage.[38]

Less Radical Views

Actually, Peter Paris suggests that, although most blacks even today reject the views of Cone as too radical and not true to the historic role of black churches,[39] it is simply not correct to say that black churches have retreated into a haven-of-rest mentality. Paris maintains that the traditional black churches are motivated by racial self-interest in a new way. He says that the members of black churches no longer feel that they are being unfaithful to "their ideal societal vision by working vigorously for such racial goals as political determinism, economic development, preservation of predominantly black schools (private and public), and construction of senior citizens homes in the black community."[40] In other words, the black militants portrayed by the 1960s Negro Preachers of Detroit and Vicinity identified earlier are winning, so to speak, yet short of Cone and Cleage's black liberation theology.

This would certainly be consistent with Paris's contention that the mission of the black churches has always transcended their own constituency, by aiming at the reform of the larger white society, that is, causing the latter to practice racial justice as an expression of genuine Christian understanding and devotion. Their mission, therefore, has had both an internal and an external dimension, in that they have sought religious, moral, and political reform in both the black and the white community, though not in the same respect.[41]

Another black theologian, Olin P. Moyd, goes further by suggesting that black theological themes not only speak to the situation of blacks but also can make important contributions to theological discussion and development generally. He suggests with pure sociological insight that principally, because American blacks have had a different experience than whites, their theology will be distinctive. He and others have further suggested that it is such black theology that will move to the forefront as theological discussion proceeds beyond the twentieth century. While Cone and others have talked about the black theology of liberation, Moyd uses the term *redemption*. In that term he incorporates three ideas:

1. "liberation" in the sense of deliverance from states of human-caused oppression,
2. "liberation" in the sense of salvation from sin, and
3. "confederation" with other people in a covenant relationship with each other and with God.[42]

J. D. Roberts certainly reflects the perspective of Moyd and Paris as he calls for black churches to fulfill both their mission and their potential in ministry to the whole person. But black churches must confront the continuing racism that surrounds the black community, as well as face head-on and realistically the "harsh realities of black life" in America.[43]

As black theologians have increasingly talked about "liberation" and liberation theology, they have interacted widely with Third World theologians from Africa, Latin America, and Asia. Cone notes that dialogue with these theologians has greatly expanded American black theologians' awareness. He notes that Africans brought knowledge of historic black culture; Latin American theologians expanded black awareness of the need for class analysis; feminist theologians exposed the sexist base of much of Christian theology, true also of black American theology; and other minorities pointed out the importance of a coalition to join in the struggle for justice in America and throughout the world.[44] Cone notes further that in return American black theology has been able to heighten significantly the awareness of Third World theologians concerning racism.[45]

In the two concluding essays of his 1999 book, *Risks of Faith*,[46] Cone clearly has not changed his mind. Rather, in his two concluding essays, he points out that both traditional white racism and a contemporary addition, termed *environmental or ecological racism,* are very much in evidence. Environmental or ecological racism is an extension or link to traditional white racism, which includes disproportionate exposure to toxic and hazardous waste in urban ghettos, rural poverty pockets, barrios, reservations, and communities nested in the shadow of massive hazardous landfills. These forms of racism may stem from governmental or corporate decisions or applications of certain regulations or policies that in the words of Bunyan Bryant quoted by Cone, "deliberately target certain communities for least desirable land uses . . . Environmental racism is the unequal protection against toxic and hazardous waste exposure and the systematic exclusion of people of color from environmental decisions affecting their communities."[47]

All this discussion and exposition by black theologians and scholars has deeply enriched the theology of liberation and produced a growing appreciation of the relevance of this theology for American blacks. In the process, "liberation" has taken on new meanings. Not only is it liberation *from* sin and slavery, as in the Negro spirituals of old, but also it is liberation *for* change in society, as all who have been subjected arbitrarily to second-rank status (notably women and ethnic/racial minorities) gain freedom and equal opportunity.

It should probably be noted that a more traditional word and concept, that is closely related to *liberation*, namely, *freedom*, has always been at the forefront of black consciousness and theology. As Lincoln and Mamiya point out, the precise meaning of freedom has depended on the exigency of the time and context. During slavery, it suggested escape from bondage; following emancipation it suggested newly won rights to an education and to employment, and authorization to move about freely in America; more recently, freedom has been defined in terms of social and political freedom, economic justice, and full civil rights.[48]

Increase in the Black Middle Class　　During this period, when black theologians were trying to raise the religious consciousness of black churchgoers, a combination of successes in the civil rights movement and general economic prosperity made a difference. The sociologist, Cheryl Townsend Gilkes, cites data reported by Bart Landry, that show the black middle class experienced significant growth as it doubled during the 1960s to 28.6 percent of the black population and then continued to grow through the 1970s and early 1980s to 37.4 percent of the black population.[49] These "new middle class" blacks brought new ideas and experiences to the black churches. They came with a college education and employment in professional and corporate America, as beneficiaries of the civil rights movement. But they, in turn, received from the established black churches they joined (in Gilkes' words) "therapeutic relief from the micropolitics of being black in a white and unpredictably hostile world."[50] Gilkes also calls these experiences they sought and found in traditional black churches "cultural comfort."[51] Certainly, those churches would change somewhat as these new middle-class blacks joined, but many features of the old would remain. In other words, in the last forty-five years, there has been a blending and evolution in many black churches, which preserves important aspects of the old, more sect-like experiences of the black religious tradition, but also absorbs some of the newer theological insights and social perspectives of the middle class, mostly white world in which many of their members were now circulating more freely.

An important change, emphasized by Andrew Billingsley in a chapter titled "New-Time Religion,"[52] is that the black churches have recently become much more active in community outreach. That is, they sponsor social welfare and service activities for their own people, independent of governmental social service programs and traditional efforts by white churches. In his research, he has found that a majority of black churches are conducting on their own one or more community outreach programs in addition to their primary religious programs. Clearly they see a dual mission and have not withdrawn into seeking personal salvation and comfort alone.

OTHER RELIGIOUS OPTIONS FOR AFRICAN AMERICANS

The new direction and changes described in the foregoing discussion, which began with traditional black religious expressions adding new dimensions and understanding, would suggest that there is much more choice within black religion in the United States than in years past. Once again, rational choice theory would tell us we should not be surprised at that; nor will the more socially conscious theology of liberationist black ministers fall on deaf ears. Religion is merely adapting to changing social conditions, thus allowing people to make religious choices that seem to them to be rational considering their needs and development.

This pattern of change and choices within the Christian tradition is further enhanced by taking note of other options available to black Americans. African-American religion has always been more diverse than what can be encompassed by Christianity. Anthony Pinn describes several major alternatives, of which we will mention two.

Voodoo   One is voodoo, which flourished in the Caribbean and was imported when slaves from islands such as Haiti, were brought to the United States as early as 1716.[53] But Pinn suggests that voodoo also was carried directly from Africa by many of the slaves who arrived in the previous century and continued to come from Dahomey and Nigeria in West Africa during the remainder of the eighteenth century.

Traditional Muslim Option   Then there is the Muslim option. The earliest Muslim contact with the New World came with the sixteenth- and seventeenth-century Spanish explorers, who traveled around the Caribbean and what became the American Southwest, as well as Spanish Florida and French Louisiana. Some were adventurers and ship captains; others were their servants.[54] But of greater significance were the thousands of black African Muslims who were brought to the United States as slaves during colonial times and in the nineteenth century until the Civil War. These people were Muslim by origin from regions of Islamic Africa. But the vast majority of the Muslim slaves brought from Africa in the seventeenth through to the nineteenth centuries were stripped of their Muslim religion and Christianized, with only small enclaves evidencing any traces of those early introductions of Islam into the United States still identifiable today. Examples are the Free Moors of the Carolina, the Malungeons of Tennessee, the Delaware Moors, and the Virginia Maroons, who have insisted that their beginnings date back to colonial times.[55]

In addition to these remnants of traditional Islam from Africa, there are the more numerous Black Muslims to whom we referred briefly earlier in this chapter. These Black Muslims are members of the Nation of Islam.

Black Muslims   The Nation of Islam was founded in the 1930s, by W. D. Fard, and continued by Elijah Muhammad (Elijah Poole), who remained head of the Black Muslims for some forty years until his death in 1975. Although the Nation of Islam split into two segments (a peaceful separation, by the way), one led by a son of Elijah Muhammad, Wallace Deen Muhammad, the other by Louis Farrakhan, the movement continues and is an option for as many as 70,000 members and affiliates today.[56]

The faction led by Louis Farrakhan receives more publicity because of his flamboyant style and his exposition of the early Black Nationalist tenets of the Nation of Islam identified earlier in this chapter. But the other branch of the Nation of Islam, led by Wallace Deen Muhammad, has modified many of the early positions of the Black Muslims as espoused by W.D. Fard and Elijah Muhammad, to the point of being officially accepted by orthodox Arabic Islam. The major modifications of the original tenets of the Nation of Islam by the Wallace Muhammad division of the Nation of Islam are: decentralization of power and authority in the group; sloughing off many of the businesses and commercial enterprises operated by the Nation of Islam through sale or closure; declaring that the founder, W.D. Fard, was mortal; instruction that the memory of Elijah Muhammad, though still accorded honor, should be reconsidered in light of his times and personal limitations; and direction that all racial considerations and the idea of black supremacy as requirements for membership in the Nation of Islam should be discarded.[57]

Black Catholics   Then there is another religious option within the Christian tradition, which until the last half of the twentieth century was relatively rarely taken by blacks. That is to become Roman Catholic. For all practical purposes, Vatican II, which concluded in 1965, opened the door to black Protestants when vernacular languages (in this case English) could be substituted for the Latin mass. It was then a short step to include some gospel music and other worship practices borrowed from the black church tradition. In 1987, a Black Catholic hymnal was published titled, *Lead Me, Guide Me: The African American Catholic Hymnbook*. M. Shawn Copeland describes *Lead Me, Guide Me* as follows: "Thoroughly Black and thoroughly Catholic, the hymnal preserves spirituals as well as Catholic standards, traditional as well as contemporary Gospel Songs, Freedom Songs as well as

African-American Catholic compositions."[58] What is rather surprising is that currently about 2.5 million African Americans are Catholic. Patrick Carey reports that they constitute 3 percent of the total Catholic population and 9 percent of the total African-American population in the United States.[59] There are now more African-American Catholics than total membership of either the African Methodist Episcopal Zion Church or the African Methodist Episcopal Church—two of the major African-American Protestant denominations.[60]

NATIVE AMERICAN RELIGION

At the beginning of any discussion of Native American religion, we need to observe that there really is no such thing as "Native American Religion." To try to speak of a religion that somehow represents Native Americans, ignores the fact that this vast group comes from many dozens of nations and cultures. The fact that they are all "Indians" or even "Native Americans," is an alien notion thrust upon them by the Europeans who settled the land, and then by Americans who pushed westward to the Pacific. Native Americans were not one people or society. Therefore, it is understandable that they would not have one religion. We should remember, too, that as independent nations, they had separate languages. While they are not all totally different, there are nine language families, each with dozens of distinctive languages within it.

It should also be noted that these languages were oral only. They were neither preserved nor taught in written form. There was, therefore, little chance that a language spanning the continent on which the Native Americans lived would develop.

Examples of such variation and the importance of oral tradition are cited by Ake Hultkrantz, who states that on both sides of the Mississippi, not only tribes and clans but also families had their unique oral traditions. By way of example, each clan among the Winnebago had its own myth of the origin of the world—not totally different, to be sure, but unique nonetheless.[61]

As we noted in Chapter 2, in describing the religions of preliterate people, Native American cultures rarely had a word for "religion."[62] What we call religion and see as a distinguishable entity that can be separated out of the rest of culture—separated from the economy, the educational system, industry, sports, and the like—most Native American societies did not have. Rather, their religion was woven into the fabric of life and prescribed activities that were accepted traditional components of life and reality. Therefore, at the moment we describe any activity, belief, or word as "religious," we have made it something different than it is, because we have made it conform to our language and our conceptions of things.

What we do know is that many Native American nations speak of things that other peoples, such as ourselves speak of but call "religion"—how the world came into being, how we should treat our fellow human beings, what happens after death, how we become and remain one of God's chosen, and so on. Yet the basic difference remains: We talk about religion as one specialized slice of life, but Native Americans would simply say "life."

Further, we cannot ignore the fact that we are already over three hundred years past the beginning of Christian missionary activity among Native Americans. Missionary work among Native Americans has been extensive—so much so that probably nothing in Native American religion is today in pure form. Nor were earlier accounts from one to two hundred years ago much better. Not only had Christian missionaries already been very active, but also those who observed and wrote about the Native Americans had strong biases toward Western culture and the Judeo-Christian heritage, so that any observation about Native American religions was filtered through a lens composed of Christian perspectives and understandings of what religion was and should be.

Therefore, our task will not be to get back to the beginnings of Native American religion and describe its manifestations, as they existed in pure form. Nor will we even attempt to be inclusive of all there was or is of Native American religion. Rather, we shall look first at some of the more central ideas in Native American religion that, while not necessarily universal nor without nuances and variations from one Native American culture to another, are frequently present in Native American nations. Second, we shall look at changing emphases in the religion of Native Americans in response to influences from the surrounding American culture.

Time

Our Western tradition tends to categorize events and history into past, present, and future. While we also recognize that some things are continuous and span past, present, and future, most of what we think and do occurs in a context of linear movement through time—that is what I did yesterday, this is what I am doing now, those will be my activities tomorrow. Everything can be placed at a point on a line of time. But Native Americans are much more likely to concentrate on cyclical time. Emphasis is not so much on when an event occurred (yesterday, today, or tomorrow), as where on its recurrent cycle it is. Whereas linear time looks toward ends and points on a continuum moving toward the end, cyclical time concentrates on a core, a center that is always there and around which we move. Thus, Native Americans, as they saw the seasons of a year, they saw a progression in a familiar cycle and repeated familiar patterns. This is in contrast with the Western pattern of keeping track of the 365 days in a year that can be marked one by one on a calendar and keep accumulating for centuries and millennia—all moving toward some future end. Native Americans see time more as a recurring cycle of experiences. Hultkrantz notes that some Native American languages have no term for past and future. Everything is present.[63] Consistent with their concept of time, Native Americans were generally uncomfortable with the dichotomies and trichotomies westerners use so much—heaven-hell, life-death, good-evil, true-false, and so on. It makes sense then that the traditions of Native Americans do not make the distinction between supernatural and natural. Everything is some of both, inasmuch as everything exists and moves in a cyclical fashion.

Circle

Such an emphasis on cyclical continuity makes the importance of the circle symbol among Native Americans quite understandable. A circle is the perfect visual representation of cycle and repetition. Black Elk, a Lakota Sioux, summarizes better than anyone what the circle means:

> You have noticed that everything an Indian does is in a circle, and that is because the Power of the World always works in circles, and everything tries to be round. In the old days when we were a strong and happy people, all our power came to us from the sacred hoop of the nation, and so long as the hoop was unbroken, the people flourished. The flowering tree was the living center of the hoop, and the circle of the four quarters nourished it. The east gave peace and light, the south gave warmth, the west gave rain, and the north with its cold and mighty wind gave strength and endurance. This knowledge came to us from the outer world with our religion. Everything the Power of the World does is done in a circle. The sky is round, and I have heard that the earth is round like a ball, and so are all the stars. The wind, in its greatest power, whirls. Birds make their nests in circles, for theirs is the same religion as ours. The sun comes forth and goes down again in a circle. The moon does the same, and both are round. Even the seasons form a great circle in their changing, and always come back again to where they were. The life of a man is a circle from childhood to childhood, and so it is in everything where power moves. Our teepees were round like the nests of birds, and these were always set in a circle, the nation's hoop, a nest of many nests, where the Great Spirit meant for us to hatch our children.[64]

Relationships

Closely allied with the perspective of the cyclical nature of time, is the Native American view of relationships, which link everyone in the family, the clan, the tribe, and the nation together with the animals and the land itself. Even the winds and the rain and the change of seasons share in the inter-relationships with the land and its resources and with animal life.

The emphasis on such inter-relationships is well illustrated by the arctic Indians or Inuit, who live a most precarious existence in a land that offers few resources. Nonetheless, they believe that their greatest risk is not from subzero temperatures or lack of food, but the omnipresent reality that their lives depend on taking the lives of other living things, whether fish and seal from the sea or four-footed land animals.[65] However, when appropriate norms and rituals are followed and the hunter is respectful of the rights of all parties, then the animals will present themselves willingly as sacrificial offerings to the hunter.[66]

The sacred pipe adds meaning to the inter-relatedness of place, people, and animal life. As the pipe is passed from one person to another, each one inhales the breath of others and, as the innumerable grains of tobacco represent all the creatures of God and thereby contribute to the unity, so each person smoking from the pipe is expressing and experiencing unity with all that exists.

In keeping with our earlier observations about the diversity among Native Americans, we need to emphasize that the tribes had varying points of emphasis, depending upon their means of making a living. Those with a hunting culture stressed their relationships with animals; those with a gathering culture emphasized their relationships with vegetation—the trees, shrubs, seeds, roots, and grasses.[67] In either case, they wanted to live peacefully and in harmony with nature, disturbing it as little as possible. So, hunters kill only so much game as is needed and will be fully consumed. The gatherers pick up nuts and fruit from the trees and the ground around them without damaging the trees, and they use only fallen wood for building and burning.[68] One can thus readily understand the outrage of Native Americans at the mass shooting of bison by travelers aboard excursion hunting trains, who left the animals to rot where they fell.

The ideas of harmony with nature and unity of all that exists, is well illustrated by the reaction of the Shahaptin Indians of the Northwest, to the suggestion by Indian agents that they cultivate the ground and begin to farm.

> You ask me to plow the ground! Shall I take a knife and tear my mother's bosom? Then when I die she will not take me to her bosom to rest.
> You ask me to dig for stone! Shall I dig under her skin for her bones? Then when I die I cannot enter her body to be born again.
> You ask me to cut grass and make hay and sell it, and be rich like the white men! But how dare I cut off my mother's hair?[69]

And thus do Native Americans see all that exists as interrelated and interdependent. Our task as human beings is to fit in and integrate with what is there—other people, other living things (both plant and animal), and inanimate matter and things—in a cooperative, mutually beneficial manner. Religious beliefs instruct us how to achieve that goal; religious ritual mobilizes us into appropriate activities and behavior.

Peyote Cult

Late in the nineteenth century, something new in Native American religion emerged, and it became the focal point of a branch of Native American religion that continues until today, namely, the *peyote cult*. Peyote is a small, carrot-shaped cactus that resembles a small pincushion when fresh, a coat button when dried. Both the "button" top and its root can be eaten for a mild hallucinogenic effect. Of its eight alkaloids, mescaline is the best known.

Peyote was not a new nineteenth-century discovery. It had been used within many Native American tribes for special purposes for centuries. Weston LeBarre discusses some nonreligious uses: to foretell the future, as a magic fetish to ward off evil, as a curative for wounds and snakebites, and to induce bravery in battle.[70] These uses were centuries old. The modern application that integrates peyote use with religion dates back to around 1870. This is a date commonly used to signal the end of the "Indian Wars" and the resignation of Native Americans to their subjugation to the white invaders of their lands.

Peyote has become an important adjunct to religious activity and worship for a substantial number of Native Americans from the Far West to the Middle West. Those who use it are participants in the Native American Church. While importation of peyote is outlawed in nine western states, its use for religious purposes is allowed. The function of peyote is not to induce visions, though on rare occasions people do experience them. Rather, as David Aberle suggests, its religious function is to provide the user with a sense of personal significance.[71] He adds that people also report improved health and experiencing a sense of power. On the medical side, peyote is a mild analgesic and modest stimulant as well. Many recipients will "feel better" for a while when under the influence of peyote. Aberle discusses the power effect in terms of something external added to the individual. He says of the Navajo, "When a person eats peyote, something external to him proves able to affect his thinking, his feelings, his perceptions, and his behavior, and to do so without his volition."[72] Aberle summarizes the function of peyote as providing a feeling of personal significance, which heightens religious experience in the assembly, because it demonstrates that something is indeed being done to and for the person, and because it is felt to be a "power."[73]

The religious ceremony, that involves peyote, must find people gathered for a purpose, whether to cure illness, avert evil/promote good, or thank God for his blessings. It is a "communion" service, in which one communicates with God and with the rest of the group. This communion is expressed by joint consumption of peyote at several points during the night, by the drinking of water at midnight and in the morning, and in the ceremonial breakfast at the end. The service begins at sundown, lasts all night, and involves prayer, singing, drumming, and eating peyote.

While the adoption of peyote use by the Native Americans probably began in the 1870s and 1880s, independent of Christian influence, by 1892 Christian elements were present.[74] The religious peyote cult spread rapidly after its probable origin among the Comanche or Kiowa Native Americans in Oklahoma. It had spread to at least sixteen tribes by 1899, and a total of seventy-seven tribes by 1955.[75] Areas where peyote ceremonies were common included the western provinces of Canada and most states west of the Mississippi. The religion of peyote did not formally incorporate until the Native American Church of Oklahoma formed in 1941; in 1945 it became the Native American Church of the United States. While opposed both by some Native Americans as an aberration from and rejection of traditional Native American beliefs and rituals, and by whites, who disliked its incorporation of "drugs" and its sectarian or cultic nature, it has become popular among Native Americans, attaining an estimated membership of approximately 250,000 people.[76]

Native American Responses to Deprivation

To locate the reason the peyote religion arose in the first place and why it appeals to many Native Americans today, we probably need to look no further than the position of Native Americans in the broader American society. The first acceptance of peyote in the late 1800s followed closely the end of the Indian Wars, with Native Americans the losers on all fronts. Aberle suggests that many Native Americans looked for something special and unique, which would set them apart as something other than losers, inferior to the victorious white Americans.

We also know that Native Americans have, as a whole, not done well since then. They are not integrated into American society; many live in poverty; alcoholism, and other drug addictions are common scourges. In short, Native Americans suffer significantly from deprivation. If you recall our discussion of the relationship of relative deprivation and the formation of sects in Chapter 4, and if we can identify a significant part of the deprivation of Native Americans after 1870 as a social deprivation, then it is not hard to understand resorting to peyote as an escape and as a way of identifying those who see themselves chosen by God, even if such a quality is not recognized by white society. As Aberle suggests, participation in peyotism "assures some Navahos that Indians are at least equal to, and in some ways superior to whites—in knowledge, in wisdom, in spirituality, and in possession of a good religion."[77]

David Chidester, following Bryan Wilson, describes several distinct responses by Native Americans to the destruction of their traditional world and their displacement from it. First, there is the introversionist response. This reaction involves an attempt to resurrect and reaffirm traditional religious values of the tribe in the face of "overwhelming encroachment of white domination."[78]

Handsome Lake, an Iroquois, exemplified the introversionist response around the turn of the nineteenth century, as he espoused a religion of the "good word" that involved ethical discipline, repentance, and mutual cooperation, which would facilitate the survival of traditional Native American religious values in a new political environment.[79] Yet while expounding traditional Native American values, such as integrity, honesty, marital fidelity, and contributing a fair measure of one's labor for the good of all, the white man's religion was having its effect also. The very name "Good Word" is obviously reminiscent of Christianity's "good news" (gospel). The introversionist response tried to make the best of a bad situation and implicitly accept defeat. But through it all was the staunch conviction that they would retain a separate, continuing Iroquois identity and someday the old ways would return.

A second response was revolution. Herein lies the popular image of the fierce, fighting Indian doing battle with settlers, cowboys, and cavalry. The religious aspects of this revolutionist response are best exemplified in the Ghost Dance religion. The basic premise is that Native Americans would be invincible in battle (a magical, powerful cloak would surround the warrior and it would repel enemy bullets and knives) if they were properly prepared by the Ghost Dance ritual. It was with this belief of Ghost Dance protection that Chief Short Bull led the Sioux into the disastrous battle of Wounded Knee in 1890, in which 370 Sioux were killed. They believed that their "ghost shirts" would shield them from harm. Joseph Jorgensen summarizes the Ghost Dance as a response of some Native Americans "to the deep poverty and ubiquitous oppression they had suffered during prolonged contact with whites.[80] They had suffered enormous losses in battle, from epidemics, and by starvation. They lost their land, were herded into reservations, and were forced into a way of life devoid of their traditional resources. Small wonder that the Ghost Dance theology would be attractive, even seductive. As Native Americans sought to transform their lives, Jorgensen suggests that not only had they rejected the *status quo* but also they had some insight into the "enormous force necessary to transform things to what they should have been."[81]

And such is the religion of Native Americans. Nowhere has it remained even close to what it had been. This is in significant part because no other people has seen more Christian missionary activity over the years than Native Americans. But Christianity did not soon triumph; nor in the end did it completely supplant the Native American religion that had come before. And certainly the reader would be correct to assume that Christian missionary activity would necessarily presume the eradication of Native American religion, if Christianization were to be fully successful. Most practitioners of Christianity view it as the single true religion to the exclusion of all others. As such, "truth" has the right and obligation to cut out all that is "false."

The Dawes Act

This view was consistent with and reinforced by the effects of the Dawes Act, enacted by the U.S. Congress and effective in 1887. While the Dawes Act did not outlaw Native American religion *per se*, the clear purpose of what has come to be known as the *Allotment Act* was to "Americanize" the Native Americans. The widely-held belief was that they would amount to nothing and would not fulfill their destiny, until they were full-fledged Americans doing what most Americans did—they tended their farms and attended the Protestant church. By definition, to Americanize the Native Americans for their own good meant to strip them of their old culture, of which religion was an important part, and replace it with Protestant American values and culture. It was the clear, expressed intent of those promoting the passage of the Allotment Act that everything distinctly Native American was to be erased: Native American languages, religious and other communal ceremonies, drumming and dancing, and traditional funeral rites.

The core provision of the Dawes Act, which was to accomplish all of the above, was to split up the tribes by allocating 160 acres to each family head for the purpose of establishing a home separated from others, engage them in typical American agrarian pursuits, and make each family responsible for itself. Actually, the land was to be held in trust by the U.S. government for twenty-five years, after which the family would receive the deed to the land and full citizenship in the United States. The remainder of Indian reservation lands (and there was a lot left over after the allocation of 160 acres for each family, with lesser amounts for single persons), would go on the general market and be withdrawn from Indian control forever. But in addition, many of those Native Americans who received land were swindled out of even their small tracts. Acreage owned by Native Americans dropped from 140 million acres in 1887 to 78 million in 1900. In 1934, the amount owned had dropped to about 55 million, when the Wheeler-Howard Act, usually called the Indian Reorganization Act, was passed by Congress to rescind the Dawes Act.

Of course, after forty-seven years under the Dawes Act, a great deal of damage had already been done to Native American culture. Yet some tribes had kept their traditional religion and ceremonies alive surreptitiously. Often their relative isolation on remote reservations helped in this regard. Vine Deloria cites another way. The Lummi tribe from western Washington preserved many ceremonies under the guise of celebrating the signing of their treaty with the United States.[82] Similarly, some of the Plains tribes kept ceremonies alive by ostensibly celebrating the Fourth of July—a grand joke on the conquering whites who did not really understand what they were seeing. The "patriotic" Native Americans were really preserving their religious customs. Also, after 1934 and the loosening of restrictions both of a formal and informal nature that had been imposed under the Dawes Act, there were still some old members of the tribes alive to remember and instruct in the former religious ways.

Concluding Observations

Despite somewhat greater freedom for Native Americans to practice the religion of their choice, there is relatively little authentic traditional Native American religion being practiced today. While there is great interest within the Native American communities in the old ceremonies, they stand and are practiced independently and are not serving the same religious function they once did. Most Native Americans are today what most other Americans are, namely, some brand of Christian. It is of interest that charismatic Christianity and Mormonism have had some notable success among Native Americans since the early 1960s.[83] The Pentecostal groups, in emphasizing ecstatic experience and what some might call visions or trances, provide some opportunities for linkage with similar experiences that had been part of traditional Native American religious practices. Mormonism, with its emphasis on compiling accurate genealogical records, going back many centuries in order to bring ancestors into the fold, will be attractive to Native Americans who, in their emphasis on community, have strong, personal feelings for the many members of their communities who have gone before.

In conclusion, while it is difficult to generalize, religion for some Native Americans, even when in Christian guise, continues to emphasize the importance of land and sacred space and place, the quest for power (mana) to deal with misfortune, and hope for an ultimate triumph—the final inheritance of themselves and all their ancestors, who will rise up to populate and tend their land again when the white man is gone.

Notes

1. Kenneth M. Stampp, *The Peculiar Institution* (New York: Knopf, 1956), p. 158.
2. Quoted in ibid., p. 160.
3. Richard C. Wade, *Slavery in the Cities: The South, 1820–1860* (New York: Oxford University Press, 1964), p. 83.
4. Ibid., pp. 162–163.
5. W. E. B. Du Bois, *The Philadelphia Negro* (Philadelphia: University of Pennsylvania, 1899), p. 201.
6. Gunnar Myrdal, *An American Dilemma* (New York: Harper & Brothers, 1944), p. 938.
7. W. E. B. Du Bois, *Economic Cooperation among Negroes* (Atlanta: Atlanta University Press, 1907), p. 54.
8. E. Franklin Frazier, *The Negro Church in America* (New York: Schocken, 1963), p. 40.
9. Ibid., p. 41.
10. Ibid., p. 42.

11. Wade, *Slavery*, pp. 173–177.

12. Frazier, *The Negro Church*, p. 43.

13. Ronald L. Johnstone, "Militant and Conservative Community Leadership among Negro Clergymen" (Ph.D. dissertation, University of Michigan, 1963), pp. 126–127.

14. Frazier, *The Negro Church*, p. 44.

15. See Ronald L. Johnstone, "Negro Preachers Take Sides," *Review of Religious Research* 11, no. 1 (1969): 81.

16. C. Eric Lincoln and Lawrence H. Mamiya, *The Black Church in the African-American Experience* (Durham, NC: Duke University Press, 1990), pp. 14–15.

17. *Aggressiveness* is understood here and in the discussion that follows in a very general sense of direct action of some kind that is perceived as likely to improve the condition of oneself or one's group.

18. Letter sent to black ministers in the Detroit area by the Negro Preachers of Detroit and Vicinity, dated November 22, 1961, in possession of the author.

19. J. Deotis Roberts, *The Prophethood of Black Believers* (Louisville, KY: Westminster/John Knox Press, 1994), p. 107.

20. Ibid., p. 75.

21. Delores Carpenter, "Contemporary Black Clergywomen" (paper presented at the 1995 annual meeting of the Society for the Scientific Study of Religion and the Religious Research Association, St. Louis, Missouri, October 27, 1995).

22. Roberts, *The Prophethood of Black Believers*, p. 76.

23. Ibid.

24. Ibid., p. 88.

25. Lee Rainwater, "A World of Trouble: The Pruitt-Igoe Housing Project," *The Public Interest* 8 (Summer 1967): 116–126.

26. Joseph R. Washington Jr., *Black Religion* (Boston: Beacon Press, 1964); idem, *The Politics of God* (Boston: Beacon Press, 1967), pp. 207–227.

27. James H. Cone, *Liberation* (Philadelphia: Lippincott, 1970).

28. James H. Cone, *Black Theology and Black Power* (New York: Seabury Press, 1969), p. 115.

29. Joseph R. Washington Jr., review of *Black Theology and Black Power* by James H. Cone, *Journal for the Scientific Study of Religion* 11, no. 3 (1972): 311.

30. Cone, *Black Theology*, p. 113.

31. Ibid., pp. 121, 125.

32. Albert B. Cleage Jr., *Black Christian Nationalism* (New York: Morrow, 1972), p. xxviii.

33. Albert B. Cleage Jr., *Black Messiah* (New York: Sheed & Ward, 1968), p. 4.

34. Ibid., p. 8.

35. Cone, *Liberation*, pp. 120–121.

36. Ibid., p. 121.

37. James H. Cone, *A Black Theology of Liberation* (Maryknoll, NY: Orbis Books, 1986), p. 63.

38. Cone, *Black Theology*, Chapter 4.

39. Peter J. Paris, *The Social Teachings of the Black Churches* (Philadelphia: Fortress Press, 1985), p. 127, fn. 22.

40. Ibid., p. 132.

41. Ibid., p. 111.

42. Olin P. Moyd, *Redemption in Black Theology* (Valley Forge, PA: Pudson Press, 1979).

43. Roberts, *The Prophethood*, p. 138.

44. James H. Cone, "Black Religious Thought," in *Encyclopedia of American Religious Experience*, eds. Charles H. Lippy and Peter W. Williams, vol. 2 (New York: Charles Scribner's Sons, 1988): p. 1186.

45. Ibid.

46. James H. Cone, *Risks of Faith: Emergence of Black Theology of Liberation, 1968–1998* (Boston: Beacon Press, 1999).

47. Bunyan Bryant, ed., *Environmental Justice: Issues, Policies, and Solutions* (Washington, DC: Island Press, 1995), p. 5. Cited in Cone, ibid, p. 140.

48. Lincoln and Mamiya, *The Black Church*, p. 4.

49. Cheryl Townsend Gilkes, "'Plenty Good Room . . .' In a Changing Black Church," in *One Nation Under God*, eds. Marjorie Garber and Rebecca L. Walkowitz (New York: Routledge, 1999), p. 167.

50. Ibid., p. 168.

51. Ibid.

52. Andrew Billingsley, *Mighty Like a River: The Black Church and Social Reform* (New York: Oxford University Press, 1999), pp. 87–101.

53. Albert Raboteau, *Slave Religion: The "Invisible Institution" in the Antebellum South* (New York: Oxford University Press, 1978), p. 76, quoted in Anthony B. Pinn, *Varieties of African American Religious Experience* (Minneapolis, MN: Augsburg Fortress Press, 1998), p. 35.

54. Pinn, ibid., p. 113, who references Ivan Van Sertima, ed., *African Presence in Early America* (New Brunswick, NJ: Transaction Books, 1987).

55. Pinn, *Varieties of African American Religious Experience*, who references Allan D. Austin, *African Muslims in Antebellum America* (New York: Routledge, 1977), p. 22.

56. C. Eric Lincoln, *The Black Muslims in America*, 3rd Edition (Grand Rapids, MI: William B. Eerdmans, 1994), p. 269.

57. Ibid., pp. 264–265.

58. M. Shawn Copeland, "African American Catholics and Black Theology," in *Down By the Riverside*, ed. Larry G. Murphy (New York: New York University Press, 2000), p. 428.

59. Patrick Carey, "Preface," in *Black and Catholic*, ed. Jamie T. Phelps (Milwaukee, WI: Marquette University Press, 1997), p. 7.

60. Ibid.

61. Ake Hultkrantz, *Native Religions of North America* (San Francisco: Harper & Row, 1987), p. 16.

62. It is very possible that the few tribes that do have a word for "religion" created the word only after contact with colonists, settlers, and missionaries. Cf. Ake Hultkrantz, *The Religion of the American Indians* (Berkeley: University of California Press, 1967, 1979), p. 10.

63. Hultkrantz, *Native Religions of North America*, p. 33.

64. Black Elk, as told to John G. Neihardt, *Black Elk Speaks* (New York: William Morrow and Co., 1932), pp. 279–280. Reprinted in paperback by the Bison Series of the University of Nebraska Press, 1961. Quoted in Joseph E. Brown, *The Spiritual Legacy of the American Indian* (New York: Crossroad Publishing Company, 1982), p. 35.

65. Brown, *Spiritual Legacy*, p. 53.

66. Ibid., pp. 6–7.

67. Think back to Chapter 2 and Guy E. Swanson's high correlations between characteristics of the social structure and the beliefs and perspectives people hold.

68. Ake Hultkrantz, *Belief and Worship in Native North America* (Syracuse, NY: Syracuse University Press, 1981), p. 121.

69. James Mooney, *The Ghost-Dance Religion and the Sioux Outbreak of 1890* (Washington, DC: Bureau of American Ethnology, 14th Annual Report, 2), p. 121.

70. Hultkrantz, *Belief and Worship*, p. 121.

71. David F. Aberle, *The Peyote Religion among the Navaho* (Chicago: University of Chicago Press, 1982), p. 6.

72. Ibid., p. 9.

73. Ibid., p. 11.

74. Ibid., p. 17.

75. Membership varies considerably from one tribe to another. Aberle estimated membership among Navahos to range from 12 to 14 percent in 1951. By 1965 he reports an increase to 35 to 39 percent (Aberle, ibid., pp. 110 and 124). Among Shoshoni, Hultkrantz estimates 75 percent in 1987 (Hultkrantz, *Native Religions*, p. 84).

76. David Chidester, *Patterns of Power: Religion and Politics in American Culture* (Englewood Cliffs, NJ: Prentice Hall, 1988), p. 133.

77. Aberle, *Peyote Religion*, pp. 193–194.

78. Chidester, *Patterns of Power*, p. 123.

79. Ibid., p. 124.

80. Joseph G. Jorgensen, "Religious Solutions and Native American Struggles," in *Religion, Rebellion, Revolution*, ed. Bruce Lincoln (London: Macmillan, 1985), p. 102.

81. Ibid., p. 107.

82. Vine Deloria Jr., *God Is Red* (New York: Grosset and Dunlap, 1973), pp. 251–252.

83. Joseph G. Jorgensen, "Modern Religious Movements," in *Native American Religions*, ed. Lawrence E. Sullivan (New York: Macmillan, 1987), p. 215.

Chapter 14

Denominational Society

Religion: So many choices.

The necessity of devoting a full chapter to a discussion of the denominational phenomenon in American religion is reinforced by an observation by the American sociologist Andrew Greeley, to the effect that the United States is nearly unique among world societies as a denominational society.[1] By *denominational society* Greeley means one characterized by neither an established church nor a protesting sect, but one in which religion and the rest of the society interrelate through a considerable number of essentially equal religious organizations. These constitute a social organizational adjustment to the fact of religious pluralism, and not a halfway house between sect and church.[2] Greeley's emphasis, which is also this chapter's, is on the social organizational aspect of denominationalism. That is, we are observing here an important social phenomenon, not simply a religious one—a type of social organization that has significant impact on social structure and social interaction in American society.

THE MULTIPLICITY OF GROUPS

The denominational character of American society is, of course, rooted in the fact that it is, among other things, a pluralistic society, particularly insofar as religion is concerned. As we pointed out in Chapter 12, the denominational society arose, not because everyone desired it, but because at the founding of our nation, no one religion was sufficiently powerful to gain predominance and also because of the various philosophical perspectives and commitments of those who framed the Constitution. The result has been one of the most obvious features of denominationalism within American society—that is, the subdivision of religion in American society into a host of independent religious groups. A society could be designated as a denominational society, with only a few different religious groups. But American society leaves no doubt as to its diverse denominational character, for it includes literally hundreds of religious groups. Note well that we are not referring here to the thousands of local congregations, but to larger groupings of individual congregations into more or less cohesive associations. That is, several, perhaps thousands, of local congregational units identify sufficiently with one another to stand under one umbrella, so to speak, to carry out some activities and functions jointly, to share perhaps a summary statement of belief, and to think of themselves as united together and distinct from other associations of congregations, who raise different umbrellas and fly different theological flags. Thus, we are talking about Baptists, Methodists, Presbyterians, Roman Catholics, Mormons, Unitarians, Orthodox Jews, Jehovah's Witnesses, Muslims, Buddhists, Hindus, and other fairly familiar religious groups or denominations, as well as a plethora of lesser-known groups, such as the Pilgrim Holiness Church, the Plymouth Brethren, the Duck River Baptists, the Free Magyar Reformed Church in America, the Macedonian Orthodox Church in America, and so on.

There are over three hundred such associations, which maintain membership statistics and report them to the National Council of Churches. J. Gordon Melton has identified over twelve hundred distinct religious groups in the United States.[3] Mainly, these are groups that consist of more than one local congregation, though Melton included single-congregation churches if they are large (two thousand or more members) or if they draw members from more than one state and beyond a single metropolitan area. In addition, there are literally thousands of individual local congregations, which we might call entrepreneurial churches, which are autonomous and begin and usually end with the entrepreneurial religious leader who founded them. These are particularly numerous in the sect-prone inner-city ghettos, though one sees such entrepreneurial groups elsewhere as well.

The Diversity of Groups

Recognizing the multiplicity of religious groups in the United States is only an introduction to the great diversity among religious organizations that is a second prominent feature of denominationalism in this country. The difference among denominations can be seen along a variety of dimensions, some of which we have alluded to earlier in this text.

The Authority Dimension

At the level of structure and organization, there is the basic distinction among episcopal, presbyterian, and congregational forms, which we referred to in passing in Chapter 3. These terms refer to the structure of authority within the denomination and the relationship of the local congregation to the larger denomination with which it is affiliated. In the *episcopal* form, authority proceeds from the top down—from the heads of the denomination (pope, archbishop, bishop, and so on) down to local representatives. In the *presbyterian* form, authority rests more in the middle range, with elected representatives, both clergy and lay, at various levels from local to national holding regulatory and disciplinary authority over the levels below them. In the *congregational* type, authority lies, as the term implies, with the local group, with the national denomination having limited authority, at least of a formal nature.

The Emotional Dimension

Another typology contrasts Apollonian with Dionysian religious orientation and worship style of liturgy.[4] The *Apollonian* style assumes that since human beings are basically rational and capable of controlling their biological and emotional urges, the person's communication with God should reflect such rationality and be characterized by moderation and gentility. The *Dionysian* emphasis rests on the observation that people are more than strictly rational beings. They have emotions and they need to express themselves individualistically. In fact, this orientation contends that an important, if not primary, feature of religion is the emotional dimension, including ecstatic, mystical experiences of the human with the divine. In religion one must and one does transcend the mundane rationality of life.

These descriptions of the Dionysian and Apollonian styles and orientations are likely to remind one of the religious sect and the denominational type of religious organization, respectively, and appropriately so. Yet neither should be considered an exclusive association. Some groups most properly classified as denominations, nevertheless exhibit Dionysian elements, either because they have only recently evolved to denominational status and retain vestiges of their old pattern or because religious leaders, particularly at the local level, are convinced of the importance of the Dionysian element in religion and encourage it. Note, for example, the practice of "speaking in tongues" and other pentecostal religious acts, which were introduced in the 1960s, to such Apollonian denominations as the Roman Catholic, Episcopal, and Lutheran churches, and that continue among some members today.

MAJOR DENOMINATIONAL FAMILIES

In an attempt to understand differences among the major denominations in America today, it is helpful to know the source and meaning of the broad, popular categories Catholic, Protestant, Jew, and Eastern Orthodox. Each of these designations is a highly-inclusive category in itself—inclusive in the sense that each has numerous subdivisions within it. We will explore some of that internal diversity in the coming pages. But here, just a few comments about the origins of these major categories.

Judaism

Judaism is, of course, the oldest and is, in fact, the source out of which Christianity grew, first as Catholicism (later divided into the Roman Catholic and the Eastern Orthodox branches), and then as Protestantism. Although we will add some detail later, we should mention that Judaism in America is itself diverse. There are six major categories of Jews: Orthodox, Conservative, Reform, Reconstructionist, Hasidic, and cultural-ethnic. Orthodox Judaism remains firmly rooted in historic Judaism, with a heavy emphasis on the Old Testament and its laws, restrictions, and rituals. Jews, who can be called Reformed, as well as the Reconstructionists and those we call cultural-ethnic, are highly-responsive to developments within contemporary society, assume that religion both does and should evolve, and have discarded much or all of the historical belief and ritual system of Judaism. Conservative Jews stand very consciously between the two extremes of Orthodox and Reform. Hasidic Judaism is a more mystical form of Judaism, truly in a class by itself.

Catholicism

Catholicism in its two major forms of Roman Catholicism and Eastern Orthodoxy came to be the designation for the religious group, which was established by Jesus Christ and his followers in the first century A.D. and was a direct descendant of historic Judaism. It was the Christian Church that spread from Jerusalem throughout the Mediterranean world and beyond, within a few generations following the death of Christ. Catholics believe that Christ's statement to the disciple Peter recorded in Matthew 16:18, "Thou art Peter, and upon this rock I will build my church" (King James Version), marked the true founding of the Catholic Church. Catholic tradition says that Peter journeyed to Rome late in life, preached there, became leader (bishop), and began to carry out Christ's directive to create one universal (catholic) church on earth. Both the catholicity and the unity were challenged by Eastern Christianity almost immediately, and in the Middle Ages[5] the Western (Roman Catholic) and the Eastern (Orthodox) Christian churches split and remain separated until this day. Actually, these divisions into Byzantine and Roman have existed from the beginning, were evident in the seven ecumenical councils, were enhanced by language differences (Greek in the East, Latin in the West), and found their political counterparts engaged in war (e.g., when in 1204 the armies of the West during the Fourth Crusade sacked Constantinople, the center of the Eastern Church).

Protestantism

Protestantism is the newest of the major categories of American religion, originating as it did in the late Middle Ages with religious reformers, such as John Huss (1369–1415), Martin Luther (1483–1546), Ulrich Zwingli (1484–1531), John Calvin (1509–64), and John Knox (1513–72), who wanted not so much to found new churches as to reform and restore what was already there, namely, the Roman Catholic Church. Thus, we have the term *reformation*. And we have the term *Protestant*, which refers both to the idea of protest against what some viewed as perversions and distortions of original Christianity within the Roman Catholic Church and, as the term came to be used in Elizabethan England, to the idea of affirming a particular set of beliefs, of "bearing witness" to a particular confession and point of view.

Jewish Denominations in America

We mentioned earlier that along religious dimensions, there are six major subgroups of Jews in the United States. We will describe each briefly.

Orthodox Judaism   The most firmly-rooted in historical Old Testament Judaism, is that of Orthodoxy. Orthodox Jews very consciously try to maintain the teachings and rituals of the Torah (the first five books of the Old Testament) and perceive themselves as the only legitimate bearers of Jewish tradition.[6] This means that they view themselves as the preservers of both traditional doctrine and ritual observances. There is a high emphasis on study of the Torah and the Talmud (the rabbinical commentary on the Torah) in the original Hebrew. The Torah is supreme and is believed to reveal that

God has chosen the Jews to be his special people, who will teach justice, peace, and love to the world. There is careful observance of festival days, such as Yom Kippur and Passover. An unqualified obligation is the keeping of a kosher house and serving kosher meals, by maintaining separate sets of dishes and utensils for meat and for dairy products, as well as using only those foods that have been slaughtered or prepared under approved rabbinical conditions. In observation of the Sabbath, from sunset Friday to sunset Saturday, the Orthodox Jew tries to put aside the secular world and enter a world of prayer and family activities that will not allow cooking, writing, buying and selling, and any number of other everyday activities, which are avoided on such a special day in the week. Orthodox Judaism continues adamantly to prohibit the ordination of women to the rabbinate, contending that Halakah (the body of Jewish law), which prohibits the ordination of women, is an immutable presentation of God's will.

Reform Judaism   Reform Judaism emerged in nineteenth-century Europe, as a very conscious attempt by some Jewish intellectuals led by Abraham Geiger (1810–74) in Germany, to bring traditional Jewish Orthodoxy more up to date and in tune with modern realities. The movement rejected many traditional Jewish laws and substituted ethics for laws. The declaration of principles, issued by the Frankfort Society of the Friends of Reform in 1843, is a fairly concise summary of their position.

> First, we recognize the possibility of unlimited development in the Mosaic religion. Second, the collection of controversies and prescriptions commonly designated by the name Talmud possess for us no authority from either the doctrinal or the practical standpoint. Third, a Messiah who is to lead back the Israelites to the land of Palestine is neither expected nor desired by us; we know no fatherland but that to which we belong by birth or citizenship.[7]

Isaac Mayer Wise (1819–1900), who is credited with establishing Reform Judaism in the United States when he founded the Union of American Hebrew Congregations in 1873, expressed confidence that this Reform Judaism would soon become the Judaism of all American Jews. While this did not happen, Reform Judaism did attract a substantial following and accounts for a little less than a third of American Jews today.[8]

Conservative Judaism   Conservative Judaism quite deliberately takes the traditionalism of Orthodoxy and the liberalism of the Reform movement and blends them. It is a distinctly American innovation for Jews who had immigrated to the United States some years earlier but were becoming highly acculturated—people who had moved out of the Jewish ghetto into neighborhoods that were predominantly non-Jewish, who wanted to use English as their religious as well as social language, yet did not want as complete a divorce from historic Judaism with its host of customs and beliefs as Reform Judaism represented. The Conservative movement devised a Sunday school program for children in conformity with the Protestants around them and developed, in the early 1900s "confirmation ceremonies"— "bat mitzvah" for girls as a ritual parallel to the bar mitzvah for boys. Thus, Jewish children could maintain a solid link with their past but also point out to the other children in their neighborhood and school that, although they were Jews, they were not that different. In 1955, women were allowed to read Torah at services, and in 1973 they could be counted as part of the quorum (minyan) for public worship.

Marshall Sklare points out that it became particularly difficult for truly Orthodox Jews to maintain their orthodoxy, when so much of their everyday life was outside the synagogue and its immediate community.[9] In other words, it was much easier to be an Orthodox Jew in a Jewish ghetto in eastern Europe than in an American city, where most of one's contacts and activities were with non-Jews.

The compromise that is Conservative Judaism quickly showed its practical wisdom, as it became the largest Jewish religious organization. This growth was particularly marked in the decades after World War II.

Reconstructionist Judaism   Reconstructionist Judaism is the newest of the Jewish denominations, emerging to full-blown denominational status only in the late 1960s. Although the founder, Mordecai Kaplan (1881–1983), did not propose a new denomination and wanted only to synthesize the best of all Jewish traditions into a meaningful program of thought and practice for the contemporary Jew, a new denomination emerged when Reconstructionists established both their own seminary to train rabbis and a central organization to aid congregations and propagate the faith. Doctrinally, Reconstructionist Jews reject all ideas of supernatural power or person. Thus, no Torah was revealed to Moses on Mt. Sinai, no Messiah should be expected, and miracles as recorded in the Bible never really happened. Instead they place heavy emphasis on the unity of Jews with a common culture and heritage despite denominational differences that separate them.

Sectarian Judaism   Sectarian Judaism consists of several small groups and movements, the best known of which is Hasidic Judaism. A *Hasid* is a mystic. Thus, Hasidic Judaism includes persons who consider themselves Orthodox but also possess an additional dimension of mysticism, emotion, and ecstasy. Their counterparts within Protestantism, in at least some ways, would be the charismatic pentecostals.

The Hasidic movement arose in Poland in the eighteenth century and spread rapidly to include nearly half of eastern European Jews in its ranks.[10] Hasidic Jews are usually distinguished by their outward appearance.

The men will likely be dressed in black, wear large, black (sometimes fur) hats, be bearded, and have long curled earlocks. They are highly concentrated in circumscribed urban areas—the Labavitcher movement, for example, located predominantly in the Crown Heights section of Brooklyn, the Satmar community of about twelve hundred families, most of whom are located in the Williamsburg and Borough Park sections of Brooklyn, and the Skvirer Hasidim in Rockland County, New York, who left Brooklyn to establish a separate community, in which they could exercise greater internal social control.[11]

Cultural-Ethnic Judaism   The final Jewish subgroup we would mention is not religious at all, strictly speaking. These are people of Jewish ethnicity who feel some kinship with others of Jewish origin but who have rejected the religious elements of Judaism—hence the designation we used earlier of *cultural-ethnic Jews.* This designation would include the more than half of American Jews who are not affiliated with a local synagogue yet will probably identify themselves as Jews and might even claim affiliation with Reform Judaism if questioned about their religious identity.[12] Of the less than half of American Jews who are affiliated with a synagogue, only about half participate at all regularly in synagogue services and activities.[13] Of that quarter of American Jews, only about half do more than participate in Passover and Hanukkah observances.[14] Gerhard Falk notes that only 22 percent of Jews light Sabbath candles every week.[15] Actually, more (28 percent) Jewish households have a Christmas tree in their home sometimes or every year. Falk also reports from the *National Jewish Population Survey of 1990* the findings that 72 percent of American Jews do not belong to any Jewish organization, and, since 1985, over half of born Jews have chosen a spouse who is not Jewish.[16]

Roman Catholicism

Roman Catholicism, in the United States, has suffered the effects of minority status since the country's beginning. Even when millions of immigrants from eastern and southern Europe and Ireland swelled the ranks of the Catholic Church in the nineteenth and early twentieth centuries, Roman Catholicism continued to be viewed with suspicion and distrust by other Americans. They saw Roman Catholic subjection to the pope in Rome as an expression of a divided loyalty that made Roman Catholics at best only half American. They also saw Roman Catholics sending their children to Roman Catholic schools, which were established explicitly to help members "keep the faith," and they marked them as under suspicion. If one adds to the list of issues, the opposition of Catholic theology to any kind of so-called unnatural birth control, the opposition to interfaith marriage and the requirement of a prenuptial agreement to educate any children in the Catholic faith, if permission to marry outside the faith was granted at all, and a retention of many Old World customs in the many Roman Catholic ethnic enclaves, and Protestant Americans became even more suspicious. Quite expectedly, though hardly helping to improve the situation, many Roman Catholics developed an "inferiority complex" and found it difficult to relate on an eyeball-to-eyeball basis with their Protestant neighbors. However, with the election of the Roman Catholic, John F. Kennedy Jr. as president, with clear signs of ecumenical openness in the person and message of Pope John XXIII, with signals of doctrinal innovation and change in the second ecumenical council (Vatican II), with fewer Roman Catholics isolating themselves in Catholic schools, with many nuns adopting average street clothing for their works of mercy and education, with the civil rights movement gaining acceptance for many minorities and not just black Americans, and above all with the practices of Catholic laypeople, with respect to such traditionally important issues of marriage and birth control rapidly approximating those of other Americans—with all these changes, we find that Roman Catholics have definitely joined and been accepted in the mainstream of American life.

Distinctive Doctrine   Yet Roman Catholic doctrine continues to be distinctive. There continues to be a high regard for Mary, the mother of Jesus, who is still believed to have been immaculately conceived; she is believed to have lived a sinless life, to have given birth to Christ with her virginity intact, to have bodily ascended to heaven before death, and to serve now as an intermediary between people and God. There continues to be a belief in papal infallibility over matters of faith and doctrine and an emphasis on penance paid by the faithful by way of partial atonement for their sinful acts. Yet on central doctrines of historic Christianity, such as the triune nature of God as Father, Son, and Holy Spirit; creation of the world by God; the existence of angels both good and evil, the sinful nature of human beings and their need for God's salvation; and salvation as coming only through the death and resurrection of God's Son, Jesus Christ, Roman Catholics join most Protestants and Eastern Orthodox Christians.

Discrepancies Between Doctrine and Lay Practice   Many areas of doctrine and practice show great discrepancies between the official doctrine and the practice of Catholic laypersons. For example, Andrew Greeley found in a 1974 sample of Roman Catholics, that only 17 percent practiced monthly confession and only 18 percent would accept the church's position on even two of three items that constituted a "sexual orthodoxy" scale (no divorce, no "artificial" methods of birth control, and no premarital sex). In each case, there was a significant decline from only eleven years earlier, when 37 percent still practiced monthly confession and 42 percent followed the church's dictates on at least two of the three items in the sexual orthodoxy scale.[17]

These trends continued, according to Gallup Poll Data gathered in 1989. For example, whereas in 1969, 72 percent of Roman Catholics disapproved of premarital sex, by 1987, only 38 percent said it was always or almost always wrong.[18] Also, in 1987, 8 in 10 (77 percent) of Roman Catholics said they relied on their conscience in making moral decisions, not the teaching of the church on such moral issues as "artificial" birth control or premarital sex, as proclaimed by the Pope.[19] Further, the proportion of Roman Catholics, who reject the church's teaching on "artificial" birth control, continues to increase. Gallup data from 1993 show 84 percent of Roman Catholics saying "Catholics should be allowed to practice artificial means of birth control, and 89 percent maintain that people who use birth control are still good Catholics."[20] Also, 58 percent of Catholics believe the "Catholic Church should relax its standards on forbidding abortions," and 78 percent say "divorced Catholics should be permitted to remarry in the Catholic Church"[21]

Reactionary Responses from the Vatican   We suggested earlier that such changed practices constitute one reason for greater acceptance of Catholics in the mainstream of American life. But probably more significant is the prediction that, as a consequence of such changing practices, doctrines will eventually change as well, although not overnight by any means. In fact, in the face of such changing behavior and practice, there have been reactionary voices within Roman Catholic officialdom.

For example, although Pope John XXIII established a special commission in 1963, to investigate whether a change in the church's traditional prohibitions against birth control could and should be brought about, and although the commission voted thirteen to two for change,[22] the closest advisors to the pope (the Vatican Curia) persuaded the successor to John XXIII, Pope Paul VI, to conserve the traditional position of the church. His encyclical letter *Humanae Vitae*, issued in 1968, reaffirmed traditional positions and was at odds with the liberalizing directions suggested by the Second Vatican Council (1962–65). Andrew Greeley, whose data on the changed attitudes and practices of Roman Catholics we reported earlier, finds the encyclical *Humanae Vitae* almost entirely to blame for the rapid decline of traditional Roman Catholic practice with respect to birth control in particular.

When Pope John Paul II succeeded Pope Paul VI, he was determined to reinforce his predecessor's encyclical letter *Humanae Vitae*. And so, although charming, diplomatic, warm, open, and well-received by most, whether Catholic or non-Catholic, liberal or conservative, he still felt obliged, in the early 1980s, to reaffirm traditional Roman Catholic positions in such areas as birth control, the ordination of women to the priesthood, and priestly celibacy. All these reaffirmations of the position taken in *Humanae Vitae* are consistent with his earlier role as a highly placed advisor to Pope Paul VI, under whose name *Humanae Vitae* was issued in 1968.

Yet Pope John Paul II seems not to have been successful in bringing back or turning around more than a very few Catholics, who had already made the move toward liberalized attitudes on the above and related issues. And every early indication from the new Pope, Benedict XVI, is that he will continue the conservative position of John Paul II. If anything, based on his record of 24 years prior to his election as Pope, when he was head of the Congregation for the Doctrine of the Faith, he might as Pope more vigorously enforce official Roman Catholic doctrine in disciplining both clergy and laypeople. It is clear that disagreements and dissensions are rife in the Roman Catholic Church in America, and many other countries today, and will continue to be so. A brief look at a few recent events and counter events will illustrate this point.

In April 1994, the Roman Catholic Church approved altar girls to function alongside altar boys. While some Roman Catholics saw this as a sign of change, Pope John Paul II quickly dashed such optimism by issuing his apostolic letter *Ordinatio Sacerdotalis*, which explicitly rejected change in the church's position on the role of women in the church and the ordination of women in particular. And if there were any doubt, in June 1994, after a two-year delay, the English translation of the *Catechism of the Catholic Church* was published. In that catechism, the formerly gender-inclusive language was changed to exclusive sexist language, in which the terms *man* and *men* were used to refer to all people, just as in days of old—at the very time that many Protestant denominations were busily changing their language to be gender inclusive.[23]

Another example of the reaction of conservative Catholicism to the liberalizing trends instituted by Vatican II, can be seen in the authorization, in 1981, by the Vatican, of a broad study and evaluation of all 501 Catholic seminaries in the United States. This action prompted a great deal of suspicion among more liberal Catholics. They saw this as a fairly heavy-handed attempt to return to more traditional educational methods, which will train more traditional priests, who will stick to their traditional ministries and avoid political and social action involvement. Some heads of American Roman Catholic seminaries fear serious infringement of hard-won academic freedom gained since the Second Vatican Council.[24]

Further evidence of Vatican attempts to reaffirm the conservatism of the encyclical *Humanae Vitae* and discredit the Second Vatican Council came in the summer of 1986, when a Roman Catholic priest, Father Charles Curran, was dismissed from his post as a professor of moral theology at Catholic University of America. He was dismissed by the Congregation for the Doctrine of the Faith at the Vatican, for his liberal views on birth control, abortion, divorce, homosexuality, and euthanasia, among other issues. Note that, as mentioned above, the Cardinal who chaired this powerful Vatican agency was, from 1981 to 2005, Cardinal Joseph Ratzinger, who became Pope Benedict XVI on 19 April 2005.

Catholic Traditionalism   The movement called "Catholic Traditionalism" should also be mentioned. These are Roman Catholics, both laity and clergy, who not only do not want to hear of a relaxation of theological prohibitions against birth control, homosexuality, marriage of priests, and ordination of women, but want Latin brought back as the worldwide language of the liturgy. Although its international leader, Archbishop Marcel Lefebvre died in 1991, the movement continues with some significant support.

Conclusion   It is clear that the Roman Catholic Church in America is not nearly so cohesive or unified as some common stereotypes would suggest. There are strong pressures from some constituencies to move in a more liberal direction; other constituencies push fervently back toward the past and a more conservative, traditionalist emphasis and practice. Roman Catholics are facing what Jews and Protestants have grappled with for a long time. We shall return to this topic in Chapter 15.

Eastern Orthodoxy

The Eastern Orthodox Church has its origins with the very beginning of Christianity, and its theologians played the leading roles in the seven ecumenical councils, which were held during the fourth through to the eighth centuries C.E. As mentioned earlier, the Christian Church split into the Western (Roman Catholic) and Eastern (Orthodox) Churches in the ninth century C.E. But while the Roman Catholic Church remained formally unified under the pope in Rome, the Eastern Church recognized four primary Patriarchs—the religious sovereign and counterpart to the pope—in Constantinople, Alexandria, Antioch, and Jerusalem. In addition, semiautonomous churches evolved in Greece, Albania, Bulgaria, Cyprus, Romania, the Soviet Union, and Yugoslavia. Immigrants to the United States from these countries brought their churches with them. The largest and best known are the Greek Orthodox Archdiocese of North and South America and the Russian Orthodox Church in America. Other Eastern Orthodox churches are the Albanian, the Bulgarian, the Romanian, the Carpatho-Russian, Serbian Orthodox, Syrian Antiochian Orthodox, the United Ukranian Orthodox churches, and many other very small groups for a total of fifty denominations in the Eastern Orthodox tradition.[25]

Although closer theologically to Roman Catholicism than is much of Protestantism, Orthodoxy differs from Roman Catholicism in several ways. It does not recognize the pope in Rome as the supreme pontiff, but only as one bishop among many; it contends that the Virgin Mary was cleansed from original sin at the annunciation rather than at her conception; it rejects the

Roman Catholic doctrine of the assumption of Mary and the doctrine of purgatory. The Orthodox groups differ from most Protestants in accepting apostolic succession, subscribing to seven sacraments (called mysteries), engaging in a dramatic liturgy, de-emphasizing the sermon, employing icons in their worship, and believing that there is a supernatural link between the icon and the person it represents.

The Orthodox churches have by and large successfully resisted the pressures of the surrounding society to "modernize" and "Americanize" their doctrine and practice. To step inside an Orthodox sanctuary is to take a longer step back in time and observe an older and more original tradition than would be the case in almost any other American religious group, except Orthodox Judaism. Consistent with such traditionalism and resistance to change, a religious feminist movement has yet to begin in the Orthodox churches.

Protestantism

The denominations and sects that comprise Protestantism are sufficiently different among themselves as almost to doom any attempt to generalize. Not only do their forms of organization run the full range from episcopal to presbyterian to congregational, but also their assent to various central orthodox Christian doctrines is far from unanimous. While some say that the Lord's body and blood are truly present in the bread and wine of the Lord's Supper, others believe that the presence is only symbolized by the bread and wine, perhaps also insisting that the wine be grape juice. While some see the virgin birth as not only unimportant but untrue, others make the doctrine one of only a handful of the most crucial beliefs of all. While some believe God created the universe in six days of twenty-four hours each in length, others accept evolutionary theories that do not presume divine creation of any kind. For further specification of the diversity, note the great diversity among Protestant denominations and Roman Catholics on several standard Christian doctrines shown in Table 14.1. Note that these data reflect what members of these denominations believe and not necessarily what the denominations might officially stand for.

Although we have emphasized the vast diversity within Protestantism and have implied that it is almost absurd to try to generalize, there are historical reasons for generalizing about Protestantism, and there are even a few generalizations that are reasonably valid today.

We suggested earlier that Protestants got their name by protesting against Roman Catholicism. In such protest there were some implicit similarities among the protesters—resentment against the pope and religious control over political agencies, reaction against the imposition of indulgences, aversion to what amounted in many cases to worship of the saints, and the like. But there were important differences among the groups that gathered around the various

TABLE 14.1 Proportion of Denominational Members Agreeing with Various Doctrinal Statements

Statement	Congrega-tionalist	Methodist	Episcopa-lian	Disciples of Christ	Presby-terian	American Lutheran	American Baptist	Missouri Lutheran	Southern Baptist	Sects	Roman Catholic
"I know God really exists and I have no doubts about it."	41%	60%	63%	76%	75%	73%	78%	81%	99%	96%	81%
"Jesus is the Divine Son of God and I have no doubts about it."	40	54	59	74	72	74	76	93	99	97	86
"Jesus was born of a virgin." (% saying: "Completely true.")	21	34	39	62	57	66	69	92	99	96	81
"Jesus walked on water." (% saying: "Completely true.")	19	26	30	62	51	58	62	83	99	94	71
"Will Jesus actually return to the earth someday?" (% answering: "Definitely.")	13	21	24	36	43	54	57	75	94	89	47
"Miracles actually happened just as the Bible says they did."	28	37	41	62	58	69	62	89	92	92	74
"There is a life beyond death." (% saying: "Completely true.")	36	49	53	64	69	70	72	84	97	94	75
"A child is born into the world already guilty of sin." (% saying: "Completely true.")	2	7	18	6	21	49	23	86	43	47	68

Source: Rodney Stark and Charles Y. Glock, *American Piety* (Berkeley: University of California Press, 1968), pp. 28, 33, 34, 36, 37, and 40. Used by permission of the University of California Press.

reformers. For example, while someone like Martin Luther thought there was much in the Roman Catholic Church that should be retained, others, such as Andreas Carlstadt (d. 1541) and Thomas Müntzer (d. 1525), insisted that everything that smacked of Romanism must go. So, while Luther thought organs and music and statues and paintings were important and must be integrated into worship and instruction, Carlstadt and Müntzer felt justified, not only in keeping such ornamentations out of their churches, but in destroying them when they could.

A more explicit tenet of all of Protestantism has been the right and the ability of individuals to be in touch with God, to learn religious truth, and to worship God as individuals, without the necessity of an intermediary or intercessor, such as a priest or the Virgin Mary. Integral to this belief is the conviction that the Bible as the sourcebook for Christianity should not only be open and available to all believers but that it can be understood by them as well. This emphasis on the Bible has led to near idolatry by some Protestants, who make much of its "verbal inspiration" and authority as the perfect and complete revelation of God for all times.

Another generalization, so far as Protestants are concerned, is a restriction on the number of sacraments to two or fewer (Holy Baptism and the Lord's Supper), certainly far fewer than the traditional seven in Roman Catholicism (Baptism, Lord's Supper, Confirmation, Penance, Ordination, Matrimony, and Extreme Unction).

We have mentioned several times the great diversity within Protestantism. We will now, as we conclude our discussion of Protestantism in general terms, identify the major groupings of Protestant religious denominations in the United States.

The Anglican or Episcopal Churches   While it has been said that Anglicanism has no "theology" in the sense of a comprehensive summary of doctrine, in a practical sense, Anglicanism actually has a very *comprehensive* theology, in that it has very deliberately retained the traditional liturgical emphasis of the Roman Catholic Church, while also incorporating an essentially Calvinist or Reformed set of beliefs. Its continuity with Roman Catholicism is reinforced by its emphasis on apostolic succession—the belief that its clergy are descendants in an unbroken line from the apostles. Further, it is a sacramental church—meaning it believes that the two primary sacraments are central to the essence of the church. These Anglican churches might also be called "Christmas churches," in the sense that they stress that God became human at the birth of the God-man Jesus Christ (the Incarnation).

The Episcopal or Anglican churches originated in the English Reformation, which saw Parliament grant independence to the Church of England around 1530 during the reign of Henry VIII. The Anglican (English) Church was transplanted to the New World with the settlement of

Jamestown, Virginia, in 1607. Following the Revolutionary War, the American Anglicans established their religious independence as the Protestant Episcopal Church in the United States.

The Lutheran Churches   The Lutheran faith might be said to have begun when Martin Luther nailed his ninety-five theses to the church door in Wittenberg, Germany, on 31 October 1517. However, it was not Luther's intent at that time to start a new church; he wanted reform of the Roman Catholic Church and had ninety-five issues or points he wanted to discuss and debate. The Lutheran movement spread rapidly through Germany and into the Scandinavian countries. It arrived early on the American scene— Dutch Lutherans in New York in 1623 and Swedes along the Delaware River in 1638. The immigration of Lutherans continued steadily during the next three centuries and resulted in the establishment of many ethnic communities and churches. The Norwegians, Swedes, Danes, Finns, and Germans all established ethnic denominations—several denominations, in fact, within each ethnic group—and the Lutherans became in the process the most ethnically divided religious family in America.[26]

But there were several mergers within American Lutheranism in the twentieth century, which reduced the number of Lutheran denominations to three major ones, though there remain several other small groups that range from a few hundred to a few thousand members.

Lutherans constitute a "confessional" religious movement. That is, they place great stress on detailed bodies of doctrine that have become official interpretations of Scripture, which are accepted because they correctly (it is asserted by Lutherans) interpret Scripture. Like the Roman Catholics and the Anglican-Episcopal traditions, they are sacramental churches. That is, they view the sacraments of baptism and the Lord's Supper as "means of grace," through which God works directly. As such, the sacraments are more than symbols; they mediate God's grace.

Their central confessional principle is the Latin expression *Sola gratia, sola fide, sola scriptura*—by grace alone, by faith alone, by Scripture alone. Or to say it differently, but with another expression frequently used by Lutherans—justification by grace through faith. Like the Roman Catholics, Episcopalians, and Eastern Orthodox, they are liturgical churches. That is, Lutherans follow a fairly elaborate ritual and pattern in their worship services—one with strong historical roots and with great uniformity from one local congregation to another.

Reformed and Presbyterian Churches   These are the denominations that most directly followed the lead of John Calvin. The various Reformed bodies originated in Switzerland, Germany, and Holland; the Presbyterian bodies started in Scotland. Prominent themes within the Calvinist tradition are the sovereignty of God, the life of piety for God's people, and predestination or eternal election (see Chapter 9). Although they too use the two primary sacraments, they are seen more as symbolic acts that bring to remembrance God's acts in the past.

The first essentially Presbyterian Church was established in the Massachusetts Bay Colony in 1629. The Reformed Church in America goes back to 1621 when the Dutch West India Company placed Reformed ministers in the New Netherlands Colony along the Hudson River.

In many ways the Presbyterian-Reformed tradition is the most centrist, "average" expression of Protestantism in America. All the traditional orthodox doctrines of Christianity are there, with little of an extreme nature, except perhaps the classic presentation of predestination. On the other hand, there are offshoots of this tradition that are not only highly conservative in theology but also in practice and have strong overtones of the Radical Reformation that we will introduce next. We are thinking here of such groups as the Dutch Reformed, Christian Reformed, Orthodox Presbyterian, and the Bible Presbyterian, among others.

Churches of the Radical Reformation The major foundations and emphases of this tradition are articulated in the seven articles of the Schleitheim Confession of 1527.[27] These articles are as follows: baptism is for adults only; excommunication is an important means of keeping the group pure; the Lord's Supper is a memorial feast for adult members; the group must be separated from all evil such as Roman Catholic and any other worship services, as well as from drinking establishments; the pastor must be a person of good reputation and integrity; church and state must be strictly separate, and individual Christians should not participate in the political process; oaths are forbidden.

In America, the original Puritans and the various Mennonite groups were direct practitioners of the Radical Reformation. Two major Protestant groupings today, that might be surprises in a list of practitioners of this track of Protestantism because they seem to be such "normal," standard Protestant denominations, are the Congregational Christian and the Evangelical and Reformed Churches, which merged to become the United Church of Christ in 1957, as well as the largest denominational cluster in the category today-the many Baptist groups.

Baptists place strong emphasis on the lordship and sovereignty of Christ who has revealed himself in the Bible, which is inerrant and the sole, authoritative source of the will of God. High emphasis is placed on individual believers and their direct access to true knowledge of God, without the necessity of intermediaries. Since the Bible is totally authoritative and a complete record of God's will, that is totally open to understanding by the faithful, written creeds and summaries of doctrine are unnecessary. The First Baptist churches in the United States date back to 1638 and 1639 under the leadership of Roger Williams and John Clarke in Rhode Island.

Methodist Churches   Methodism is certainly the youngest of the major Protestant denominations. Founded in the eighteenth century by John and Charles Wesley, as a movement within the Church of England, it did not become a separate body until after John Wesley's death in 1791. Its origin was in the pietistic revival movement that swept Europe, the British Isles, and America in the early 1700s. Wesley held to the authority of Scripture and the centrality of faith but emphasized more than some Protestants the fruition of that faith in a life of love and good works. He talked much about the "life of perfection," which he believed was attainable by true Christians, who felt God at work within them and had the experience of true conversion burning within them. Thus, knowing the moment of one's conversion became a trademark of Methodists. Also, the methodical attention in one's life to attain perfection became not only a trademark but also the source of their name.

Holiness and Pentecostal Denominations   An outgrowth of Methodism, in the late 1800s, was the Holiness movement, which, in turn, provided the soil out of which the Pentecostal movement grew around the turn of the twentieth century. These are all Arminian groups with their theology rooted in the teachings of Jacob Arminius (1560–1609), who stressed both the universality of God's grace and the freedom of people to choose for or against salvation—an emphasis implying a cooperative, human element in salvation that Lutherans and others viewed as undercutting the doctrine of salvation by God's grace alone.

The Holiness movement developed in classic sectarian form (see Chapter 4) as some among American Methodists felt that both the goal and method of attaining Christian perfection were being neglected. As Arthur Piepkorn says so succinctly, "[They] sought to recapture Wesleyan perfectionism in order to make American Methodists into holy people."[28] They stressed the sanctified life, renounced unholy practices such as the use of alcohol and tobacco and membership in secret societies, and encouraged continuation of the Methodist-inspired camp-meeting approach to instruction, conversion, and spiritual reinforcement.

The Pentecostal movement, in most simple terms, was holiness religion to which had been added the special gift of glossolalia (speaking in tongues) as evidence of Pentecostal experience. Although the holiness people, as well as what we might call the classical Methodists, were not pleased with the development of Pentecostalism, Ignacio Vergara's statement that "Pentecostalism is Methodism carried to its ultimate consequences"[29] is quite accurate.

Other Religions

There are, of course, many other religious groups in America. We have discussed only the major ones—major in terms of numbers and visibility. But
there are others, including Islam and the major Asian religions; Buddhism
and Hinduism. We shall look at the presence of all three in the United States.

Most of the influx of immigrants, who professed these other, non-
Western religions, came after World War II, particularly after the 1965 relaxing
of the highly restrictive immigration limits that addressed Asians in particular.
These hundreds of thousands of individuals and families, who have come,
brought their religion with them just as earlier Poles brought their
Catholicism, Swedes brought their Lutheranism, and Russian Jews brought
their Judaism. More recently, the refugees from Vietnam and Cambodia have
come, bringing their Buddhism and other religions with them. Many students
from India and Pakistan have come to study and have stayed or have come
back after a brief return to their country of birth, bringing their Muslim faith
and practice with them. Immigrants from Lebanon, Turkey, Iran, and Yemen
have come, just as millions of immigrants before them, looking for employment and a better life for themselves and their children. They too have brought
their Muslim religion with them.

Islam   We wrote in the last chapter about the Muslim heritage of some
black slaves (about 10 percent of all slaves) brought to this country in the
eighteenth and nineteenth centuries. Mostly isolated from one another and
faced with the active deculturation practiced by their white owners, only a
few could retain their religious heritage and only a few pockets of
descendants, that we mentioned in Chapter 13, remain today.

But there were other Muslim immigrations, well before 1965. There
was substantial immigration from Syria, including what we know today as
Jordan and Lebanon, beginning in the 1870s and continuing until the early
1900s and picking up again right after World War I, and yet again in the
1930s[30] as many Lebanese, some of whom were Christians, came to
Dearborn, Michigan to work for the Ford Motor Company. And then there
was substantial immigration to Iowa, with many Muslims coming to Cedar
Rapids, Iowa, beginning in 1895. In fact, the designated "mother mosque"
for American Muslims is in Cedar Rapids.[31]

After World War II, there was what Diana Eck calls a third wave of
Muslim immigration, principally Palestinians displaced by the re-establish-
ment of Israel by United Nations mandate on 15 May 1948. In addition, there
were Egyptians and Iraqis fleeing turmoil in their homelands, as well as
Albanian and Yugoslavian Muslims fleeing the onrush of Communism.[32] The
"fourth wave" came after 1965, from throughout the Muslim world, as many
Muslim professionals sought greater opportunity in America, as professors
and medical doctors.[33]

Diana Eck makes the point that the United States is now part of the Arab world. Not only is there the homegrown Nation of Islam (the Black Muslims) but the millions of other Muslims who have immigrated or are descendants of immigrants, or are American converts to Islam.[34] There were, in 2001, more than 1,400 mosques spread throughout the United States,[35] even 200 Islamic full-time schools, where some or all K-12 grades were taught.[36] Included in this fourth wave, are the many Muslim immigrants from India and Pakistan, who outnumber any other subgroup simply because of these countries' large populations from which to draw. The 2000 United States census identified slightly over one million (1,007,000) Asian Indians living in the United States.[37]

It is not too surprising then that today, estimates of the Muslim population in the United States stands in excess of four million, perhaps as much as six million.[38] John Esposito notes that there are more Muslims in America than in Kuwait, Qatar, and Libya. And Islam is the second largest religion in France as well as the third largest in Britain, Germany, and North America. In a few years Islam will replace Judaism as the second largest major religion in the United States. Note that he is considering major religions only—Christianity, Judaism, Islam, Buddhism, Hinduism, and perhaps Confucianism and Shinto—not the individual denominations within Christianity.[39] Islam vies with Evangelical/Pentecostal Protestant Christian groups, as the most rapidly growing religious group in America today. Certainly Islam has become a major religion in the United States today.

Hinduism   Ralph Waldo Emerson and Henry David Thoreau were the first prominent Americans to delve somewhat seriously into Hinduism, partly through reading about Hinduism, but also through their contact with Swami Vivekananda. The Swami had come to America in 1893 to attend what became a very significant event in American religion—the World's Parliament of Religions in conjunction with the 1893 Chicago World's Fair. He stayed two years lecturing and teaching throughout the east and Midwest and returned to India having sown the seeds of what would become an American Hindu organization, the Vedanta Society, which still exists but with small numbers and little influence today.

However, more recently, Hinduism has attracted considerable attention and an increasing following. We think of the Maharishi Mahesh Yogi (later known simply as Maharishi), who introduced Transcendental Meditation (TM), which began in the 1950s and subsequently quite popular and remains viable today.

Other gurus also came and attracted followings. Of the longest lasting in America, whom Diana Eck calls the "senior statesman," is Swami Satchidananda, who came in 1969 and attracted a following of hippies after his appearance at Woodstock that same year.

The Hare Krishna group, that became familiar to many urban Americans and airport visitors in the 1970s and 1980s, though clearly not the largest, became the most visible Hindu subgroup in America. Although it still exists, its expression of Hinduism has been replaced by more traditional Hinduism, for which temples are built by devotees and where families worship, to provide religious socialization for their children, as they observe traditional Hindu rites. Yet Hinduism remains the numerically smallest major Eastern religion in the United States, with about a million adherents.

Buddhism   Buddhism is represented in the United States by many more followers. Buddhism is quite visible in America today, though nowhere more so than Los Angeles, with its more than 300 Buddhist temples.[40] Buddhism, like both Islam and Hinduism, trace beginnings in the United States at least to the nineteenth century and perhaps earlier. There was a significant influx in the 1800s, as many Chinese Buddhists arrived to work on the railroads and in service occupations, as well as some Japanese Buddhists, who arrived as early as 1868. But paralleling these and other Asian immigrations, was an interest on the part of American intellectuals and others who began to study Buddhism and adopted its teachings as their own, with adaptations of course. Early inquirers were Emerson and Thoreau, who explored Buddhism as well as Hinduism. Thoreau (d. 1862) at one point wrote: "I know that some will have hard thoughts of me, when they hear their Christ named beside my Buddha."[41] Others were more enthusiastic about Buddhism, notably Helena Petrova Blavatsky and Henry Steele Olcott, who together, in 1875, founded the Theosophical Society—a name familiar to many Americans even today.[42] The Theosophical Society was far from pure Buddhism. It incorporated ideas from Hinduism and the ancient world of Egypt and Persia, yet Olcott particularly strove to unify Buddhism, both statewide and in Asia, by stressing the simple early teachings of the Buddha.[43] The 1893 World's Parliament of Religions provided an important infusion of Buddhism, just as it did Hinduism. In particular, Zen Buddhism gained an audience and some converts. The modern day revival of Zen probably began with the 1957 conference on Zen and psychoanalysis in Cuernevaca, Mexico and continued during the period of widespread religious experimentation in the 1960s and beyond. Many Zen groups followed various leaders and as with all religions, there are many branches (shall we call them "sects?"). The most familiar Buddhist in recent years has been the Dalai Lama, the spiritual head of the Tibetan Buddhist Gelugpa tradition. According to Diana Eck, if we include the whole spectrum of American Buddhism, their numbers could be around four million.[44]

Resumption of Asian Immigration in 1965   It is clear that followers of Buddhism, as with followers of both Islam and Hinduism, did not become numerous in the United States until the relaxation of restrictions on Asian immigration began in 1965. Following that date, hundreds of thousands of Buddhists from Vietnam, Sri Lanka, Korea, Taiwan, Cambodia, and Thailand began to arrive. As a consequence, Buddhism in an American form (actually many ethnic American forms) became yet another major religion in the rich pluralism for which the United States is justifiably notable.

But there is one more statement to make. We have emphasized the huge impact religiously that the opening of America's doors in 1965 to large-scale immigration of Asians has produced. It provided robust reinforcement of the numbers of Muslims, Hindus, and Buddhists who were already here, albeit on a fairly small scale in each case. Yet it needs to be said that some of those who came were already Christians and either joined local Christian congregations here or established their own ethnic congregations, sometimes with their own ethnic pastors, within the denomination with which they identified. For example, many of the immigrants from Korea were Protestants, and many from the Philippines were Roman Catholic. And certainly some, particularly those in the second and third generations, have converted to a traditional American denomination or sect that has appealed to them, having made what for them was a *rational choice* in a surrounding American culture that is still predominantly Christian.

It is of considerable significance, that between 1981 and 2000, over three million persons immigrated to the United States from Asia.[45] One result of this massive immigration is that Hindus, Buddhists, and Muslims, like other ethnic Americans, have easily found others of the same faith so they could transplant their religion complete with temple or mosque, hire one of their own as leader, and maintain a Western version of their religion and culture. In total, as of the 2000 U.S. Census, there were 10,243,000 persons of Asian descent resident in the United States.[46] All of this adds new dimensions to the meaning of religious diversity and pluralism in America.

SPECIAL INTEREST RELIGIOUS GROUPS

While stressing the importance of denominationalism in American religion, we will discuss at least briefly two developments that might counter, to some degree, the dominant pressure toward denominationalism and suggest that denominationalism is not quite so dominant a condition of American religion as it once was. The major qualification is the factor of ecumenism, which we shall discuss in the next section. But there is another pattern that is stressed by Robert Wuthnow. That is an increase in special interest religious groups that transcend denominational boundary lines.

While many of these groups focus on issues of concern to the new religious right[47] and thus draw from a somewhat narrow range on the denominational spectrum, some of them find their support among the religious left, and some draw from all along the denominational spectrum. Drawing from the religious left was particularly noticeable during the civil rights movement, the Vietnam War protest movement, the movement for nuclear arms control, and, more recently, collective action for support for AIDS research and acceptance of homosexuality. Robert Wuthnow points out that all these special interest religious groups "take their legitimating slogans from religious creeds" and "they draw their organizational resources, leadership, and personnel largely from churches and ecclesiastical agencies."[48]

Wuthnow's point, in discussing special interest religious groups, is not to suggest this is totally new to American religion. In fact, the Women's Christian Temperance Union and the Anti-Saloon League are perfect examples of special interest religious groups, that date back to the last quarter of the nineteenth century. He simply suggests that such groups, which span denominational lines, but seem not to reflect them, appear to be increasing in numbers. Wuthnow notes that there are currently approximately eight hundred nationally organized voluntary associations that have religious purposes (meet Internal Revenue Code definition as religious organizations) yet are not churches or denominations.[49] Groups, such as the American Bible Society, the Fellowship of Christian Athletes, the Christian Business Men's Association, and the Americans United for Separation of Church and State, it should be noted, tend not to draw from only one end of the religious or political spectrum.

ECUMENISM

Early Years of Mostly Peaceful Coexistence

Despite the theological diversity we have just scanned, American denominations have shown considerable facility at coexisting peacefully. Historically, this is true of Protestants primarily with other Protestants. It has been suggested that, for Protestants at least, different denominations are regarded by most citizens as equally valid ways of being a religious American. In fact, the principal occasion for Protestant religious groups, to become suspicious of other Protestant groups, has been when the actions or beliefs of those others suggested less than wholehearted commitment to the American Republic. As we mentioned in Chapter 12, German Lutherans, for example, were prodded and occasionally harassed during World War I, as many of them continued to use the German language in their churches and schools and as some openly supported the German "fatherland." Jehovah's Witnesses have repeatedly felt legal and social pressure, because of their stands against saluting the flag and serving in the armed forces. Amish fathers, who refused to allow their children to attend school beyond the eighth grade, were periodically jailed for their convictions until 1972, when the Supreme Court ruled in their favor. Choosing not to use the English language, refusing to salute the flag, and questioning the value of formal education, raise doubts in many citizens' minds about a group's loyalty and commitment to basic American principles. It hardly needs mentioning that both the Jehovah's Witnesses and the Amish are sectarian groups, which protest not simply against what they view as religious error but against prevailing social structures as well.

Despite some exceptions, such as those just referred to, and the Anti-Catholicism and Anti-Semitism we discussed in Chapter 12 under the heading "The Ordeal of Pluralism," we can say that for most of the United States' history, most religious groups have felt relatively secure and have been able to pursue their business unhampered by government, other religious groups, or fellow citizens. In short, the constitutional provision for free exercise of religion has been in fairly effective operation, though we shall revisit this issue in the final chapter as we introduce some words of caution.

There is, of course, a fairly certain way for a religious group to bring down the wrath of other groups upon itself, and that is to proselytize actively and seek converts from other religious groups. Actually, except for a few groups, such as the Mormons and Jehovah's Witnesses and a few small conversionist sects, this has been no serious issue. Not that most groups have not been willing to make converts to their faith. But they have tended to concentrate on those who were not affiliated with any religious groups, those who voluntarily knocked on the door, and those with whom the group has been put in contact because of marriage with a group member. In fact, most major Protestant groups, concerned lest they inadvertently overstep the bounds of others and be accused of proselytizing, commonly establish comity arrangements with one another; particularly in expanding communities, denominations typically divide the territory among themselves so that each has designated areas in which to work and establish new congregations, without competing with other denominations.

Rise of Ecumenism

The context of cooperation and peaceful coexistence just described, is an important background factor in the rise of *ecumenism*—not simply greater cooperation but joint efforts that might lead ultimately to the organic merger of two or more denominations. The ecumenical movement is essentially a phenomenon of the twentieth century and has involved much discussion and commentary.

Few Mergers   Yet despite the great volume of literature and discussion, relatively few actual mergers have taken place. There have been mergers among Lutheran denominations from various Scandinavian countries, once the groups had become "Americanized," began conversing in English, and realized they all subscribed to the same confessional and creedal statements. Specifically, there have been four of these—the formation of the United Lutheran Church in America in 1917, the American Lutheran Church in 1960, the Lutheran Church in America in 1962, and the Evangelical Lutheran Church in America in 1988. In the last merger, the Lutheran Church in America, the American Lutheran Church, and a smaller group, the Evangelical Lutherans in Mission, joined forces and now constitute the largest Lutheran and the third largest Protestant denomination in the United States.

Other Protestant Mergers and Discussions   In 1957, the Congregational Christian Churches merged with the Evangelical and Reformed Church to form the United Church of Christ. And in 1968, a merger was effected between the Evangelical United Brethren Church and the United Methodist Church. In 2001, two small Mennonite groups (the Mennonite Church and General Conference Mennonite Church) approved a merger to form the Mennonite Church USA.

Stimulated by Eugene Carson Blake's dramatic suggestions in 1960, for a merger of most of the major Protestant denominations in the United States, discussions went on for over four decades within the Consultation on Church Union (COCU), which was formed to facilitate discussion and possible ultimate merger itself. Twelve denominations originally entered the discussions of COCU. By 1972, four had withdrawn, the latest being the United Presbyterian Church, which, however, voted in 1973 to rescind its action of the previous year and rejoin the discussion.

The eight denominations (African Methodist Episcopal Church, African Methodist Episcopal Zion Church, Christian Methodist Episcopal Church, Christian Church [Disciples of Christ], Episcopal Church, Presbyterian Church U.S.A., United Church of Christ, and United Methodist Church) and one federation (International Council of Community Churches) that remained, continued to meet but consummated no mergers. They found that differences in views of the ministry and the church, ordination, and other doctrinal and practical matters kept them from the dramatic ultimate step of mergers.

Then, during the evening of 19 January 2002, COCU voted itself out of existence, only to reconstitute itself the next day as a new ecumenical organization called Churches Uniting in Christ (CUIC). It was not mere coincidence that CUIC constituted itself on Martin Luther King Day in Memphis at the Lorraine Motel where Dr. King was assassinated on 4 April 1968. The new group will focus less directly on formal mergers of denominations, perhaps implicitly granting the futility of effort to attain full organic mergers, and will put its major energies into the elimination of racism, both within Christendom and the surrounding society as well. Note that three of the nine groups listed above, that constituted COCU during most of its 42 years, are primarily black denominations. A few other denominations have already become "partners in mission and dialogue" and have expressed interest in joining CUIC. These are the Evangelical Lutheran Church in America, the Moravians, and the American Baptists.

Christian Churches Together in the USA   A very recently-formed ecumenical organization is the Christian Churches Together in the USA, which formally constituted itself in late Spring 2005. There are several distinctive features of this organization. First, it is fairly large (around 30 denominations with others waiting until their next church body convention to make the decision). Second, it has the broadest representation of any ecumenical association. Even the National Council of Churches does not include Roman Catholics and Eastern Orthodox bodies. Even some Evangelical groups have joined, in addition to many of the usual participants in ecumenical dialogue, such as Episcopal, United Methodist, United Church of Christ, and Evangelical Lutheran Church in America. Its purpose is traditional ecumenism: "To enable churches and national Christian organizations to grow closer together in Christ in order to strengthen Christian witness in the world."[50]

Ecumenism a Challenging Task   Blending religious groups that have unique histories, distinct theologies, and different social constituencies is extremely difficult. Here, in a real sense, the theological differences reflected by the data in Table 14.1, become evident and important. Issues involving forms of church government (episcopal, presbyterian, or congregational), differing views of the ministry, the nature and function of the two most common Christian sacraments of baptism and holy communion (Lord's Supper), and a host of other issues, make agreement and compromise extremely difficult to achieve.

It also needs to be mentioned that ecumenical discussion has not been limited to Protestantism or Christianity. Increasingly, after 1950, Jews have been included in discussions and, particularly at local levels, where there are population concentrations of Muslims and followers of Buddhism, Hinduism, Sikhism, and other Eastern religions, ecumenical discussions and even some joint activities among a wide range of religious groups have taken place. Probably no one expects such conversations to ever break down the walls that separate the major religions, so that any unification and mergers can take place. But there is growth in mutual understanding, respect, and occasionally statements of agreement on certain social or religious freedom issues ensue.

Sociological Interest   Certainly ecumenism has been an absorbing subject for religious leaders and groups. But sociologists have also been interested, for ecumenism is a sociological phenomenon, not simply a religious one. Sociological interest has focused less on what is going on than why ecumenical interest has developed at all. What, if any, are the social sources of this phenomenon? Peter Berger has suggested that one primary reason is economic—that is, rising costs, particularly for buildings and staff, suggest joint effort and cost sharing.[51] It appears that denominations have become increasingly aware that duplication of effort is not only wasteful, but ultimately impossible to continue forever. Pooling resources, using one missionary governing board to supervise forty missionaries, rather than two boards each supervising twenty missionaries, building one church edifice instead of two in a new subdivision—ideas such as these have begun to make economic sense to denominations. Such recognition would probably not have come so quickly, had religious membership expansion continued past the early 1960s at its post-World War II pace. But as we will discuss in Chapter 15, by the 1970s, membership growth in the major denominations had either ceased or, in fact, had begun to decline. In the face of declining membership and a concomitant decline in contributions, denominations have been forced to become cost-conscious and to look for ways to economize and increase efficiency. At this point, groups began regarding the theological justification for ecumenism as more convincing than ever before.

A prime factor underlying the problem of stable or declining membership, is that while church membership in this country has shown a fairly steady increase for nearly two centuries, the growth of churches was closely tied to population growth in the nation generally. It is very possible that denominations have "converted" and brought into their folds proportionately nearly all the people they can ever expect to. Few of those not yet convinced to join are likely to be convinced in the future. Thus, one of the activities that before the mid-1960s absorbed much of the energy of local churches and of denominations—namely, home missionary activities (the establishment of new congregations to meet the demands of population shifts)—has declined and no longer commands the attention it once did. What, then, are church leaders at all levels within the structure, as well as laypeople in the congregations, to do by way of church work? What kind of religious frontier is left to explore and conquer? One option that excites the imagination of many is to try to break down ancient barriers that have kept denominations apart. A divided Christendom is defined as a "scandal." What with the recent emphasis in American society on overcoming prejudices, tolerating differences among people, and compromising old absolutes regarding what is good and what is evil, it is only natural that religious groups should begin to work at cleaning up their houses, so to speak, by relating to other religious groups. Ecumenical discussion and activity have become popular as a consequence. The challenge for the churches, during the twenty-first century, will be for many the ecumenical goal of a united Christendom. Yet at this point we need to state again that enthusiasm and commitment to ecumenism, in theory, have not been enough to effect much notable success since 1968.

Another factor that undoubtedly fostered ecumenism in the two decades following the close of World War II, was the long-term trend toward autonomous bureaucracies in the major denominations. As numerous sociological studies have shown, those persons in high-level positions in organizations are the most tolerant, accepting, and understanding of competing organizations. High-level labor union officials, for example, often interact more harmoniously with their counterparts in management, from whom they will ultimately be trying to extract concessions to union demands, than they do with the rank-and-file union members they represent. It has been suggested that such leaders may even have difficulty demanding certain things that they have come to believe, through their contacts with management, the employer cannot afford. Similarly, officials of church bureaucracies tend to interact with comparable officials of other denominations, whom they find to be much like themselves. They find it easy to get along with them and therefore counsel that the denominations themselves ought to be able to get along as well. These church bureaucrats tend to be more liberal than the rank-and-file clergy in the denominations in the first place—a fact that may in itself go far in explaining why there is so much discussion of ecumenism by religious leaders but why relatively little of a concrete nature in terms of denominational mergers and extensive cooperation seem to occur. The local churches are most likely not so interested or convinced as their representatives in the denominational bureaucracies.

Suffice it to say, in summarizing our discussion to this point, that during the twentieth century, ecumenism has paralleled denominationalism. That is to say, both have thrived, even though this would seem to involve an inherent contradiction. Denominationalism appears to be as viable as ever, and ecumenism is also alive and at least fairly well. Part of the answer to this seeming contradiction, is that in ecumenical conversations and activities denominations have found themselves looking more closely, not only at others, but at themselves, their heritage, and their uniqueness. This analysis may have led them to a new and stronger appreciation of themselves in their uniqueness. In fact, the United States is a pluralistic society that today encourages its subgroups to celebrate and preserve their uniqueness, as long as they support the fundamental values of the society. The upshot is that denominations may not be particularly ready to give up their identities. Yet they see much value in cooperation and certainly no value in cut-throat competition. Hence ecumenism remains viable also. While not going the whole ecumenical route and effecting outright organizational mergers, denominations feel free to cooperate and engage in joint tasks while each retains its identity.

Postdenominationalism   A variant on the ecumenical theme is called *postdenominationalism* in Canada. The strong push for regional and provincial independence, so strongly held by many in Quebec, but also with a great deal of support in western Canada, has spilled over into religion. Canadians are beginning to question the value of centralized, national denominational structures. Not only is there traditional ecumenical cooperation among denominations, but at the local level, a community of people from a variety of denominations have decided to join together to worship under one minister, in effect forsaking former denominational affiliations.[52]

This pattern is most likely observed in western and northern Canada, where relatively sparse populations find it difficult to support the traditional variety of denominational choices. In a sense, such "postdenominationalism" is a more advanced stage of churches responding to the circumstance of relatively sparse population, as on the American frontier nearly two hundred years ago. Traditional denominations, with a station in every community, may well be a luxury people can no longer afford. As part of this, one must also assume that the voluntary financial contributions of church members have not kept pace with inflation, so that it is extremely difficult for a small group of congregants to support a full-time pastor. Several small congregations, linking together around one pastor from one of the denominations represented, becomes expedient and pragmatic, doctrinal issues, tradition, and old loyalties aside.

THE MEGACHURCH PHENOMENON

The term "megachurch" has been coined to identify very large churches—large in members and attendees and large in size of sanctuary and physical plant. The consensus definition is a ministry of 2,000 or more worship attendees per week. Also they exhibit rapid growth to have reached this status, growing by the hundreds every year. But large is not new. In fact, once the United States had developed large urban centers, some church buildings became large and memberships did as well. This occurred fairly early in U.S. history. There were definitely some engaging, charismatic preachers at work in the eighteenth century, gathering together large congregations. Anne Loveland and Otis Wheeler describe an evolution of large church buildings from the open-air revival gatherings (camp meetings), where thousands assembled for days of religious revival services (though in the open air), to the early large barn-like structures and tabernacle tents, to the large urban auditorium churches that eventually could be found in nearly every city and town, with some still standing today.[53]

Characteristics   But many of today's new large churches are indeed **mega**-churches, seating thousands—as many as 15,000 and more. What is probably America's largest church facility—Lakewood Church in Houston. Texas—held its first Sunday services in its new building, the former Compaq Center that had been the home of the Houston Rockets, on 17 July 2005. This remodeled building seats 16,000. Even without the new facility, Sunday services were averaging 32,500 per Sunday, spread among four services.[54] Yet the size of the worship facilities in these megachurches is but the beginning. It is the ancillary buildings and spaces that make these churches so visually distinctive: gymnasiums, ball fields, lounges and dining facilities seating hundreds, nursery schools, exercise facilities, classrooms and meeting rooms by the score, Starbucks coffee lounges, McDonald's restaurants, credit unions, and electronic media installations that rival commercial television studios, to name but some of the facilities one might expect to find in a megachurch complex. Their grounds are measured not in city lots, or even city blocks, but in scores of acres.

These megachurches tend to be located in suburbia, or even increasingly in exurbia, where their vast land requirements for expanding facilities and providing acres of parking spaces can be met. They begin with the assumption that religion needs to be relevant and contemporary, free from traditional patterns of music, art, and liturgy. The goal is to meet the modern person with messages relevant to their daily life and enhanced by contemporary Christian musical arrangements. While nearly all these churches profess a conservative Christian theology with most considered Evangelical, Charismatic, or Fundamentalist,[55] there is major emphasis on preaching that is relevant to the needs and life situations of today's middle classes. Lee McFarland, pastor of Radiant Community Church in Surprise, Arizona, 45 minutes from Phoenix, focuses on "successful principles for living—'how to discipline your children, how to reach your professional goals, how to invest your money, how to reduce your debt, even how to shake porn addiction.'"[56] Yet the goal of such preaching to the needs of people, for help in living successfully, is to become immersed in the many Christ-based programs of the church and, in the words of David Travis, head of a consulting firm for megachurches "to become a more passionate follower of Christ, not just in the church, but in your community, your workplace and your home."[57]

Scott Thumma speaks of three general approaches guiding these churches. The first is the "Nontraditional" approach, used specifically to attract religious "seekers" and the "unchurched." In the words of one megachurch pastor, the approach is straightforward: "We're trying to create an environment here so that the unchurched person can come in and say, 'This is church like I have never known church.'"[58]

The approach of a second category of megachurch Thumma designates "Conventional." These tend to be older, established congregations that have grown to megachurch size and complexity and retain the images of traditional Protestant Christianity. They want to portray to people that this is the religion of your childhood, with parents and grandparents at your side, but bigger and better. The choirs, perhaps augmented by contemporary musical instrumentation is superb, the preaching is excellent and moving, and ancillary offerings of the church are diverse, with something of interest to just about everyone.

The third category of megachurch Thumma identifies as "Composite" churches, which retain a visual connection to traditional religion, with a traditional church exterior or façade, but have shaped the interior as a theater with a performance stage to feature musicians, dynamic preacher, and perhaps charismatic healing sessions.

Membership in these megachurches, based on Thumma's study tends to be relatively young, with an estimated median age of 38, and a high proportion of women (60 to 70 percent).[59] Members tend to be middle class, and are fairly highly-educated (studies of individual congregations suggest about 40 percent are college educated). Because of the suburban/exurban geographic areas, many of the megachurches serve, they tend to Caucasian membership, though some congregations are highly-integrated racially and ethnically, and several megachurches are affiliated with traditional black denominations.

The characteristics of the ministers of these churches are, of course, crucial. They tend to be highly gifted, often charismatic men that are excellent motivational preachers who also possess the strong organizational skills of a successful C.E.O. In many cases, they started the congregation from nothing and brought it along in but a decade or two to its present membership of 2,000, 4,000, or 10,000 and more members. Thumma describes these pastors as visionaries and "innovative spiritual entrepreneurs."[60]

We mentioned earlier the size of megachurches as their most obvious characteristic, though we must now note size is not their most important characteristic. More important are the program and what is increasingly being called the post denominational character of these churches.

Megachurch Program   First, Program. A commonly heard description of these churches is that of a shopping mall, because of their wide array of consumer-driven ministerial and service offerings,[61] where traditional core ministries, such as inspirational sermons, Bible study, baptisms, counseling, and like are provided, serving like the anchor stores in a shopping mall. The specialty shops that abound in a mall are represented in a megachurch as health fairs, divorce recovery groups, addiction recovery groups, political action groups, teen and youth groups of all kinds, auto repair clinics, parenting classes, dance academies, groups for sports enthusiasts, exercise classes for new mothers, and so on. Such specialization requires a large staff, much larger than that found in the large churches of the last two centuries. In fact, some of the megachurches have as many as twenty assistant ministers and over 250 full-time staff members.[61] Herein lies an important part of the uniqueness of the megachurch, in that it can provide service and contact with members and attendees far beyond the Sunday morning worship service. This small-group contact provides more intimacy among members and enhances commitment and identity on the part of parishioners, thereby helping to overcome the anonymity that is inherent in a Sunday worship service involving thousands of people. Also, many megachurches create cell-groups or friendship circles to promote connectedness and friendship among members. Of course, not all of those thousands who attend a megachurch become a part of small group and cell group ministries of these churches. A participation rate of 20 percent is common, rarely breaking 30 percent according to Eddie Gibbs, a professor at Fuller Theological Seminary.[62]

Post Denominational Character   The second primary distinguishing mark of the megachurch phenomenon is its post-denominational character. That is, old denominational labels and attachments do not apply. Most of these congregations began as small non-denominational "community" churches, without denominational affiliation; some have gradually pulled away from an original denominational base; and approximately a third actually continue with a denominational affiliation. The largest denominational representation is Southern Baptist, with about 20 percent of the megachurches, followed by the Assemblies of God with 9 percent, and a sprinkling of other denominations contributing about 4–5 percent.[63] It should be noted that the largest denominational representation—the Southern Baptist—is a congregationally-based denomination, which gives much autonomy to each independent congregation.

Some of the most successful megachurches, such as Willow Creek, Calvary Chapel, and Vineyard Christian Fellowship, have actually become mini-denominations themselves, with hundreds of branches throughout the world. Some are stand-alone churches, which share the mother church name. Others are satellite churches, where people in other communities, even other states and countries, can hear the same gifted preacher and inspirational music, and sing the same songs and hymns, but be rooted in a church facility in the local community where they live. These satellite churches must have on-site pastors and perhaps other religious professionals, who provide person-to-person ministries. But through the satellite connection, they also have benefit from some of the features of the megachurch host that attracted so many people in the first place. Some have called this branching process "church franchising." This idea fits well with the shopping mall imagery we mentioned earlier. These are not intended to be terms of ridicule. In fact, a *Los Angeles Times* story in 1996, quoted the pastor of Faith Community Church in West Covina, California, as saying, "We did not want a traditional church atmosphere. What we were aiming for was the feeling of a mall. A place that's familiar, a real gregarious place."[64] This "franchising" phenomenon appears to be growing, with well over a thousand of these branch or satellite congregations attached to a host megachurch, such as those named above. As such, each of these host churches, with its branches, creates a very large, geographically dispersed megachurch, which, strictly speaking, is an association of individual congregations forming a small new denomination.

A Protestant Phenomenon   The megachurch phenomenon is Protestant (Catholic parishes can be as large as some of these Protestant megachurches, but the large Catholic parish is of long standing and does not reflect the diversity of program and size of professional staff and where its numerical standing is based on parish membership, not number of Sunday worshippers). And the Protestant megachurch that we have been describing, is relatively new. John Vaughn, at the Megachurch Research Center, notes that in 1970 there were but 10 Protestant megachurches, but by 2005 there were 282 in the United States alone.[65] There are also some of these megachurches in other countries around the world. They have shown particular success in Central and South America, where Evangelical Protestantism is growing rapidly, in part because of the extreme shortage of priests to take care of the very large parishes in these traditionally Catholic countries. Great numbers of members are severely under-served, as priests have become circuit riders along the lines of the Methodist circuit riders in eighteenth-century North America described in Chapter 12. Many Catholics gravitate to Evangelical missions, where they hear preached a gospel of salvation as well as a gospel of coping and success for people in Third World countries who seek improvement in both their spiritual and material condition. These Evangelical missions are growing rapidly and some have already become megachurches.

THE CONTINUED VIABILITY OF DENOMINATIONALISM

But after our diversion above to the post-denominational megachurch phenomenon, we now return more explicitly to the denominational phenomenon with which this chapter is primarily concerned and discuss additional sociological reasons why the denominational phenomenon has remained so dominant a feature of American religion—of American society, for that matter. In the face of strong pressures, both theological and sociological, toward ecumenism, and given yet another unifying tendency (which we discussed in Chapter 7)—the phenomenon of civil religion, which at least implicitly would replace traditional religion with a religion focusing on the society itself, why is American society still divided into so many distinctive religious groups? It is not enough to point out, as we have already, that important doctrinal differences divide denominations, or that another factor keeping denominations distinct is the type of organizational tradition or liturgical emphasis, or the differences between Apollonian and Dionysian orientations. All of these are significant, and all represent a combination of theological and sociological factors and pressures. But two other factors, which are primarily sociological, reinforce the denominational heritage that American society continually updates.

The Ethnic Factor

The first factor reinforcing denominationalism that we want to discuss—one strongly emphasized by Andrew Greeley—is the important ethnic function that religion in American society continues to serve. That is, one's religious affiliation represents for a great many people, much more than commitment to a set of religious beliefs, symbols, and rituals. Religious affiliation may also become a means people use to define their identity—"who they are and where they stand in a large and complex society."[66] Greeley mentions that this definition and location of self may be the most important function religion performs for some people. For others, it is intermixed with the belief system and ethical code that the religious group stands for.

Origin of the Ethnic Factor   The origin of religion as an American ethnic phenomenon, rests with the fact that most of the nationality groups that immigrated into the United States brought their churches with them and transplanted them on American soil. The Norwegians, Swedes, Finns, and Danes brought their Lutheran churches. Some Germans brought their Lutheran Church; other Germans brought their Catholic church; the Italians and Poles did likewise. The Vietnamese brought their Buddhist traditions, and so on. But there is more to it than that. The religious organization for these immigrants was immediately an important source of identification. In many cases it was a safe place for people to use their native tongue, and it linked them in their present insecurity in a new environment to a secure tradition or heritage. As so many of the immigrants left the old cohesive communal relationship of the peasant village, with its primary relationships and awareness of who one was in relation to others, and entered a strange land of secondary relationships, they clung to their ethnic group, in order to preserve some semblance of identity and a linkage with people who could provide empathy. Some of these people may not have been particularly "religious" before and perhaps would not have scored high on certain measures of religiosity in the new land, yet many found in the religious group an opportunity to meet those with whom they shared a heritage, people who spoke their language in both a literal and figurative sense. Andrew Greeley says that denominational membership makes available to Americans "a fellowship which is highly important in compensating for those intimate relationships of life which seem to have been lost when the peasant village was left behind."[67] Clearly, we see religion performing the "belonging" function emphasized by Max Weber.

Ethnicity Factor Enhanced by the Ideal of Pluralism   It should be noted that the opportunity for religion to serve an ethnic function, particularly for immigrant groups, was in part made possible by the religious pluralism that had existed in some of the American colonies and was reinforced in the Constitution. In some of the colonies and certainly as an important part of the Constitution itself, religious diversity (pluralism) was valued and encouraged. Therefore, immigrants could turn to their religious group, as a source of belonging, without undue fear of reprisal. Not that the established Americans were always happy with the religious-ethnic enclaves. But they could do little about them and still be true to the American religious heritage and precedent. That resentment and suspicion did erupt in harassment and violence, is attested to in the discussion of the "Protestant Crusade" in Chapter 12; the point to be made here is that not only was anti-Catholicism being expressed, but also anti-Irish and anti-cheap urban labor sentiments as well.

Limitations on the Melting Pot Hypothesis   Acknowledging the ethnic nature and function of religion in the United States raises some serious questions about the melting-pot hypothesis—the idea that the United States has accommodated and homogenized peoples from a diversity of cultures and backgrounds. It is hardly even the triple melting pot of Protestants, Catholics, and Jews that some have suggested. Historically, it was Dutch Reformed, German Lutheran, Scottish Presbyterian, and so on, for the Protestant immigrant groups; Polish Catholic, Serbian Catholic, Irish Catholic, and so on, for the Catholic groups. It was even, to some extent, Russian Jew, German Jew, and so on—not simply Jewish—for the third major religious family in America. That is, Americans were not only ethnically "hyphenated" as citizens (Irish-Americans, German-Americans, Polish-Americans), but they were ethnically hyphenated as members of religious groups as well. The ethnic factor has thus been more important in patterning American religion than has often been recognized.

Continuing Impact of the Ethnic Factor   One final comment in connection with our discussion of the ethnic feature of religion in America, is that the numerical strength of American religion is in significant degree related to the ethnic factor. Because the religious group was able to serve as an ethnic rallying point, to provide an identity for people and a sense of belonging to something more intimate and meaningful than the diffuse, cold, and distant society, people gained a religious commitment that, though perhaps less intense for many as the importance of ethnic identity fades for them, they are still reluctant to cut themselves off from completely. Religion has served and does serve an important social function as an ethnic community, which exists in addition to any strictly "religious" function it may serve. In many cases, people have even been able to live out their entire lives, while only rarely leaving the religious-ethnic community. Scattered throughout the land, are ethnic-religious communities where nearly 100 percent of the citizens are of a single national origin and a single religious persuasion, and where the public schools become almost parochial ones. But one need not be a farmer or a shopkeeper in such a community to live out one's life in an ethnic subcommunity. One may be a city dweller and a medical doctor, or an accountant, or an attorney, or an academician—and still serve only or almost exclusively members of the ethnic community into which she or he was born.

The Social Class Factor

The second additional factor that reinforces denominationalism in American society, is social class. We spent considerable time in Chapter 10, discussing the relationship between religion and social class, and will, therefore, do little more than mention it again here. Yet it is of considerable relevance to our present interest in denominationalism. Religion does reflect the class structure. Denominations are disproportionately constituted of different social classes, sects are almost universally a lower social class phenomenon, and social mobility sometimes results in change in religious group affiliation that corresponds more appropriately in the eyes of the community with one's newly achieved social status.

The fact that religion reflects the class structure of the society is, of course, not unique to American society. Differences in religious orientation and practice have been observed in less complex societies, which have religious systems at an earlier stage on Bellah's continuum of religious evolution.[68] A distinctive feature of the "archaic" state of religious evolution, according to Bellah, is a clearly stratified society and fairly distinctive religious expressions according to class level. The upper-status people, who control the political and military power, usually claim superior religious status as well. Bellah states that noble families are proud of their divine descent and often have special priestly functions.[69] We can point, for example, to ancient Greece, where there appears to have been a fairly clear distinction between the religion of the plebeians and that of the patricians. The plebeians related to gods associated with agriculture, gods of local concerns, and gods related to magical animal symbols. The patricians were absorbed with the Olympian gods, such as Zeus, Apollo, Aphrodite, Athena, and Hermes, who oversaw broader areas of life, universal principles and emotions, and broader societal concerns. Another example is the Hindu religion. The major beliefs and practices associated with the Vedas and Upanishads and the concepts of Brahma and Brahman, are largely unknown to the lower castes, who, in fact, have traditionally been deemed unworthy of being given the sacred truths. Instead, the lower castes learn the elemental Hindu ideas of samsara, karma, and dharma, and relate to a variety of local gods and spirits.

In American society, we have fairly clear evidence of Weber's *theodicy of escape* and of Marx's and Freud's *compensation for deprivation* function of religion for the lower classes, on the one hand, and the *theodicy of good fortune* for the economically and socially successful members of the society on the other hand. The upshot is that various denominations and religious groups appeal disproportionately to different social classes. The fact that the United States has been and continues to be a highly stratified if somewhat mobile society, has tended to reinforce and preserve denominational and religious diversity as different religious groups provide different things to different people.

Regional Differences

We must not leave our discussion of denominationalism and pluralism, without a quick look at regional differences in denominational affiliation. While pluralism would perhaps suggest an idea of fairly equal dispersion of religious groups across the landscape as each tolerates the others, such is really not the way it is. There are, in fact, distinct regional concentrations of particular denominations. One is the Southern Baptist denomination in the South. The vast majority of counties in the southern states have 25 percent or more of the church membership affiliated with the Southern Baptist Convention, with many of those counties actually at 50 percent or more. The major exceptions are the southern tips of Florida, Texas, and Louisiana. Those exceptions show large concentrations of Catholics, who are also dominant in most of the Northeast and in many urban centers. In addition, Martin Marty points out that in only five of the counties that border a Great Lake, do Catholics not make up at least 25 percent of the religious population.[70] Lutherans show a distinct concentration in the upper Midwest—southern Wisconsin, Minnesota, the Dakotas, and in western Iowa and eastern Nebraska. And, of course, the most dramatic concentration is that of Mormons in the state of Utah (in no county are Mormons outnumbered by any other religious group). Their concentration extends also to contiguous areas: eastern Nevada, southern Idaho, western Wyoming, northern Arizona, and northwestern Colorado.

NOTES

1. Andrew Greeley, *The Denominational Society* (Glenview, IL: Scott, Foresman, 1972), p. 1.
2. Ibid.
3. J. Gordon Melton, *The Encyclopedia of American Religion* vols. 1 and 2 (Wilmington, NC: McGrath Publishing Company, 1978).
4. See Greeley, *The Denominational Society*, p. 23.
5. There is no consensus among historians on either a date or an event to mark the formal division into a Roman Catholic and an Orthodox division of Christianity, though a prime candidate would be the ninth century mutual excommunication exchanged by

St. Photius, patriarch of Constantinople, and St. Nicholas of Rome. Other suggestions range all the way to 1439 A.D., with a commonly accepted date being 1054, when another mutual excommunication took place. Cf. Arthur C. Piepkorn, *Profiles in Belief*, vol. 1 (New York: Harper & Row, 1977), pp. 32–33.

6. Charles S. Liebman, "Orthodoxy in American Jewish Life," in *The Jewish Community in America*, ed. Marshall Sklare (New York: Behrman House, 1974), p. 134.

7. Quoted from G. F. Moore, *History of Religions*, vol. 2 (New York: Scribner's, 1946), p. 94.

8. A Boston survey found that 27 percent of Jews identify themselves as Reform, 44 percent Conservative, 14 percent Orthodox, 15 percent with no preference or consider themselves as nonreligious. Cf. Morris Axelrod, Floyd J. Fowler, and Arnold Gurin, *A Community for Long Range Planning—A Study of the Jewish Population of Greater Boston* (Boston: Combined Jewish Philanthropies of Greater Boston, 1967), p. 119. A survey in Providence, Rhode Island, found 21.2 percent Reform, 19.8 percent Orthodox, 54.1 percent Conservative, and 4.9 percent other self-designations. Cf. Sidney Goldstein and Calvin Goldscheider, *Jewish Americans: Three Generations in a Jewish Community* (Englewood Cliffs, NJ: Prentice Hall, 1968), p. 177.

9. Marshall Sklare, *Conservative Judaism: An American Religious Movement* (New York: Schocken Books, 1972), pp. 45–46.

10. Martin Buber, *Hasidism and Modern Man*, ed. and trans. Maurice Friedman (New York: Harper & Row, 1958), p. 10.

11. Marshall Sklare, *America's Jews* (New York: Random House, 1971), pp. 49–50.

12. Charles S. Leibman and Eliezer Don-Yehiya, *Religion and Politics in Israel* (Bloomington: Indiana University Press, 1984), p. 9.

13. Ibid.

14. Ibid., p. 11.

15. Gerhard Falk, *American Judaism in Transition* (Lanham, MD: University Press of America, 1995), p. 4.

16. Ibid.

17. Andrew M. Greeley, "Council or Encyclical?" *Review of Religious Research* 18, no. 1 (Fall, 1976): 11.

18. George Gallup, Jr. and Jim Castelli, *The People's Religion* (New York: Macmillan Publishing Company, 1989), p. 79.

19. Ibid., p. 18.

20. George Gallup, Jr. and D. Michael Lindsay, *Surveying the Religious Landscape: Trends in U.S. Beliefs* (Harrisburg, PA: Morehouse Publishing Company, 1999), p. 85.

21. Ibid.

22. Andrew Greeley, "The Making of the Pope, Part Four," *Detroit Free Press* (August 17, 1978), p. 11a.

23. Catherine Wessinger, "Women's Religious Leadership in the United States," in *Religious Institutions and Women's Leadership: New Roles inside the Mainstream*, ed. Catherine Wessinger (Columbia, SC: University of South Carolina Press, 1996), pp. 25–26.

24. Harry Cook, "Is the Vatican Out to Change the Education of Its Priests?" *Detroit Free Press* (October 4, 1981).

25. J. Gordon Melton, *Encyclopedia of American Religions*, vol. 1 (Wilmington, NC: McGrath, 1978), pp. 57–87.

26. Other ethnically identified religious groups would be the Dutch Reformed and informal subgroups within American Catholicism—Irish Catholics, Polish Catholics, Italian Catholics, Hispanic Catholics, and so on.

27. Arthur C. Piepkorn, *Profiles of Belief*, vol. 2 (New York: Harper & Row, 1978), p. 363.

28. Piepkorn, *Profiles of Belief*, vol. 3, p. 3.

29. Ignacio Vergara, *El Protestanismo En Chile* (1961), pp. 126–127, quoted in the Introduction by Vinson Syman to Arthur C. Piepkorn, *Profiles of Belief*, vol. 1, p. xvi.

30. Diana L. Eck, *A New Religious America* (San Francisco: HarperSanFrancisco, 2001), pp. 243–248.
31. Ibid., p. 246.
32. Ibid., p. 248.
33. Ibid.
34. Ibid., p. 260.
35. Ibid., p. 262.
36. Ibid., p. 284.
37. *Statistical Abstracts of the United States 2001*, 121st Edition (Washington, DC: 2001), p. 55.
38. Ibid., p. 265.
39. John L. Esposito, "Introduction: Muslims in America or American Muslims?" in *Muslims on the Americanization Path?*, eds. Yvonne Yazbeck Haddad and John L. Esposito (Oxford, England: Oxford University Press, 2000), p. 3.
40. Eck, ibid., p. 142.
41. Ibid., pp. 180–181.
42. Ibid.
43. Ibid.
44. Ibid., p. 3.
45. *Statistical Abstracts of the United States 2001*, ibid., p. 11.
46. Ibid., p. 24.
47. Groups such as the Moral Majority, Religious Roundtable, National Federation for Decency, Christian Voice, and the National Christian Action Coalition.
48. Robert Wuthnow, *The Restructuring of American Religion* (Princeton, NJ: Princeton University Press, 1988), p. 101.
49. Ibid., p. 108.
50. Chris Herlinger, Press Release, Ecumenical News International, March 11, 2005, through Internet access (www.christianchurchestogether.org).
51. Peter Berger, "A Market Model for the Analysis of Ecumenicity," *Social Research* 30, no. 1 (1963): 77–93.
52. Reported in *Religion Watch*, ed. Richard P. Cimino, vol. 9, no. 5 (March, 1994): pp. 6–7, from *Faith Today* Jan./Feb., 1994, Willowdale, Ontario, Canada.
53. Anne C. Loveland and Otis B. Wheeler, *From Meetinghouse to Megachurch* (Columbia, MO: University of Missouri Press, 2003).
54. Associated Press, "America's Largest Church Will Open Where Rockets Played," *Muncie Star Press*, July 16, 2005, p. 2D.
55. Scott Thumma, "Exploring the Megachurch Phenomena: Their Characteristics and Cultural Context." C. 1999, p. 6, paper published on the internet: www.sthumma@hartsem.edu.
56. Jonathan Mahler, "The Soul of the New Exurb," *New York Times*, March 27, 2005, p. 3.
57. Ibid., p. 4.
58. Kimberly Winston, "That Old-time Religion No Longer," Tri-*Valley Herald*, April 7, 1996, p. A1, A10, quoted in Thumma, "Exploring the Megachurch Phenomena," ibid., p. 6.
59. Thumma, ibid., p. 16.
60. Ibid, p. 13.
61. Ibid., p. 14.
62. Mahler, "The Soul of the New Exurb," ibid., p. 6.
63. Thumma, ibid., p. 5.
64. Quoted in Anne C. Loveland, *From Meetinghouse to Megachurch*, ibid., p. 131.
65. Mahler, "The Soul of the New Exurb," ibid., p. 4.
66. Greeley, *The Denominational Society*, p. 108.
67. Ibid., p. 114.

68. Robert Bellah outlines five stages of religious evolution: the primitive, the archaic, the historical, the early modern, and the modern. Robert N. Bellah, "Religious Evolution," *American Sociological Review* 29, no. 3 (1964): 358–374, reprinted in Bellah, *Beyond Belief* (New York: Harper & Row, 1970), Chapter 2.

69. Bellah, *Beyond Belief*, pp. 30–31.

70. Martin E. Marty, "The Career of Pluralism in America," in *Religion in America, 1950 to the Present*, eds. Jackson W. Carroll, Douglas W. Johnson, and Martin E. Marty (San Francisco: Harper & Row, 1979), p. 52.

Chapter 15

The Future of Religion

A broad spectrum of religious persistence into the future.

Those who might have predicted in the past, that by the beginning of the twenty-first century, religion would be a defunct institution, would have to be quite surprised at what they can see almost anywhere in the world today. Not only are many traditional signs of religion in abundance, but also new manifestations emerge almost daily. In the United States, not only does one continue to observe bumper stickers proclaiming "Jesus Saves," political candidates expressing religious clichés, and freshly-painted church spires dotting both countryside and town, but one observes amazing new sights and sounds that daily bombard the consciousness. One sees in both newspapers and the evening television news, vivid pictures of one or another unusual if not outright bizarre activity of a religious cult, Christian pop music sales skyrocketing and beginning to rival jazz, rock, soul, and country in popularity, fundamentalist religious groups deliberately and openly trying to affect U.S. elections and move members of Congress to their point of view, picketers and paraders on both sides of the abortion issue trying to solicit more popular support for what many define as a religious issue, and people called Islamic fundamentalists plotting to destroy the United States.

In other words, there is a great deal of religious activity that attracts the attention and interest of multitudes around the world. Some of these developments will give us clues as to what kind of future religion might have, particularly in the United States. Certainly they will influence people's thinking about the future of religion. Therefore, as we try to look into that future, we shall focus on several major religious developments that seem to have particular sociological relevance.

LEVEL OF RELIGIOUS ACTIVITY

Two commonly used measures of religious activity, which tell us something about the vitality of religion and about people's commitment to religion, are church/synagogue membership, and church/synagogue attendance.

A Gallup poll sampling of the U.S. adult population reveals a very slight erosion of church and synagogue membership between 1940 and 1995, when membership declined from 72 percent to 70 percent. Yet this decrease is clearly too small to be significant. We are left with the conclusion that church and synagogue membership, as reported by people when queried by a Gallup pollster, has not changed significantly in the past sixty years! The change from year to year, or even decade to decade, is nothing more than the fluctuations simply from sampling error that we would expect in any poll.

When we consider church/synagogue attendance as a measure of religious vitality, we find that the proportion of Americans who say they attended their place of worship during the seven days preceding the pollster's posing of the question, has ranged between 37 percent in 1940 to a high of 49 percent in 1955, only to drop back to 40 percent from 1975 through to 1987, increasing again to 43 percent in 1997. The average overall attendance from Gallup poll data is clearly in the low 40s on a percentage basis and has not changed significantly or in a pattern of either growth or decline in sixty years.

Yet there is one difference in church/synagogue attendance that needs to be pointed out. This difference is observed in Table 15.1, where we note no change for Protestants over a thirty-year period, but a fairly dramatic *decrease* for Roman Catholics, who started out significantly higher than Protestants in church attendance but decreased fairly precipitously to approximately equal Protestant attendance. There is a story here to which we shall return at the end of this section.

But before we make too much of attendance figures, we need to point out recent evidence, which strongly suggests that the attendance figures we have relied on for several decades might be incorrect, that is, overstated.

Church attendance figures have been based on polling data, done year after year by the Gallup poll. But a landmark study by Hadaway, Marler, and

TABLE 15.1   Protestant and Catholic Church Attendance Rates for Selected Years

Year	Protestant Attendance (%)	Catholic Attendance (%)
1958	44	74
1978	40	52
1980	39	53
1982	41	51
1984	38	52
1987	38	52
1988	45	48
1998	42	46

Sources: George Gallup Jr. and Jim Castelli, *The People's Religion: American Faith in the 90's* (New York: Maxmillian Publishing Company, 1989), Tables 2.5, 2.6, and 2.7, pp. 30–32,

Frank Newport, ed., *The Gallup Poll Monthly* No. 364 (January, 1996), p. 22,

George Gallup, Jr. and D. Michael Lindsay, *Surveying the Religious Landscape: Trends in U.S. Beliefs* (Harrisburg, PA: Morehouse Publishing, 1999), p. 15.

Chaves suggests that the polling data might consistently be overstating rates of church attendance for all faiths, because the people in the samples recall and report their frequency of attendance at a higher frequency than is really the case. Hadaway, *et al.*, suggest that for Episcopalians, as one representative group from American denominationalism, actual church attendance seems to be approximately only 16 percent, instead of the 35 percent that gets tallied from the polls as the weekly attendance rate for Episcopalians.[1]

To begin to provide data to test the accuracy of poll data on church attendance, Hadaway and his associates checked actual attendance at all 172 Christian churches in Ashtabula County in northeastern Ohio. Essentially, all Christian churches in the county were identified through church and telephone directories, denominational yearbooks, newspaper advertisements, tax-exempt property listings, and by actually driving the length of every road in the county looking for churches not identified through standard listings. Of the 172 Christian churches in the county, 44 were discovered by looking beyond the reports made by denominations and fellowships.[2]

Average actual church attendance figures were obtained from 137 Protestant churches. For the remaining 22 Protestant churches, attendance was either estimated on the basis of the number of cars in the parking lot or by actually counting those in attendance on Sundays during February and March, 1992.[3] Using such figures, which in most cases were averages of actual counts of people in attendance, Hadaway and associates calculated that only 19.6 percent of Protestants attended Sunday (or Saturday) services during an average week in Ashtabula County, Ohio. This attendance rate compares with 42 percent estimates of Protestant attendance based on Gallup poll sampling.

For Catholics, national diocesan data were used—data gathered from each Catholic parish during October of each year and compared with the data reported by Catholics in Gallup polls. The finding is nearly as dramatic as for Protestants. True Catholic attendance on an average Sunday is closer to 25 percent than the 46 percent that comes out of the polls.[4] A follow-up study that increased the number of dioceses from the eighteen in the Hadaway study to forty-eight, confirmed the data almost exactly—a weekly attendance rate for Catholics of 26.7 percent.[5]

If we accept the lower percentages from the Hadaway study as more accurate than the polling data, evidence of the vitality of religion is somewhat less convincing than it might otherwise be. And it provides reinforcement for hypotheses about secularization in American society—a topic for discussion later in this chapter. While such data might require some modification of opinions about the depth of religiosity, the data show the United States less dramatically out-of-line with respect to church attendance and involvement of people in other Western countries (about the same level as in Australia, Canada, Belgium, and Holland, and only twice the 10 percent attendance level in the United Kingdom).[6] The lower attendance figures, suggested by the Hadaway study, also mesh a little better with the perceptions of people who are active in churches and know a little by first-hand observation of the numbers and rates of member attendance in their local houses of worship.

While such data would hardly support anyone's contention that religion is on the ascendancy in America, the data do not necessarily suggest the opposite, either. There are still a high proportion of citizens who hold membership in churches and attend worship services fairly often. Further, church attendance is a far from clear indicator of vital religiosity in the first place. Recalling our discussion in Chapter 5, religiosity is multidimensional. Frequency of church attendance is only one measure and possibly not a highly valid measurement, when all is said and done.

So much for total, national figures and trends. We have to consider also that there might be differences, possibly even substantial ones, among the various groups that in total constitute the summary figures. That is to say, some religious groups could be declining, perhaps dramatically, but others could be growing, perhaps as dramatically or even more dramatically than others are declining. If we find it is so (and it certainly is), then we are likely to ask another question as well: What are the reasons that might account for these differences—some churches growing, some declining?

THE GROWTH AND DECLINE OF MEMBERSHIP

By way of a very general summary, we can observe that some of the standard, mainline Protestant churches have been declining fairly noticeably since the 1960s. For example, some of the most dramatic declines, over the period of

1965 through to 1993, were registered by the Episcopalians with a decline in membership of 27 percent, the United Methodist Church with a decline of 22 percent, and the United Church of Christ with a decline of 26 percent.[7] These were not the only losers, but they tended to have the more dramatic percentage losses.

On the other hand, several religious groups have not only been growing, but growing at a substantial rate. For example, between 1965 and 1993, the Church of the Nazarene grew by 72 percent, the Seventh-Day Adventists increased by 109 percent, the Church of Jesus Christ of Latter-Day Saints added 153 percent, and the Assemblies of God grew by 297 percent.[8] Others are, of course, in between, with only small fluctuations one way or the other, or alternating between small decreases some years but increases in other years.

Declining Membership in Mainline Denominations, Growth in Conservative Churches

In a controversial book, published in 1972 (with a second edition in 1977), *Why Conservative Churches Are Growing*, Dean M. Kelley analyzed the data on growth for some, decline for others, and suggested that one explanatory factor stood out in particular: The growing religious organizations were the strict ones. These demand high commitment and loyalty from their members; they exert church discipline over members' beliefs and lifestyles; they tend to be absolutist and clear-cut about true and correct beliefs.[9] In fact, Kelley has since said that, although overruled by his publisher, he had wanted as his title not *Why Conservative Churches Are Growing*, but *Why Strict Churches Are Strong*.[10] These strict churches demand firm allegiance, tireless devotion to proclaiming the Gospel, obedience to authority, and stoic acceptance of ridicule from the outside.

In a similar vein, is the explanation for conservative growth and liberal decline proposed by George LaNoue, who notes that the conservative churches offer people a scarce commodity for which religion is the nearly unique source—namely, salvation—while the liberal churches have been trying to offer a plethora of goods and services that are also available from a host of other sources—entertainment, intellectual stimulation, and discussion and activity centering around social issues, for example. Because many secular groups can often do a better job of delivering such goods and services within their areas of specialization, liberal religious groups are likely to lose out in the competition. Small wonder, then, that conservative groups that promise delivery of a scarce commodity should grow, and liberal groups that must compete with numerous secular groups in the same business, so to speak, should be shrinking.[11]

Understandably, there was consternation among the mainline denominations. Was their decline real? And, if so, why? Was it their theology? Or was it something else? And was the growth of the conservative churches really their conservative, demanding theology that was attracting so many people or were other factors at work? Such questions and the membership changes that precipitated the questions immediately attracted the attention of researchers. And thirty years of research has ensued. We will summarize some of the more interesting and significant findings. First we will look at two studies that trace the actual movement of people in a sample who relate the changes they have made in their religious affiliations over a period of time. A distinct disadvantage of both Kelley's and LaNoue's work is that their data represent total membership figures only and thus cannot be used to trace the movements of individuals from one religious group to another. In fact, we cannot necessarily infer from these data any movement at all. For example, if the birth rate were higher among members of the more conservative religious groups (which is quite likely, in fact), then the growth of these groups, through natural reproduction alone, might account for some, perhaps even all, of their increasing numerical advantage over the liberal denominations. Or again, perhaps the conservative groups are gaining strength by picking up the nonaffiliated person with little or no religious background, not necessarily the dropouts from liberal denominations.

Other Analyses of Data

Rodney Stark and Charles Glock conducted such research in their important San Francisco Bay Area study, in the mid-1960s. They found that nearly half of the Protestant respondents (46 percent) reported having changed denominational affiliation at some time in the past.[12] In seeking patterns away from and toward certain denominations, Stark and Glock conclude that the general tendency for those who change religious affiliation is to move from more conservative bodies to those that are more liberal theologically.[13] This would quite directly contradict the observations of Kelley and LeNoue. Samuel Mueller, analyzing the same data, reached different, though not diametrically opposed, conclusions. Through the application of factor-analytic techniques, he found that switches of religious affiliation occur essentially without reference to the liberal or conservative stance of the groups involved, but are made in such a way as to preserve similarity along as many dimensions as possible; that is, people tend to affiliate with a religious group similar in a sociological sense to the one they are leaving. The relevant similarities do not seem to be so much doctrinal or creedal, as they are related to such factors as social status and liturgy. In other words, people seem to look for another religious group that has members like themselves and that has a form of worship similar to what they have known and practiced in the past. Some of these religiously mobile people wind up in more liberal denominations, but usually for other than theological or doctrinal reasons or motivations. And the same is true for those who move to more conservative denominations.[14]

Where does this leave us, then, with regard to the issue of the relative growth and decline of conservative and liberal churches? And at an even more general level, where do these trends fit into the observation with which this chapter began—namely, that there has been a small decline in denominational religion in the United States since peaks of activity in the 1950s and 1960s?

For one thing, the analyses offered by Mueller, and by Stark and Glock, cast some doubt on Kelley's hypothesis. Since we do not know the source of the new members in the conservative groups, for which Kelley gives data—whether they are defectors from liberal denominations, converts from irreligion, or simply a result of above-average natural reproductive increase—we cannot infer that doctrinal motivations cause the discrepancy between liberal and conservative denominational growth rates, as both Kelley and LaNoue at least implicitly suggest. In fact, Stark and Glock's data, as well as National Opinion Research Center data that they also examined, suggest that denominational mobility proceeds in both directions between liberal and conservative groups—moreover it proceeds, according to Mueller's analysis, in a nearly random fashion, insofar as theological stances of the gaining and losing denominations are concerned.

Other Factors in Church Growth and Decline

Wade Roof and C. Kirk Hadaway provided very helpful information on the issue a decade later, using National Opinion Research Center General Social Survey data from 1973 through to 1976, which involved a merged sample of nearly six thousand adults. One important qualification of the earlier Stark and Glock findings, is that many who defect from the mainline denominations do not move to the more liberal denominations, as a sort of way station to religious agnosticism and dropping out altogether, but go directly from membership in mainline denominations to nonmembership in any religious group. For example, as high a proportion as 20.4 percent of former United Presbyterians describe themselves as religious dropouts. Corresponding proportions of Lutherans, Methodists, Baptists, and Disciples of Christ were 17.8 percent, 13.4 percent, 13.8 percent, and 9.1 percent, respectively. Among the Presbyterians and the Lutherans, those who dropped out constituted more than those who switched to any other specific religious group.[15]

Furthermore, at least somewhat in line with what Kelley and LaNoue have been saying, Roof and Hadaway found considerable switching out of mainline Protestant denominations into what they term the "religious fringe"— the small Protestant denominations, sect and cult groups, Mormons, and various non-Christian, non-Jewish groups. By way of example, of Presbyterians who left the United Presbyterian Church, 16.8 percent went to small Protestant bodies, 9 percent to sectarian groups, and 3.6 percent to non-Christian groups; of Baptist defectors, 15.6 percent went to small

Protestant denominations, 18.2 percent to sects, and 1.4 percent to non-Christian groups; of Methodist defectors, 14.7 percent went to the smaller Protestant denominations, 10.4 percent to various sects, and 1.0 percent to non-Christian groups.[16]

So it was certainly clear that mainline Protestant denominations were losing members. The data were clear. And we know something about where they were going. Some were dropping out of organized religion; some went to smaller, fringe groups, including some to more sectarian, conservative groups. Further, there was some switching from one mainline group to another. They made such a switch for the same reasons that members of mainline Protestant denominations have switched denominations for generations: They found no local church of their former denomination within convenient driving distance of their new home; new colleagues or friends attended and liked the other church and brought them along; they were attracted to the minister and his preaching; the new church had outstanding programs for children and youth; and so on. Such switching, however, probably evened out, as mainline churches exchanged members in fairly equal numbers, as mobile people found a church in their new community that was similar in so many ways to their former one, but in a different mainline Protestant denomination.

Differential Birth Rates an Important Factor   But churches grow, not only because people switch or transfer from one church to another. There are three other very important sources that are as old as the history of churches. One is births of children to parents who are already members. Here the question is, are there differences in relative birth rates among denominations? Another source of additional members is immigration of members of the same faith into the host country, the United States, for example. A third source is conversion of those who have not been church members. Perhaps the birth rate within conservative churches is higher than in mainline Protestant denominations. Perhaps immigrants are more attracted to conservative churches than to mainline congregations or more immigrants have conservative church backgrounds. Perhaps conservative churches have more successful strategies to attract the unchurched.

Subsequent research did indeed find that different birth rates accounted for some of both membership decline and growth, as the birth rate in the growing conservative churches was higher, birth rates in mainline congregations was lower. Wade C. Roof and William McKinney observed in 1987, that the more conservative denominations did indeed have higher birth rates than the mainline Protestant denominations. Their data for white women born before 1935, show that the birth rate of conservative Protestant women was 17 percent higher than that of women from moderate denominations and 37 percent higher than that of women from liberal denominations.[17] This higher birth rate was one significant factor in the rapid growth of conservative denominations in the last four decades of the twentieth century.

Michael Hout, Andrew Greeley, and Melissa Wilde[18] have recently presented additional strong evidence in support of this fertility differential between conservative and mainline Protestants. In fact, they found that higher fertility, combined with earlier childbearing, accounts for most of the differential, with the rest traceable to another dramatic finding. That is, that the old pattern of upward mobility of lower-status people, leading to dropping one's membership, in a more sectarian, conservative religious group and joining a higher status mainline Protestant denomination, which was popular with middle- and upper-class people, such as those who were upwardly mobile, has become relatively rare in recent decades.[19] This is an extremely important finding, because the relative absence of these membership transfers to mainline denominations by the upwardly mobile, explains much of the declining membership of the mainline groups. That is, the decline was not so much **losing** members to conservative churches but not gaining some from conservative denominations as used to occur. But then there is also the factor of defection from organized religion altogether by some members of mainline churches, as well as the conversion to Roman Catholicism by other mainline Protestant members.

In summary, four factors are involved in the parallel growth of conservative churches and declines among mainline Protestant churches:

1. higher birth rates among conservative church members, lower birth rates among mainline denominational members,
2. continuing defections from organized religion altogether on the part of some mainline church members,
3. fewer members of conservative churches transferring to mainline denominations as their personal social status rises, and,
4. some conversions of mainline members to Roman Catholicism.

But the original inferences, drawn by many from the Kelley revelation of the dramatic growth of conservative denominations and the parallel declining membership of mainline groups, that many of those dropping out of mainline groups were then joining the more conservative groups and thereby contributing significantly to the membership growth of conservative churches, turned out not to be true.

Despite the qualifiers that sociologists have added in the discussions of the original observations by Kelley, about the decline of mainline Protestantism and the gain in conservative Protestantism, the growth and declines themselves remain correctly observed. And the trends have remained, though at a slower rate and have actually, probably stabilized. What has been at issue, is the interpretation that there were dramatic switches of members from liberal mainline Protestant denominations to more conservative groups. No, hordes of mainline Protestants did not defect to conservative groups during the last four decades of the twentieth century.

Yet, both trends of growth in conservative denominations and loss in more liberal denominations really happened. And we certainly have to be aware that the rapid growth of conservative Protestantism is a striking fact of modern American religion and is a fascinating phenomenon to explain. It is particularly fascinating, in the context of the widespread belief, that secularization and some kind of movement away from traditional religion has been going on for many decades. Nonetheless, the growth and the decline among Protestant denominations is fact and is succinctly portrayed in Table 15.2. These data provide the context to consider some theories by Rodney Stark and Roger Finke,[20] about some reasons in addition to those we have already discussed (e.g., higher birth rates among conservative Protestants), for the attraction and success of conservative Protestantism.

Return to the High Cost/High Reward Factor in Rational Choice Theory Stark and Finke are major spokesmen for the application of rational choice theory in the sociology of religion. In the context of membership gains and losses, they and others speak of a continuum from ultra-strict through to ultra-liberal niches that religious groups occupy.[21] Hypothetically at least, these niches would most likely be arranged much like pictured in the bell shaped curve in Figure 15.1. They are arranged in the curve according to their degree of tension with the culture within which they function. At one end are

TABLE 15.2   Membership Gains and Losses among Lower Tension and Higher Tension Protestant Denominations between 1970 and 2000

	Percent Gain or Loss (%)
Lower Tension*	
Episcopal Church	−30
United Church of Christ	−30
United Methodist	−22
American Baptist Churches (USA)	−2
Higher Tension*	
Jehovah's Witnesses	+157
Mormons	+151
Assemblies of God	+142
Seventh-Day Adventists	+89
Church of the Nazarene	+66
Southern Baptist Convention	+37

*Lower Tension and Higher Tension concepts and sample groups from Rodney Stark and Roger Finke, *Acts of Faith* (Berkeley: University of California Press, 2000), pp. 142–154.

Source: *Yearbook of American and Canadian Churches 2002*, ed. Eileen W. Lindner (Nashville, TN: Abingdon Press, 2002), Table 2, pp. 347–358

Statistical Abstracts of the United States 1970, 91st Edition (Washington, DC: 1970), pp. 44–45.

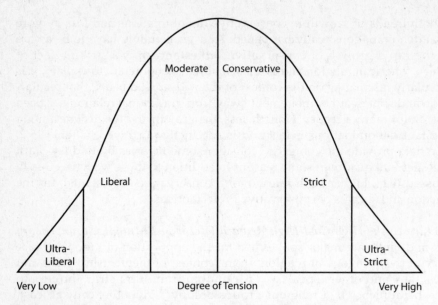

FIGURE 15.1 **Hypothetical Distribution of Tension across Religious Niches**
Source: Rodney Stark and Roger Finke, *Acts of Faith* (Berkeley: University of California Press, 2000), p. 197.

the ultra-strict sects, which demand a great deal from their adherents—strict rules against smoking, drinking, "loose" sexual behavior, card playing, and the like, as well as expectations of a high degree of time commitment and involvement in the group's activities for both worship and social activities. There is "high cost" to belong to such a group, because it demands strong allegiance by its members, such that time that remains for adult members after employment and basic family responsibilities, are often consumed by activities dictated by the religious group with which they are bonded. Members may be given additional requirements that set people apart from the surrounding culture, such as clothing styles (Amish), rejection of the activities and trappings of holidays, such as Christmas and Halloween (Jehovah's Witnesses), or worship on a day other than Sunday (Seventh Day Adventists).

The mainline Protestant denominations are at various points on the left side of the curve, that is, in relatively low tension with the surrounding culture, despite in an earlier day residing on the other slope of the curve, perhaps even fairly far down that slope at a point of "strict" or "ultra-strict." Evolution of the religious group (denomination), both officially concerning doctrine and practice and at the level of personal practice by the majority of members, finds some members no longer satisfied and therefore making decisions to leave, either going to a stricter group, branching off with a few others of like mind as a new small sect or, at the other extreme, deciding if religion is really little more than good citizenship and ethics, then I can practice those virtues outside of religion altogether.

What has become clear is that some people desire strict, high-cost religious groups and are willing to contribute not only their money but also their time, as well as perhaps endure some ridicule by others. Similarly, others desire less demanding churches, in which only modest commitments of time and talents are required and a fairly open, liberal theology and world-view are proclaimed. At this point, we cannot help but remember our earlier discussion of sects in Chapter 4, where we identified their key feature of **protest** against changes in both religion and society. Such protest, of course, implies tension, as persons go against the tide or direction of dominant religion and culture.

The end result is a very dynamic religious scene in the United States, aided by an already existing commitment to the value and desirability of religious pluralism, which results in the continual breaking off of religious sects from the more satisfying affiliations with other religious groups.

IMPENDING PROTESTANT LOSS OF MAJORITY RELIGIOUS POSITION

But there is one more observation about membership changes involving Protestants that needs some discussion. That is a somewhat recent overall decline of Protestantism in the United States—decline at least in proportional position relative to other groups, if not actual decline in numbers. Actually, the numerical dominance of Protestantism, which has existed since the original colonists arrived from Europe, is about to end. The historic domination of Protestantism has been dramatic and is succinctly summarized in Table 15.3.

TABLE 15.3   Percent of All Religious Adherents in Major Protestant Denominations

Denomination	Year	
	1776	1850
Congregationalists	20.4	4.0
Episcopalians	15.7	3.5
Presbyterians	19.0	11.6
Baptists	16.9	20.5
Methodists	2.5	34.2
Total:	74.5	73.8

Sources: Adapted from Joseph B. Tamney, *The Resilience of Conservative Religion* (Cambridge, UK: Cambridge University Press, 2002), p. 49

Adapted from Roger Finke and Rodney Stark, *The Churching of America* (New Brunswick, NJ: Rutgers University Press, 1992).

The data in Table 15.3 show that the five historically largest Protestant groups constituted approximately 75 percent of religiously affiliated citizens at the birth of the nation and in mid-nineteenth century. Actually, there were even more Protestants, who belonged to smaller groups that are not listed or included here. During the nineteenth century, the Protestant majority remained strong, as Reformed and Lutheran Protestants emigrated from Northern Europe and many new Protestant sects and denominations formed and flourished on U.S. soil (Pentecostal groups, Mormons, and many others). Small wonder, as an aside, that many citizens have, for three centuries, referred to the United States as a Protestant Christian society and have maintained that traditional Protestant values should rule. But Catholics and Jews also came in large numbers, as they fled famine and persecution in Europe and Russia, and reduced the size of the Protestant majority just a little.

We mentioned earlier the majority status that Protestants had held from colonial days. Until the early 1900s the Protestant majority had held at around 62.8 percent. But between 1993 and 2002, occurred a fairly precipitous decline. In 2005, Tom Smith and Seokho Kim reported that between 1993 and 2002, the Protestant majority declined nearly 11 percentage points from 63.1 percent to 52.4 percent.[22] Again, a dramatic finding that is so close to dipping below 50 percent, that it undoubtedly will before 2008. There are several reasons for this dramatic change.

Reasons for the Protestant Decline

First, Smith and Kim report that an increasing proportion of younger representatives in the sample, who now report no religious allegiance, were reared in homes where the parents, who might earlier have been Protestants, had themselves joined the ranks of the non religiously affiliated.[23]

Second, there is what we have discussed earlier—the dropping away of substantial numbers of members from the large mainline denominations, which began showing up in the last four decades of the last century. We have earlier observed that many of these did not reaffiliate with any other religious group, Protestant or otherwise. Hout, Greeley, and Wilde note that 60 percent of those who have left mainline Protestant churches, have dropped away from organized religion of any kind.[24] So they constituted a real net loss to Protestantism. It is equally important to note that this number of religious dropouts (not just Protestants, of course) has increased quite substantially recently. In fact, Michael Hout and Claude Fischer found that those who claimed no religious affiliation at all, had held steady for many years at around 7 percent. But after 1991, that percentage began a doubling to 14 percent by 1998, and was projected to be over 15 percent already by the year 2000.[25]

Third, Roman Catholic membership in the U.S. continues to grow, and some of this growth is directly at the expense of Protestantism. Here we recall the discussion in Chapter 13, of significant growth of black Catholics. And, of course, some of the Catholic growth has come from immigration of Catholic South and Central American immigrants. But some of that growth in Roman Catholicism is from some of the dropouts from mainline Protestantism. Hout, Greeley, and Wilde suggest that about 40 percent of recent mainline Protestant dropouts have joined the Roman Catholic Church.[26]

Fourth, there is continuing immigration of Muslims, Buddhists, Hindus, Sikhs, and people of other world religions. Such immigration ultimately erodes the old Protestant majority as their numbers become smaller proportionately to the entire U.S. population, even if they have no further defections from their ranks.

Two Predictions and An Observation

As we try to make some predictions or projections from the data discussed in this latter section, dealing with membership changes, particularly among Protestantism, we will make two predictions and one observation. First, mainline Protestant membership will probably continue to erode somewhat, though the dramatic decline of the last several decades is probably over. That is, the majority position of Protestantism in the United States will disappear. Smith and Kim suggest, in their 2005 article, that was based on data up to 2002, that the event of losing majority status could already have occurred. Second, other religions may not gain much in this process, because a major reason for Protestantism's loss of its majority position has been losing members to irreligion. Not all of Protestantism's losses will be picked up by other religious groups.

Now, by way of observation, if conservative Protestantism (the "strict churches") were to continue the gains they experienced in the last several decades of the twentieth century, they could potentially make up the difference and keep Protestantism above 50 percent of the U.S. population. But there is little likelihood of this occurring. We noted in Chapter 8, that these Evangelicals and the fundamentalists particularly have gained about as high a proportion of church members as they are likely to acquire. Despite newfound political power gained by the New Christian Right, they are unlikely to gain significant numbers of new members.

THE DILEMMAS OF ROMAN CATHOLICISM

Earlier in the chapter we introduced the reader to some significant changes in Roman Catholicism, in terms of church membership and attendance. From the Catholic perspective, this could be alarming. It would be particularly alarming to traditional, conservative Catholics because, at first glance, there appears to be a connection in timing between the decline in rates of Catholic religious participation and the pronouncements of the Second Vatican Council (Vatican II) in the early 1960s, which relaxed many traditional Catholic obligations. Vatican II moved the Catholic Church down a more liberal path. Garry Will's analysis at the time was that Vatican II let the "dirty little secret" of Catholicism out of the bag, so to speak.[27] That secret was simply the admission that the Catholic Church could and does change.

Mixed Doctrinal Messages

While Vatican II certainly has had some influence, at least in the sense that the Catholic populace has been introduced to the possibility of change so far as some previously immutable doctrines are concerned, the more immediate, precipitating cause likely has been the *Humanae Vitae* encyclical letter on birth control, issued by Pope Paul VI in 1968. As we described in Chapter 14, this was a reiteration and reinforcement of very traditional Catholic prohibitions against "artificial" methods of birth control, such as condoms and birth control pills. The encyclical was an abrupt reversal of the direction that many Catholics saw their church taking following Vatican II. And it came only three years after the conclusion of Vatican II, in 1963.

This reversal "turned off" a great many Catholics, so much so that some dropped out and, if not withdrawing their membership, ceased attending church services. Andrew Greeley says categorically: "Catholic church attendance declined because of birth control . . ."[28] Nonetheless, many continued to attend church, though not necessarily as frequently, out of old loyalties. Greeley describes the behavior of Catholics, who would not accept the reaffirmation of traditional Catholic doctrine on birth control, and were carrying out their own "quiet revolution," in which they decided to remain Catholic "on their own terms."[29] Their loyalty stems in part from the minority status of Catholics in the Protestant-dominated United States for so many decades, as well as the close link of Catholicism with ethnic cultures and enclaves (Poles, Ukrainians, and Italians, for example). The Catholic Church is more than *just* a church. It is a link with one's ethnic heritage and has been a place of refuge in an occasionally hostile Protestant society. Such loyalties limited the disengagement of Catholics from their church. And so, many Catholics remain loyal to their church and continue to attend with some frequency, although privately they hold to a non-Catholic ethic on birth control and rationalize that God "understands" even if church leaders do not.[30]

Data compiled by the Gallup polling organization certainly reinforces that observation. In 1993, Gallup found that, contrary to the directive of the encyclical, 84 percent of Catholics believed that "Catholics should be allowed to practice artificial means of birth control."[31] In a national poll of Catholics, by researchers at Purdue University in 1996, that focused on the two-thirds who not only define themselves as Catholics but are actually registered as current members of a Catholic parish, found that only 9 percent of their sample of Catholics believed "artificial" means of birth control are always wrong.[32] In addition, 72 percent of Catholics agreed that priests should be allowed to marry (up from 53 percent in the 1970s); and 63 percent agreed that women should be ordained as priests (up from only 35 percent in the 1970s).[33]

Priest Pedophilia Crisis

Most readers will be aware too that the Catholic Church has recently faced another serious threat to maintaining the continuing commitment of its members, in the widely-publicized scandal involving pedophilia by a significant number of its diocesan priests. But the problem is not only the impact of such behavior coming from its respected religious élite and now after many years being exposed and authenticated, often in courts of law, but also the mounting evidence of deliberate cover-ups and denials by those high in the religious hierarchy (at the Archbishop level).

Most widely-publicized has been activity in the Archdiocese of Boston. There, after many individuals who alleged sexual abuse by priests had come forward, many lawsuits had been filed and judgments won. Also, as allegations mounted of culpability at the archbishop level, in glossing over the complaints by parishioners of sexual abuse by priests, that covered a period of many years, Cardinal Bernard Law of the Archdiocese of Boston finally admitted he had indeed covered up many allegations in the past, by transferring priests from one parish to another, perhaps with a bit of counseling and therapy for the priests, though seldom for the abused and their families. The next parish seldom had an inkling of the problem, until sexual abuses began in their parish also. Records of complaints filed by lay members go back at least as far as 1967, against a priest who apparently was transferred many times, never removed from the priesthood, and remains a priest to this day, though, now in his 70s, he no longer has parish responsibilities.

Similar allegations of molestation of children by priests have been made in most all parts of the United States, with a familiar "solution" practiced by the clerical authorities, namely, calming down the local agitation among parishioners, by transferring the offending priests to other parishes. All 195 U.S. dioceses have by now been scrutinized and at least 325 priests have either been suspended or resigned. The most infamous diocese has become Boston, both because of very vocal and well-organized groups of Catholic laypersons and Catholic clergy, all of whom called repeatedly for Cardinal Bernard Law's resignation or removal as Archbishop, and fairly strenuous resistance to stepping down by Cardinal Law. However, after nearly a year of public protests by the lay groups—the national Survivors Network of Those Abused by Priests (SNAP) and the local Voice of the

Faithful—Cardinal Law did resign his leadership position on 13 December 2002. This came after a private consultation with Pope John Paul II, who accepted Law's resignation. It is of at least passing interest that, although Cardinal Law had to resign his position of Cardinal in Boston, he was subsequently given responsibility at the level of the Vatican itself and played a prominent, public role in the funeral ceremonies for Pope John Paul II in April 2005. Needless to say, this was a disappointment to many families in Boston, who had suffered harm from Cardinal Law's failure to deal forthrightly with the problem-priests in the diocese.

It is of further interest that, what was for many years considered by Vatican officials as American sensationalism, a localized "American problem," or part of a strategy against the Roman Catholic Church's requirement of celibacy for its priests, was not confined to the United States. In January 2002, the Catholic Church in Ireland agreed to a "landmark $110 million payment to children sexually abused by clergy over decades."[34] Over 20 priests, brothers, and nuns had been convicted of molesting children. Between 1995 and 1999, 21 Catholic priests in England and Wales were convicted of sexual abuse of children.[35] And in Australia, a Roman Catholic bishop, accused of covering up sexual abuses by a priest using the familiar tactic of transfer from parish to parish, was forced to resign in 1997.[36] The problem has surfaced in many other countries as well.

This is a worldwide problem for the Roman Catholic Church, that is as old as the church itself, but for centuries has been mostly submerged under church hierarchy cover-up strategies and a fairly cooperative public press. But the cover has been fully removed and, as such, even with reform and restitution, the scandal in its ignominious detail will probably have some long-term effect on Catholic membership, particularly within the context of rational choice theory, as some members choose other religious options. Short-term impact is already evident. By April 2002, Catholic Charities of Massachusetts reported a severe decline in giving to its $40 million annual budget on behalf of 150 social service agencies.[37] The Gannett News Service reported, in August 2002, that at least five protest groups had sprung up recently in several cities. For example, a Catholic attorney organized Catholics Opposed to Pedophile Priests and urged Catholics to withhold contributions to the Archdiocese of Palm Beach; and in Chicago, a Catholic bank executive formed the Catholics for Prevention of Sex Abuse by Clergy and similarly urged withholding funds.[38]

It is of interest that the partial alienation from their church, which is evident among the membership, carried over into voluntary financial contributions. In the early 1960s, Protestants and Catholics both contributed about the same amounts to their churches ($141 from Catholics, $138 from Protestants). By the mid-1980s, both groups had increased their contributions, but Catholics had fallen far behind Protestants ($320 from Catholics, $580 from Protestants). The proportion of contributions, as compared to income, had been 2.2 percent for both Catholics and Protestants in 1969, but by 1983 Catholics were giving half their former rate (1.1 percent of income), whereas Protestants contributed the same percentage as in 1969.[39]

Priest Shortage

Exacerbating the loosening of member ties and commitment to traditional Catholic parishes, is what some are calling an alarming decline in the priestly ranks. A substantial study by Richard Schoenherr and Lawrence Young, of the shrinking number of diocesan priests, found a decline of about 20 percent between 1966 and 1984, with a like decline predicted for the twenty following years. In other words, by 2005, the number of active diocesan priests was predicted to have decreased by 40 percent (from 35,000 in 1966 to approximately 21,000 in the year 2005).[40] Tim Unsworth notes that some close observers believe the decline would be as much as 50 percent by 2005. Also, almost 46 percent of the Roman Catholic clergy will be fifty-five or older and only 12 percent will be younger than thirty-five by 2005.[41] In addition to normal attrition through deaths and retirements, fewer men are entering the priesthood. In this connection Andrew Greeley relates the following telling statistics: in 1965 1,500 priests were ordained in the United States, but in 2002 only 450; in 1965 there were 49,000 seminarians, in 2004 only 4,700.[42] These are declines of 70 and 90 percent, respectively.

This has become a very serious problem for the Roman Catholic Church throughout the world. The priest shortage is worldwide and numbers of men in training for the priesthood have also declined significantly. In many countries, vast geographic areas and tens of thousands of parishioners are assigned to a single priest who becomes like the Methodist circuit-riding ministers on the American frontier, visiting individual congregations but a few times a year. As we mentioned earlier, in South America, for example, this lack of attentiveness to parishioners has left vast territories open to Evangelical and Pentecostal Protestant missionary activity, which now provides highly successful competition to traditional Catholic religious dominance.

While current priests maintain that the priesthood is a highly satisfying profession and few cite celibacy as a significant source of personal dissatisfaction (with relatively few thinking of resigning), others cite the rigid persistence of the celibate rule as a major contributing reason for the unattractiveness of the priesthood for young (and older) Catholic men.[43] Perhaps even more significant, is the refusal by the Church to ordain women to the priesthood or even the diaconate. While no one knows how significant the celibacy issue is, in discouraging men from entering the priesthood today, we do know that a significant number of Catholic women have been and are being trained in Catholic theological schools and many have secondary leadership positions in Catholic churches, as we discussed earlier in Chapter 11.

Some kind of compromise on the prohibition of the ordination of women to the priesthood would probably have a quicker and more significant impact on the priest shortage than removing the requirement of celibacy. But neither action by the Catholic hierarchy is at all likely to occur, at least for decades.

CONTINUITY IN THE TRADITIONAL SOCIAL FUNCTIONS OF RELIGION

Here we wish to expand a little on observations made by Émile Durkheim (see Chapter 2), that much of the time and in most societies, religion serves as an integrating influence in society. We refer to this observation again and, in fact, expand on it, because we believe there are several important functions that religion will continue to provide for society in the future.

Normative Reinforcement

First, religion serves a reinforcement function in society to the degree that it teaches and emphasizes the same norms and values as the society at large. This may be at the very general level of teaching such values as human dignity and freedom, equality before the law, respect for legitimate authority, and faithfulness to one's role. Or it may be more specific, such as, "Thou shalt not kill, steal, or procreate illegitimate children." In a direct sense, religion is here viewed as a socializing agent in the society. Although allowing that religious groups, just as all other kinds of groups, socialize their members into some norms unique unto themselves, we are speaking of religion as one among several institutions involved in socializing citizens to the core norms of the society. Educational agencies, families, peer groups, mass media, and various voluntary associations are all involved in this process. Religion is but one such agent. But it is one that touches a majority of people with some regularity.

At a second level, with respect to the reinforcement idea, we observe that religion not only socialized people in the "thou shalts" and "thou shalt nots" of society in a reinforcing sense, but occasionally pushed those norms even further. For example, society has norms against murder, but does not usually try to control what you think about your neighbors, so long as you do not harm their persons or property or infringe on their rights. A religious system may go further by teaching, for example, "Whosoever hateth his brother is a murderer," "Love your neighbor," and "Bless those who persecute you." If a religion is successful in inculcating norms more stringent than those the society imposes and thereby creates a "super-Christian" (or "super-Buddhist," or "super-Hindu,"), to that degree one may also see a "supercitizen." That is to say, society would be even better off if people not only avoided destroying their neighbors but also actually loved them and went out of their way to help them. The key here, of course, is discovering whether and to what degree religion actually produces such superior people. Undoubtedly there are some—they tend to be called "saints," and they may even be societal heroes and models for behavior. But there is no clear evidence that, on the average, religion produces a great number of such people. Yet we must again observe: To the degree that it happens, the society would benefit and would be getting citizens with a level of commitment and dedication that they might not have in the absence of religious influence and training.

Integration into Meaningful Relationships

An exceptionally important function performed by religion is that of bringing individuals into meaningful relationships with others in a group. Religious groups bring immigrants, social isolates, various minorities, and some socially maladjusted persons into a group where they are in contact with others. Not that religion reaches every such person or is successful in integrating all of those with whom it establishes contact. Nor is religion unique in performing this task or function for society—so do labor unions, fraternal lodges, newcomers' clubs, political parties, and innumerable other voluntary associations and groups of all sizes, constituencies, and purposes. However, religious groups, in large part because of their reputation for being concerned about life purposes and adjustment, as well as for raising a person's sights beyond current mundane problems, attract relatively large proportions of persons in need of meaningful interpersonal contact. Society needs such groups to do this. Society needs members who can function well in their roles. People function better when they feel they have some personal worth and have meaningful, satisfying relationships with other people. To the extent that religious groups provide this service to some who feel isolated and who are not being relieved of their anxieties and problems elsewhere, religion is serving the society.

While it is important to note that, with increasing immigration from Asia and the Middle East, there are growing numbers of U.S. residents and citizens who hold commitments to such major world religions as Islam, Buddhism, Hinduism, Sikhism, and others, some of these immigrants ultimately convert to Christianity. In the process, they illustrate the integrating function of religion. In fact, Barry Kosmin and Seymour Lachman make special note that a major reason for a significant number of conversions is that the religion of the host culture is a major source of social cohesion and integration for immigrant people. While there is a strong tendency for the religion of their origin to be a continuing source of internal cohesion for their subculture and something from the past to hold on to, Western religion can serve as an important point of entry to American culture for these immigrant groups. American churches replace the public school as an acculturating melting pot for many of these recent immigrants.[44]

Catalyst and Symbol for Reaffirming Societal Values

Another way, in which religion contributes to the integration of society, is by serving as a focal point or symbol—in a sense, as a catalyst—for the society to reaffirm some of its basic values. Religion everywhere does this through festivals. Think, for example, of what happens in our society in connection with the religious festival called Christmas. Although there is plenty of growling about gifts yet to buy, overdrawn checking accounts, and crass commercialism conspiring to do us all in, there is something else as well. There is a pervasive spirit in the air of good will and joviality. There are increases in gifts to charities. There is more attention given to those less fortunate than the majority. Not that what emerges is particularly enduring. Yet periodically, through such rites and festivals that reach out beyond the religious group itself, some of the fundamental values of the society are dramatized for people, and they reaffirm them at least intellectually and momentarily. Certainly not every Scrooge does an about-face, much less one that lasts beyond the festival itself; yet some do, and most citizens are at least temporarily affected.

Aid in Adjusting to Personal Crises

Another integrating function of religion, that some feel is actually getting close to the fundamental purpose or essence of religion itself, is the help it gives to people facing various crisis situations in their lives. To the degree that religion helps people grapple with emotional crisis, with death and bereavement, with uncertainties and disappointments of all kinds, religion is performing an important service for society. We introduced the idea of relativizing suffering and crisis in Chapter 2. Religion attempts to relativize human problems, by placing them in an eternal perspective, interpreting events as God's will ("All things work for good to those who love God"), and providing "answers" for irrational events. Whether the answers and explanations are "true" is for our purposes—and for society's—beside the point. What is important is whether people feel better as a result of what religion does for them in periods of crisis and imbalance. The society needs functioning members who fill their social roles with skill and attention. Society cannot afford to have great numbers of members incapacitated for extended periods of time. To the extent that religion helps with this task, society is greatly aided.

Source of Social Welfare

A final fairly major function, performed by religion in society, is its service as a welfare institution. Religious groups were in the forefront of the nineteenth-century movement for establishing orphanages, schools for the deaf, blind, and mentally retarded, adoption and family-service agencies, hospitals, and similar welfare and service institutions. Earle E. Cairns has documented the significant impact of numerous Christian groups on drives for prison reforms, the abolition of slavery, humane treatment of the mentally ill, and improved working conditions for industrial workers in the wake of the Industrial Revolution.[45] Even today, lists of United Way agencies include organizations that either retain a religious name or were founded by a religious organization. Today, most of these agencies derive the major portion of their monetary support from nonreligious sources through fees, voluntary contributions and solicitations from the general public, and governmental subsidy. But initially they were religiously motivated and funded and represented a direct response of religious groups to human need. Although the majority of funds in social welfare areas today are collected and distributed by the government, much of the original stimulus and effort in these directions was religious.

And then there is the dramatic recent example of the continuing function of religious social welfare efforts as religious communities and organizations stepped up so quickly and in such a significant way in rescue and sustenance for victims of hurricanes Katrina and Rita in the days following those Gulf Coast disasters in August/September 2005. Religious organizations responded immediately and abundantly with substantial sums of money, life saving supplies, services, and shelter when governmental agencies delayed, stumbled, and got lost in bureaucratic bungling.

The President's Faith-Based Initiatives   President George W. Bush's recently established Faith-Based Initiative program has added both new dimensions and new questions about the relationship of governmental funding for community and social welfare programs that are connected to religious organizations. The Faith-Based Initiative proposal had been a prominent part of candidate George W. Bush's campaign agenda, prior to his election to his first term as President in 2000. Therefore, it was no surprise that as soon as nine days after his inauguration on 20 January 2001, he announced his Faith-Based Initiative program and made clear it was of highest priority on his agenda. But the proposal immediately encountered difficulties in Congress and faced challenges from many other groups as well—enough that the President decided to implement the program by issuing two executive orders nearly two years later in December 2002. The first established the White House Office of Faith-Based and Community Initiatives, the second formed centers in five cabinet agencies—Justice, Housing and Urban Development, Labor, Education, and Health and Human Services. Parenthetically, we should mention that Amy Black, Douglas Koopman, and David Ryden suggest that this quick introduction of his Faith-Based Initiative was a strategic mistake by President Bush and his advisers. There was not enough attention to detail and normal legislative process and it appeared there was little serious consideration of potential political challenges and backlash, all of which created an unsteady launching pad for the proposal.[46]

In reviewing and reacting to the Faith-Based proposals, the concern of members of congress and others was not over Federal monies going to religious organizations, which carry out functions and services needed by society. Such cooperation was already of long-standing. But the fairly standard pattern of many years standing was to channel governmental funds through fairly large sub-agencies of religious groups, specifically set up for welfare work, whose budgets and administration were clearly separated from the parent religious entity. Prominent examples are Jewish Social Services, Catholic Charities, World Vision, and Lutheran Social Services, all of which had developed contractual relationships with government and were paid for services rendered. The new Faith-Based Initiative would be more decentralized, be spread among many more individual religious groups, often in relatively small amounts of several thousand dollars per grant, and be administered by people who had little or no experience in handling grants, creating annual reports, and responding to governmental audits.

But, according to Black, Koopman, and Ryden, more fundamental to the proposal and therefore at the heart of its opposition, was President Bush's desire to bring into the fold of federally supported religious social service programs, three types of providers. First, were highly evangelical providers that would, from deep commitment, urge clients to join with them in a particular faith. Second, were the providers that based their services on "traditional moral beliefs and behavior," rather than from a base of prior development within the professional helping professions. Third, were explicitly religious-based agencies that employed professional social service workers but had been traditionally denied federal assistance because of their close ties to a local church group, despite offering services that would otherwise be regarded as professional and not religiously biased.[47]

Early questions from Congress and the general public included: What would happen when the religious group with a federal grant goes to hire people to carry out the program? Can the group give preference to those of their own faith, just as they can when a denomination hires professors to teach at their seminaries? Will it be permissible to use the contact with people who use the services of the religious group's programs as an opportunity to proselytize and "spread the faith" to such persons?

Of course, the answers to such questions must be that, with governmental money and backing involved, the religious group must be committed to non-discrimination in hiring and cannot use the contact to attempt to indoctrinate the client through religious counseling, Bible study, prayer sessions, chapel attendance, or other means of trying to enlighten the client with the theology of the serving group.

The fundamental issue here, then, is separation of church and state, which we discussed in Chapter 7. As challenges have been raised, concerning Faith-Based Initiatives and individual cases taken to court, the U.S. Supreme Court" decision (1971) in the *Kurtzman v. Lemon* case, has been brought to bear. Out of that decision, has come what is now called the "Lemon test" of four parameters within which religious or faith-based groups must function. These are:

1. avoid either direct or indirect proselytizing,
2. provide services to clients without regard to religious affiliation or commitment,
3. keep the religious group's funds separate from governmental grant funds, with the latter spent only according to governmentally mandated procedures and subject to audit, and
4. comply with other applicable laws against discrimination in hiring or service.

Although the Faith-Based Community Initiatives program did not develop exactly as President Bush envisioned (e.g., there is less flexibility than the President hoped there would be for the religious groups to express their full message, because of limitations inherent in the Lemon text), several billion dollars have already moved through the program—$1.17 b in 2003 alone.

It should be noted, before leaving this topic of religiously based social welfare, that there is significant disagreement among religious groups over what is appropriate practice on their part with respect to social issues and welfare—should their emphasis be on spiritual matters or on social concerns? We will pursue this topic later in this chapter. But now we must consider the concept of "secularization." It may well be that the changing responsibility for dealing with social welfare is but one manifestation of a fundamental change in society called secularization.

THE FACTOR OF SECULARIZATION

A concept that has been widely-discussed for several decades and must be understood if we are to hope, at one level, to make sense out of contemporary developments in religion and, at a second level, to project the future of religion, is that of *secularization*. As this concept is commonly understood and used by rank-and-file citizens and some scholars as well, it is assumed that there has been a displacement of religious interpretations of reality and religious orientations toward life, by an orientation that seeks explanations for and justifications of human behavior and other phenomena in scientific and rational terms. One has undergone a secularization process if, for example, instead of asserting that marriages are made in heaven and for eternity, one says that marriages are made by human beings, in time, on the basis of propinquity, and in response to biological and psychological needs. The results of secularization are that, instead of more or less automatically "explaining" much that happens—death of loved ones, floods, plane crashes, drought, war, peace—as "God's will," more and more people are seeking explanations in the laws of physical science and in the social scientific "laws" of human interaction, or perhaps simply as the result of chance or pure accident. In other words, secularization is as much a state of mind as it is a specific, measurable development.

Andrew Greeley is very much on target when he says that secularization, as discussed in the United States today, means essentially that religion is less important now than it was in the past.[48] If this is, in fact, what people mean when they refer to the secularization process at work in American society, then the decline of religion in general, and not just in its institutional manifestations, is an empirical question that clamors for sociological investigation and documentation. Much will rest on how religion is defined—whether in terms of its "essence," or as a particular traditional package of beliefs and principles (such as "our Judeo-Christian heritage"), or in terms of the vitality of its institutional forms (membership, attendance, new construction, and so on).

Definition I: Replacement of Religion

This problem of achieving a consensus, so far as a definition of religion is concerned, surfaces in many discussions of the issue of secularization, where one person's understanding of religion does not coincide with the understandings of others. Larry Shriner implies as much, when he shows how secularization has been defined in half a dozen ways in the past.[49] Although each of these definitions has its own nuances, two basic connotations of secularization can be distilled from them. First, many see secularization as a process of *replacement* of religious faith by faith in scientific principles. This concept goes back to the beginnings of modern Western science, when scientists first dared to set aside religion's view of reality, at least temporarily, in order to consider and evaluate data objectively. Thus, Copernicus and Galileo were secularists in that they repudiated the belief—then a religious doctrine—that the earth is the center of the universe.

The logical extreme of secularism, in this view, is refusing to grant credence to any assertion about people, the world, or the universe, that cannot be empirically verified. While some view with alarm and others with joy such a displacement of religious faith by the scientific method, many on both sides see such secularization as a trend in which people manifest less and less interest in sacred and supernatural phenomena, as religious doctrines and institutions lose prestige and influence, with the possible ultimate result of a religionless society emerging.

Note, however, that no simple dichotomy exists of secular scientists hailing the replacement of religious faith, with scientific faith versus religionists decrying such replacement. The popular Protestant theologian of a generation ago, Harvey Cox, for example, welcomed secularization and saw it as a fulfillment of biblical themes and sources. He defined secularization in terms of "emancipation"— as the "liberation of man from religious and metaphysical tutelage, the turning of his attention away from other worlds and toward this one."[50] Thus, Cox's view may be regarded as a distinct variation on the "secularization-as-replacement" theme, one in which fulfillment is emphasized as a form of replacement.

Definition II: *Differentiation* Between Religious and Secular Spheres

The second general understanding of secularization is that it is a process of increasing differentiation between the religious and the secular (nonreligious) spheres of life—a process, moreover, coinciding with and perhaps in part resulting from increasing specialization within society, as it grows and becomes more urbanized and industrialized.[51] Some, who hold to the differentiation definition of secularization, cite the increasing "privatization" of faith—the process of compartmentalizing the religious and the secular, of regarding religion as a mystical, personal phenomenon that one does not share with others.

The haunting question that pervades this discussion and a myriad of other allegations of spreading secularization, is whether such signs reflect gains by "secular" forces and points of view at the expense of religion, or whether religion in its basic sense has remained essentially unaffected. Conceivably the essence of religion may be enjoying greater strength and influence today than during the heyday of the church type of religious organization in Europe or the early days of state churches in the United States. Further, "privatization" of religion need not mean that religion is not in evidence in people's actions, attitudes, and decisions. Also, many former public manifestations of religion, which are no longer in evidence, may have been ritualistic, pro forma actions that signified little and influenced people even less.

The point we are making is that before undertaking any analysis of secularization, one must specify one's operational definitions of the variables under discussion, for the conclusions one reaches about secularization are inevitably influenced by what one regards as the valuable features of religion and whether these features are perceived as threatened or disappearing, as well as by what one understands religion to be in the first place. That is, does the focus and concern center on the preservation of the institution as presently constituted? Or is one concerned about what might be happening to the "essence" of religion, apart from its institutional manifestations?

All we wish to do at this point is to raise the issue of secularization, not to resolve it. For one thing, the information and discussion in this chapter will help to "flesh out" the issue before trying to answer the question. Second, establishing operational definitions of religion and secularization will be more helpful in understanding both the current status and the future of religion in the United States, than will premature conclusions about secularization.

Paradoxes in Contemporary Religion

One reason that definitive conclusions about secularization are so difficult to reach is that contemporary American religion evinces numerous seeming paradoxes. While total church membership has declined somewhat from mid-1960s highs, and many mainline denominations have been experiencing membership losses, some religious groups have been advancing with firm strides, if not leaps and bounds, so far as membership is concerned. There is evidence of growing disenchantment with traditional religious forms among young people, yet a broad-based attempt to capture the "real Jesus" and "authentic Christianity" constituted the Jesus movement—a movement primarily of young people; and many young people today hold firmly to traditional beliefs about Jesus and Christian doctrine.

In 1966, many Protestant theologians were busy proclaiming the "death of God," yet by 1980, some religious leaders were organizing to take over political parties and processes, as they joined the Moral Majority and other successor groups. And by 2000, evangelical and fundamentalist Christians, through a variety of organizations such as the Christian Coalition, continued to push their political agendas and support pro-life political candidates. A strong movement among Christian men called the Promise Keepers in the mid- to late 1990s, attracted large crowds to their gatherings in many cities. Yet as the year 2000 dawned, their numbers were dwindling sharply and the group's continued viability was in doubt. Finally, there is much emphasis within denominations on employing modern techniques of management, cost accounting, and computer technology, yet one observes only a little progress in eliminating duplication of effort by putting ecumenical ideology into practice. Such paradoxes (or seeming paradoxes) simply highlight the importance of one's decisions regarding which phenomena to consider in reaching conclusions about secularization on the one hand or "religionization" on the other. We do indeed have to be concerned about what operational definitions and what measures of these concepts we adopt.

Bellah's Fifth Stage of Religious Evolution: *Differentiation*

One of the best definitions of secularization from the differentiation perspective, is Robert Bellah's, in his account of the historical evolution of religion through five stages. A dominant theme within this evolutionary process, according to Bellah, is the process of making increasingly more sophisticated differentiations between the sacred and the secular. This process has culminated, in the fifth stage (the modern period), in a breakdown of the dualistic distinction between the sacred and the secular, and its replacement by a multidimensional view of life and reality.[52] At this final stage, everything, including religion, is seen as revisable (though not all people see it this way, of course). Removed, or in the process of being removed, are such "either-or" dualistic descriptions of reality as *this world–other world, sacred–profane, good–evil, salvation–damnation*. Absolutism is replaced with relativity. The search by people for meaning is no longer confined within religious institutions or limited to traditional religious formulations. Such concepts as *situation ethics* and *process theology* typify the modern period. Certain traditional concepts and approaches from the past (*orthodoxy, sin,* and *moral law,* for example), are nevertheless retained by some and apparently will not disappear completely in the near future. This latter observation, of course, only reinforces Bellah's point, for a diversity of approaches and expressions and a broad range of views and interpretations are characteristic of religion in the modern period.

Historical Context

As we attempt to understand secularization, it is important to look back and become aware of the context out of which the concept grew. That is, what had happened and what was going on that gave rise to the concept known as secularization? There are four major factors that need to be recognized. First, there was the explosive growth of scientific knowledge and technology that continues to expand and conquer the unknown at a breathtaking pace. This is the modernization and technological development that are both praised and decried in discussions about secularization. Second, following the birth of social science a century and a half ago, came the optimism of its early practitioners (unabashed optimists that they were) that people could and would create an essentially perfect society, when at last we understood the laws of social interaction and organization. This was a clearly linear process leading to an attainable goal of full understanding and rational organization in a future time. Third, there was a widespread belief, particularly among the scientists, that religion was a product of ignorance (insufficient knowledge and understanding) and superstition that would become unnecessary in the future. This view of religion, of course, overlooks the important function of religion that centers around dealing with the emotional discomfort and sadness that are universal in human experience and for which science has no better answers today than it ever did. Fourth, as would be expected, there has been strong reaction on the part of religious leaders, which has taken two quite different alternative paths. One was a conscious attempt to adapt and incorporate findings of science, both natural and social, into religion. The other was a reaction against much of the new learning and methods, and it became an attempt to "hold the line" and beat down the new learning that threatened to lure people away from the eternal verities.

At this point we must hasten to observe that both of these somewhat polar approaches to religious expression remain viable today. Neither approach is nearing extinction. And there are many nuances of each approach, as well as a panoply of alternatives already flourishing in nations around the world. What this all suggests is that not only does religion live on, but it will continue to survive, offering as it does a great many choices. This brings us to two contributions to sociological theory that will be helpful in understanding where religion is headed and will, in a sense, "rescue" the concept *secularization* that some social scientists have for some time been suggesting needs to be abandoned. One is the by now fairly familiar *rational choice theory*. The other, while not a part of *rational choice theory*, is compatible with it and elaborates a set of ideas that both advances our understanding of what *secularization* is and retains it as a useful term in our sociological vocabulary.

Application of Rational Choice Theory

First, *rational choice theory* alerts us to the immense religious universe that is open to people who decide that the religious groups with which they have been affiliated are no longer serving them well. These run the gamut, for Christians, from linking up with an entirely new world religion, such as Buddhism or Islam, to joining an existing Christian group of either a more conservative or a more liberal stripe, depending on the nature and direction of their dissatisfaction, or going the sectarian route to try to recover what these dissatisfied Christians no longer see featured in their group. But the point is, religion is not in the process of self-destructing here. It is simply that religious people, who find that some of their religious needs are not being well addressed, either find or help create a group that does provide what they believe they need religiously.

Focus on Changes in Religious Authority

The second set of ideas is by Mark Chaves, who helps us find our way through the maze that the concept *secularization* often seems to be. He makes the point that most of the endless discussion of *secularization*, over the centuries since the Enlightenment, has been about "religion" when what was really at issue should have been "religious authority."[53] That is to say, religion is not disappearing but there are changes in its authority. But to understand that distinction, we need to look at three distinct levels or areas in which *secularization* can occur. Chaves overlays his distinction between "religion" and "religious authority" on Karel Dobbelaere's three dimensions of secularization,[54] to which Chaves then attaches the labels *laicization, internal secularization, and religious disinvolvement*. While the meanings of these terms are not inherently evident, they are easy to distinguish.

First, laicization. We quote Chaves as follows: "Laicization refers to the process of differentiation whereby political, educational, scientific, and other institutions gain autonomy from the religious institutions of a society. The result of this process is that religion becomes just one institutional sphere among others, enjoying no necessary primary status."[55] This kind of secularization is what occurred in Europe in the late Middle Ages, when societal institutions, such as politics and education over which the Roman Catholic Church had ruled, began to operate more independently. Political leaders, such as kings, reserved political decision-making for themselves and their secular (non clergy) advisors and enforcers. Such laicization is now commonplace and seems to us most natural. Nonetheless, it is a manifestation of secularization, though without any necessary conclusion that religion is on the road to extinction. There has simply been some reduction of religious authority as religion now stands in a row of other societal institutions, each with areas of service to the broader society. Just as the political system and the economy continue to perform important societal functions, so religion continues to perform its societal functions. Religious authority has decreased; but the services that religion provides citizens continue to operate.

Chaves continues with a description of "internal secularization," which occurs when religious organizations accommodate teachings and practices in varying degrees to the secular world.[56] A classic example would be the medieval church finally accepting the Copernican view of a heliocentric universe in the face of compelling scientific evidence. Or, much more recently, the decision by dozens of Christian denominations to accept women into the ranks of the clergy through ordination. This is but one of many accommodations to societal change accepted by religious groups— decisions not accepted by all members, some of whom withdraw and change their religious affiliation (making what they believe to be a rational choice) because their original group has become "secularized." That is, it has changed some of its teachings and practices.

The third dimension (*religious disinvolvement*) is at the level of the individual religious adherent, and occurs when members change their personal religious beliefs to be more in line with what science shows them.[57] For example, they might reject the six-day creation story to accept some form of evolutionary theory with respect to the formation of mother earth. Or perhaps they decide that God's people might include, not only those who bear the religious identify they happen to hold, but could also encompass all Protestants or all Christians or even all those believers world-wide who believe in a monotheistic god—also including Muslims, for example.

Summary and Concluding Comments

To summarize, *secularization* is a concept worth retaining, so long as we make clear our meaning of the term. After all, changes in religion have taken place. The concept "secularization" recognizes and encompasses such change so long as we speak of religious authority having lost some control, while religion in its multitudinous forms remains in the hearts and minds of most people.

But there is one more set of comments we need to make before we leave the topic of secularization. As mentioned earlier, some social theorists have recently called for the death of the concept of secularization as a descriptive and explanatory factor that influences religion. They have a point, if what they oppose is the utilization of secularization theory to presage the demise of religion. But religion is not going to disappear. So if that is all there is to secularization theory, the concept should be discarded.

However, secularization, as presented in this text, is used to describe a far less dramatic impact on religion than outright annihilation. We have suggested that the main effect of secularization has been to encourage specialization. It is true that many religions have a narrower range of influence than they used to enjoy. Religion does not exert so much influence over the political and economic systems as it once did. True enough. But then most would say that is not its central function anyway, though it may have been powerful in these areas in the past and though, in some societies, the dominant religion still has strong influence, particularly on the political structure. Of course, everyone is well aware that many religious groups today want to regain religious and political power of old and work quite single-mindedly to impact politics. In the United States, individuals and groups of a conservative religious persuasion are exerting substantial pressure on the political system to overturn the *Roe v. Wade* abortion decision made by the U.S. Supreme Court in 1973. In Iraq, some Muslim clerics and citizens exhort the faithful to use violence to rid their soil of Americans and those Iraqi public servants they believe have been duped by American propaganda.

Another mistake of some secularization theorists in the past, as Rodney Stark and William Bainbridge have pointed out, is that they equated religion with a particular set of existing religious groups and failed to consider the possibility of new religious groups developing in response to changing social environments. Or they did not consider that the reaction of some persons to the secularization tendencies, which they saw and experienced in religion, would be to pursue *revival* of the "old-time religion" with others of like mind and that even the old religion, which in some sectors was experiencing change, would be rejuvenated by others.[58] These true sectarians find marvelous opportunities to return to what they perceive to be their religious roots, and traditional religion survives—both in a remodeled form that has responded to change in the surrounding culture, and in a more or less traditional form that some from the religious group have either held onto or recaptured.

THE CONFLICT OVER THE PURPOSE OF RELIGION

A final feature of contemporary American religion, which adds a dimension to our consideration of the future of religion, is the controversy over its purpose. Is it for the personal benefit of its practitioners—that is, for the sake of their possible ultimate eternal salvation, in addition to their feelings of well being, comfort, and reinforcement of lifestyle? Or is religion primarily a vehicle of social change, as it tries to combat poverty, discrimination, sexism, and other social ills?

This debate over religion's functions and purposes, pitting social service versus self-service, is certainly not new. It represents a dilemma in American society, at least as old as the Social Gospel movement that emerged in the last half of the nineteenth century and the counterchallenge by fundamentalism that followed. Yet the issue has been updated. Not that either perspective or emphasis ever disappeared. Both have remained viable, and in fact have in many instances coexisted within the same denomination. But the original social gospel or social service emphasis became institutionalized, in the sense that denominations established specialized commissions, boards, and subsidiary institutions to handle that aspect of their work. It may have been a part of the annual budget of both the local congregation and the national denomination and called "benevolences." It supported orphanages, hospitals, schools for the physically or mentally handicapped, and the like. Or it may have been supported through annual fund-raising drives, as people's hearts were touched by an emotional appeal and they made a contribution. In any case, once a religious group's social service and welfare concerns became primarily the responsibility of specialized personnel and agencies operating in the group's name, these same concerns were easily relegated to a peripheral dimension of most church members' lives.

Resurgence of Social Service Emphases

However, with the emergence of the civil rights movement in the late 1950s and early 1960s, with the Vietnam War in Southeast Asia, and amid growing publicity and concern over such domestic social issues as poverty, capital punishment, abortion, nuclear power, and environmental pollution, individual church members and *ad hoc* religious groups began involving themselves in the issues. They urged their religious groups to become similarly involved and in a real sense forced an issue that had long lain dormant. Protestant, Catholic, and Jewish clergy began participating in civil rights marches, sit-ins, and demonstrations; administrators of denominational social service programs began to urge more substantial support for existing and additional programs; Martin Luther King Jr. challenged church people of all colors to support the struggle of black citizens for freedom and dignity. Seminaries intensified their efforts by offering new courses in social ethics and concerns and by implementing social action fieldwork programs. Denominations began issuing position statements supporting, at least in general terms, the rights of minority and disprivileged groups. Young seminary graduates, assuming the leadership of congregations, began preaching a gospel that included more than personal comfort and salvation. A "new breed" began to enter the ministry.

Crisis of Purpose

The outcome of all this was a crisis of direction or purpose, so far as organized religion was concerned. That is, organized religion was caught in the middle of the agonizing confrontation of individual versus social concerns, personal comfort and salvation versus social welfare and help for the disprivileged.

   Not that those who championed the social concern emphasis always saw these as polar alternatives. Certainly most people who emphasized social service in the name of religion, spoke of it as a concomitant of traditional individual salvation and comfort emphases, though some at least implicitly urged social service emphases at the expense of individual ones. It all became an issue when the idea left the seminaries and the resolution-forming conferences and conventions and began confronting the local congregations. Then the allegations and accusations implied by such book titles as *The Suburban Captivity of the Churches* and *The Comfortable Pew* became meaningful.[59] The message of these and similar analyses of organized religion, in the 1960s, was that churches not only were self-serving but also probably would not change. The direct implication was that large numbers of both laypersons and clergy sought to retain the individual emphasis of the church at all costs—perhaps out of ideological commitment to the idea that salvation is the only true concern of churches, or perhaps because of inertia related to the comfort and security and meaningful interpersonal relationships the church provided many people.

   In *The Gathering Storm in the Churches* (1969), Jeffrey Hadden provided data from various studies, to support his contention that a wide gap existed between many laypersons and growing numbers of clergy on the salvation versus social service issue. Centering his discussion on support for the civil rights issue, Hadden pointed out that, although a great majority of Americans interviewed in one study (86 percent) agreed that "the best mark of a person's religiousness is the degree of his concern for others," nearly half (49 percent) of the same sample felt that "clergy should stick to religion and not concern themselves with social, economic, and political questions." Further, nearly three-fourths (72 percent) admitted they would be upset if their minister, priest, or rabbi were to participate in a picket line or demonstration. Only slightly more than a third (37 percent) professed being "basically sympathetic with Northern ministers and students who have gone to the South to work for civil rights." By way of contrast, on this last issue, 64 percent of the clergy interviewed expressed sympathy for such active civil rights involvement.[60]

Such data reflected not only the conflict over the purpose of religion and the proper aims of the church, in which denominations have tended to lean strongly in one direction or the other, but also the conflict between clergy and laypeople within a given denomination, particularly those denominations that have tended to emphasize salvation. As a result of the latter conflict, Hadden felt, the traditional authority of clergy was gradually eroding as laypeople began to "think for themselves" when their personal views of the purpose of religion were challenged. Such intradenominational conflicts are not new in themselves. Because the number of people involved became greater, however, the traditional techniques religious groups had used for handling internal diversity became inadequate. Agencies, "special ministries," and monastic orders with a social service emphasis no longer provided enough openings to accommodate the number of clergy and serious laypersons committed in this direction. Thus, the "segmentation of radicalism" technique, which Phillip Hammond and Robert Mitchell suggested had been widely used by religious groups, could no longer contain the challenge to tradition as it had in the past.[61] While radicals at one time could be "kicked upstairs" into administrative positions or directed into campus or social welfare ministries, where contact with rank-and-file laity in standard congregations was minimal, such tactics became less effective. It is interesting that falling back on such options assumes the group is not particularly interested in facing directly the problems that the challengers are raising.

Crisis Abated

In general, however, the crisis of the salvation versus social concern issue has abated. Many of the major objectives of the civil rights movement have been achieved, at least regarding legislation; the Vietnam War has ended; social problems and solutions that appeared simple have been recognized as complex; considerable backlash against social welfare programs has set in; and new issues continue to surface that make a dichotomy of salvation versus social concern not so simple to maintain. Concentrating on a single, specialized issue, such as women's rights, gay rights, or abortion reform, need not place a protagonist at total odds with a congregation that pursues its own comfort, especially if they do not expect much participation or commitment from the congregation.

The whole issue of why there has been a reduction of such pressures is exceedingly complex, however, and so the following observations are perhaps only a few of the factors that need to be considered:

1. Social service-oriented clergy have made up the bulk of those who have left the ministry—and their numbers have been substantial in all faiths—apparently feeling that they could "do their thing" better in a secular setting. Moreover, the departure of such ministers may itself indicate that the salvation emphasis is still dominant.

2. Financial pressures have forced denominations to eliminate some of the administrative positions, which formerly served as sources of and encouragement for dissidence.

3. In some denominations, controversy has shifted to more traditional theological issues. There has been a significant resurgence of traditional conservative theology in many denominations.

4. Some laypersons, who objected most strongly to what they defined as at best a dilution and at worst a perversion or betrayal of the proper purpose of the church, have left their denominations for more conservative ones that still emphasize salvation and personal goals.

5. A well-organized countermovement, of which the so-called Moral Majority was a prominent early example (replaced by the Christian Coalition today), arose within the ranks of Christian denominations. Such groups explicitly aim to undo some of the earlier efforts of more liberal religious social service efforts, in the areas of welfare and abortion reform, liberalization of rights for homosexuals and women, and curtailment of the military machine.

It appears that the first wave of the most recent salvation versus social action controversy is past. There is some indication that the interest in social concerns has fallen victim to the mood of the nation, as people have become more concerned with such urgent personal goals as keeping a job when others are losing theirs, maintaining financial solvency when inflation or deflation threaten, and staying healthy as new dangers from cancer-inducing agents are constantly made public. Further, the stridency of many of the victims of social inequities who have shouted "Black Power," "Gay Rights," and "Women's Liberation," has tended to discourage some of the more faint hearted—they did not intend to go to "war," but only to help the helpless.

It is interesting that the "social service" churchpeople of a liberal stripe and the Christian Coalition churchpeople of a conservative stripe, though far apart ideologically and theologically, proceed from a similar premise. That is, religious organizations can be used to apply political and social pressure to help bring about the social change the group desires.

It is also worth noting that what has been most often described as a clash of perspectives between liberals and conservatives, has been challenged by what might be called "religious centrists." These are people in all denominations, who have sided with neither the right- nor the left-wing groups and have remained relatively silent. They are the people we referred to earlier in this chapter who, despite holding membership in liberal denominations, espouse traditional orthodox doctrine.

CONCLUSION

By way of conclusion, we shall introduce the reader to some interesting observations made by James Duke and Barry Johnson, about what seems to happen to religion and its institutional forms as time goes on. These observations will stimulate our thinking about where religion might be going in the future. They used voluminous data compiled by David Barrett on the religious commitment and affiliation of people in 224 nations throughout the world in the mid-1970s.[62]

The context is traditional, popular secularization theory, in its most common themes, which Duke and Johnson summarize as follows:

1. Secularization is linear or progressive in the sense that it moves forward down the road more or less inexorably in contradiction and opposition to traditional religion
2. Once underway, secularization is inevitable
3. The cause of secularization is modernization and, as such, is of recent origin
4. Secularization is, in the main, a Western phenomenon.[63]

Duke and Johnson assert that the data they analyzed from Barrett's compilation suggest five rather different observations or conclusions:

1. Religious change can be and often is cyclical, rather than always linear. This cyclical pattern is often repeated, as a dominant or established religion begins to lose influence and new religions begin, or already existing minority religions gain adherents and power and challenge the old dominant forms. These challengers grow and become dominant. But they, too, can be seen ultimately to peak, then decline. They are challenged and give way to something new, and the cycle is repeated.
2. What is, of course, of absolutely paramount importance is the fact that religion itself does not disappear or even necessarily lose influence or adherents as this cycle repeats time after time. What changes is simply the form or structure it takes, as it addresses the same needs for comfort, belonging, explanation for the mysterious, and authentication of the significance and importance of the individual that religion addresses everywhere in every age.
3. Religious reformations occur fairly frequently. That is, the cycle gets repeated as a dominant religion is displaced by an alternative.
4. Such religious change is observed everywhere and in records both ancient and modern.
5. Such religious changes are expectedly joined and influenced by changes in other features of the culture.[64]

Although change in religion is universal, and although particular religions can wane to the point of losing their leadership position in a given society never to regain its former level of influence, the phenomenon of religion in one form or another does not disappear. While it may be in a new form with changes of emphasis and message that might be quite radically different, it is still what religion always is—namely, an expression of people's ultimate concerns and their basic needs for reassurance about their future—both eternal and in the here and now.

Ubiquity of the Religious Factor

It is of far more than casual significance that almost all major events in recent world history have a major religious connection or ingredient. Jose Casanova notes that, whereas religion had appeared to be primarily a private matter for individual attention, suddenly in the 1980s religion thrust itself dramatically and forcefully into the public arena. He cites four occasions when this happened. He says that "four seemingly unrelated yet almost simultaneously unfolding developments gave religion the kind of global publicity which forced a reassessment of its place and role in the modern world."[65] He identifies these as the Islamic revolution in Iran, centering around the Ayatollah Khomeini, the rise of the Solidarity movement in Poland, the involvement of Catholicism in the Sandinista revolution and other political conflicts in Latin America, and the return of Protestant Fundamentalism to the political scene in America.[66]

If we come even closer to the present and focus on the impingement of religion into the public sphere of American life, we will note that a great many of the events and issues that have absorbed public attention and/or shocked public consciousness recently, are incidents and events that had strong religious overtones or connections. We think of the ethnic/religious war in Bosnia, to which we sent twenty thousand American troops in 1995, the NATO air attack in Bosnia in 1999, to stop the genocide of Slobodan Milosevic's soldiers and followers against the Muslim citizens of Kosovo, the bombing of the World Trade Center by Muslim extremists, the "Million Man March" in Washington, DC, the killing of Roman Catholic citizens in East Timor by Indonesian troops, the Branch Davidian tragedy in Waco, the mass suicides in San Diego of thirty-nine members of the Heaven's Gate cult, the murder of abortion clinic personnel by individual Christian extremists, the 9/11 airplane missiles crashing into the World Trade Center towers, the Pentagon, and the Pennsylvania field, and the rise of Islamism and its blending of Islamic religious principles and concepts with political and national objectives and strategies (Osama bin Laden style of terrorism in the name of one's God, for example).

We make reference to these events to dramatize the highly visible presence and significance of religion in societies today, as well as to emphasize that this presence is worldwide. We believe also that the distribution of these events gives evidence of the importance of religion to people worldwide and suggests that religion is and will be important to people in the future. People continue to ponder, not only who and what they are, but from whence they came and where they are going. Is there any meaning and purpose in the world around them and, above all, is there any meaning and purpose for them as tiny, individual specks in the universe? Religion attempts to deal with such questions. As such, religion has a future. In fact, it has a future to the extent that humanity has a future, because religion is an expression of the confrontation of people with their environment, both physical and social, and with each other. It is a reflection both of the precariousness of human existence and of the imperfections with which people relate to people. As such, religion in some form—or rather, in a variety of forms—not only is a part of society but will remain so.

NOTES

1. C. Kirk Hadaway, Penny Long Marler, and Mark Chaves, "What the Polls Don't Show: A Closer Look at U.S. Church Attendance," *American Sociological Review* 58, no. 12 (December 1993): 741–752.

2. Ibid., p. 744.

3. Ibid.

4. Ibid., p. 747.

5. Mark Chaves and James C. Cavendish, "More Evidence on U.S. Catholic Church Attendance," *Journal for the Scientific Study of Religion* 33, no. 4 (1994): 376–381.

6. Hadaway et al., "What the Polls Don't Show," p. 749.

7. Percentages computed from data in Constant H. Jacquet, Jr., ed. *Yearbook of American and Canadian Churches* (Nashville, TN: Abingdon, 1984), pp. 246–247; and Kenneth B. Bedell, ed. *Yearbook of American and Canadian Churches, 1995* (Nashville, TN: Abingdon, 1995), pp. 265–272.

8. Ibid.

9. Dean M. Kelley, *Why Conservative Churches Are Growing* (New York: Harper & Row, 1972).

10. Dean M. Kelley, "Commentary: Is Religion a Dependent Variable?" in *Understanding Church Growth and Decline: 1950–1978*, eds. Dean R. Hoge and David A. Roozen (New York: Pilgrim Press, 1979), p. 340.

11. Cited in Kelley, *Why Conservative Churches Are Growing*, pp. 92–93.

12. Rodney Stark and Charles Y. Glock, *American Piety* (Berkeley: University of California Press, 1968).

13. Ibid., p. 187.

14. Samuel A. Mueller, "Dimensions of Interdenominational Mobility in the United States," *Journal for the Scientific Study of Religion* 10, no. 2 (1971): 76–84.

15. Wade Clark Roof and C. Kirk Hadaway, "Denominational Switching in the Seventies: Going beyond Stark and Glock," *Journal for the Scientific Study of Religion* 18, no. 4 (1979): 372.

16. Ibid.

17. Author's calculations from data presented by Wade Clark Roof and William McKinney, *American Mainline Religion: Its Changing Shape and Future* (New Brunswick, NJ: Rutgers

University Press, 1987), p.161, and confirmed by Michael Hout, Andrew Greeley, and Melissa J. Wilde, "The Demographic Imperative in Religious Change in the U.S.," *American Journal of Sociology,* vol. 107, no. 2 (Sept. 2001), p. 471.

18. Hout, Greeley, and Wilde, "The Demographic Imperative in Religious Change in the U.S.," ibid.

19. Ibid., p. 486.

20. Rodney Stark and Roger Finke, *Acts of Faith: Explaining the Human Side of Religion* (Berkeley: University of California Press, 2000).

21. Ibid., pp. 195–217.

22. Tom W. Smith and Seokho Kim, "The Vanishing Protestant Majority," *Journal for the Scientific Study of Religion* 44, no. 2 (June, 2005), pp. 214–215.

23. Ibid., p. 218.

24. Hout, Greeley, and Wilde, "The Demographic Imperative in Religious Change in the U.S.," ibid., p. 488.

25. Michael Hout and Claude S. Fischer, "Why More Americans Have No Religious Preference," *American Sociological Review* 67, no. 1 (2002), p. 167.

26. Hout, Greeley, and Wilde, "The Demographic Imperative in Religious Change in the U.S.," ibid.

27. Garry Wills, *Bare Ruined Choirs* (Garden City, NY: Doubleday, 1972), p. 21.

28. Andrew M. Greeley, *Religious Change in America* (Cambridge, MA: Harvard University Press, 1989), p. 47.

29. Ibid.

30. Ibid., p. 52.

31. George Gallup, Jr. and D. Michael Lindsay, *Surveying the Religious Landscape: Trends in U.S. Beliefs* (Harrisburg, PA: Morehouse Publishing Company, 1999), p. 85.

32. James D. Davidson, Andrea S. Williams, Richard A. Lamanna, John Stenftenagel, Kathleen Maas Weigert, William J. Whalen, and Patricia Wittberg, *The Search for Common Good: What Unites and Divides Catholic Americans* (Huntington, IN: Our Sunday Visitor, 1997), p. 47.

33. Ibid.

34. Victor L. Simpson, "Vatican Changes Views on Pedophilia," Associated Press News Story, December 5, 2002, p. 1, published on the Associated Press website.

35. Ibid.

36. Ibid.

37. *Star Press*, Muncie, IN, April 13, 2002, p. 4D.

38. Gannett News Service, *Star Press*, Muncie, IN, August 3, 2002, p. 3C.

39. Comparative data on financial contributions by Catholics and Protestants from Andrew M. Greeley, *Religious Change in America* (Cambridge, MA: Harvard University Press, 1989), p.68.

40. Richard Schoenherr and Lawrence Young, *Full Pews and Empty Altars* (Madison: University of Wisconsin Press, 1993), p. 25.

41. Tim Unsworth, *The Last Priests in America* (New York: Crossroad Publishing Company, 1991), p. xii.

42. Andrew M. Greeley, *Priests* (Chicago: University of Chicago Press, 2004), p. 7.

43. Ibid., pp. 68ff.

44. Barry A. Kosmin and Seymour P. Lachman, *One Nation under God* (New York: Harmony Books, 1993), p. 116.

45. Earle E. Cairns, *Saints and Society* (Chicago: Moody Press, 1960).

46. Amy F. Black, Douglas L. Koopman, and David K. Ryden, *Of Little Faith: The Politics of George W. Bush's Faith-Based Initiatives* (Washington, DC: Georgetown University Press, 2004), p. 105.

47. Ibid., p. 18.

48. Andrew M. Greeley, *The Denominational Society* (Glenview, IL: Scott, Foresman, 1972), p. 127.

49. Larry Shriner, "The Concept of Secularization in Empirical Research," *Journal for the Scientific Study of Religion* 6, no. 2 (1967): 207–220.

50. Harvey Cox, *The Secular City* (New York: Macmillan, 1965), p. 17.

51. Talcott Parsons, "Christianity and Modern Industrial Society," in *Sociological Theory, Values, and Socio-Cultural Change*, ed. Edward A. Tiryakin (New York: Free Press, 1963), pp. 33–70.

52. Robert N. Bellah, "Religious Evolution," *American Sociological Review* 29, no. 3 (1954): 358–374.

53. Mark Chaves, "Secularization as Declining Religious Authority," *Social Forces* 72, no. 3 (March, 1994): pp. 754–757.

54. Ibid., p. 757 and Karel Dobbelaere, "Secularization: A Multi-Dimensional Concept," *Current Sociology* 29 (1981).

55. Chaves, ibid., p. 757.

56. Ibid., p. 766.

57. Ibid., p. 768.

58. Rodney Stark and William Sims Bainbridge, *A Theory of Religion* (New York: Peter Lang, 1987), pp. 301ff.

59. Gibson Winter, *The Suburban Captivity of the Churches* (Garden City, NY: Doubleday, 1961); Pierre Berton, *The Comfortable Pew* (Philadelphia: Lippincott, 1965).

60. Jeffrey K. Hadden, *The Gathering Storm in the Churches* (Garden City, NY: Doubleday, 1969), pp. 132, 134, 136.

61. Phillip E. Hammond and Robert E. Mitchell, "Segmentation of Radicalism: The Case of the Protestant Campus Minister," *American Journal of Sociology* 71, no. 2 (1965): 133–143.

62. David B. Barrett, ed., *World Christian Encyclopedia* (New York: Oxford University Press, 1982).

63. James T. Duke and Barry L. Johnson, "Religious Transformation and Social Conditions: A Macrosociological Analysis," in *Religious Politics in Global and Comparative Perspective*, ed. William H. Swatos Jr. (New York: Greenwood Press, 1989), p. 76.

64. Ibid., pp. 77ff.

65. José Casanova, *Public Religions in the Modern World* (Chicago: University of Chicago Press, 1994), p. 3.

66. Ibid.

Photo Credits

Chapter 1: Page 1, Eugene Gordon/Pearson Education/PH College.

Chapter 2: Page 21, Pearson Education/PH College.

Chapter 3: Page 40, (left) Scott Cunningham/Merrill Education and (right) Ken Karp/Pearson Education/PH College.

Chapter 4: Page 60, (left) Ken Karp/Pearson Education/PH College and (right) Laimute E. Druskis/Pearson Education/PH College.

Chapter 5: Page 91, (left) Silver Burdett Ginn and (right) Silver Burdett Ginn

Chapter 6: Page 122, Laima Druskis/Pearson Education/PH College.

Chapter 7: Page 145, David Mager/Pearson Learning Photo Studio.

Chapter 8: Page 179, Teri Leigh Stratford/Pearson Learning/PH College.

Chapter 9: Page 206, Teri Leigh Stratford/Pearson Learning/PH College.

Chapter 10: Page 221, Laimute Druskis/Pearson Education/PH College.

Chapter 11: Page 243, Richard Hutchings/Silver Burdett Ginn.

Chapter 12: Page 288, Louis R. Linscott and S. B. Goddard & Sons Co./Pearson Education/PH College.

Chapter 13: Page 311, Marc Anderson/Pearson Education/PH College.

Chapter 14: Page 344, Laima Druskis/Pearson Education/PH College.

Chapter 15: Page 384, (left) Silver Burdett Ginn and (right) Teri Leigh Stratford/Pearson Education/PH College.

Index